Achieving Quality in Software

IFIP – The International Federation for Information Processing

IFIP was founded in 1960 under the auspices of UNESCO, following the First World Computer Congress held in Paris the previous year. An umbrella organization for societies working in information processing, IFIP's aim is two-fold: to support information processing within its member countries and to encourage technology transfer to developing nations. As its mission statement clearly states,

> IFIP's mission is to be the leading, truly international, apolitical organization which encourages and assists in the development, exploitation and application of information technology for the benefit of all people.

IFIP is a non-profitmaking organization, run almost solely by 2500 volunteers. It operates through a number of technical committees, which organize events and publications. IFIP's events range from an international congress to local seminars, but the most important are:

- the IFIP World Computer Congress, held every second year;
- open conferences;
- working conferences.

The flagship event is the IFIP World Computer Congress, at which both invited and contributed papers are presented. Contributed papers are rigorously refereed and the rejection rate is high.

As with the Congress, participation in the open conferences is open to all and papers may be invited or submitted. Again, submitted papers are stringently refereed.

The working conferences are structured differently. They are usually run by a working group and attendance is small and by invitation only. Their purpose is to create an atmosphere conducive to innovation and development. Refereeing is less rigorous and papers are subjected to extensive group discussion.

Publications arising from IFIP events vary. The papers presented at the IFIP World Computer Congress and at open conferences are published as conference proceedings, while the results of the working conferences are often published as collections of selected and edited papers.

Any national society whose primary activity is in information may apply to become a full member of IFIP, although full membership is restricted to one society per country. Full members are entitled to vote at the annual General Assembly, National societies preferring a less committed involvement may apply for associate or corresponding membership. Associate members enjoy the same benefits as full members, but without voting rights. Corresponding members are not represented in IFIP bodies. Affiliated membership is open to non-national societies, and individual and honorary membership schemes are also offered.

Achieving Quality in Software

Proceedings of the third international conference on achieving quality in software, 1996

Edited by

Sandro Bologna
ENEA CRE Casaccia
Rome
Italy

and

Giacomo Bucci
University of Florence
Florence
Italy

SPRINGER-SCIENCE+BUSINESS MEDIA, B.V.

First edition 1996

Originally published by Chapman & Hall in 1996
MyCopy version of the original edition 1996

DOI 10.1007/978-0-387-34869-8

A catalogue record for this book is available from the British Library

∞ Printed on permanent acid-free text paper, manufactured in accordance with ANSI/NISO Z39.48-1992 and ANSI/NISO Z39.48-1984 (Permanence of Paper).
www.springer.com/mycopy

CONTENTS

FOREWORD

Software quality is a generalised statement difficult to agree or disagree with until a precise definition of the concept of "Software Quality" is reached in terms of measurable quantities. Unfortunately, for the software technology the basic question of:

- what to measure;
- how to measure;
- when to measure;
- how to deal with the data obtained

are still unanswered and are also closely dependant on the field of application.

In the past twenty years or more there have been a number of conferences and debates focusing on the concept of Software Quality, which produced no real industrial impact. Recently, however, the implementation of a few generic standards (ISO 9000, IEEE etc.) has produced and improved application of good practice principles at the industrial level. As a graduate in Physics, I still believe it is a long way before the concept of Software Quality can be defined exactly and measured, if ever.

This is way I think the AQuIS series of conferences is important, its object begin to provide a platform for the transfer of technology and know how between Academic, Industrial and Research Institutions, in the field of Software Quality. Their objects are:

- to provide a forum for the introduction and discussion of new research breakthroughs in Software Quality;
- to provide professional Software Quality engineers with the necessary exposure to the results of current research;
- to expose the research community to the problems of practical application of new results.

In line with the general trend in the area of Software Quality, AQuIS'96 as many other conferences focus on the aspects of quality modelling, quality measurements and process improvement. What we believe is new, and important, is the attempt to investigate:

- potential relations between conventional software systems quality and knowledge-based system quality;
- the impact of formal methods to software quality;
- the impact of object-oriented approach to software quality

Of course we do not pretend to provide an answer to all these issues but we hope at least to encourage further motivation to participate in AQuIS'96 and enjoy reading their proceedings.

Last but not least I want to thank all, who have devoted their work to AQuIS'96 and made it possible to prepare this volume.

The Program Chair
Sandro Bologna

GENERAL CHAIR'S MESSAGE

AQuIS '96 is the third in series of international conferences on "Achieving Quality in Software". AQuIS has been established by Qualital and IEI-CNR in the aim of providing a forum in which theoretical and practical results in the field of software quality could be discussed and compared.
Previous AQuIS conferences have been held in Pisa (1991) and in Venice (1993).

There are many factors that contribute to the success of a conference, the quality of the program being the first. The program includes three invited paper by three leading software quality experts, plus twenty-eight contributed papers presented by authors belonging to Europe, USA and Japan.
These papers cover areas ranging from Formal Methods to Process Improvement, thus providing a significant picture of the state-of-art in software quality.
For the first time a session is dedicated to the quality of Knowledge-Based Systems (KBS).
In structuring the program we deliberately avoided parallel sessions, to favour discussion and interaction among the attendees.

I wish to acknowledge all the authors who have submitted their papers to AQuIS '96 and the large number of anonymous referees as well as the members of the Program Committee.
I wish to thank Qualital, IEI-CNR and CESVIT for their support in organising the conference. CESVIT deserves a special acknowledgement for the constant support it has provided in solving the big and the little problems that are brought about by the organisation of an international conference.
In this sense, I greatly appreciated the dedication of Maurizio Campanai and Silvia Lucci, and the work they have done to make the conference successful.
I also acknowledge IFIP, the sponsor of AQuIS '96, all the co-sponsors and the supporting organisations.

It is with great pleasure that I welcome in Florence all AQuIS '96 participants. After all, the choice of this town should be a further factor making the conference successful.

The Conference Chair
Giacomo Bucci

CONFERENCE COMMITTEE

General Chair
Giacomo Bucci, U. of Florence - I
Program Chair
Sandro Bologna, ENEA - I
Program co-Chairs
Motoei Azuma, Waseda U. - Japan
Edward Miller, Software Research - USA
Program Committee

V.	*Ambriola*	*Italy*	*M. Giromini*	*Italy*
P.	*Ancilotti*	*Italy*	*R. Glass*	*USA*
P.	*Asirelli*	*Italy*	*J. Hemsley*	*UK*
G.	*Bazzana*	*Italy*	*B. Henderson-Sellers*	*AUS*
A.	*Bertolino*	*Italy*	*B. Lepape*	*Belgium*
F.	*Brito e Abreu*	*Portugal*	*P. Meseguer*	*Spain*
M.	*Campanai*	*Italy*	*P. Nesi*	*Italy*
A.	*Davis*	*USA*	*S. Nocentini*	*Italy*
C.	*Debou*	*Austria*	*M. Pivka*	*Slovenia*
G.	*Di Lucca*	*Italy*	*A. Preece*	*UK*
G.	*Dipoppa*	*Italy*	*St. Robinson*	*UK*
W.	*Ehrenberger*	*BRD*	*T. Rout*	*AUS*
N.	*Fenton*	*UK*	*J. Souquieres*	*France*
K.	*Fruhauf*	*CH*	*T. Stålhane*	*Norway*
T.	*Furuyama*	*Japan*	*J. Tepandi*	*UES*
M.	*Fusani*	*Italy*		

Organization Chair
Piero De Risi, QUALITAL - I

Organizing Committee

A	*Facchini*	*CESVIT - I*
O.	*Morales*	*CESVIT - I*
M.	*Traversi*	*CESVIT - I*
C.	*Franceschi*	*QUALITAL - I*
V.	*Lami*	*IEI, CNR - I*

Scientific Conference Secretariat
S. Lucci CESVIT - I

General Conference Secretariat
C. Franceschi QUALITAL - I

PART ONE

Invited Papers

Evolving and Packaging Reading Technologies

V.R. Basili
Department of Computer Science
and Institute for Advanced Computer Studies
University of Maryland, College Park, MD 20742 U.S.A.
(301)405-2668, (301)405-6707 FAX, basili@cs.umd.edu

Abstract

Reading is a fundamental technology for achieving quality software. This paper provides a motivation for reading as a quality improvement technology, based upon experiences in the Software Engineering Laboratory at NASA Goddard Space Flight Center and shows the evolution of our study of reading via a series of experiments. The experiments range from the early reading vs. testing experiments to various Cleanroom experiments that employed reading to the development of new reading technologies currently under study.

Keywords

Reading scenarios, cleanroom, experiments, inspections, quality improvement paradigm

1. INTRODUCTION

Reading is a fundamental technology for achieving quality software. It is the only analysis technology we can use throughout the entire life cycle of the software development and maintenance processes. And yet, very little attention has been paid to the technologies that underlie the reading of software documents. For example where is "software reading" taught? What technologies have been developed for "software reading"? In fact, what is "software reading"?

During most of our lives, we learned to read before we learned to write. Reading formed a model for writing. This was true from our first learning of a language (reading precedes writing and provides simple models for writing) to our study of the great literature (reading provides us with models of how to write well). Yet, in the software domain, we never learned to read, e.g., we learn to write programs in a programming language, but never learn how to read them. We have not developed reading-based models for writing.

For example, we are not conscious of our audience when we write a requirements document. How will they read it? What is the difference between reading a requirements document and reading a code document? We all know that one reads a novel differently than one reads a text book. We know that we review a technical paper differently than we review a newspaper article. But how do we read a requirements document, how do we read a code document, how do we read a test plan?

But first let us define some terms so that we understand what we mean by "reading". We differentiate a technique from a method, from a life cycle model. A technique is the most primitive, it is an algorithm, a series of steps producing the desired effect. It requires skill. A method is a management procedure for applying techniques, organized by a set of rules stating how and when to apply and when to stop applying the technique (entry and exit criteria), when the technique is appropriate, and how to evaluate it. We will define a technology as a collection of techniques and methods. A life cycle model is a set of methods that covers the entire life cycle of a software product.

For example, reading by step-wise abstraction [Linger, Mills, and Witt, 1979] is a technique for assessing code. Reading by stepwise abstraction requires the development of personal skills; one gets better with practice. A code inspection is a method, that is defined around a reading technique, which has a well defined set of entry and exit criteria and a set of management supports specifying how and when to use the technique. Reading by stepwise abstraction and code inspections together form a technology. Inspections are embedded in a life cycle model, such as the Cleanroom development approach, which is highly dependent on reading techniques and methods. That is, reading technology is fundamental to a Cleanroom development.

In what follows, we will discuss the evolution and packaging of reading as a technology in the Software Engineering Laboratory (SEL) [Basili, Caldiera, McGarry, Pajerski, Page, Waligora, 1992] via a series of experiments from some early reading vs. testing technique experiments, to various Cleanroom experiments, to the development of new reading techniques currently under study.

In the SEL, we have been working with a set of experimental learning approaches: the Quality Improvement Paradigm, the Goal Question Metric Paradigm, the Experience Factory Organization, and various experimental frameworks to evolve our knowledge and the effectiveness of various life cycle models, methods, techniques, and tools [Basili - 1985, Basili and Weiss - 1984, Basili and Rombach - 1988, Basili - 1989]. We have run a series of experiments at the University of Maryland and at NASA to learn about, evaluate, and evolve reading as a technology.

2. READING STUDIES

Figure 1 provides a characterization of various types of experiments we have run in the SEL. They define different scopes of evaluation representing different levels of confidence in the results. They are characterized by the number of teams replicating each project and the number of different projects analyzed yielding four different experimental treatments: blocked subject-project, replicated project, multi-project variation, and single project case study.

The approaches vary in cost, level of confidence in the results, insights gained, and the balance between quantitative and qualitative research methods. Clearly, an analysis of several replicated projects costs more money but provides a better basis for quantitative analysis and can generate stronger statistical confidence in the conclusions. Unfortunately, since a blocked subject-project experiment is so expensive, the projects studied tend to be small. To increase the size of the projects, keep the costs reasonable, and allow us to better simulate the effects of the treatment variables in a realistic environment, we can study very large single project case studies and even multi-project studies if the right environment can be found. These larger projects tend to involve more qualitative analysis along with some more primitive quantitative analysis.

Because of the desire for statistical confidence in the results, the problems with scale up, and the need to test in a realistic environment, one approach to experimentation is to choose one of the multiple team treatments controlled experiments to demonstrate feasibility (statistical significance) in the small, and then to try a case study or multiproject variation to analyze whether the results scale up in a realistic environment - a major problem in studying the effects of techniques, methods and life cycle models.

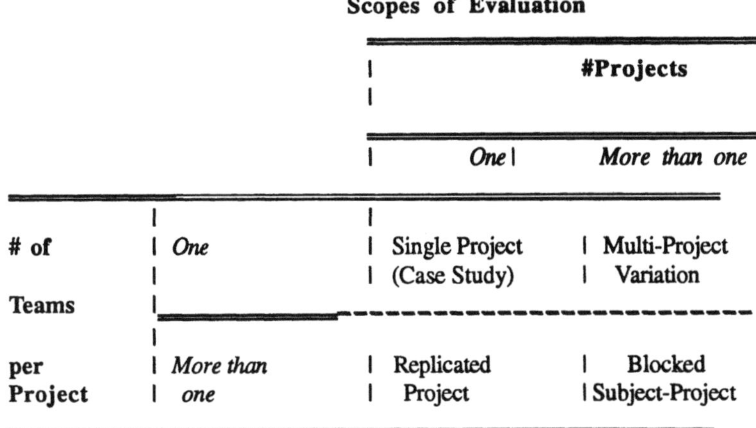

Scopes of Evaluation

		#Projects	
		One	*More than one*
# of Teams per Project	*One*	Single Project (Case Study)	Multi-Project Variation
	More than one	Replicated Project	Blocked Subject-Project

Figure 1: Classes of Studies

2.1 Reading by stepwise abstraction

In order to improve the quality of our software products at NASA, we have studied various approaches. One area of interest was to understand the relationship between reading and testing in our environment. Early experiments showed very little difference between reading and testing [Hetzel - 1972, Myers - 1978]. But reading was simply reading, without a technological base. Thus we attempted to study the differences between various specific technology based approaches. Our goal was to analyze code reading, functional testing and structural testing to evaluate and compare them with respect to their effect on fault detection effectiveness, fault detection cost and classes of faults detected from the viewpoint of quality assurance [Basili, Selby - 1987]. The study was conducted in the SEL, using three different programs: a text formatter, a plotter, and a small database. The programs were seeded with software faults, 9, 6, and 12 faults respectively, and ranged in size from 145 to 365 LOC. The experimental design was a blocked subject-project, using a fractional factorial design. There were 32 subjects.

Specific techniques were used for each of the three approaches studied. Code reading was done by stepwise abstraction, i.e., reading a sequence of statements and abstracting the function they compute and repeating the process until the function of the entire program has been abstracted and can be compared with the specification. Functional testing was performed using boundary value, equivalence partition testing, i.e., dividing the requirements into valid and invalid equivalence classes and making up tests that check the boundaries of the classes. Structural testing: was performed to achieve 100% statement coverage, i.e., making up a set of tests to guarantee that 100% of the statements in the program have been executed.

As a blocked subject-project study, each subject used each technique and tested each program. The results were that code reading found more faults than functional testing, and functional testing found more faults than structural testing. Also, code reading found more faults per unit of time spent than either of the other two techniques.

Other conclusions from the study include the fact that the code readers we better able to assess the actual quality of the code that they read than the testers. And in fact, the structural testers were better able to assess the actual quality of the code they read than the functional testers. That is, the code readers felt they only found about half the defects (and they were right), where the functional testers felt that had found about all the defects (and they were wrong). Also, after the completion of the study over 90% of the participants thought functional testing worked best. This was a case where their intuition was clearly wrong.

Based upon this study, reading was implemented as part of the SEL development process. However, much to our surprise, reading appeared to have very little effect on reducing defects. This lead us to two possible hypotheses:

Hypothesis 1: People did not read as well as they should have as they believed that testing would make up for their mistakes

To test this first hypothesis, we ran an experiment that showed that if you read and cannot test you do a more effective job of reading than if you read and know you can test. This supported hypothesis 1.

Hypothesis 2: There is a confusion between reading as a technique and the method in which it is embedded, e.g., inspections.

This addresses the concern that we often use a reading method (e.g., inspections or walk-throughs) but do not often have a reading technique (e.g., reading by stepwise abstraction) sufficiently defined within the method. To some extent, this might explain the success of our experiment over the ones by Hetzel and Myers.

Thus we derived the following conclusions from the studies to date:

- Reading using a particular technique is more effective and cost effective than specific testing techniques, i.e., the reading technique is important. However, different approaches may be effective for different types of defects.
- Readers needs to be motivated to read better, i.e., the reading motivation is important.
- We may need to better support the reading process, i.e., the reading technique may be different from the reading method.

2.2 The Cleanroom approach

The Cleanroom approach, as proposed by Harlan Mills [Currit, Dyer, Mills - 1986], seemed to cover a couple of these issues, so we tried a controlled experiment at the University of Maryland to study the effects of the approach.

The goal of this study was to analyze the Cleanroom process in order to evaluate and compare it to a non-Cleanroom process with respect to the effects on the process, product and developers [Selby, Basili, Baker - 1987]. This study was conducted using upper division and graduate students at the University of Maryland. The problem studied was an electronic message system of about 1500 LOC. The experimental design was a replicated project, 15 three-person teams (10 used Cleanroom). They were allowed 3 to 5 test submissions to an independent tester. We collected data on the participants' background, attitudes, on-line activities, and testing results.

The major results were:

- With regard to process, the Cleanroom developers (1) felt they more effectively applied off-line review techniques, while others focused on functional testing, (2) spent less time on-line and used fewer computer resources, and (3) tended to make all their scheduled deliveries
- With regard to the delivered product, the Cleanroom products tended to have the

following static properties: less dense complexity, higher percentage of assignment statements, more global data, more comments, and the following operational properties: the products more completely met the requirements and a higher percentage of test cases succeeded.
- With regard to the effect on the developers, most Cleanroom developers missed program execution, modified their development style, but said they would use the Cleanroom approach again.

2.3 Cleanroom in the SEL

Based upon this success, we decided to try the Cleanroom approach in the SEL [Basili and Green - 1994]. This was the basis for a case study and we used the Quality Improvement Paradigm to set up our learning process. The QIP consists of 6 steps and we define them here relative to the use of Cleanroom:

<u>Characterize:</u> What are the relevant models, baselines and measures? What are the existing processes? What is the standard cost, relative effort for activities, reliability? What are the high risk areas? (Figure 2)
<u>Set goals:</u> What are the expectations, relative to the baselines? What do we hope to learn, gain, e.g., Cleanroom with respect to changing requirements? (Figure 2)
<u>Choose process:</u> How should the Cleanroom process be modified and tailored relative to the environment? E.g., formal methods hard to apply, require skill; may have insufficient data to measure reliability. Allow back-out options for unit testing certain modules.
<u>Execute:</u> Collect and analyze data based upon the goals, making changes to the process in real time.
<u>Analyze:</u> Try to characterize and understand what happened relative to the goals; write lessons learned.
<u>Package:</u> Modify the process for future use.

There were many lessons learned during this first application of the Cleanroom approach in the SEL. However, the most relevant to reading were that the failure rate during test was reduced by 25% and productivity increased by about 30%, mostly due to fact that there was a reduction in the rework effort, i.e., 95% as opposed to 58% of the faults took less than 1 hour to fix. About 50% of code time was spent reading, as opposed to the normal 10%. All code was read by 2 developers. However, even though the developers were taught reading by stepwise abstraction for code reading, only 26% of the faults were found by both readers. This implied to us that the reading technique was not applied as effectively as it should have been, as we expected a more consistent reading result.

During this case study, problems, as specified by the users, were recorded and the process was modified.

Based upon the success of the first Cleanroom case study, we began to define new experiments with the goal of applying the reading technique more effectively. The project leader for first project became process modeler for the next two and we began to generate the evolved version of the SEL Cleanroom Process Model. Thus we moved our experimental paradigm from a case study to a multi-project analysis study. Figure 3 gives an overview of the projects studied to date. A fourth project has just been completed but the results have not yet been analyzed.

Cleanroom has been successful in the SEL. Although there is still some room for improvement in reading and abstracting code formally, a more major concern is the lack of techniques for reading various documents reading, most specifically, requirements documents. This provided our motivation for the continual evolution of reading techniques both inside and outside the Cleanroom life cycle model. Specific emphasis is on improving reading technology for requirements and design documents.

	Sample Measures	Sample Baseline	Sample Expectation
PROCESS	Effort distribution Change profile	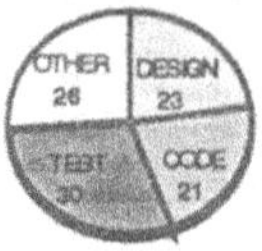 OTHER 26, DESIGN 23, CODE 21, TEST 30	Increased design % due to emphasis on peer review process
COST	Productivity Level of rework Impact of spec changes	Historically, 26 DLOC per day	No degradation from current level
RELIABILITY	Error rate Error distribution Error source	Historically, 7 errors per KDLOC	Decreased error rate

Figure 2: Sample Measures, Baselines, and Expectations

Technology Evaluation Steps	Off-line Reading Technology Controlled Experiment	Off-line Cleanroom Controlled Experiment	SEL Cleanroom Case Study 1	SEL Cleanroom Case Study 2	
				project 2A	project 2B
Team Size	32 individual participants	3-person development teams (10 Cleanroom teams, 5 control teams)	3-person development team, 2-person test team	4-person development team, 2-person test team	14-person development team, 4-person test team
Project Size and Application	small (145-365 LOC) sample FORTRAN programs	1500 LOC electronic message system for graduate lab course	40 KDLOC FORTRAN flight dynamics production system	22 KDLOC FORTRAN flight dynamics production system	160 KDLOC FORTRAN flight dynamics production system
Results	*reading techniques appear more effective than testing techniques for fault detection*	*Cleanroom teams use fewer computer resources, satisfy requirements more successfully, make higher percentage of scheduled deliveries*	*project spends higher percentage of effort in design, uses fewer computer resources, achieves better productivity and reliability than environment baseline*	*project continues trend in better reliability while maintaining baseline productivity*	*project reliability only slightly better than baseline while productivity falls below baseline*

Figure 3. Multi-Project Analysis Study of Cleanroom in the SEL

The experiments to date convinced us that reading is a key, if not ***the*** key technical activity for verifying and validating software work products. However, there has been little research focus on the development of reading techniques, with the possible exception of reading by stepwise abstraction, as developed by Harlan Mills.

The ultimate goal here is to understand the best way to read for a particular set of conditions. That is, we are not only interested in how to develop techniques for reading such documents as requirements documents, but under what conditions are each of the techniques most effective and how might they be combined in a method such as inspections to provide a more effective reading technology for the particular problem and environment.

The idea is to provide a flexible framework for defining the reading technology so that the definer of the technology for a particular project has the appropriate information for selecting the right techniques and method characteristics. Thus, the process definition will change depending on the project characteristics. For example, if the problem and solution are well understood, we might choose a waterfall process model; if a high number of omission faults are expected, we might emphasize a traceability reading approach embedded in design inspections; when embedding a traceability reading in design inspections, we might make sure a traceability matrix exists.

As stated in the introduction, we believe there are many factors that affect the way a person reads, e.g., the reviewer's role, the reading goals, the work product. Based upon these studies, we also believe that (1) techniques can be developed that will allow us better define how we should read, and (2) using these techniques, effectively embedded in the appropriate methods, can improve the effects of reading. For example, end-users read software requirements differently than do software testers, developers read for interface defects differently than they read for missing initialization. The more I know about what kinds of defects each of the views is most effective in tracking, the better I am able to promote and manipulate that kind of reading technique in the method I am using.

We need to improve the reading of all kinds of documents and more deeply understand the relationship between techniques and methods and the dimensions of both. For example, consider the following dimensions of a reading technique:

Input object: Requirements, specification, design, code, test plan,...
Output object: set of anomalies
Approach: Sequential, path analysis, stepwise abstraction, ...
Formality: Reading, correctness demonstrations, ...
Emphasis: Fault detection, traceability, performance, ...
Method: Walk-throughs, inspections, reviews, ...
Consumers: User, designer, tester, maintainer, ...
Product qualities: Correctness, reliability, efficiency, portability,..
Process qualities: Adherence to method, integration into process,...
Quality view: Assurance, control, ...

We have spent some energy trying to develop and evaluate reading techniques based upon the dimension and historical data. The goal is to define a set of reading technologies that can be tailored to the document being read and the goals of the organization for that document. The technology should be usable in existing methods, such as inspections.

2.4 Scenario-Based Reading

We have defined an approach to generating a family of reading techniques. It consists of building operational scenarios based upon combining two dimensions of the technique. An operational scenario requires the reader to (1) create an abstraction of the product (based on one dimension) (2) answer questions based on the abstraction (based on another dimension). The choice of abstraction and the types of questions asked may depend on the document being read, the problem history of the organization or the goals of the organization. The scenarios try to take advantage of the dimensions of a technique (Figure 4).

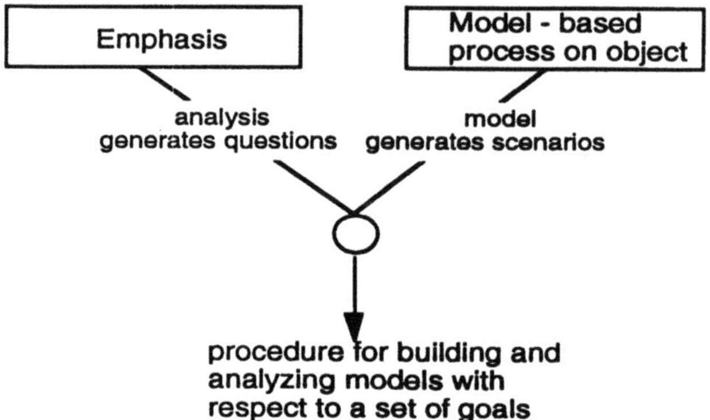

Figure 4. Building Focused Tailored Reading Techniques

Two different reading techniques, within the family, have been defined for requirements documents: defect based reading and perspective based reading

For our study, defect based reading was defined for reading SCR style documents. Defect based reading focuses on modeling different defect classes, creating three different scenarios based upon the data type consistency, safety properties, and ambiguity/missing information. The analysis questions were generated by combining/abstracting a set of checklist questions for requirements documents.

For our study, perspective based reading was defined for reading natural language requirements documents. Perspective-based reading focuses on different product customer perspectives, e.g., reading from the perspective of the software designer, the tester, or the end-user. The analysis questions were generated by focussing predominantly on various requirements type errors, e.g., incorrect fact, omission, ambiguity, and inconsistency.

To provide a little more detail into scenarios in general, and perspective based reading reading in particular, consider as an example, test-based reading.

Reading Procedure: For each requirement, make up a test or set of tests that will allow you to ensure that the implementation satisfies the requirement. Use your standard test approach and test criteria to make up the test suite. While making up your test suite for each requirement, ask yourself the following questions:

1. Do you have all the information necessary to identify the item being tested and to identify your test criteria? Can you make up reasonable test cases for each item based upon the criteria?
2. Is there another requirement for which you would generate a similar test case but would get a contradictory result?
3. Can you be sure the test you generated will yield the correct value in the correct units?
4. Are there other interpretations of this requirement that the implementor might make based upon the way the requirement is defined? Will this effect the test you made up?
5. Does the requirement make sense from what you know about the application and from

what is specified in the general description?

Each of the techniques aims at being (1) associated with the particular document (e.g., requirements) and notation (e.g., English text) in which the document is written, (2) tailorable, based upon the project and environment characteristics (3) detailed, in that it provides the reader a well-defined set of steps to follow, (4) specific, in that the reader has a particular purpose or goal for reading the document and the procedures support that goal, (5) focused, in that a particular technique provides a particular coverage of the document, and a combination of techniques provides coverage of the entire document, (6) studied empirically to determine if and when it is most effective.

Each of the techniques has been studied experimentally. The first series of experiments are aimed at discovering if scenario based reading is more effective than current practices. A second series will be used to discover under which circumstances each of the various scenario based reading techniques is most effective.

In the defect-based reading study, the goal was to analyze defect-based reading, ad-hoc reading and check-list based reading to evaluate and compare them with respect to their effect on fault detection effectiveness in the context of an inspection team from the viewpoint of quality assurance. The study was applied using graduate students at the University of Maryland. The requirements documents were written in the SCR notation. They were a water Level Monitoring System and a Cruise Control System. The experimental design is a blocked subject-project: Partial factorial design, replicated twice with a total of 48 subjects [Porter, Votta, Basili - 1995].

Major results were that (1) the defect-based readers performed better than ad hoc and checklist readers with an improvement of about 35%, (2) the defect-based reading procedures helped reviewers focus on specific fault classes but were no less effective at detecting other faults, and (3) checklist reading was no more effective than ad hoc reading.

Perspective-based reading is currently under study. The goal for the perspective-based reading evaluation was to analyze perspective-based reading, NASA's current reading technique to evaluate and compare them with respect to their effect on fault detection effectiveness in the context of an inspection team from the viewpoint of quality assurance. Two studies have been performed in the SEL environment using generic requirements documents written in English (ATM machine, Parking Garage) and NASA type functional specifications (Two ground support AGSS sub-systems). The experimental design is again a blocked subject-project using a partial factorial design. It has been applied twice, with a total of 25 subjects [Basili, Green, Laitenberger, Schull, Sorumgaard - 1995].

Preliminary indications for perspective based reading are also positive. Where there is any statistical significance, perspective-based reading appears to be more effective in uncovering defects and teams consisting of perspective based readers appear to do better than the standard reading techniques used.

3. CONCLUSION

Defect-based reading has been evaluated in experiments and has so far been shown to be superior to existing current practices. Perspective-based reading is being evaluated in experiments and the results so far appear promising.

Specifically we have run the experimental gamut from blocked subject-project experiments (reading vs. testing) to replicated projects (University of Maryland Cleanroom study) to a cased study (the first SEL Cleanroom study) to multi-project variation (the set of SEL Cleanroom projects) and now back to blocked subject project experiments (for scenario based reading). See Figure 5.

Scopes of Evaluation

		#Projects	
		One	*More than one*
# of Teams per Project	*One*	3. Cleanroom (SEL Project 1)	4. Cleanroom (SEL Projects, 2,3,4, ...
	More than one	2. Cleanroom at Maryland	1. Reading vs. Testing 5. Scenario Reading vs. ...

Figure 5. Series of Studies

In the future, we plan to replicate these experiments in many different environments. Various groups at different sites are already replicating some of the earlier experiments. Most of these are members of ISERN, the International Software Engineering Research Network, whose goal is specifically to perform and share the results of empirical studies.

We will continue to develop operational scenario reading techniques (e.g., design reading, etc.) and test their effectiveness in experiments. Future work also includes the consideration of tool support for the technologies developed.

4. REFERENCES

Basili, V.R. (1985) Quantitative Evaluation of Software Methodology, Keynote Address, *First Pan Pacific Computer Conference*, Melbourne, Australia.

Basili, V.R. (1989) Software Development: A Paradigm for the Future, *COMPSAC '89*, Orlando, Florida, pp.471-485.

Basili, V.R., Caldiera, G., McGarry, F., Pajersky, R., Page, G., Waligora, S. (1992) The Software Engineering Laboratory--An Operational Software Experience Factory, *14th International Conference on Software Engineering*, Melbourne, Australia.

Basili, V.R. and Green, S. (1994) Software Process Evolution at the SEL, *IEEE Software*, pp 58-66.

Basili, V.R., Green, S., Laitenberger, O.U., Schull, F. and Sorumgaard, S. (1995) To be published) The Empirical Investigation of Perspective-Based Reading (in progress).

Basili, V.R. and Rombach, H.D. (1988) The TAME Project: Towards Improvement-Oriented Software Environments, *IEEE Transactions on Software Engineering*, vol.14, no.6.

Basili, V.R. and Selby, R. (1987) Comparing the Effectiveness of Software Testing Strategies, *IEEE Transactions on Software Engineering*, pp.1278-1296.

Basili, V.R. and Weiss, D.M. (1984) A Methodology for Collecting Valid Software Engineering Data, *IEEE Transactions on Software Engineering*, pp.728-738.

Currit, P.A., Dyer, M. and Mills, H.D. (1986) Certifying the Reliability of Software, *IEEE Transactions on Software Engineering*, vol.SE-12, pp. 3-11.

Hetzel, W.C. (1972) An Experimental Analysis of Program Verification Problem Solving Capabilities as They Relate to Programmer Efficiency, *Computer Personnel*, vol.3, pp.10-15.

Linger, R.C., Mills, H.D. and Witt, B.I. (1979) *Structured Programming: Theory and practice*, Reading, MA: Addison-Wesley.

Myers, G.J. (1978) A Controlled Experiment in Program Testing and Code Walkthroughs Inspections, *Communications ACM*, pp.760-768.

Porter, A.A., Votta, L.G. and Basili, V.R. (1995) Comparing Detection Methods for Software Requirements Inspections: A Replicated Experiment, *IEEE Transactions on Software Engineering*, vol.21, no.6, pp.563-575.

Selby, R., Basili, V.R. and Baker, T. (1987) Cleanroom Software Development: An Empirical Evaluation, *IEEE Transactions on Software Engineering*, pp 1027-1037.

2

Analysis of fault generation caused by stress during software development

Tsuneo FURUYAMA, Yoshio ARAI, and Kazuhiko IIO
NTT Software Laboratories
9-11, Midori-cho 3-chome, Musashino-shi, Tokyo 180, Japan
Tel. +81-422-59-2540 Fax. +81-422-59-3712 E-mail: furuyama@slab.ntt.jp

Abstract
The effects of stress on fault generation in both structured and functional design methodologies were quantitatively determined through a controlled experiment. Two teams developed the same software program under the same stressed conditions, except for design methodologies. The degree of stress was measured by inner metrics we proposed (Furuyama, 1994-b). The results of the analysis show that (1) the generation rate of faults caused by mental stress of the team who developed a software program using functional design methodology was higher than that of the other team, which used structured design methodology; (2) among the faults caused by human nature, many seemed to be correlated to stress at higher stress levels, so that faults caused by stress were considered to be generated by developers much more than they reported them; and (3) physical stress could generate faults at a higher rate than mental stress when it appeared even for a short period, independent of design methodology.

Keywords
Quality improvement, Fault analysis, Quantitative quality evaluation, Mental stress, Physical stress, Stress metrics, Design methodology, Software engineering

1 INTRODUCTION

Estimating and improving reliability is one of the most important areas in software development management. In the early history of software development, techniques for detecting and eliminating faults during the test phase and estimating the remaining faults were important. Later, the importance of estimating and improving reliability during the design phase was recognized. Design review techniques, such as formal inspection, were developed and became widely used in actual software development.

The purpose of these techniques, however, is to detect and eliminate existing faults and to estimate the remaining faults. A more effective approach to improving reliability would be to prevent faults during the early stages of development. One proposed way to reduce faults is to decrease software complexity, which is a significant factor in fault generation (Basili, 1984 and Takahashi, 1984). In this approach, however, human factors are generally not explicitly considered because it is difficult to measure and analyze human behavior.

Human factors have been discussed in the area of mechanical engineering for a long time as one of the major influences on system reliability. However, most research into human error has focused on operational aspects (Reason, 1987 and Lee, 1988). Among them, Rasmussen et al., in their distinguished work, used cognitive science techniques in their model and produced a comprehensive framework to describe the mechanisms behind the cause of human errors (Rasmussen, 1987).

In the area of software development, however, human factors have been little discussed, despite the fact that human factors seem to affect software reliability, and it is therefore important to develop methods that minimize the impact of human factors to improve reliability.

Nakajo and Kume, in their systematic description, stated briefly that fault generation is the result of human factors, that is, human misunderstandings as well as the circumstances in which faults are likely occur and the generation of faults is related to the system interface or system functions. However, their fault generation model does not clearly define such factors as the mental state of the programmer, making it difficult to draw conclusions regarding the prevention of faults.

One of the reasons that clarifying the effect of human factors during software development is so difficult is that they are concerned only with human thought, which, unlike mechanical operations, is invisible and hence difficult to measure.

To clarify the effect of human factors during software development, we first proposed a fault generation model (Figure 1) for software development taking human factors into consideration, based on our interviews with developers (Furuyama, 1994-a). Then, we estimated that about a third of the generated faults could have been avoided by identifying the factors causing them and removing those factors. Our finding was that mental stress greatly affects fault generation.

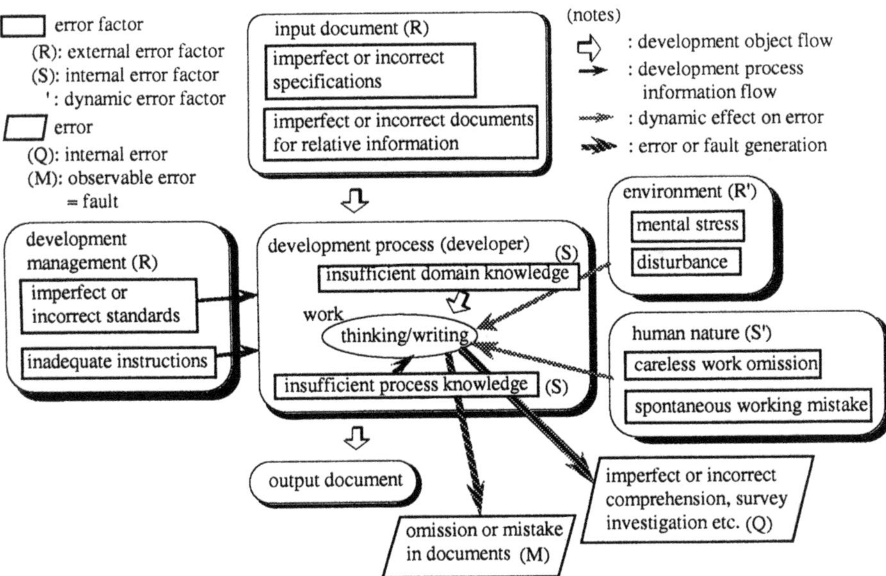

Figure 1 Abstract Model of Fault Generation (modefied from Furuyama, 1994-a).

Software developer stress factors such as short development times were earlier researched by Fujigaki, based on questionnaires sent to software specialists and her analysis of developer dialogs during the design phase (Fujigaki, 1992). However, her data included many factors that could not be clearly separated, making it difficult to isolate the effects of stress on fault generation.

Next, we conducted controlled development experiments to isolate and measure quantitatively the mental stress effect on fault generation, developing metrics that measure mental stress easily and objectively in actual software development. Two teams developed software based on the same specifications under nearly the same circumstances, except for mental stress. The team skill levels were nearly equal. Our 'inner stress metrics' system was used by the developers to report their mental conditions in predefined formats. These metrics were collected every day. The results of our analysis showed that this metric system is effective for predicting how many faults might be generated according to the mental stress level (Furuyama, 1994-b).

Takahashi, et. al. compared the data obtained from two teams developing the same software but using different design methodologies, and found that the software reliability of the team using structured design methodology was higher than that of the team using functional design methodology (Takahashi, 1995). However, in their experiment, no consideration was given to the development environment, especially to the mental and physical stress which usually occur in an actual development environment.

To clarify further details of the effect of stress, not only mental but also physical, on software development -- in particular, the difference between design methodologies -- we again carefully designed the controlled experiment with the aim of quantitatively determining the difference of stress effect on fault generation between design methodologies.

2 EXPERIMENT

In our experiment, two teams developed the same software under the same mental stress conditions, except for design methodologies. During the development process, the degree of the developers' mental and physical stress, the number of generated faults and their characteristics, and general working condition data were collected every day. The experiments were designed so that such factors as developer skill and work environment were nearly the same for both teams.

2.1 Outline of development

System developed

The system each team developed was a 'library management system' to support such functions as searching, lending, returning, and registering libraries. The program size was about 5 KLOC in C language.

Design methodologies

Two different methodologies were examined, functional design and structured design. Table 1 compares the two methodologies. Their main differences are as follows.

(a) In the functional design phase, the functional design team was required to make only functional specifications narratively described, while the structured design team was additionally required to produce more rigorously structured documents, such as data flow and data structure diagrams. These additional documents required much efforts though their volume was smaller than that of the functional specifications.

(b) In the detail design phase, the functional design team was required to make only a module structure chart, while the structured design team was additionally required to produce a structure chart showing data flow between modules. Both teams were required to produce a Hierarchical Compact (HCP) chart.

Team organization
Each team consisted of two developers, who were instructed to design the system collaboratively, except for the documentation, within each team. To minimize the differences between both teams in terms of development ability and skill, the developer with the highest development skill and the developer with the lowest were assigned to one team (Team A), which used functional design methodology, and the two intermediate-skill developers were assigned to the other (Team B), which used structured design methodology.

Though both teams had experience in functional design methodology, Team B had no experience in structured design methodology. Therefore, Team B received training in that methodology.

Table 1 Comparison of products between the two methodologies

Phase	*Functional Design Methodology*	*Structured Design Methodology*
FD	Functional design document	Functional design document
	-	Data flow diagram
	-	Data structure diagram
DD	Module structure chart	Module structure chart with data flow between modules
	HCP chart	HCP chart

Work environment
To equalize the physical development circumstances and to avoid team interactions, the teams were placed in separate rooms with nearly the same space, lighting, and noise level. The developers were forbidden to speak with the members of other teams about the development work.

Table 2 Development efforts

Phase	*Team A* *(mon-hours)*	*Team B* *(mon-hours)*
FD	119	192
FD review	98	70
DD	250	321
DD review	100	59
M/DB	180	158
Total	747	800

Development schedule
The total development time was about three months. Based on the report that design time between the two design methodologies varies (Oka, 1993), we determined the standard design schedules of the two teams such that the schedule of Team B was longer than that of Team A by 50% in the functional design (FD) phase and by 30% in the detail design (DD) phase respectively. Table 2 shows the actual development efforts of both teams.

2.2 Creation and measurement of mental stress

Creation of mental stress
During the software development, stress factors in terms of 'work contents' such as schedule pressure and too much work are the major factors (Fujigaki, 1992, Furuyama, 1994-a and Furuyama, 1994-b). To analyze the effects of these factors in detail, the following stresses were given to both teams during both the FD phase and DD phase:

- Design time was reduced by 30% less than the standard schedule, and
- Specification changes were imposed three times in both design phases.

Metrics for mental stress

Stress is generally measured physiologically (by electroencephalograph, electrocardiogram, heart rate, respiration volume), biochemistrically (by catechol amine in urine or in blood), and psychologically (by subjects' answers to questions about stress-related conditions). Among these measurement metrics, psychological metrics are effective and easily applied to actual software development. In particular, the 'schedule pressure' metric was the most effective for detecting the degree of mental stress, and the 'workload' metric had the highest correlation coefficient to the number of stress-caused faults (Furuyama, 1994-b). Based on these results, these metrics were selected for measuring the degree of mental stress of all developers in this experiment.

Metrics for physical stress

Besides mental stress, another type of stress directly affects developers' intellectual conditions and therefore leads to fault generation. For example, catching a cold lowers developer working efficiency. To analyze the effect of this type of stress, a 'physical condition' metric was also selected to measure physical stress. Since other types of physical conditions such as fatigue caused by overwork seemed to be correlated to mental stress, we did not identify them as separate physical metrics.

Measurement of stress

Metrics values from -6 to +6 were recorded by the developers themselves at the end of their work every day in a questionnaire (Figure 2), though the scale endpoints in the previous experiment were at -5 to +5.

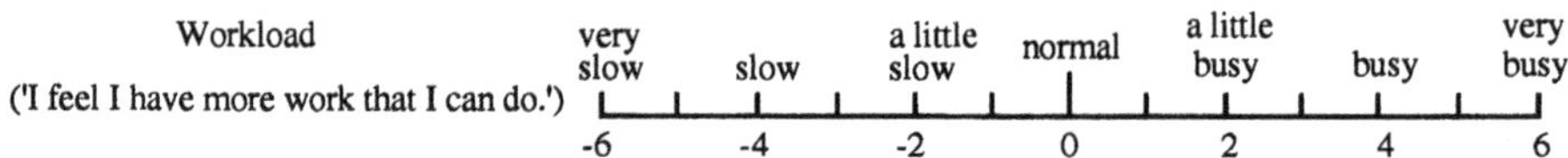

Figure 2 Example of stress questionnaire item.

2.3 Recording works and fault report

All developers recorded their work in detail in daily work diaries so that all faults detected could be easily tracked and the moment and the causes of fault generation could be accurately identified from the fault phenomena.

The faults report recorded fault occurrences, the error factors causing the faults, and the fault generation date. It also recorded the stress metric values so that the relationships between the error factors and the stress metrics could be easily discerned. Faults detected during design were counted, as well as those detected during design review and testing. Spelling mistakes were excluded.

3 RESULTS

3.1 Degree of stress

Figure 3 shows the degree of mental and physical stress of all developers measured with 'schedule pressure,' 'workload,' and 'physical condition' metrics. All metrics values were equal to zero when developers felt no stress, such as a few days before starting this experimental project. We assumed that the same metric values among developers means that they were loaded with the same degree of stress.

Table 3 shows the result of the F-test of mean stress level between the two teams.

Analysis of the results as shown in Figure 3 and Table 3 leads to the following conclusions.
(a) On the whole, both teams suffered from the same level of stress during the FD phase.
(b) Team A suffered from much more stress than Team B during the DD phase, but if developer B2, whose stress level was significantly lower than others, is excluded, stress levels of both teams become equal.
(c) Only developer A2 and developer B2 were suffering from poor health during both the FD and the DD phase.

Table 4 shows the correlation coefficients between all three metrics values. From Table 4, the following conclusion is also obtained.
(d) Two mental stress metric values were highly correlated to each other, while physical metric values had little correlation to either of the mental stress metrics values, as we assumed in 2.2.2.

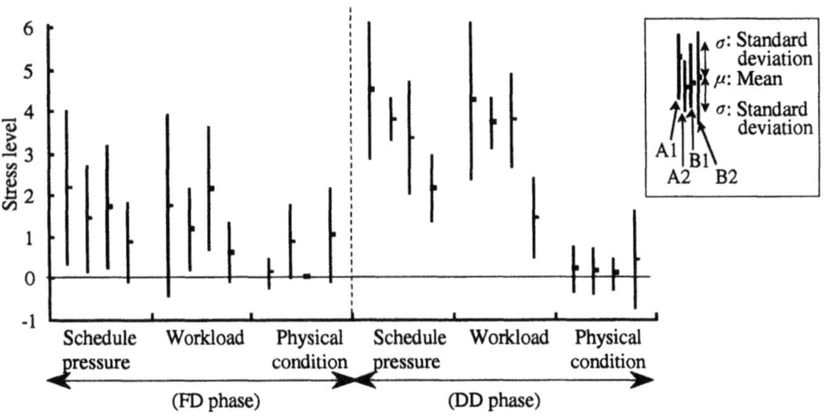

Figure 3 Stress metrics values.

Table 3 F-test of mental stress metrics between Team A and Team B

		Team A			*Team B*				
Phase	*Stress Metrics*	*Mean*	*Variance*	*Points*	*Mean*	*Variance*	*Points*	*d.f.*	*t*
FD	Schedule pressure	1.81	2.544	32	1.35	1.721	52	56.3	1.39
	Workload	1.47	2.838	32	1.38	1.888	52	55.9	0.24
DD	Schedule pressure	4.16	1.547	62	2.75	1.534	68	126.8	6.48*
	Workload	4.03	1.999	62	2.62	2.449	68	128.0	5.42*

(*) 1% significance

Table 4 Correlation coefficient between three metrics

	Schedule pressure and Workload		*Schedule pressure and Physical condition*		*Workload and Physical condition*	
Developer	*FD phase*	*DD phase*	*FD phase*	*DD pahse*	*FD phase*	*DD pahse*
A1	0.98*	0.92*	--	--	--	--
A2	0.95*	0.86*	--	--	--	--
B1	0.85*	0.81*	--	0.36**	--	--
B2	0.77*	0.72*	--	0.71*	0.48**	0.62*

(*) 1% significance, (**) 5% significance

3.2 Fault classification

Generated faults were classified into those caused by static factors and those caused by dynamic factors due to human error, or 'dynamic error factors' for short, as shown Figure 1, based on the fault reports in which error factors of all faults had been determined by developers. The former consists of faults caused by inadequate input documents, such as imperfect or incorrect input specifications (*what* to be developed); by inadequate development management, such as imperfect or incorrect work standards (*how* to develop); and by developers' lack of knowledge needing supplementation when designing software. The dynamic error factors consist of faults caused by stress, and faults caused by human nature.

The faults were classified according to the following priority: faults caused by static factors > faults caused by stress > faults caused by human nature. For example, if a fault apparently resulted from incorrect specifications, it was classified into 'faults caused by static factors,' regardless of the level of stress conditions. Similarly, if a fault was apparently caused by strong stress conditions, it was classified into 'faults caused by stress,' even if the developer overlooked a necessary part of his work because of his overconfidence -- a human nature error. Therefore, 'faults caused by human nature' can be said to be those whose error factors are not necessarily clear.

3.3 Generated faults

Table 5 shows the distribution of the fault generation patterns classified according to the two teams (two design methodologies), development phases, and fault-causing error factors. Since only four faults were considered to be caused by physical conditions, we decided to analyze them separately in detail (discussed later in 4.3) and excluded them from Table 5.

Table 5 Distribution of fault generation patterns

	FD phase			*DD phase*		
Error Factors	*Team A*	*Team B*	*Total*	*Team A*	*Team B*	*Total*
Static	14	15	29	8	13	21
Stress	20	14	34	85	42	127
Human nature	22	15	37	10	23	33
total	56	44	100	103	78	181

General trends of the generated faults were as follows.

Difference between teams and between design phases

(a) Both teams generated twice as many faults during the DD phase as during the FD phase.

(b) The number of faults generated by Team B (the structured design team) was less than that of Team A (the functional design team) by about 30% during both the FD and the DD phase (A : B = 53 : 40 during the FD phase and 103 : 78 during the DD phase). This will be discussed in detail in 4.1.

Faults caused by static factors

(c) No statistical significance was found between the two design methodologies in terms of faults caused by static factors generated during the FD phase (A : B = 14 : 15). Though there is little statistical significance between them (8: 13) in the kind of faults during the DD phase, the main reason that Team B generated more faults than Team A was their inexperience with the HCP chart used during the DD phase compared to Team A, and the HCP chart was considered to be a problem specific to Team B.

(d) In both teams, most of the faults caused by static factors were due to lack of domain knowledge in the FD phase (A : B = 11/14 : 11/15) and lack of design knowledge in the DD phase (5/8 : 10/13). This is because domain knowledge is an important element in the functional design, and design knowledge is an important element in the detail design phase.

Faults caused by dynamic error factors
(e) Faults caused by stress accounted for a high proportion of all generated faults. More than a third of the faults generated during the FD phase (A: 36%, 20 faults; B: 32%, 14 faults) and more than a half of all faults generated during the DD phase (A: 82%, 85 faults; B: 54%, 42 faults) were due to mental stress.
(f) The number of faults caused by human nature was nearly equal to that caused by mental stress in the FD phase, and lower than that in the DD phase, which was a stressful development environment.

The results of (e) and (f) were consistent those of our previous report (Furuyama, 1994-b): stressful conditions over time shifted some of the developers' attribution of faults from the human nature category to the stress category.

4 ANALYSIS

Figure 4 shows a model of the relationships between stress, mental and physical conditions, fault generation, and their measurement. Physical stress was measured in addition to mental stress. Both stresses are considered to seriously affect human intellectual behavior.

Using this model, the collected data were analyzed from the following viewpoints.

- Are there any differences, in terms of fault generation, between functional design methodology and structured design methodology in stressful circumstances?
- In addition to mental stress metrics, is a 'physical condition' metric related to fault generation?

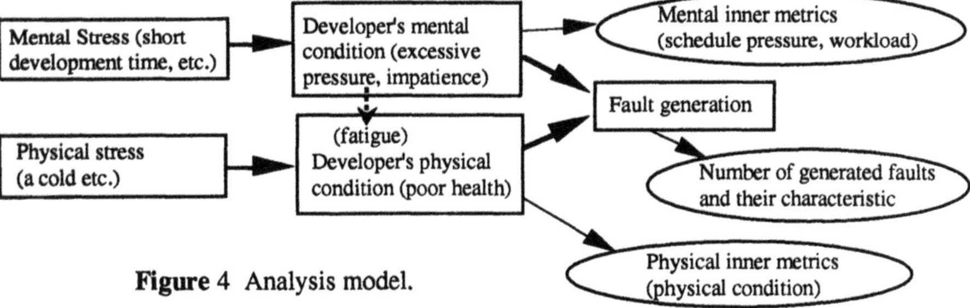

Figure 4 Analysis model.

4.1 Mental stress effect on fault generation between two design methodologies

Calculation of fault generation rate
Since there was occasional overtime work and working time varied widely every half-day (morning and afternoon), to merely count and compare the raw number of faults generated in every-half day as a unit for measuring stress level was inadequate. Therefore, we accumulated working time for calculating efforts and generated faults level by level, and compared the fault generation rate obtained by dividing accumulated faults by accumulated working time level by level (Table 6).

'Workload' metric values were used as representative to classify the faults level by level, because both mental stress metric values were correlated to each other as shown in Table 4, and 'workload' had a little higher correlation to fault generation than 'schedule pressure' (Furuyama, 1994-b).

There were two types of fault generation rate each level: the faults per actual effort in man-hours, and the normalized rate by total design effort. These differed both between the two design methodologies and between the FD and the DD phases. The latter type was derived from the concept that the fault generation rate should be normalized by the effort needed to complete the same function, such as the Function Point concept. In other words, the fault generation rate should be calculated as faults generated per working steps, to build up a unit function. We adopted the normalized rate to compensate for the difference in efforts between the two teams. Speaking more concretely, each fault generation rate of Team A was calculated by dividing the number of faults by the actual effort themselves, and that of Team B was compensated by multiplication of the ratio of total efforts of Team B to that of Team A after dividing the number of faults by actual efforts. For example, in the FD phase, every fault generation rate at each level for Team B in the FD phase was compensated by the value 191.5/119 obtained from Table 2. (Hereafter, 'normalized fault generation rate' is expressed as 'fault generation rate' for short).

Table 6 Faults caused by dynamic error factors and the generation rate classified by mental stress level

		Team A			*Team B*		
			Generated faults			*Generated faults*	
Phase	*Stress level (Work-load)*	*Accumulated effort (man-hours)*	*Caused by stress*	*Caused by human nature*	*Accumulated effort (man-hours)*	*Caused by stress*	*Caused by human nature*
FD	0	41.25	2 (0.05)	6 (0.15)	49.75	0 (0.00)	3 (0.10)
	1	24.75	1 (0.04)	2 (0.08)	66.50	1 (0.02)	5 (0.12)
	2	16.50	1 (0.06)	2 (0.12)	31.25	2 (0.10)	0 (0.00)
	3	9.50	2 (0.21)	6 (0.63)	0.00	--	--
	4	19.00	9 (0.47)	6 (0.32)	44.00	11 (0.40)	7 (0.26)
	5	0.00	--	--	0.00	--	--
	6	8.00	5 (0.63)	0 (0.00)	0.00	--	--
	Total	119.00	20 (0.17)	22 (0.18)	191.50	14 (0.07)	15 (0.08)
DD	0	4.25	0 (0.00)	0 (0.00)	21.75	0 (0.00)	1 (0.06)
	1	2.00	0 (0.00)	0 (0.00)	54.75	11 (0.26)	7 (0.16)
	2	28.00	7 (0.25)	0 (0.00)	83.75	15 (0.23)	5 (0.08)
	3	18.00	1 (0.06)	0 (0.00)	31.75	1.5 (0.06)	1 (0.04)
	4	144.50	65 (0.45)	6 (0.04)	107.25	13.5 (0.16)	7 (0.08)
	5	0.00	--	--	8.75	0 (0.00)	0 (0.00)
	6	53.00	12 (0.23)	4 (0.08)	13.25	1 (0.10)	2 (0.19)
	Total	249.75	85 (0.34)	10 (0.04)	321.25	42 (0.17)	23 (0.09)

( ): fault generation rate (faults/man-hour); Team B is normalized by the ratio of total effort of Team B to that of Team A.

Comparison of fault generation rate between two teams

Our analysis led to the following conclusions.

(a) Faults caused by mental stress (hereafter sometimes expressed merely as 'stress') of Team A in the FD phase (0.17 faults per man-hour) were much more numerous than those of Team B

(0.07 faults per normalized man-hour) even after normalization, as shown Table 6. To clarify the differences of fault generation between the two teams in detail, we investigated faults and generation rate at each mental stress level. The difference was found to be due to five faults generated at level 6 of Team A as shown in Table 6, while Team B did not attain stress level 6 at all and therefore had no faults at that level. If we exclude these faults at level 6, **there is no difference in normalized fault generation rate at all between the two teams in FD phase**, in that the normalized fault generation rate of Team A was a little higher than that of Team B at stress level 1, a little lower at stress level 2, and nearly equal at stress level 4.

(b) **In the DD phase, faults caused by stress per actual and per total design time of Team A were both much more numerous than those of Team B.** The overall difference was derived from the extreme difference of generated faults at level 4 between the teams.

(c) In the FD phase, no significant differences of normalized fault generation rate for faults caused by human nature were found between the teams, except for the difference at stress level 3, where the fault generation rate of Team A was very high while there was no data at the level of Team B, thus making comparison impossible. The difference at level 3 is discussed in detail in 4.2.

(d) In the DD phase, total faults caused by human nature of Team A (10) were less than those of Team B (27). This seemed to derive from the shift from the human nature category to the stress category, as described earlier.

(e) **The total number of faults caused by dynamic error factors of Team A was much greater than those of Team B**, even considering the difference of stress level between the teams. This means that using structured design methodology rather than functional design methodology can improve reliability not only in non-stressed circumstances, as reported by Takahashi et. al (Takahashi, 1995), but also in stressed circumstances.

Stress level and fault generation rate

Table 7 shows the correlation coefficients between stress level and fault generation rate.

Table 7 Correlation coeffficients between stress level and generated faults

Phase	*Team*	*Faults caused by stress*	*Faults caused by human nature*
FD	A	0.94*	0.01
	B	0.96**	0.58
DD	A	0.63	0.89**
	B	-0.22	0.09

(*) 1% significance, (**) 5% significance

(f) In the FD phase, faults caused by stress increased proportionate to stress level. A high correlation was found between stress level and generated faults caused by mental stress (Table 7). The regression coefficients were nearly equal to each other: 0.109 and 0.104 respectively (Table 8 and Figure 5).

(g) In the DD phase, Team A's generation rate of faults caused by stress was correlated to stress level, though it was not statistically significant, while that of Team B had no correlation to stress level.

Table 8 Analysis of variance of stress level and faults caused by mental stress during FD phase

Team	*Factor*	*d.f.*	*Sum of square*	*F-value*	*Contribution rate*	*Regression coefficient*	*Constant*
A	Regression	1	0.2783	32.6*	0.891	0.109	-0.048
	Residual	4	0.0341				
B	Regression	1	0.0952	24.6**	0.925	0.104	-0.050
	Residual	2	0.0077				

(*) 1% significant, (**) 5% significant

(h) In the FD phase, there seemed to be correlations between stress level and generated faults caused by human nature in both teams; Team A could have had a higher correlation coefficient if the fault generation rate at level 3 whose value was much higher than others were ignored, and Team B had correlation coefficient 0.58.
(i) In the DD phase, there was significant correlation between stress level and faults caused by human nature for Team A, while there was no correlation in Team B as to faults caused by stress. Detail analysis will be described below in 4.2.

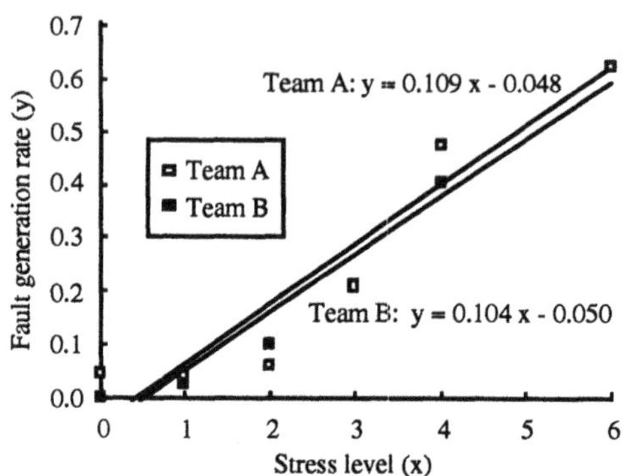

Figure 5 Generation rate of faults caused by mental stress in the FD phase.

Discussion
An unexpected result was that in the FD phase, there was no difference in the normalized generation rate of faults caused by stress between the two methodologies ((a) and (f)). One reason for this result would be, as described above, that faults may be generated according to the amount of work done to accomplish a unit function, because in other respects the working or thinking steps would be similar within a family of design methodologies, as in the case of our experiment, even if the documents to be made were different.

The better effect of using structured design methodology to reduce faults caused by stress appeared, instead, in the DD phase((b)). The reason may be due to 'structured and sufficient input documents' made during the FD phase.

As a whole, faults caused by dynamic error factors of Team B were fewer than those of Team A, slightly in the FD phase and appreciably in DD phase, and consequently throughout all the design phase. Therefore, it becomes clear that **structured design methodology is much more suitable for developing reliable software, even in a stressed environment, than functional design methodology.** One significant reason that structured design methodology is highly tolerant of a stressed environment may be that developers using it design software in a more deliberate, orderly way and write the results in comprehensive documents in an earlier design phase than is done in functional design methodology.

For the increasing rate of fault generation in the FD phase as the stress level increases, the result of 0.109 per hour was consistent with the previous result, 0.86 per (8-hour) day, which was obtained by a team also using functional design methodology (Furuyama, 1994-b), even considering the difference of maximum scales of stress metrics between +6 and +5. This means **these controlled experiments can have consistent results** even though they deal with human factors heretofore considered too difficult to investigate.

The reason that the fault generation rate of both teams was less correlated to stress in the DD phase than in the FD phase seemed to be that the work in the DD phase was more procedural than that in the FD phase. In particular, Team B had no correlation to stress level, though they generated many faults caused by stress. This was due to the input documents used in the DD phase that were written rigorously in the FD phase.

Though Team B spent more time in the design phase (in particular, in the FD phase nearly twice as long), compared to Team A, their total effort was nearly equal as shown Table 2. However, in this experiment, almost all of the faults were detected at the end of the DD phase by experimenters and hence correcting efforts for remaining faults were almost eliminated. If the fault detection rate of both teams by design review had been equivalent, the remaining undetected faults of Team A would have been much greater than those of Team B, and more efforts would have been needed than was the case in this experiment. This means that it is important to design software in a structured way, to reduce fault and development effort.

4.2 Indirect stress effect on fault generation caused by human nature

By definition, faults caused by human nature are to be considered as not dependent on stress. In fact, they tend to decrease as a whole as stress increases, because the period time when developers are conscious of schedule pressure may decrease. However, as described in 4.1, it was observed that most of generation rate of faults caused by human nature seemed to have correlation to stress level. In this section, we analyze the reason in detail.

Table 9 shows the classification of fault generation according to whether two types of faults were generated alone or together when stress was loaded on the developers. If the generation of both types of faults are independent, co-generation factor η, as defined by the following expression:

$$\eta = (P1/P2)/(P3/P4) = (P1*P4)/(P2*P3)\,, \tag{1}$$

is equal to one, where P1 is the probability that neither faults caused by stress nor by human nature are generated, P2 and P3 are the probabilities that only one type of fault is generated, and P4 is the probability that both types of faults are generated together in a unit time.

All half days were assumed to be equal. In each of the tabulations in Table 9, P1 is the lower right, P2 and P3 are the upper right and lower left items, and P4 is the upper left item respectively. Table 9 also shows that η was mostly much greater than one. This means there was strong dependence between the two types of fault generation. In other words, **in their overconfidence and not fully aware of their level of stress, developers might have misattributed stress-caused faults to human nature instead.**

Table 9 Co-generation of faults caused by stress vs. those caused by human nature

(a) Team A in the FD phase

Faults caused by human nature	*Faults caused by stress* Generated	Non-generated
Generated	16 (8/14)	6.75 (--/2)
Non-generated	20 (10/--)	35
(η=4.2)		(hours)

(b) Team B in the FD phase

Faults caused by human nature	*Faults caused by stress* Generated	Non-generated
Generated	21.5 (12/9)	9 (--/13)
Non-generated	8 (2/--)	103.25
(η=30.1)		(hours)

(c) Team A in the DD phase

Faults caused by human nature	*Faults caused by stress* Generated	Non-generated
Generated	24.25 (8/9)	5.25 (--/1)
Non-generated	118.75 (77/--)	97.25
(η=3.8)		(hours)

(d) Team B in the DD phase

Faults caused by human nature	*Faults caused by stress* Generated	Non-generated
Generated	73.75 (27/15)	25 (--/7)
Non-generated	79.75 (15/--)	121
(η=4.5)		(hours)

Note: Data from stress level zero is excluded
Legend: (faults caused by stress/faults caused by human nature)

This assumption was reinforced by the following example. Since so many faults caused by human nature in Team A were generated at level 3 in the FD phase, as described in 4.1 (c), we analyzed this in detail and found that developer A2 had generated two faults caused by stress followed by six faults caused by human nature in a half-day while suffering from mental stress at level 3. Considering only the FD phase, this was the only day that he suffered from such a high level both of stress and of fault generation. He might have been unaware of his mental stress at stress level 3. In spite of his report, the six faults caused by human nature should have been classified into those caused by mental stress.

This conclusion seems to contradict the results that stress causes the number of faults caused by human nature to decrease, as described in 3.3 (f) and 4.1 (d). However, it can be resolved with consideration that above conclusion means that more of the faults caused by human nature already reduced by stress should be included in the total caused by stress.

4.3 Effect of physical stress on fault generation compared to mental stress

To clarify the effect of physical stress on fault generation, we counted the number of faults caused by dynamic error factors generated by developers A2 and B2 at each physical stress level (Table 10), since only these two suffered from poor physical condition in this experiment, as shown in Figure 3. By calculating the fault generation rate, we found that only developer A2 seemed to generate faults due to physical stress at physical stress level 3. He had a poor health at physical stress level 3 in the middle of the FD phase, while his mental stress (schedule pressure) values during this period were lower than or equal to his physical stress values (Figure 6). An interview with developer A2 disclosed that he had caught a cold during that period, and his poor health caused by the cold was the main factor for generating four faults during that time. Therefore, we categorized these four faults as faults caused by physical stress and excluded them from Table 4. On the other hand, developer B2 also had a poor health for a few days, but there was no correlation between physical stress levels and the number of faults during that period.

Table 10 Faults caused by dynamic error factors classified by physical stress level

		Developer A2			*Developer B2*		
			Generated Faults			*Generated Faults*	
Phase	*Stress Level (Physical Condition)*	*Accumulated Effort (man-hours)*	*Caused by Stress*	*Caused by Human Nature*	*Accumulated Effort (man-hours)*	*Caused by Stress*	*Caused by Human Nature*
FD	0	15.25	2 (0.13)	6 (0.39)	27.50	0 (0.00)	1 (0.06)
	1	31.50	1 (0.03)	4 (0.13)	37.50	2 (0.09)	0 (0.00)
	2	7.75	1 (0.13)	2 (0.26)	14.00	1 (0.11)	2 (0.23)
	3	**3.00**	**4 (1.33)**	0 (0.00)	12.00	0 (0.00)	0 (0.00)
	4	--	--	--	2.00	0 (0.00)	0 (0.00)
	Total	57.50	8 (0.14)	12 (0.21)	93.00	3 (0.05)	3 (0.05)
DD	0				143.25	26.5 (0.24)	13 (0.12)
	1				1.50	0 (0.00)	0 (0.00)
	2				3.75	0 (0.00)	0 (0.00)
	3				0.00	--	--
	4				9.00	1 (0.14)	2 (0.29)
	Total				157.50	27.5 (0.22)	15 (0.12)

( ): fault generation rate (faults/man-hour); Team B is normalized by the ratio of total effort of Team B to that of Team A

While high mental stress is considered to be 'constantly' loaded on developers throughout the software development cycle, whether accidentally or, as in the case of this experiment, intentionally, high physical stress tends to appear suddenly and accidentally for a short period. In this experiment, physical stress measured with the 'physical condition' metric appeared with two developers only for a short period. Although poor health possibly derived from both 'inner' factors such as fatigue and 'outer' factors such as catching a cold, the latter is considered to be the dominant factor, as shown in this experiment.

From these observations, we conclude as follows:
(a) Constant mental stress is one of the most significant factors for generating faults, and
(b) Physical stress can generate faults at a higher rate than mental stress when it appears even for a short period. It may be possible to use a physical metric for estimating faults caused by physical stress, taking into consideration the individual differences of the effect.

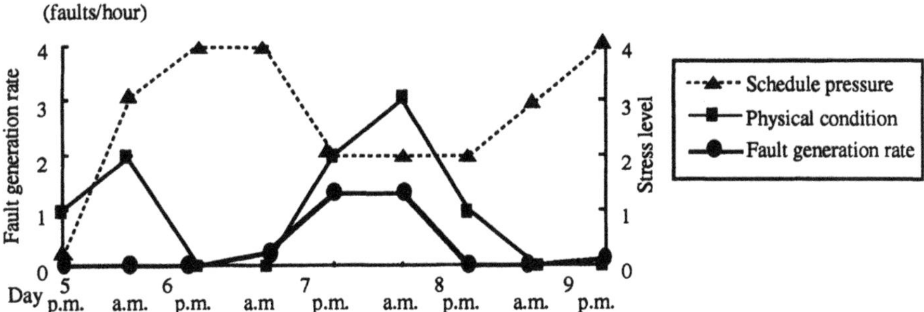

Figure 6 Physical condition and generation rate of faults caused by stress of Developer A2 in the FD phase.

5 CONCLUSIONS

As too much stress causes serious fault generation, it is important to remove it during software development to improve software reliability. The effect of stress may vary depending on factors in the development environment such as design methodology, working space, noise level around developers, and so on. To clarify the difference in stress effect depending on the development environment, we investigated the effect of mental and physical stress between different design methodologies. A controlled software development experiment was used to quantitatively determine the effect. The results are as follows.

(a) In the functional design phase, there was no difference in fault generation caused by mental stress between Team A, which used functional design methodology, and Team B, which used structured design methodology.
(b) In the detail design phase, however, Team A generated many more faults due to mental stress (hence, faults caused by dynamic error factors) than Team B, though Team A generated fewer faults by human nature than Team B.
(c) Among the faults caused by human nature, many seemed to be correlated to stress at higher levels, though developers themselves were not aware of it. Therefore, faults caused by stress were considered to be generated much more often than they were actually reported by developers.
(d) Physical stress could generate faults as well as mental stress, and it sometimes caused fault generation at a higher rate than mental stress when it appeared even for a short period.

These results lead to the conclusion that it is important not only to establish better development circumstances, but also to use more structured design methodology rather than functional design methodology to improve reliability even under sometimes inevitable stressful circumstances.

REFERENCES

Basili, V.R. and Perricone, B.T. (1984) Software errors and complexity: an empirical investigation. *Communications of the ACM*, **27**, 42-52.

Fujigaki, Y. (1992) Mental workload of software engineers. *Institute for Science of Labour Publishers* (in Japanese)

Furuyama, T., Arai, Y. and Iio, K. (1994-a) Fault generation model and mental stress effect analysis. *J. Systems and Software*, **26**, 31-42.

Furuyama, T., Arai Y. and Iio K. (1994-b) Metrics for measuring the effect of mental stress on fault generation during software development. *Int. J. Reliability, Quality and Safety Eng.*, **1**, 257-75.

Lee, K.W., Tillman F.A. and Higgins, J.J. (1988) A literature survey of the human reliability component in a man-machine system. *IEEE Transs. Reliability*, **R-37**, 24-34.

Nakajo, T. and Kume, H. (1991) A case history analysis of software error cause-effect relationship. *IEEE Trans. Software Eng.*, **SE-17**, 830-7.

Oka, A., Yamamoto, S. and Isoda, S. (1993) An experimental evaluation of structured analysis and design methodology. *Trans. of Information Processing Society of Japan*, **34**, 2543-51 (in Japanese).

Rasmussen, J., Dunkan, K. and Leplat, J. (ed.) (1987) New Technology and Human Error. *John Wiley & Sons Ltd.*

Reason, J. (1990) Human Error. *Cambridge Univ. Press* .

Takahashi, K., Oka, A., Yamamoto, S. and Isoda, S. (1995) A comperative study of structured and text-oriented analysis and design methodologies. *J. Systems and Software*, **28**, 69-75.

Takahashi, M and Kamayachi, Y. (1985) An empirical study of a model for program error prediction. *Proc. 8th ICSE*, 330-6.

BIOGRAPHY

Dr. Tsuneo Furuyama is a Senior Research Engineer of NTT (Nippon Telegraph and Telephone Corp.) Software Laboratories. He received the B.S. degree, the M.S. degree and the Ph. D. degree in measurement engineering from the University of Tokyo in 1968, 1970 and 1974, respectively. He has been working at NTT Electrical Communication Laboratories since 1973 and was engaged in developing programming language processors. He is now researching on software metrics. He is also a Visiting Professor of the postgraduate course of the University of Electro-communications. He is a regular member of the Information Processing Society of Japan, the Institute of Electronics, Information and Communication Engineers of Japan.

Mr. Yoshio Arai is a Senior Research Engineer of NTT software Laboratories. He received the B.S. degree in Electrical Engineering from Muroran Technical University, Japan, in 1970. He has been working at NTT Electricasl Communication Laboratories since 1970. He is now researching Software Quality Metrics. His interests include Programming Language, Software Reuse, Software Tools and Software Metrics. He is a member of the Information Processing Society of Japan.

Mr. Kazuhiko Iio is a member of NTT Software Labotratories. He received the B.S. degree in Electronics and Communication Engineering from Waseda University, Tokyo, 1989. Since 1989, he has been with Software laboratories. His current research interest whthin the Software Engineering area include the complexity of Software Metrics and Human Factors involved in Software Development. He is a member of the Information Processing Society of Japan, the Japan Society of Software Science and Technology and Japanese Society for Artificial Intelligence.

3

EC Projects and Efforts in the Field of Software Quality

Brice Lepape
European Commission - DG III / F4
200 rue de la Loi - B-1049 Bruxelles
Tel: 32.2.296 80 97 - Fax: 32.2.296 83 64
E-mail: ble@dg13.cec.be

Abstract

Software quality has been and still is a continuous concern in the software technology area and numerous projects have contributed to state the art and to improve best practice: results span from contribution to world standards to methods tools and techniques covering various aspects of software quality.

Production of high quality software needs to be tackled from different angles according to the software development process (from user requirements to the product and its evolution) and to the actors involved (users, developers, managers, ...).

The presentation will give a structured overview on how the various issues leading to software quality have been addressed as well as some examples of significant results achieved and on going work in the context of the European RTD programmes.

Keywords

Software Quality - Software Best Practice - ESPRIT

EXTENDED SUMMARY

Since the beginning of the 80's the European Commission has launched RTD programmes with the objective to reinforce the technological base and competitiveness of European industry. The flagship programme ESPRIT addresses the Information Technology domain where Software Technology is one of the essential components. In this area more than 300 projects have been launched covering the whole spectrum of advanced methods, tools, and techniques to develop and put in use software intensive systems. (CEC Summaries, 1993), (Kuntzmann-Combelles, A., 1989), (Kuntzmann-Combelles, A., 1993).

ESPRIT has evolved and is still evolving, from its first phase which was mainly technology push to its current status where a market driven approach is taken. During this last decade IT has evolved from a sectoral activity towards a pervasive and generic technology which has become a key asset for the whole economic and social activity. Moreover the convergence of IT and Telecommunications is leading to a profound revolution with the foreseable emergence of the Information Society as described in (CEC White Paper, 1993).

In this fast evolving context Software Technology plays a central role being the means to animate and provide intelligent behaviour of any IT&C-based systems. The software production demand is broadly outstripping the available resources and the growth of population daily exposed to software based components (often hidden) and applications is accelerating rapidly. It is therefore of paramount importance to develop methods and techniques that enable the software developpers to operate in a more predictable, more user relevant and cost effective manner. Software quality of both product and development process have been a continuous concern since the inception of the programme.
The strategy adopted to address software quality has been pragmatic and evolving, tackling various activities in achieving software quality. From a software product perspective, significant achievements and ongoing work deal with formal methods (eg. LACOS, LOTOSPHRE), user requirements analysis (eg. F3, ORDIT), software metrication and test (eg. MERMAID, MUSIC, COSMOS) and software assessment (eg. SCOPE Bache, R., Bazzana, G. 1994). From a software development perspective, process modelling and improvement (eg. PERFECT, BOOTSTRAP, SQUID), software evolution (eg. MACS, RECYCLE), rapid prototyping (eg. IPTES <Bologna, S., 1993>) and development methods and tools for emerging technologies (e.g. CommonKADS for KBS <Steels, L., Lepape, B., 1992>) have been and still are on the agenda. It is also worthmentioning that the software reuse paradigm (eg. SCALE, REBOOT, EUROWARE), when correctly implemented, will have a significant impact on both software process and products.

Since the beginning of the 90's, due to the rapid evolution of the demand for Software Technology, we are facing a dual dilemma: the current techniques are inadequate to deal with new challenges (e.g. more complexity, more reliability) on one side, and on the other side current practice in software development makes inadequate use of available technologies.
Moreover a smooth transition between new RTD results and their best practice needs to be secured.

The current activities and workprogramme address this dilemma in order to achieve better software quality:
RTD is focusing on the mid-term software quality improvements with a particular emphasis on process modelling and improvement, reuse, user centered developments and safety critical aspects.

Best Practice (European Software and System Initiative) is dedicated to improving the software development process by means of assessments of current practice, process improvement experiments, training and dissemination.
Trial Applications aim to secure the early adoption of emerging results from RTD by advanced users.

REFERENCES

CEC White Paper: *Growth, Competitiveness, Employment* (1993) - Office for Official Publications of the European Union - Luxembourg

CEC *Summaries of Projects in Software and Advanced Information Processing (1993)* - Office for Official Publication of the European Union - Luxembourg

Kuntzmann-Combelles, A, *ESPRIT: Key results of the first phase* - IEEE Software, Vol. 6, N°6, (1989)

Kuntzmann-Combelles, A., Luqui, *Advancing Europe's Fortunes*, IEEE Software, Vol. 6, N°6, (1993)

Steels, L., and Lepape, B., *Enhancing the knowledge engineering process*, Contributions from ESPRIT, North-Holland, Amsterdam, (1992).

Bache, R., and Bazzana, G., *Software metrics for product assessment*, McGraw-Hill, London, (1994).

Bologna, S., *Incremental prototyping technology for embedded real-time systems*, Special Issue of Real-time Systems Journal, Vol. 5 N°2/3, Kluwer Academic Publishers, (1993).

4

Verification and Validation of Knowledge Based Systems

Marc Ayel
Universitè de Savoie-Aderias-Lia F-73376
Le Bourget du Lac-France
Tel:0033-79758845, Fax:0033-79758785

Abstract

The goal of this talk is to show that the set of available Validation and Verification (V&V) tools could be larger for Knowledge-Based Systems (KBSs) than for classical software. All the tools which use a black box approach may be applied on KBSs and a great number of glass box tools can be adapted to KBSs. For example the test-data generation is really effective with KBSs.

Moreover, the KBSs have more or less a declarative part and V&V requirements can be checked on the corresponding Knowledge Bases (KB). The KB consistency can be one of these requirements.

Some of the V&V requirements are very difficult to check on KBSs. The reason is not in the nature of a KBS or in the nature of the checking. The KBS approach is used to solve complex problems and then the V&V checkings are obviously also complex problems.

PART TWO

Process Improvement

5

Process improvement through Root Cause Analysis

G. Damele, G. Bazzana§, F. Andreis*, F. Aquilio*, S. Arnoldi*, E. Pessi°*

* *Italtel SIT, 20019 Settimo Milanese (Italy)*
Tel: +39 2 43 88 1; Fax: +39 2 43 88 87 05

§ at the time of writing: *Etnoteam SpA*
at the time of final submission: *Onion Srl, 25020 Brescia (Italy)*
Tel: +39 30 3581510; Fax: +39 30 3581525; email: gb@onion.it

° *Etnoteam SpA, via A. Bono Cairoli 34, 20127 Milano (Italy)*
Tel: +39 2 261621 Fax: +39 2 261 107 55; email: epessi@etnoteam.it

Abstract

Italtel SIT BUCT Linea UT has been conducting a software process improvement program since 1991, following some of the most widespread paradigms, including: process certification in accordance with ISO 9001, Process Quality Management and Improvement (PQMI), process assessment in accordance with Bootstrap. After four years, the improvement program has brought to tangible quantitative benefits and to the reaching of a stable maturity level 3. Among the lines of actions that have been set up to feed and care the continuous improvement program, a particular emphasis has been put on the experimentation of defect prevention techniques. In this context, a Root Cause Analysis (RCA) program has been implemented, focusing both on failures and on scheduling slippages.

The paper is focused on the experiences matured, dealing with the following topics:

- basics of the Italtel SIT BUCT Linea UT process improvement program;
- summary of the benefits achieved and of the challenges set for the next future;
- the adoption of Root Cause Analysis techniques for the sake of defect prevention;
- the results from the application of RCA to the failures found in operation;
- the extension of RCA to the investigation of scheduling slippages;
- the feed-back on the development process.

The goals, the activities, the results and the findings are presented in adherence with a Plan-Do-Check-Act (PDCA) paradigm and are supported by quantitative data. The conclusions of the study can be summarised as follows:

- From a technical point of view, RCA has contributed to a better understanding of the development/ testing practices and to the adoption of a number of corrective actions.
- From a methodological point of view, RCA has proven to be powerful in singling out improvement opportunities; for this reason the software producing unit is aiming at its extension and standardisation.

Keywords

Process improvement, RCA, PDCA, Bootstrap.

1. THE PROCESS IMPROVEMENT PROGRAM UNDERGOING AT ITALTEL SIT BUCT LINEA UT

Italtel designs, manufactures, markets and installs systems and equipment for private and public networks. This software producing unit is committed, among other products, to the development and maintenance of the Linea UT telecommunication switching system (Italtel, 1995). At the end of 1994, over 15 million Linea UT lines, 1000 exchanges and 2000 RSU (Remote Subscriber Units) were operating in 18 countries world-wide.

As part of a company wide quality program (Maggi, 1995), Italtel SIT BUCT is strongly committed to the excellence of quality in delivered products and internal processes, in adherence to Process Quality Management and Improvement (PQMI) principles (AT&T, 1989). In this context the main goal of the improvement program was to adopt a Plan-Do-Check-Act (PDCA) scheme able to check and measure the products and the development process in a quantitative way in order to single out, implement and monitor the improvement opportunities. The improvement program has its roots in the Quality Management System (Italtel, 1993) and is supported by quality planning activities and by a measurement system that has been applied since 1991 (Damele, 1993).

Italtel SIT BUCT holds ISO 9001 certification (ISO, 1990) since April 1992; since 1993 the certificate has been recognised at European level by ITQS (Souter, 1992). Now the company is moving towards Total Quality Management assessment schema recognised world-wide (ASQC, 1995).

In order to drive and monitor process improvement also in software, process assessments (performed with the Bootstrap methodology) take place at regular time intervals. Bootstrap (IEEE, 1993) (Kuvaja, 1994) is an European assessment method, based on the Software Engineering Institute Capability Maturity Model - SEI CMM (Paulk, 1993) reference scheme and questionnaire, but extended with concepts widely adopted by European companies, namely: ISO 9000 quality standards and the European Space Agency's process models. The resulting assessment approach yields capability profiles at a fine granularity level and can be applied to both organisations and projects. Maturity levels are divided into quartiles, and maturity determination can be applied to a wide set of capability factors divided into three groups: organisation, methodology, technology. For the most part, the SEI's maturity levels are still recognisable and the assessments are largely compatible with CMM ones.

The latest process assessment (Damele, 1995), undertaken in 1994, concluded that Italtel SIT BUCT Linea UT has progressed to a maturity level 3.5 at Software Producing Unit (SPU) level and 3 at project level, with many activities reaching level 4 grading. Improvements include almost all areas with respect to the baseline of the first assessment, indicating that the SPU has reached a good positioning, as detailed in Fig. 1, that shows the maturity levels of the various practices both from a global (or in other terms: SPU or QMS) perspective and a project perspective, with details also of the maximum maturity level of each area, in order to highlight the difference between the current status and the optimising level (the highest grading).

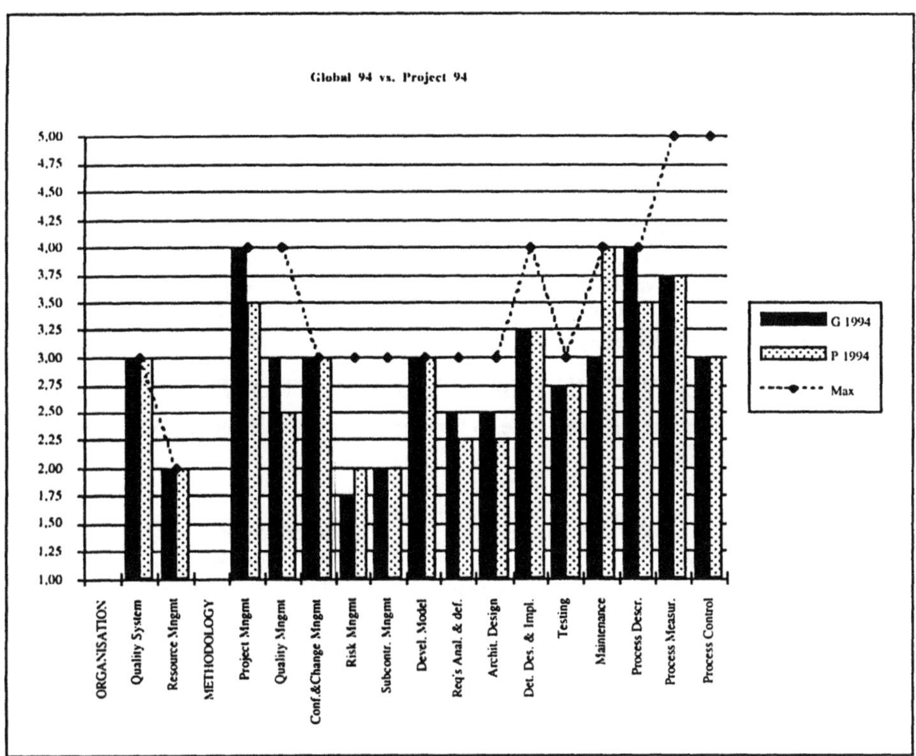

Figure 1 - Italtel SIT BUCT Linea UT Assessment results in 1994 according to Bootstrap.

2. RESULTS ACHIEVED FROM THE IMPROVEMENT PROGRAM

The process improvement program has given valuable contributions in reaching the goals of the software producing unit; results have been tracked and analysed in a quantitative way, thanks to the early adoption of a measurement system. The metrics have been defined in accordance with the goals of the SPU: timeliness, reliability, documentation, resources. Indicators are collected and analysed from two different points of view: the customer and the project. Table 1 summarises the indicators defined at customer and project levels and their relationships with the goals of the SW producing unit (for a detailed definition of indicators and basic data, the interested reader is referred to (Damele, 1993)).

Table 1 - Relationships between indicators and goals of the metrics program

Goal	*Indicators relevant for the customer*	*Indicators relevant for the project*
Timeliness	• Timeliness for the customer	• Timeliness for the project • Efficacy
Reliability	• Fault Rate in operation • Testing Effectiveness	• Fault Rate in testing • Fault Density
Documentation	• Documentation for the customer	• Documentation for the project
Resources		• Productivity

As detailed in (Damele, 1995), the following results can be reported after four years of process improvement:

- Timeliness for the customer has always been achieved; moreover, if we consider the contribution of process improvement it can be shown that timeliness capabilities have been improved by 10%.
- Reliability in operation has reached a fault density of less than 1 fault per 10 KLOC, with an improvement of 54%; the net contribution of process improvement is tracked by the 'testing effectiveness' indicator, that has increased by 7%.
- Documentation for the product is quickly increasing and has reached its goals, without negatively affecting other indicators (in particular: timeliness issues).
- Productivity goals have been largely reached and we can observe better performance by a factor of around 65% even if, considering the difference between expected values and actual ones, we come to the conclusion that this is the area where benefits from process improvement are less tangible.

3. ROLE OF RCA WITHIN THE IMPROVEMENT INITIATIVE

Fig. 2 shows the path that has been done so far in terms of activities undertaken and maturity levels reached since 1990.

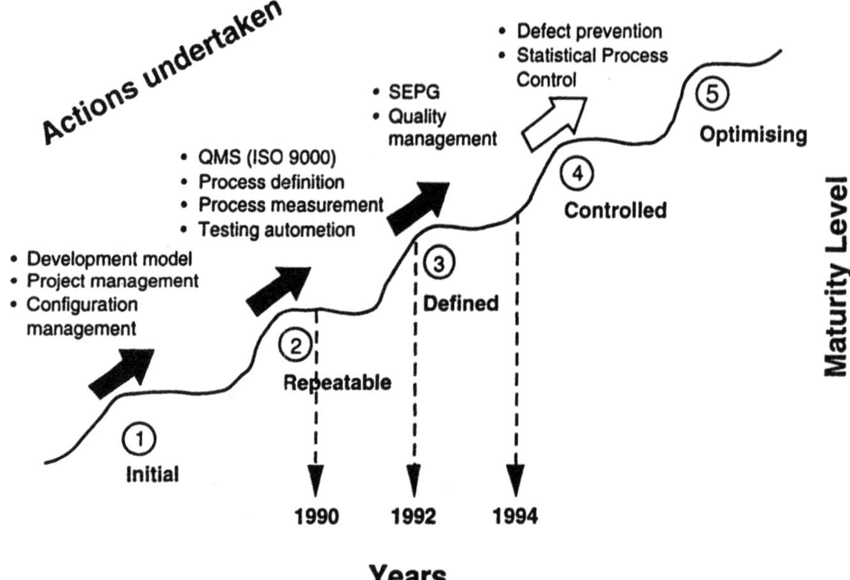

Figure 2 - Italtel SIT BUCT Linea UT path towards process improvement.

Defect prevention is, together with Statistical Process Control, the current challenge for growing the capabilities of the producing unit. As a consequence, Root Cause Analysis has been investigated for adoption.

4. BASICS OF ROOT CAUSE ANALYSIS

4.1 Goals of RCA

As well described in (Briand, 1995), casual analysis (or, in other terms, Root Cause Anlaysis) is a technique appropriate to identify the causes and inner mechanism that lead to costly or risky problems related to the quality of the delivered products or the efficiency of the development process. As a consequence, Root Cause Analysis (RCA) has been chosen as the technique supporting cause-effect modelling, in conjunction with the well-known classifications proposed by Ishikawa (Ishikawa, 1991). The goal of RCA is the analysis of the problem occurred for evaluating why it happened, in order to identify the root causes of the problem, not simply the symptoms. In so doing we can derive a diagnosis for fixing the defects in the process or materials that caused the problem in the first place. RCA techniques are based on the observation that SW problems (faults, scheduling slippages, budget overheads) are not only symptoms of a problem in the product, but also in the process that created it; as a consequence, the root cause might involve the processes, inputs, environment or people involved. In order to get the knowledge and remove the root cause (thus preventing future problems of a similar nature) what is needed is an extra effort to go back and determine why the problem was created in the first place.

The aim of RCA is the improvement of the process through the analysis of problems, by means of a set of activities including:

- Investigation of where and why problems have been introduced.
- Investigation of where the problems have been detected and why they were not detected earlier.
- Formulation of recommendations to eliminate or reduce the incidence of similar errors in subsequent development projects.

The preliminary condition for the application of RCA is the traceability of the processes. In fact, for an objective approach, the processes shall be defined and described in order to perform analysis on the project documentation.

A second condition for the application of RCA is that it must be supported by an ad-hoc group, that has the duty of classifying the possible causes and to support developers in performing the analysis; as a matter of fact you must not stop at the first cause but you have to go back to the root cause, by means of repetitive "Why?" (as taught by Japanese approaches to RCA, known as "Naze-Naze", that simply means "Why? Why?").

4.2 RCA in the context of PDCA

Whenever a process improvement initiative is decided, it should be driven in accordance with a PDCA strategy (Ishikawa, 1991).

The PDCA problem-solving approach is very simple in its foundations:

- Plan: identify and analyse the problem;
- Do: deploy countermeasures;
- Check: verify root causes decreased and targets met or exceeded;
- Act: sustain improvements and make them part of the QMS.

The application of the overall PDCA scheme for the RCA activities is quite time-consuming and will be tracked by the measurement system applied to the projects that will benefit of the countermeasures decided after the analysis of RCA findings.

But a PDCA scheme can be applied also to the RCA activity itself; in particular, adapting the general procedures to perform casual analysis (Collofello,1993) (Nakajo, 1991), the various steps have to be intended in the following way:

- Plan:
  - analysis of quality indicators in order to single out improvement opportunities;
  - selection of the data sample onto which RCA should be applied;
  - definition of the set of possible causes to investigate;

- Do:
  - data collection;
  - validation of collected data;
- Check:
  - analysis of data with usage of Ishikawa diagrams;
  - interpretation;
  - cost-effectiveness analysis of possible actions aiming at eliminating root causes;
- Act:
  - evolution of the QMS in order to incorporate process improvement actions agreed.

In the following such PDCA scheme will be used for describing the application of RCA to failures, that is to say:
- planning RCA of failures;
- doing RCA of failures;
- checking the results from RCA;
- acting in adherence with RCA recommendations.

5. ROOT CAUSE ANALYSIS OF FAILURES

5.1 Planning RCA of failures

5.1.1 Analysis of quality indicators in order to single out improvement opportunities

Table 2 details the values in 1992 and 1994 for the indicators of the measurement system referring to reliability issues. For each indicator, the metrication unit is stated, together with the goal that was established at the beginning of the improvement program.

Table 2 - Values for the customer-relevant indicators affecting reliability

Indicator	*Unit*	*Goals*	*1992*	*1994*
Fault density in operation	Faults/Kloc	<0.12	0.149	0.08
Fault rate in operation	Faults/Week	<10	4.02	6.22
Testing effectiveness	% of faults pre-release	>80	77	84.1

The indicators can be interpreted in the following way:
- the challenging goals of the improvement program have been attained;
- fault density in operation has significantly improved;
- testing effectiveness has also improved;
- failure rate has worsened (keeping in any case its goal).

The last point is worth discussing: despite the fact that the process has significantly improved, the customer perceives in field more failures per week; this is due to the fact that the size of released products grows so much that improvement in fault density is overridden. This means that process improvement has to continue and even to accelerate in order to compensate the unavoidable growth of applications released!

Hence the need to understand, by means of RCA, where to focus the additional improvement efforts, that should concentrate on bettering fault density up to the point that the fault rate becomes at least stable.

5.1.2 Selection of the data sample onto which RCA should be applied

The RCA was applied to a set of failures coming from the field and selected on the basis of their severity.

The reasons for this choice are:

- The field failures are the most relevant aspect of the quality perceived by the customer.
- The field failures are the most important to analyse because they have not been captured neither by internal tests nor by validation tests with the customer.
- In accordance with an analysis made in the specific environment, the cost to found, fix and validate failures from field is 70 times more than the cost to found, fix and validate failures found during system test (Tosi, 1994).

On the bases of severity and of fair distribution across development areas, 98 failures out of 313 were selected for analysis.The sample is thus considered to be fairly representative and of statistical validity.

5.1.3 Definition of the set of possible causes to investigate

In order to keep full control of the experiment, the analysis focused only on the internal processes, while processes mastered by external entities (such as: technical assistance, system requirement specification, acceptance) were not analysed.

A team of experts in the different activities of the development process was set-up with the aim to prepare a questionnaire including the possible causes of errors; in particular, a distinction was made between the causes for the injection of the error and the causes for not detecting the problem.

A questionnaire was prepared for each phase of the development life-cycle for a total of several hundreds of questions. It has to be underlined that, in order not to influence the subsequent collection of results, questions were not clustered in accordance with root causes but presented in a flat format.

5.2 Doing RCA on failures

5.2.1 Data collection

The data was collected by means of direct interviews with designers involved in development, testing and fixing of the faulty features. Interviews fully adopted a back-tracking strategy: each time a selected cause had roots in a previous phase of the development life-cycle, the analysis jumped on that activity, starting a new interview with the appropriate questionnaire together with the people in charge of the activity under analysis. For this reason, starting from 98 failure, more than 300 interviews were done, involving 200 persons at varying responsibility levels. In order to select the right people to interview, the planning documents were taken into account.

5.2.2 Validation of collected data

Before analysing the data collected, a validation step was performed. The goal of validation was not to review the results in order to pre-process them but rather to allow the possibility of uncovering additional causes. For this reason the development area managers were asked to give their view of the causes onto which designers had already expressed their point of view. It was not seldom the case in which opinions differed, sometimes also utterly. In these cases, the analysis of inconsistencies between the different points of view proved invaluable in suggesting additional causes.

5.3 Checking the results from RCA

5.3.1 Analysis of data with usage of Ishikawa diagrams

The results of the interviews were stored into a database; the data was then analysed with usage of SAS, a statistical analysis tool. In order to identify the root causes of the introduction and the missing detection of failures, "cause-effect" Ishikawa diagrams were adopted (Ishikawa, 1991). Such diagrams are very useful for presenting RCA results since they show the relationships between the effects (that is to say, the symptoms observed) and the causes. They are also called fishbone diagram owing to the resemblance to a fish's skeleton, with the head being the effect and the bones the cause at various levels of nesting.

5.3.1.1 Root causes for error injection

The first analysis step consisted in the identification of the process where the error was injected in the first place. Figure 3 shows the percentage distribution across the various processes identified.

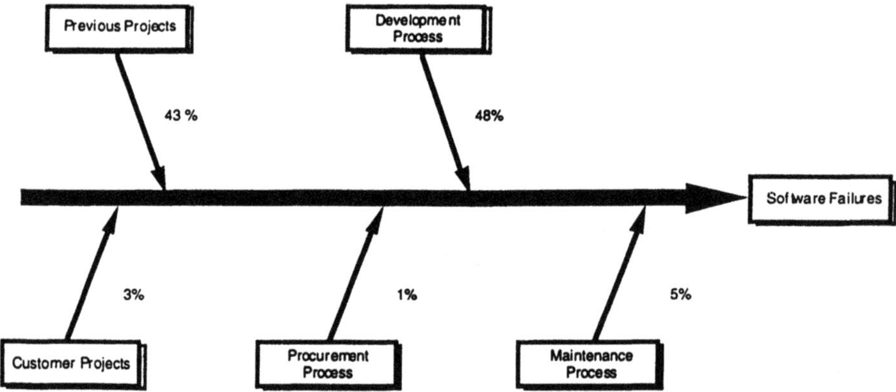

Figure 3 - Processes responsible for fault injection.

This step brought to an interesting result:

- The biggest contribution comes (as expected) from development activities.
- About 43% of problems were due to failures injected in the previous project and inherited in the current one; this was interpreted as due to the fact that the previous release experienced a modest usage on field and thus many problems were not observed and detected.
- Very few problems were due to change management.
- The impact of external processes (procurement and definition of requirements) is negligible.

Zooming into the development activities, the biggest contribution was found from the coding activities (83%), far exceeding the impact due to errors injected during functional specifications (17%). Within coding activities (known also as 'block design') the causes were grouped into four categories: People, Methods, Documentation, Development Environment & Tools. From the analysis of the percentage of errors assigned to each category (see Figure 4) for a simplified representation the most critical category was identified as "Method", with lack of time as the most recurrent cause (as already reported by similar experiences, see (Furuyama, 1993)). "People" issues were the second cause of errors, with aspects like "human factors", "no adoption of coding rules" and "wrong interpretation of specs" as the prevailing typologies.

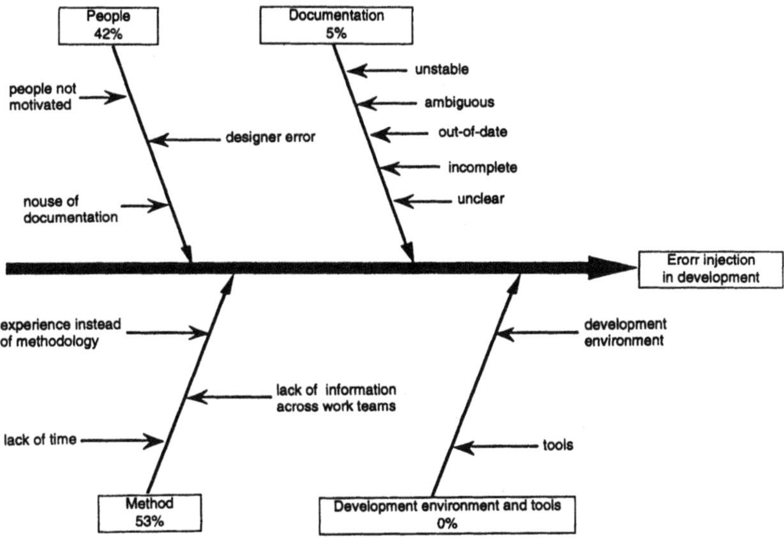

Figure 4 - Categorisation of causes for error injection during coding.

5.3.1.2 Root causes for missed error detection

Concerning the reasons for not being able to discover the errors, 57% of faults should have been discovered during system test (also known as function test) and 33% in integration (component) test, with the remaining 10% that ought to have been discovered during change management activities. The following picture shows the categorisation of causes as far as system test is concerned.

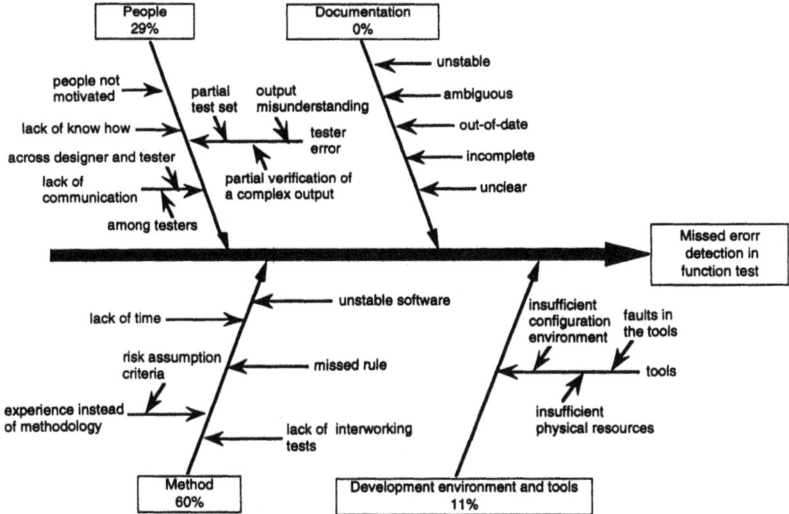

Figure 5 - Categorisation of causes for missed error detection during system test.

5.3.2 Interpretation of results

The following Pareto chart summarises in the overall the root causes of failures clustered across the four identified categories.

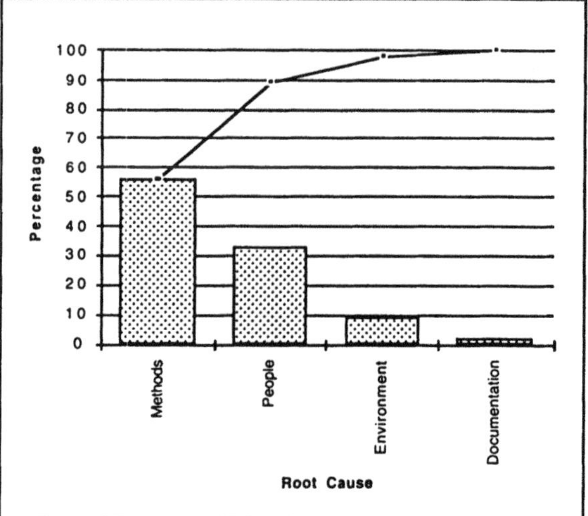

Figure 6 - RCA of failures: overall aggregation of results.

Several interpretations were very useful, among which:

- the high impact of problems injected in previous projects;
- the major role of coding in error injection;
- the major role of system test in missed error detection;
- the clusters of "method" and "people" causes;
- the high impact of the following causes, in decreasing order of priority: "lack of time", "lack of adoption of coding rules", "test case selection strategy", "usage of experience instead of rules", "missing reviews".

Such causes were elaborated in order to take preventive and corrective actions, as described in the "Act" paragraph.

5.3.3 Cost-effectiveness analysis

The following table summarises the effort spent in performing RCA of failures, including data collection, data analysis, meetings, interviews, reporting and all other kinds of activities.

Table 3 - Effort spent in RCA of failures

Activity	*Effort in person-days*
Plan - analysis of quality indicators	5
Plan - selection of the data sample	10
Plan - definition of possible causes	40
Do - data collection	400
Do - validation	80
Check - data analysis	100
Check - interpretation	50
Check - cost-effectiveness analysis	15
Act - evolution of QMS	not available yet
TOTAL	700

Such figures correspond to about 1,5% of the overall effort spent for the project to which RCA was applied. Part of the effort is due to the lack of previous specific experiences in RCA (especially in the definition of possible causes), but the biggest part (around 70%) was spent in data collection and validation. The effort needed for such activities might be largely reduced in case RCA is performed as soon as the failure is detected, using SW factory tools for declaring the root cause.

Even if precise effort estimates for the 'Act' phase are not yet available, first analyses show that a positive Return On Investment will be reached in case the resulting preventive actions will bring to a 2% improvement in the indicator 'Testing Effectiveness' and to a stabilisation of the indicator 'Failure Rate'. In any case, RCA is likely to be introduced steadily in the working practices only if it will be possible to run it as part of the daily routine work, with an effort overhead limited to 0,5% of the overall project budget.

5.4 Acting in adherence with RCA recommendations

The ultimate goal of RCA is process improvement. For this task an expert working group was set-up to evaluate and propose a set of process improvement actions. Improvement actions have been decided at three levels:

- improvement to the development/ testing process;
- improvement to specific technical aspects;
- improvement to the mechanics of RCA.

As far the development/ testing process are concerned, the following improvement actions were decided:

- More careful co-ordination between integration testing and system testing activities, in order to ensure the maximum synergy and the minimum overlap.
- Widening of test automation, in order to overcome scheduling problems during test execution and to force the application of standard rules instead of personal experiences.
- Controlled adoption of the risk management criteria used in deciding the accuracy of integration tests and in selecting system test cases, by means of the adoption of process waivers that have to be authorised by appropriate management levels (for a detailed presentation of this method and of the related "Process Standardisation" indicator, the interested reader is referred to (Damele, 1995)).

Concerning specific technical aspects, the following actions have been agreed:

- extension of training on coding practices and testing guidelines;
- review of system test documents in order to include non-regression tests aiming at covering the most frequently emerged issues.

As far as tuning of RCA mechanisms is concerned, in order to improve its effectiveness and its pragmatic feasibility within the budget constraints described before, the following actions have been devised:

- Application of RCA as soon as the failure is detected, instead of 'post-mortem' project analysis; this will be accomplished enhancing the defect tracking system used, so that it will be possible to declare and store the 'cause' chosen from a list of pre-defined motivations.
- Extension of RCA also to the failures found during system test, in order to benefit of the feedback before the release is shipped to First Office Application.
- Extension of RCA to scheduling slippages (the activity is currently in progress).

ACKNOWLEDGEMENTS

Our thanks go to S. Dal Monte and U. Ferrari who supported and sponsored the initiative. The improvement activities described in this paper were conducted with the support of the Software Quality Research Team and of external consultants. Special mention has to be devoted to: M.C. Aletti, F Aprigliano, M.G. Corti, L. De Domenico, M.L. Giovanelli, M; Giunchi, M.T. Graziani, F. Marziliano, G. Panzeri, F. Pilla, G.F. Pisano, F. Pompili, G. Ru, D. Scrignaro, T. Tucci, G. Vailati.

REFERENCES

(Arthur, 1992) L.J. Arthur, Improving Software Quality - An insider's guide to TQM. *Wiley* (Internet = http://www.wiley.com/ProductInfo.html)

(ASQC, 1995) American Societ for Quality Control, 1995 Malcolm Baldrige Award Criteria, (Internet = http://www.asqc.org)

(AT&T, 1989) AT&T, Process Quality Managemet and Improvement Guidelines. *AT&T Quality Steering Committee*, Issue 1.1 (Internet = http://www.att.com/infocenter/infores.html)

(Briand, 1995) L. Briand, K. El Emam, W.L. Melo, An inductive Method for Process Improvement: Concrete Steps and Guidelines. *Proceedings of ISCN Conference*, Wien

(Collofello, 1993) J. Collofello, B. Gosalia, An application of casual analysis to the software production process". In *Software Practice and Experience*, 23 (10)

(Damele, 1993) G. Damele, G. Bazzana, M. Giunchi, G. Rumi, Setting-up and using a metrics program for Process Improvement. *Proceedings of AQUIS Conference*, Venice

(Damele, 1995) G. Damele, G. Bazzana, M. Giunchi, G. Caielli, M. Maiocchi, F. Andreis, Quantifying the Benefits of Software Process Improvement in Italtel Linea UT Exchange. *Proceedings of XV International Switching Symposium*

(Furuyama, 1993) T. Furuyama, Y. Arai, K. Iio, Fault Generation Model and Mental Stress Effect Analysis". *Proceedings of AQUIS Conference*, Venice

(IEEE, 1993) Members of the BOOTSTRAP project team (Editor: D. Card), BOOTSTRAP: Europe's Assessment Method. *IEEE Software*, May (Internet = http://www.etnoteam.it/bootstrap/index.html)

(Ishikawa, 1991) K. Ishikawa Guida al controllo di qualità. (A guide to quality control) *F. Angeli*

(ISO, 1990) International Organization for Standardization, Quality Management and Quality Assurance Standards - Part 3: Guidelines for the Application of ISO 9001 to the Development, Supply and Maintenance of Software. *ISO/IS 9000-3* (Internet = http://www.iso.ch)

(Italtel, 1993) Italtel-SIT-BUCT-Linea UT, Iter di progetto software - Manuale di qualità del processo di produzione di una release software per le centrali della linea UT. Version 04

(Italtel, 1995) Internet www Server location = http://www.italtel.it

(Kuvaya, 1994) P. Kuvaia, J. Simila, L. Krzanik, A. Bicego, S. Saukkonen, G. Koch. Software process assessment & improvement. *Blackwell*

(Maggi, 1995) A. Maggi, Il percorso della qualità Italtel (Italtel path to quality).Qualità, N° 1/95

(Nakajo, 1991) T. Nakajo, H. Kume, A case history analysis of software error cause-effect relationship. In *IEEE Transactions on Software Engineering*, 17 (8)

(Paulk, 1993) M.C. Paulk, CMM for Software - Version 1.1. CMU/SEI-93-TR-24, *SEI*, (Internet = http://www.sei.cmu.edi)

(Souter, 1992) J.B. Souter, D.P. Cheney, Information Technology Quality System Certification in Europe. *Proceedings of 3rd European Conference on Software Quality*, Madrid,

(Tosi, 1994) L. Tosi, Analisi dei costi connessi alla qualita' del software (Analysis of costs related to software quality). Graduation thesis University of Milan

BIOGRAPHY

G. Damele is Head of the Linea UT Sw Laboratory of Italtel SIT BUCT. He is also Quality Manager for the development projects that have been experiencing Root Cause Analysis.

G. Bazzana is Partner and Consulting Director of Onion, a private company active in the field of communications, technologies and consulting.

F. Andreis is Head of Sw Quality Research for all the business units of Italtel SIT.

F. Aquilio is Manager of the DataBase Sw development area of the Linea UT Sw Laboratory; she is responsible for process improvement activities concerning root cause analysis.

S. Arnoldi is a Senior Researcher at Italtel SIT; he has given continuing support to the definition, implementation and analysis of the RCA program.

E. Pessi is a Senior Consultant at Etnoteam SpA, a major private company that has been supporting the overall process improvement program of Italtel SIT BUCT Linea UT.

6

A Process Improvement Experiment through Process Modelling Technology

P. Coppola, P. Panaroni
Intecs Sistemi s.p.a.
Via Gereschi 32, - 56127 Pisa - Italy
Tel.: *+39.50.545.111*
Fax.: *+39.50.545.200*
e-mail: *paolo@pisa.intecs.it*

Abstract

Intecs Sistemi is an Italian software company deeply engaged in software developments for space systems. The growing role being assigned to software in the control of complex and/or critical functions of space system raised the need of a well defined and disciplined software production process to reach the required software quality.

This need is usually faced by the definition and regulation of the software process through Standards. However Standards have not solved the problem, and, to some extent, have even worsened it: thick documents, vague, ambiguous or incomplete are often hampering or slowing down production without actually assuring a better quality.

Process Modelling Technology is emerging as a set of models, techniques and tools to support effectively and efficiently a well defined and disciplined software production process through the notion of Process Centered Software Development Environments.

This paper reports a Process Improvement Experiment in a space on-board project through the adoption of Process Modelling Technology. The experiment is sponsored by the European Strategic System Initiative (ESSI). The tool Process Weaver, recently adopted by the DoD in its I-CASE initiative, was the selected process tool.

A formal BOOTSTRAP assessment was conducted at the beginning of the experiment, and repeated at the end, to reveal areas of improvement.

The paper will present and critically discuss these main topics:

1) industrial maturity of the Process Modelling Technology and corresponding support tools
2) ease of migration from traditional standards to process models
3) management and engineers acceptance/resistance to tools enforcing the process.
4) BOOTSTRAP assessments as a mechanism to monitor and measure improvement.

Keywords

Standard, quality, process modelling, process visualisation.

1 OBJECTIVES OF THE EXPERIMENT

The experiment has been aimed at assessing application of process modelling technology to an industrial software development project by overcoming the limitation and troubles incurred by the use of traditional software development standards based on natural language.

The focus of the assessment has been on three main items:

1) maturity of the process modelling technology and corresponding support tools
2) ease of migration from traditional standards to process models
3) management and engineers acceptance/resistance to tools enforcing the process.

2 THE CASE STUDY PROJECT

The experiment has been based on a real industrial project. Identification of a suitable project was not an easy task and was constrained by various criteria:

- suitable for the technology to be experimented,
- feasible for transferability of results,
- in the right time frame,
- without affecting costs and schedule,
- carried out by motivated people.

2.1 Selection criteria

Suitable for the technology to be experimented

The project has been selected in order to be representative of a class of project for which Process Technology deployment is best suited. We then focused our search among the projects of our on-board software group where the applicable development standards are the more demanding and complex.

Transferability of results

We also looked at one project where adopted Standards were not excessively "unique" (ad hoc) to that project but, as far as possible, based-on/derived-from more generally applied standards. Since most space projects are now adopting the ESA PSS-05-0 Software Engineering Standard (ESA, 1992), a Process Model based on it will facilitated the transfer of experiment results to other project.

In the right time frame

It was not easy to match the ESSI experiment time frame with that of the on-going or planned projects but, fortunately, we could apply the experiment to a project from its start up to completion.

Without affecting costs and schedule

The funding from ESSI was rather effective to mitigate resistance on the extra costs induced by the experimentation, but a real hard resistance came from the perceived risks of project delays. Almost all software project are under tight schedule pressure, driven by external constraints. Application of a new technology is always perceived as a potential threat. Actually even good technologies (e.g. the Ada language) often provide tangible benefits only from the second project on. The use of Process Technology presented too many novel aspects (including organisational and psychological) and is of some concern to many managers.

Motivation of people
People acting as the object of an experiment, usually do not feel much "comfortable".

Fortunately we found a high motivation both from top management (that encouraged the on-board group to embark in the experiment) and project staff.

Moreover the project run in parallel of a company effort for ISO 9000 certification and Process Technology was clearly perceived as a fundamental step for achieving a well "defined" process.

2.2 The selected project

The selected project is a space software development of a critical on-board application. This class of applications is characterised by strong management requirements, thus matching the selection criteria of its appropriateness for deployment of Process Technology.

Furthermore, since the applicable development standards (covering the whole life cycle) were based on a slight "variation" of the ESA PSS-05-0 Software Engineering Standards, the modelling of the Process for this project was expected to be reusable also for other projects.

The selected project was not in a critical path and the risk of a little slippage was tolerated. However much care was continuously devoted to avoid any unnecessary "perturbation" that might cause a delay.

The application is the Input/Output Subsystem of the Fault Tolerant Computer Pool (FTCP) for a Guidance Navigation and Control (GNC) Avionics Test Bench. This pool of computer is composed of three replicated computers (based on SPARC and 1750A processors) linked by an Inter Processor Network and connected to several GNC busses based on the MIL-STD-1553B protocol.

It is sized about 10 KLOC of Ada code and involved an average of 4 persons for 15 months.

The project is carried out by Intecs Sistemi as principle software subcontractor of Matra Marconi Space, which, in turn, acts as prime contractor on behalf of the CNES (Centre Nationale D'Etudes Spatials). It is part of the Manned Spacecraft Technology Programme (MSTP), whose purpose it to prepare future European manned space missions.

While the hardware computers are triplicated (with a voting mechanism) the software is not diversified and the same version runs in parallel on the 3 computers in hot redundancy. Giving the safety requirements for a GNC system, the software is a highly critical components and in particular the Input/Output Sub-Systems is categorised as "safety critical" (class A software in ESA classification).

The major development methods in use have been the "Structured Analysis and Design Technique" (SADT) during the Requirement Analysis phase, the "Hierarchical Object Oriented" method (HOOD) during the Architectural and Detailed Design phases and Ada as implementation language.

The development environment included tools such as ASA (from Verilog), HOODNice (an Intecs Sistemi own commercialised CASE toolset), and two Ada Compilers: Verdix (native compiler) and TLD 1750A (cross compiler). The development environment is based on SUN SPARCStations (running Unix Sun OS).

3 THE EXPERIMENT

The project started on February 1994 for a duration of about 15 months (BEST-PM, 1995).

The major activities performed were centered around the following major areas:

1) rigorous modelling of the process
2) ProcessWeaver Tool
3) the 'Virtual Desk' metaphore
4) enacting the process on the case study
5) BOOTSTRAP assessment

3.1 Modelling the process

Our first concern was to define the Process Model with the major constraints of being compatible with the applicable standards and feasible for being implemented with Process Weaver. It was soon realised that the modelling power of ProcessWeaver presents some weaknesses. In fact the only available diagrammatic notation available to express process models is a tree of activities providing a plain Work Breakdown Structure (WBS).

We strongly missed a comprehensive high level diagrammatic notation capable to capture also data flow, activity dependencies, recursive and iterative activities, roles involved, etc. In addition this notation should have been easy enough for being understandable by Managers, Quality Engineers and in general all staff performing the process. Cap Gemini Innovation proposed an ad-hoc notation they have developed (not supported by the tool) (PROMESSE, 1995). Intecs Sistemi decided to adopt the notation resulting from the ESPRIT project SCALE (SCALE, 1993). The adopted process notation was an original improvement over SADT (Ross, 1977) (Ross, 1985) (Shepard, 1992) by adding concurrency, recursion, multiple perspectives and an implicit mechanism for backtracking to previous steps in the process (to model re-work).

The full life-cycle process has been rigorously modelled using this notation at a reasonable level of detail. The "model" was a good basis for clarification, improvements and training. Its rigorous and compressed form, made it much more effective than the thick narrative standards available.

This modelling effort represented a major achievement. An internal document, titled IMPROVE, reporting the full process description, was produced and is being maintained as the "master process". This maintenance can be seen as a kind of "continuous" process improvement. A consolidate version of the IMPROVE document will be proposed to become integral part of the company Quality Manual. This activity will parallel our transition from ISO 9000:1987 certification to ISO 9000:1984 certification that requires the revision/extension of some of our processes.

It is finally worth to mention that the adopted notation is independent from ProcessWeaver, therefore it could be used, in different contexts, in conjunction with other process enactment tools (e.g. Life*Flow, ProcessWise, etc.).

3.2 The tool Process Weaver

The tool Process Weaver, developed by Cap Gemini (Fernstrom, 1993), is supporting a rather novel technology compared to traditional CASE tools. More than a tool it can be perceived as an "environment" supporting "Process Centred Software Development".

The adoption of the tool had to be preceded by familiarisation of the staff involved on the basic principles of Process Modelling. The tool was quite easily installed and process toy examples were made running in a few hours. However full mastering of the tool required significant effort, including a formal course held by Cap Gemini experts.

3.3 The 'Virtual Desk' metaphor

The process modelling approach can be conveniently exposed with the so called 'Virtual Desk' metaphor. A metaphor is often an effective way to synthesise a complex new concept by exploiting its resemblance with a common and familiar concept.

The concept of Virtual Desk is very similar to that of Work Context used in the process modelling literature. However Desks can be more easily visualised and conceptually grasped.

A process is seen as the cooperative execution of several activities aimed at a common goal. Each activity is associated with one desk. Every time one activity is started a new desk is created exactly with the purpose of performing that activity. We may have a desk for the design, one for the coding of module A, one for the testing of module A, one for coding of

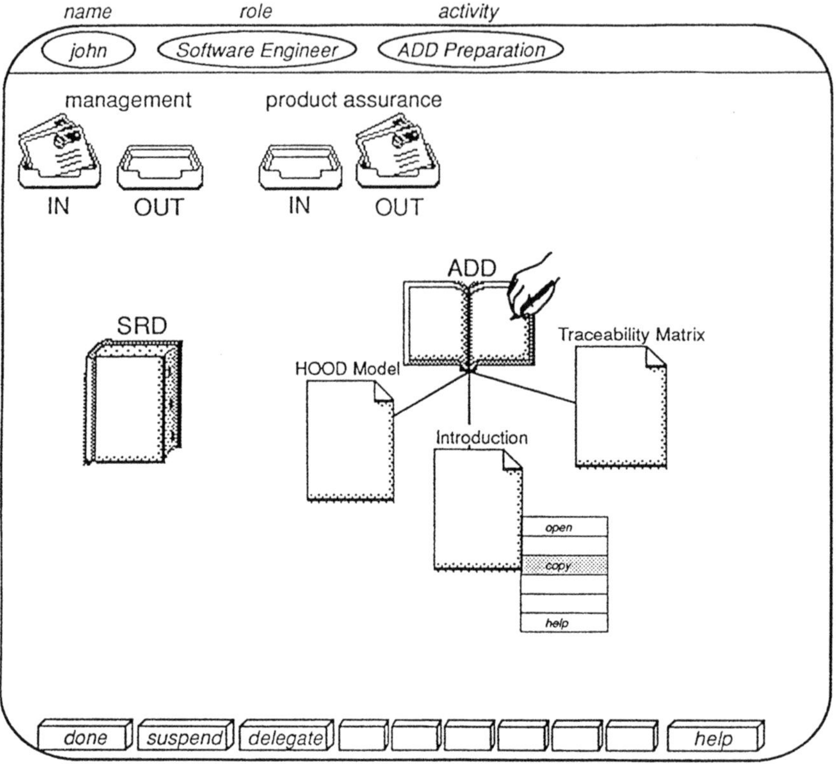

Figure 1 The Virtual Desk.

module B, etc. The desks for coding of module A and B will share the same type, but, are at all effects, different desks.

The whole process is then seen as a set of cooperating desks. A human can sit at a desk and perform part or all the activity, according to his/her role in the project and scheduled/authorized tasks. The same human can move over several desks or different humans can be assigned to the various desks. In principle, a human is responsible of the work performed while sitting at a desk.

An example of Virtual Desk is shown in Figure 1.

Virtual desks are not isolated "work islands" but cooperation among desks takes place through two basic mechanisms:

- exchanging of artefacts (document producer/consumer paradigm);
- exchanging of messages (conversation paradigm).

The distinction between artefacts and messages is rather fuzzy. One may claim that any artefacts can be exchanged by a message or viceversa that any message is a kind of artefact delivered to the other party. Common sense encourages to use the concept of artefacts for relevant and relatively stable pieces of information (e.g. artefacts usually are documents or source files managed under configuration control). At the opposite, messages should be used to model small and volatile pieces of information (e.g. a software problem report, a notification of completion, a request for delay, etc.).

The virtual desk supports these two paradigms of cooperation by:

1) automatically load on top of the desk all the input artefacts necessary to accomplish the activity. As soon as the activity has completed its output artefact/s is/are loaded on top of other desks according to the process rules. This implements the flow of artefacts from desk to desk (and the corresponding synchronisation).

   The desk "knows" what are the expected input artefacts, output artefacts and the allowed operators (e.g. tools) necessary to produce the output starting from the input.

   The desk supports the user by identifying all (and only those) artefacts and operators necessary to accomplish the activity. The user is not concerned about the selection of inputs, their completeness, their availability, selection of operators, applicability of operators to the input, etc. Everything is prepared on top of the virtual desk. The user mental load is reduced: all is creative energy is spent on the activity to be performed rather than on a quest for input and tools.

   Even more, the desk "knows" which operator is applicable to what artefact (e.g. a compiler on a source, a speller on a document, etc.) and even has knowledge to support proper sequencing of application of operators (e.g. first lint, only after compilation). The user is then warned against illegal sequencing of operators (e.g. first print, after spell) that might affect quality or productivity.

2) the exchange of messages between desks is supported by a strong paradigm well beyond and much powerful than the plain e-mail-like paradigm.

   Each desk has pre-defined a set of communication channels with other desks with which a communication can take place. Not every desk can communicate with any other desk: the process model defines a well predefined network of communication. A channel connect two desks. A protocol is associated with a channel such that communication on that channel shall stick to the defined protocol. Messages are named and typed. The respect of the protocol is controlled. The same message can even be broadcasted through many channels as long as it is compatible with the protocols of those channels.

An example of channel (e.g. status account) is one between the manager desk and the programmer of module A desk. Through that channel the manager may send a request for status report and the programmer shall respond with a status report.

The channel mechanism is able to discipline communication among the desks. If the manager is waiting for a status report the desk warns that such channel is pending waiting a response. Concurrent communications (conversations) can then occur between one desk and many others: each will have its own channel and its own "status of the communication".

Let's imagine a desk for a marketing staff member with a series of channels with each of the customers. New channels are dynamically created (on top of the desk) as new customers are identified. For each customer a communication is established (first contact, presentation letter, product brochure, offer, response, if positive answer, delivery, invoice, else make a discount, etc.). The human sitting on the marketing desk is supported by the desk that keep track of all open channels and their status. A new hired marketing person, "sitting" at that virtual desk, will easily take over the job, by proper continuation of message exchange always respecting the protocol imposed by the process model.

3.4 Enacting the process on the case study

Automatic enactment of the process by the staff of the on-going space project occurred incrementally according to the following steps:

Process tracking

The actual on-going process was manually tracked so that actual process events (e.g. start of an activity, review, re-work, etc.) could be used to validate the process being defined.

Implementation of the Virtual Desks

The various virtual desks needed to support the process were identified (more than 60) and designed. The design included:

a) definition the desk composition: input documents, output documents, tools, applicable standards, applicable plans, relevant reference documents, relevant reuse materials or good examples, etc.
b) definition of the desk layout (e.g. iconic representation of a source a test, etc.).
c) inter-desks relationships (which documents will flow from one desk to another).
d) definition of roles and staff enabled to work on the various types of desks (e.g. programmer, tester, QA, manager, etc.).

Process Weaver provided a nice user friendly and interactive interfaces to implement these virtual desks.

Model exercise

As soon as first fragments of the process model and corresponding virtual desks were available these were exercised by the project Quality Assurance Engineer to validate them against typical process patterns previously tracked.

Process Control

Once the whole process and all virtual desks were available, they have been used by the Quality Engineer only, to control and guide the process execution.

The QA engineer was actually "sitting" at the various virtual desks and used the information on the desk to "direct" the engineers in their daily activity in order to assurance conformance of the executed process with the model.

Manually the QA engineer gave (physically) the right documents at the right person at the right time and waited for the expected results. This manual activities was driven by the virtual desks.

In other words only the Quality Engineer was using the tool. The tool was then acting as an assistant to the Quality Assurance Role supporting the identification of what has to be done, with which dependencies, by whom, with which tools, on what input data, etc. Manually the Quality Engineer assured that the "real" process was enacted in accordance with the tool suggestions/prescriptions.

This phase of the experiment was called as "off-line" phase. It was useful to minimise interferences and perturbations on the on-going project while consolidating both the process model definition and it implementation through Process Weaver.

Model application

Then the experiment entered in its "on-line" phase. In "on-line" mode the tool directly interacts with the various roles of the process (manager, designer, programmers, tester, etc.) providing directly to them assistance on what has to be done. Thus the process was directly enacted by the tool without any "mediation" of the QA role: software engineers were working directly within the virtual desk.

Metrics collection
As long as the Process Model has been used, a tight monitoring of the enactment of the Process on the selected Case Study was performed. Monitoring included systematic metrics collection covering both process attributes (e.g. effort per activity, rate of re-work, etc.) and product attributes (e.g. size, complexity, quality of many artefacts including specifications, design, code, etc.).

3.5 Evaluating the results

In the context of the ESSI Application Experiment, the need for a "quantitative", further than "qualitative", evaluation and measurement of results was emphasized. In order to accomplish to this requirement, we decided to perform before the start of the experiment a BOOTSTRAP assessment and a "delta" assessment after its completion (BOOTSTRAP, 1993) (Kuvaje, 1995).

The formal assessment according to the BOOTSTRAP Scheme was conducted by 2I-Synspace (Friburg - Germany) .

The assessment evaluated at first Intecs Sistemi as a whole Software Producing Unit (SPU) by analysing standards, methods and practices at corporate level as evidenced by internal Quality Manual and associated procedures. The resulting score 3.0 placed Intecs Sistemi at the "defined" maturity level.

A second step of the assessment was the evaluation of two on-board space projects (similar to the one being under experimentation) to assess their project maturity. The resulting score was 2.8 for the best project and 2.0 for the worst, with an average of 2.4.

This was a clear indication that maturity of projects was lagging behind maturity of the SPU, and that an improvement was necessary to assure greater compliance of projects with applicable standards and norms.

The BOOTSTRAP assessment was not delivering just final scores (though important) but a full set of indications on weak areas and recommendations for improvement. All of them have been passed to the Quality Office as input for revision of internal Quality Manual and associated procedures.

The "delta" assessment, conducted after the completion of the experiment and centered on the FTCP project, resulted with a score of 2.6 . As far as the Intecs Sistemi as a SPU is concerned, we also experienced a small step forward at organization level (also due to the ISO 9000 certification obtained in the meanwhile). The obtained scores were under our initial expectation, even though, as long as the experiment was being carried on, we perceived that a significant improvement does not depend on the modelling of the process and its application on just one project but can be only consequence of a higher maturity level reached by both management, technical and QA staff. However, the "delta" assessment showed that we are on the right path.

It is worth to mention that, beside the measurement of process status and improvement, the BOOTSTRAP assessment was a useful exercise to better understand, with the support of external and independent experts, the company strengths and weaknesses. The wide set of technical areas covered was comparable or even superior to the SEI Assessment schema (for which we had a self-assessment experience). Coverage of ISO 9000 areas, for which there was some interest as the certification process was underway, was globally unsatisfactory: there were many ISO 9000 areas not well covered by BOOTSTRAP. We found very useful a score assigned to individual technical areas and a comparison with European averages.

4 LESSONS LEARNED

In general we can assert that the results of the experiment was positive, since it allowed us to better monitor and control the progress of each single task performed during the project development, including both technical, management and QA ones. Nevertheless some points which need further improvement have arisen. In the following the major lessons learned during the experiment are presented.

4.1 The Process Model

The issue of Process Granularity is central: to which level of detail the process has to be decomposed and modelled? How many virtual desks are necessary?

While it is difficult to provide a general answer to this issue (Mittermeir, 1992), a pragmatic approach has been followed: the process has been decomposed up to terminal activities; a terminal activity, by norm, has few inputs, one single output and is performed by one single role using a small number of tools. When such a terminal activity revealed to be effort critical (i.e. it spend a significant percentage of the overall project effort), or quality critical (i.e. it generate a significant percentage of overall defects in the project) the activity has to be further refined.

The underlying philosophy is that a process model should be refined driven by the criticality (effort and quality) of the activities being modelled: there is no need for a very detailed breakdown of those activities which do not consume man/power and do not generate defects. On the other hand, critical activities, must be better understood in terms of their internal steps (sub-activities) and better controlled by rigorous enactment.

4.2 The tool

We found ProcessWeaver a useful tool for process "enactment", since it is easy to use and allows to efficiently track the ongoing activities. It is also worth to mention that it is satisfactorily reliable as we did not experienced serious problems during its usage. Nevertheless, at the time being, it is still naive for process "modelling".

A tool supporting the editing of process models using the selected diagrammatic notation was strongly missed. This lack was acknowledged by Cap Gemini that experienced the same problem in other similar projects (PROMESSE, 1995). This tool should also provide basic consistency analysis of the model being edited.

In addition it still lacks of some basic mechanisms to support advanced process modelling issues such as backtracking, early starting, etc.

4.3 The Process Enactment

By adopting the incremental approach presented above, a rather smooth introduction of this novel technology was possible.

In off-line mode the technology was only perceived by the QA Engineer and the first reaction from QA Staff was positive. They found in the tool a good and rigorous assistance for their day-by-day work of assuring that the process is executed as it is prescribed by the process model.

In on-line mode, when the tool directly and automatically drove the various roles in the execution of the process, people suffered of being too much constrained on what they had to do and when. In a typical process there are a lot of circumstances where activities are started, trying to met tight schedules, before they formally should be, in a sort of concurrent engineering (Frailey, 1993) (Petri, 1990). In addition the on-line mode was not capable to properly handle what has been called "process backtracking", that is the re-execution of the process from a previous activity (e.g. revision of specifications) in order to fix a problem or accommodate a change request (Suzuki, 1993).

On the other hand, there is a very positive reaction on the assistance given by the tool in terms of reducing the mental load (one task at a time), to identify the input and tools to be used and, last but not the least, synchronise activities between the various roles involved.

6 REFERENCES

BEST-PM, (1995) *BEST-PM - Beyond the Standards: Process Modelling.* ESSI Application Experiment nb. 10841, Final Report

BOOTSTRAP, (1995) Europe's Assessment Method. *IEEE Software*, May 1993

ESA (1992) *Software Engineering Standards.* PSS-05-0, issue 2,

Fernstrom C., (1993) Adding Process Support to Unix. IEEE Software, September 1993

Frailey D. (1993) Concurrent Engineering and the Software Process. in *Proceedings of the 2nd International Conference on Software Process*, Berlin,

Kuvaje P., (1995) BOOTSTRAP: a Software Process Assessment and Improvement Methodology. in *Objective Quality Software Symposium,* Florence, May 1995

Mittermeir R.T. et al. (1992) Stepwise Improvement of the Software Process in a Multidimensional Framework, *Annual Review of Automatic Programming*, **vol. 16**

Petri J., Pulli et al. (1990) Concurrent Engineering for Real Time Systems, *IEEE Software*, November 1993

PROMESSE, (1995) *Final Report.* ESA contract nb. 10081/92

Ross D.T., (1977) Structured Analysis (SA): A Language for Communicating Ideas. *IEEE Transaction on Software Engineering*, January 1977.

Ross D.T., (1985) Applications and Extensions of SADT. *COMPUTER*, April 1985

SCALE, (1993) *Process Modeling Formalism Definition*, ESPRIT project nb. 6334

Shepard T. et al. (1992) A Visual Software Process Language, *Communication of the ACM*, April 1992

Suzuki M. et al. (1993) A Formal Method of Re-execution in Software Process, in *Proceedings of the 2nd International Conference on Software Process*, Berlin, 1993

BIOGRAPHY

Paolo Coppola
Paolo Coppola is the head of the Special Systems Section of INTECS Sistemi. He is responsible of the development of critical software systems, in particular for spacecraft on-board applications.

Paolo Panaroni
Paolo Panaroni is the head of the QA & Methodologies Section of INTECS Sistemi. He is responsible for the overall Company Quality Management and of internal Quality Manuals in compliance of ESA, NATO and ISO software standards. He is currently President of the Ada-Italy Association.

7

Process Maturity - Growing older and wiser? Using *Process Advisor* for Process Assessment

A Bryant and J Grogan

Tony Bryant, Professor of Informatics, Leeds Metropolitan University, Leeds LS6 3QS; email A.BRYANT@lmu.ac.uk; fax +44 113 283 3182

John Grogan, Research Assistant, Leeds Metropolitan University, Leeds LS6 3QS; email J.GROGAN@lmu.ac.uk; fax +44 113 283 3182

Abstract

The idea of process maturity has a particular allure for software developers: Not only does it support the argument that there is a central development architecture for software construction; but it also lends an air of credibility to the efforts at improvement that have characterized earlier periods and now extend into the present and future. The software crisis may be no more than symptoms of growth: process puberty and adolescence. Maturity will bring with it a wider and deeper set of foundations for general software practise; and in the not too distant future the period from 1968 to approximately 1998 will be seen in a more favourable light, as a period which had to be endured, but has now been surpassed. Whether this happy situation comes to pass is dependent on a variety of factors and forces, not least of which is the ability of organizations and practitioners to come to terms with their own shortcomings, for instance as demonstrated by the findings of indicators such as those designed to assess process or capability maturity. What follows is based on our initial use of one such indicator.

Keywords

Software Engineering, Process Improvement, Process Maturity, Capability Maturity

1 INTRODUCTION & BACKGROUND

The concept of process maturity is an inherently appealing one, but also derives great strength from an understanding that the route to improvement and perfection consists of many small steps and stages, rather than a single leap. The general idea of maturity, in a quality sense, derives from the work of Deming and Crosby, although the central figure for *software process improvement* is Watts Humphrey and his work on the Software Process Maturity Model (SPMM) which developed into the current programme at the Software Engineering Institute (SEI).

In fact the concept of maturity with regard to IT, if not exactly software engineering, dates back a little further to the work of Gibson and Nolan. Their model of technological maturity was focused more on the application of the technology, but they employed the terminology of growth and a process of development in a fashion similar to that now used with regard to process improvement and maturity. (See Bryant, 1995 chapters 3 and 4 for a more extended discussion of the links between these models.)

Any growth model immediately evokes a number of questions -

- Is it necessary to pass through all the stages in a defined sequence?
- How quickly does the maturation proceed, and can it be accelerated or retarded in any way?
- How can one assess where one is along the route of maturity?

The wide variety of applications modelled around SPMM all seek to offer responses to these questions. The general SPMM model was initially offered as a basis for assessment; internally by the development organization itself. Later variations such as the Capability Maturity Model (CMM) were oriented towards external, customer-based assessment. But the mere existence of such models does not necessarily assist an organization in moving from assessment to improvement. There is also the issue of how applicable the model actually is, given that there is such a wide range of software development contexts. Does a particular model apply only to very specific forms of software development - e.g. real-time or safety critical systems? These issues have been recognized by those developing the maturity models, and much of the innovation and refinement over the last 5 years has been concerned with developing various forms of guidance, extension, specialization and so on.

In the commercial world Process Advisor (PA) has been available for some time as 'a self-directed system for software process improvement' It is clearly derived from the SPMM approach, but is marketed in a slightly different way as 'a low-cost, multimedia product' Pressman, 199.).

If SPMM is like a health check from your family practitioner; CMM is more like a health check demanded by your insurance company before they will renew your policy: PA is a little like a *Do-It-Yourself* health check that can be done in the comfort of your own home. Given that a large proportion of software is developed in-house by fairly small development departments, or by independent software companies with fewer than 50 employees, the relatively informal, low-cost PA approach can be seen to have an obvious market.

Some organizations probably have used PA in precisely this way. It is certainly cheaper and less externally visible than employing a consultant to do the assessment. On the other hand, there are many who would argue that without some external and disinterested party to such an assessment there is little value to the findings. At Leeds Metropolitan University (LMU) we have been interested in process maturity for some time, both in itself and as part of our work on standards and quality for information systems.

We have used PA as part of our teaching, but have also been keen to show students how PA is used in practice. One way in which we have begun to accomplish this has been to apply PA to the development department of a large organization with whom we collaborated previously. This has demonstrated the practical issues which arise in a process assessment project, and has also provided insight into the PA package itself. In what follows we describe the PA package, before giving a description of the context in which we used it, and then offer some insights into its use and the general lessons which we drew from the experience.

2 *PROCESS ADVISOR*

Process Advisor (PA) is a software process improvement method developed in 1992 by Roger Pressman. It consists of a number of stages designed to guide a company through a phased approach to software process improvement. Pressman uses the term 'Software Engineering Implementation Life Cycle' (SEILC) to refer to the six stages he identifies and his advocated progression through those stages.

The philosophy of PA is similar to that of the Software Process Maturity Model (SPMM) developed by Humphrey (1989) and later used to underpin the Capability Maturity Model (CMM) from the Software Engineering Institute (SEI). In summary this philosophy states that in order to improve and sustain the quality of software *products*, the software development *process* must be improved. The overall ideas are drawn from a variety of sources, such as Deming and Crosby; and Humphrey's application of them to software development has spawned a large number of software process improvement and assessment initiatives, including CMM (1993), Bootstrap (1994), Trillium (1994) and SPICE. PA does not directly implement the SEI approach, although many of the questions used in PA have been openly adapted from the CMM questionnaire.

One of the findings of the early uses of SPMM and like was that 80-90% of organizations assessed were at the two lowest levels of the 5 point scale. This proportion has not altered dramatically during that time, and it is for this reason that PA has been designed particularly for organizations at maturity levels 1 and 2 of the CMM; although it can also be used by more advanced organizations. The strategies developed as a result of using PA are also said to be consistent with the philosophy behind general quality standards such as the ISO 9000 series (1991). PA has been marketed as a low-cost alternative to - or basis for - the CMM.

2.1 The Process Advisor Method:

PA is described as a 'self-directed system for software process improvement', which means that it is expected to be utilized by the developers themselves to improve their own software development process. PA aims to offer guidance for users, charting a route through the 'Software Engineering Implementation Life Cycle'. This consists of six stages starting with an initial assessment of current process practices, through selection and justification stages, to eventual implementation of improved practices. The stages are defined as follows:

Assessment:

Objective - Assess the current state of Software Engineering Practice within the organization, a 'look in the mirror'. The software process assessment is used to determine the strengths and weaknesses of current practices. This is accomplished through use of a detailed questionnaire, followed by evaluation of the responses.

Education:

Objective - Increase the level of knowledge of software engineering methods, procedures and tools by those involved with development. An 'Education Planning Matrix' is coupled with the results of the software process assessment, providing the basis for an education strategy to be developed.

Selection:

This encompasses three elements:
1 - establishment of overall goals and criteria for selecting methods, procedures and tools
2 - identification of the particular methods, procedures and tools that have a high probability of improving the existing software engineering practices
3 - choosing, justifying and acquiring software engineering and CASE technology

Justification:

Use of the Justification Model provided enables previously collected baseline metrics to be used for productivity and quality projections for later assessment of decisions and selections.

Installation:

A Transition Plan is created which identifies the strategy chosen to implement the software engineering methods, tools and procedures and CASE technology selected earlier. This involves the definition of tasks, milestones and deliverables, and also the assignment of responsibilities for the individuals involved.

Evaluation:

Another 'look in the mirror'. Initially at a macro level, by focusing on the success and acceptance of early transition tasks, and finally by undertaking a technical evaluation once an improved process has been applied to one or more projects.

The overall sequence of stages may be altered so that some run in parallel. Following the final evaluation stage, the process is iterative.

For our assessment of PA we devised an action research project involving the use of PA to undertake an assessment of an organization's current software development practices. Therefore we focused almost exclusively on the first stage of the SEILC.

2.2 Process Advisor contents

The PA package consists of three main elements

- a workbook, supported by a disk containing questionnaires, automated models, and standard reports, to take the user through the SEILC stages
- a video of sessions that support the main SEILC stages and activities
- a text book 'A Manager's Guide to Software Engineering'.

The workbook is aimed at the person handling the PA exercise, and it seems to be taken for granted that this would be a (senior) manager of some sort. The workbook contains a detailed description of each of the stages and activities in the SEILC. It also contains the questionnaires, models and reports that are used at the various stages. The intention is that the workbook guides the user through the SEILC, directing the activities, advising on what to look for and making suggestions on how to handle the results. The workbook is also supported by a computer disk containing automated support aids for the questionnaires and models used, together with a number of templates for the resulting reports.

The video provides sessions on each of the stages of PA, helping the user to prepare for each before it is begun. It also contains a question and answer section on each stage providing help for the most common questions. The book also uses a question and answer format to providing further advice on adopting the PA approach.

3 STUDY OVERVIEW

The application of PA came about as a result of LMU approaching a local financial organization, with whom we had previously collaborated, with the suggestion that we use the PA package to assist them in their own internal deliberations regarding process improvement. The work was not done on a consultancy basis, but on the understanding that we could use the experience of our use of PA for our teaching and research. The organization is the headquarters of a group of financial companies, with a centralized software development staff of around seventy people, dealing with systems and projects for the group. Many of the systems involve large daily volumes of transactions. One of the development personnel had previously used part of the SPMM; seeking to incorporate ideas of 'best practice' in a specific project and then producing a report rating the actual practices used, and giving an overall calculation of the 'cost of quality'. The results of this indicated that the processes used on that project could be rated at level three of the SPMM, and that the payback expressed in the form of a ratio of 'expected rework' to 'actual rework' was in the order of 10:1. (The approach used to measure 'rework' was based on Error Source Accounting, see Bryant & Chan, 1992). These fairly impressive results had raised the visibility of process improvement issues amongst the personnel, and probably acted as a deciding factor in the organization's decision to allow outsiders to apply the PA assessment.

The initial task was to identify the organization personnel who would liaise with the external project team (the authors). Although the bulk of the effort would be supplied by the external team, an internal group was required to initiate and oversee the project. Three internal staff were selected, including a senior manager and the staff member who had previously applied SPMM to a project. The group met and decided on a project schedule. The internal members were responsible for selecting interviewees, and arranging a briefing meeting at which the aims and objectives of the project could be discussed with all those involved. The scope of the project was to be limited to the first task of PA; the assessment stage of the SEILC. This involved assessing the current practices, tools and methods of the organization, using the questionnaires provided by PA as the main instrument for data gathering. The PA Workbook advises that this, like all other stages, should involve a team of managers and technical staff to ensure different perspectives are taken into account, and also to promote involvement by the staff generally.

It was decided that a team of ten people would be asked to complete the questionnaires and be interviewed. Their job functions included -
Project Leader
Senior Development Manager
Analysis & Design
Program and Build
Development (Quality) Manager

Business Development Manager
The team also included two senior managers from user areas of the company, to represent the customer view of the products resulting from the software development process. This combination provided a wide range of views from those participating in the software development process.

4 ASSESSMENT EXERCISE

The interviews were conducted by one of the authors, who also undertook the processing of the results from the questionnaires. The assessment exercise involves responding to three questionnaires; one being done in the respondent's own time, with the results recorded on paper, and two completed during individual face-to-face interviews. The paper questionnaire consists of a number of questions requiring either "Yes" or "No" responses - "Don't Know" and "Not Available" are also allowed. All ten participants completed this: They did this prior to the interviews, so that they knew the sorts of topics that the later interviews would cover. The questions are quite detailed and are designed to elicit information concerned with whether various activities are performed or standards followed. These questions are similar to those of the CMM (Humphrey 1987), and cover a number of aspects including 'Organizational policies' and 'Training and software development'. Since the answers are either Yes or No, they can be combined for all respondents, and give an overall score for each section. (PA includes, on disk, a template for a spreadsheet which produces the relevant ratings when the scores are entered.)

A qualitative set of questions is put to the interviewees to gain further details of the practices, methods and tools currently in use. This is an extension of the comment provision in the CMM questionnaire, which itself is mostly in a Boolean Y/N form. Each interview for this section took about one hour, and resulted in a great deal of information complementing the earlier responses. PA also offers guidance for follow-up questions and inferences to be drawn from the detailed information that is acquired.

Finally, there is a set of quantitative questions regarding matters such as budgets and future plans. It was felt that this required specialized knowledge not available to most of the target group. Only the Senior Development Manager, who was responsible for most of these areas, answered these questions. Again, a set of inferences and follow-up questions are supplied to guide the PA user.

The interviewing itself caused some anxiety on the part of the target personnel, but this was dissipated when the confidentiality of their answers was emphasized: But this had to be restated a number of times. Respondents expressed some difficulty in deciding upon their answers to the Boolean questions, but the PA guidelines account for this, suggesting that such questions should only be answered with a 'Yes' if -

> 'A - The question is true for a significant majority of the cases or situations (normally 70% or more); B - the majority of knowledgeable people within your organization would also respond 'yes'; C - an independent party could substantiate that the answer is true by using specific project evidence.'

As is common with projects requiring co-ordination of many people, with different priorities and objectives apart from those of the project itself, the project faltered at this interview stage. The project team had been keen to work to a tight schedule. It had been hoped to be able to go from the initial briefing, through to completion of the interviews in a three week period: And completion of this first stage project within one month of that. The idea was to demonstrate to participants that their efforts had been useful, and the overall results of the project would yield meaningful results and tangible effects. Unfortunately various people were unavailable at the pre-arranged interview times, and the period for this activity had to be extended. The Senior Development Manager was the hardest to get hold of, an early indication perhaps of lack of management commitment to the project.

5 PROCESSING THE RESPONSES

Upon completion of all the questionnaires and interviews the results were then processed. For the Boolean questions PA does not state whether the overall ratings should be reached by consensus or by averaging across all the results. The project team decided that an average should be taken, although the range of responses would be noted. The average is then plotted against scores supplied by PA for 'common' and 'best practice'. (These scores derive from Pressman's use of PA on a range of software development organizations.)

The attributes measured by this particular questionnaire correspond roughly to the sections covered by the CMM. (CMM for instance uses terms such as 'organizational and resource management', 'training, standards & procedures', 'software engineering process metrics' and so on.) An average score for each process attribute is obtained, which results in a grade corresponding to the maturity rating for that attribute. A summary of the scores obtained in our example is shown in Figure 1. The column headed '*actual*' gives the average score attained for that process attribute, or sub-section. The CP column indicates 'common practice'; the BP column 'best practice'.* The resultant grade for each aspect is shown in the final column.

Pressman warns against using the attribute scores and the overall ratings too simply. Each software development company is unique, has different demands from its own customers and its own management structure and personnel. Scores and comparisons must not be treated as absolute and objective measures, but at best as indicators. They can provide a guideline, but should not be allowed to form the focus of the exercise, with the sole aim of improvement being to reach a higher score as an end in itself.

Using PA for a group drawn both from users (customers) and developers is slightly problematic. It is unrealistic to expect users to have detailed knowledge of the software development process. Therefore many of their responses will be "don't know". But for PA scoring a "don't know" scores '1', the same as that for a "no". The net result of a large proportion of "don't knows" would be poor comparison for that attribute against common or best practice. PA offers no suggestions to deal with this, probably on the assumption that users/customers are not expected to be involved. In our case study there were a large number

* Common practice is typical of most software development. Best practice represents the top 10-15 per cent of software developers. Common practice is inadequate in the software industry today, whilst best practice is still short of state-of-the-art practices and thereby has scope for improvement

	Section	Actual	CP	BP	Grade
1	**Organizational Policies**	**1.35**	**1.8**	**3**	**E**
2	**Training**	**1.49**	**2.2**	**3.7**	**E**
3	**Software Development Process***	**2.17**	**1.4**	**3.1**	**D**
4	**Quality Assurance Activities**	**1.93**	**1.4**	**3.1**	**D**
4.1	Documentation	2.78	1.6	3.9	
4.2	Reviews & analysis of results	1.77	1.4	2.6	
4.3	Quality assurance functions	1.23	1.3	2.8	
5	**Project Management***	**2.0**	**2.0**	**3.6**	**D**
5.1	Organizational resources	2.56	1.6	4.4	
5.2	Oversight	2.33	2.7	3.7	
5.3	Planning	1.67	2.0	3.1	
5.4	Monitoring & tracking	1.84	1.4	3.4	
5.5	Configuration management	2.12	2.0	3.8	
5.6	Subcontracts	1.61	2.5	3.0	
6	**Methods and Techniques**	**1.98**	**2.3**	**3.8**	**D**
6.1	Customer communication	1.85	2.7	4.5	
6.2	Software engineering methods	2.1	2.2	3.1	
7	**Tools**	**1.9**	**1.4**	**3.0**	**D**
7.1	Categories	2.5	1.7	3.3	
7.2	Environment	1.38	1.0	2.8	
8	**Metrics & Measurement**	**1.09**	**1.0**	**2.4**	**E**
	Overall	**1.74**	**1.69**	**3.21**	**D**

Figure 1 Grading Software Engineering Practice.

*** denotes an average score based on a wide range of individual scores**

of "don't knows", which did affect scores for some attributes; but did not alter the grade for that attribute, or the overall grade.

The attribute grade gives an indication of the organization's current practice for that attribute, and also an intimation of how best to start to improve it. The overall grade is based on the profile of all the attributes. PA suggests that a grade 'D' indicates that the organization has -

- few controls in place
- a relatively informal software development process
- some procedures in use, but these are incomplete, not fully defined, and allow a range of interpretations across and within projects
- some methods have been identified, but they are not always used (correctly)
- some CASE tools might be in use, but are not integrated into the development process

This is a fairly accurate description of the situation existing in the organization studied.

The descriptions of the five possible grades offered by PA are not meant to be more than broad approximations. They are based initially only on the one form of questionnaire. But this does permit a simple form of validation, since there should be some correspondence between the description offered by PA, and the context in which the questionnaire has been applied. In our case the project team were satisfied that the 'D' rating was reasonably accurate.

For each process attribute PA offers an outline of initial improvement activities. For example, with regard to the grade 'E ' for 'Organizational Policies': PA suggests that this indicates a lack of top down direction for software engineering practices. This is usually because senior management has not identified such practices as a critical aspect. The suggested remedies include: educating senior management on the importance of software to their business; affirming this view to middle and line management; getting senior management to commit resources to process improvement initiatives. These suggestions from PA are then combined with the findings from the other two questionnaires; the 'qualitative' and 'quantitative' interviews.

5.1 Sample Findings

The processing of the interview results is time consuming, and requires skill and judgement on the part of the project team. The disinterestedness of people external to the organization itself is critical: Both earlier in the interviews themselves, and in this processing of the responses. Essentially what is required at this stage is for the interview material (tapes, notes, etc.) to be analyzed, highlighting key points and issues. If this were to be done by someone within the organization, there would be a high possibility that individual prejudices would interfere with the process. One of the authors worked through all the interview material, and produced a draft report with a number of findings.

The initial list of findings was then used as a basis for a second pass through the material; correlating responses to the findings, whether they supported that finding or not. (It can be as useful to know that people are unsure or differ about something as it is to know if something is working well or not.) The attribute scores were also a useful guide, particularly where there were a wide range of individual scores. A total of 40 findings resulted as shown in Figure 2.

FIGURE 2 - Findings from PA Assessment

Organizational Policies

1. Lack of management commitment to improving the development process.
2. No clearly defined software development process exists.
3. No clearly identified quality and productivity improvement program exists.

Training

1. Training is ad-hoc for staff when new practices, methods or tools are implemented.
2. The lack of a training strategy is having a detrimental effect on staff.
3. Training is not clearly specified for software engineers and project managers.
4. Project planning does not take into account training requirements for project staff.
5. Staff find it hard to keep up-to-date with latest developments in the industry.
6. Project managers are seen as having little experience of handling large-scale projects.
7. Management are seen as requiring training in staff management and motivational skills.

Software Development Process

1. The development process is not defined and monitored to ensure consistency of approach.
2. Standards that have been established are not followed by all staff.
3. Testing seems to be planned for some projects and not for others.
4. Projects on different platforms employ different testing methods.
5. Requirements capture is seen as an area that is not given great enough emphasis.

Quality Assurance Activities

1. There are specific documentation formats defined, but not all staff are aware of this.
2. Configuration management is not used for all documentation.
3. Formal technical reviews are neither formal nor conducted regularly.
4. There is no analysis of the review data.
5. The Q. A. procedures are not applied consistently.

Project Management

1. The estimating process does not identify risk areas.
2. Timescales for projects are not seen in the same way by users and developers.
3. Project management is not consistent over all projects.
4. Project initiation stems from a number of sources, projects vary in importance and size.
5. The project management process is seen as de-motivating staff.
6. Users do not understand their role in the project management process.
7. There is little emphasis on a review of projects upon completion.
8. Project Management of subcontracted work is seen as managed differently.
9. The development effort spent on maintenance activities is 23.8% of the total workload.

Methods and Techniques

1. No established team to monitor and assess the development process on a long-term basis.
2. The user is not involved regularly during the development process.
3. The methods employed are not as comprehensive as they could be or utilized consistently.
4. Software developers are lacking in knowledge of best practices in software engineering.
5. Development staff have different views upon who the customer is.

Tools

1. CASE tools are not being used to any great extent.
2. Some tools are not being used to their fullest capabilities.
3. There is no strategy for the evaluation, purchase and implementation of tools.
4. Prototyping is sometimes used, but not often.

Metrics and Measurement

1. Metrics are employed but have only recently been introduced.

Staff are largely unaware of the benefits to be gained from the use of metrics.

Each finding was then stated in the assessment report, together with a discussion and recommendation. An example entry for the Software Engineering Process attribute is given below.

FINDING: The software development process is insufficiently defined and monitored to ensure consistency of approach.

DISCUSSION: *The software development process is partially defined in that procedures exist for certain elements, e.g. configuration management. These elements are not always employed as they should be, e.g. independent software quality assurance is not employed on all projects, through lack of publication, auditing and management commitment in varying degrees. It is interesting that the score given for this section by the users involved in this exercise was markedly lower than that given by the development staff who participated. Even development staff who identified the development methods employed as being a strong point in the company's favour also pointed out that these methods were not consistently employed.*

RECOMMENDATION: *There is a need for the software development process to be defined and documented. The documented process should identify milestones, deliverables (and their assessment) and control points (i.e. reviews, review procedures, user involvement) that ensure consistency of approach across all projects. Then a quality management system should be applied to the whole software development process. This would give a process based on established procedures, a manual that all staff could have access to, or copies of the relevant parts, and a solid base for auditing projects. It would also provide a good platform for decisions on how to improve the process, methods and tools employed.*

At this stage Pressman recommends that all the findings are prioritized, forming the basis for an action plan for later stages of PA. The prioritization was carried out by the entire project team, since some internal steering was essential. The team, however, had great difficulty in accomplishing a list of priorities based on the findings; and found it easier to focus on the recommendations. This was a slight departure from the prescribed PA route which provides a template for the prioritization report. One of the key factors in the decision to present the results in this way was that it would enhance the accessibility to those unfamiliar with the technicalities of the exercise, particularly senior management. This change in emphasis caused the project to overrun, but resulted in an assessment report that met with the approval of all of the project team, with a prioritized list of recommendations that would provide a strategy for process improvement for the next eighteen months (a time frame recommended by PA).

6 ASSESSMENT EXERCISE COMPLETION & RESPONSES

The exercise was completed with briefings to senior management and the participants; outlining the findings and recommendations. The assessment report was made available to both groups. At the outset, there had been the expectation that the earlier 'level 3' rating for the individual project would be matched across the department as a whole. The 'D' roughly equates to the lower level 2, and some attributes only rated 'E' (or roughly level 1). This failure to match expectations had extensive repercussions. The senior development manager who had initiated the project, and was part of the project team, was in a particularly difficult position. The findings showed that recent initiatives to create a more open and quality-minded organization had proved ineffective. Also that improvements in methods and practices had been introduced, but there had not been any check to see if they were understood, working effectively, or indeed being used properly or at all.

This meant that the process envisaged by PA was undermined. Instead of continuing to the education and selection phases, the report led to an overall questioning of recent policy and control. Various personnel felt threatened by the findings, and many questioned the wisdom of allocating resources to accomplish what should already have been achieved by earlier initiatives. Rather than providing a mechanism for increased awareness and resource commitment, the assessment stage threatened to subvert the whole idea of process improvement.

At the time of writing, this combination of factors has meant that there is no immediate prospect of continuing the project to later PA stages. Officially this hiatus is caused by the arrival of a manager responsible for all quality matters. Internally some have seen this as indicating that management have started along the path to process improvement, but again demonstrated that they are not yet fully committed to allocating the necessary effort and resources. The effect of this failure to act on the software development staff, and particularly those involved in the exercise, has been severe. The danger is that any future attempts will be clouded by this negative experience. This aspect has been grasped by the Information Systems Director, who seems determined to maintain some momentum, and so the project may progress in the near future. If it does so, the intention is to continue with PA, and our case study will move on to the Education and Selection stages.

7 EVALUATION OF PROCESS ADVISOR - ASSESSMENT STAGE

PA is marketed as a self-directed system for software process improvement. The workbook and video are meant to guide people through this, and their structure and content are well suited to the purpose. On the other hand, the earlier metaphor of a *Do-It-Yourself* kit is valid. It may be cheaper to use a DIY approach, but it does not obviate the need for adequate preparation, sufficient resources, and a critical assessment of progress and results. Although we have a few criticisms of PA, from our limited use of the assessment stage, our conclusion is that more thought needs to be given to the pitfalls of using a self-directed approach to something as important as process assessment. PA does not come with any 'health warnings', and it would be naive to expect it do so. On the other hand, many of the points we make below apply to any process improvement project, whether done with PA, CMM or similar.

The importance of management commitment to the exercise itself cannot be over-emphasized. PA does not really stress this, perhaps assuming that purchase of the product is a useful indication of commitment; although this is unlikely since it is not expensive. The case study exemplifies the problems of failing to elicit and *sustain* commitment. The project was initiated by the senior development manager, with encouragement from above. But this may have been because there was the expectation of a high rating. Even before the findings were produced, there was a lack of visibility by management as the project progressed; and this was seen by some as evidence of a lack of interest. The delay in producing the report, and the absence of senior management from the de-briefing session for participants were also unfortunate aspects. Now that the assessment stage has been completed, but with no obvious progression, there is a danger of a loss of credibility, with participants wondering what all the fuss was about.

PA cannot be held to blame for this: On the other hand we do not believe that our experience is unique in this sort of project. Perhaps PA should devote more attention to the pitfalls of a self-directed program, with guidance on how best to avoid some of the more likely problems. It is ironic that PA stresses the importance of management commitment to the software engineering process, but does not stress that this is equally essential to the success of using PA itself. Moreover this cannot be an initial enthusiasm, but must be sustained throughout the project. The problem the case study organization will have is in re-gaining the enthusiasm of those involved if and when it is decided to continue with the process. Rather than having shown continued commitment to improving the situation, which impressed everybody at the beginning, management have prevaricated and seemed to indicate that they do not wish to improve, or feel incapable of improving, the software development process. Perhaps a cautionary note to the effect that management might not come out of the exercise as well as they expected might have eased the way for reception of the actual findings and so prevented the loss of momentum.

Another aspect not emphasized by PA is the importance of selecting the personnel to take part in the assessment exercise. PA suggests that a team of managers and technical staff complete all the stages together. This does not help identify the specific staff to involve, nor the qualities they should have. The project team for the case study decided that staff at all levels in the software development process should be involved, and this was reflected in the roles of the ten people who completed the questionnaires and were interviewed. It was also decided that people with both a positive and a negative attitude to the process should be included. With no prior knowledge of the individuals involved, it is difficult for the authors to say whether they were representative in this respect; but it is true to say that their contributions were not always what the organization may have expected.

Another decision we took was to ensure that users (customers) were represented. This was done by involving senior managers from external departments, since it is they who initiate most development projects. At first they were a little unsure of their role, but it was made clear that it was their responses as users of the software, and their involvement in the development process itself that were required. Both those selected contributed greatly to the findings and certainly widened the view obtained of the current state of software development within the organization. PA does not stress this user involvement, possibly because users are thought of as external to the organization; although some of the attributes assessed clearly involve users - e.g. customer communication.

One area where the project team failed was in not involving all senior managers involved in software development. It was suggested at the beginning that all relevant senior managers should be briefed, and should take part in the questionnaires and interviews. However, only one 'friendly' senior manager, apart from the two user senior managers, did actually take part. While nothing may have been lost in terms of their contribution, they may well have provided more impetus to the whole project and prevented the subsequent loss of momentum.

PA fails to highlight that the interview findings will be imprecise, and are likely to derive from the feelings of the respondents involved. This means that parts of the assessment report are not backed up by evidence, but may reflect general sensitivities, and will need further investigation in some areas. Although we were prepared for this, we were surprized at the opinions that were expressed. There was some discussion of the validity of these results, and how best they could be included in the report. The project team felt it was important to note and respond to such findings, since process improvement is as much a cultural change as it is a technical one.

One of the great strengths of PA is the advice given on what to do once the results are known. The descriptions of each grade provide a useful starting point for identifying the findings, and the associated questions are useful in obtaining supporting information. The comparison with common and best practice, whilst not being all-important, is also useful. Another point in the assessment stage is the identification of comparators for later use. These include the percentage of people working on maintenance, the turnover rate for software personnel, and also various annual budgets. These are useful figures in a general sense, but are often not used at all despite being easily available, as was found in the case study organization.

8 COMPARISON OF PA WITH CMM

In comparison with the CMM from the SEI (CMM, 1993), PA is a low-cost alternative. It does not give the specific measure that the CMM gives for process maturity; the figure it gives is a grade rather than the score. PA also goes further in its investigations than the CMM through use of the qualitative and quantitative questionnaires. This does widen the view of the process and so aid a better understanding of the current situation. (It is the use of the qualitative questionnaire that brought out many of the feelings from the respondents, as described earlier.)

CMM does, however, have advantages, the main ones being that it is a de facto standard within the industry, and also that it mandates use of independent personnel. Many of those involved in the case study, from the organization itself, felt that the objectivity and weight added to the project by the presence of the authors contributed greatly to the assessment exercise. It was felt that the presence of these independent personnel helped to create a true picture of the current software development process and how to improve it. But PA itself does not insist on this.

CMM is very expensive because of the use of SEI or SEI-accredited assessors. The benefit of this is that a rating can be obtained that, if favourable enough, can be made use of in marketing. PA on the other hand is purely for internal purposes. Another issue to go with the cost of CMM is that the investment prompts the organization to do something about the situation. Investing a lot of money and then not using the results would not be seen to be a good decision. In the case study example, perhaps the fact that the exercise involved costs in terms only of time and resources coupled with the poor showing of management in the results, made it easy to drop the project. The lack of investment in the exercise may well have contributed to its loss of momentum.

9 CRITIQUE OF PROCESS ADVISOR - AND OF PROCESS ASSESSMENT IN GENERAL

There are many available approaches to process assessment. Most of them involve great expense and high degrees of risk. PA, as a 'self-directed system' appeals to those organizations who want to, or are impelled to, embark on the route of process improvement; but who are uncertain what the progression will entail, and where they are starting from. PA offers a low cost, low risk starting point. On the other hand a PA project must be undertaken with careful thought and planning. The process of gathering the information must be well planned, and although it can be done by internal personnel, there are clear advantages in using disinterested, external people. What must also be realized is that there should be some thought given to the processing of the results, based perhaps on a small number of scenarios - e.g. the expected results, and a range of 'worst cases'.

This study only undertook the first stage of PA, Assessment. It proved very successful in providing a picture of the current software development process and helped to identify recommendations on how to improve it. Nevertheless, PA does have its pitfalls, notably that it is meant to be self-directed and that this may cause problems in terms of the integrity of the results and how they are handled. Independent personnel would not only be useful but may be necessary to ensure project success. It does however, provide a good starting point for any organization wishing to gain experience in process improvement at low cost.

Despite the problems encountered by our target organization, we hope to continue the project to the later stages of PA. Furthermore we hope to extend our work to investigate the practical issues surrounding the application of other forms of process assessment and improvement, including CMM, Trillium, SPICE and Bootstrap.

REFERENCES

Bootstrap(1994), Bootstrap: Fine-tuning process assessment, Haase, V., Messnart, R., Koch, G., Kugler, J., Decrinis, P., *IEEE Software*, volume 11, no. 14, July 1994

Bryant, A. (1995), *Standardizing SSADM: Methods, Standards & Maturity*, McGraw Hill

Bryant, A. and Chan, D.(1992) 'Error Source Accounting - An Approach to Measuring Information Systems Quality', *Software Management*, February 1992

CMM (1993), *Key Practices of the Capability Maturity Model*, Version 1.1, Paulk, M., Weber, C., Garcia, S., Chrissis, S., Bush, M., CMU/SEI-93-TR-25, Software Engineering Institute

Humphrey, W. S. (1989) *Managing the Software Process*, Addison-Wesley

Humphrey, W. S. (1987) A Method for Assessing the Software Engineering Capability of Contractors, *Software Engineering Institute Technical Report*, CMU/SEI-87-TR-23

ISO (1991), *ISO 9000-3: Guidelines for applying ISO 9001 to Development, Supply, and Maintenance of Software*, ISO

Pressman, R. S. (1992), *Process Advisor: A Self Directed System for Improving Software Engineering Practice*, R.S. Pressman & Associates, Inc

Pressman, R.S. (1993), *A Manager's Guide to Software*, McGraw-Hill, 1993

TRILLIUM (1994), *TRILLIUM A Model for Telecom Product Development & Support Process Capability*, Release 3.0, Internet edition, Bell Canada

Tony Bryant is currently Professor of Informatics within the Faculty of Information & Engineering Systems at Leeds Metropolitan University. Since 1989 he has initiated a series of projects aimed at incorporating the strengths of different methods and specification techniques under the general heading of 'methods integration'. The work of his Methods Research Group now extends into formal specification, process maturity, standardization, and IS methodologies. Originally a social scientist, Professor Bryant obtained his first degree from Cambridge University in 1975, and his PhD from the London School of Economics in 1980. In 1982 he obtained his MSc in Computing from Bradford University and then worked for a number of years in commercial software development before taking a post at Leeds Polytechnic (now Leeds Metropolitan University).

Following a BSc in Computing, John Grogan became a Research Assistant at Leeds Metropolitan University working on "Total Quality and Information Systems Development and Operations". Initially from an engineering background he later moved into system development and operations. His experience in project/quality management, and information systems development has been utilized by commercial organizations in both the engineering and IT industries. He is a Licentiate of the Institute of Quality Assurance, a Graduate Member of the British Computer Society, a member of the UK Academy of Information Systems, and also a Member of the British Computer Society Quality Special Interest Group.

PART THREE

Quality Practices

8

Software quality: Perceptions and practices in Hong Kong

J. M. Verner, T. T. Moores** and A. R. Barrett*
Department of Information Systems, City University of Hong Kong, 83 Tat Chee Avenue, Kowloon Tong, Hong Kong.
Fax: +852 2788 8694
*Tel: *+852 2788 7560 **+852 2788 8529*
*Email: *isjune@cityu.edu.hk **ismoor@cityu.edu.hk*

Abstract

The extent to which software quality is seen as an issue by IS professionals in Hong Kong, and the practices employed to achieve quality is investigated. One-hundred and seventy-five IS professionals were surveyed to obtain answers to the following questions: What definition of "quality" is being used? What, if any, techniques are being used to ensure a quality product? It will be shown that "quality" is defined chiefly in terms of reliability and maintainability. However, there are few techniques in common use by those respondents that claim to be following a software quality assurance (SQA) approach. When asked about the problems in employing a SQA approach the main reason given was that it is time consuming, with some support for the view that SQA is costly and lacks management support. This research clearly defines the problems Hong Kong IS professionals perceive in pursuing SQA, and sets the groundwork for the initiatives by major industrial organisations in Hong Kong for quality improvement.

Keywords

Software development, software quality, software quality assurance, survey, Hong Kong.

1 INTRODUCTION

Producing and maintaining software is a major challenge for the software industry in this decade and beyond. Up front effort spent on quality is said to be repaid: directly, in time saved on debugging and rework, and in reduced software maintenance; and indirectly, in better relationships with customers. Before software developers can receive this benefit, however, there are a number of problems to be faced. First, there is no clear definition of what "quality" is. Some organisations may have no actual definition, while in other cases the definition may depend on the occupation of the person making the definition or the maturity of the software development process. Secondly, there are no commonly accepted measures of good quality so that there may be no way of showing that a quality product has been produced. Finally, the customer may not be prepared to pay for quality. Budgetary, staffing and schedule constraints may force many organisations to forgo the development of a quality product and settle instead for a product that is simply "acceptable".

With its close relationship with China, Hong Kong is in an ideal position to tap the huge manpower resource that China represents and to become a major player in world software development. If this is to be achieved, Hong Kong developers must be able to assure that the product developed will be of an acceptably high standard. As a result, the issue of software quality has gained in importance. For instance, the Hong Kong Productivity Council (a Government funded organisation which provides advice and consulting to many industrial sectors) recently helped to form a Software Process Improvement Network group. The same council is also active in the Software Process Improvement and dEtermination (SPICE) initiative, and in running courses for ISO9000 accreditation. Furthermore, international conferences in the area of quality management are being held in Hong Kong with major Hong Kong industrial and government sponsors, such as the Industry Department, Hong Kong Telecom, and the transport corporations. This suggests that the issue of quality has now been recognised by institutions in Hong Kong.

1.1 Definitions of software quality

The first problem with software quality is that it can be defined from many points of view, depending on the role taken by the definer in the development process and the type of system being developed (Arthur, 1985; Deutsch and Willis, 1988; Wallmuller, 1994). These include (but are not limited to): the developer (looking for a stable set of clear requirements); the buyer (looking for value-for-money and delivery on-time); the user (looking for a bug free system that performs according to their expectations); and, the maintainer (looking for a bug free system with clearly structured documentation). Other important viewpoints from which further definitions of quality may be derived include the project manger, the accountant and other specialists (such as lawyers). In some cases the view taken is quantitative, such as the number of defects per thousands of source lines of code (Jones, 1978; Grady, 1992); while in others, it is qualitative with a focus specific aspects, such as the functionality, product, market, development process or end-user.

An early and widely quoted definition of quality is that of Boehm *et al* (1978) who suggested that quality has seven important attributes: portability, reliability efficiency, human engineering, testability, understandability and modifiability. Other definitions of quality take a slightly different point of view but include many overlapping quality characteristics. Some definitions are quite narrow and are from a single viewpoint, such as: the ability to deliver on time and within budget; absence of defects and errors; or, the degree of conformance to standards. Other definitions are more generally stated and may include aspects related to users of the system and their needs, such as: the degree of conformance of the product to its stated requirements (Rook, 1986; Crosby, 1979); the degree to which the attributes of the software enable it to perform its intended end use (Gillies, 1992); fitness for use (Juran, 1979); an assessment of how well the software helps users do their work; and, the degree of users satisfaction according to their expectations (Denning, 1992).

1.2 Questions regarding software quality

This research investigates the current state-of-the-practice for software quality in information systems (IS) departments in Hong Kong. A survey of software development professionals was conducted to obtain their definition of software quality and the methods used to achieve it. The survey was not intended to study views on the use of specific software quality standards such as ISO9000, since it was known that few organisations (10%) conform or are certified to any quality standards (Ko, 1995). Rather, the focus of this study was to ask more fundamental questions about what IS professionals actually think 'quality' is. With the aid of a questionnaire we asked about our respondents' backgrounds, their definition of quality, and what standards their information systems department are in conformance with. Other questions were included in order to determine:

1. The definition of quality used in Hong Kong by different industrial sectors.
2. How practitioners in different occupations in Hong Kong define quality.
3. The techniques (if any) being used in Hong Kong to ensure a quality product.
4. The additional techniques or methods (if any) practitioners would like to include in the development (and maintenance) process to ensure a quality product.
5. The problems practitioners meet when applying software quality assurance in their organisations.
6. The major reasons for, and problems in applying a software quality approach.

In the next section we report on the characteristics of the organisations employing our respondents, their business sector, size of the IS departments, respondents' occupation and their experience in IS. In the following section we discuss our major findings with regard to the definition of quality. We then look at the software quality practices in organisations, noting where the responses differ by business sector, by size of IS department or by occupation of the respondents. We conclude with a discussion of the state-of-the-practice in Hong Kong and note the changes we expect to see in Hong Kong in the near future.

2 RESPONDENT'S BACKGROUNDS

Our 175 respondents come from the IS departments of many of the major industries important in Hong Kong. The greatest number (see Figure 1) are from the insurance/financial/banking sector (21%) and the software industry (21%). These groups are followed by government/utilities (16%), manufacturing (12%), and transportation (10%). Over 80% of our respondents are employed by organisations in these five sectors. Smaller groups come from communications, wholesale/retail and the education/research sectors.

Seventy-one percent of our respondents are involved in the technical aspects of systems development, identifying themselves as programmers (17%), analysts (13%), analyst/programmers (38%), and software engineers (3%). A further 7% identify themselves as project managers, 6% as IS managers, and 3% as project leaders. The remaining 13% is made up of small groups from quality assurance, database administration, business analysts and other. The "other" group is mainly made up of support personnel, such as technical support officers. Most (72%) have between 2 and 9 years' experience (38% between 2-4 years; 34% between 5-9 years). A sizeable group (18%), have ten or more years' experience; the smallest group (10%), have less that two years' experience.

Approximately half (51%) work in either very small (less than 10 IS staff), or large IS departments (100 or more IS staff); 19% of respondents work for IS departments with 10-29 staff; 15% in IS departments with 30-49 staff; and 15% are in departments with between 50 and 99 staff. The small IS departments are mainly involved in software development, the manufacturing sector, or the wholesale/retail sector. The large departments are from the government/utilities sector or from the insurance/banking/financial sector. Only two quality assurance personnel answered the questionnaire and both are from large IS departments, one from the government/utilities sector and the other from the insurance/banking/financial sector.

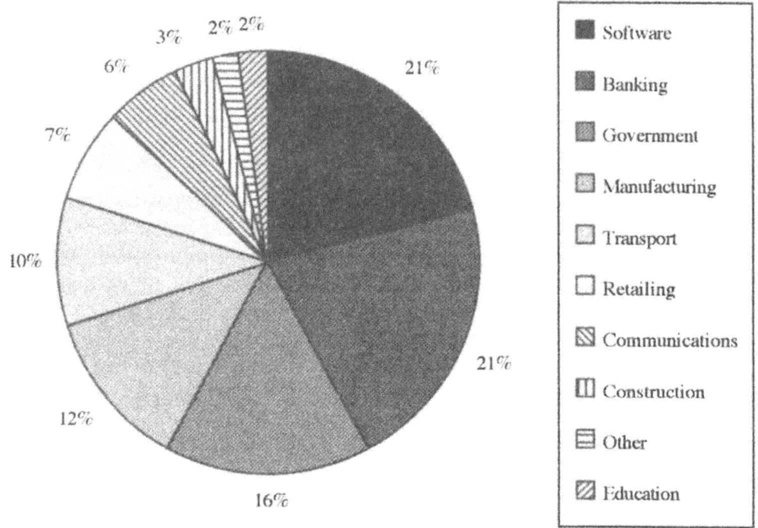

Figure 1 Classification of respondents by industry (N=175).

3. QUALITY ASSURANCE ISSUES AND PRACTICE

3.1 Definition of quality

Our respondents define quality as *reliable*, *maintainable*, *functionally correct*, *well documented*, *efficient*, *easy to use*, *flexible* and *usable*. This definition was obtained by asking the question: "Please tick four of the following that best fit your idea of software quality". The list provided was derived from a number of the widely quoted quality attributes, including the hierarchical four level definition of quality suggested by Boehm *et al* (1978). The full list and the response to this question is shown in Table 1.

In general our respondents agreed with Boehm *et al*'s (1978) definition of quality. However, there are two attributes on their list not rated highly by our respondents (*portability*, and *testability*) and one attribute highly rated by our respondents and not on their list (*functionally correct*). We believe that functional correctness is an essential part of quality. Boehm *et al*'s *human engineering* and *understandability* (each is chosen by 10% of our respondents) are replaced by most of our respondents with *well documented* and *easy to learn to use*. These attributes cover in some sense many of the same ideas. *Portability* and *testability* are also rated quite low by our respondents (10% and 8%), with more concern expressed over a product being *flexible* rather than *testable*. Lowest rated items were *technically advanced* (2%) and *resilient* (2%).

Table 1 Quality attributes

	Quality attribute	*Frequency*	*%*
RELI	*Reliable	132	75
MAIN	*Maintainable	91	52
FCT	Functionally correct	81	46
DOC	Well-documented	67	38
EFFI	*Efficient	64	37
LRN	Easy to learn to use	58	33
FLEX	Flexible	45	26
USAB	Usable	37	21
CORR	Correct	33	19
RUSE	Reusable components	26	15
DATA	Good data security	25	14
ROB	Robust	24	14
ENG	*Good human engineering	18	10
UND	*Understandable	18	10
PORT	*Portable	17	10
TEST	*Testable	14	8
SIMP	Simple	13	7
VERI	Verifiable	13	7
UNIF	Uniform	8	5
RESI	Resilient	4	2
TECH	Technologically advanced	4	2
OTH	Other	2	1

*From Boehm *et al* (1978)

3.2 Attributes of quality by industry

Table 2 shows the quality attributes chosen by respondents in the five main industrial sectors. All groups chose *reliable* as the most important quality attribute. The manufacturing sector respondents see *reliable* and *maintainable* as equally important, with *functionally correct* rated a relatively poor third. The software industry rate *functionally correct* top equal with both *reliable* and *maintainable*. The banking/finance/insurance sector rank *reliable* first, *maintainable* second, while *functionally correct* and *well documented* are equal third. The concern that this industry sector has with customers, who may interact directly with the software, is shown by the fact that both *easy to learn to use*, and *usable* are included in their top seven quality attributes.

The transport and government industries clearly see *reliable* as being the dominant quality attribute. Reliability is understandably crucial for these industries. For instance, imagine the chaos at Hong Kong's Kai Tak International Airport - one of the busiest passenger airports in the world - if the software on the computers used for immigration control was unreliable. The other attributes seen as important include *maintainable* for the transport industry, and *efficient* for the government. *Functionally correct* follows closely for the transport industry. Efficiency is, of course, a key issue for Government departments handling large numbers of inquiries, e.g., immigration, where a large number of customers are dealt with in a short space of time.

Table 2 Quality attributes (in %) by industrial sector

	Manu.	*Software*	*Banking*	*Transport*	*Govern.*
RELI	81	50	81	89	86
MAIN	76	50	56	56	43
FCT	52	50	44	50	43
EFFI	38	39	28	39	57
DOC	48	28	44	28	36
LRN	38	28	29	22	36
FLEX	29	33	14	22	29
USAB	19	19	22	33	25

3.3 Quality attributes by occupation

Table 3 shows the top seven attributes by occupation group, ordered by popularity of the attribute. When we consider the quality attributes chosen by the different occupation groups we observe a number of differences. Although two occupation groups (programmers and software engineers), include all the overall top seven attributes in their list, no two groups are in complete agreement with the ordering. Most respondent groups differ by one or more quality attributes, although all the groups include *reliable*, *maintainable*, and *functionally correct*, the top three quality attributes overall. Other quality attributes also included are: *efficient* (cited by 6 of the groups), *well documented* (6), *usable* (3), *easy to learn to use* (3), *flexible* (2) (all from the top seven list), and *correct* (2), *data secure* (1), *robust* (1), *understandable* (1), *verifiable* (1), and *reusable* (1).

Table 3 - Top 7 quality attributes by occupation group

IS manager	*Project leader*	*Analyst/ prog.*	*Project manager*	*Software engineer*	*Pro-grammer*	*Analyst*
RELI	MAIN	RELI	RELI	MAIN	RELI	RELI
MAIN	FCT	FCT	FCT	RELI	MAIN	MAIN
EFFI	RELI	EFFI	VERI	FLEX	FCT	LRN
CORR	CORR	MAIN	MAIN	DOC	FLEX	DOC
DATA	ROB	DOC	DOC	EFFI	LRN	FCT
FCT	UND	LRN	RUSE	LRN	EFFI	EFFI
USAB	DOC	USAB	EFFI	FCT	DOC	USAB

Analyst/programmers and analysts also have the same list of attributes but with a different ordering. Both have replaced *flexible* with *usable*. Presumably because they deal with users in their day-to-day jobs, analyst/programmers are more aware of the problems that users can have when using software systems.

IS managers include one attribute not present on any other occupation list: *data secure*. The IS manager is in the front line if the system fails to be data secure. This group are also more concerned with the system being usable in the long term, than it being easy to learn to use in the short term, and replace *easy to learn to use* with *usable*. Another concern is that the systems developed are both *correct* and *functionally correct*. Attributes replaced are *well documented*, and *flexible*.

The importance of technical correctness in the view of project managers is evident by their inclusion of *verifiable* as the third most commonly cited quality attribute. Further worries over the cost, schedule and possible long term cost improvement is shown by their inclusion of *reusable*. *Verifiable* and *reusable* replace *flexible* and *easy to learn to use*.

Project leaders are concerned with integrating their part of the development with other parts and not surprisingly are the only group that choose *understandable*. They include both *correct* and *functionally correct* - probably on the grounds that they want to get it right - and are the only occupation group to include *robust*. These three attributes replace *easy to learn to use*, *flexible*, and *efficient*.

4 QUALITY APPROACH

The benefits and problems companies in Hong Kong perceive with SQA were investigated by two questions. The first question asked whether the respondents think that a software quality approach is in place in their organisations and the perceived benefits of SQA. Six possible benefits were given as prompts and ranged from *To reduce maintenance* to *For better project management*. An *Other (please specify)* option was given in order to capture any new or novel views. The second question asked specifically for the problems associated with SQA. A list of six possible problems as well as an "other" option was provided. The problems ranged from *Not enough software support* to *Poor guidelines*. The results were as follows.

4.1 Reasons for employing a SQA approach

To the question "Do you think your company deploys a software quality assurance approach when it develops software?", 49% answered *Yes*, while 51% answered *No*. Higher proportions of positive responses were given by those working in the software industry (61%), and the media/communication (64%) industrial groups. Note that these two industrial sectors are more likely to show conformance to ISO9000 than the other industrial groups within our sample.

To the question "In your opinion, why do you think a company would employ a software quality approach?", on average each respondent choose 1.6 of the available options. Although the question did not encourage the respondents to give multiple answers, this suggests there is no single reason for employing a SQA approach. The distribution of responses are given in Table 4.

Table 4 Reasons for employing a SQA approach

Reason	*%*
To improve reliability	51
To reduce maintenance	33
To increase user/customer satisfaction	27
For better project management	23
To detect errors early	21
To increase profit	5
Other (please specify)	1

To improve reliability is the only option chosen by the majority of the respondents. Clearly, *To increase profit* is not seen as a motivation, while the other four options seem to be secondary motivations for software quality. It would seem from these results, therefore, that there is no dominant reason for employing a SQA approach. The lack of a coherent response might also suggest a certain confusion over the nature of SQA approaches. This confusion is exemplified by the fact that 22% of respondents who said a SQA approach was in place did not believe any staff had special responsibility for software quality, while 33% of respondents who said no SQA approach was in place claimed there were staff with special responsibility for software quality.

4.2 Problems in applying a SQA approach

To the question "In your opinion, what problems are there in applying software quality assurance in an organisation?", on average each respondent choose 2.6 of the available options. Unlike the earlier question, the respondents were here encouraged to tick as many options as they liked. The results are given in Table 5. As can be seen, *Time consuming* is cited by 71% of the respondents and is clearly the greatest problem for SQA approaches. Respondents are clearly bothered about the "up front" work required to deliver quality systems. The reasons given under *Other* included resource limitations (4), lack of understanding and commitment (4) and lack of control (2). Some of these fit in with the reasons already given in the above table. The other options gained some support, with *Costly* and *Lack of management support* being cited by almost half the respondents. These issues are similar as those expressed as problems with gaining official certification to quality standards, such as ISO9000 and ISO9126 (e.g., Bazzana *et al*, 1993).

Table 5 Problems in applying a SQA approach

Reason	*%*
Time consuming	71
Costly	46
Lack of management support	45
Poor guidelines	38
Not enough software support	29
No short term benefits	27
Other	7

Combining the results from these two sets of questions, it would seem that while the move towards a software quality approach has taken root in Hong Kong, there are still well-recognised problems in making the approach work. Confirming the results from the previous section, SQA is seen as generally helping deliver more reliable and maintainable systems, although assuring such quality is seen as delaying the overall progress of the project. For this reason, SQA is still seen as being both time-consuming and costly. Clearly, what is needed here are concrete examples to show Hong Kong companies that the time spent on SQA has demonstrable pay-offs in quality, or, a demand from the larger customer organisations such as the Government for quality to be an element in the development of products. Without such examples or customer-push, it is hard to see how a genuine commitment to software quality can be sustained in Hong Kong.

5 TECHNIQUES USED FOR QUALITY ASSURANCE

We asked our respondents about five techniques they may use to ensure a quality product. The techniques were: documentation standards and controls; code inspections; testing strategies; collecting and recording errors found during development; and, testing team used to test the software. Against each technique respondents were asked to tick whether the technique was *always*, *frequently*, *sometimes*, or *never* used in their organisation. A *don't know* option was also provided. Taking *always* and *frequently* to denote a high frequency of use, the degree to which each technique is used with a high frequency is given as follows: documentation standards, 58%; testing strategy, 53%; errors recorded, 46%; testing team, 37%; and, code inspections, 21%.

Documentation standards emerged as the most frequently used technique in the organisations employing our respondents, while code inspections is clearly not a popular method for ensuring quality. A number of respondents who said that a testing team was used in their installation did not know if a testing strategy was used. This would seem to show a lack of communication between members of the development team.

In order to further investigate the perception of what software quality is, and what needs to be done to achieve it, we gave our respondents the opportunity to include practices that they believe contribute to quality assurance in their organisations that we had not asked about. Only a small percentage (15%) responded; of these, over 50% mentioned practices that include users, e.g., user walkthroughs. This fits in with the overall definition of quality which does seem to be user oriented. We also gave our respondents the opportunity to tell us which single practice, not currently done in their organisation, they would like included in their development practices. Thirty percent responded and nearly 50% of these mentioned practices related to either testing, or with quality assurance and development standards. This is quite a high percentage of responses for a written answer and suggests that many developers are unhappy about the approach to software quality taken in their organisations.

If we take a closer look at the size of the IS departments involved and classify the organisations by industry sector we get a better idea of what strategies are used by the different sectors.

5.1 By size of IS department

A comparison of responses to the five questions on methods to help with quality assurance by size of IS department is shown in Figure 2.

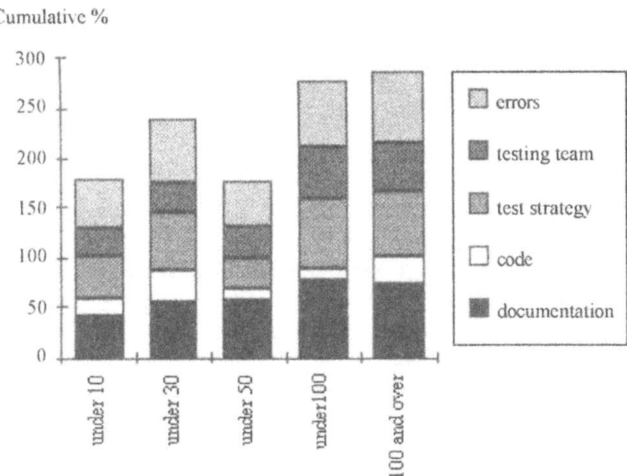

Figure 2 SQA practices by department size.

It can be seen that documentation standards are used less frequently in IS departments with fewer than 10 staff; that code inspections are used much less often in departments with between 30 and 99 staff; and that the use of a testing strategy or testing team is least in departments with between 30 and 49 staff. This figure shows that overall the departments with under 50 staff are doing less of everything. There are probably a number of reasons for this but we would speculate that it is probably to do with the relative ease of managing small IS departments, where informal management strategies are effective in departments of less than 30. By the time the department reaches 100, good management practices must already be in place and Figure 2 shows that the larger departments are overall doing substantially more towards SQA. The possibility that management practices must change as the size of the department increases, and how this change manifests itself, may provide an interesting area of further research.

5.2 By industry sector

Figure 3 shows how the surveyed SQA practices are spread across the five largest industry sectors. The other groups are too small to be of significance here. As can be seen, the banking/finance/insurance sector appears to be the most advanced, with the majority of respondents practising each of the SQA techniques except for code inspections. Few respondents from any sector carried out code inspections.

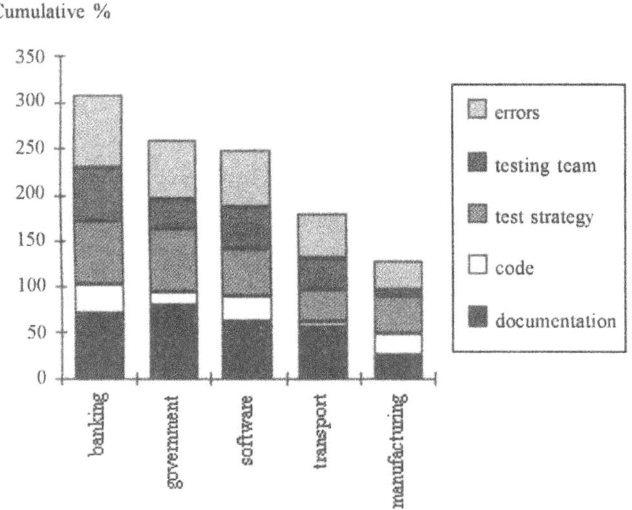

Figure 3 SQA practices by industry.

The government sector is notable for having more than 75% of respondents using documentation standards. The majority of the respondents from the software industry are in organisations that employ all the SQA techniques we asked about except, again, for code inspections. The construction sector, although too small to appear in Figure 3, is interesting in that those who contract to the government must show ISO9000 conformance. As a result, the construction industry scores high for documentation standards (60%). Manufacturing and Transport are doing rather less in SQA than the other sectors. The Transport sector is more likely to be recording errors, using a testing team, and using documentation standards than Manufacturing. This is probably because the Transport sector is more concerned with customer relations.

6 CONCLUSIONS

In general our respondents view quality as relating to both customer-oriented as well as technical factors. The key attributes of quality identified by this survey show that practitioners in Hong Kong relate quality to a *reliable*, *maintainable* and *functionally correct* product, that is *well-documented*, *efficient* and *easy to learn to use*. Other attributes of quality advocated by Boehm *et al* (1978), however, are seen as less important. The attributes *good human engineering*, *understandable*, *portable* and *testable* are seen as important by no more than 10% of the respondents. The most frequently used software quality techniques are documentation standards, testing strategies, and errors recorded. To a lesser extent testing teams are used. Code inspections are used infrequently.

Consistent with our respondents' overall definition of quality, the most cited reason for employing a quality approach is to improve reliability. However to make this improvement in reliability there are problems with the perception of SQA that must be overcome in Hong Kong. Specifically, quality assurance is seen as being time consuming, with almost half the respondents supporting the view that SQA is costly and suffers from a lack of management support. This is perhaps consistent with any highly dynamic business centre, such as Hong Kong, where both time and money are seen as important resources. Perhaps as a direct result of the increased interest in software quality in Hong Kong, we find that some of our respondents are already unhappy about the development practices in place. Respondents see a need for more testing, quality assurance and development standards to be in place.

Clearly, the change of sovereignty in 1997 will change Hong Kong's business outlook and bring her closer to China and her vast resources of potential software developers. In the near future, we expect to see even greater interest in software quality in Hong Kong and a great deal of improvement in the quality practices in common usage. The Hong Kong Government is aware of the current situation and has recently begun promoting a software process improvement program. The Industry Department of Hong Kong has commissioned the Hong Kong Productivity Council to carry out a project:"Software process improvement programme for the software industry in Hong Kong" (Verner & Ko, 1995), in order to promote awareness of the software process, quality improvement and to assist companies in Hong Kong to achieve better quality software. We feel that such programmes are undoubtedly the way forward for Hong Kong, and the entire Asia-Pacific region.

7 REFERENCES

Arthur, L. J (1985) *Measuring programmer quality*. John Wiley & Sons, New York, NY.

Bazzana, G., Andersen, O. and Jokela, T. (1993) ISO 9126 and ISO 9000: Friends or foe? In Proceedings, IEEE Software Engineering Standards Symposium, Brighton, UK, September 1993.

Boehm, B. W. *et al* (1978) *Characteristics of software quality*. North Holland, New York.

Crosby, P. B. (1979) *Quality is free: The art of making quality certain*. McGraw-Hill, New York.

Denning, P. W. (1992) What is software quality? *Communications of the ACM*, **35**(1), pp13-15.

Deutsch, M. S. and Willis, R. R. (1988) *Software quality engineering*. Prentice-Hall, Englewood Cliffs, NJ.

Gillies, A. (1993) *Software quality: Theory and management*. Chapman & Hall, London.

Grady, R. B. (1992) *Practical software metrics for project management and process improvement*. Prentice-Hall, Englewood Cliffs, NJ.

Ko, R. (1995) Status of software engineering practices in Hong Kong. *Hong Kong Productivity Council Consultancy Report*.

Jones, C. (1978) Measuring programming quality and productivity. *IBM Systems Journal*, **17**(1), pp39-63.

Juran, J. M. (1979) *Quality control handbook* (3rd edition). McGraw-Hill, New York.

Rook, P. (1986) Controlling software projects. *Software Engineering Journal*, **1**(1), pp7-16.

Verner, J. and Ko, R. (1995) Status of software engineering practices in Hong Kong. In *Proceedings, Asian Software Engineeering Workshop*, Seattle, USA, April 1995, pp8.1-8.5.

Wallmuller, E. (1994) *Software quality assurance: A practical approach*. Prentice-Hall, Englewood Cliffs, NJ.

9

Controlling side-effects in maintenance

*G. Canfora** *G. A. Di Lucca*** *M. Tortorella***

**Dept. of 'Ingegneria dell'Informazione ed Ingegneria Elettrica'*
University of Salerno, Faculty of Engineering at Benevento
***Dept. of 'Informatica e Sistemistica' - University of Naples 'Federico II'*
via Claudio, 21 - 80125 Napoli, Italy
Tel.: +39 81 7683199 Fax: +39 81 7683186
E-mail: canfora/dilucca/martor@nadis.dis.unina.it

Abstract

Each time a maintenance operation is performed on a program the overall quality of a software system can rapidly decrease because of the introduction of side effects. Such side effects are due to the relationships existing between the components of a software system, and these can be classified into potential relationships and actual relationships. Successful maintenance requires knowledge of both actual and potential relationships in order to avoid, or at least reduce to a minimum, the introduction of side-effects.

A method is proposed to analyze both potential and actual relationships existing in programs coded by a language with strict scope and visibility rules. The method is based on the definition, use and computation of some Boolean matrices and allows the identification of the software units that will be affected by a modification involving data references in a software unit.

Keywords

Software Engineering, Software Quality, Software Maintenance, Impact Analysis, Side-effects

1 INTRODUCTION

Software maintenance is not only one of the most expensive phases in the software life cycle (Lientz *et al.*, 1980; Nosek *et al.*,1990) but it is also one of the most critical as far as quality is concerned since a bad maintenance phase can rapidly decrease the overall quality of a software system. One of the reasons why maintenance is so critical is that changes made at any one point in a system may have side effects at other points (Schneidewind, 1987). Therefore, each time a maintenance operation (whether corrective, adaptive, or perfective) has to be performed, the introduction of side effects is a considerable hazard.

Such side-effects consist of undesirable and unforeseen (but not necessarily unforeseeable) erroneous behaviours that occur as a result of a modification, in parts of the system not directly modified and possibly 'geographically' far from the point where the modification has been made (McClure *et al.*,1978; Freedman *et al.*, 1982). Side effects stem from the relationships existing between the components of a software system (software units, variables, named-constants, control structures and data-types) and usually propagate across several software units (modules, routines, etc.). These relationships mainly derive from intra- and inter-unit control-flow, data-flow, data-dependence, and data-binding.

The side-effects most frequently introduced in a software system, and which are also the most difficult to detect, are generated by changes to variable references in statements. Such changes may modify the data-flow, data-dependence and data-binding that actually exist or can potentially exist between software units according to the scope-rules of the coding language.

Relationships between software units can be divided into two classes: (i) potential relationships, which potentially exist between two units because, according to the language scope and visibility rules, a unit may refer to any component in the other unit; and (ii) actual relationships, which actually exist between two units because the code of one of them contains direct or indirect references to some components of the other. Obviously, actual relationships are a sub-set of potential relationships (Cimitile *et al.*, 1990).

Any given maintenance operation affects the actual relationships and can also transform potential relationships into actual ones.

Successful maintenance requires knowledge of both actual and potential relationships. In particular, a deep knowledge, understanding and analysis of potential relationships can help to avoid, or at least to reduce to a minimum, the introduction of side-effects.

Potential and actual relationships have to be identified, represented and analysed before any change can be implemented in a maintenance operation. A document that represents these relationships is the main source to which the maintainer will refer to obtain the information he needs in order to evaluate the impact of a change. Static code analysis can identify the components of a software system and the actual relationships existing among them. It can also provide the information needed to identify the potential relationships.

In this paper we propose a method to: (i) represent the potential and actual relationships between the software units in a system; (ii) analyse these relationships in order to identify automatically which other software units are affected by a change in the code of a unit.

The method is based on a matrix representation of the relationships, both potential and actual, existing between the various software units and due to the sharing of global data, the exchange of data through their interfaces and the activations of one unit by the others. The information needed to achieve this representation and the subsequent analysis is extracted from code by static analysis. This means that the data flow analysis is static and flow-insensitive, and only refers to the data references in the various software units and not also to the way in which they are arranged.

The method is described with reference to such languages as Ada, Pascal, and Modula-2, which have strict scope and visibility rules limiting the reference to components from the various units. Although these languages allow structured coding and information-hiding, they also make it more difficult to identify the potential and actual relationships.

In order to simplify the exposition, but without affecting its general nature, reference will be made to a software system made up of a single monolithic program that is in turn made up of various software units (procedure- and function-like units) rather than to a system composed of several separate software units (programs, packages, units, etc.).

2 BACKGROUND AND MOTIVATIONS

The changes typically made in a program concern the structure of the control-flow (introduction of new control structures and modification or deletion of existing ones), the data structure, and references to variables (their definition and use).

These changes introduce logic, semantic and performance variations regarding both the lines of code that are going to be directly modified, and thus the software units containing them, and the other parts of code (and relative units) having some relationship with the modified ones.

In actual fact the impact of a modification extends to all the artefacts of a software product (Turver *et al.*, 1994; Queille *et al.*, 1994), but here we will only deal the impact on code.

Before making a modification, therefore, it is essential to assess, and be aware of, the impact that this might have on the code. This entails identifying all the software areas, both inside the software unit directly affected by the change and in the others which have a relationship with it, that will be affected by the modification in order to reduce the possibility of side effects occurring. This will also enable a better assessment of the maintenance effort needed to implement the required change.

The effects that may be introduced by a modification of the control-flow (e.g. the introduction of a new control structure, the deletion of an existing one, or the substitution of one or more existing structures with other ones) are generally limited to the inside of the software unit in which this modification is made and do not affect the relationships with the other software units. Whereas it is much more difficult to identify areas of code affected by the modification of references to variables, for instance the modification of an expression defining the value of a variable with the addition or deletion of a reference to a variable. This type of modification may involve more than one software unit and in particular all the units that, according to the language rules, reference or can reference the variables affected by the modification and all the other variables that have a dependence relationship with them.

The impact on the code also depends on the coding language used, especially for effects due to modifications on the variable references. For instance, the impact that may arise in a program coded with a language that only allows use of global variables for all the software units of which it is made (e.g. COBOL in which the various SECTIONs and PARAGRAPHs can refer to all the variables declared in the DATA DIVISION) is different from the impact obtained with languages (such as PASCAL, ADA, PL1) that enable the declaration of variables in each of the various software units making up the program and which have rigid scope and visibility rules to discipline the possibility to reference them, according to where they have been declared. In the former case, in order to identify the regions of code that may be affected by the modification of references to variables, in an initial analysis it may be worthwhile using a cross-reference-lister which makes it possible to identify the lines of code referring to the variables involved in the modification and thus the software units affected (which may potentially be all of them). Then, use of a slicer makes it possible to further define, inside the unit, the code affected by the modification. On the contrary, in the latter case, if there is any homonymy, due to the possibility for variables declared in different units to have the same name, or any synonymity due to the exchange of actual/formal parameters in the activation of software units, this considerably reduces the utility of a cross-reference-lister. It will then be necessary to have tools that make possible a univocal identification of each variable (or other entity declared in the program), distinguishing between the various homonyms and grouping together the various synonyms. Only in this way we can be sure that more than one software unit actually references the same variable or different variables and, thus, be able to identify the units that may actually be affected by a modification in the code. Here too, intra- and inter- procedural slicing can be used to give a better definition of the areas of code affected by the modification.

Arnold (1993) defines a framework that enables comparisons to be made between the various approaches used for conducting Impact Analysis and assesses the tools currently available. One of the main characteristics that should be satisfied is that the estimation of the areas, i.e. of the software units, affected by a modification must be as close as possible to the actual one. This degree of accuracy should be reached as soon as possible so as to enable an early estimation of the modification's complexity and the resources to be dedicated to it and also to identify regions in which side effects might occur and thus reduce the possibility of their occurring.

In literature there are a number of contributions on Impact Analysis, most of which aim to establish measurements of Program Stability (Yau and Collofello, 1980), i.e. 'the resistance of a program to the amplification of changes in the program'. Yau and Collofello (1980) define metrics for assessing the resistance of a program's software units to a logic change. The metric is based on a complexity metric and on the probability that a change in a unit might affect a given variable. Yau and Chang (1984) describe a technique that is similar but more straightforward to apply for large systems. Haney (1972) presents a technique for modelling the stability of large systems based on the use of a matrix which reports the probability with which a modification in one unit will entail modifications in others. Yau and Collofello (1985) describe a stability measurement based on the counting of assumptions made on the software unit interfaces and the global data structures.

However, these techniques are not always able to satisfy the requisite of identifying, as quickly and accurately as possible, the set of software units affected by modifications regarding variations to the variable references. To achieve this, we must first define and identify the potential and actual relationships existing between these units as a result of the type of implementation made, and thus also according to the coding language used.

3 REPRESENTING POTENTIAL AND ACTUAL RELATIONSHIPS

The relationships existing between the various program units making up a software system are of two fundamental types: (i) those defined by the Inter-Modular Data-flow (IMD), produced by the set of links established between pairs of units that respectively define and use the same data; (ii) those defined by the Inter-Modular Relationship (IMR), i.e. by the set of links established between pairs of units when one of the two activates the other. These relationships must be known and fully understood in order to control the effects deriving from their modification in a maintenance operation. However, these relationships are not always adequately identified by classic high level design documents, such as Structure Charts and/or Data Flow Diagrams, mainly because they are highly dependent on the programming language adopted and on the way in which the programmer has integrated the various software units according to the rules made available by the adopted language.

With reference to the two categories of actual and potential relationships and to the IMD and IMR, we can distinguish between:

- Potential Data-Flow (PDF): the set of links due to the possibility to define and use data in different program units. These links are not necessarily actually implemented in the code but knowledge of them is nevertheless important as they can be produced directly or as side effects in subsequent maintenance interventions.
- Actual Data-Flow (ADF): the set of links actually implemented in the code through the definition and use of data in different program units. We are interested in these links both for the exact identification of the effects deriving from their changes and for the side effects due to variations that do not involve them directly.
- Potential Modules Relationship (PMR): the set of links due to the possible activation of program units by other program units. These links are not necessarily actually implemented in the code but can be achieved subsequently and can produce new sequences of program unit execution directly or as side effects.
- Actual Modules Relationship (AMR): the set of links actually implemented in the code through the activation of program units by other program units. We are interested in these links both for the analysis of the consequences of variations in such links and for the side effects that their presence might produce following variations that do not involve them directly.

3.1 Potential Relationships

The PMR existing between two program units is generally defined by the declarative section of the program. In particular, with reference to the languages with strict scope/visibility rules it is defined by the declarative nesting of the software units of which it is made and by the visibility rules. The declarative nesting can be represented with a tree whose root is the main program; every remaining node 'n' is associated to a software unit, and an edge from n_i to n_j indicates that the unit n_j is declared in the declarative section of n_i. This tree, called MDT (Module Declaration Tree), can be represented through a squared Boolean matrix MDT_mat of order n, where n is the number of software units making up the program.

Rows and columns are associated to the program units; the order of association coincides with the lexicographical order with which the declarations follow each other in the source text (and thus the first row and first column will correspond to the main program, the second to the first unit declared in it, and so forth).

If we use MDT_mat(i,j) to indicate the generic element of this matrix, we will have:
- MDT_mat(i,j)=1 if the unit i contains the declaration of the unit j;
- MDT_mat(i,j)=0 if the unit i does not contain the declaration of the unit j.

Also the PDF depends on the declarative structure of the program: it depends on the declarative nesting of the various software units, on the data declarations made in each of these units and by the language's scope/visibility rules.

The structure of the data declarations made in the various software units can be represented by a data declarations matrix DD_mat: a Boolean (n x m) matrix, where n is the number of units making up the program and m is the number of variables with different names declared in it.

Rows and columns are associated to program units and variables, respectively; the order of association coincides with the lexicographical order with which the declarations follow each other in the source text. In the event of homonymy, i.e. declarations (in different units) of different variables with the same name, the variables are made to correspond to the same column (the one for the first declaration). In our discussion, homonyms will be univocally identified by a dot notation (unit_name.variable_name).

If we use DD_mat(i,j) to indicate the generic element of this matrix, we have:
- DD_mat(i,j)=0 if the unit i does not contain the declaration of the variable j;
- DD_mat(i,j)=1 if the unit i contains the declaration of the variable j.

Therefore, row i will indicate all the variables (including the formal parameters) declared in unit i while column j will indicate in which units a variable assigned to it is declared.

3.2 Actual Relationships

The AMR is made up of the activations actually implemented in the code. It can be represented by a tree whose root is the main program. Every remaining node n is associated to a software unit, and an edge from n_i to n_j indicates that the unit n_j is activated at least once by the unit n_i. This tree, called MCT (Module Call Tree), can be represented through a squared Boolean matrix MCT_mat of order n, having the same structure and composition as MDT_mat.

If we use MCT_mat(i,j) to indicate the generic element of this matrix, we have:
- MCT_mat(i,j)=1 if the unit i activates the unit j;
- MCT_mat(i,j)=0 if the unit i does not activate the unit j.

The ADF is due to the actual data references made in the various software units. These references can be represented through the Data Reference Matrix, DREF_mat, a Boolean matrix (n x m) with the same structure and composition as DD_mat.

If we use DREF_mat(i,j) to indicate the generic element of this matrix, we have:
- DREF_mat(i,j)=0 if the unit i does not reference the variable j;
- DREF_mat(i,j)=1 if the variable j is referenced in the unit i.

Row i therefore indicates all the variables referenced by the unit corresponding to it; similarly, column j will indicate in which units the variable associated to it is referenced.

With reference to the Pascal-like program scheme of Figure 1, the relative MDT and MCT are illustrated in Figure 2 and the MDT_mat, MCT_mat in Figure 3, while DD_mat and DREF_mat matrices are illustrated in Figure 4.

4 THE REPRESENTATION OF POTENTIAL AND ACTUAL RELATIONSHIPS DUE TO DATA REFERENCES

Information on the Potential and Actual Data-Flow is important as we have to know which of the already existing links are modified or which of the possible new links are created through a maintenance operation involving the reference to a variable. In the following we show how this information can be represented using the matrix notation.

```
Program EXAMP;
 {decl.: pk, pz, pr, pq, pt, pa, px}
 procedure A(k, w);
 {decl.: am, at}
 begin {A}

   {def.: am,at}
   {used: am,at,k,w}

 end; {A}
 procedure B(s, v, z);
  {decl.: bm, ba, bo}
  procedure C(q);
  {decl.: cc}
  begin {C}

   {def.: cc}
   {used: cc,q}

  end; {C}
  procedure D(n, r);
  {decl.: dk, df}
   procedure E(z);
   {decl.: em}
   begin {E}

   {def.: em,z}
   {used: em,z,bo,px}

   A(em, z);

   end; {E}
  begin {D}

   {def.: dk,n,bo}
   {used: dk,n,bo,df,r,v}

  dk = n + df;

  E(r);
  E(df);
  C(v);

  end; {D}
 begin {B}

   {def.: bo,ba,z,s}
   {used: bm,ba,v,bo,z,px}

   C(bm);
   A(ba, z);
   D(bm, z);

 end; {B}
 procedure F(z, g);
 {decl.: fk, fi, fg}
   procedure G(i);
   {decl.: gu, gk}
     procedure H(b);
     {decl.: hh}
     begin {H}

     {def.: hh}
     {used: b, fg}
     end; {H}
   begin {G}

     {def.: i,gk,gu,fg}
     {used: gu,gk,i}

     H(gu);
     A(gk,i);

   end; {G}

   procedure I(y, w);
   {decl.: it, fg: integer;
     procedure L(c);
     {decl.: le}
     begin {L}

     {def.: le}
     {used: c, fg}

     end; {L}
     procedure M(d);
     {decl.: mn, mq}
     begin {M}

     {def.: mn, mq}
     {used: mn, d, mq, pa}

     end; {M}
   begin {I}

   {def.: y, it, fg}
   {used: y, it, fg, w}

     L(y);
     M(it)

   end; {I}
 begin {F}

 {def.: fk, fi,g}
 {used: fk, g, z, pa}

   G(g);
   I(g, fk);

 end; {F}
begin {P}

 {def.: pa, pk, pq, pz, px}
 {used: pa, pk, pq, pz, px, pt}

 B(pk, pq, pz);
 F(pr, pz);
 F(pr, pt);
end.
```

Figure 1 The scheme of the program EXAMP.

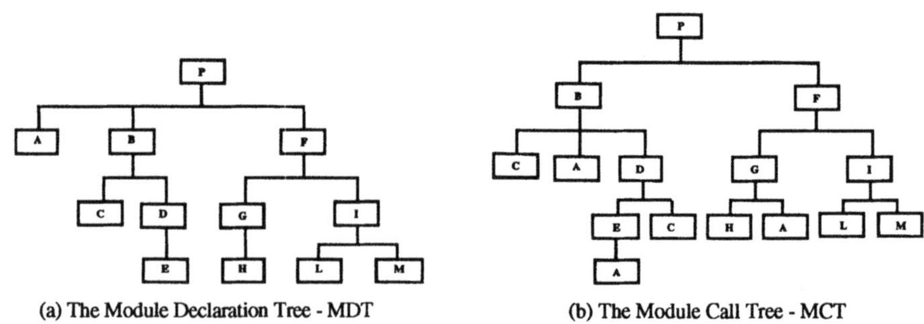

(a) The Module Declaration Tree - MDT

(b) The Module Call Tree - MCT

Figure 2 The MDT and MCT of the program EXAMP.

The scope/visibility matrix, VIS_mat

This is a Boolean matrix (n x n) with the same structure and composition as the MDT_mat matrix, from which it can be obtained. The matrix has the peculiarity that VIS_mat(i,j) = 1 if, and only if, on the basis of the programming language's scope/visibility rules, the unit corresponding to row i can reference the variables declared in the unit corresponding to column j. VIS_mat can be determined as follows:

$$\text{VIS\_mat}\ (i,j)=((\text{MDT}+I)^T)^+$$

where I is the unity diagonal matrix and A^T and A^+ indicate the transpose and the transitive closure of matrix A respectively.

Figure 3 shows the VIS_mat matrix for the program in Figure 1. Figure 3 also points out that the VIS_mat matrix shows the existence of subtrees identifying the declaration scope in each unit, and the units belonging to each subtree: these are identified by the sequences of values 1 along the columns of the VIS_mat matrix and the root of each of them corresponds to the first row of the chain containing the value 1.

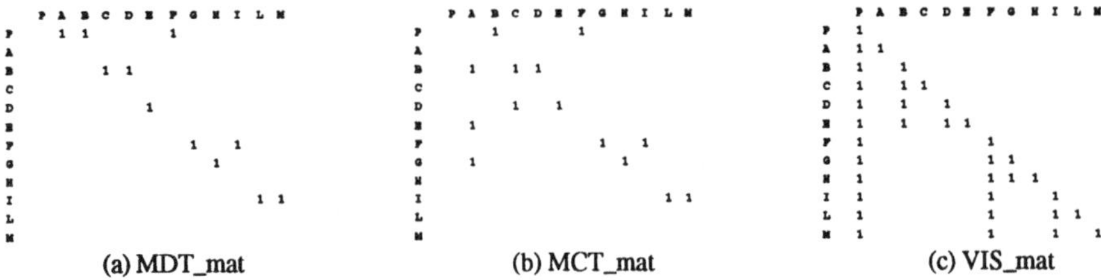

Figure 3 The matrices MDT_mat, MCT_mat and VIS_mat of the program EXAMP.

The potential data reference matrix, PDR_mat

PDR_mat is a Boolean matrix (n x m) with the same structure and composition as the matrix DD_mat. PDR_mat can be obtained from the following matricial product:

$$\text{PDR\_mat} = \text{VIS\_mat} \times \text{DD\_mat}$$

If we use PDR_mat(i,j) to indicate the generic element of this matrix, we have:

PDR_mat(i,j)=1 if, and only if, the unit i can reference the variable corresponding to column j (i.e. the declaration of variable j is visible to unit i).

If the variable j has been declared just once in a unit (i-k) which is visible to unit i, unit i can reference it. Otherwise, if the variable j has been declared more than once, unit i can reference the last declaration, i.e. the declaration performed in the closest unit (i-k) that lexicographically precedes unit i and is visible to it.

Let x_j be a variable declared one or more times and P_i be a unit that can reference it, i.e. PDR_mat(i,j)=1 where i is the row corresponding to the unit P_i and j the column corresponding to the variable x_j. The variable x_j which P_i is referencing to is the one declared in a unit P_{i-k} (corresponding to the row i-k) for which the following is true:

$$\text{DD\_mat}(P_{i-k},x_j)|_{k=0,i-1} = 1 \ \text{.and.}\ \text{VIS\_mat}(P_i,P_{i-k})|_{k=0,i-1} = 1$$

where k is equal to the first value that satisfies the above rule.

Thus, the generic row i of the PDR_mat matrix gives information on the variables that can be referenced by unit i, while the generic column j indicates the units that can reference variable j. Figure 4 shows the PDR_mat matrix for the program in Figure 1.

The actual data flow relationships matrix, ADF_mat

ADF_mat is a Boolean matrix (n x n), where n is the number of units making up the system, and having the same structure and composition as the matrix MDT_mat.

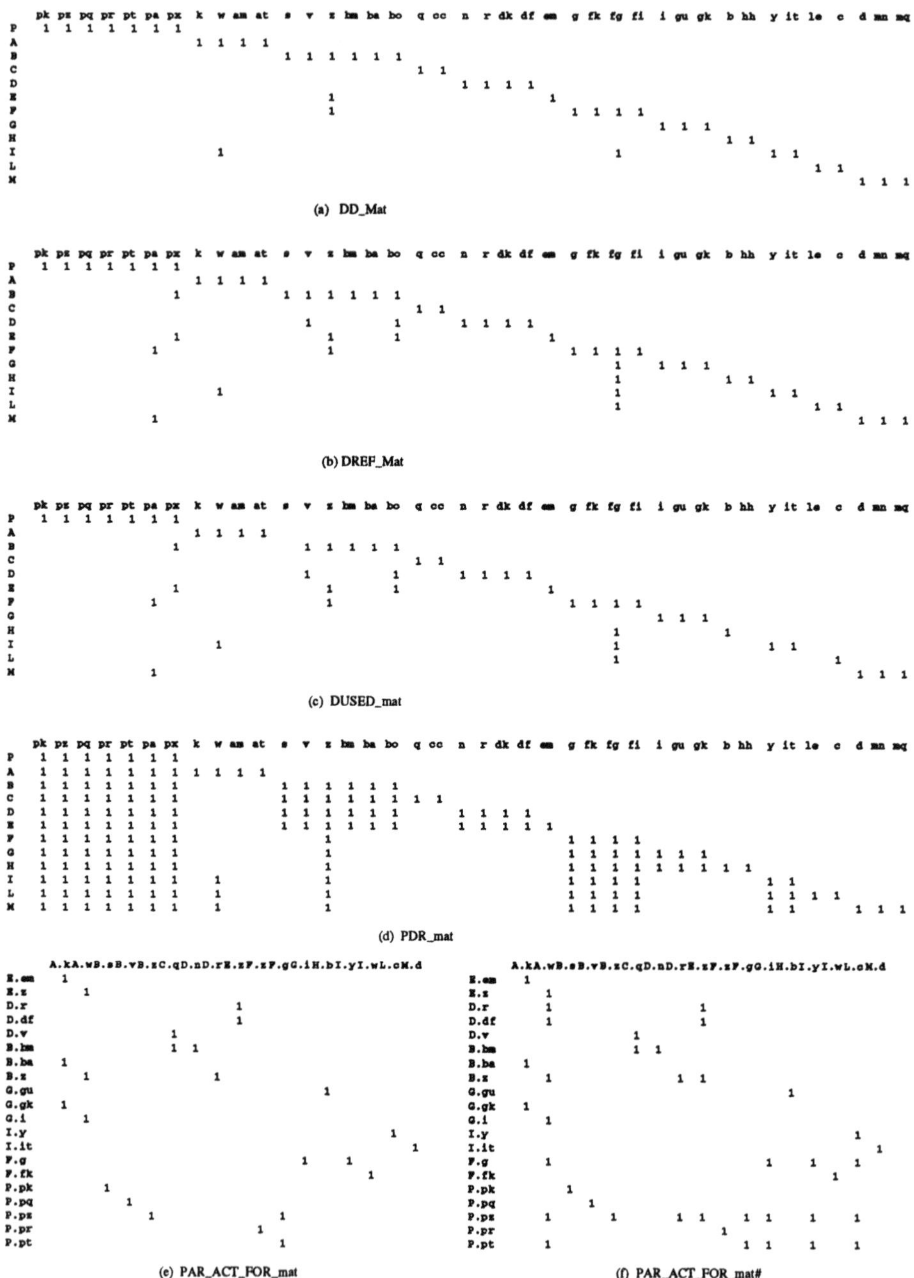

Figure 4 The matrices relative to the program EXAMP.

We have:

ADF_mat $(P_i,P_w) = 1 \iff \exists\ j \in (1,n)$ satisfying the following conditions:

1. DREF_mat (P_i, x_j)=1.and.DREF (P_w, x_j)=1;
2. DD_mat $(P_{i-k}, x_j)|_{k=0,i-1}$=1.and.VIS_mat $(P_i, P_{i-k})|_{k=0,i-1}$=1;
3. DD_mat $(P_{w-y}, x_j)|_{y=0,w-1}$=1.and.Vis_mat $(P_w, P_{w-y})|_{y=0,w-1}$=1;
4. $P_{i-k}=P_{w-y}$.

where k and y are equal to the first value that makes true the conditions 2 and 3.

The conditions 1, 2, 3 and 4 solve the problem caused by the homonymy between the variables.

The ADF_mat matrix is symmetrical; it represents the relationships between the various units because of the actual data flow existing between them. The generic element ADF_mat (P_i,P_w)=1 indicates that there is a relationship, due to the reference to the same variable, between P_i and P_w. Thus the generic row i (or column) of the ADF_mat matrix indicates the software units related to the unit P_i because of their references to the same variables, and, therefore, they may be directly affected by a change made on the unit P_i. Figure 5 shows the ADF_mat matrix determined using the other matrices shown in the Figures 3 and 4 and the above rules.

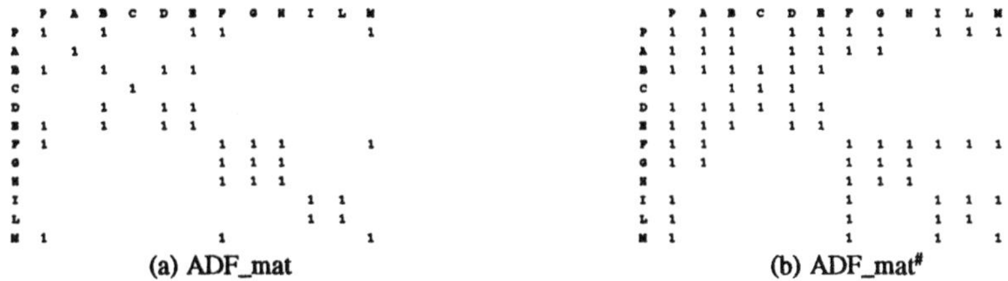

(a) ADF_mat (b) ADF_mat#

Figure 5 The ADF_mat and ADF_mat# matrices of the program EXAMP.

The actual/formal parameter matrix, PAR_ACT_FOR_mat

This is a Boolean matrix (p x q) where p is the number of actual parameters exchanged in the various activations and q is the number of formal parameters declared in the interface of the software units. Each actual/formal parameter is identified by its name and the name of the calling/called unit, i.e. if p_x is an actual/formal parameter and P_u a calling/called unit then we refer to it as $P_u.p_x$. Each row of the matrix corresponds to an actual parameter identifier (even if an identifier is used in more than one call, only one row represents it), while each column corresponds to a formal parameter identifier.

For the generic element PAR_ACT_FOR_mat(i,j), we have:

- PAR_ACT_FOR_mat(i,j) = 0 if the actual parameter $P_u.p_i$ is not exchanged with the formal parameter $P_v.p_j$;
- PAR_ACT_FOR_mat(i,j) = 1 if the actual parameter $P_u.p_i$ is exchanged with the formal parameter $P_v.p_j$.

Synonymity problems, due to the aliasing between the formal and actual parameters, make it difficult to identify the actual variables referred in the various units. This can be overcome by actualizing the data flow for the parameter exchange between the various units. This can be achieved by substituting each reference to the formal parameters with one to the respective actual parameter (Canfora *et al.*, 1992). The use of the PAR_ACT_FOR_mat matrix helps to solve this problem as the values '1' indicate a correspondence between the actual parameter corresponding to the subject row and the formal parameter related to the subject column. More difficult is the situation in which a formal parameter of a unit P_u becomes in turn an actual parameter because it is exchanged along a sequence of activations. In this case, the same identifier appears both on the rows and on the columns of PAR_ACT_FOR_mat, i.e. if $P_g.a_i$

and $P_d.f_j$ indicate the names of the actual parameter corresponding to row i and the formal parameter corresponding to column j respectively, it may happen that $P_g.a_i = P_d.f_j$. To know which is the actual parameter corresponding to the formal parameter to whom is passed, as the actual one, a formal parameter of another unit, we use the following matrix PAR_ACT_FOR_mat#, a Boolean matrix having the same structure and composition of PAR_ACT_FOR_mat; we have:

1. PAR_ACT_FOR_mat (i,j) = 1 => PAR_ACT_FOR_mat# (i,j) = 1;
2. $\forall$ $i^+ \in (1,p)$, $j^+ \in (1,q)$: $P_g.a_{i+} = P_d.f_{j+}$ find the values $j*$ that satisfy PAR_ACT_FOR_mat(i^+,$j*$)=1, indicating that the formal parameter $P_d.f_{j+}$ of a unit is used as the actual one in the activation to another unit, i.e. the formal parameter $P_d.f_{j+}$ is passed to the ones corresponding to the columns $j*$ as the actual parameter $P_g.a_{i+}$;
3. $\forall j*$ set PAR_ACT_FOR_mat#(i ,j*)$|_{i=1,p}$ =1 <=> PAR_ACT_FOR_mat#(i ,j^+)$|_{i=1,p}$ =1

The last operation reports the values of the column $P_d.f_{j+}$ in the column $P_h.f_{j*}$, thus establishing a direct correspondence between the actual parameter $P_k.a_k$, passed to $P_d.f_{j+}$, and the parameter $P_h.f_{j*}$.

In such a way we can know which are the actual variables that a unit refers to when it is referencing to a formal parameter.

The synonymity problems, due to the aliasing between actual and formal parameters, are solved referring to the PAR_ACT_FOR_mat#.

From the matrix PAR_ACT_FOR_mat# we can compute the matrix ADF_mat#, which is a Boolean matrix (n x n) having the same structure and composition of ADF_mat. In ADF_mat# we have the same kind of information that is in ADF_mat but it also gives us information about the relationships among the units due to the aliasing of formal parameter.

Let P_i and P_j be the units corresponding to row i and column j respectively, we can compute ADF_mat# by applying the following rules :

1. ADF_mat (i, j) = 1 => ADF_mat# (i, j) = 1;
2. ADF_mat# (i,j) = 1 <=> $\exists$ (k, q) : PAR_ACT_FOR_mat# (k, q) = 1 .and. P_i is the unit whose actual parameter, corresponding to the row k of the last matrix, reaches the formal parameter, corresponding to the column q, of the unit P_j along a sequence of activations.

Figure 4 shows the PAR_ACT_FOR_mat and PAR_ACT_FOR_mat# matrices for the program in Figure 1, while in Figure 5 is the ADF_mat# matrix for the same program.

5 THE IDENTIFICATION OF THE SOFTWARE UNITS AFFECTED BY A CHANGE

We use the matrices defined in the previous sections to identify the software units that may be affected by a change to be made in a unit P_i. Let us denote with:

- P_i , the software unit to be modified in order to make a change;
- MV, the set of the variables v_j involved by the change. We can get the MV set by:

$$MV = IV \cup DV \cup AV \cup FV$$

where:

  - IV is the set of the variables directly involved in the change, i.e. the ones referred to in the statement to be changed:

$$IV = \{v_i : \text{reference to } v_i \text{ in } P_i \text{ to be modified}\}.$$

  - DV is the set of the variables having a dependence relationships, inside the unit P_i, with the ones in the set IV.
  - AV is the set of actual parameter corresponding to any formal one of P_i being in $IV \cup DV$:

$AV = \{v_a : \exists v_i \in (IV \cup DV), v_a \in AP : PAR\_ACT\_FOR\_mat^{\#} (P_a.v_a, P_i.v_i)|_{a=1,p} = 1\}$
where AP is the set of actual parameters, corresponding to the rows of the matrix PAR_ACT_FOR_mat.

- FV is the set of formal parameters to which any variable in $IV \cup DV$ is passed:
  $FV = \{v_f : \exists v_i \in (IV \cup DV), v_f \in FP : PAR\_ACT\_FOR\_mat^{\#} (P_i.v_i, P_f.v_f)|_{f=1,q} = 1\}$
  where FP is the set of formal parameters, corresponding to the columns of the matrix PAR_ACT_FOR_mat.

Let P_REF_ALL be, the set of all the software units that have a relationship with P_i because they reference the same set of variables:

$$P\_REF\_ALL = \{P_k : ADF\_mat^{\#}(P_i , P_k)|_{k=1,n;\, k\neq i} = 1\}$$

we have to determine the sub-set $PV \subseteq P\_REF\_ALL$ made up of the software units referencing only the variables in the set MV.

The set PV will thus be made up of all the units $P_j \in P\_REF\_ALL$ that make true at least one of the following conditions:

- for each variable $v_j \in (IV \cup DV)$ all the following conditions must be true:
  1. $DREF\_mat (P_i, v_j)=1.and.DREF\_mat (P_j, v_j)=1;$
  2. $DD\_mat (P_{i-k}, v_j)|_{k=0,i-1}=1.and.VIS\_mat (P_i, P_{i-k})|_{k=0,i-1}=1;$
  3. $DD\_mat (P_{j-y}, v_j)|_{y=0,j-1}=1.and.VIS\_mat (P_j, P_{j-y})|_{y=0,j-1}=1;$
  4. $P_{i-k}=P_{j-y}$.

  where k and y are equal to the first value making conditions 2 and 3 true.
- for each variable $v_a \in AV$ and $v_j \in (IV \cup DV)$ all the following conditions must be true:
  1. $DREF\_mat (P_i, v_j)=1.and.DREF\_mat (P_j, v_a)|_{j=1,n}=1;$
  2. $PAR\_ACT\_FOR\_mat^{\#} (P_j.v_a, P_i.\ v_j)|_{j=1,p} = 1$.
- for each variable $v_f \in FV$ and $v_j \in (IV \cup DV)$ all the following conditions must be true:
  1. $DREF\_mat (P_i, v_j)=1.and.DREF\_mat (P_j, v_f)|_{j=1,n}=1;$
  2. $PAR\_ACT\_FOR\_mat^{\#} (P_i.\ v_j, P_j.v_f)|_{j=1,q} = 1$.

The set PV has been computed under the hypothesis that the change to be made will not insert into P_i new references to variables not already referenced in it before, and it will not delete any of the existing references, i.e. the change will not modify the values of the DREF_mat matrix and it will thus not create new actual relationships between the software units.

New actual relationships between software units will, however, be created if the change inserts new references to variables not referenced before. This means that in the DREF_mat matrix some values of some elements $DREF\_mat(P_i, v_j)$ will change from 0 to 1 for some $v_j \in MV$. We can identify the new software units affected by the change, before changing the code, by modifying the DREF_mat matrix, setting $DREF\_mat(P_i , v_j) = 1$ where v_j is the new referenced variable, and computing from this the new ADF_mat' matrix and the matrix $ADF\_mat^{\#'}$, in which the new actual links created by that change are shown. The new actual links can be computed by: $ADF\_mat^{\#'} - ADF\_mat^{\#}$.

In order to insert into a software unit P_i a reference to a variable v_j not previously referred in it, we must first make the following considerations:

1. check that the unit P_i can refer the variable v_j and this is possible if and only if:
   1.1. $PDR\_mat(P_i, v_j)=1;$
   1.2. $DD\_mat(P_{i-k},v_j)|_{k=0,i-1} =1.and.\ VIS\_mat(P_i ,P_{i-k})|_{k=0,i-1} =1;$

   that is P_i has the visibility of the variable it has to reference.
2. check that the variable v_j is declared in P_i itself, or it is a global variable for P_i:
   2.1. $DD\_mat(P_i, v_j)=1;$
   2.2. $(PDR\_mat(P_i, v_j)=1).and.(DD\_mat(P_i, v_j)=0).$

In the case of 2.1, if the unit P_i is a leaf in the Module Declaration Tree (P_i does not declare any other software unit), i.e.MDT_mat $(i,j)|_{j=1,n}= 0$, the insertion of the new reference into P_i does not create new actual links and thus ADF_mat$^{\#'}$ = ADF_mat$^{\#}$.

In the case of 2.2 or 2.1, but where P_i is not a leaf in the Module Declaration Tree, we have to identify the new actual links that exist between P_i and the other software units referencing the same variable v_j, by analyzing the matrix ADF_mat$^{\#'}$ and computing the set PV.

We can make similar considerations if the change to be made entails the deletion of a reference to a variable v_j. Here too we have to modify the DREF_mat matrix, this time setting the value of the element DREF_mat(P_i, v_j) from one to zero, and then compute the ADF_mat$^{\#'}$ matrix and evaluate the set PV.

The set PV includes all the software units referencing the same set of variables referred in P_i, but this does not mean that there is necessarily an ADF link between all the pairs (P_i, P_j): there will be an ADF link only if one of the two units references a variable v_i to define its value, and the other unit references v_i to use its value.

Our analysis does not allow the computation of the sequences of definitions and uses of a variable v_j but we can only know in which software units v_j is referenced. Thus we cannot determine when a variable is defined or used in a unit (i.e. whether it is first defined and then used or vice versa, or whether it is defined and/or used more than once, and so on) but only if it is defined and/or used and if it is only defined or only used in a unit. Therefore, we can only know which are the pairs (P_i, P_j) where a variable is only defined or only used in both the units and in this case we delete the unit P_j from the set PV. When, on the other hand, a variable v_j is both defined and used in the units P_i and P_j we do not know if its use in one unit follows or precedes its definition in the other, i.e. whether we have a sequence def(P_i, v_j) - def(P_j, v_j) - use(P_j, v_j) or a sequence def(P_i , v_j) - use(P_j , v_j) - def(P_j , v_j). In this case we cannot know if there actually is an ADF link between the units (P_i, P_j) so we assume the worst case, that is we assume that an ADF link exists between (P_i, P_j) due to v_j .

In order to delete from the set PV the units that do not have an ADF link with P_i, for the above mentioned reasons, we define the following two matrices:

- the used variables matrix, DUSED_mat, a (n x m) Boolean matrix, with the same structure and composition as the DD_mat matrix; it will be:
  DUSED_mat (i,j)=1 if and only if in the unit corresponding to row i there is a 'use' (the variable is referenced without changing its value) of the variable corresponding to column j at least once.
- the defined variables matrix, DDEF_mat, a (n x m) Boolean matrix, with the same structure and composition as the DD_mat matrix; it will be:
  DDEF_mat (i,j)=1 if and only if in the unit corresponding to row i there is a 'definition' (the variable is referenced and its value is changed) of the variable corresponding to column j at least once.

Of course, DREF_mat = DDEF_mat $\cup$ DUSED_mat.

Figure 4 shows the matrix DUSED_mat of the program in Figure 1.

We have to remove from the set PV all the units $P_j \in$ P_NOT_IMP where P_NOT_IMP is the set defined as follows:

P_NOT_IMP =
{P_j: DDEF_mat(P_i, v_i)=1 .and. (DUSED_mat(P_j , v_i)=0 .and. DDEF_mat(P_j, v_i)=1)
.or. DDEF_mat(P_j, v_i)=1 .and. (DUSED_mat(P_i, v_i)=0 .and. DDEF_mat(P_i, v_i)=1)
.or. DUSED_mat(P_i, v_i)=1 .and. (DUSED_mat(P_j, v_i)=1 .and. DDEF_mat(P_j, v_i)=0)
.or. DUSED_mat(P_j, v_i)=1 .and. (DUSED_mat(P_i, v_i)=1 .and. DDEF_mat(P_i, v_i)=0) }

where $v_i \in$ MV and $P_j \in$ PV.

The unit P_j is in P_NOT_IMP if the variable v_i , or any actual/formal parameter corresponding to it in P_j, is only defined or only used both in P_i and P_j.

In all the other cases we consider to have an ADF link between the pairs (P_i , P_j).

Finally, we can define the set P_IMP as:

P_IMP = PV - P_NOT_IMP

which is the set made up of the software units referencing the variables in MV and that are affected by the change to be made in P_i .

Once the set P_IMP has been defined, we have useful information for estimating the impact of the change to be made and the resources to dedicate to it. The estimate will depend on the number of affected units and on the complexity of each unit. Moreover we have to consider that the change may have repercussions, passing from the units in the set P_IMP to other units having a relationship with the ones in P_IMP but not with P_i. Thus, for each unit in P_IMP, we have to make an analysis similar to the one made above regarding P_i .

As an example, we apply the method to the program whose scheme, in a Pascal-like format, is in Figure 1.

Let us suppose to have to modify, in the unit D of the Program EXAMP, the statement

```
dk = n + df;
```

by adding the variable bo, that is the changed statement will be:

```
dk = n + df + bo;  .
```

As it results by the matrices PDR_mat, DD_mat and VIS_mat, the unit D can refer to the variable bo . Thus it is possible to make the desired change. In order to estimate its impact, we have to identify which are the units affected by the change.

We have that the sets IV, DV, FV and AV are:

IV ∪ DV = {B.bo, D.dk, D.n, D.df}
FV = {A.w, E.z}
AV = {B.bm}

so that the set MV will be:

MV = {B.bo, D.dk, D.n, D.df, A.w, E.z, B.bm}.

From the matrix ADF_mat# we obtain the set

P_REF_ALL = {P, A, B, C, E}

of the units that have a relationship with D because they reference the same variables referred by D. By applying the rules we told about above, we can determine the set

PV = {A, B, E}

of the units in P_REF_ALL that reference the variables in MV, and the set

P_NOT_IMP = {A}

and, finally, we can determine the set P_IMP = {B, E} that will be the units affected by that change in the unit D.

6 CONCLUSIONS

Every time we have to make a change in a program we must carefully evaluate its impact on the code by means of a thorough understanding of the software to modify in order to reduce the considerable hazard of generating side-effects. Side-effects stem from the relationships existing between the components of a software system and depend on the implementation structure and on the programming language used. The links and relationships that can exist between the several software units of a program differ according to the different syntactic, scope and visibility rules of each language. For these reasons there are a number of different reasons why a side-effect arises. Therefore, the way a program is represented is important and this representation must also take into consideration the language rules that make it possible to establish relationships between the various software units.

In the paper we have proposed a method that allows the representation of both potential and actual relationships existing in a program coded by a language with strict scope and visibility rules (such as ADA, PASCAL, MODULA-2, PL1). The proposed representation is based on the definition, use and computation of some Boolean matrices and it allows us to identify the software units that will be affected by a change involving data references in a software unit. The method makes it possible to identify the set of units that will be directly affected by the change, before it is actually made, and to have information to estimate the impact of the change on the code and the resources to devote to achieve it.

REFERENCES

Arnold, R. S. and Shawn, A. B. (1993) Impact Analysis - Towards a Framework for Comparison, in *Proc. of the IEEE Conference on Software Maintenance* (IEEE Comp. Soc. Press), Montreal, Canada, 292-301.

Canfora, G. and Cimitile, A. (1992) Reverse Engineering and Intermodular Data Flow: A Theoretical Approach. *Software Maintenance: Research and Practice*, **4**, 37-59.

Cimitile, A., Di Lucca, G. A. and Maresca, P. (1990) Maintenance and Intermodular Dependencies in Pascal Environment, in *Proc. of the IEEE Conference on Software Maintenance* (IEEE Comp. Soc. Press), San Diego, California, 72-83.

Freedman, D. and Weinberg, G. (1982) A Cheklist for Potential Side Effects of a Maintenance Change, in *Techniques of Program and System Maintenace*, (ed. G. Parik), Winthrop Publishers.

Haney, F. M. (1972) Module Connection Analysis, in *Proc. AFIPS Joint Computer Conference*, **41** (5), 173-9.

Lientz, B. P. and Swanson, E. B. (1980) *Software Maintenance Management.* Addison Wesley.

McClure, C. (1978) *Managing Software Development and Maintenance.* Van Nostrand Reinhold Company, New York.

Nosek, T. J. and Palvia, P. (1990) Software Maintenance Management: Changes in the Last Decade. *Journal of Software Maintenance*, **2** (3), 157-174.

Queille, J. P., Voidrot, J. F., Wilde, N. and Munro, M. (1994) The Impact Analysis Task in Software Maintenance: A model and a Case Study, in *Proc. of the IEEE Conference on Software Maintenance* (IEEE Comp. Soc. Press), Victoria, Canada, 234-242.

Schneidewind, N. (1987) The State of Software Maintenance. *IEEE Trans. on Software Engineering*, **SE-13**, 303-310.

Turver, R. J. and Munro, M. (1994) An Early Impact Analysis Technique for Software Maintenance. *Software Maintenance: Research and Practice*, **6**, 35-52.

Yau, S. S. and Collofello, J. S. (1980) Some Stability Measures for Software Maintenance, *IEEE Trans. on Software Engineering*, **SE-6**, (6), 545-552.

Yau, S. S. and Chang S. C. (1984) Estimating logical stability in Software Maintenance, in *Proc. IEEE C.S. Computer Software and Application Conference* (IEEE Comp. Soc. Press), 109-119.

Yau, S. S. and Collofello, J. S. (1985) Design Stability Measures for Software Maintenance. *IEEE Trans. on Software Engineering*, **SE-11** (9), 849-856.

10

The short but interesting life of small software firms

Mario Raffa, Giuseppe Zollo, Renata Caponi
ODISSEO-DIS, Dept. of Computer Science & Systems, University of Naples "Federico II"
Via Diocleziano 328, 80124 Naples, Italy, phone: +39 81 5704498, fax: +39 81 5704498, e-mail: zollo@nadis.dis.unina.it

Abstract

The paper analyses the organizational transformations of small innovative firms and the influence of the entrepreneurial know how on the growth path of the firms. A sample of 32 software firms has been investigated for more than fifteen years by the research group. From the raw data the authors derived 103 different organizational profiles, resulting in seven configurations. The results of the research show complex growth paths. Most of firms are not able to sustain a competition, mainly based on technological innovation. While the firms based on an initial technical know-how shows a variety of trajectories, the firms based on an initial orientation to market are forced to renounce to the software development as the main business. Most of the surveyed firms stop to exist as small software firms. For most of them their life as software producers lasted from three to seven years.

Keywords

Entrepreneurial know-how, growth path, organizational configurations

1 THE KNOW-HOW OF ENTREPRENEURIAL FIRMS

Start-ups are common in emerging industries, such as personal computers, software, industrial control, biotechnology, and so on. Those sectors are interested by the presence of many competing and often redundant companies, created under the double pressure of availability of resources and growing market demand. A wide range of strategic and organizational choices are available for those firms, because traditions, habits, culture, standard process technology and reference examples are quite completely absent (Kao, 1991). In such conditions the organizations must deal with a high degree of uncertainty both internally and externally. The original culture, vision, skills of the entrepreneur is the unique factor which can turn the original ambiguity, uncertainty and disorder into a successful organization (Filion, 1991).

Increasing number of studies refer to the personal characteristics of entrepreneur the success of the firm in the early stages of its life (Miller *et al.* 1988; Lefebvre and Lefebvre, 1992). Roberts (1991) presents a schematic model which assumes that new companies are dependent at their formation upon the technological base learned by the entrepreneur from the incubating source, i.e. former companies, university laboratories, engineering departments. Personal abilities and individual attitudes are seen to be critical factor of successful entrepreneurial technology transfer.

This does not imply that the firm's performances should be attributed to the entrepreneurial characteristics alone. During the passage from organizational infancy to adulthood the firm undergoes the crises of control and directions (Greiner, 1972), due to the necessity to reduce the central role of the entrepreneur. After the first critical event, the firm's innovative abilities are based on a complex range of interacting factors (Acs and Audretsch, 1990; Rothwell, 1988; Pavitt, 1988; Storey and Johnson, 1987; Gibb and Scott, 1985; Kelly and Brooks, 1991):

a) structural incentives to innovate;
b) internal technological resources;
c) resources of the network within which the firm is included.

The literature shows the picture of a small growing firm that, for supporting successfully its innovation capability, must have a minimum size, hold internal skills, maintain a network of stable linkages with external economic agents.

The in-firm/out-firm relationships are crucial to support small firms' innovation capabilities in the growth stage. This is due to two reasons: a) the small firms' difficulty to finance long-term internal technological developments (Greiner, 1972; Huppert, 1981; La Belle *et al.*, 1980); b) the difficulty of sustaining their technological capabilities when loosing the inventor-founder-manager's support increasingly concerned with the firm management (Meyer and Roberts, 1986).

Summing up the current knowledge, the founder-entrepreneur plays a crucial role during the first stage of firm's life, while, during the growth stage a more complex set of resources is necessary to sustain the firm's activities. According to Roberts (1991), fewer articles focus upon detailed aspects of technical base of new firms during the both stages. It has been developed a detailed analysis on small software firms, including several case-studies, in order to point out the evolution of firms founded by entrepreneurs with strong scientific and technical background.

Software small firms were chosen for two reasons:

a) in the software industry manufacturing technology is basically made up of technician-embodied professional skills. In spite of the remarkable development of the software engineering in the last ten years, and notwithstanding the early availability of advanced development environments such as the CASE, professional skills will still be crucial in the next years. For this reason software firms are an excellent laboratory to analyze the organizational implications of person-embodied technologies;
b) in the last decade the small firm was really prevailing in the industry development. However the competitive situation is changing due to the higher focus by traditional information technology leaders (hardware producers) on software manufacturing. This, together with the strong technological dynamics and the new demand characteristics, is rapidly changing the small firms' room of maneuver.

2 THE ENTREPRENEURIAL KNOW-HOW IN SOFTWARE FIRMS

Software production is characterized by *applied know–how* (Werner, 1983; OECD, 1982, 1986). The know-how is, however, very complex to be acquired and it often requires the contribution of technical entrepreneur and a large number of skilled personnel (Weinberg, 1982). Applied know-how is basically made of three elements (Raffa and Zollo, 1988): 1) *basic technology visibility*, i.e. the knowledge of the performance of the basic products and their full use; 2) *different technologies integration capacity*, i.e. technical ability not related only to a given sector but to a wide range of disciplines, so that a complex system can be made; 3) *market visibility*, i.e. the capability of following demand trends and market opportunities opened up by applied technologies.

In order to understand how this know-how is formed and developed it is necessary to refer to the know-how of the *neighboring sectors*, i.e. those sectors where entrepreneurs come from. Within these neighboring sectors four types of know-how can be detected: *basic know-how (group 1)*, which includes scientific and technological skills forming the nucleus of the sector technologies. These skills are learnt in various places such as universities, research centres, large information technology and electronics firms, large EDP user firms, all of which are characterized by their specific and complex technological development. *Know-how of related goods* (alternative and complementary goods) *(group 2)*, which consists of a deep knowledge of the customer needs (business consultancy, EDP consultancy), of the firms' software problems (information services, hardware producers). *Market know-how (group 3)*, which consists of a knowledge of the demand trends and characteristics and of the marketing channels (hardware and software sellers). *User know-how (group 4)*, i.e. the knowledge required to introduce the software products into existing organizations. This know-how starts from a detailed knowledge of the user needs (a firm, a production department, a class of business) so as to define the software product's characteristics, and, hence, to attempt the switch to software production, firstly to serve the captive market and then the open market.

Given the articulated nature of software technology, the software industry growth can be seen as a colonization of the adjacent sectors through a widening of their technological horizons (Mintzberg, 1985, 1987; Rothwell and Zegveld, 1982).

3 THE SAMPLE

The outcomings illustrated in this paper are grounded on a fifteen years research starting from 1979. During the years 1983-84, 132 software firms were studied, representing 84% of the software firms in Southern Italy, the less developed area of the country. The core of the software industry in Southern Italy was made up of small firms: 58.27% of the sample have less than 10 employees, and 21.26% have between 11 and 20 employees, while only 4.72% have more than 100 employees. The medium-sized firm range is very narrow in this sector (15.75%). For many of those firms detailed case studies are developed, and several firms are analyzed in different stages of their life. In the years 1989-90 and 1993-94 new field surveys was carried out regarding small firms out of the firms sample studied in the years 1983-84. The new survey was aimed at analyzing organizational changes, development paths, product strategies and firms' performances. It was difficult to contact every single firm studied in the first survey: some of them ended up their activities, some changed location and address, others changed their name. At present, 80 firms are studied. However the investigated sample is sufficiently meaningful and some considerations can be made as to the relation between initial know-how and firm development. A large number of indications emerged from the research, but the present paper summarizes only the outcomes related to 32 small firms, which are considered a typical example of how the original culture of the entrepreneur affected the growth path of the firms.

4 THE FIRMS' FORMATION

In Italy the software sector began to develop from 1979 onwards. More than 70% of the firms operating in '84 first appeared between '79 and '84. Firms established before this date carried out related activities such as data processing for third parties and hardware sales, and some of them later on diversified into software production. It is important to stress at this point that most of the small software firms do not produce only software, but have a mixed output.

4.1 The entrepreneurial know-how

In order to analyze differences in the initial know-how during the establishment stage, references is made to the three initial development stages of the Italian software industry: *incubation* (up to 1978), *takeoff* (1979-80) and *growth consolidation* (1981-84) (Table 1). The development of the software sector is closely bound to the acquisition of its know-how. The research revealed that 34.4% out of 132 firms entered the sector with basic know-how (group 1). This know-how is basically held by technicians who have left large firms operating in the information technology and electronics sector, or having a university background. Basic know-how was conspicuous in the three periods analyzed, and it played a particularly important role in the sector take-off period (1979-80), where it was responsible for the establishment of 40% of the firms.

Table 1 % of firms according to the know-how of their establishment or of their diversification into software sector

Neighboring	*Period of establishment/diversification*			*Total*
know-how sectors	*up to 1978*	*1979-'80*	*1981-'84*	*of firms*
Basic know-how sector (group 1)	25.71	40.00	36.36	34.40
Related goods know-how (group 2)	25.71	22.86	16.36	20.80
Market know-how (group 3)	20.00	22.86	30.92	25.60
User know-how sector (group 4)	28.58	14.28	16.36	19.20
Total	100.00	100.00	100.00	100.00

A given share of the firms (19.20%) entered the software sector with user know-how (group 4). It is important to note how this know-how was crucial in the sector's first period of incubation (in 28.58% of the firms), while its role declined in the following periods. This was due to the fact that users started producing software by themselves because of inability or nonexistence of supply to meet user needs. Consequently the know-how, acquired for internal production, was then utilized for the market. In the subsequent periods the appearance of an adequate supply reduced the need for self developed software. Finally, 46.40% of the firms entered the software sector with users' needs and market know-how, which can be divided into two large groups (groups 2 and 3 of Table 1). The group 2 includes competencies on software applications and information technology (organizational consultancy, EDP consultancy, services firms, hardware assembly) and represents 20.80% of the firms. The group 3 concerns the knowledge of demand characteristics as a result of the activities carried on (software and hardware selling) and accounts for 25.60% of the firms. The role of this know-how increases as the market develops.

5 ORGANIZATIONAL TRANSFORMATIONS IN SMALL INNOVATIVE FIRMS

The life of the small innovative firms is marked by changes that can give rise to different outcomes, such as growth, survival, or death (Raffa and Zollo, 1994). In any case the small innovative firms have to cope with external changes (competitors, market, technology) and internal changes (professional skills, organization, management). Several field researches performed in the United States, in Great Britain and in Italy, highlighted that, while in the mature industries, many firms do not experience any growth, in the innovative industries the small firms have many options. The high development rate of those industries drives the small firm to focus its attention on growth issues. This in order to follow the market expansion, to have access to new market segments and, ultimately, to acquire market and technological skills through the collaboration with other firms or the acquisition of new firms.

5.1 The original know-how and firm's transformations

The life of the small innovative firms is usually typified by a technology-oriented stage and by a marketing-oriented stage (Greiner, 1972; Brandt, 1981). The technology-oriented stage is characterized by an internal focus: the firm develops its key technologies and identifies its strengths and weaknesses. In the marketing-oriented stage the firm focuses its attention on the market and on formal management and planning methods. The organizational and managerial crisis experienced when shifting from the first to the second stage gives rise to a distinction between management and development functions and to a leading group in which different skills are combined (Kao, 1991).

While in the large firm most of the uncertainties are overcome through full and visible changes in the organization pattern (creation of new firm functions, new responsibilities, new hierarchies, new communication lines) (Kay, 1984), in the small firm (where the organizational pattern is less structured) most of the uncertainties are overcome through responsibility changes, differentiation and rearrangements of the firm's activities. The new relations amongst the firm's subjects are heuristically experimented through a set of trials for new development paths. In this context - typified by a high uncertainty typical of innovative industries - targets and tools for their achievement are ambiguously perceived. Moreover, given the limited rationality of the firm's actors, the missing information is supplemented by individual creativity. For this reason small innovative firms can give rise to different development paths, even though they have similar internal requirements and operate within the same competitive environment.

The entrepreneur's technical role is crucial for the firms' development. Several empirical studies has demonstrated that in small firms technological entrepreneurs play a central role to influence the successful technological innovations and firm's strategies (Miller and Toulouse, 1986a, 1986b; Roberts, 1991). Entrepreneur's characteristics, such as professional and technical background, are considered the most important resource associated with the ability of the firm to innovate and to growth (Roberts, 1991). On the other side, several authors report situations where the entrepreneur blocks the growth potentiality of small firm (Meyer and Goes, 1987). The ambivalence concerning the role of the entrepreneur seems to be related to the fact that the firm goes through various organizational stages during its growth process (Churchill and Lewis, 1983; Kimberley and Miles, 1980). At each stage a particular combination of resources is requested in order to success.

A sample of 32 software firms has been investigated for more than fifteen years, and the research group collected several questionnaires and case studies for each firm. The field data have been analyzed in the light of configurational theory (Meyer *et al.*, 1993), resource-based theory (Grant, 1991; Prahalad and Hamel, 1990), and growth-stage theory (Greiner, 1972; Kimberly and Miles, 1980). The growth process of the firm has been considered as a change process and the life of the firm as a sequence of developmental stages. A organizational profile corresponds to every stage. From the raw data 103 different organizational profiles have been derived. Each profile was defined by the values assumed by a set of resources. The set of resources was gathered from literature of small innovative firms (Reid and Jacobsen, 1988; Kelley and Brooks, 1991; Quinn, 1979; Garden, 1992), and from the literature on software firms (Barocci *et al.*, 1983). A set of 16 resources were identified, grouped in three subsets:

i) *resources related to the entrepreneurs* (individual know how, experience, personal network, involvement in software development). These resources concern the background experience of the entrepreneurial group and the involvement of the entrepreneurs in the technical and managerial aspects of the firm;
ii) *resources related to professionals* (technical abilities, professional skills, variety of competencies). These resources concern the competencies of the professionals of the software firms. The level and the diversification of competencies are very important to sustain the competitiveness of the small firm;
iii) *resources related to the organization and technology* (firm size, cooperation with external subjects, internal methodologies). These resources concern the technical and market experience of the firm, that is the presence of organizational routines, technology, structured relationships with the environment.

6 MAIN CONFIGURATIONS

On the basis of the variables identified as resources, 103 organizational profiles have been identified. The close analysis of the profiles led to the definition of seven organizational configurations. The configurations were derived through the identification of a small subset of resources influencing each other and forming a self-supporting cycle of relationships. For example, the high technical competencies of the entrepreneur influences positively the level of involvement of the entrepreneur in software development activities. The resulting focus on technical problems influences the prevalent competencies of the employees, who are technicians. The development group is dominated by the entrepreneur, and the technical information come from the entrepreneurial personal network. These stable and mutual reinforcing relationships are the core of the configurations. According to the configurational approach, a configuration is established when each resource acts as catalyst to reproduce the others. The identified configurations are the followings:

C1 *Configuration based on technical know how of entrepreneurial group* (# of configurational profiles: 17). The entrepreneur is a technician coming from other firms or from university. He dedicates attention and time almost exclusively to product development. The non-technical competencies are poor, while organizational structure of development group is informal. The firm is constituted by one or more software project groups.

C2 *Configuration based on professionals* (# of organizational profiles: 13). This configuration is characterized by new competencies, both technical and marketing, and by collaborations with external consultants and professionals, who have a part-time relationships with the firm.

C3 *Configuration based on network (collaborations with larger firms, sw and services firms, technical environment and university)* (# of organizational profiles: 18). The competitive capability of the firm is based on relationships with other external subjects, particularly large hardware firms. These relationships allow the small firm to acquire new managerial and market skills, that integrate initial technical abilities.

C4 *Configuration based on organizational routines and development methodologies* (# of organizational profiles: 8). This configuration marks the shifting from an organizational structure focused on entrepreneur to a structure regulated by a set of procedures and standard, for both development and managerial activities.

C5 *Configuration based on market relationships* (# of organizational profiles: 14). The competitive capability is based on entrepreneurial market knowledge, that allows the firm to response rapidly to needs of the market.

C6 *Configuration based on integrated and specialized products/services* (# of organizational profiles: 9). Firm's competitiveness is based on firm's capability to response to needs of market supplying complementary services to the basic product. Collaborations with customers are generally limited to local market. This configuration is also characterized by new competencies market oriented.

C7 *Configuration based on systems' commercialization* (# of organizational profiles: 24). This configuration is characterized by several activities: hardware and software commercialization, training activities, organizational consultancy. Generally, software development is only a support to the other activities.

7 FIRMS' EVOLUTION

The growth path of firms could be considered a sequence of moves from one configuration to another. *At their beginning firms have two possible configurations: C1, based on technical entrepreneurial know-how, and C5, based on market entrepreneurial know-how. Consequently, firms are polarized on technology or on market.* Among analyzed firms, 17 belong to first group (Cl configuration based on technical know how of entrepreneurial group), and 15 to second group (C5 configuration based on market competence of the entrepreneur). Both those firms' groups have to complete their initial know how to develop their activities. Consequently each firm after few years modifies its initial organizational configuration.

7.1 The growth path of the firms based on technical entrepreneurial know-how

The 17 firms based on technical entrepreneurial know how (Cl configuration) have to complete their capability by expanding market competencies. The pattern of growth shows very diversified paths, which indicates the necessity for the firms to explore a variety of opportunities. It is very important to underline that this initial variety at the end converges to a small number of organizational solutions.

This occurs through different ways:

i) relationships with other firms, which determine the passage from Cl configuration (technical-firms) to C3 configuration (network-firms);
ii) collaborations with professionals and consultants, which determine the passage from Cl configuration (technical-firms) to C2 configuration (professional-based firms);
iii) new market abilities realized by a diversification of entrepreneur activities or by new employees market oriented. Those firms, generally, are focused on local market and develop strong relationships with their clients. Close collaborations with customers allow the firms to develop several services around their basic software products. This fact determines the passage from Cl configuration (technical-firms) to C6 configuration (services-orientated firms);
iv) organizational structure regulated by a set of procedure and standards, for both development and managerial activities, which determine the passage from Cl configuration (technical-firms) to C4 configuration (procedures-based firms);
v) finally, some firms strongly modify their initial vocation, increasing market competencies and focusing on hardware and software commercialization. This fact determines the passage from Cl configuration (technical-firms) to C7 configuration (commercialization-based firms).

These passages from Cl configuration to other configurations can occur directly, or through other intermediate configurations. From a statistical point of view we can observe that the most important paths that the firms follow are those depicted in Figure 1.

We have that 24% of the firms starting with Cl configuration pass to the C2 configuration, and successively to C4 configuration (12%) and to C7 configuration (12%); while the 29% to C3 configuration and successively to C7 configuration. The others pass strictly to C6 configuration (12%) or to C7 configuration (23%); only one remain in Cl configuration (6%) and only one passes directly to C4 configuration (6%). With reference to Figure 1, the passage from Cl initial configuration (technical-firms) to C4 configuration (procedures-based firms) determines an organizational transformation involving both technological resources (technical standards adoption) and organizational resources (engagement of new employees).

Since these resources become internal firm's resources we say that the passage from C1 configuration (technical-firms) to C4 configuration (procedures-based firms) is characterized by an *internalization strategy of technological and organizational resources.*

The passage from C1 configuration (technical-firms) to C2 configuration (professional-based firms) is mainly characterized by a *product diversification strategy* and by a *strategy of complex networking with professional resources* (new technical competencies acquisition), *with different degrees of membership in the firm.* Instead, the passage from C1 configuration (technical-firms) to C6 configuration (services-orientated firms), is mainly characterized by a *networking strategy* (collaborations with customers) and by a *vertical market strategy*, while the passage from C1 configuration (technical-firms) to C3 configuration (network-based firms) is characterized by a *networking strategy* (concessionaire of large hardware firm, jobbing, leveraged buy-out by large firms, collaborations with other firms to develop package).

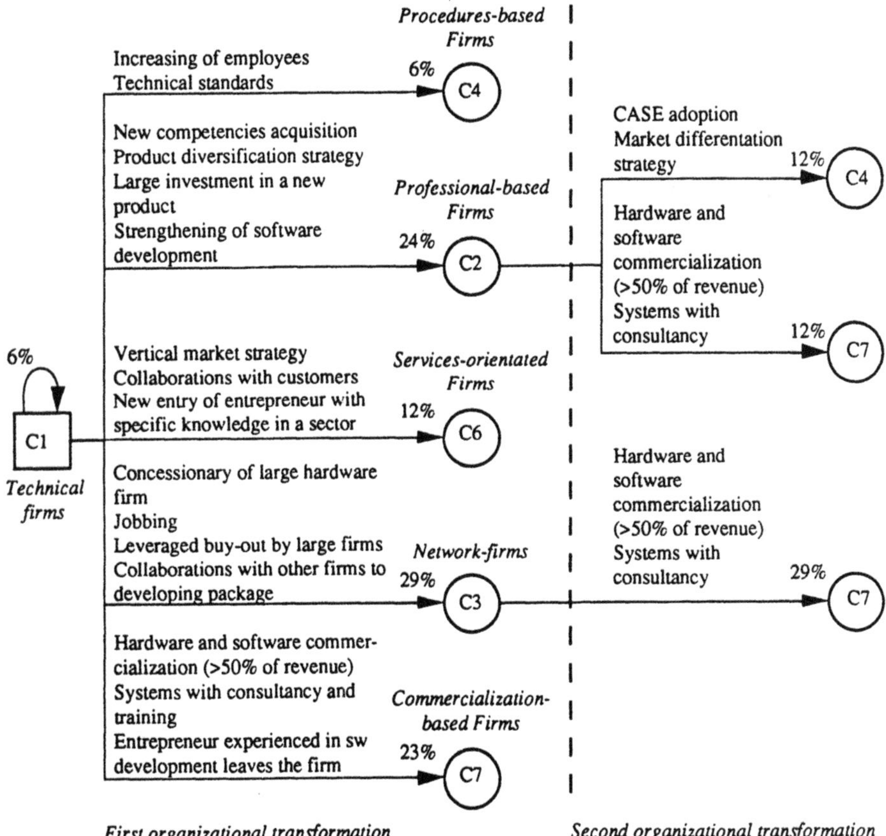

Figure 1 Organizational transformations of technical-firms.

Finally, the passage from C1 configuration (technical-firms) to C7 configuration (commercialization-orientated firms) is characterized by a *commercialization strategy* (hardware and software commercialization activities >50% of revenue).

With reference to the part of the Figure 1 that shows the second organizational transformations, we have that the passage from C2 configuration (professional-based firms) to C4 configuration (procedures-based firms) is characterized by a *market differentiation strategy* and by an *internalization strategy of technological resources* (CASE adoption), while the passage from C2 configuration (professional-based firms) to C7 configuration (commercialization-orientated firms) and from C3 configuration (network-based firms) to C7 configuration (commercialization-orientated firms) are characterized by a *commercialization strategy* (hardware and software commercialization activities >50% of revenue).

In conclusion, most transformations led the firms to reduce their involvement in software development. Only the development path from C1 (technical-firms) to C2 (professional-based firms) to C4 (procedures-based firms), regarding only 12% of the firms, led them to strengthen their software competencies. This path was supported by a strategy that allow the passage from an initial subset of resources, constituted by the entrepreneurial know-how, to a second subset of resources, constituted by a network of professionals, and at last, to a third subset of resources, constituted by internal and/or external technologies of software development and a more structured organization.

7.2 The growth path based on market entrepreneurial know-how

The firms originated from a configuration based on market entrepreneurial know-how (C5 configuration) have different growth paths:

i) most of those firms strongly reduces software development, giving rise to a variety of activities, within which software development is only a complementary activity. This fact determines the passage from C5 configuration (market-orientated firms) to C7 configuration (commercialization-based firms);

ii) some firms establish close collaborations with other firms (generally commercial collaborations). This fact determines the passage to C3 configuration (network-firms). The passage from C5 configuration (market-orientated firms) to C3 configuration (network-firms) and to C7 configuration (commercialization-based firms) can be occur directly, or through other intermediate configurations.

From a statistical point of view we can observe that the most important paths that the firms follow are those depicted in Figure 2.

We have that 20% of the firms starting with C5 configuration pass to the C2 configuration, and successively to C7 configuration (13%) and to C3 configuration (7%), while 35% of the firms starting with C5 configuration pass to C3 configuration and then to final C7 configuration (20%). The others remain in C3 configuration (15%) or pass strictly to C7 configuration (38%); only one passes directly to C4 configuration (7%). With reference to Figure 2, the passage from C5 configuration (market-orientated firms) to C4 configuration (procedures-based firms) is characterized by an *internalization strategy of technological resources* (CASE adoption) *and of organizational resources* (engagement of new employees), and by a *market differentiation strategy*.

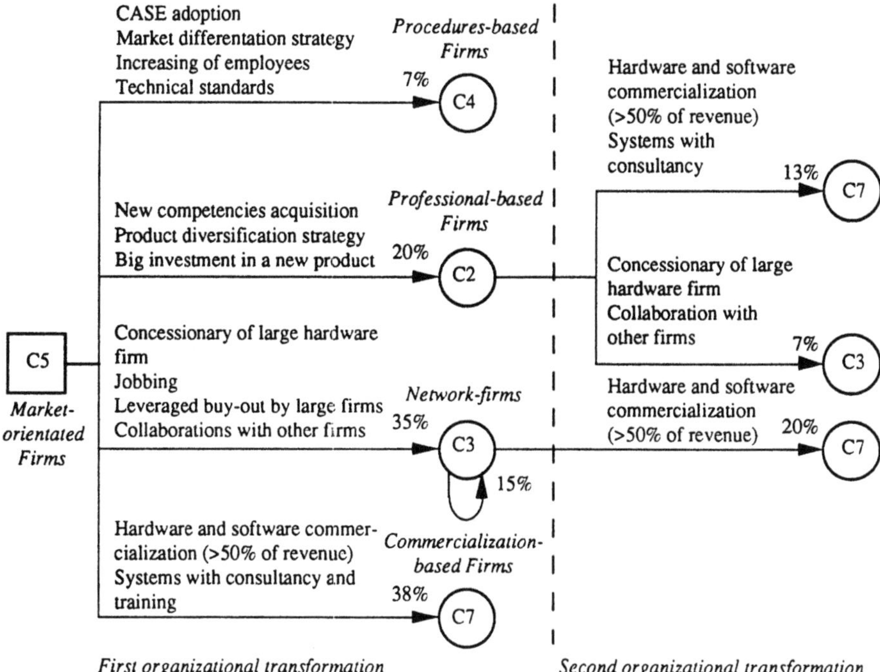

Figure 2 Organizational transformation of market-orientated firms.

The passage from C5 configuration (market-orientated firms) to C2 configuration (professional-based firms) determines an organizational transformation characterized mainly by a *product diversification strategy* and by a *strategy of complex networking with professional resources* (new technical competencies acquisition) *with different degrees of membership in the firm.*, while the passage from C5 configuration (market-orientated firms) to C3 configuration (network-based firms) is characterized by a *networking strategy* (concessionaire of large hardware firm, jobbing, leveraged buy-out by large firms, collaborations with other firms).

Finally, the passage from C5 configuration (market-orientated firms) to C7 configuration (commercialization-orientated firms) is characterized by a *commercialization strategy* (hardware and software commercialization activities >50% of revenue).

With reference to the part of the Figure 2 that shows the second organizational transformation, we say that the passage from C2 configuration (professional-based firms) to C3 configuration (network-based firms) is characterized by a *networking strategy* (concessionaire of large hardware firms, jobbing, collaborations with other firms), while the passage from C2 configuration (professional-based firms) to C7 configuration (commercialization-orientated firms) and from C3 configuration (network-based firms) to C7 configuration (commercialization-orientated firms) are characterized by a *commercialization strategy*.

In conclusion, the development path of the market-orientated firms has some significant differences with the development path of the technical-firms. The most important aspect is that C2 configuration (professional-based firms) did not evolve towards a specialization in software production but it evolved towards hardware and software commercialization. Only 7% of firms reached C4 configuration (procedures-based firms) through the internalization of technologies and methodologies, together with the hiring of new software employees.

8 CONCLUSIONS

At their very start firms have two possible configurations: firms based on technical entrepreneurial know-how, and firms based on market entrepreneurial know-how. Consequently, firms are polarized on the technology or on the market. The lack of initial configurations showing both competencies of market and technology is mainly due to the small size of the entrepreneurial group, usually one person who influenced the initial competencies of the firm.

Both those firms' groups have to complete their initial know how modifying the set of their resources. The firms with initial configuration based on technical entrepreneurial know-how have to complete their capability, expanding their market abilities. This occurs through different ways: i) collaborating with large firms; ii) collaborating with professionals and consultants; iii) using external competencies, both technical and market; iv) acquiring new market competencies through diversification of entrepreneurial group's activities, or through new market-oriented employees.

The firms with an initial configuration based on strong market entrepreneurial knowledge face several difficulties to complete their initial know how with technical competencies. Generally, those firms: i) reduce software development activity, diversifying towards services and hardware commercialization; ii) establish relationships with other firms.

The empirical evidences show that an important difference is present between the two firms' groups in the initial stages of their life. The firms with a strong technical know-how explore a wider set of possibilities than the firms of the other group, and their trajectory is more complex. Anyway, after few intermediate transformations, most of technical firms falls prevalently in the same configuration of the firms based on market competencies, that is they reach the configuration based on systems' commercialization (C7). This fact could be explained with the difficulty of both groups of firms to answer to the same competitive environment, which requires or a radical improvement of quality of products and services or to shrink the involvement in software development.

It is worthwhile to notify that few technical firms are able to realize this improvement (that is, to reach configuration C6), while this alternative appear more difficult to realize for firms based on market know-how. In any case the firms reaching this configuration develop a strong focus on a niche market.

In conclusion, it seems that most of firms are not able to sustain a competition mainly based on technological innovation, independently from their original know-how, and that the most important difference between the two groups is that the technical firms possess a set of resources that let them explore a wider set of possibilities than other firms. *Most of the surveyed firms are forced to significantly reduce their involvement in software development and to shift their strategic focus to the commercialization and other information services. In other words, they stop to exist as software houses and as small software firms. For most of them their life as software producer lasted from three to seven years.*

From the entrepreneurial point of view the knowledge of the configuration is important to understand the key resources sustaining the competition and the alternatives available to grow. From the public policy point of view, the knowledge of configurations and developmental trajectory provide information about the firms' specific weakness and help to define appropriate services supporting the competitiveness of the firm.

9 NOTES AND ACKNOWLEDGMENTS

Although the paper is based on a joint research between the three authors, of this version M. Raffa and G. Zollo wrote §1, §2, §3 and §4, R. Caponi §5, §6 and §7. The research has been supported by CNR Strategic Project "Trasferimento delle tecnologie dei progetti finalizzati", and by MURST 60% and 40% 1992 - 1993.

10 REFERENCES

Acs, Z.J. and Audretsch, D.B. (1990) *The Economics of Small Firms. A European Challenge.* Kluwer, Dordrecht.

Barocci, T.A., Wever, K.R. and Lahey, R.A. (1983) *Human Resource Planning for Information Systems Personnel: Skills Mixes and Technological Trends,* Working Paper 1478-83, MIT, Sloan School of Management.

Brandt, S. (1981) *Strategic Planning in Emerging Companies.* Addison Wesley, Reading (MA).

Churcill, N.C. and Lewis, V.L. (1983). The Five Stages of Small Firm Growth. *Harvard Business Review,* **63**, 30-50.

Filion, L.J. (1991) *Vision et relations: clefs du succès de l'entrepreneur.* Les éditions de l'entrepreneur, Montréal.

Garden, A.M. (1992) Potential Reasons for Software Employees in Small Companies to Leave Their Present Company. *IEEE Trans. Eng. Manag.*, **39**, 246-53.

Gibb, A. and Scott, M. (1985) Strategic Awareness, Personal Commitment and the Process of Planning in the Small Business. *Journal of Management Studies,* **22**, (6).

Grant, R.M. (1991) The Resource-Based Theory of Competitive Advantage: Implications for Strategy Formulation. *California Management Review*, **33**.

Greiner, L.E. (1972) Evolution and Revolution as Organizational Growth. *Harvard Business Review*, **50**, July-Aug.

Huppert, R. (1981) Stratégies de développement des PMI françaises. *Revue d'economie industrielle*, **17**.

Kao, J. (1991). *The Entrepreneurial Organization.* Prentice Hall, London.

Kay, N.M. (1984) *The Emergent Firm.* MacMillan, London.

Kelley, M.R. and Brooks, H. (1991) External Learning Opportunities and the Diffusion of Process Innovations to Small Firm. *Technological Forecasting and Social Change*, **39**, (1-2).

Kimberly, J.R. and Miles, R.H. (1980) *The organizational life cycle.* Jossey-Bass, San Francisco.

La Belle, C.D., Shaw, K. and Hellenack, L.J. (1980) Solving Turnover Problem. *Datamation*, April.

Lefebvre, E. and Lefebvre, L.A. (1992) Firm innovativeness and CEO characteristics in small manufacturing firms. *Journal of Engineering and Technology Management*, **9**, 243-77.

Meyer, M.H. and Roberts, E.B. (1986) New Product Strategy in Small Technology-Based Firms: a Pilot Study. *Management Science*, **32**, (7).

Meyer, A.D. and Goes, J.B. (1987) How organizations adopt and implement new technologies, in *47th Annual Meeting of the Academy of Management,* New Orleans, LA.

Meyer, A.D., Tsui, A.S. and Hinings, C.R. (1993) Configurational Approaches to Organizational Analysis. *Academy of Management Journal*, **36**, 1175-95.

Miller, D., Droge, C. and Toulose, J.M. (1988) Strategic process and content as mediators between organizational context and structure. *Academy of Mangement Journal*, **31**, 544-69.

Miller, A.D. and Toulouse, J.M. (1986a,) Chief executive personality and corporate strategy and structure in small firms. *Management Science,* **32**, 1389-409.

Miller, A.D. and Toulouse, J.M. (1986b.) Strategy, structure, CEO personality and performance in small firms. *Am. J. Small Bus..* Winter, 47-62.

Mintzberg, H. (1985) Of Strategies, Deliberate and Emergent. *Strategic Management Journal*, **3**.

Mintzberg, H. (1987) Crafting Strategies. *Harvard Business Review*, July-Aug.

OECD, (1982) *Innovation in Small and Medium Firms.* Paris.

OECD, (1986) *Software: A New Industry.* Paris.

Pavitt, K. (1988) The Size and Structure of British Technological Activities: What We Know and Do Not Know. *Scientometrics*, **14**, 329-46.

Prahalad, C.K. and Hamel, G. (1990) The Core Competence of the Corporation. *Harvard Business Review*, **68**, 79-91.

Quinn, J.B. (1979) Technological Innovation, Entrepreneurship and Strategy. *Sloan Management Review,* **20**, (3).

Raffa, M. and Zollo, G. (1988) *Software: tecnologia e mercato.* Il Mulino, Bologna.

Raffa, M. and Zollo, G. (1994) The Role of Professionals in Small Italian Firms. *Journal of Systems Software*, **26**, 19-30.

Reid, G.C. and Jacobsen, L.R. (1988) *The Small Entrepreneurial Firm.* Aberdeen University Press, Aberdeen.

Roberts, E.B. (1991) The technological base of the new enterprise. *Research Policy*, **29**, 283-98.

Rothwell, R. (1988) Small Firms, Innovation and Industrial Change. *Small Business Economics,* **1**, (1).

Rothwell, R. and Zegveld, W. (1982) *Innovation and the Small and Medium Sized Firm.* Frances Pinter, London.

Storey, D.J. and Johnson, S. (1987) *Job Generation and Labour Market Changes.* MacMillan, London.

Weinberg, G.M. (1982) *Understanding the Professional Manager.* Little Brown, Boston.

Werner, F.L. (1983) *Critical Issues in Software.* Wiley, New York.

11 BIOGRAPHICAL NOTES

Mario Raffa, graduated at the University of Naples "Federico II", is professor of Business Economics and Organization at the Faculty of Engineering of Naples. He is also the scientific director of ODISSEO, the Centre for organization and technological innovation, Department of Computer Science and Systems, University of Naples "Federico II". He has published in several journals and has presented papers at international conferences on innovation management, organization, small innovative firms and relationships between small and large firms. In 1991 he received the "Award of Excellence" in Vienna for the best contribution presented to the 36th ICSB World Conference. In the last years he carried out a research project on small innovative firms in Italy and other European countries.

Giuseppe Zollo, graduated at the University of Naples "Federico II", is an associate professor of Business Economics and Organization at the Faculty of Engineering of Naples. During the years 1985-86 he has been Visiting Research Associate at Dept. of Economics of Northeastern University, Boston, MA. At present, he is a coordinator of a research unit of CNR (National Research Committee). In 1992 he received the "Entrepreneurship Award" in Barcelona for the best contribution presented to the 6th EIASM Workshop "Research in Entrepreneurship".

Renata Caponi, graduated at the University of Naples "Federico II" in Electronic Engineering, is junior researcher for ODISSEO-DIS. She is also research fellow at University of Rome "Tor Vergata". In 1993 she has won a scholarship ATA (Associazione Tecnica dell'Automobile) on the management of human resources in the small innovative firms. At present she makes research activities on small innovative software firms.

PART FOUR

Software Testing

11

Static Analysis of VHDL Source Code: the SAVE Project

M. Mastretti
ITALTEL–SIT– Central Research Labs
Settimo Milanese (MI) – ITALY
phone: +39.2 43888582
fax: +39.2 43888593
e–mail: mastrett@settimo.italtel.it

M. L. Busi, R. Sarvello,
M. Sturlesi, S. Tomasello
Universita' degli Studi di Milano – Computer Science Dept.
Milano – ITALY
e–mail:
busi@ghost.sm.dsi.unimi.it, sarvello@ghost.sm.dsi.unimi.it
sturlesi@ghost.sm.dsi.unimi.it, tomasell@ghost.sm.dsi.unimi.it

Abstract

VHDL (Very High Speed Integrated Circuits Hardware Description Language) is one of the most popular languages (IEEE standard) for building software models of hardware systems. While the typical VHDL–based design environment provides tools for code simulation and logic synthesis, no support is given in order to cope with the increasing complexity of VHDL descriptions and the widespread demand for their quality evaluation and improvement.

Automated source code analysis is a valuable approach to develop, measure and compare models in order to assure the satisfaction of quality requirements of VHDL descriptions before adding them to model libraries. Therefore a static analyzer may assist the user in the challenging task of introducing significant modifications and improvements into source code so that, assuring that VHDL code is developed according to some well–founded guidelines, a relevant impact on the quality of the overall design process may be achieved.

The goal of this paper is to summarize the activities carried out within the SAVE project, leading to the development of a collection of quality analysis tools in order to improve modifiability, reusability, readability of models reducing the VHDL descriptions complexity.

Keywords
complexity metrics, quality, CAD/CASE environment, static analysis, hardware design flow.

1 INTRODUCTION

The design methodology for hardware systems (in particular integrated circuits) is migrated from interactive capture of electrical schematics to software modeling. This is the reason why software engineering techniques begin to become strategic also within hardware design centers.

The VHSIC (Very High Speed Integrated Circuits) Hardware Description Language is an industry standard language (IEEE 1076) used to describe hardware from the abstract to the concrete level. Computer–aided engineering workstation vendors throughout the industry are standardizing on VHDL as input and output for their tools which include simulation and automatic synthesis (Perry).

VHDL allows to describe the functionalities of design components (like memory cells, chips, logic ports and so on) in an algorithmic way without assumptions about the technology of a device or the methodology used to design it and, by the synthesis phase, it is possible.

It is based on ADA language principles and it supports some characteristics such as information hiding, components instantiation (like objects instantiation) and the possibility of declaring new data structures and functions enclosed in a package. Currently some committees are trying to extend it towards an object oriented methodology. Moreover, its concurrent computational paradigm is based on processes and signals concepts.

VHDL simulation is the modeling and behavior analysis of an electronic design in order to verify the design functionality. This type of analysis, when performed before the logic design phase, ensures design quality earlier in the engineering process, where errors are easier and cheaper to fix. With a simulator it is possible to analyze the design on a test bench, with stimulus, probes, and waveform displays. With a top–down design method employing VHDL synthesis, functional changes can be made rapidly and verified through simulation.

Synthesis is the process of automatically generating a logic level representation, i.e. the traditional circuit representation where basic components (logic gates, flip–flops, etc.) are connected together with wires and buses, from an algorithmic description. According to different constraints introduced in the VHDL description, the synthesis process can produce various implementation alternatives. A typical design flow is represented in Figure 1.

While the typical VHDL–based design environment provides tools for code simulation and logic synthesis , no support is given in order to cope with the increasing complexity of VHDL descriptions and the widespread demand for their quality evaluation and improvement. Furthermore, some high–level design tools (similar to CASE environments) are able to generate VHDL source code in an automated way, but in some cases the resulting code may be too large and complex for the human reader.

Therefore, automated source code analysis is a valuable approach to develop, measure and compare models managed by all the above methodologies and tools in order to satisfy quality requirements of VHDL descriptions before adding them to model libraries.

If enhanced with advising capabilities, a static analyzer may also assist the user in the challenging task of introducing significant modifications into source code to improve simulation performances to make project maintainability easier and to create an efficient link with hardware synthesis results.

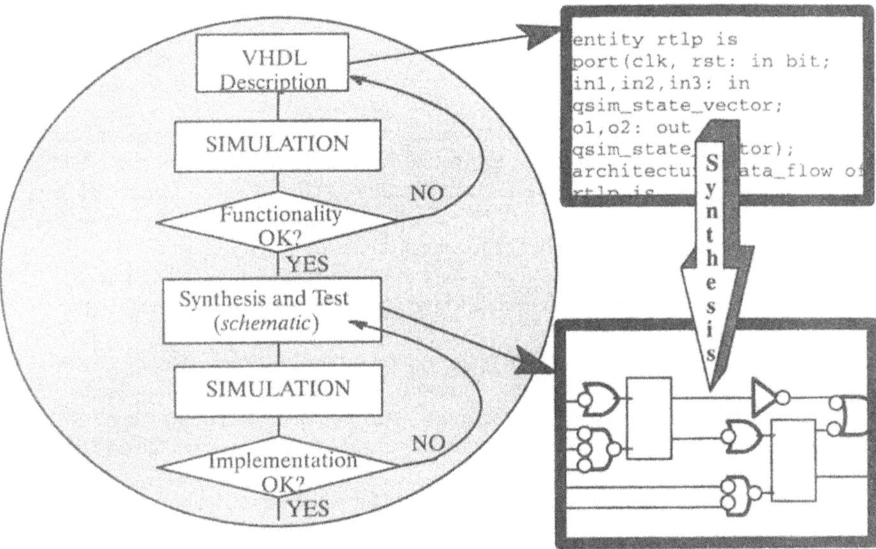

Figure 1 Design Flow.

This paper describes the activities carried out within the SAVE project. Starting from software engineering principles, SAVE consists in some tools which assist designers in writing high quality VHDL code, that means easily readable, modifiable and reusable code.

Qualitative analysis of VHDL source code, in fact, is a completely unexplored research field and results from software engineering can provide some interesting suggestions that need to be extended to some particular aspects strictly related to hardware design concepts (simulation and synthesis). Because of the intrinsic complexity of the problem, heuristic techniques (giving approximate results) look very promising.

If code is written following some guidelines enclosed in the SAVE expert system, the time spent in functional verification can be reduced. Furthermore synthesis evaluation shows in advance if code can be synthesized and if it is optimized to make synthesis more efficient.

These tools give additional advantages like advising designers about models not conforming to corporate standards and the possibility of improving code style and project documentation.

From the theoretical point of view, existing software metrics have been analyzed in order to apply the most suitable ones to a single VHDL module (process, procedure, function) and develop higher level metrics based on cost functions. Moreover, some new metrics and guidelines have been discovered on experimental basis.

The goal of the approach followed in the SAVE project is to produce not only a numerical quality measure, but mostly give to the designer a set of textual and graphical suggestions to improve the description quality itself.

2 SAVE PROJECT ANALYSIS

2.1 VHDL code complexity analysis

In Software Engineering literature the term *quality* means the degree to which software satifies a selected combination of attributes. A distinction between internal and external attributes can be made like in (Fenton, 1991): internal attributes are related only to the features of the model itself (number of execution paths, data size, etc.); external attributes depend on how the model relates to its environment (readability, maintainability, etc.).

In quality evaluation, external attributes tend to be the ones that managers would most like to evaluate and predict in order to estabilish the cost–effectiveness of some processes or the productivity of their personnel.

Unfortunately, by their own nature, external attributes cannot be measured as directly as internal ones: for instance, maintainability costs depend on different factors like number of errors or designer expertise and so on, while the model size is evaluated simply counting lines of instruction code. Nevertheless, there is a wide consensus that good external quality depends on good internal structure.

For example, (Robillard, 1991) shows an interesting method for evaluating software based on metrics. Users may define a range of values for each metric. The method consists in the collection of metric measurements, determining the metrics distribution for each module of the project. The groupings of the various metrics constitute quality factors like testability, that can be evaluated

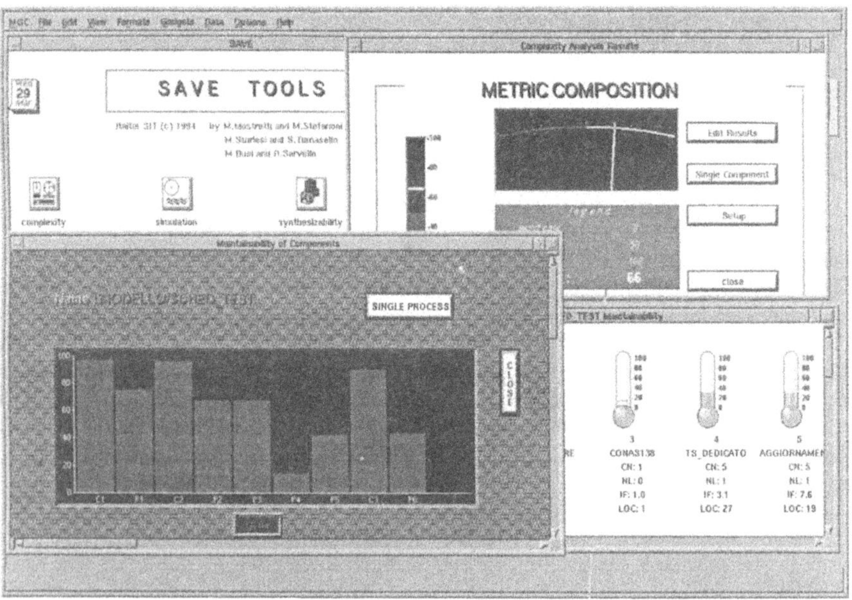

Figure 2 Example of some SAVE tools.

using some metrics (number of independent paths, number of loops, etc.) within the given ranges. The percentage of modules meeting the metrics ranges represents a good indication of this quality factor. The resulting profile provides a quick visualization of the overall project. High level management can easily interpret such a profile.

Therefore, VHDL model features like low maintainability costs, high simulation performances and good synthesis results can be estimated measuring some internal attributes inside descriptions and respective metrics can evaluate the presence of these indicators. However, it should be pointed out that defining suitable complexity measures for hardware description languages such as VHDL, involves specific aspects which may have no direct counterpart in the more assessed field of software design (mixed behavioral/structural paradigms, event–driven behavior, ...).

While static analysis techniques for concurrent programs are emerging (Gannon, 1986), (Ramamoorthy, 1985), (Shatz, 1988), (Cha, 1993), several theoretical and practical issues still make VHDL analysis a very complex task. In fact the concurrent model of VHDL is different at a large degree from the ADA model (from which many VHDL language constructs have been derived).

The result of this study is the application of existing software metrics which have been chosen and modified to adapt them to the particular nature of VHDL.

Some metrics represent a combination of some adapted traditional ones like Mc Cabe' s cyclomatic number (McCabe, 1976), nesting level and information flow. Because of VHDL relevant complexity, a main problem is to determine the most suitable metrics.

Finding only a single evaluation standard may not be a correct approach; in fact VHDL language, with respect to other programming languages, provides many different description styles (imperative, data–flow and structural).

The SAVE solution is to compose different metrics by means of a weighted sum, adjustable by the user, following the team typical design style. Users can easily change metrics coefficients to obtain a custom evaluation of the project: different profiles will result mainly based, for example, on nesting level and cyclomatic number or process size and information flow (Figure 3).

Of course, the traditional metrics have undergone adaptations for the particular language to analyze. For example, information flow has been adapted to the VHDL communication mechanism. Its goal, in this context, is to measure the information exchange between processes. A high value in this measure can indicate a non optimal process partitioning without a well defined functionality. The definition adopted is the following:

$$Inf\_Flow = a_1 \cdot R_{sgn} + a_2 \cdot W_{sgn}$$

where R_{sgn} and W_{sgn} stand for the number of signals read and the number of signals written respectively with $a_1 < a_2$ (more importance has been given to written signals as they wake up all processes sensitive to them).

A further metric adopted in VHDL code complexity evaluation is the concurrency level. In a VHDL description, concurrent processes have a sensitivity list, i.e. a list of signals whose changes activate processes; the concurrency level is defined as the number of times signals in a sensitivity list are written in other processes. This metric gives an estimation of the number of times a process is activated. This measure is only an estimation, because in the SAVE approach the analysis is made by a static analyzer, while the actual value can be obtained only by dynamic analysis.

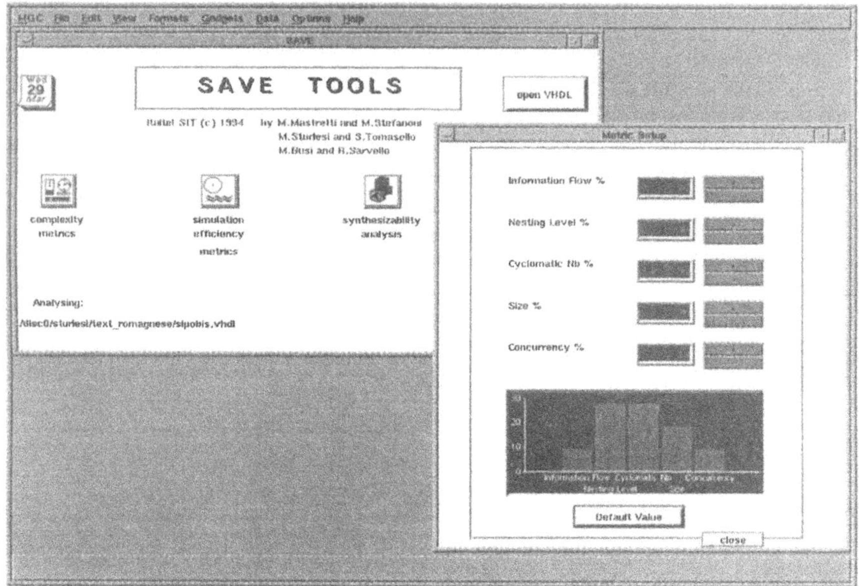

Figure 3 Users can easily change metrics coefficients to obtain a custom evaluation.

The global evaluation of the whole VHDL description is then obtained by averaging the complexity values of single processes. The results are presented graphically through a histogram that represents each process with its evaluation.

It is very difficult to determine the relation between VHDL code complexity and maintainability effort, because of the lack of historical archives for this kind of software.

To reduce maintenance costs, designers should try not only to decrease the number of errors in the design but also to create a readable and easily modifiable source code; so another kind of metrics are related to VHDL coding style, i.e. how designers use VHDL statements to achieve readability in their descriptions. They can improve code by following some general guidelines.

In order to give a general evaluation of the coding style, a description is divided into single modules and the readability degree of each one is measured on a value scale obtained by heuristic methods. The descriptions are evaluated through the application of metrics expressing the number of guidelines followed.

This kind of analysis is twofold: first of all it gives an evaluation (from 0 to 100) of the metrics composition discussed above; second it permits to evaluate readability of the VHDL source code giving some useful guidelines regarding identifier names, lack of comments, module separators and so on and obtaining a rank (from 0 to 100) according to the followed guidelines. The output of these analysis is both textual and graphical (Figure 1), enabling the designer to focus own work on critical modules.

A standard format of the source code assumes a strong relevance in an industrial context because of the need for maintaining control on a hardware design in spite of designers' turn–over.

This approach could increase the VHDL description readability.

If the header does not exist or does not complain to a standard template, it is possible to interactively insert the missing fields: Title, Engineer, Company, Project, Filename, Purpose, Simulator, Synthesis, Revision and optionally Limitations and Note. If some of these fields are not present, the tool automatically inserts the informations available from the VHDL file as default and asks for the others to the user. Only one statement per line, separators and comments presence, uniform indentation and uniform casing for VHDL reserved words are verified and automatically applied.

Additional algorithms under development include the extraction of particular code sections translatable into procedures, by means of pattern recognition techniques.

2.2 Synthesis and simulation efficiency analysis

A set of guidelines to possibly increase the simulation speed of VHDL descriptions, has been discovered on an experimental basis (with tests on various commercial simulators such as Vantage of ViewLogic, QuickSim II and QuickVhdl of Mentor Graphics) searching for constructs which are semantically equivalent but with different simulation performances. One of such guidelines advises that replacing many concurrent processes with a sequential one loads to a compression of the simulation time up to 20% (Stefanoni, 1994). These results agree with (Hueber, 1991) and partially with (Levia, 1991).Tests have shown that static sensitivity lists are more efficient than dynamic ones at the bottom of the process and without conditions. Moreover, in order to create a fast code, it is suggested to the designer to avoid resolved signals whenever possible, to limit the use of attributes returning signals, to reduce the number of functions, procedures and generics and so on. Besides if in some examples with simulators QuickSim II and Vantage, applying suggestions has led to a gain up to 50% in simulation time (Figure 4) while the gains obtained with the more efficient QuickVhdl are not so evident.

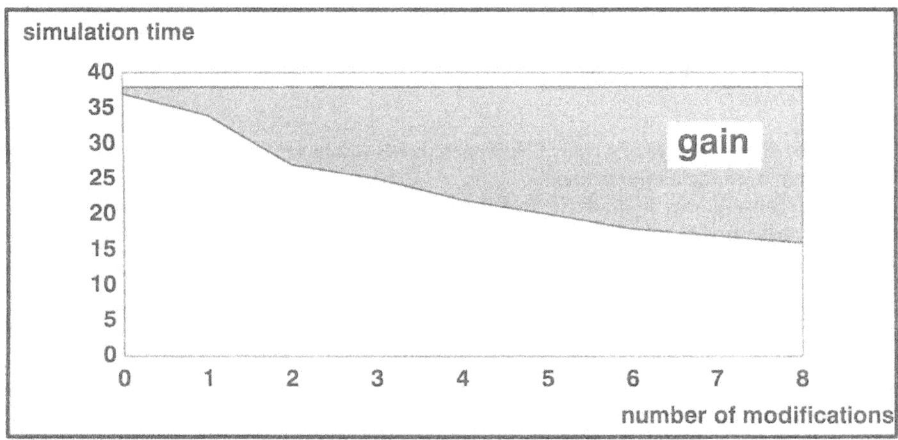

Figure 4 Benefits achieved following the SAVE suggestions.

Moreover, an analysis from the synthesizer point of view, has been developed in order to reduce the time spent in the synthesis phase and to guarantee better results. SAVE tools can also give the designer some suggestions about a more quickly synthesizable coding style (currently related to AutoLogic synthesizer of Mentor Graphics) or perform some checks to avoid synthesis of bad descriptions. All the warnings obtained from these tools suggest some code replacements that designers can choose to apply in an automatic way.

An example of the synthesizability guidelines is large CASE structures where the same signals are assigned in all the branches changing only for few bits. If code is written so that the only assignments to the changing bits are made, the synthesis tool will run much faster and with less memory. For instance, the following code will generate, with the synthesis tool, an intermediate result of 28 generic gates:

```
p1:PROCESS (sel)
  BEGIN
   CASE sel IS
     WHEN "00" => y <= "0001";
     WHEN "01" => y <= "0010";
     WHEN "10" => y <= "0100";
     WHEN "11" => y <= "1000";
   END CASE;
 END PROCESS;
```

that can be reduced to about 6 gates in the following way:

```
p1:PROCESS (sel)
  BEGIN
   y <= "0000";
   CASE sel IS
     WHEN "00" => y(0) <= '1';
     WHEN "01" => y(1) <= '1';
     WHEN "10" => y(2) <= '1';
     WHEN "11" => y(3) <= '1';
   END CASE;
 END PROCESS;
```

These two different ways of writing CASE statements will have the same result, but the second one does not need logic optimization.

The SAVE usefulness is to advise designers of this (and many others) situations before the synthesis phase saving a lot of time; synthesis takes a long time and SAVE can predict some results letting designers to modify code (sometimes automatically) avoiding unwanted synthesis results.

In a structured design, SAVE is also able to recognize Gated Clock and Gated Latch Enabled Signals (Figure 5) and this capability is extended recoursively in the overall design structure. First of all SAVE recognizes all the clock implemented in the design, then there is an automatic verification about the existence of assignment of the clock value to another clock (Gated Clock) or to a signal (Gated Latch Enabled Signals).

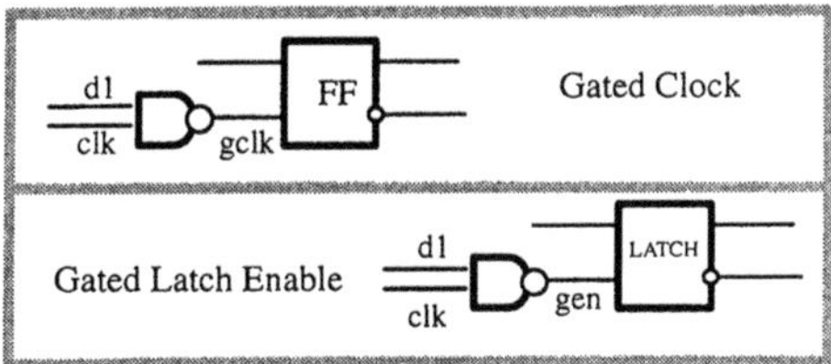

Figure 5 Gated Clock and Gated Latch Enable Signals.

This verification is made, in the beginning, analyzing the same file in which the clock has been implemented and then analyzing the others files always respecting the design hierarchy.

3 THE SAVE IMPLEMENTATION

The metrics and methodologies discussed in the previous sections have been implemented in the SAVE tools: complexity analysis, simulation efficiency analysis and feasibility of the synthesis process. Moreover an integrated expert system provides the user with suggestions to improve source code. An architectural scheme of the prototype environment is depicted in Figure 6.

The developed tools assist designers to create standard and easily modifiable descriptions and to improve their ability to create models. It is important that designers use these tools during the

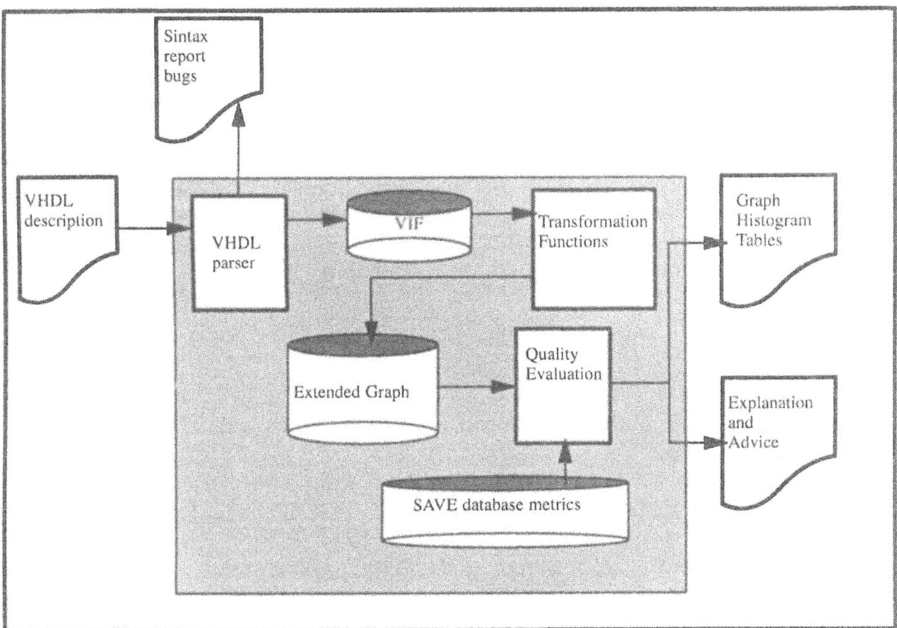

Figure 6 The SAVE Project Architecture.

development process as they use tools as compilers, simulators and so on. In fact, starting from the suggestion reports and graphs which improve the capabilities of the designer to write efficient code, he can evaluate the code, possibly deciding for appropriate modifications.

The LVS (Leda VHDL System) tool supports the parsing step of VHDL source files, including semantic analysis concerning the standard language definition. LVS is also able to build an intermediate representation within an object–oriented database according to VIF (VHDL Intermediate Format) specifications. Starting from the results of the parsing step, a custom tool (Preprocessor) builds a new representation more suitable for further processing by exploiting the LVS support for user–defined extensions to the basic VHDL schema.

Such an enriched representation collects all data needed for the computation of simulation efficiency, complexity and synthesizability analysis.

The designer can choose to evaluate the project in term of these aspects and the analysis is performed activating different tools that compute the metrics embedded in the rule base.

A graphical interface module (Presentation Manager) enables the display of the above characteristics by using graphs, tables and diagrams.

4 CONCLUSION

The SAVE goal consists in creating support tools to measure, check and generate suggestions with an automatic replacement of pieces of code in order to improve the quality of VHDL models.

In fact, designers should utilize SAVE not to obtain a mere hardware ability evaluation, which is often unappreciated, but to learn to write good quality code.

Users do not need only to know results about software or statistical metrics, they have to recognize the existing relationsships among attributes measure, written code and the possible pratical effect on final design quality.

As much metrics are difficult to understand, as more they will be improbably utilized. That is the reason why simple measures are better than complex ones and why starting with a small set of metrics, increasable during the design development, is the best approach.

Designers will verify the real activity control usefulness and will be more persuaded to analyze their products. All the measures have to be applied in an automatic way using suitable tools and this approach results in minimizing the necessary resources.

5 REFERENCES

A.Balboni, M.Mastretti, M.Stefanoni (1994) Static Analysis for VHDL model Evaluation, EURO VHDL, Grenoble.

A.Balboni, P.Cavalloro, M.Mastretti, A.Bonomo, E.Paschetta, G.Buonanno, D.Sciuto (1994) A set of tools for VHDL–Code Quality Evaluation, VHDL–FORUM for CAD in EUROPE IEEE, Tremezzo.

A.Balboni, M.Mastretti, A.Bonomo, E.Paschetta, G.Buonanno, D.Sciuto (1994) Tool–supported quality evaluation in VHDL–based design, *EDAC 94*, Paris.

A.Bonomo, P.Garino, G. Ghigo, A. Balboni, M.Mastretti (1993) VHDL optimization techniques for coding and simulation. *Rapporto Tecnico CSELT.*

T.J.McCabe (1976) A complexity measure, in *IEEE Trans. Software Engineering,* **vol. SE–2**, 308–12.
S.Cha, I.S.Chung, Y.R.Kwon (1993) *Complexity measures for concurrent programs based on information–theoretic metrics.*
N.E. Fenton (1991) *Software metrics: a rigorous approach*, Chapman & Hall, Norwich.
J.D. Gannon, E. Katz, V Basili (1986) Metrics for ADA packages: an initial study. *Communication of the ACM.*
M.Hueber (1991) VHDL experiments on performance. *Euro VHDL.*
M.Mastretti, M.Sturlesi, S.Tomasello (1995) Quality Measures and Analysis: a way to improve VHDL models. *Workshop on Libraries, Component Modeling, Model Verification and Quality Assurance*, Nantes.
M.Mastretti, M.Sturlesi, S.Tomasello (1995) Static Analysis of VHDL Model Evaluation: Simulation Efficiency and Complexity. *VHDL International User's Forum*, San Diego.
B.A. Kitchenham, S.J. Linkman (1990) Design metrics in practice, in *Information and software technology.*
O.Levia (1991) Writing high performance VHDL models. *Euro VHDL.*
S.Midkiff , D.Padua (1990) Issues in the optimization of parallel programs. *International Conference on Parallel Processing.*
P.Oman, J.Hagemeister (1992) Metrics for assessing a Software system's maintenability. *IEEE Transaction on software engineering.*
L.Ott, J.Bieman (1992) Effects of software changes on module cohesion. *IEEE Transaction on software engineering.*
B.Paulsen O.Levia (1992) Techniques for Writing High Performance and High Quality VHDL Models. *Euro VHDL.*
D.L.Perry *VHDL.* McGraw–Hill, Inc.
J.Ramamoorthy, W.Tsai, T. Yamaura, A.Bhide (1985) Metrics guided methodology. *Proc. 9th Computer Software and Application Conf.*, **11**.
P.N.Robillard, D.Coupal, F.Coallier (1991) Profiling Software Through the Use of Metrics. *Software–Practice and Experience vol.21(5)*, **507**.
S.Shatz (1988) Towards Complexity Metrics for ADA tasking. *IEEE Transaction on software engineering.*
M. Shepperd (1990) Design metrics : an empirical analysis , *Software Engineering Journal.*
M. Stefanoni (1994) *SAVE: analizzatore statico di codice VHDL.*
S.N.Woodfield, H.E.Dunsmore, V.Y. Shen (1981) The effect of modularization and comments on program comprehension. *5th International Conference on Software Engineering.*

6 AUTHORS

Mirella Mastretti received the doctoral degree in Computer Science from the University of Milano in 1989.
She joined Italtel in 1989 as member of the technical staff of Central Research Labs. She has worked since then on electronic design automation, developing methodologies and tools to support hardware design flow.
Her main current interests are in the fields of HDL languages, high level synthesis and object–oriented programming.

Maria Laura Busi Since 1989 she joined the Computer Science Department of University of Milano as a computer science degree student. She is currently in stage at the Central Research Labs of Italtel.
Her main interests concern synthesizability and testability of VHDL designs.

Roberto Sarvello After the military service he joined the Computer Science Department of University of Milano as a computer science degree student. He is currently in stage at the Central Research Labs of Italtel.
His main interests concern software quality and artificial intelligence.

Maurizio Sturlesi received the doctoral degree in Computer Science from the University of Milano, in 1995, working in the electronic design automation area at the Central Research Labs of Italtel.
His main interests concern software quality, object–oriented programming and HDL languages.

Sergio Tomasello received the doctoral degree in Computer Science from the University of Milano, in 1995, working in the electronic design automation area at the Central Research Labs of Italtel.
His main interests concern software quality, object–oriented programming and HDL languages.

12

Metrics and Analyses in The Test Phase of Large-Scale Software

E. Obara, T. Kawasaki, Y. Ookawa, and N. Maeda
NTT Telecommunications Software Headquarters

2-1-1 Nishi-Gotanda, Shinagawa-Ku, Tokyo 141, Japan
Tel. +81-3-5487-9143   Fax. +81-3-5487-9790
E-mail: obara.eiji@d70.tsh.cae.ntt.jp

Abstract

To predict the time needed for a test case, four factors that characterize test cases were extracted and the time needed for actual test cases was measured. This paper describes (1) the formula for predicting the number of test MM (Man-Months) from these factors, (2) the development of the skill curve in the test phase, and (3) the modeling of the evolution process for groups of software engineers. These results can be used to predict and improve test productivity. This paper also reports how to extract factors effective in characterizing the testing processes and measuring the MM of test cases. It then discusses a prediction formula, efficient curricula derived from the skill curve in the test phase, and a model of the evolution of software development factories.

keywords

test phase, metrics, measurement, skill curve, model, estimate, curriculum

1 Introduction

Large-scale switching software must have a failure rate so low that the software is out of service less than one hour in 20 years (Ishii, 1991.) The quality of the software also needs to be improved in order to maintain such a low failure rate and to enable 200 K-lines for new services to be accommodated annually throughout the software lifetime. Because the number of these additional services is huge, they will eventually amount to 15% of the entire system. It is therefore especially important to increase the productivity of the test phase.

Few studies have focused on the productivity of the test phase, possibly because the skills in testing factories are extremely diversified and the application of test-equipment is very complex. Very little has been done to identify the relationship between the test productivity and the time required to develop the technical skills of testing engineers.

Several metric methods have been used to measure the productivity and complexity of software testing, but according to Beizer (1990) none have been successful. Many methods have been suggested to measure the entire life-cycle of the software development, but none have been found to be particularly effective for a specific phase, such as the test phase.

McCabe (1976) studied the measurement of program complexity. The complexity measured in his method is related to the productivity of the design and implementation phases but is not directly related to the productivity in the test phase. Though the productivity in the test phase depends on whether or not the test case needs terminal simulators, McCabe dealt with the complexity of the program by examining the program structure.

Walston and Felix (1977) measured 29 factors related to the complexity of the user interface between the software system and the user, and they discovered the relationship between these factors and software productivity. DeMarco (1982,) however, pointed out the possible influence of measured engineers upon the measurement results. Measured engineers tend to think that their poor productivity is due to the complexity of the user interface and consider this complexity to be greater than it actually is. This is a psychological aspect of the measurement of complicated phenomena, and the metrics factors must therefore be selected independently of the desires of the testing engineers.

The present study is therefore intended to shed light on this complex issue, with a view to improving the productivity of the software in the test phase. To identify the issues and problems in test productivity, the authors applied the quantification 1 analysis of test productivity. Since software development is undertaken in the ten NTT factories scattered all over the country, the complexity of testing the new services to be conducted in the test phase was addressed first. Then the ten factories were analyzed so that they could be categorized with regard to factors most likely to affect test productivity. Each of the factories was then categorized into a model and then curricula for educating unskilled engineers were developed.

To further improve the data base, care was taken to avoid the influence of measurement engineers when extracting factors in the test phase.

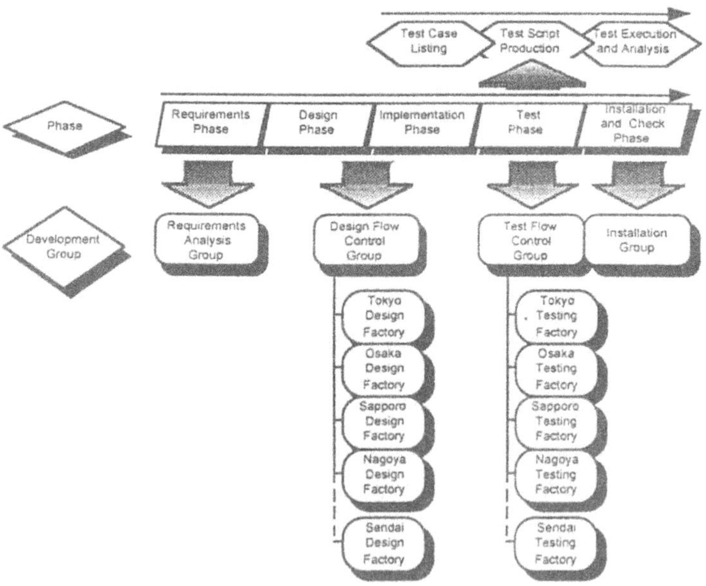

Figure 1 Flow and organization of D70 switching software development.

2 Environment and Classification Method of Test Cases

2.1 Environment of Switching Software Development

In the case of the D70, one of NTT's major switching machines, 60-80 new services that are equivalent to about 200 K-lines are added annually. The total volume of new services amounts to about 15% of the entire D70 system, and about 700 software engineers are engaged in developing these services.

The D70 development system is divided into several phases. In the test phase, about 300 testing engineers are charged with work ranging from Unit Testing to Installation Checking. The design factories and the testing factories are located in ten major cities in Japan. This nationwide development system enables NTT to supply all factories with many well-selected engineers.

New service features to be added are thoroughly studied and defined by the requirement analysis group and are then, for detailed design, sent to any of the design factories. The design groups are charged with all the tasks from basic design to compilation and linkage. The subsequent test phase may be performed at any testing factory.

Table 1 Factors and their values

Factors Identifying the Services	Factor Values & Items			
Service IDs	3ba01, 3ba02, 3ba03, 3ba04, 3ba05, 3ba06, 3ba07, 3ba09, 3ba11, 3ba12, 3ba13, 3ba14, 3ba16, 3ba17, 3ba18, 3ba19, 3ba21, 3ba22, 3ba23, 3ba25, 3ba27, 3ba50, 3ba51, 3ba60, 3ba61, 3ba62, 3ba63, 3ba64, 3bc01, 3bc02, 3bc50, 3bd05, 3bd30, 3bd31, 3bk01, 3bl01, 3bp01, 3bz50			
Classes of Services	Originating Call Service		Terminating Call Service	
	Restart Feature		Construction Feature	
	Command service		Fault Recognition Feature	
	Common Channel Signal Feature		System Configuration Feature	
	Diagnosis Feature			
Other Node Simulator	Needed		Not Needed	
Program Route	Normal Route		Abnormal Route	
Office Data Change	Change		No Change	
New Equipment	New		Old	
Software Reusability	Reusable		New Software	
Method of Testing	Automation		Manual	
Terminal Simulator	Needed		Not Needed	
Factories	Hiroshima	Kanazawa	Kumamoto	Matsuyama
	Nagano	Nagoya	Osaka	Sapporo
	Sendai	Tokyo		
Skill of Test Script	<1	1-2	3-4	>5
Skill of Executing Test	<1	1-2	<1 & 1-2	3-4
	<1 & 3-4	1-2 & 3-4	<1 & 1-2 & 3-4	>5
	<1 & >5	1-2 & >5		

The flow of the test phase consists of (1) the extraction of the test cases from the specification of the new services to be added and their codes, (2) the production of test scripts for each test case, (3) the execution of test cases, and (4) the analysis of the results of the executed test cases. The production of the test scripts and the execution of the test cases make up approximately 60% of the tasks of the entire test phase. Accordingly, this paper concerns mainly these two tasks (Figure 1.)

2.2 Classification Method of Test Cases

The complexity in the test phase depends not on the structure of the software program but on a complicated test system consisting of numerous and diversified test elements with different levels. To work out a new rational test system, we initiated the study by sequentially raising the following basic questions:

- Does a test case need new equipment?
- Does the protocol with other nodes need any changes?
- Does a test case contain features of originating or terminating call service?

Considering past experience in software development, we chose the 12 factors listed in Table 1 to characterize the structure of the test cases.

Table 2 Example of Test Case IDs vs. factors

	Factors											
Test Case ID	*Service ID*	*Classes of Services*	*Other Node Simulator*	*Program Route*	*Office Data Change*	*New Equipment*	*Software Reusability*	*Method of Testing*	*Terminal Simulator*	*Factories*	*Skill of Script*	*Skill of Executing Test*
3ba01-0201cnp001-001	1	1	2	1	2	2	2	1	2	7	2	2
3ba01-0201cnp124-001	1	1	2	1	2	2	2	1	2	7	2	4
3ba01-0201toa027-001	1	1	2	1	2	2	2	1	2	7	2	4
3ba01-0201toa044-001	1	1	2	1	2	2	2	1	2	7	2	4
3ba01-0201toa064-001	1	1	2	1	2	2	2	1	2	7	2	4
3ba01-0201gan043-001	1	1	1	2	1	2	2	2	2	7	4	4
3ba01-0209toa022-001	1	1	2	2	2	2	2	2	2	7	1	1
3ba02-0101ton001-008	2	7	1	1	2	2	2	1	1	1	2	2
3ba02-0101ton001-048	2	7	1	2	2	2	2	1	1	1	2	2
:						..						
3ba03-0206aan907-015	3	1	2	1	2	2	2	1	2	5	4	4
:						..						
3ba12-0301aan326-221	10	1	2	1	1	2	2	2	2	4	1	1
:						..						

These items are numbered in accordance with quantification 1 analysis. As can be seen in Table 2, for test case ID *3ba01-0201cnp001-001*, the entry in the column for the *Classes of Services* factor is 1 and so this test case has the feature of *Originating Call Services*.

Table 3 Example of GTC data

GTC ID						Test Script (min.)					Test Execution (min.)				
Class of Services	Method of Testing	Skill of Script	Software Reusability	Terminal Simulator	Factories	Number of GTC's Members	Test Script Preparation	Test Script Description	Others	Total of Production of Test Scripts	Machine Setting	Test Execution	Test Execution Analysis	Total of Execution of Test Cases	Total
1	1	2	2	2	7	11	17.0	36.6	1.3	54.9	30.0	69.3	12.6	111.9	166.8
1	2	2	2	2	7	6	36.7	34.2	6.7	77.6	15.2	30.0	10.8	56.0	133.6
7	1	2	2	1	1	9	23.5	21.4	1.3	46.2	15.2	26.4	13.7	55.3	101.5
		:						:					:		
7	1	2	2	1	2	5	5.4	18.1	0.0	23.5	20.4	9.0	7.5	36.9	60.4
		:						:					:		
7	2	2	1	1	6	6	26.5	39.2	0.0	65.7	15.2	30.5	0.0	45.7	111.4
		:						:					:		

Each factor consists of several items, and one item characterizes a test case. For example, for *New Equipment* there are two items: *New* and *Old*. A group of test cases that have common items is called a GTC (Group of Test Cases). For example, a GTC may consist of 11 test cases with common items. They are *Originating Call Services* for the factor *Classes of Services*, *Automation* for *Method of Testing*, *1-2* (Year) for *Skill of Test Script*, *New Software* for *Software Reusability*, and so on. These test cases belong to the same GTC because they have items common to each of the factors. A test case is classified into a GTC for a set of items. If the MM (Man-Months) needed for a test case is measured, then the test productivity of the GTC may be estimated. In applying the GTC method, the productivity of a test may be predicted. This approach is called the GTC method.

Table 3 is an example of the data actually measured. According to this table, the GTC is identified by six factors: *Classes of Services*, *Method of Testing*, *Skill of Script*, *Software Reusability*, *Terminal Simulator*, and *Factories*. Each row of Table 3 indicates a GTC and the values of its productivity, which are the averages of test cases that belong to the GTC. The GTC-ID of the first row in Table 3 is *1-1-2-2-2-7*. Each number represents items for each of the six factors.

In Table 3, six factors and their items provide the scheme of the GTCs. Accordingly, it will become possible to predict how many factors and their items will provide an accurate scheme of the GTCs. For example, if the 12 extracted factors are reduced to ten factors, the scheme of the GTCs will change. And the scheme of the GTCs will also change if the nine items of *Classes of Services* increase to 11.

The scheme must be adjusted to obtain the best prediction.

Test Case/MM (Man-Months), on how many test-cases a testing engineer can handle in one month, is used as a unit of productivity in the test phase. We chose Test Case/MM as an index of productivity in the test phase for two reasons: One is that the performance time of test cases is easy to measure, and the other is that Test Case/MM is nearly equivalent to Function Point/MM (since one test case checks about one function). In other words, the number of test cases is closely related to the number of function points.

Figure 2 Example of worksheet.

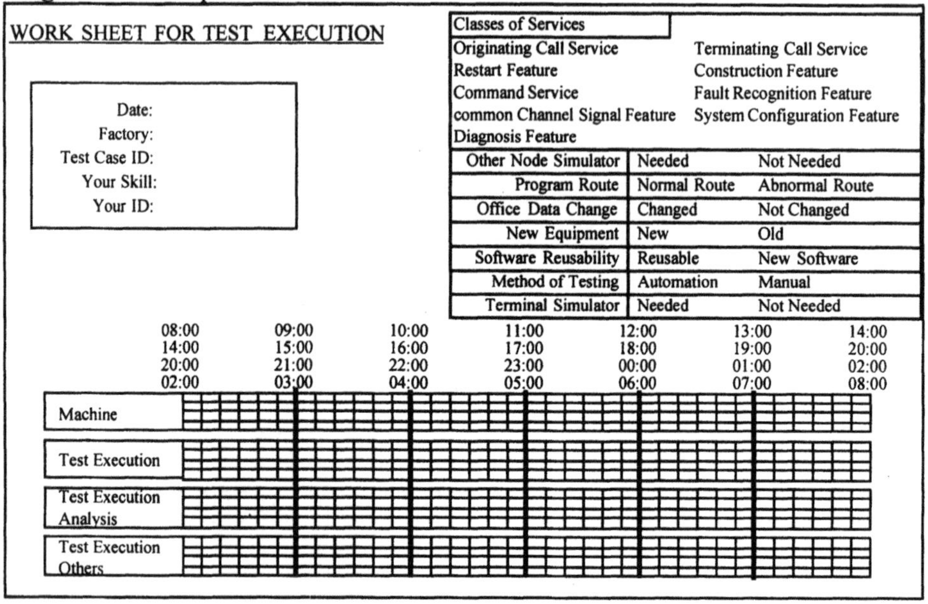

WORK SHEET FOR TEST EXECUTION

Date:
Factory:
Test Case ID:
Your Skill:
Your ID:

Classes of Services

Originating Call Service	Terminating Call Service
Restart Feature	Construction Feature
Command Service	Fault Recognition Feature
common Channel Signal Feature	System Configuration Feature
Diagnosis Feature	

Other Node Simulator	Needed	Not Needed
Program Route	Normal Route	Abnormal Route
Office Data Change	Changed	Not Changed
New Equipment	New	Old
Software Reusability	Reusable	New Software
Method of Testing	Automation	Manual
Terminal Simulator	Needed	Not Needed

	08:00 14:00 20:00 02:00	09:00 15:00 21:00 03:00	10:00 16:00 22:00 04:00	11:00 17:00 23:00 05:00	12:00 18:00 00:00 06:00	13:00 19:00 01:00 07:00	14:00 20:00 02:00 08:00
Machine							
Test Execution							
Test Execution Analysis							
Test Execution Others							

3. Measurement in Factories

The measurement process has four steps: (1) the selection of the test cases to be measured, (2) the examination of the GTCs, (3) measurement of MM for each test case, and (4) the gathering and analysis of the MM data.

The details of these steps are as follows: (1) In selecting test cases to be measured, 1200 of the entire 29 000 cases were selected. The 29 000 test cases were numbered, and then 1 was selected from every 24. (2) The 1200 selected were examined to determine the GTC of each. Testing engineers to whom selected test cases were to be assigned were asked to fill out a worksheet (Figure 2) every day during the test period. The worksheet contained columns for the MM of the test case, the items of the test case, and information about the testing engineer (e.g., engineer's skill and the factory he belongs to). (3) Testing engineers measured the MM of their test cases during the period from October 1993 to April 1994. (4) The worksheets were collected at the end of every month and thoroughly checked to ensure their reliability.

4. Analysis

The measurements described in sections 2 and 3 made it possible to evaluate the measurements in the test phase in quantifiable terms and also enabled the following three analyses:

1. The formula of the MM as a function of the items of each test case;
2. Determining what kind of curriculum is effective for improving test skills; and

3. The development of a model for the evolution of factories.

4.1 MM as a Function of Test Case Items

The formula for MM as a function of the items of each test case was derived by applying quantification 1 analysis (Honda, 1993.) 1,200 test cases were classified into 160 GTCs provided with 12 factors. Logically speaking, 12 factors can make more than 160 GTCs, but many of them have no test cases. The MM of GTCs that are vacant, however, can be estimated by applying quantification 1 analysis.

Quantification 1 analysis is not strictly accurate since there are more factors than are necessary. The number of factors and their items must be properly selected for accurate prediction. In this study, 12 factors were selected, which resulted in the coefficient of determination relating Total Test Time (Total time of the time of the production of a test script and the execution of a test case) to the 12 factors being about 12%. The coefficient of determination to predict Total Test Time from the 12 factors and 85 items and samples of 1,200 test cases is not sufficient for accurate prediction because the itemization of the individual factors was too detailed. According to the quantification 1 analysis, ineffective factors can be eliminated and items that have few members can be combined into one item for accurate prediction. The 12 factors were therefore reduced to the following seven factors:

1. Classes of Services,
2. Method of Testing,
3. Software Reusability,
4. Terminal Simulator,
5. Factories,
6. Skill of Test Script, and
7. Ratio of Test Script Production to Execution (RPE.)

Ratio of Test Script Production to Execution (RPE), indicating the ratio of the time spent producing the test script to the time spent executing the case, gives us *Test Style*. Both producing a test script and executing the case are closely related to the complexity of the case. For example, a test case that is assigned to a person who is precise in running tests tends to have a large RPE value. And when a testing engineer is not well prepared for the test, the RPE of his test cases may be smaller than that of others.

Although RPE was not included in the 12 factors selected in the study, it was treated as an example of the factors that indicate the test style. Of the 12 factors and their items selected at the onset of the study, some were found not to contribute adequately to the test productivity. This led to the reexamination of the number of factors and their items to be further studied, and a reduction of the 12 factors to 7 by combining some and discarding others. There were some GTCs that have few test cases, and some test cases that showed abnormal results were ignored. Some similar items, such as some factories that bear resemblance in their environments and testing engineers, are combined to increase their contribution to the prediction. These were cases that;

1. had less than five Test Cases in a GTC, and
2. had Total Test Time (for production of the test script and execution of the test case) of more than 300 minutes.
3. Furthermore, three factories (Kumamoto, Matsuyama, and Sapporo) were integrated into one, and
4. two factories (Nagoya and Tokyo) were integrated into one.

As a result of this reexamination process, 55 GTCs were left being classified by seven factors and integrated items. By calculating the mean value of MM for test cases in each GTC and analyzing them by applying quantification 1 analysis and focusing on the four factors as listed below, a formula for accurate prediction could be derived.

1. Method of Testing
2. Software Reusability
3. Factories
4. Ratio of Time of the Production of the Test Script (T_{ps}) to Time of the Execution of the Test Cases (T_{ec}).

The coefficient of determination for the four factors is 58.4%. The test productivity was then obtained using the following formula:

$$T = 40.1 \times RPE + [0 \quad 114.0 \quad 41.9 \quad 82.6 \quad 48.6 \quad 57.9] \begin{bmatrix} F_1 \\ F_2 \\ F_3 \\ \vdots \\ F_n \\ \vdots \end{bmatrix}$$

$$+ [0 \quad 23.8] \begin{bmatrix} S_1 \\ S_2 \end{bmatrix} + [0 \quad -37.6] \begin{bmatrix} M_1 \\ M_2 \end{bmatrix},$$

where T is Total Test Time ($T_{ps} + T_{ec}$), RPE is the Ratio of T_{ps} to T_{ec}, **F** is the vector that represents *Factory* (e.g., $\mathbf{F} = \begin{bmatrix} 1 \\ 0 \\ \vdots \\ 0 \end{bmatrix}$ means *Hiroshima*, $\mathbf{F} = \begin{bmatrix} 0 \\ 1 \\ \vdots \\ 0 \end{bmatrix}$ means *Kanazawa*), **S** shows whether software is reusable or not (e.g., $\mathbf{S} = \begin{bmatrix} 1 \\ 0 \end{bmatrix}$ means *reusable* and $\mathbf{S} = \begin{bmatrix} 0 \\ 1 \end{bmatrix}$ means *new software*), and **M** shows the method of the test (e.g., $\mathbf{M} = \begin{bmatrix} 1 \\ 0 \end{bmatrix}$ means *automation test* and $\mathbf{M} = \begin{bmatrix} 0 \\ 1 \end{bmatrix}$ means *manual test*).

For instance, if a test case uses an *automation* method and its software is not *reusable* and if it is executed at *Hiroshima* factory and its RPE is equal to *1.2*, the MM of the test case can be predicted by

$$T = 71.9 \pm 11.3 \text{ (min.)}$$

Thus, the formula and the model for the prediction of the productivity in the test phase were obtained. In this model, four factors characterize the test phase and the necessary man-power can be estimated. According to estimated the work load, each of the factories and testing engineers will be re-assigned with the proper amount of tasks.

4.2 Effective Curriculum for Improving Test Skills

Factor *Skill of Production of Test Script* and *Skill of Execution of Test Case* indicate the skill. Figures 3 and 4 show the relationship between the skill and the test productivity.

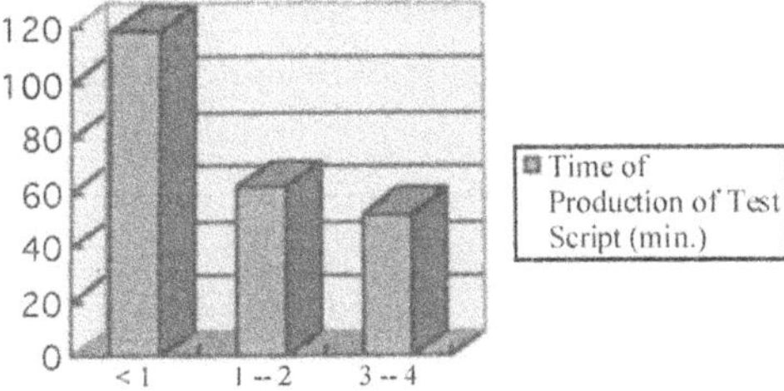

Figure 3 Script skill vs. time of production of test script.

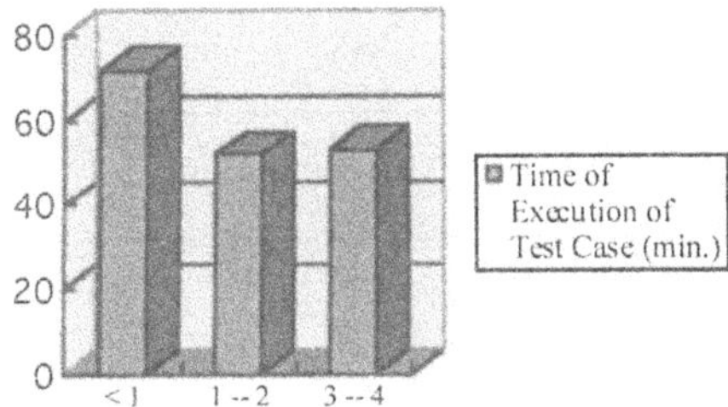

Figure 4 Execute skill vs. time of execution of test case.

These figures show that after *one* year of training, untrained engineers have acquired skills equivalent to those of engineers with four years of experience. In this connection, it should be noted that one year corresponds to the period of two life-cycles of new services.

Inspecting Figures 3 and 4, we should note that (1) the efficiency and effectiveness of on-the-job-training could be best achieved by selecting the engineers with less than one year of experience as the target group, and (2) to improve the testing skills of engineers with more than one year of experience, we need to develop different curricula.

4.3 Model of Evolution of Factories

This section addresses the issues related to the model for the evolution of factories, analyzing qualitatively the relationship between factors and the time required for Production of Test Script and for Execution of Test Case.

The two factors that have the largest F-values with regard to the Time of Production of Test Script (T_{ps}) and the Time of Execution of a test case (T_{ec}) were selected. According to the data listed in Tables 4 and 5, these factors are *Skill of Test Script* and *Classes of Services*.

Table 4 Influence of factors on T_{ps}.

Factors	F-Value
Skill of Test Script	25.6
Terminal Simulator	13.7
Software Reusability	13.6
Method of Testing	9.7
Classes of Services	5.9

Table 5 Influence of factors on T_{ec}.

Factors	F-Value
Classes of Services	8.2
New Equipment	6.5
Skill of Executing Test	6.3

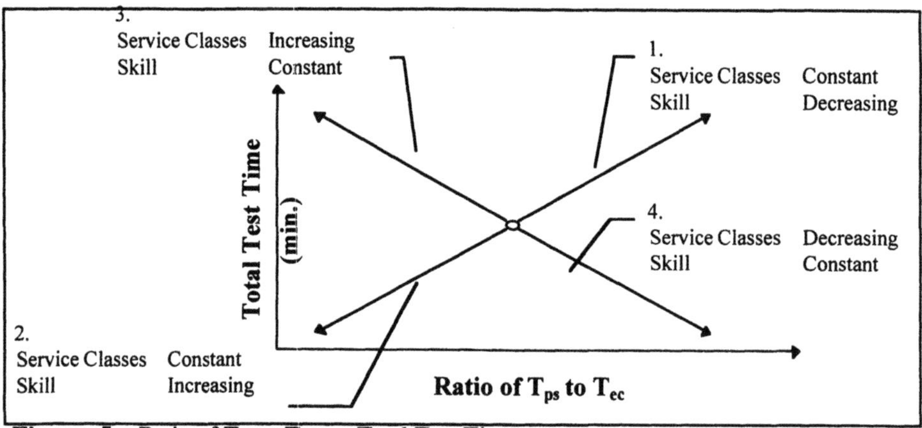

Figure 5 Ratio of T_{ps} to T_{ec} vs. Total Test Time.

Figure 5 illustrates the relationship between Total Test Time and RPE. Here $\mathrm{RPE} = \frac{T_{pc}}{T_{ec}}$, where T_{ps} means Time of Production of Test Scripts and depends mostly on *Skill of Production of Test Script* and T_{ec} means Time of Execution of Test Cases and depends mostly on *Classes of Services.*

The hypothesis, that in order to examine how the point of a test case moves as the items of a test case change under the following rules, is considered.

1. **Classes of Services constant, Skill of Production of Test Script decreasing.** RPE increases because T_{ps} (the numerator of RPE) is more sensitive than T_{ec} (the denominator of RPE). Total Test Time also increases. Therefore, the point moves toward the upper right.
2. **Classes of Services constant, Skill of Production of Test Script increasing.** Both RPE and Total Test Time decrease. Therefore, the point moves toward the lower left.
3. **Classes of Services increasing, Skill of Production of Test Script constant.** Because T_{ec} (the denominator of RPE) is more sensitive than T_{ps} (the numerator of RPE) RPE decreases, and Total Test Time increases. Therefore, the point moves toward the upper left.
4. **Classes of Services decreasing, Skill of Production of Test Script constant.** RPE increases and Total Test Time decreases. Therefore, the point moves toward the lower right.

In Figure 6, the values of T_{ps} and T_{ec} obtained for each of the factories are plotted against the scale of RPE vs. Total Test Time.

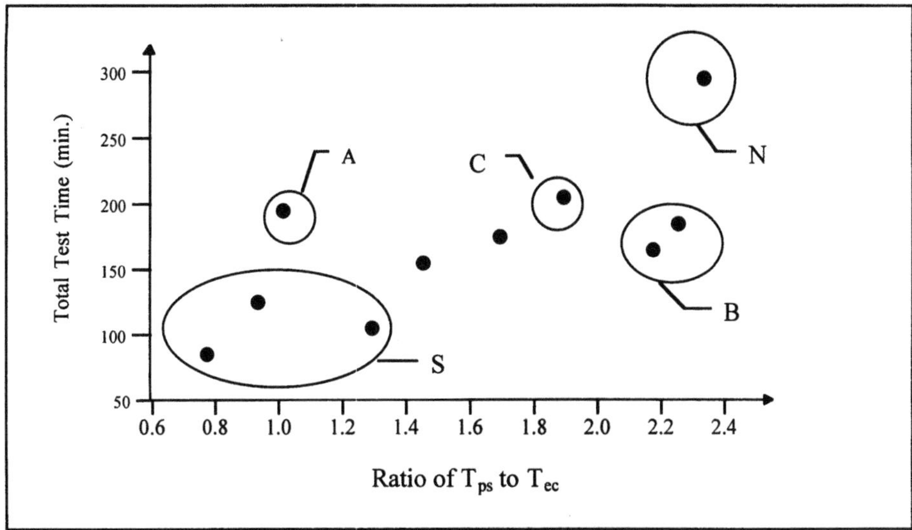

Figure 6 Ratio of T_{ps} to T_{ec} vs. Total Test Time in factories.

While some factories are newly built and the overall skills there are yet to be improved, others factories are old and skills there are well established. In this paper, these two groups of factories are called the NFG (New Factories Group) and the SFG (Skilled Factories Group). Many engineers in the NFG are newcomers and unskilled whereas many engineers in the SFG are experienced and highly skilled.

As can be seen in Figure 6, the plotted points tend to be located along a positive linear curve, and the point indicated at the upper right corresponds to the NFG (area N in the figure) whereas the points in the lower left correspond to the SFG (area S). Moreover, there is a point A in the upper left part of the figure and there are points B in the lower right part. The factories that fell into the A and B groups are thought to have been assigned services that differ greatly from those assigned to the others.

According to the hypothesis, two factories that have the same average value of Total Test Time are easily identifiable from the others. Factory A and Factory C in Figure 6 are such factories. Factory A is thought to have many test cases of difficult services, and Factory C is thought to have many unskilled engineers.

Each of the factories is expected to evolve into an advanced one through experience. The evolution stage of each of the factories can be visually assessed by using RPE vs. Total Test Time value and plotting them as shown in Figure 6. Efficient development plans which will increase the efficiency of the test phase in each of the factories can then be worked out.

5. Conclusion

With a view to measuring the MM of test cases of new services in the test phase, four factors that characterize the services are identified and used in measuring many actual test cases. By analyzing the information thus obtained, we developed a formula for predicting the MM of test cases, effective curricula in the test phase, and a model for the efficient evolution of each of the factories in the test phase.

The following three areas need to be further improved:
(a) measurement in the design phase,
(b) successive measurement in the test phase, and
(c) detailed analysis of the measurement results.

Because only a part of the entire development process is measured, serious problems may be transferred to other phases without being recognized. Therefore, all the phases should be targeted for measurement. In that sense, this study should be furthered to find satisfactory solutions for enhancing the productivity of the test phase of large scale software.

6. Acknowledgments

Throughout the entire period of this study, we have greatly benefitted from the advice and suggestions of Mr. Ishii, Executive Vice President and Director of the NTT Telecommunications Software Headquarters, and of Mr. Yamaguchi, Executive Manager. Mr. Shidara, Project Manager, also was instrumental in conducting the study by providing us with very helpful advice and direction. Finally, without the support and cooperation of all the testing engineers in all the factories, this study could not have been accomplished, therefore, we would like to express our sincere appreciation to them.

References

Ishii, K. and Goto, T. (1991) Development Telecommunication Software. *NTT R&D*, Vol. 40, No. 11, (In Japanese).
Walston, C. E. and Felix, C. P. (1977) A method of programming measurement and estimation. *IBM Systems Journal*, Vol. 16, No. 1.
DeMarco, T. (1982) *Controlling Software Projects*. Youhan Inc., New York.
Beizer, B. (1990) *Software Testing Techniques*. Van Nostrand Reinhold.
McCabe, T. A. (1976) A Complexity measure. *IEEE Transactions on Software Engineering*, Vol. 2.
Jones, C. (1991) *Applied Software Measurement*. McGraw-Hill Professional Publishing Group.
Boehm, B. W. (1981) *Software Engineering Economics*. Englewood Cliffs, N. J., Prentice-Hall.
Honda, M. (1993) *Actual Multivariable Analysis for Information Analysts*. Sannou Univ. Print, (In Japanese).
Bergman, M. (1991) The Evolution of Software Testing Automation. *Testing Computer Software Proceedings*, June 17-20.
Tomono, K., Takeuchi, E., and Tokoyoda, T. (1991) Functioned Technology for Development of Telecommunications. *NTT R&D*, Vol. 40, No. 11, (In Japanese).

Biography

Eiji Obara (head author): Bachelor of Science, University of Tokyo, 1988. Assistant Manager, Telecommunications Software Headquarters, NTT. As a team leader, the author has been working on software engineering in the test phase of D70, one of the major switching machines of the NTT network, for six years. He is a member of the Institute of Electronics, Information, and Communication Engineers.

13

Automated Testing of Safety Requirements with the Support of a Deductive Database

Patrizia Asirelli, Antonia Bertolino, Stefania Gnesi
Istituto di Elaborazione della Informazione - CNR
Via S. Maria, 46, I-56126 Pisa

Abstract

We present an approach to the implementation of an automated test oracle. The oracle is built on a Deductive Database Management System, called Gedblog. The oracle is partial, in the sense that it checks the correctness of the test outputs with respect to a set of necessary conditions derived from the functional specifications, but does not know the correct output for each possible test input. We identify a set of requirements, called "safety requirements", that is deemed to be essential for the safe behaviour of the system under test. We express these safety requirements as a set of formulae by using the ACTL logic. We then incorporate these ACTL formulae in Gedblog. Assuming that the program has been previously tested apart, according to some test plan, and that the test outputs have been collected then, by means of the Gedblog mechanisms, we are able to automatically check the test outputs against the safety requirements. We illustrate the approach by means of a simple example.

Keywords

Automated Testing, Safety Requirements, Modal Logic, Deductive Databases

1 INTRODUCTION

Given the high-level specification of a safety-critical system, we can derive a set of programs, possibly at different levels of abstraction, that provide an implementation of such a system. Then, we need to verify that these implementations are consistent with the specification: in fact, this is a necessary requisite of safe and reliable software.

Testing is the dynamic verification of the consistency between the program under test and the specification. Indeed, testing has a fundamental role for both the achievement and the assessment of software reliability and safety (Laprie, 1992).

The testing activity essentially consists of checking the actual behaviour of the software

---

Work supported by CNR-Committee 12 - Project "Use of deductive databases to support software development" and by OLOS HCM Network - EC Contract No. CHRX-CT94-0577 product against the specified, or *expected*, behaviour. For this purpose, the program is executed on a collection of suitably selected inputs, the "test cases".

The problem of the selection of a subset of test inputs from the (usually infinite) input domain is a crucial one and has received great attention in the past research. The selection may be done systematically, according to one of the several test data selection strategies available, (Beizer, 1990) and (Myers, 1979), or may consist of randomly drawing an appropriate sample from a given input distribution (Musa, 1987), (Thevenod-Fosse, 1991). Whichever approach is followed, after having executed the program on the selected test inputs, the equally critical problem remains of analysing the outputs obtained and of deciding for each test whether it is approved or rejected. Unfortunately, this problem has been neglected by researchers.

In fact, most part of the testing literature is based on the assumption that once the inputs have been selected and the program has been executed, then the task of determining whether or not the test results are correct with respect to the specification can always be done in a straighforward manner. A mechanism that routinely decides whether or not a test output is correct is generically called an *oracle*, and the assumption that an oracle is always available is the *oracle assumption*. However, it would be more realistic to speak rather of the "oracle problem". Indeed, the situation is not much changed since Weyuker (1982) recognized more than a decade ago, that confidence in the oracle assumption is not justified, neither in theory nor in practice. In most cases, an oracle is not available, e.g., because the correct output can't be known exactly in advance or because building such a mechanism would be impractical; thus, the tester is faced with the problem of devising a useful substitute.

An oracle consists of two components (Richardson, 1992): the *oracle information*, that is the specification of the correct behaviour for the program under test, and the *oracle procedure*, that is the process followed by the oracle to check the obtained test outputs against the oracle information.

The oracle information can be implemented into one (or more) independent program version(s) intended to accomplish the same specifications as the program to be tested. In this way, each program version provides the complete oracle information to the other version. A simple comparison program then implements the oracle procedure. This approach is however highly expensive and is used just for critical software.

More often, in practice, the test results are inspected manually, i.e., the oracle information is provided by an expert of the application. To help the human oracle, the program is generally executed on a simplified set of test inputs, for which the correct output is known or can be determined easily. In some cases, the oracle information that is available is not complete. For instance, the person who is examining the test outputs cannot know the correct output of the program under test exactly. He can usually say that a test has failed, when he sees an incorrect output, but clearly the risk that he accepts plausible, yet incorrect, tests always exists.

On the other hand, if it can be still admissible to pretend that a human being can examine every result when the execution of comparatively few tests is considered, in the more realistic case that many tests, even thousands or millions, are needed, it is clear that the oracle must be automated. To allow the realisation of an automated mechanism, the oracle information is reduced to a set of conditions. These are usually only necessary conditions, so that incorrect runs may go undetected.

When the oracle information is not complete, we speak of a *partial* oracle. For a partial oracle, the information consists only of a set of correctness, or *plausibility*, conditions; if a test output does not satisfy these conditions the oracle rejects the test. But, the partial oracle does not know exactly the correct result: so a test that satifies the oracle conditions will be approved, but, even though plausible, the test result might actually be incorrect.

In other words, an automated, high-level oracle can be used to check whether the results of the testing satisfy at least the "type" (if not the"value") of the expected results, where the "type" is derived from the (formal) specifications of the system. To better explain the idea, let us provide the following, trivial, example. Suppose we have to design, and test, a program that implements a multiplier for relative integers. Then, for instance, we could build an automated oracle that only checks whether the sign of the multiplication is correct. That is, if the two factors have the same sign, the oracle checks that the result is positive, or, otherwise, that it is negative. In the special case that one of the factors is zero, the oracle checks that the result is zero. This oracle however does not provide the exact numerical result for the multiplication.

Several approaches have been recently suggested to develop oracles from specifications expressed in formal languages, e.g., Richardson (1992), Gorlick (1990) and Bernot (1991). Among formal languages, logic is a good candidate for expressing the high-level specification of systems, since it permits to describe system properties. Different types of logics have been proposed for this purpose. In particular, modal and temporal logics, due to their ability to deal with notions such as necessity, possibility, eventuality, etc., have been recognised as a suitable formalism for specifying properties of reactive systems (Manna, 1989). Among them, we recall the action based version of CTL (Emerson, 1986), ACTL (De Nicola, 1990). This logic is suitable to express properties of safety-critical systems defined by the occurrence of actions over time. Moreover, a set of ACTL formulae can be used to express those requirements that a safety-critical system must necessarily satisfy. Specification-based oracles provide different degrees of automation, both for the derivation of the oracle information and for the implementation of the oracle procedure. The cost of such oracles increases with the level of detail of the information, which here consists of formally specified conditions. In our approach, the oracle information consists of a set of plausible conditions, which are expressed using the ACTL formalism (see section 2). The oracle procedure is realised by implementing the ACTL formalism using the logic database and integrity checking features of the Gedblog system (Asirelli, 1994) (see section 3). Gedblog is based on a logic language extended with the capabilities of handling graphical and non graphical information, in a uniform way, and the possibility of defining and verifying integrity constraints (Asirelli, 1985). Our automated oracle consists of an environment built on Gedblog according to a formal high-level specification in ACTL of the safety requirements for the system under test. More precisely, from the functional specification of the system we derive in ACTL the safety requirements. These safety requirements are then incorporated in Gedblog and constitute the basis from which the oracle verdict is derived. We suppose that an implementation of the given safety-critical system is tested apart accordingly to some test plan, anyhow derived, and that the test outputs are collected. Gedblog then, allows us to automatically check these test outputs against the ACTL safety requirements.

Table 1 ACTL operators

Action formulae		
$\chi ::=$	*true*	"any action"
	false	"no action"
	α	"α action"
	$\neg\chi$	"not χ"
	$\chi \mid \chi'$	"χ or χ'"
State formulae		
$\phi ::=$	T	"any behaviour"
	F	"no behaviour"
	$\sim \phi$	" not ϕ"
	$\phi \& \phi'$	"ϕ and ϕ'"
	$E\gamma$	"there exists a path in which γ"
	$A\gamma$	"for all paths γ"
Path formulae		
$\gamma ::=$	$[\phi\{\chi\}U\{\chi'\}\phi']$	"ϕ is true for the states of the path until a state that satisfies ϕ' is reached by executing an action satisfying χ'. Before it, only actions satisfying χ or τ can be executed."
	$X\{\tau\}\phi$	"the next state of the path satisfies ϕ and is reached by executing a τ action"
	$X\{\chi\}\phi$	"the next state of the path satisfies ϕ and is reached by executing an action satisfying χ"

2 THE ACTL LOGIC

Process algebras and their semantic models, i.e., Labelled Transition Systems (or, state automata), Milner (1989), are generally recognized as a convenient tool for describing sequential or concurrent safety-critical systems at different levels of abstraction. They rely on a small set of basic operators, which correspond to primitive notions of concurrent systems, and on one or more notions of behavioural equivalence or preorder. The operators are used to build complex systems from more elementary ones. The behavioural equivalences are used to study the relationships between descriptions of the same system at different levels of abstractions (e.g., specification and implementation). The concept of a Labelled Transition System and of computation paths over it is formally defined below.

A *labelled transition system* (or simply *transition system*) TS is a quadruple (S, T, D, s_0), where S is a set of states, T is a set of transition labels, $s_0 \in S$ is the initial state, and $D \subseteq S \times T \times S$. A transition system is finite if D is finite. An element of D is denoted by $s \xrightarrow{\mu} s'$.

A *finite computation* of a transition system is a sequence $\mu_1\mu_2..\mu_n$ of labels such that $s_0 \xrightarrow{\mu_1} .. \xrightarrow{\mu_n} s_n$.

ACTL is a temporal logic of state formulae (denoted by ϕ), in which a path quantifier prefixes an arbitrary path formula (denoted by γ) whose models are Labelled Transition Systems. Also, it includes the logic for the definition of action formulae (denoted by χ). The ACTL operators and their informal semantics over TS's are reported in Table 1, while the formal semantics is described in (De Nicola, 1990).

Several logic operators can be defined starting by the basic ones. Let χ, χ' range over action formulae, E and A be path quantifiers, X and U be the "next" and "until" operators, respectively. We will write:

• $EF\phi$ for $E[true\{true\}U\phi]$ and $AF\phi$ for $A[true\{true\}U\phi]$: these are called the *eventually* operators;

• $EG\phi$ for $\sim AF \sim \phi$ and $AG\phi$ for $\sim EF \sim \phi$: these are called the *always* operators.

The ACTL logic allows to simply express *safety* and *liveness* properties in terms of the actions a system can perform. Safety properties claim that nothing bad can happen; liveness properties claim that something good eventually happens (Manna, 1989).

When an ACTL formula is given and a system is described by means of a TS, it is possible to check if the TS is a model for such a formula. In this case we say that the system satisfies the property the formula expresses. On the other hand, it may be also interesting to perform to opposite step: given a formula that represents a system requirement, to look for a model that satisfies such a formula. In (Asirelli, 1995), we have presented a method that, for each given ACTL formula, derives a particular TS that satisfies such formula.

3 THE GEDBLOG SYSTEM

The Gedblog system, (Asirelli, 1994), (Aquilino, 1994), is a uniform environment which supports the fast prototyping of applications that can take benefit from a declarative specification style. For instance, applications which demand for:

- a support for knowledge management (according to the given data-model this knowledge is based on);
- a support for the graphic representation of knowledge;
- a support for the interactions, to make the knowledge manageable at the graphic level.

Gedblog is based on logic databases theory. It is a deductive (logic) database, that can deal with basic knowledge management functionalities (storing, retrieving, quering), and besides it is enriched with several additional features: i) Integrity Constraints and Checks, to define the data model entities must fit in; ii) Transactions, to enter the operational framework; iii) Input/Output graphic model (declarative, based on prototypes), to define graphics and interactions with graphic objects.

Gedblog can manage logical theories that consist of different kinds of clauses:

• *Facts* - "unit" clauses, considered to be the Extensional component of the DB (EDB);

• *Rules* - considered to be the Intensional component of the DB (IDB);

• *Integrity Constraints* (ICs) - their syntax is: $A >> B_1, ..., B_s$. Informally speaking their meaning is that: each time A is true, then B_1 and ... and B_s must be true. ICs are managed following the method of the *modified program* (Asirelli, 1985) and they automatically inhibit the deduction of inconsistent information;

• *Checks* - their syntax is: $A_1, ..., A_m ==> B_1, ..., B_n$. These formulae are checked only on user request and do not modify the knowledge expressed by the theory, as integrity constraints do; their meaning is analogous to ICs.

• *Transactions*, in the form T := Precondition # $B_1, ..., B_n$# Postcondition. The goals in the body can modify the extensional component of the theory (facts). Modifications are recorded only if Postcondition succeeds.

By means of the system-defined predicate *theory*, it is possible to perform inclusion among theories. In this way, given a *starting* theory Th, the associated Gedblog theory can be defined as the set-theoretic *union* of all the theories in the inclusion tree rooted in Th.

Gedblog includes a graphic specification language, integrating the features of Motif and X11 in the Gedblog theories.

4 DESCRIPTION OF THE APPROACH THROUGH A SIMPLE EXAMPLE

In this section, we shall illustrate our approach to derive an oracle from an ACTL specification and to implement it within the Gedblog system. To help exposition, we shall describe our approach while walking-through a simple example.

4.1 The *search* program

The example program we shall refer to is a simple C program, *search*. It is the demonstration program given with the SMARTS tool (Sostware Test Works, 1991), which we used to automatically run the testing session (see 4.2).

Search accepts two arguments: the name of a textfile and a string (up to 20 characters long) and searches the textfile for the string. Then:

- if the program finds the string in the textfile, it returns a message saying "Match found on line i";
- if the program does not find the string, it returns a message saying "No match";
- if the program was not launched with exactly two arguments, the program returns either of the two messages: "Not enough command line arguments" or "Too many command line arguments", depending on which is the appropriate case;
- if a textfile with the given name does not exist, the program returns the message "File does not exist".

4.2 The test session

In our approach for the derivation of a partial oracle, we are not concerned with the strategy followed to select the test cases. We assume that the program has been tested according to a certain test plan, and that we have the test inputs and the produced outputs available. Thus, for this specific example, a set of about one hundred test inputs was generated randomly using an automatic test generator tool, TDGEN (Software Test Works, 1991). Then, we supplied these inputs to a test driver, the SMARTS tool (Software Test Works, 1991), which automatically executed the *search* program and registered the test outputs on a file. In order to verify the functioning of the Gedblog oracle, we introduced a bug in the program: we have commented out the source lines that verify whether the arguments provided are more than two and output the error message "Too many command line arguments".

4.3 Safety requirements for the *search* program

We now want to derive a formal description of the expected behaviour for the program *search* and use this to derive our automated oracle. More precisely, we want to excerpt from the informal requirements given in 4.1 a set of conditions that we believe essential for the safe behaviour of the program, i.e., those that we deem are the *safety requirements* for this program. This phase is the most critical, because it is the phase in which the contents of the oracle information is decided. Obviously, the decision relies on the tester's sensibility. Different users might identify different conditions as their own safety requirements. For instance, in our example, we decided that the oracle must necessarily detect errors in the input phase. That is, the oracle will reject those tests that will not output an error message "Not enough command line arguments" or "Too many command line arguments" when less or more, respectively, than exactly two input parameters are passed to the *search* program.

We now describe more explicitly how we derived the safety requirements. We have identified in the informal requirements some key actions. They are: the launch of the search operation; the input of the file name and the input of the string. For the sake of simplicity, we have identified each of them with a keyword: *check*, *read_file* and *read_string*, respectively. Moreover, we have identified the possible output messages of the system and again we have assigned to them a set of overlined keywords: $\overline{error1}$ (for "not enough command line arguments"), $\overline{error2}$ (for "too many command line arguments") , $\overline{file\_not\_found}$, $\overline{match}$, $\overline{nomatch}$.

Hence, we have expressed our safety requirements as follows:

• Only a *check* operation is expected after a sequence of a *read_file* and a *read_string* (or viceversa). Afterwards, the system may return any * of $\overline{file\_not\_found}$ or $\overline{match}$ or $\overline{nomatch}$.

• When a *check* operation precedes a *read_file* or a *read_string* operation then the system returns $\overline{error1}$.

• If after a sequence of a *read_file* and a *read_string* (or viceversa) another *read_file* or a *read_string* is performed then the system returns $\overline{error2}$.

From these requirements expressed by natural language sentences we derived the following set of ACTL formulae.

• $AG([read\_file][read\_string][check] < \overline{match}|\overline{nomatch}|\overline{file\_not\_found} > true)$

• $AG([read\_string][read\_file][check] < \overline{match}|\overline{nomatch}|\overline{file\_not\_found} > true)$

• $[check] < \overline{error1} > true$

• $AG([check][read\_file|read\_string] < \overline{error1} > true)$

• $AG([read\_file][read\_string][read\_file|read\_string] < \overline{error2} > true)$

• $AG([read\_string][read\_file][read\_file|read\_string] < \overline{error2} > true)$

Finally, from this set of formulae we derived in figure 1 a finite TS (Asirelli, 1995) that represents the minimal TS satisfying the conjuction of the above formulae: this TS will be the basis on which the oracle is built. In 1, we have denoted with a double circle the final states.

---

*Note that our partial oracle is not able to judge whether any of these 3 outputs is correct.

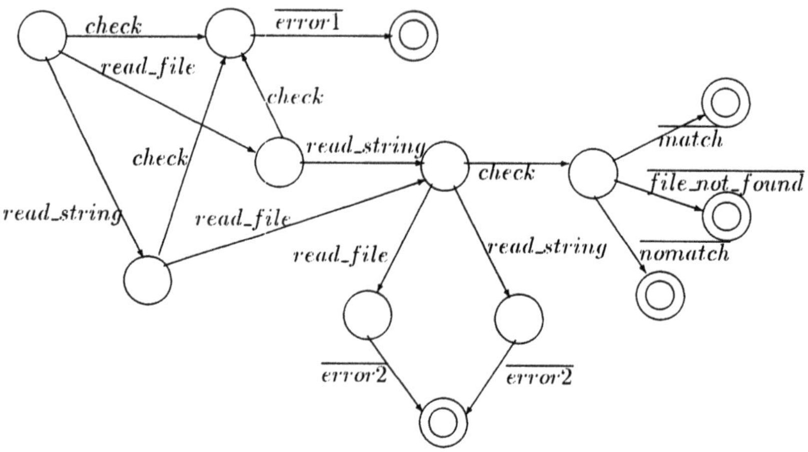

Figure 1 A TS for the Search Program

4.4 Implementation of the oracle

The oracle implementation in Gedblog consists of three theories:
- *oracle_info*: that contains the specification in clausal logic of the program under test. That is, the translation into clausal logic of the ACTL specification of the safety requirements for the *search* program;
- *test_outputs*: that contains the test outputs in form of unit clauses;
- *oracle_proc*: it is defined as the union of the two theories *oracle_ info* and *test_ outputs*, plus a set of definitions that can be considered of two kinds:

  - one is the specification of the syntactic transformation of the *test_outputs* so that they can be handled by the *oracle_ proc*, i.e., it specifies the mapping between the specification and the output of the test;

  - the other is the definition of two predicates: *correct_proof* and *wrong_proof* that realize the oracle itself; i.e., they identify which *test_output* (called "proof") is correct and which is wrong, respectively.

In particular:
- the *oracle_info* theory consists of three sets of facts:

  1) the set of states of the model of the program, e.g.,:
  $state(s0)$.
  $state(s1)$.
  ⋮

  2) the set of facts that defines which are the initial and the final states, e.g., :
  $initial\_state(s0)$.
  $final\_state(sfin1)$.

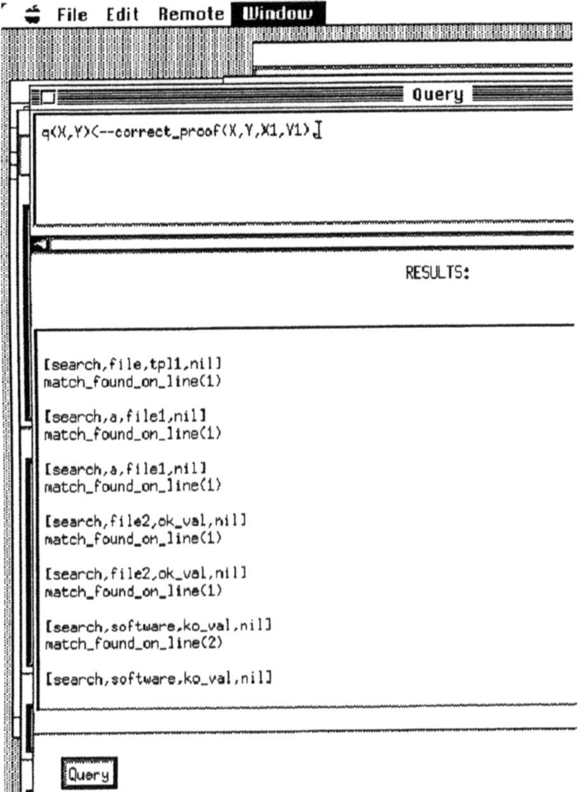

Figure 2 Correct test outputs

⋮

3) the set of transitions among the states, e.g.,: $transition(s0, s1, search)$.
$transition(s0, s2, read\_file)$.
$transition(s0, nil, nil)$.

⋮

The following are the rules to define a correct behaviour of a process as a possible path in the transitions net:
$correct\_behave(X, Y, Out) \longleftarrow path(X, Sfin, Y, Out) \& final\_state(Sfin)$.
$path(Sin, Sout, [], Out) \longleftarrow transition(Sin, Sout, Out)$.
$path(Sin, Sout, [X, Y], Out) \longleftarrow transition(Sin, Sinter, X) \& path(Sinter, Sout, Y, Out)$.

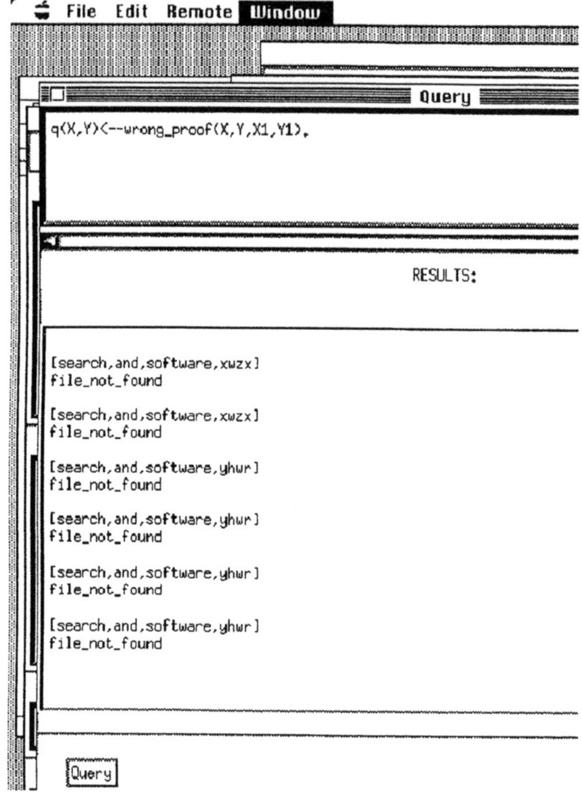

Figure 3 Wrong test outputs

Finally, there are the "checks", i.e., integrity constraints that can be periodically run to check that the model satisfies them.

$final\_state(X)\&transition(X, Y, Z) ==> Y = nil.$
$initial\_state(X)\&transition(Y, X, Z) ==> fail.$
⋮

- The theory *test_outputs* appears as follows :
  $proof([search, nil, nil, nil], not\_enough\_command\_line\_arguments).$
  $proof([search, file1, abcd, file2], too\_many\_command\_line\_arguments).$
  ⋮
- Finally, the theory *oracle_proc* includes:
  - the two theories above described, by means of clauses:
  $theory('oracle\_info').$

$theory('test\_outputs')$.

- the definition of the mapping of the input/output parameters between the two theories, e.g.,:

$convert([search, nil, nil, Z], [search, []])$.

$convert([search, Y, nil, Z], [read\_file, [search, []]]) \longleftarrow not(Y = nil)$

⋮

$final\_msg(error1, not\_enough\_command\_line\_arguments)$.

$final\_msg(file\_not\_found, file\_not\_found)$.

$final\_msg(error2, too\_many\_command\_line\_arguments)$.

⋮

the definition of $correct\_proof$ and $wrong\_proof$ that implement the oracle:

$correct\_proof(X, Y) \longleftarrow proof(X, Y)\&$
$convert\_proof(X, Y, X1, Y1)\&correct\_behave(s0, X1, Y1)$.

$wrong\_proof(X, Y) \longleftarrow proof(X, Y)\&$
$convert_proof(X, Y, X1, Y1)\¬(correct_behave(s0, X1, Y1))$.

which states that the result of a test is correct if, given the syntactic, pre-defined, mapping of the input /output of the test (defined by the $convert\_proof$ predicate), there is a correct behaviour, in the specifications, starting from the state s0 (the initial state).

We have executed the oracle on the set of produced test outputs. As expected, the oracle could automatically indentify those test outputs that were correct and those not correct with respect to our TS (figure 1). The correct and wrong test outputs were found by running two different queries as shown in figure 2 and figure 3 respectively. In particular, 13 test outputs were rejected.

5 CONCLUSIONS

We have introduced an approach to implement an automated oracle for a subset of the specification requirements for a given system. The oracle has been implemented in Gedblog and is running on a Sun 4 station under Unix.

We have illustrated our approach by means of an example program. The example described is of course too simple to allow us to draw general conclusions.

However, our goal in this paper was to verify the feasibility of the approach. Our preliminary study seems to confirm the validity of our ideas. Now, experimentation on more significant case studies is necessary to investigate if the approach is viable in more realistic development environments.

Several enhancements on this preliminary implementation of an oracle are planned. The oracle implementation here described relies only on the support of the deductive database capabilities. We are now implementing the ACTL Graphic Formalism Modelling System, which will allow us to derive the TS from a set of ACTL formulae in a completely automated way. Hence, we should be able to exploit the full power of Gedblog in the near future. Moreover, we believe that such an approach can be used to deal with more complex applications, in particular concurrent programs, which can be easily expressed in the ACTL formalism.

6 REFERENCES

Aquilino, D., Asirelli, P. and Inverardi, P. (1994) Gedblog: a Multi-Theories Deductive Environment to Specify Graphical Interfaces. In *Proc. GULP-PRODE'94 Joint Conf. on Declarative Programming.* Peniscola, Spain.

Asirelli, P, De Santis, M. and Martelli, M. (1985) Integrity Constraints in Logic Databases. *Journal of Logic Programming*, **3**, 221-232.

Asirelli, P., Di Grande, D., Inverardi, P. and Nicodemi, F. (1994) Graphics by a Logic Database Management System. *Journal of Visual Languages and Computing*, **5**, 365-388.

Asirelli, P., Gnesi, S. and Magnani, S (1995) Syntesis of Temporal Logic Formulas: an Approach to Software Design. IEI-Internal Report., 1995.

Beizer, B. (1990) *Software Testing Techniques.* Second Edition. Van Nostrand Reinhold, New York.

Bernot, G., Gaudel, M.C. and B. Marre (1991) Software Testing based on Formal Specifications: a Theory and a Tool. *Software Engineering Journal*, **6**, 387-405.

De Nicola, R. and Vaandrager, F. W. (1990) Action versus State based Logics for Transition Systems. Proceedings Ecole de Printemps on Semantics of Concurrency. *Lecture Notes in Computer Science*,**469**, Springer-Verlag, 407-419.

Emerson, E. A. and Halpern, J. Y. (1986) Sometimes and Not Never Revisited: on Branching Time versus Linear Time Temporal Logic. *Journal of ACM*, **33 (1)**, 151-178.

Gorlick, M. M. , Kesselman, C. F., Marotta D. A. and Parker, D. S. (1990) Mockingbird: A Logic Methodology for Testing. *Journal of Logic Programming*, **8**, 95-119,

Laprie, J. C. (1992) Dependability: Basic Concepts and Terminology. *Dependable Computing and Fault-Tolerant Systems*, **5**, Springer-Verlag.

Manna, Z. and Pnueli, A. (1989) The Anchored Version of the Temporal Framework, in Linear Time, Branching Time and Partial Order in Logics and Models for Concurrency, *Lecture Notes in Computer Science*,**354**, Springer-Verlag, 201-284.

Milner, R. (1989) *Communication and Concurrency.* Prentice-Hall International, Englewood Cliffs.

Musa, J. D., Iannino, A. and Okumoto, K. (1987) *Software Reliability Measurement, Prediction, Application.* McGraw-Hill, New York.

Myers, G. J. (1979) *The Art of Software Testing* John Wiley & Sons, New York

Richardson, D. J., Aha, S. L. and O'Malley, T. O. (1992) Specification-based Test Oracles for Reactive Systems. *Proceedings of the 14th Int. Conference on Software Engineering*, 105-118.

Software TestWorks (1991) Test Regression Tools: CAPBAK, SMARTS, EXDIFF, TDGEN. SR Software Research, Inc. San Francisco.

Thevenod-Fosse, P. and Waeselynck, H. (1991) An Investigation of Statistical Software Testing *J. of Software Testing, Verification and Reliability*, **1(2)**, 5-25.

Weyuker, E. J. (1982) On Testing Non-testable Programs. *The Computer Journal*, **25(4)**, 465-460.

7 BIOGRAPHY

Patrizia Asirelli graduated in Computer Science at the University of Pisa, Italy. Since 1978 she has been a researcher of the Italian National Research Council (CNR), Pisa, Italy, in the Programming Languages and Operating Systems group for wich she is responsible since 1991. Her research interests include logic programming, deductive databases and software engineering.

Antonia Bertolino graduated cum laude in Electronic Engineering at the University of Pisa. Since 1986 she has been a researcher of the Italian National Research Council. Her research interests are in software engineering, particularly in testing theory and techniques and in testing automation. She is an Associate Editor of the Journal of Systems and Software.

Stefania Gnesi, graduated cum laude in Computer Science at the University of Pisa, Italy. Since 1984 she has been a researcher in the Programming Languages and Operating Systems group of the Italian National Research Council (CNR), Pisa, Italy. Her current research interests include methods and tools for the high-level specification and formal verification of concurrent systems, and applications of temporal logic.

PART FIVE

Numerical Assessment

14

Poisson Models for Subprogram Defect Analyses

Dr. William M. Evanco
The MITRE Corporation
7525 Colshire Drive
McLean, Virginia 22101-3481
e-mail: evanco@mitre.org
Fax: (202) 863-2970

Abstract

For Ada systems, the hierarchy of subprograms compose a layered virtual machine within an object-based framework. Poisson analyses are proposed for the identification of the determinants of defects in these subprograms. Software complexity (measured during design or implementation) as well as characteristics of the software development environment influence the number of defects identified during the testing phase. The Poisson models are calibrated on the basis of measures extracted from the code of Ada projects and data from software change reports. One of the models is used to estimate defects at the subprogram and project levels for the calibration data, and these estimates are then compared to the actual defects. To demonstrate cross-language applicability, defect predictions are made at the subsystem level for a project coded in the C programming language and compared to the actual subsystem defects. Notable results from the analysis are that extensively modified reused subprograms (>25% changed) have substantially more defects than new code of otherwise comparable characteristics and that software development environment volatility (as measured by non-defect changes per thousand source lines of code) is a strong determinant of subprogram defects.

Keywords

Software metrics, software quality, multivariate analysis, prediction models, reliability modeling, Poisson analysis

1 INTRODUCTION

A wide variety of metrics characterizing software and the software development process have been identified in the research literature (for reviews, see Cote et al., 1988; Zuse, 1990). Of particular interest are measures of software complexity, many of which have been related to software quality factors such as reliability or maintainability (Agresti and Evanco, 1992; Agresti et al., 1990; Kafura and Reddy, 1987).

Most of these software complexity metrics can be collected relatively early in the development life cycle (e.g., during design or implementation). On the other hand, indicators of software quality generally emerge later in the life cycle (e.g., during testing or operation). Thus, software complexity measures provide early indications of software quality.

However, as has been pointed out by a number of authors, no single metric can adequately capture the complexity of software (Basili and Rombach, 1988; Evanco and Agresti, 1992; Munson and Khoshgoftaar, 1992; Selby and Porter, 1988). Rather, software complexity can be characterized along different dimensions, each dimension being measured by at least one metric. The problem then becomes one of deciding how to integrate the metrics to determine their joint contributions to software quality. Methodologies to accomplish this integration of metrics are a topic of current research interest.

1.1 Discriminant Analysis

For example, Munson and Khoshgoftaar (1992) propose that many of the available metrics can be clustered into correlated groups. Each group represents a domain of software complexity such as control flow or data structure complexity. A principal components analysis identifies these groups from which a smaller number of orthogonal domain metrics can be defined. Each domain metric has an associated eigenvalue representing the relative amount of variance explained by the domain. Multiplying the domain metrics by their eigenvalues and summing the products provides a unitary metric for the relative complexity of a software component. This relative complexity may then be used to identify, for example, defect-prone software modules.

Selby and Porter (1988) propose a classification tree methodology to identify defect prone or difficult-to-maintain modules. A tree generation algorithm produces a classification tree using various software metrics for a group of previously developed modules. The classification tree is then applied to a new set of modules in order to identify potentially troublesome ones based on their metric characteristics.

Both of these approaches rely on some form of discriminant analysis. For example, an integer value is selected as a cutoff and modules with defect numbers exceeding this value are regarded as defect prone. Unfortunately, these methodologies do not provide quantitative estimates of the numbers of module defects.

The argument made for the use of discriminant analysis is its appropriateness for analyzing relatively small software components such as subprograms typically having few defects. In fact, a substantial number of subprograms may have zero defects, yielding a defect distribution skewed toward zero. Additionally, defects are measured on an integer scale and for small defect numbers the integer scale cannot be adequately approximated by a continuous one. These conditions rule out the use of a statistical technique such as ordinary least squares, which requires that the dependent variable (i.e., defects) be continuous and normally distributed.

1.2 Quantitative Defect Analysis

There is a need, nevertheless, for an approach that integrates a variety of software metrics into models to provide a quantitative measure of software defects for small software components. Such methodologies have a clear advantage over discriminant analyses that only provide classification capabilities. For example, during the design phase, defect prediction models may be used to evaluate the impact of design changes on defect numbers. Prior to testing, components at risk of being under-tested could be identified by comparing the planned test coverage with the predicted defect distribution. During testing, additional test cases may be identified by comparing the actual defects revealed through testing with the predicted defects. And, finally, a decision to stop testing could be made when the actual defect numbers approach the predicted defects.

One such technique for integrating metrics was proposed by Evanco and Agresti (1992). Using an ordered response model, a composite complexity measure was calibrated. This composite complexity measure, expressed as a linear combination of basic software complexity metrics (e.g., calls per subprogram) and measures of the development environment complexity (e.g., non-defect changes), is an order statistic. Assuming a probability distribution for the composite complexity, probabilities were estimated for membership in one of the n+2 categories: no defects, one defect, two defects,..., n defects, and greater than n defects, where n is a positive integer chosen so that few modules have more than n defects. These probabilities were then used to calculate the expected number of defects at the library unit aggregation level for Ada programs.

In this study, another approach based on Poisson analysis is presented. Poisson models treat the defect number as a random variable that can assume any non-negative integer value. The Poisson methodology is applied to analyze the determinants of defects in Ada subprograms.

1.3 Subprograms in Ada Systems

Software analyses have been conducted at the level of physical modules such as subprograms (Kafura and Reddy, 1987) in FORTRAN or C, or some rollup of physical modules such as library unit aggregations (Evanco and Agresti, 1992), subsystems (Agresti and Evanco, 1992; Agresti et al., 1990), or projects (Card and Agresti, 1988). However, within the Ada programming language, a subprogram is not the natural physical unit of encapsulation. The compilation unit plays this role and may encapsulate a package specification or body, a subunit, and, sometimes, library unit subprograms. Typically, though, subprograms appear as program units encapsulated within package library units and such subprograms may be regarded as submodules.

The hierarchy of subprograms (expressed as a call tree) can be viewed as a layered virtual machine (LVM). Nielson and Shumate (1988) combine the concepts of the LVM and object-oriented design (OOD) into a design methodology whereby a software system is decomposed into a hierarchy of virtual machines (i.e., Ada subprograms) and objects (e.g., Ada packages, types, and objects of the types). While the version of Ada, namely Ada83, considered in this study does not fully support the object-oriented paradigm, it nevertheless has some features of an object-oriented language. Ada83 allows for information hiding through its packaging constructs to ensure the reliability and modifiability of software by controlling dependencies. Ada83 also supports data abstraction through abstract data types. Ada95 is, however, a fully object-oriented language supporting in addition, dynamic binding and inheritance. Because Ada83 does not support all of the features of an object-oriented language it is sometimes referred to as an *object-based* language.

In previous work (Agresti and Evanco, 1992; Agresti et al., 1990 ; Evanco and Agresti, 1992), we focused on some of the object-based features of Ada83 (e.g., context coupling of packages) expected to influence defects. In this study, our attention is turned to the analysis of the characteristics of the LVM that may affect defects. Future work will focus on merging the LVM and the object-based features into an integrated framework.

For Ada systems, subprogram level analyses have a number of advantages over analyses of library unit aggregations. A library unit aggregation, encapsulating multiple subprograms, averages about 650 source lines of code for the Ada programs used in this study. On the other hand, a subprogram averages about 100 source lines of code. Therefore, the identification of defects can be better localized for subprograms.

Second, subprograms rather than packages may be a more natural unit for analysis with respect to the testing process. A functional profile can be derived when testing is conducted according to some operational profile (Musa, 1993). The functional profile identifies those functional capabilities of interest and value to end-users along with their usage probabilities. Since subprograms embody the functionality of the system, the ability to predict subprogram defects provides a means for monitoring and controlling the progress of testing. Actual defects may be compared to predicted defects in order to identify potentially under-tested subprograms.

Third, the Ada subprogram level analyses in this study can be extended to procedural languages such as FORTRAN or C. The explanatory variables for the Ada subprogram defect prediction models discussed below are generic to procedural languages since no reference is made to Ada-specific constructs. Thus, subprogram level analyses enable us to handle systems with mixed programming languages such as Ada systems with calls to FORTRAN or C subprograms.

Finally, subprogram level analyses can facilitate the reengineering of a system from a procedural language such as FORTRAN or C to the object-based language of Ada. Measurements of the system can be made at each stage of the reengineering process. Reverse engineering of the procedural language system provides "views" from which metrics can be derived to evaluate software components for restructuring. For example, the call tree and logic control flow views are characterized by fan-out and cyclomatic complexity metrics, respectively. These metrics can help to identify excessively complex components for restructuring. Similarly, measurements of the reengineered system allow comparisons to the original system to evaluate whether or not it is an improvement.

In the next section, the Poisson methodology is presented and the determinants of subprogram defects used in this study are discussed. In Section 3, we discuss the characteristics of the empirical data. In Section 4, the empirical results are presented. Section 5 demonstrates the cross-language applicability of the LVM results by predicting defects for a C language system. Finally, Section 6 presents the conclusions.

2 POISSON DEFECT MODEL

In order to conduct subprogram level analyses, we use a Poisson model* (Evanco and Lacovara, 1994). As discussed previously, since subprograms are relatively small units, the discrete nature of the defect number becomes apparent. Thus, least squares regression analyses, relying on assumptions of normality and continuity of the dependent variable, are ruled out. Instead, the defect number can be represented by a Poisson distribution given by

$$P(\text{Defects}=r_i;\, i) = \exp(-\lambda_i)\frac{(\lambda_i)^{r_i}}{r_i!} \qquad (1)$$

where $P(\text{Defects}=r_i;\, i)$ is the probability of r_i defects ($r_i=0,1,2,\ldots$) and λ_i is the expected number of defects for the ith subprogram. λ_i is a non-negative function of both the complexity characteristics of the ith subprogram and the development environment characteristics that can be expressed in log-linear form as:

$$\ln(\lambda_i) = a_0 + a_1{*}\ln(1+NSC) + a_2{*}\ln(1+NP) + a_3{*}\ln(CC) + a_4{*}\ln(1+ND) + a_5{*}\ln(1+NCH) + a_6{*}NCI + a_7{*}EMC \qquad (2)$$

* Non-homogeneous Poisson models have been used previously for reliability growth analyses (Goel and Okumoto, 1979). In such models, the parameter is a function of time and the units of observation typically have been projects. In this study, the subprogram is the unit of observation and the parameter is a function of subprogram characteristics. The number of defects is the total number accumulated throughout the testing phase.

where "ln" is the natural logarithm and $a_0, a_1, \ldots, a_m$ are parameters to be estimated. The explanatory variables are defined as:

- NSC = number of subprogram calls
- NP = number of parameters
- CC = cyclomatic complexity
- ND = average nesting depth
- NCH = non-defect changes per source line of code
- NCI = new code indicator (equals one if subprogram is completely new code and zero otherwise)
- EMC = extensively modified reused code indicator (equals one if subprogram is reused but extensively modified and zero otherwise).

The first four variables represent characteristics of the software design/code. These characteristics are not Ada-specific and may also be obtained for procedural languages such as FORTRAN or C. The *number of subprogram calls* and the *number of parameters* may be derived through the analysis of system design documentation. Using design documentation to determine these complexity attributes provides useful information about potential determinants of defects early in system development. On the other hand, the *cyclomatic complexity* and the *average nesting depth* may be available late in the design stage but generally are available at some point in the implementation phase.

One way of characterizing the structural complexity of a software system is by means of a subprogram call graph. The nodes of the graph represent subprograms and the directed arcs represent subprogram calls. The *number of subprogram calls* is a measure of the contribution by a subprogram to the structural complexity of a software system. This measure is an indicator of a subprogram's connections to its external environment through calls to other subprograms and is a major component of the fan-out measure introduced by Henry and Kafura (1981). We hypothesize that increasing a subprogram's external complexity will tend to increase its defects.

Parameters are data items that are manipulated by the executable code of subprograms. These parameters serve as inputs to or outputs from other subprograms. The process of mapping from a set of inputs to a set of outputs may be interpreted as the computational workload of a subprogram. Adding parameters to a subprogram tends to increase its computational workload and, hence, its internal complexity, leading to potentially more defects. Therefore, the *number of parameters* is an indicator of the workload performed by a subprogram (Card and Agresti, 1988). We establish the convention that parameters which are data structures such as vectors or matrices increment the parameter count by one.

The McCabe *cyclomatic complexity* has been proposed in the literature as an important determinant of defects (McCabe, 1976; Walsh, 1979). It is a measure of a subprogram's internal complexity from the perspective of logic control flows. A directed graph can be derived to represent these control flows. The cyclomatic complexity is the number of independent paths in the directed graph. Equivalently, the cyclomatic complexity can be calculated by counting the simple Boolean conditions in the control statements (e.g., while statements, do loops, etc.). We hypothesize that the number of subprogram defects tends to increase as the use of control statements to implement a subprogram's workload increases. The cyclomatic complexity measure generally becomes available later in the development process when a subprogram body is implemented in terms of its control flow logic.

The *average nesting depth* is the final indicator of the internal complexity of a subprogram. This measure complements the cyclomatic complexity measure which varies with the number of program predicates but is not sensitive to the complexity associated with nesting structures. The average nesting depth measure is explicitly concerned with program nesting structures and their contribution to complexity. To compute the average nesting depth, each statement of the subprogram is assigned a nesting depth. This depth is incremented by one when entering or decremented by one when leaving, for example, a block declarative region, a begin-end block, a logic control flow block (e.g., loop, case, or if statements), and exception handler alternatives. The average nesting depth is obtained by summing the nesting depths of the statements and dividing by the total number of statements.

The remaining variables represent features of the development environment. These variables are not collected by means of a software analyzer, but rather through additional data provided by the developer about software changes and the reuse of software components.

The *number of non-defect changes per source line of code* made to a subprogram is an indicator of development environment volatility. This variable has been shown to influence subsystem level defect densities in a previous study (Agresti and Evanco, 1992). The non-defect changes may be a result of new or unanticipated requirements that emerge during the development process. New requirements may be poorly communicated or inadequately understood, leading to implementation defects. In addition, the new requirements may be difficult to implement in the framework of the original design since these requirements were not initially anticipated. In any case, the resulting changes contribute to development complexity and we hypothesize that the changes may lead to additional defects.

The ability of an organization to reuse previously developed code is expected to influence the number of defects. Code that is reused verbatim (without any modifications) exhibits very few defects in our data (14 defects in about 50,000 source lines of code). Therefore, we restricted the analyses to new code, reused but slightly modified code, and reused but extensively modified code.

The *new code indicator,* NCI, is a dummy variable equal to unity for a subprogram consisting of new code and zero otherwise. Similarly, the *reused but extensively modified code indicator,* EMC, equals unity for a subprogram developed from reused code with extensive modifications and zero otherwise. If more than 25% of a subprogram's code has been changed, then it is regarded as having been extensively modified. Thus, the (NCI,EMC) values are (1,0) for new code, (0,1) for extensively modified code, and (0,0) for slightly modified code (i.e., less than 25% modified). The effect of the dummy variables, NCI and EMC, is to shift the constant term, a_0, of equation (2) by a_6 and a_7 respectively. Our working hypothesis is that slightly modified reused code will have fewer defects than either new code or extensively modified reused code. Thus, we expect a_6 and a_7 to have positive values.

From the probabilities in equation (1), the values of the coefficients, a_j, can be estimated using a maximum likelihood approach. Given N empirical observations, the likelihood function is expressed as:

$$L(a_0, a_1, ..., a_7) = \prod_{i=1}^{N} \exp(-\lambda_i) \frac{(\lambda_i)^{r_i}}{r_i!} \quad (3)$$

where the λ_i are functions of the parameters, $a_0, a_1, ..., a_7$, as indicated in equation (2). Taking the derivatives of (3) with respect to the parameters, setting the derivatives equal to zero, and solving for the parameters yields solutions for the parameters optimizing equation (3).

3 EMPIRICAL DATA

The subprograms were obtained from four flight dynamic and telemetry simulation programs written in Ada83 by the NASA Software Engineering Laboratory (NASA/SEL). These programs were analyzed using the Ada Static Source Code Analyzer Program (ASAP) (Doubleday, 1987). The raw outputs of ASAP were input to a number of tools and utilities to extract subprogram level data. The subprograms include both library units and program units contained within library units.

A total of 1013 new, reused but slightly modified, and reused but extensively modified subprograms were obtained from the four projects. Reused subprograms with no modifications were not considered since they contain very few defects. About 81% of the code is new while 19% is reused with some modifications. About 6% of the subprograms are library units while the rest are program units contained within library units. About 14% of the subprograms are at the bottom of the call tree, making no calls to other subprograms.

Change report data were tabulated for defects and for non-defect changes and component origination forms were analyzed to extract data on software reuse. Additional summary statistics for the subprogram data are shown in Table 1.

Table 1 Characteristics of Subprogram Data

Variable	Mean	Standard Deviation	Minimum	Maximum
Defects	1.02	1.54	0	11
Source lines of code	93	97	5	927
Subprogram calls	11.5	18.2	0	142
Parameters	2.7	3.3	0	48
Cyclomatic complexity	23.3	29.8	1	249
Average nesting level	1.6	.77	0	6
Non-defect changes	1.5	1.8	0	18

4 ANALYSIS RESULTS

Estimates of the parameters in equation (2) are shown in Table 2 for three different models. The standard deviations of the parameter estimates are the numbers in parentheses. The first column gives the names of the variables associated with the parameters. The second column shows the analysis results for Model A which involves only those software complexity metrics that are expected to be available at design time: the number of subprogram calls and the number of parameters. Model B, shown in the third column, incorporates the additional software complexity measures available during implementation: the cyclomatic complexity and the average nesting level but excludes the number of parameters count. Finally Model C includes all of the variables of Model B plus the number of parameters count. In the three models, all of the variables are at least at the 5% level of significance.

The last row of Table 2 shows the correlations of the predicted defects calculated from equation (2) with the actual defects for the different models. Model A has a correlation coefficient of .41. The correlation coefficient of Model B is .46, while that of Model C is .48.

Table 2 Poisson Model Estimates of Subprogram Defects

Variable[1]	Model A	Model B	Model C
Intercept	-1 .63 (.14)	-2 .17 (.16)	-2 .28 (.16)
Subprogram Calls[2]	.48 (.03)	.25 (.04)	.26 (.04)
Number of Parameters[2]	.14 (.04)		.11 (.05)
Cyclomatic Complexity		.27 (.04)	.27 (.04)
Average Nesting Depth[2]		.47 (.16)	.39 (.16)
Non-Defect Changes/ Source Lines of Code[2]	4.8 (1.3)	5.6 (1.4)	5.7 (1.4)
New Code Indicator	.41 (.11)	.34 (.11)	.37 (.11)
Extensively Modified Code Indicator	.73 (.16)	.62 (.16)	.67 (.16)
Coefficient of Correlation	.41	.46	.48

[1] All variables are entered in logarithmic form with the exception of the indicators for new and extensively modified code.

[2] One is added to the value of the variable to prevent zero-valued arguments in the logarithm.

Taking the differential of equation (2) with respect to one of the software complexity variables, X, on the right hand side yields:

$$\frac{\Delta\lambda}{\lambda} = a_j * \frac{\Delta X}{X} \tag{4}$$

Since λ is the expected number of defects, the parameter a_j is interpreted as the *elasticity* of the expected number of defects with respect to the corresponding variable, X. For example, in Model C a 10% decrease in cyclomatic complexity leads to a 2.7% decrease in defects.

The elasticities associated with the four software complexity measures are all substantially less than unity. Taking the anti-logarithm of equation (2), the contribution of subprogram calls to predicted defects is given by $(1+NSC)^{a_1}$ where from Table 2, a_1 equals .48 for Model A, .25 for Model B, and .26 for Model C. These empirical results do not support assumptions made in other studies (Card and Agresti, 1988; Henry and Kafura, 1981) that the number of defects varies as the square of subprogram calls.

Most notable in Table 2 is the very high elasticity associated with development environment volatility as measured by non-defect changes per source line of code. For example, in Model C, a 10% increase in (1+NCH) increases defects by 57%.

The results in Table 2 also indicate that reused slightly modified code (NCI=0, EMC=0) exhibits the fewest defects since the parameters associated with NCI and EMC are positive. Reused extensively modified code (NCI=0, EMC=1) has more defects than new code (NCI=1, EMC=0), since the parameter for EMC is greater than the parameter for NCI.

Taking reused slightly modified code as a baseline, in Model C new code is expected to have about 45% more defects ($e^{.37}=1.45$), while extensively modified reused code is expected to have about 95% more defects ($e^{.67}=1.95$). Thus, if a potentially reusable subprogram requires that more than 25% of its code be modified then it may be better to develop new code if the objective is to minimize defects. However, tradeoff analyses are needed to compare the costs of new development with the costs of extensively modifying reused code and correcting the additional defects.

These results for reuse are related to the large impact that non-defect code changes have on defects. Adapting code for reuse in a new system involves non-defect changes (however, these changes are not included in the counts of non-defect changes per source line of code). The analysis results for reuse and for non-defect changes support the view that adapting code to account for new or modified requirements is an important risk factor contributing to software defects.

In addition to the variables shown in Table 2, we also examined the impact on expected defect numbers of a subprogram being either a library unit or program unit. A dummy variable was introduced equal to unity for a library unit and zero for a program unit. The associated coefficient was small and statistically insignificant, indicating that this distinction was not an important factor in determining defects.

The predicted and actual defects for the four projects in this analysis were rolled up to the subsystem level to graphically demonstrate the fit of the model. These rollups are plotted in Figure 1 for Model C. Perfect predictions would lie on the forty-five degree line. The actual and predicted defects fit well with the exception of one outlier. The correlation between actual and predicted defects is .93.

Project level rollups for the four projects used in the analysis are shown in Table 3. The predicted defects and the defect densities (expressed as defects per thousand source lines of code) compare well to the actuals except for Project D. This project involves mostly verbatim reuse and the remaining subprograms that were used in this analysis constitute only 2800 source lines of code.

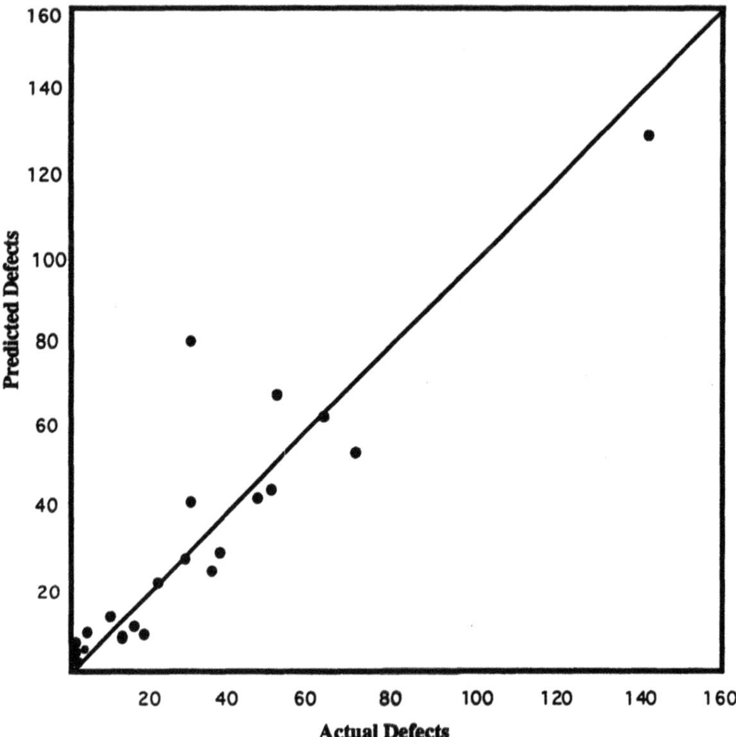

Figure 1 Actual Defects vs. Predicted Defects (subsystem rollups)

Table 3 Project Level Aggregations

Project	Actual Defects	Predicted Defects	Actual Defect Density	Predicted Defect Density
A	425	434	9.4	9.6
B	182	179	10.3	10.2
C	419	398	13.5	12.8
D	12	26	4.3	9.3

5 MODEL APPLICATION

In this section, Model B of Table 2 is applied to a project coded in the C programming language. The purpose of this exercise is to demonstrate the cross-language applicability of the results for Ada subprograms. The project involves 2221 subprograms in fourteen subsystems comprising about 184,000 source lines of C code. The analyzer used to extract the subprogram level software complexity characteristics did not provide a count of the number of parameters, hence necessitating the use of Model B. Also, defect data for this project was available only at the subsystem level, requiring the aggregation of subprogram level predictions to the subsystem level. The reuse was measured in terms of the fraction of code reused within a subsystem denoted by FREUSE.

Because of these dissimilarities, several adaptations of Model B in Table 2 were required. Using the coefficients from Table 2 associated with the software complexity measures, we defined a software complexity term, ICV, given by:

$$\ln(ICV) = .25*\ln(1+NSC) + .27*\ln(CC) + .47*\ln(1+ND) \quad (5)$$

From this equation, the ICV was computed for each of the 2221 subprograms. The ICV's were summed to the subsystem level, yielding subsystem complexity levels denoted by TICV. The correlation between the TICV measure and the numbers of defects at the subsystem level was found to be .83.

Next a Poisson model for the expected number of defects at the subsystem level, λ_S, was defined as a logarithmic function of TICV and FREUSE, and estimated on the basis of the subsystem level defect data yielding:

$$\ln(\lambda_S) = \underset{(.55)}{-2.86} + \underset{(.08)}{.93}*\ln(TICV) - \underset{(.41)}{1.36}*\ln(FREUSE) \quad (6)$$

The coefficient estimates enter with the appropriate signs and are significant to within the 5% level of significance.

Equation (6) was used to calculate the predicted defects at the subsystem level which was then correlated with the actual subsystem defects yielding a coefficient of correlation of .86. The plot of predicted vs. actual defects is shown in Figure 2.

6 CONCLUSIONS

A prime objective of this study was to demonstrate the feasibility of a methodology to integrate metrics and provide defect predictions for small software components such as subprograms. Previous approaches based on discriminant analyses have been capable only of identifying defect-prone components as indicated by some defect number cutoff. The use of Poisson analysis overcomes this limitation.

The analyses have led to some insights for software development policy when employing reuse and for software development taking place in highly volatile environments. Changes in software not anticipated in the original design have a strong impact on defect numbers. These changes may result from the need to adapt previously developed software components for reuse or from volatile software requirements. In any case, software components subjected to such changes should be targeted for additional testing.

The analyses were based on data from projects, some of which reused software components developed in other projects. However, we may consider using the models to predict defects for:

- software development projects involving multiple builds
- software maintenance projects involving enhancements
- software integration efforts

For phased software projects involving builds, defect prediction models can be calibrated on the basis of one or more previous builds. The models can then be applied to predict defects for future builds. Software components from previous builds may be regarded as reused and are classified as being used verbatim, with slight modifications, or with extensive modifications. The software components developed for the new build are regarded as new code. Unanticipated changes in requirements from build to build resulting in non-defect changes may also be taken into account.

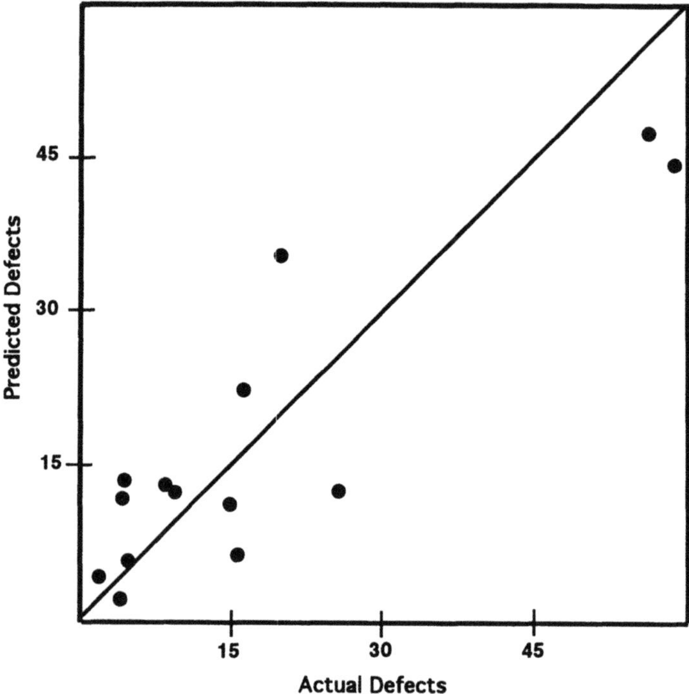

Figure 2 Actual Defects versus Predicted Defects for C Code

For software maintenance projects involving enhancements, the original software components may be regarded as reused. Some of these reused components may require modifications. Any additional software components required to effect the enhancements are regarded as new code. Software defect models may be calibrated on the basis of the original software and then applied to the enhancement project.

Large system development projects often involve the integration of subsystems consisting of COTS software products and developed software subsystems. Their integration may require software component modification at the interfaces while most of the software components "internal" to the COTS subsystems remain unchanged. In addition, some new components may be required to effect the integration. Once again, defect models can be applied to the integration effort and can aid in the development of test strategies.

Future extensions of these models will be concerned with their calibration for other programming languages such as FORTRAN and C to further demonstrate the cross-language applicability of the models. Within the Ada software system context, attention will be focused on the merging of the LVM results with the object-based features of Ada83 and the object-oriented features of Ada95. Also, a continuing validation of these models will be conducted to assess their applicability to a variety of development contexts.

7 REFERENCES

Agresti, W., and W. Evanco (1992), Projecting Software Defects from Analyzing Ada Designs, *IEEE Transactions on Software Engineering*, **18**, 988-997.

Agresti, W., W. Evanco, M. Smith (1990), Early Experiences Building a Software Quality Prediction Model, in *Proceedings of the Fifteenth Annual Software Engineering Workshop*, NASA/GSFC.

Basili, V. R. and Rombach, H. D. (1988) The TAME Project: Towards Improvement-Oriented Software Environments, *IEEE Transactions on Software Engineering*, **6**, 758-773.

Card, D. and W. Agresti (1988), Measuring Software Design Complexity, *Journal of Systems and Software*, **8**, 185-197.

Cote, V., P. Bourque, S. Oligny, and N. Rivard, (1988), Software Metrics: An Overview of Recent Results, *Journal of Systems and Software*, **8**, 121-131.

Doubleday, D. L. (1987), *ASAP: An Ada Static Source Code Analyzer Program*, Technical Report 1895, University of Maryland, College Park, Maryland.

Evanco, W. and W. Agresti (1992), Statistical Representation and Analyses of Software, in *Proceedings of the Seventeenth Symposium on the Interface of Computer Science and Statistics*, College Station, TX., 334-347.

Evanco, W. and R. Lacovara (1994), A Model-Based Framework for the Integration of Software Metrics, *Journal of Systems and Software*, **26**, 77-86.

Goel, A. L. and K. Okumoto (1979), Time Dependent Error Detection Rate Model for Software Reliability and Other Performance Measures, *IEEE Transactions on Reliability*, **28**, 206-211.

Henry, S. and D. Kafura (1981), Software Structure Metrics Based on Information Flow, *IEEE Transactions on Software Engineering*, **7**, 510-518.

Kafura, D. G., and G. R. Reddy, (1987), The Use of Software Complexity Metrics in Software Maintenance, *IEEE Transactions on Software Engineering*, **13**, 335-343.

McCabe, T. J., (1976), A Complexity Measure, *IEEE Transactions on Software Engineering*, **2**, 308-320.

Munson, J. C., and T. M. Khoshgoftaar (1992), The Detection of Fault-Prone Programs, *IEEE Transactions on Software Engineering*, **18**, 423-432.

Musa, J. D. (1993), Operational Profiles in Software Reliability Engineering, *IEEE Software*, **10**, 14-32.

Nielson, K. and K. Shumate (1988), *Designing Large Real-Time Systems with Ada*, McGraw-Hill Book Company, New York, New York.

Selby, R. W. and A. Porter (1988), Learning from Examples: Generation and Evaluation of Decision Trees for Software Resource Analysis, *IEEE Transactions on Software Engineering*, **14**, 1743-1757.

Walsh, T. J. (1979), Software Reliability Study Using a Complexity Measure, in *Proceedings of the National Computer Conference,* New York: AFIPS, 761-768.

Zuse, H. (1990), *Software Complexity: Measures and Methods*, Walter de Gruyer and Company, New York, New York.

8 ACKNOWLEDGEMENTS

The author thanks Mr. Frank McGarry and Mr. Jon Valett of the Software Engineering Laboratory at the NASA Goddard Space Flight Center for their cooperation in providing the data used in this analysis. This research was conducted through funds provided by the MITRE Technology Program.

9 BIOGRAPHY

William M. Evanco received the B.S. degree in physics from Carnegie-Mellon University, Pittsburgh, PA, and the Ph.D. degree in theoretical physics from Cornell University, Ithaca, NY. He has been with the MITRE Corporation since 1987. His primary research interests are software metrics and software performance modeling.

15

Early Estimation of Software Reliability through Dynamic Analysis*

Anders Wesslén and Claes Wohlin
Dept. of Communication Systems, Lund Inst. of Tech., Lund University, Box 118, S-221 00 Lund, Sweden, Phone: +46-46-2223319, Fax: +46-46-145823, E-mail: (wesslen, claesw)@tts.lth.se

Abstract

Early estimations and predictions of software quality attributes are essential to be in control of software development and to allow for delivery of software products which fulfil the requirements put on them. This paper focuses on a method enabling estimation and prediction of software reliability from the specification and design documents. The method is based on dynamic analysis of a well-defined high level description technique, and by applying usage-oriented analysis, it is illustrated, through a case study, how the reliability can be controlled. Furthermore, it is described how the output from the analysis can be used as an acceptance criterion of the design, as support in the planning process for the test phases to come and finally as a method to enable estimation and prediction of the reliability in the testing phase and operational phase. The method is still being evaluated and improved, but it can be concluded that so far the results are inspiring for the future.

Keywords

Software reliability, statistical usage testing, dynamic analysis, usage modelling.

---

* This work is supported by National Board for Industrial and Technical Development (NUTEK), Sweden, Reference Dnr: 93-2850.

1 INTRODUCTION

A key issue in achieving quality software is the ability to ensure the software quality attributes, for example reliability, throughout the software life cycle. In particular, this implies that quality attributes must be assessed early in the life cycle. Assessment during the early phases of software development is the only way to be able to influence the software process in the on-going project, and hence also the final quality of the product. Therefore, this paper focuses on the ability to perform reliability estimation and prediction from software specifications and designs in a high-level description technique.

These early indications of software quality are essential for planning and controlling the further development as well as obtaining a quality check of the final software product. A method for a usage-oriented analysis approach, which enables software reliability estimation and prediction from specification and design documents, was originally proposed by Wohlin (1992). The method has since then been further elaborated and a number of problems have been solved. The method and its potential are here presented through a case study, where the actual implementation of the method is presented. The solutions to some technical problems that occur when implementing the method are highlighted to enable people to adopt the proposed method.

2 OBJECTIVES

A major problem to obtain quality control of software is the inability to obtain early and objective measures of quality. Thus, methods for early estimation and prediction of quality attributes are essential (Musa, 1990). The objective here is to provide such a method for early software reliability estimation and prediction.

Statistical usage testing (Mills, 1987) and (Runeson, 1995a) or operation profile testing (Musa, 1993) is an emerging technology. The objective with this test technique is to resemble the actual usage to allow for reliability certification. It is, however, not enough to improve the test phase, similar procedures are needed at earlier stages in the software life cycle.

The objective is to illustrate how a usage-oriented approach can be applied early, through:

- usage modelling;
- generation of usage cases;
- dynamic analysis from a usage perspective of a software specification or design;
- estimation of software reliability for dynamic failures identified by the available tool support;
- prediction of software reliability in general, which can be used to plan the forthcoming test phase and also determine when it is likely that the reliability requirement is fulfilled.

These issues are presented through a case study of a software design. It is shown how the data obtained from the dynamic analysis can be used both to control the subsequent development and testing phases and as an estimator and predictor of the final software reliability. Furthermore, it illustrates that achieving quality software must mean that high-level specification and design techniques are applied. These techniques do not only provide a better development environment, they provide actually also new opportunities to perform early analysis of different software quality attributes.

3 THE CASE STUDY

The case study used in this paper is a small telecommunication system. The system is called SPOTS and controls a small digital telephone exchange. This system is a part of an educational development system at the department of Communication Systems, see (Yeh, 1989). The basic functionality of SPOTS is to provide services for plain ordinary telephone calls. SPOTS is used in an undergraduate project course which is held to teach the students about system development for large and complex systems. In this project course the students modify and extend the basic SPOTS with the following new telephone services:

- Charging
  This service contains two parts. The first part is the actual charging of the calls and the second contains functions to read and to reset the charging.
- Take Call
  This service provides the user with the ability to take a telephone call from a different telephone than the ringing one.
- Call Forwarding
  This service moves the incoming telephone calls to another telephone.
- Maintenance functions
  These functions can only be ordered from the operator terminal. The maintenance functions are:
  - Installation of a new subscriber
  - Removal of a subscriber
  - Change the telephone number for a subscriber.

The design and implementation of the new services are made using SDL (ITU-T, 1988) and the development tool SDT* (SDL Development Tool). SDL (Specification and Description Language) is a standardized specification and design technique, and an introduction to the technique can be found in, for example, (Belina, 1991).

4 USAGE MODELLING

The system described briefly in the previous section is the basis for the case study. The services should be modelled from the user perspective, hence it is mostly necessary to model ordering and cancellation of services and not the actual behaviour as it is transparent for the user of the system. For example, it means that a subscriber phoning to another subscriber where the latter has forwarded his calls does not know that the call is forwarded, hence the actual behaviour is invisible and it should not be modelled in a usage model. This is the explanation of the mapping of the services in the previous section to the usage model in Figure 1.

The usage of the system is modelled with a hierarchical state model. This type of model is described by Runeson (1992, 1995a) and Wohlin (1994). The model is illustrated in Figure 1. The lowest level in the hierarchy is a description of the services. This level is described with a Markov chain, which is not shown in the figure.

---

* SDT is a registered trademark of Telelogic AB, Malmö, Sweden.

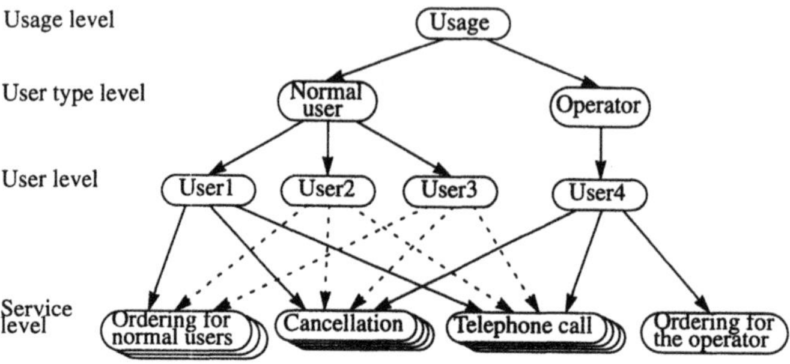

Figure 1 The hierarchical part of SPOTS's usage model.

The usage model is then complemented with a usage profile, which describes the usage frequency of different services and different events. As an example, probabilities are assigned to the possibility that the next event is generated by a normal user or by the operator. It is possible to make the probabilities dynamic, i.e. dependent on the actual state of different services in the system. It is, however, outside the scope of this presentation to elaborate on this issue any further. The details are presented in (Runeson, 1992 and 1995a) and (Wohlin, 1994).

The state hierarchy model is transformed into SDL, see (Runeson, 1995b). The model could have been transformed into other representations as long as they support state machines, but SDL was chosen due to the available tool support and that the system to be assessed was implemented in SDL. One advantage with transforming into a standardized technique is that it was not necessary to spend a lot of time developing a tool, which means that the focus could be on the quality issues.

5 USAGE GENERATION

The usage specification, i.e. usage model and usage profile, forms the basis for generating usage cases which are representative of the anticipated usage of the system.

The usage specification is now available in the tool environment and usage cases are generated by running through the hierarchy according to the assigned usage profile. The person generating the usage cases must act as an oracle at this stage and answer the usage specification with the responses expected of the system when it has been developed. The expected answers are obtained by using the requirements specification. This is illustrated in Figure 2.

The generation is made semi-automatically in the sense that the person generating the usage cases must act as an oracle, but the usage cases are logged automatically on a file. The log includes both the usage and the expected answers from the system, which are provided by the person generating the usage cases. Fault handling can also easily be incorporated, hence allowing for automatic execution of the generated usage cases and it is thus possible to log the failures that occur, i.e. deviations from the expected behaviour. The usage generation procedure is further described by Runeson (1995b) and Wesslén (1995).

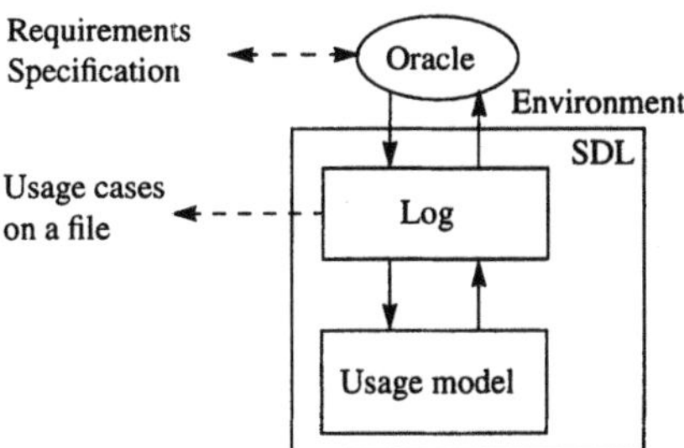

Figure 2 Generation of usage cases.

The usage cases are input to the dynamic analysis, which means that the analysis can be made from a usage perspective, hence supporting the objective of early estimation and prediction of software reliability.

6 DYNAMIC ANALYSIS FROM A USAGE PERSPECTIVE

6.1 Dynamic analysis

In the tool environment SDT there is a dynamic analyser which is called the Validator. The objective of the Validator is to support the specifier and the designer to avoid unwanted dynamic properties in the specified behaviour. The prototype of the Validator is described by Ek (1991). When the specified system interacts with the environment the analysis can be guided by using an SDL model of the interaction or a Message Sequence Chart, MSC (ITU-T, 1993), which describes the wanted exchange of signals between the system and the environment.

The Validator automatically detect some sorts of faults. The types of faults that the Validator can detect are, for example, MSC violation, deadlocks, more than one receiver of a signal, output faults. The analysis is made by using a tree expansion procedure and is halted when a fault is detected. When the analysis is halted a report is generated, which contains the type of fault, location of the fault and the number of passed states during the analysis. If the analysis of an MSC does not detect any faults an MSC Validated report is generated with the number of analysed states.

When using usage cases described as MSCs, the results can be used in reliability estimation and prediction, because the usage cases fulfil the assumptions of the reliability models and the Validator's results can be viewed as a measurement of the time between failures. If the Validator is guided by the SDL model of the usage specification the results can not be used in reliability models as the usage specification describes the whole usage and not a sample of it. Therefore, the usage cases are generated from the usage specification in SDL and stored as MSCs.

6.2 Implementation decisions

The Validator is guided by the usage cases described as Message Sequence Charts (MSCs). The result from the analysis of a usage case is a report containing the type of fault and the number of analysed states since the last report. The number of analysed states between failures are then a measure of the time between failures. The number of analysed states is then mapped into real time, see Section 6.3.

There are some different procedures that can be identified which have different effects of the results of the dynamic analysis. The following procedures have been identified and investigated:

- Same start point vs. continuation
  The same start point for all usage case leads to that a start period is included in every usage case. This leads to longer times between failures than during operation. If the starting point for the usage cases is redefined as the ending point of the previous case, the usage cases seem to be a very long usage case and the starting period is excluded. For the dynamic analyser which is used in this paper, the starting point is redefined by saving the system state when the previous usage case ends.
- Short vs. long usage cases
  If the usage case is long and erroneous, a long sequence is discharged or need to be regenerated. This problem is less if the usage cases are short. The result is not depending on how long the usage cases are because the cases follow on each other when the starting point is redefined.

Another problem which arises is what to do with the usage case when a fault is discovered. There are two possible solutions:

- Continue with the same usage case
  The result of this is that the usage case after the failure is depending on the usage case before and this contradicts the assumptions in statistical testing (or analysis). In statistical testing the times between failures are considered as independent, i.e. the usage cases are independent of each other. In these cases the reanalysis of the system with the same usage case serves as a regression analysis.
- Continue with a new usage case
  If the usage case which finds the failure is discharged and a new is used after the discovery the usage cases are independent and the result can be used in statistical testing. In this case there is no regression analysis made. It is obvious that in this case, it is better to have short usage cases, otherwise there is a risk that long sequences have to be thrown away.

When a fault is discovered there are two alternatives what to do with it. The alternatives depend on what kind of result the dynamic analysis aims at. The alternatives are:

- Correct the fault and proceed with the analysis
  If the faults are corrected as they are discovered the failure data can be used in reliability growth models, and in prediction of the reliability in the future.

- Leave the fault and proceed with the analysis
  If the faults are not corrected the failure data can only be used to estimate the current reliability, and the analysis must continue with a new usage case as the dynamic analyser can not continue after a discovered fault.
  The dynamic analysis in the case study has been performed as follows:
- Each new usage case is a continuation of the preceding.
- Short usage cases are analysed after each other.
- When a failure occurs, the fault is removed.
- The analysis continues with a new usage case after the fault is removed.

6.3 Results

The analysis from a usage perspective gives us a number of times between failures, where the time is measured in the number of executed process states in the SDL description until a failure occurs during analysis. The result from the analysis of the case study, SPOTS, is presented in Table 1.

Table 1 Failure data from dynamic analysis

Failure number	*1*	*2*	*3*	*4*
Number of states between failures	984	795	1802	>3394

The measure of number of states between failures are then mapped into real time with an expansion factor, see Wohlin (1992). For example, the expansion factor can be that 1000 states corresponds to 3 hours in operation. This is a hypothetical value for illustration purposes and a realistic value must be determined for each specific organisation and application. In Table 2, the times between failures are shown after mapping the failure data from dynamic failures into real time.

Table 2 Failure data in real time

Failure number	*1*	*2*	*3*	*4*
Time between failures (minutes)	177	143	324	>611

7 RELIABILITY ESTIMATION AND PREDICTION OF DYNAMIC FAILURES

The intention of the method in (Wohlin, 1992) was to use the dynamic failures in a reliability growth model that can estimate and predict the reliability of the software system for the dynamic failures that the tool environment could identify. The objective was to use the model described by Currit (1986). The number of failures which occurred in the dynamic analysis of the case study is however too small for using these types of models.

The failure data collected during the dynamic analysis can be used in a number of ways, for example:

- certify the reliability of the specification or design;
- estimate and predict the reliability for all failure types based on the expansion of dynamic failures to arbitrary failures;
- planning and controlling purposes, for example:
  - a decision basis whether or not to leave the specification or design phase;
  - planning of test resources based on the prediction of the reliability;
  - as an early prediction of the release time;
  - as a means to control the reliability of the system in a software project.

As it was impossible to use a software reliability growth model, a reliability demonstration chart, (Musa, 1987), is used instead. The purpose of this chart is to demonstrate that the software system meets the reliability objective with a given confidence. The assumptions made for this reliability demonstration chart are that the usage cases are derived from an operational profile and that no faults are removed. The first assumption is met, see Section 5, but the second is not met because the faults are corrected when they are discovered. If the faults are corrected the software's reliability will increase and the actual reliability is underestimated, i.e. the estimate is on the safe side. If corrections are made, it is proposed here to use the rejection line, see Figure 3, as a reset line, as after the correction it can actually be viewed as a new and improved software product and therefore it is not reasonable to reject it.

The objective of the reliability demonstration for the case study is that the mean time between dynamic failures are greater than 4.5 hours. The objective is used to normalize the failure times from the analysis. To calculate the rejection and acceptance lines in Figure 3 three other parameters are needed. The calculation of the lines is described by Musa (1987). The three parameters are as follows:

- The probability, α, to say that the objective is not met when it is, is 0.10, i.e. the probability to reject a product fulfilling the reliability requirement.
- The probability, β, to say that the objective is met when it is not, is 0.10, i.e. the probability to accept a product not fulfilling the reliability requirement.
- The discrimination ratio, γ, is 2. This value is recommended by Musa (1987).

The resulting reliability demonstration chart is shown in Figure 3. It can be seen that the objective is met during the analysis of the fourth usage case.

8 DYNAMIC FAILURES TO ARBITRARY FAILURES

The dynamic analyser can only find faults for which it is designed and these are only a subset of all failures that can occur during operation. To be able to estimate and predict the reliability during operation the dynamic failures must be mapped into arbitrary failures. The mapping of the dynamic failures into arbitrary failures are based on two assumptions:

- The set of failures found during dynamic analysis is a subset of all possible failures.
- The failures found during dynamic analysis are randomly spread among all failures, i.e. the ratio between the number of arbitrary failures and the number of dynamic failures during a certain period is an expansion factor called C.

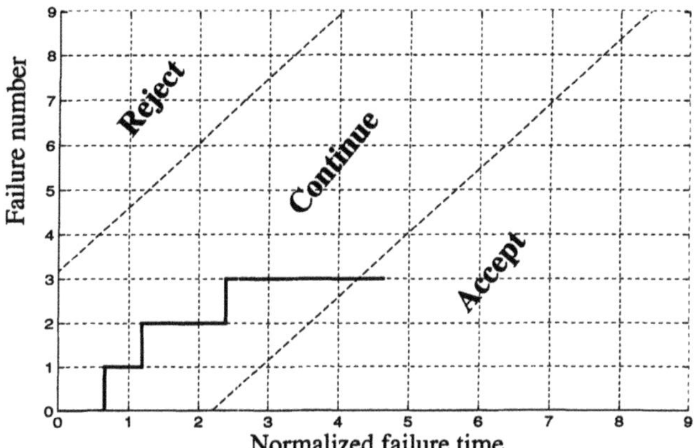

Figure 3 Reliability demonstration chart.

The expansion factor C is assumed to be known based on experience. The objective is to identify a realistic expansion factor between dynamic failures and arbitrary software failures. This is, however part of the future research and hence we use a hypothetical expansion factor here to illustrate how the information from the dynamic analysis can be used.

For the case study, the expansion factor is assigned the hypothetical value of 2.4, which means that for every dynamic failure there are 2.4 arbitrary failures in average during testing. The value of 2.4 is chosen by random to illustrate the method.

To map the dynamic failures into arbitrary failures, there are two things that must be done. First determine how many new failures that should occur in every interval from the dynamic analysis and the second is to place the new failures on the time scale.

The number of new failures in every interval is determined by the expansion factor C. If C is not an integer, the number of new failures to occur in every interval is determined from a two-point distribution with the possible values, trunc(C-1) and trunc(C), with the mean of C-1. If C is an integer, then C-1 new failures occur in each interval. If the last interval is open, i.e. the time between failures is not found, trunc(C/2) new failures are placed in this interval. A uniform distribution is used to place the new failures in the interval. This procedure is used to illustrate the method, but a realistic placement procedure must be determined as more experience is gained.

For the case study, the expansion factor of 2.4 implies that in every interval there should occur 2 new failure with the probability of 0.4 and 1 new failure with the probability of 0.6. In the last interval 1 failure is placed. The mapping to arbitrary failures for the case study is shown in Table 3.

Table 3 Arbitrary failures for the case study

Failure number	*1*	*2*	*3*	*4*	*5*	*6*	*7*	*8*
Time between failures (minutes)	100	22	55	87	56	22	302	237

9 RELIABILITY ESTIMATION AND PREDICTION

In Section 8, the dynamic failures were mapped into arbitrary failures. The arbitrary failures are failures that should have occurred if the system had been in test or operation. The arbitrary failure data can now be used in different ways, for example:

- estimate the reliability of the software when it is released for testing;
- estimate and predict the reliability when the software is in test and operation, which in particular includes the release time.

This information can be used to plan the test resources so that the software can be released at the right time with the required reliability.

From the failure data in Table 3, it is possible to estimate and predict the reliability in the case study at different points of time. The model used is presented in detail in (Currit, 1986), and it is a model to estimate the current reliability as well as to predict future reliability growth. The model is based on the following formula:

$$MTBF_k = A \times B^{k-1} \quad (1)$$

with $A = MTBF_1$ and k is the failure number. The variables A and B can be determined using linear regression to the log of the times between failures. The resulting graph is presented in Figure 4, although the number of data points is limited. From the graph it can be seen that the system in the case study has an estimated *MTBF* of 145 minutes at the release time. It is also possible to predict the *MTBF* for the system during the operational phase. The *MTBF* is predicted to be 175 minutes when the first failure have been discovered and corrected during operation. After the second failure is corrected the *MTBF* is predicted to be 210 minutes. These predictions can be made many steps ahead using the growth model when the variables A and B are determined.

The reliability requirement to release the software must be connected to the acceptance criterion of the design, i.e. the criterion based on the dynamic failures. Thus, the acceptance criterion can be derived from the overall reliability requirement and the two expansion factors described above.

10 CONCLUSIONS

The method presented can be used to estimate and predict software reliability from specification and design documents written in a well-defined high level description technique. It has been shown, through, a case study, that the usage-oriented approach to analysis is feasible and that valuable information can be extracted from the failure data obtained.

In particular, the data can be used for several purposes:

- acceptance of a particular specification or design;
- planning and controlling of the test phases, with particular emphasis on the system test when it is carried out as a statistical usage test;
- estimation and prediction of the reliability as the software enters the testing phase and also as a means for predicting when the reliability requirement is fulfilled.

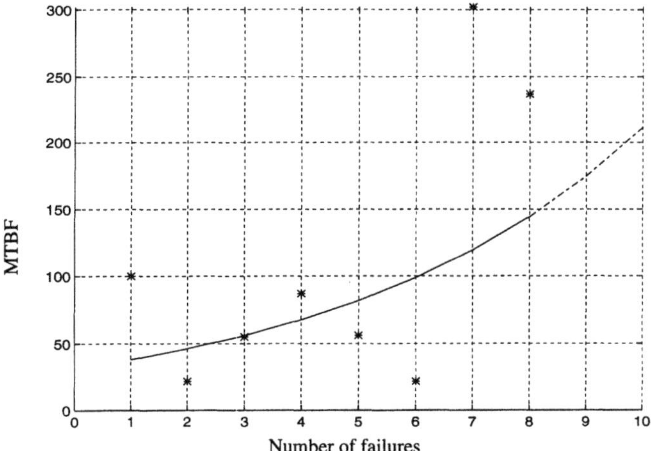

Figure 4 Reliability growth for the case study.

The method is based on two important expansion factors, which must be determined for each organization and application adopting this technique, namely time expansion from design states to real time and fault expansion from the dynamic failures that the tool can find to arbitrary software failures. The determination of these factors for the case study is part of the future work. The research objective is to take the case study through both the test phase and into operation to evaluate the proposed early software reliability estimation and prediction method.

The method ought to be a valuable tool in the future to stay in control of the software quality attributes, and to get early indications of the software reliability status. Thus, the method will help to achieve quality software.

11 REFERENCES

Belina, F., Hogrefe, D. and Sarma, A. (1991). *SDL with Applications from Protocol Specifications*. Prentice-Hall, London.

Currit, P.A., Dyer, M. and Mills, H.D. (1986) Certifying the Reliability of Software. *IEEE Transactions on Software Engineering*, **11(12)**, pp. 1411-23.

Ek, A. and Ellsberger, J., (1991) A Dynamic Analysis Tool for SDL, in *SDL '91: Evolving Methods* (ed. R. Reed and O. Færgemand), Elsevier Science Publisher B V (North Holland), pp. 119-34.

ITU-T Recommendation (1988) *Z.100: Specification and Description Language, SDL*, Blue book, Volume X.1.

ITU-T Recommendation (1993) *Z.120: Message Sequence Chart (MSC)*.

Mills, H. D., Dyer, M. and Linger, R. C. (1987) Cleanroom Software Engineering. *IEEE Software*, **September**, pp. 19–24.

Musa, J. D., Iannino, A. and Okumoto, K. (1987). *Software Reliability, Measurement, Prediction and Application.* McGraw-Hill Int.

Musa, J. D. and Everett, W. W. (1990) Software Reliability Engineering: Technology for the 1990s. *IEEE Software*, **November**, pp. 36-43.

Musa, J. D. (1993) Operational Profiles in Software Reliability Engineering. *IEEE Software*, **March**, pp. 14-32.

Runeson, P. and Wohlin, C. (1992) Usage Modelling: The Basis for Statistical Quality Control. Proceedings 10th Annual Software Reliability Symposium, Denver, Colorado, USA, pp. 77–84.

Runeson, P. and Wohlin, C. (1995a) Statistical Usage Testing for Software Reliability Control. *Informatica*, **19(2)**, pp. 195-207.

Runeson P., Wesslén A., Brantestam J. and Sjöstedt S. (1995b) Statistical Usage Testing Using SDL", Accepted for publication, to appear in Proceedings SDL Forum, Oslo, Norway, September 1995.

Wesslén, A. and Wohlin, C. (1995) Modelling and Generation of Software Usage", Accepted for publication, to appear in Proceedings International Conference on Software Quality, Austin, Texas, USA, October 1995.

Wohlin C. and Runeson P. (1992) A Method Proposal for Early Software Reliability Estimations", Proceedings 3rd International Symposium on Software Reliability Engineering, Raleigh, North Carolina, USA, pp. 156-163.

Wohlin, C., and Runeson, P. (1994) Certification of Software Components. *IEEE Transactions on Software Engineering*, **20(6)**, pp. 494-499.

Yeh C., Reneby L., Lennselius B. and Sixtensson A. (1989) An Educational Development System Employing SDL Design and Automatic Code Generation, Proceedings SDL Forum, Lisboa, Portugal.

12 BIOGRAPHY

Wesslén, Anders - Mr. Wesslén is Ph.d. student at the department of Communication Systems, Lund University, Lund, Sweden and he has an MSc in Computer Science and Engineering from the same university. His research is focused on requirements engineering, statistical usage testing and to quantify software quality attributes early in the development process.

Wohlin, Claes - Dr. Wohlin is associate professor at the department of Communication Systems, Lund University, Lund, Sweden. He has five years of industrial experience from software projects with object orientation techniques, quality assurance, simulation techniques, test methods, and prediction of system and organizational qualities. Claes Wohlin is currently responsible for the education and research in the area of software engineering in telecommunications at the department. His research interest includes methods and modelling techniques to achieve quality software, statistical usage testing and process improvement. Dr. Wohlin has published more than 35 papers in technical journals and at international conferences.

PART SIX

Quality Measurement

16

Software Quality Classification Model based on McCabe's Complexity Measure

Ryouei Takahashi
NTT Information and Communication Systems Laboratories
Yokosuka - shi, Kanagawa, 238 - 03, Japan
(TEL)+81 - 468 - 59 - 8312 (FAX)+81 - 468 - 59 - 3726

Abstract

A software quality classification model based on McCabe's complexity measure is investigated. It is experimentally shown using regression and discriminant analyses that program fault density (number of faults per 1000 source lines of code) depends on the complexity of the functional unit rather than on that of each of the modules. To identify the best model, stepwise selection method improved by AIC (Akaike Information Criterion) is applied to regression and discriminant analyses. A functional unit is the partitioning unit of the software function and consists of several modules that are combined with data that is commonly referred to or updated. This partitioning is done in the early phases of the software life cycle and experiments show that interfaced complexity among functional units is associated with software faults. The concept of an "extented cyclomatic number (S_1')" - an extension of McCabe's design complexity measure S_1 from an inner - functional - unit control structure to a between - functional - unit control structure - is proposed taking this complexity tendency into consideration and is experimentally studied. It is well known that S_1 is equal to the number of predicates + 1. In the metric S_1', the nesting depth of predicate nodes for invoking module path selection is taken into consideration. The number of predicates whose scope is confined to a functional unit can be separately counted from the predicates whose scope extends to different functional units. This software quality classification model with the extended cyclomatic number enables project managers to control software quality.

Keywords

Software quality classification, McCabe's complexity measure, regression analysis, discriminant analysis, AIC

1 Introduction

The relationship between software quality and complexity metrics has been researched for many years [Li, Cheung, 1987]. These experiments have shown that complexity metrics are interrelated with each other and several complexity metrics are related to software quality to some degree. Taking the relationship between complexity metrics and software quality into consideration, various software quality prediction models have been developed [Takahashi, Wakayama, 1994; Munson, Khoshgoftaar,

1992; Rodriguez, Tsai, 1987].

Complexity metrics, such as the cyclomatic number for measuring the complexity of the software control structure [McCabe, 1976], are used as indicators for program modularization, revising specifications, and test coverage. In addition, they have been used in software quality prediction models, whose purposes include predicting fault numbers through multivariate regression analysis and identification of error-prone modules based on discriminant analysis. Those models, however, are based on metric data and quality data contained in the program modules themselves and do not sufficiently take the functional relations between modules into consideration. Here, a module is defined as the lowest level unit of hierarchical functional partitioning [De Marco, 1986] and corresponds to a function in C-coding [Richie, Kernighan, 1978], and module's size was experientially shown to be of the order of $10^1 \sim 10^2$ SLOC (source lines of code).

In our experiments, on the contrary, the relationship between complexity metrics and software quality were investigated using multivariate regression analysis. The results show that program fault density (fault number per 1000 SLOC), which we use as a measure of software quality, does not depend on the complexity density (ex. cyclomatic number per 1000 SLOC) of every fault module but on the complexity of the functional unit with modules functionally related to the fault module. In other words, variance analysis shows that program fault density is mostly characterized by functional units. A functional unit is a program unit partitioned in the early phases of software development from the standpoints of data structure or process and corresponds to a certain hierarchical level of partitioning software. Each unit consists of several modules (coincident with functions in C-coding) and functional unit's size is experientially shown to be of the order of 10^3 SLOC, which is suitable for a programmer to design, to code and to test. Since a software quality control unit should be a manageable comprehensible evaluation unit, it generally accords with a functional unit.

The next phase of our investigation was characterization of functional units with complexity metrics, using the techniques of discriminant analysis with stepwise selection method improved by AIC (Akaike Information Criterion) estimates [Takahashi, Wakayama, 1994; Akaike, 1974], but unfortunately the ratio of correct classification-ratio was not very high. In the work reported here, we used 12 complexity metrics obtained from the viewpoints of source lines of code [Yu, Smith, Huang, 1991], the cyclomatic number that measures the number of predicates [McCabe, 1976], the fan-in and fan-out that measures the complexity of information flow [Henry, Kafura, 1981], the number of external variables [Halstead, 1977], and comment lines [Woodfield, Dunsmore, Shen, 1981]. The main reason the missclassification ratio was high in the previous work is probably that these 12 complexity metrics could not sufficiently represent the functional relationship among the modules that compose a functional unit. Agresti has measured the interfaced complexity among modules by the the "context-coupling" metric [Agresti, Evanco, 1992] and "relative complexity" metric [Card, Agresti, 1988]. The former metric counts the number of data commonly used among modules to measure the interconnection of modules and the latter metric counts the number of invoking modules and I/O variables. But data obtained by using these metrics represent interfaced complexity from every module's viewpoint and can't sufficiently represent the complexity of a functional unit. On the other hand, McCabe proposed integration complexity measure S_1 [McCabe, Butler, 1989] to measure complexity of an inner-functional-unit control structure in the design phase and to count the number of predicates that select the invoking module path. But our experiments using regression analysis have shown that the correlation coefficient between S_1 and program fault density is not so high (R^2 =0.10) and only the interfaced complexity among modules in a functional unit is not thorough enough to represent the complexity tendency of a functional unit.

To solve this problem, the "extended cyclomatic number" S_1' is proposed, considering the relationship among functional units, and the validation of this metric is empirically and statistically studied. The proposed cyclomatic number extends the concepts of integration complexity measure S_1. The applied area of McCabe's complexity metric is extended from an inner-functional-unit control structure to a between-functional-unit control structure. A functional unit control structure is represented by a gragh. In the graph, S_1 is defined as number of edges - number of nodes + 2, where nodes correspond to invoking functions or invoking predicates and edges correspond to executing sequences of nodes. It is well known that S_1 is equal to the number of predicates + 1. In the metric S_1', nesting depth of predicate nodes for invoking module path selection is taken into consideration. In it, the number of predicates whose scope is confined to a functional unit can be separately counted from those predicates whose scope extends to different functional units. Consequently, the interfaced complexity among different functional units can be obtained using the metric S_1' and the accuracy of software quality evaluation model can be increasingly improved. In fact, our experiments on regression analysis applied to a small scale program (about 10 thousand of SLOC) have shown that the correlation coefficient between S_1' and the program fault density is very high (R^2 =0.70). This software quality classification model with the extended cyclomatic number that shows the interfaced complexity among functional units enables project managers to control software quality.

2 The extended cyclomatic number

2.1 The applied area of the metric S_1'

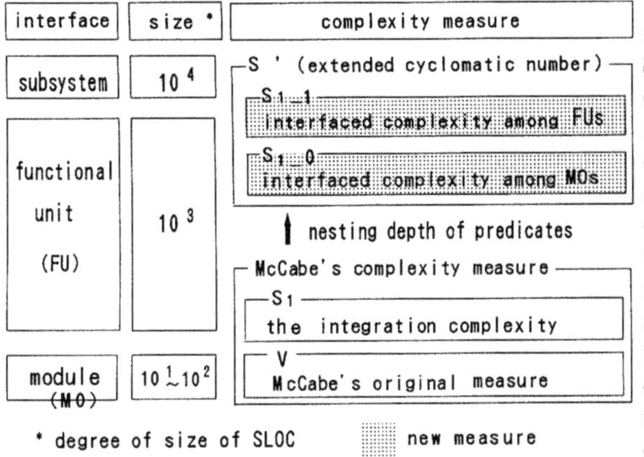

Fig. 1. Background

The applied area of the extended cyclomatic number S_1' is shown in Fig. 1. S_1' is expressed as the thin hatched areas. To measure interfaced complexity among software quality evaluation units of a certain hierarchical level partitioning, complexity metrics are divided into three classes: an inner-module level complexity metric (to measure complexities of an inner module whose size is of the order of $10^1 \sim 10^2$ SLOC and McCabes's original complexiity metric is part of this class), an inner-functional-unit level complexity metric (to measure complexities of an inner functional unit that has the size of the order of 10^3 SLOC, where a functional unit consists of several modules and McCabe's design complexity measure S_1 belongs to this class), and an inner-subsystem level complexity metric (to measure complexities of an inner subsystem that has the size of the order of 10^4 SLOC, where a subsystem consists of several functional units). The metric S_1' is an inner-subsystem level metric that measures interfaced complexity among functional units. In S_1', nesting depth of predicate nodes for invoking module path selection is taken into consideration. This metric extends the concepts of integration complexity measure S_1 proposed by McCabe. The purpose of S_1 is to measure the complexity of an inner functional unit control structure and it is well known that it is equal to the number of predicates + 1. With S_1, inner logic of every module is not taken into consideration; a path that does not influence the interrelationship between modules is eliminated. The metric S_1 itself is an extended metric of McCabe's original cyclomatic number V from an inner-module-control structure to a between-module-control structure. In this reseach, the applied area of McCabe's complexity metric is extended from an inner-functional-unit control structure to a between-functional-unit control structure. In the metric S_1', the number of predicates whose scope is confined to a functional unit can be separately counted from those predicates whose scope extends to different functional units. A software control unit corresponds to a software functional unit, and a software functional unit corresponds to a subtree of a hierarchical module control structure [De Marco,1986]. We call this tree call & called module tree. The partitioning function correponds to a call & called module tree decomposed into several subtrees.

2.2 Concepts of the metric S_1'

(1) Re-definition of integration complexity metric S_1 (G)

Before we describe the concepts of S_1', the concepts of McCabe's design complexity measure S_1 are reviewed. The metric S_1 is an extension of McCabe's original complexity metric from an inner-module control structure to a between-module (an inner-functional-unit) control structure. A module is assumed to correspond to a function in C coding. The metric S_1 (G) measures the complexity of a functional unit graph G. A node in G not only corresponds to a function in C-coding but also to a predicate for invoking function path selection. An edge in G corresponds to an invoking function or invoking function path selection. S_1 (G) does not reflect the inner logic complexity of every function. Hence, S_1 (G) is defined as

$S_1(G) = e_1 - n_1 + 2$,

where e_1 is the number of edges and n_1 is the number of nodes in graph G. On the other hand, the purpose of the original McCabe's complexity metric [McCabe, 1976] V(F) is to measure the complexity of the inner-logic of every function F, and V(F) is defined as e-n+2, where e is the numer of edges and n is the number of nodes in graph F. In graph F, a node corresponds to an instruction statement or a decision statement in C-coding, and an edge signifies the execution of sequences of nodes. It is well known that V(F) is equal to the number of predicates plus one in structured programming, and is equal to the number of regions (Euler's formula in a connected plane graph). The

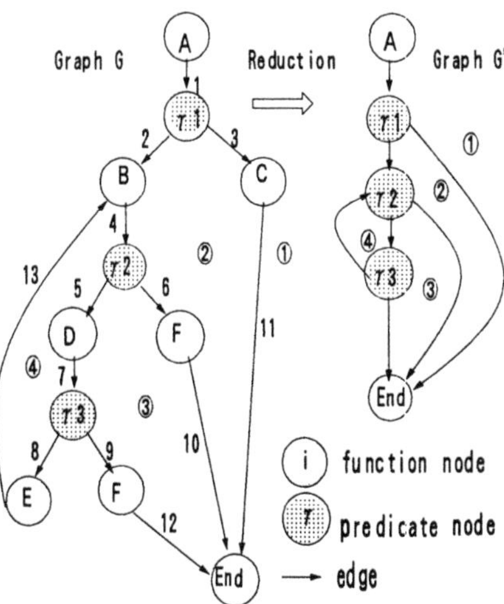

Fig. 2. McCabe's integration measure $S_1(G)$.

graph theory is also applicapable to a between-module control structure S_1, so the metric S_1 is considered to be an extention of McCabe's original complexity metric V and it is proved that $S_1(G)$ equals the number of predicates (plus 1) for invoking function path selection.

[An application of S_1]

An example of $S_1(G)$ is illustrated in Fig. 2. This graph consists of six functions denoted A, B, C, D, E, F, an end node, and 3 predicates, $\gamma 1$, $\gamma 2$, and $\gamma 3$. A invokes C when $\gamma 1$ is satisfied, and invokes B when $\gamma 1$ is not satisfied. B invokes F when $\gamma 2$ is satisfied, and invokes D when $\gamma 2$ is not satisfied. D invokes F when $\gamma 3$ is satisfied, and invokes E when $\gamma 3$ is not satisfied. E invokes B recursively. Then $S_1(G)$ = number of edges - number of nodes + 2 = 13 - 11 + 2 = 4 and is equal to the number of predicates (3) + 1. Furthermore, as you can see in the graph, $S_1(G)$ is equal to the number of regions (①~④). You can also see that S_1 in a reduced graph G' is consistent with S_1 in the original graph G, where a reduced graph G' includes predicate nodes but not function nodes.

(2) Defnition of the extended cyclomatic number S_1'

The extended cyclomatic number S_1' extends the concepts of integration complexity measure S_1, considering the effects of interfaced complexity among functional units. The metric S_1'(G) classifies predicate nodes into S_1_0(G) and S_1_1(G), taking the nesting depth (i.e. scope) of predicate nodes for invoking module path selection into consideration [Howatt, Baker, 1989]. The number of predicates whose scope is confined to a functional unit can be separately counted from those predicates whose scope extends to different functional units. The scope of predicate node X includes a set of functions whose executions are controlled by decision statement X, where nesting of predicate nodes is taken into consideration. When a predicate node Y is directly or indirectly controlled by predicate node X, not only functions whose executions are directly controlled by predicate X, but also functions whose executions are controlled by predicate Y are included in the scope of X.

[Defnition of S_1']

The metric S_1' is divided into two metrics.

(A) S_1_0(G): The extended cyclomatic number of inner quality control unit subtrees ••• This class consists of predicates in G whose scope is confined to functions defined in a functional unit G. S_1_0(G) is the number of predicates (plus + 1) belonging to this class.

(B) S_1_1(G): The extended cyclomatic number among different quality control unit subtrees ••• This class consists of two sets of predicates. The first set consists of predicates in G whose scope includes functions defined in another functional unit G'. The second set consists of predicates in another functional unit G' whose scope includes functions defined in G itsef. S_1 _1(G) is the summation of the number of predicates that belong to the first set and the number of predicates that belong to the second set.

S_1 _0(G) measures the complexity of an inner-functional-unit control structure and S_1 _1(G) measures the complexity of a between-functional-unit (i.e. an inner-subsystem-unit) control structure.

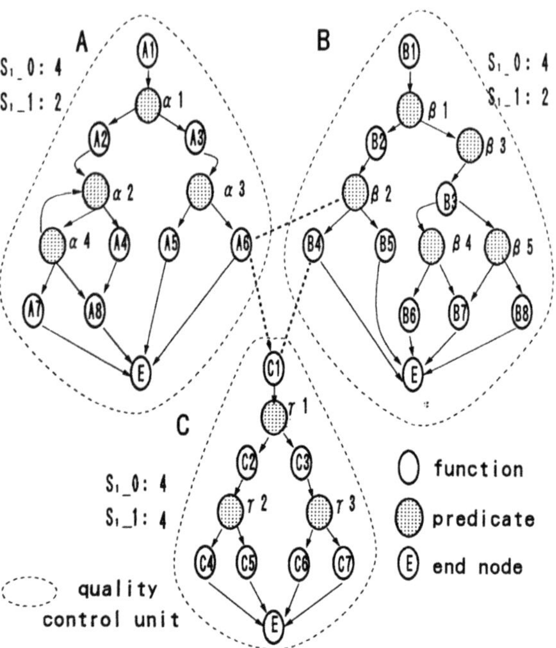

Fig. 3. An application of S_1'.

[An application of S_1']

An example of S_1'(S_1 _0,S_1 _1) is shown in Fig. 3, where the graph indicates information flow among functions including predicates for invoking function path selection, and → denotes the invoking function or invoking predicate in an inner-quality-control subtree, and ···> denotes the invoking function among different quality control-unit subtrees. This example has three software quality control units, A, B, and C. In the graph the end node of every quality control unit is also shown. Subtree A is connected with subtree C by arc A6 -> C1, where A6 and C1 are functions. Subtree B is connected with subtree A by arc $\beta 2$ -> A6 and is also connected with subtree C by arc B4 -> C1, where $\beta 2$ is an executing condition (predicate) of function A6 and B4 is a function. From subtree C's standpoint, as the scope of three predicates $\gamma 1$, $\gamma 2$, $\gamma 3$ includes only functions C2, C3, ••• C7 defined in C itself, it follows that S_1 _0(C)=3+1=4. In addition, as the execution of function C1 is controlled by predicates $\alpha 1$, $\alpha 3$, $\beta 1$, and $\beta 2$ in functional units A, and B, it follows that S_1 _1(C)=4. Similarly from subtree A's standpoint, predicates $\alpha 2$ and $\alpha 4$ ($\alpha 4$ has three branches so the number of predicates of $\alpha 4$ is 2) only control execution of functions A4, A7, and A8 defined in A itself, so it follows that S_1 _0(A)=3+1=4. Since the scope of predicates $\alpha 1$, $\alpha 3$ not only includes functions defined in A itself but also includes function C1 defined in functional unit C, it follows that S_1 _1(A)=2. Similarly, S_1 _0(B),S_1 _1(B) are counted. The calculation is summarized as follows:

- S_1_0(A) = 4 = $\{\alpha 2, \alpha 4^*\}$ + 1, S_1_1(A) = 2 = $\{\alpha 1, \alpha 3\}$
- S_1_0(B) = 4 = $\{\beta 3, \beta 4, \beta 5\}$ + 1, S_1_1(B) = 2 = $\{\beta 1, \beta 2\}$
- S_1_0(C) = 4 = $\{\gamma 1, \gamma 2, \gamma 3\}$ + 1, S_1_1(C) = 4 = $\{\alpha 1, \alpha 3, \beta 1, \beta 2\}$.

Here { } is a set of predicates, $\alpha 4$ * has 3 branches and is counted as two predicates, $S_1\_0(X)$ = number of elements of set X plus one, and $S_1\_1(X)$ = number of elements of a set X.

3 A case study

3.1 Sample spaces

Metric and quality data were obtained from the DBMS (Database Management System) maintenance program developed by NTT Information and Communication Systems Laboratories. This program is a subsystem of the DBMS. Our program is written in C and consists of 10 KDSI (thousands of delivered source instructions). Its function is to change DB attributes and directories during online operations. It consists of seven excluded software quality control units. Each quality control unit consists of several routines, and a routine coincides with a compliled file designated by *.c in UNIX. Each file consists of several functions in C coding. Overall, the DB maintenance program consists of 50 routines, and 144 functions. The sample spaces of the seven units are scribed as follows: the 1st group (the initializer/terminator is designated by● in Figures 4, 5, and 7) and consists of 7 routines, 21 functions, 1.4 KDSI (shortened to (●,7,21,1.4) hereafter); the 2nd group (the SQL analyzer) consists of (○,9,39,2.8); the 3rd group (the garbage collector), (×,7,3,0.5); the 4th (the data transporter) of (△,42,10,2.4); the 5th (the SQL parameter generator), (□,19,8,1.6); the 6th (the SG parameter reformalizer), (■,6,6,0.6); and the 7th (common modules), (▲,10,7,0.9).

3.2 Complexity metrics

In this investigation, we used 12 complexity metrics obtained from the viewpoints of source lines of code [Yu, Smith, Huang, 1991], the cyclomatic number that counts the number of predicates [McCabe, 1976], the fan-in and fan-out that measures the complexity of information flow [Henry, Kafura, 1981], the number of external and static variables [Halstead, 1977], and comment lines [Woodfield, Dunsmore, Shen, 1981]. A summary is given in Table 1.

Table 1. Summary of complexity metrics used in the case study

Complexity metrics class and its subclasses		abbreviation: Defnition in C [8]
McCabe's complexity measure		CC0: cyclomatic number without case
		CC1: cyclomatic number with case
fan-in & fan-out	subsystem level evaluation (includes debug-macro & common module)	FA1: (call to * call from)^2
		FA2: (to num * from num)^2
	subsystem level evaluation (excludes debug-macro & common module)	FA3: (call to * call from)^2
		FA4: (to num * from num)^2
	functional level evaluation (excludes debug-macro & common module)	FA5: (call to * call from)^2
		FA6: (to num * from num)^2
soure lines of code		EXEC: instruction lines + declare lines + SQL lines
		DEB: debug lines
global variables		REF: occurrence of external and static variables
comment lines		COM: comment lines + blank lines

[The metric "fan - in & fan - out"]

The metric "fan - in & fan - out" investigated in this study is not consistent with what Henry & Kafura originally proposed. In this paper, "fan - in & fan - out" is confined to the local flow [Henry, Kafura, 1981] of function invoking, and is classified into 6 patterns by the combination of three conditions: whether common modules or debug macros are excluded or not in every quality control unit, whether invoking functions among different functional units are taken into consideration or not, and whether total occurrences of invoking functions are taken into consideration or not. In the table,

- call to = number of distinct functions that call to other functions
- call from = number of distinct functions that are called from other functions
- to num = total numbers of function calling
- from num = total numbers of function called

3.3 Relationship between program fault density and module complexity density

The software control units were the 50 routines mentioned in section 3.1. Experiments show that correlation coefficients between fault number and software complexity metrics are high, and the complexity metrics are interrelated [Takahashi, Wakayama, 1994]. Faults are detected and corrected after the implementation phase of the software cycle. However, a relationship between program fault density (fault number per 1000 source lines of code) and program module complexity density was not found. As a typical example, the cyclomatic number without case (CC0) per 1000 source lines of code versus program fault density is shown in Fig. 4. The determinant coefficients R^2 of the model was low (=0.07).

3.4 Analysis of program fault density variance from the program function viewpoint

To identify the most suitable regression model, stepwise selection method [SPSS, 1991] improved by AIC (Akaike Information Criterion) [Akaike, 1974] was applied to

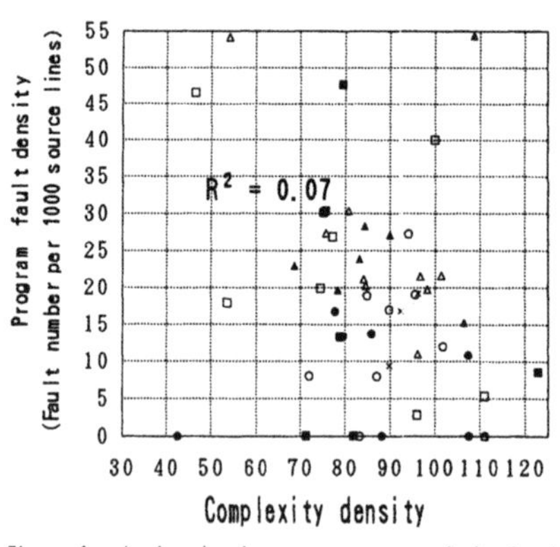

Fig. 4. Complexity density versus program fault density.

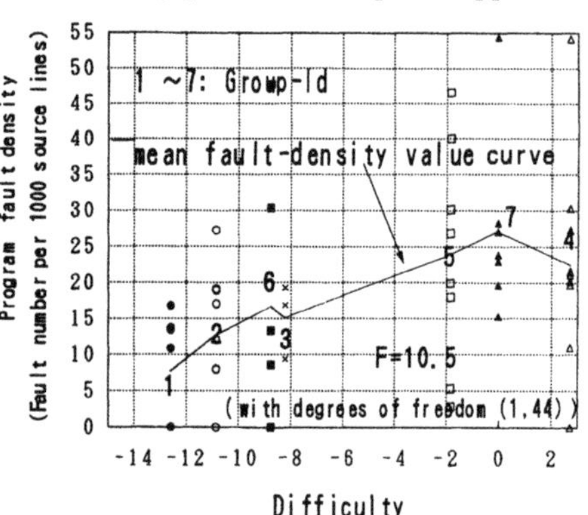

Fig. 5. Analysis of fault density variance.

select the main complexity - metric factors (the procedure to select complexity - metric factors is based on AIC estimates and details are explained in section 3.5, because the idea is the same between regression analysis and discriminant analysis). The AIC procedures are based on the maximum likelihood estimation method and the least number of complexity metrics. The results of the minimum AIC estimated model were as follows: R^2 was 0.44. The F - test value was 10.52 for the "software function", 7.04 for the "distinct functions number density", 6.28 for the "comment lines (COM) density", 3.12 for the "global variables (REF) density", and 2.56 for the "cyclomatic number with case's (CC1) density". The item "software function" has the highest F - test value, indicating it is the primary factor affecting program density. These results mean we need a complexity metric that can distinguish software functional units. The results of regression analysis is illustrated in Fig. 5. The y - axis is for program fault density. The x - axis represents software quality control unit "difficulty", whose values are item scores obtained from the minimum AIC regression model. The item score of "software function" agrees with a partial regression coefficient. If the item score increases, program fault density tends to increase, which is why we call this item "difficulty". Each sample item score is equal if the sample belongs to the same functional unit. The set (1,2,••,7) in the Fig. 5 signifies the functional units, and each functional unit's mean fault density value curve is also presented.

3.5 Discriminant analysis to classify software functional units by complexity metrics

The most suitable software quality classification model can be obtained by the stepwise selection method [SPSS, 1991] with AIC estimates [Akaike, 1974]. This method, which takes the number of complexity metrics into consideration [Takahashi & Wakayama, 1994], is thought to be an improvement on the Wilks Λ criteria [Rao, 1973]. The relationship between the AIC estimate and Wilks Λ is discussed in detail in [Takahashi, Wakayama, 1994]. The procedure begins with the selection of the metric with which the lowest AIC estimated discriminant model M1 can be constructed. Then, the second metric is selected among the residual metrics, and by adding it to M1, the lowest AIC estimated model M2 can be obtained. The AIC estimate of M2 is smaller than that of M1. This procedure of locating the next added metric continues until metrics can no longer be added or until the adding of any residual metric to the last model AIC estimate no longer gets smaller. The most suitable discriminant model obtained in this study was with an F - test value of 7.42, an AIC estimate of 364, and a ratio of correct classification of 0.16=(23/144), where 23 F - test (AIC estimate) trials were performed with the stepwise selection method, and the last selected complexity metric was "fan - in & fan - out (FA1)". The complexity metrics are interrelated (multicollineality), so we could not establish the unique contribution of every metric to the discriminant model. As a consequence, only the "fan - in & fan - out number FA1" was selected among the 12 complexity metrics. The main reason the missclassification ratio was high is probably that these 12 complexity metrics can not sufficiently represent the functional relationship among the modules that compose a functional unit. In an attempt to solve this problem, we applied our extended cyclomatic number and the validity of the metric was experimentally verified as described in section 3.6. The result shown in this section, i.e., that functional units can be classified by the metric "fan - in -

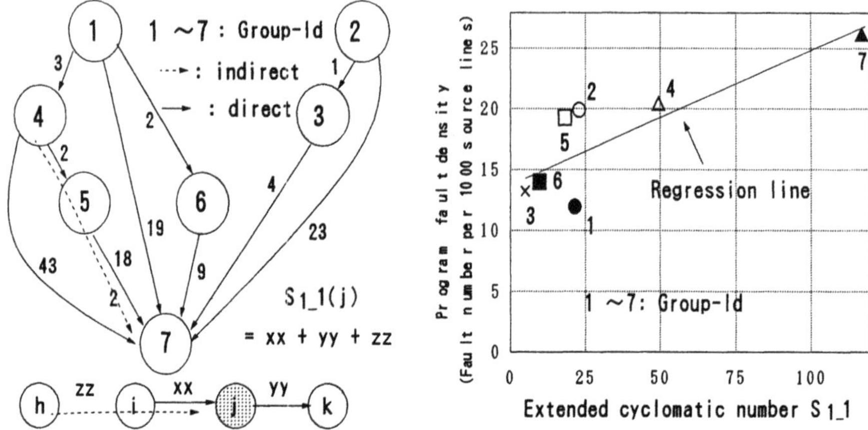

Fig. 6. S_1_1 in the case study. Fig. 7. S_1-1 versus program fault density

& fan-out" that measures the interfaced complexity among modules is consistent to the result represented in section 3.6, i.e., that program fault density has a high correlation with extended cyclomatic number S_1 _1 that measures the interfaced complexity among functional units, although the classification ratio of the most suitable discriminant model is not very high and the evaluation level of software quality is different between the model in this section and that in section 3.6.

3.6 Extended cyclomatic number S_1' and program fault density

The correlation between McCabe's integration complexity metric S_1 and program fault density (fault number per 1000 SLOC, where fault number is the summation of each module's fault number and SLOC is the summation of each module's SLOC) is not very high (R^2 of the model was 0.10). We assume that program fault density mainly stems from interfaced complexity among functional units. The measurement of interfaced complexity among seven software quality control units is summarized in Fig. 6, where ○s represent quality control units (QUs), and values on the arrows denote the degree of the effects of the predicates (i.e. number of predicates) in a certain QU whose scope occupies functions defined in another QU. In this sample, not only predicates that give effects directly (denoted by ⟶, which indicates interfaced complexity between two QUs) but also predicates that give effects indirectly (denoted by -->, which indicates interfaced complexity among more than two QUs) are taken into consideration. S_1 _1(X) is the summation of values on input arrows to a certain quality control unit X and values on output arrows from X and can be thought as an indicator of the total interfaced complexity of X. Through Fig. 6, it has been seen that group-id 7 (a group is a functional unit) has the highest interfaced complexity among the seven functional units. The relationship between program fault density and the metric S_1 _1 is shown in Fig. 7. The determinant coefficient R^2 between program fault density and S_1 _1 was very high (R^2 =0.70), indicating that the more accurate software quality classification model could be obtained by taking nesting of predicates nodes into consideration. But, the correlation coefficient between program fault density and S_1 _0 was low-

(R^2 =0.0006) in this case study.

4. Conclusion

The extended cyclomatic metric S_1' for measuring the interfaced complexity among functional units has been proposed for the purpose of evaluating software quality (program fault density) and its validity has been experimentally verified. S_1' is an extention of McCabe's integration metric S_1 from an inner-functional control structure to a between-functional control structure, taking the scope (nesting depth) of predicate nodes among functional units into consideration. The metric S_1' was applied to a DBMS maintenance program developed by NTT whose volume is about 10 thousand source lines of code (KSLOC) written in C language. The results of our experiments are summerized as follows:
(1) The correlation coefficient between program fault density and cyclomatic complexity density is not very high, where the software evaluation unit is a module, (i.e., the function or routine with the size of the order of $10^1 \sim 10^2$ SLOC) which is the lowest level of hierarchical partitioning of software functions.
(2) It has been shown using the minimum AIC estimate regression model that the "software function" is the main factor that causes program faults, where "software function" is classified into several categories coincident to the above functional units. A functional unit consists of several interrelated modules and has the size of the order of 10^3 SLOC and is a certain hierarchical-level partitioning unit of the software function.
(3) Even with the minimum AIC estimate discriminant model, the "software function" could not be characterized by complexity metrics that measure module-level complexity.
(4) Although classification ratio of the most suitable discriminant model is not very high, the metric "fan-in & fan-out", which measures the interfaced complexity among modules, is the most effective factor for the discrimination of the "software function".
(5) The correlation between McCabe's integration complexity metric S_1 and program fault density is not very high.
(6) The determinant coefficient R^2 between program fault density and our extended cyclomatic number S_1_1 was very high (R^2 =0.70), indicating that a more accurate software quality classification model can be obtained by taking the scope of predicates nodes among functional units into consideration.

To construct a more accurate software quality classification model, it is necesarry to extend sample spaces in order to confirm model validity, to investigate the conditional variable complexity (i.e., these variables are used for invoking function paths [McClure, 1978]), and to evaluate stepwise selection method to reach the minimum AIC estimate discriminant model. All of these remain for future work.

References

[1] Agresti, W. W. and Evanco, W. M. (1992) Projecting software defects from analyz-

ing Ada designs," IEEE Trans. Software Eng., 18, 11, 988 - 97.
[2] Akaike, H. (1974) A new look at the statistical identification: IEEE Trans. Automatic Conrol, AC - 19, 6, 716 - 23.
[3] Card, D. N. and Agresti, W. W. (1988) Measuring software design complexity: The Journals of Systems and Software, 8, 185 - 97.
[4] De Marco, T. (1986) Structured analysis and system specification (translated into Japanese by Takanashi,T. and Kuroda,J., and published by Nikkei BP Inc.).
[5] Halstead, M. H. (1977) Elements of Software Science: Elsevier North - Holland,Inc.
[6] Henry, S. and Kafura, D. (1981) Software strucreture metrics based on information flow: IEEE Trans. Software Eng.,SE - 7,5, 510 - 18.
[7] Howatt, J. W. and Baker, A. L. (1989) Rigorous defnition and analysis of program complexity measures: An example using nesting: The Journal of Systems and Software,10,139 - 50.
[8] Li, H. F. and Cheung, W. K. (1987) An empirical study of software metrics: IEEE Trans. Sottware Eng., SE - 13, 6, 697 - 708.
[9] McCabe, T. J. (1976) A complexity measure: IEEE Trans. Software Eng.,SE - 2, 4, 308 - 20.
[10] McCabe, T. J. and Butler, C. W. (1989) Design complexity measurement and Testing: Communications of ACM, 32, 12, 1415 - 25.
[11] McClure,C.L.(1978) A model for complexity alnalysis: 3th ICSE, 149 - 57.
[11] Munson, J. C. and Khoshgoftaar, T. M. (1992) The detection of fault - prone programs: IEEE Trans. Software. Eng., 18, 5, 423 - 33.
[12] Rao, C. R. (1973) Linear statistical inference and its applications 2nd edition: John Wiley & Sons, 244 - 47 and 556 - 7.
[13] Richie, D. M., Johnson, S. C., Lesk, M. E. and Kernighan, B. W. (1978) The C programming language: The Bell System Technical Journal, 57, 6, 1991 - 2019.
[14] Rodriguez, V. and Tsai, W. T. (1987) A tool for discriminant analysis and classification of software metrics: Information and Software technogology, 29, 3, 137 - 150
[15] SPSS Inc. (1991) SPSS Statistical Algorithms 2nd Edition: 76 - 80 and 230 - 32.
[16] Takahashi, R. and Wakayama, H. (1995) Discriminative efficiency methodology for validating software quality classification models: Systems and Computers in Japan, 26 , 5, 1 - 18.
[17] Woodfield, S. N., Dunsmore, H. E. and Shen, V. Y. (1981) The effects of modularization and comments on program comprehension: 5th ICSE, 215 - 23.
[18] Yu, W. D., and Smith, D. P. and Huang, S. T. (1991) Software Productivity measurements: COMPSAC'91, 558 - 64.

Ryouei Takahashi
received his B.S. and M.S. degrees in 1974 and 1976, respectively, from Waseda University, and then joined NTT. He has been engaged in DIPS real - time software development of maintenance systems, and software quality and productivity evaluation system. His research interests are in software complexity metrics, quality, and statistical modeling. Currently, he is a senior research engineer at NTT Information and Communication Systems Laboratories. He is a member of the I.E.I.C.E and Information Processing Society of Japan.

17

Combining Knowledge and Metrics to Control Software Quality Factors

Jordi Álvarez, Núria Castell, and Olga Slavkova
Universitat Politècnica de Catalunya
*Departament de Llenguatges i Sistemes Informàtics, UPC, Pau Gargallo, 5, Barcelona 08028, Spain. Telephone: 34-3-4017015. Fax: 34-3-4017014. email:*castell@lsi.upc.es

Abstract
The LESD project (Linguistic Engineering for Software Development) aimed to develop computing tools for analysis and reasoning on functional or preliminary specifications of aerospace software written in English. These tools help to control the quality of software written during the first stage: specification. The factors considered relevant to the quality of specifications in the LESD project are: traceability, modifiability, completeness, consistency, and verifiability. This paper deals with completeness and modifiability. In the case of completeness we present a symbolic approach to control this factor, using a Knowledge Base. Checks are based on *metarequirements* that try to ensure structural completeness. The concept of modifiability is based on the level of interconnection between the requirements of the specifications. Two metrics have been defined in order to measure global and local levels of interconnection.

Keywords
Software quality factors, quality of natural language specifications, completeness factor, modifiability factor, software metrics, metaknowledge–based control.

1 INTRODUCTION

The work presented in this paper is a continuation of a project (LESD) carried out in collaboration between French and Spanish researchers. The LESD project (Linguistic Engineering for Software Development) (Borillo et al.,1991) was initiated in the ARAMIIHS centre, Toulouse (France). Researchers taking part were drawn from IRIT–CNRS (Institut de Recherche en Informatique de Toulouse), the Université Paul Sabatier, the Université de Le Mirail, MATRA MARCONI SPACE, and from the Universitat Politècnica de Catalunya (under the terms of a joint Franco–Spanish initiative, maintained during 3 years). The aim of the LESD was to develop computing tools for the analysis and reasoning employed in drawing up functional or preliminary specifications for aerospace software written in English. These tools help to control the quality of software written during the first stage: specification. LESD selected this stage because, as stated in (Pressman,1992), it is really important to detect errors as soon as possible. The quality control is based on two aspects: the writing norms and the software quality factors. In this paper we only deal with the second aspect.

The LESD architecture (Castell et al.,1994) comprises two parts: the first consists of the syntactic–semantic and the domain analysis of the specifications, from which a conceptual representation of such specifications is obtained; the second takes in reasoning mechanisms relating to the representation of requirements. Therefore LESD falls in the fields of Linguistic Engineering and Knowledge Based Systems.

The work carried out so far on the LESD project has consisted of developing syntactic and semantic analysis tools for such specifications, a study of the knowledge required to interpret those specifications, the design of a suitable knowledge representation system (using a frame–based formalism) and the implementation of reasoning mechanisms for evaluating the quality factors in the specifications at a symbolic level, within the space field. The requirements making up a specification are successively analyzed and interpreted and subsequently incorporated in the Requirements Base while taking the domain representation (Knowledge Base) into account.

The typology of the objects and activities of the domain were defined, as were the relationships for structuring the lexicon and the entities of the domain: taxonomic relationships (the is–a relationship), meronomic relationships (decomposition of an object into its components), temporal relationships (particularly between activities), characterization (for example, status characterizes system) and thematic functionality (agent, object, etc).

In addition to symbolic control of quality, measurement algorithms are currently being added for measuring the five quality factors considered in LESD: traceability, modifiability, completeness, consistency, and verifiability. Evaluation of these factors at a symbolic level requires the development of reasoning algorithms applied to the conceptual representation of specifications expressed in natural language.

The traceability factor has been developed to date, this being of particular importance in software design (Borillo et al.,1992). In defining this factor in LESD, an interactive approach has been adopted in which the engineer investigates by specifying a set of entities which are interconnected by relationships. The system responds by providing a list of requirements whose conceptual representations contain these entities and relationships. The algorithm developed for analyzing enquiries and calculating responses is based on the notion of type. Calculation of the responses involves activating an inference mechanism operating on the Knowledge Base. A detailed description may be found in (Toussaint,1992).

At present, the Spanish group works in the research subjects left open by LESD. We are studying the other selected quality factors, following the mentioned knowledge–based approach and adding a metrics–based approach. In particular we are dealing with the control of completeness factor at symbolic level (Álvarez et al.,1994) and with metrics to measure the modifiability factor (Castell et al.,1995b). The work related to these two factors is explained in this paper. A hierarchical model of software quality control based on software measurement has been developed and applied to the traceability and the modifiability factors (Castell et al.,1995c). Also we are developing an assistance system for writing software specifications in natural language (Castell et al.,1995a).

This paper is organized in two main sections. Section 2 is devoted to the completeness factor: definition, kinds of completeness, and symbolic control of this factor. Section 3 is devoted to the modifiability factor: its definition, definition of adequate measurements, and experimental work.

2 THE COMPLETENESS FACTOR

The problem of generating complete specifications is crucial to software development life cycle. Incomplete specifications are a big source of misunderstandings between the client and the software engineer. When there are some pieces of information that are needed but missing from the specification, the persons who take information from it (designers, programmers, formal specification writers or anyone else; hereafter called specification–readers) tend to fill these holes with their own surmises. As specification–writers have generally a different point of view from specification–readers, these surmises differ at least a little from what specification–writers took for granted when writing the specification. This would cause the final system behaviour being different from the one that was initially thought. Therefor these gaps in the specification can result in problematic design and code changes. Checking automatically whether a specification is complete or not will avoid correcting errors in later stages of the software development process.

2.1 Problem Definition

To get inside the problem we will start by defining it. The (IEEE,1984) standard states that *a specification is complete when all the requirements relative to functionality, performance, constraints on system structure, attributes and external interfaces are written and if all the terms used in these requirements are defined.*

This definition is too concrete and says too many things to reason in an abstract manner about it. We prefer to give our own definition. But before doing that, we must first remember that a specification is a document to allow information interchange between different persons involved in a software engineering project. That is, the purpose of the specification is to ensure conceptual completeness among software engineers. Then, if we assume that the aim of this software engineering project is to construct a system to achieve some goals, we can say *a specification is complete if all the information needed to construct the specified system is stated.*

To deepen into the given definition, we must state several questions. The first one, *which information do we need in order to construct a system?* This question brings up the problem of deciding which pieces of information are relevant. Answering it establishes a link between the needed information and the purpose of the specification. As the system is specified through the specification, the information a specification needs in order to be considered complete depends on the specification itself.

By other hand, the action of constructing the system implies that the persons who will construct it know the exact expected behavior of the system. So, this definition implies the specification contains all the information needed to know the exact behavior of the system. This raises another question: *what do we understand as exact behavior?* The answer relates to the kind of specification we are dealing with. If it is a preliminary specification (as it is the case), we cannot expect every detail of the system to be present in it. The more detailed is considered to be the specification, the more information we must check to be present in it.

Finally, as the specification will be read by human persons and these persons will have a background and common-sense knowledge, a third question must be answered: *which part of the relevant information must be stated explicitly in the specification and which part can be taken for granted?* Background and common-sense knowledge makes needed information a subset of relevant information.

More precisely, taking into account the (ESA,1991) and (IEEE,1984) standards, and the paper (Cordes et al.,1989), the characteristics a specification must have in order to be complete are:

1. All system relevant characteristics must be present in the specification. No mind they relate functionality, performance, design constraints...
2. Every object that is referenced in the specification must also be defined. This feature could be thought as a special case of (1), so the mentioned standards do not specify it.
3. No information is left unstated or to be determined. The use of TBDs (to be determined) must be avoided.
4. The system response must be specified for all realisable classes of input data in all realisable classes of situations.
5. All figures, tables and diagrams in the document must be full labelled and referenced.

The first three characteristics constitute structural completeness, the fourth one refers to logical completeness and the last one defines documental completeness. In this paper we deal with structural completeness. For a general discussion about different kinds of completeness see (Tuells et al.,1993).

We must consider two kinds of structural completeness: external and internal. Point 1 is referred as external completeness so we have the hint to the incompleteness in the system, external to the specification itself. Points 2 and 3 are referred as internal completeness so we get the pointer to the incompleteness in the specification itself.

2.2 External completeness

Obviously, external completeness is harder to detect than internal one. The reason is that we only have the specification to detect missing information from the specification itself. As has been said in the previous section, we would find pointers to this missing information in the system; but the only knowledge we have about the system comes from the specification. We can try to supply this lack of information with an extensive domain Knowledge Base that can give some hints about possible incompletenesses. In this way, we can use this domain Knowledge Base to convert some external incompletenesses to internal ones; i.e. using *metarequirements* as explained in the next section.

If we have no domain knowledge, we can check whether an object is defined, but no more can be done. As stated in (Reubenstein et al.,1991), there is no way to detect the absence of information that is orthogonal to the knowledge we have about the system. The more domain knowledge we have, the less incompletenesses will be orthogonal to the knowledge we have.

For example, if we are specifying a library management system, the library could have been defined as a repository of books. We could know from our domain knowledge that an element of a repository must have a unique identifier. As our system manages a library, books in it will be elements of a repository and must have a unique identifier. Therefore we must check the definition of book for a unique identifier. If we do not find it, we can assure that the definition of book is incomplete for this problem.

Of course, we cannot guarantee that every incompleteness will be catch. So, as stated in (Reubenstein et al.,1991), the end–user has to be the final arbiter of completeness.

2.3 Internal completeness

The internal completeness ensures that all the information present in the document is completely defined. Cordes and Carver (1989) propose a simple algorithm to check this kind of completeness. What they do is mainly to check a minimum set of properties for each object and event that appears in the specification. In the Requirements Apprentice (Reubenstein et al.,1991) we also see this minimum set of properties: when instances are linked to clichés, a set of expectations in the form of roles that must be filled is generated. It also maintains a list of undefined things.

In addition to this minimum set of properties, we propose checking some properties resulting from the reasoning about the conjunction of the domain knowledge and the overall knowledge we have about the specification ; i.e. the Requirements Base. These properties are intended to express specification quality factors.

Our initial idea is to establish the set of properties that must be checked through the use of *metarequirements*: requirements about the knowledge we have about the system; that is, about the specification itself*. These *metarequirements* specify the quality properties we are talking about in the same way system requirements specify an activity. That is, the domain knowledge can contain some requirements that must be checked over the specifications. As a result of this, we will have requirements that refer to the system and requirements that refer to the specification. In this sense, the set of *metarequirements* could be seen as the *standard* the program follows to check the structural completeness or to check another quality factors if they are defined.

No distinction will be made between requirements and *metarequirements*. This way, the specification can also contain *metarequirements* conditioning its completeness. For example, the requirement "Every system needs an I/O device in order to be controlled" is, in fact, a *metarequirement* that forces the definition of controlled systems to have an I/O device.

This is quite easy. More interesting is the possibility to deduce *metarequirements* from system requirements. For example, if we are talking about an emergency system and we read the requirement "Each audio emergency signal shall have a tone specific to each condition", we will know that every audio emergency signal defined may have some conditions defined and each one of these conditions must have a specific tone†.

As we have seen earlier, it is very difficult to find incompletenesses. Only a few incompletenesses will be noticed by the user if we only report those we are sure about. Instead, a better approach can be to report also some possible incompletenesses. The modality of a requirement, used in (Toussaint,1992) to give an idea about the importance of the requirements (needed, desirable, in future plans...), can be used to do this work. So, a

---

*We call them *metarequirements* because in some way they are requirements over the requirements that define the system we are specifying.

†Although the specificity of the tone relates to consistency, its presence is a completeness issue.

metarequirement can tell us about a definite incompleteness or can warn about a possible one.

2.4 Computing internal completeness

A first thought to compute internal completeness can be to check every completeness property expressed through a *metarequirement*. The idea is similar to that of metarelationships in the KAOS system (Lamsweerde et al.,1995), but applied specifically to completeness specification validation.

We have requirements referring the specification (that we call *metarequirements*) and requirements referring the system we are specifying. Completeness properties will always be specified in *metarequirements*, but these properties can be influenced by any kind of requirement in the specification. In this way, system requirements can also participate in completeness checking.

In the library example, we will check for the book unique identifier (*metarequirement*) whenever the library management system performs any operation that requires books having a unique identifier. When there is no operation that requires books having a unique identifier, no check must be done.

The completeness check for the overall specification can be computed easily checking the completeness for each entity referenced in the specification. Looking at the Knowledge Base as a whole, the specification will be complete if it provides enough knowledge for the requirements activities to be performed. Looking at each entity, we can say its definition is complete in the context of the specified system if it provides enough knowledge for any related requirement activity to be performed.

Completeness properties constitute the knowledge we will use to check if there is enough knowledge to perform an activity. As these properties will refer to one or several entities, the overall specification completeness can be deduced from completeness checks over all entities related to it. Going on with this idea, there are two ways we can check for incompletenesses concerning an entity: in a *static* way and in an *operational* way.

The first way consists in checking every property related to an entity that must also be accomplished in order to allow every requirement in the specification to be feasible. For example, going on with our library management system, the static completeness check for book would result in looking for every related property. We would find a property saying: "Repository elements must have a unique identifier". As the specified system must manage a library, and a library is a repository of books, we know that books are repository elements. The next step is deciding whether the specified system needs this property to be accomplished. So, we search any activity that needs that property to be accomplished. We would find for example a reference to the operation of checking out repository elements. Then, as the library management system must be able to check out books (we have a system requirement specifying it) and checking out books is a special case of checking out repository elements (because in out problem, books are repository elements), books must have a unique identifier. So, this *metarequirement* is checked against book definition.

The second way is more ingenious, and is based on checking that an entity is able to perform any action it needs to perform. For example, we want to check operatively our library management system. We would find (among others) a requirement saying that the library management system must check out books. The activity checking out books is more specific than checking out repository elements, and this activity needs repository elements having a unique identifier. So, we must check book definition for unique identifier.

Checking completeness in a static and operational way can be very useful sometimes, but not for an interactive system that wants to check the requirements completeness when it receives them. If we check the completeness for every referenced entity in the requirement we would be repeating a lot of checks.

It is important to note that the checks that are carried out for a requirement depend on both the requirement and the Requirements and Knowledge Bases we have in the moment we incorporate to it. By other hand, it must be noticed that the introduction of a new requirement into the Requirements Base can result in the combination of three different situations that require only specific completeness checks for each one. Taking advantage of this fact, we can manage to perform all checks only once. The skeleton of the algorithm is as follows, for a more detailed explanation see (Álvarez et al.,1994):

1. Retrieve the main activity associated to the requirement (it can be either a system requirement or a *metarequirement*).
2. Perform the following checks over the activity:
   - Static: if the activity represents a property (so, the requirement is in fact a *metarequirement*) and it is needed to perform another activity, the property is checked.
   - Operational: check if the activity can be done (this implies checking properties that condition the activity).
3. For any new entity referenced, perform all operational and static completeness checks.

About completeness properties, by the moment, the implemented prototype only treats two different properties: to have an attribute and to be a concept. The first one checks the entity definition for the corresponding attribute and the second one checks the entity to be an instance of a specified class (or a subclass of it).

3 THE MODIFIABILITY FACTOR

The approach to specifications modifiability in LESD has to address two tasks: first, analyze the level of complexity in the modifications with regard to both the requirements taken as a whole (global measurement) and for each individual requirement (local measurement) and, second, select the list of requirements which may be affected by a given modification. Automating the approach to the modifiability of specifications allows both the global and local evaluation objectives to be achieved and avoids missings in the list of requirements to be reviewed as a result of an implemented modification.

3.1 Definition

In (IEEE,1984) the modifiability of specifications is defined in relation to the level of redundancy involved and the simplicity, completeness, and consistency of the modifications. The redundancy involved and the simplicity of carrying out modifications within a set of specifications in LESD are characterised by the level of interconnection between the requirements of the LESD specifications. The intuitive idea is evident: the greater the level of modification, the greater the difficulty of making the modification and the greater the possibility of detecting redundancy in the requirements. The complexity and consistency of the modifications depend on the level of propagation of a given modification in all requirements affected by that modification. Thus we have formalized the basis of the concept of modifiability in LESD in function of the level of interconnection between the specifications requirements. The interconnection between different requirements is defined by common use of entities defined in the LESD domain (i.e. by common information).

The measurement model of modifiability, in addition to indicate the global modifiability of the requirements taken as a whole, must be appropriate for defining the local level of modifiability in case of a specific modification and indicate the subset of requirements which may require modification as a result of such an alteration.

The most suitable mathematical model for calculating the quantity of the common information in a set of requirements expressed through entities (defined in the domain of LESD) in common use, is described in (Emden,1970). The model has been adapted for calculating the level of complexity of a program in (Robillard et al.,1989). In this model the interconnections in a set of predicates via objects in common use are represented by an interconnection table defined as follows:

$$table(object_i, predicate_j) = \begin{cases} X, & \text{if the predicate contains the object,} \\ 0, & \text{if this is not the case.} \end{cases} \quad (1)$$

In the next subsections we describe how looks our interconnection table and the new metrics we have defined, following Emden's model, to measure the modifiability factor.

3.2 The Interconnection Table

We have defined the interconnection table for a set of specifications requirements as follows: each row in the table corresponds to the identification of a requirement and the columns correspond to the various LESD domain entities (i.e., objects, activities, temporal relationships). The interconnection table is obtained automatically using a reasoning algorithm applied to the Requirements Base and its construction is carried out by analyzing each of the requirements in turn.

The $Table(row_i, column_j)$ values may be 0, 1, $\neg 1$, 2, $\neg 2$ or 3 according to the level of entity$_j$–requirement$_i$ dependence and its type (asserted or negated). A detailed explanation of the process to construct the interconnection table, as well as the process to define a m–partition of a set of requirements (m mutually independent subsets), can be found in (Castell et al.,1995b,1995c)

3.3 Global Measurement of Modifiability

The amount of common information in a set of elements is an indicator of the level of interconnection of the elements within this set and is called in (Emden,1970) *excess – entropy* defined as a difference between *entropies*. The formulas for calculating the entropy H and the excess–entropy C proposed in (Emden,1970) for an m–partition of a set of n elements, and the entropy H_i of a partition$_i$, are:

$$H = \log_2 n - \frac{1}{n} \sum_{i=1}^{m} n_i \log_2 n_i \quad (2)$$

$$C = \sum_{i=1}^{m} H_i - H \quad (3)$$

In order to apply Emden's mathematical model to the set of specifications requirements under LESD, let us consider an m–partition of the set of n requirements in mutually independent subsets of requirements such that n_i requirements of each subset$_i$ $(i=1,m)$ are inter–linked by common entities and

$$\sum_{i=1}^{m} n_i = n \tag{4}$$

Let us associate the set of non negative numbers $\{\frac{n_1}{n}, \ldots, \frac{n_m}{n}\}$ to m partitions;

$$\sum_{i=1}^{m} \frac{n_i}{n} = 1 \tag{5}$$

Clearly each number $\frac{n_i}{n}$ indicates the probability that a requirement belongs to the partition$_i$. We shall now define the link between two requirements in terms of the interconnection table.

Two requirements **i** *and* **j** *are inter–linked if at least one entity* **k** *is present so that Table (i,k) ≠0 and Table(j,k) ≠ 0*

The entropy H_i is calculated considering only n_i requirements in the subset$_i$. In general there may exist a k–partition in the subset$_i$. In this case the measurement of H_i is performed using the following formula:

$$H_i = \log_2 n_i \; - \; \frac{1}{n_i} \sum_{j=1}^{k} n_{ij} \log_2 n_{ij} \tag{6}$$

Should there be no partition in the (sub)set of k requirements, the formulas for calculating the entropy and the excess–entropy will be the same as the calculation formulas proposed by (Robillard et al.,1989):

$$C = \sum_{i=1}^{k} H_i \; - \; H \tag{7}$$

$$H_i = \log_2 n_i \; - \; \frac{1}{n_i} \sum_{j=1}^{l_i} p_j \log_2 p_j, \tag{8}$$

where l_i is the number of different configurations of the rows values in the interconnection table$_i$ and p_i is the number of times the configuration$_i$ is repeated. To calculate l_i and p_i let us consider the following definition:

Two requirements **i** *and* **j** *have the same configuration if the following holds true for all the columns of the subtable corresponding to the subset of requirements: Table(i, column) ≠0 ⟺ Table(j, column) ≠0*

If all the values in the rows coincide in addition to having the same configuration, we can say that there is *redundancy* in the requirements set.

In order to measure the level of interconnection independently of the size of the set of requirements a new *Interconnectivity Level* metric is defined:

$$IL = \frac{C}{C_{max}} \tag{9}$$

The quantity C_{max} represents the maximum excess–entropy of a set of requirements (when all requirements are inter–linked) and thus logically normalizes the quantity C. The range of the values of IL metric will be $[0 \ldots 1]$. 0 indicates that there is not common information between the requirements of a set, and 1 indicates that all requirements are inter–linked.

Table 1 *Interconnectivity level* values

	set_1	set_2	set_3	set_4	set_5
n	16	13	13	13	18
m	2	2	3	2	1
n_1	15	12	9	11	-
n_2	1	1	3	2	-
n_3	-	-	1	-	-
IL	0.055	0.066	0.075	0.079	1

3.4 Local Measurement of Modifiability

To locally evaluate modifiability of a requirement another metric – *Individual Interconnectivity Level* – is defined which reflects the relationship between the individual interconnectivity level of a requirement$_i$ (C_i) and the level of global interconnectivity (C) of the set.

$$IIL = \frac{C_i}{C} \tag{10}$$

The range of the values of IIL metric will be $[0 \ldots 1]$. The IIL metric values near to 0 indicate that the influence of a requirement on the global modifiability of the set of requirements is small. In calculating C_i, two cases can be distinguished:

– if we are interested in the interconnectivity level of the requirement, considering all its entities (both directly referenced ones and related ones), C_i is calculated on the subtable of the subset to which the requirement$_i$ belongs;

– if we are interested in the interconnectivity level of requirement$_i$, considering a subset of such entities, the subtable is constructed following the same steps but substituting the definition of the link between two requirements:

Two requirements i *and* j *are inter–linked if for each entity* k *of a subset the following conditions are met: Table (i,k) $\neq 0$ and Table(j,k) $\neq 0$*

3.5 Experimental work and discussion of results

The measurement model of global modifiability has been tested with real data to demonstrate its sensitivity to the interconnectivity level: an improvement of the modifiability in a set of requirements lowers the metric value. A data set of metric values has been obtained from five sets of requirements. For a detailed description of these sets, the interconnection tables and the results see (Castell et al.,1995b). Table 1 summarizes the obtained results.

In (Kitchenham et al.,1990] a robust statistics method is suggested to describe software data sets, thus we have applied this method to identify the range of metric acceptable values: [0.066, 0.079]. From the view–point of measuring the modifiability, one IL metric value within the range of acceptable values is better in comparison with another IL metric value within the range of acceptable values if it is lower. The applied statistical method suggests a quick review of sets with metric values within [0, 0.066[and]0.079, 0.12], and more stringent review of sets with values within]0.12, 1].

4 CONCLUSIONS AND FUTURE WORK

The work carried out in the LESD project consisted in developing the tools for analyzing specifications written in natural language. Five factors concerning quality of specifications were dealt with (traceability, completeness, consistency, verifiability, and modifiability). The techniques for evaluating traceability had already been developed. Currently work deals with completeness and modifiability.

In the case of completeness we have followed a knowledge–based approach. The control is based on *metarequirements* which are represented in a similar way as requirements. The reasoning mechanism operates on the Knowledge Base and the Requirements Base. As a further work, we will explore the relation between traceability and completeness.

On the other hand, we have develop and implement the modifiability measurement applicable to conceptual representation of specifications. We have formalized the basis of the concept of modifiability in function of the level of interconnection between the specifications requirements. Two metrics have been defined: *Interconnectivity Level* and *Individual Interconnectivity Level.* The measurement model is based on the notion of *excess – entropy*, and a robust statistics method has been used to identify the range of metric acceptable values. In order to validate the proposed model, it is necessary to test empirically whether the modifiability measures are good valuations of the actual time and cost of further modifications of the specifications.

Acknowledgements

This work is partially supported by CICYT Spanish institution (TIC93-420) and by CIRIT Catalan institution (GRQ93-3.015 and a postgraduate grant for the first author).

REFERENCES

Álvarez, J. and Castell, N. (1994) An Approach to the Control of Completeness Based on MetaKnowledge. *Research Report* LSI–94–50–R. Dept. LSI, Universitat Politècnica de Catalunya, Barcelona, Spain.

Borillo, M., Castell, N., Latour, D., Toussaint, Y. and Verdejo, M.F. (1992) Applying Linguistic Engineering to Software Engineering: The traceability problem, in *Proceedings of 10th European Conference on Artificial Intelligence - ECAI'92* (ed. B. Neumann), John Wiley & Sons.

Borillo, M., Toussaint, Y. and Borillo, A. (1991) Motivations du project LESD, in *Proceedings of Linguistic Engineering Conference'91*, Versailles, France.

Castell, N. and Hernández, A. (1995a) Filtering Software Specifications Written in Natural Language, in *Proceedings of 7th Portuguese Conference on Artificial Intelligence – EPIA'95, Lecture Notes in Artificial Intelligence*, Springer–Verlag.

Castell, N. and Slavkova, O. (1995b) The modifiability Factor in the LESD Project: Definition and Practical Results. *Research Report* LSI–95–7–R. Dept. LSI, Universitat Politècnica de Catalunya, Barcelona, Spain.

Castell, N. and Slavkova, O. (1995c) Metrics for Quality Factors in the LESD Project, in *Proceedings of 5th European Software Engineering Conference - ESEC'95, Lecture Notes in Computer Science*, Springer–Verlag.

Castell, N., Slavkova, O., Tuells, A. and Toussaint, Y. (1994) Quality Control of Software Specifications Written in Natural Language, in *Proceedings of 7th International Conference on Industrial & Engineering Applications of Artificial Intelligence & Expert Systems - IEA/AIE'94* (eds. F.D. Anger, R.V. Rodriguez, M. Ali), Gordon and Breach Science Publishers.

Cordes, D.W. and Carver, D.L. (1989) Evaluation method for user requirements documents. *Information and Software Technology*, **31**(4), 181–8.

van Emden, M.H. (1970) Hierarchical Decomposition of Complexity. *Machine Intelligence*, **5**, 361–80.

European Space Agency (1991) ESA software engineering standards, Issue 2, February.

IEEE (1984) Guide to Software Requirements Specifications, ANSI/IEEE Std. 830–1984.

Kitchenham, B.A. and Linkman, S.J. (1990) Design Metrics in Practice. *Information and Software Technology*, **32**(4).

van Lamsweerde, A., Darimon, R. and Massonet, P. (1995) Goal–directed elaboration of requirements for a meeting scheduler: Problems and lessons learnt, in *Proceedings of 2nd International Symposium on Requirements Engineering*, IEEE CS Press.

Pressman R.S. (1992) Software Engineering: A Practitioner's Approach. Mac Graw Hill, New York.

Reubenstein, H.B. and Waters, R.C. (1991). The Requirements Apprentice: Automated Assistance for requirements acquisition. *IEEE Transactions on Software Engineering*, **17** (3), 226–40.

Robillard, P.N. and Boloix, G. (1989) The Interconnectivity Metrics: A New Metric Showing How a Program is Organized. *The Journal of Systems and Software*, **10**, 29–39.

Toussaint, Y. (1992) Méthodes Informatiques et Linguistiques pour l'aide a la Spécification de Logiciel. *Ph.D. Thesis.* Université Paul Sabatier, Toulouse, France.

Tuells, A. and Castell, N. (1993) The Completeness Problem in LESD. *Research Report* LSI–93–26–R. Dept. LSI, Universitat Politècnica de Catalunya, Barcelona, Spain.

BIOGRAPHY

Jordi Álvarez is graduate in Computer Science by the Universitat Politécnica de Catalunya (1993). At present he is a Ph.D. student in the Artificial Intelligence Program of the LSI Departament (UPC). His main research interests are knowledge representation, neuronal networks, and machine learning.

Núria Castell is graduate in Computer Science by the Universitat Autònoma de Barcelona (1981) and received her Ph.D. degree in Computer Science from the Universitat Politécnica de Catalunya (1989). At present she is "Profesora Titular de Universidad" (similar to Associate Professor) in the LSI Departament (UPC). Her research interests include knowledge representation, and natural language processing.

Olga Slavkova is graduate in Computer Science by the Universidad Central de las Villas, Cuba (1987). Presently on leave of research. She was "Profesora Asociada" (hired Teacher) in the LSI Departament (UPC) and at the same time Ph.D. student in the Software Program of the LSI Departament. Her main research interest is software metrics.

18

Software quality evaluation from research to industry: The Qseal Consortium approach

V. Asnaghi[4], P. Caliman[3], M. Campanai[1], W. Chiarottino[2], G. Di Capua[6], F. Fabbrini[7], M. Fusani[7], A. Jeanrenaud[6], S. Mitolo[1], D. Pina[5], G. Rumi[4], P. Salvaneschi[5], I. Tsiouras[3]

1-Cesvit, v.le Strozzi 1, 50129 Firenze (Italy), Tel. +39 (0) 55 4796425; Fax. +39 (0) 55 4796363; email: Campanai@fi. nettuno. it

2-Cimeco, v. Battistotti Sassi 11, 20138 Milano (Italy), Tel. +39 (0) 2 747601; Fax. +39 (0) 2 719055

3-Etnoteam, v. A. Bono Cairoli 34, 20127 Milano (Italy), Tel. +39 (0) 2 261621, Fax: +39 (0) 26110755, email:itsiuoras@etnoteam.it/pcaliman@etnoteam.it

4-IMQ, v. Quintiliano 43, 20138 Milano (Italy), Tel. +39 (0) 2 5073320; Fax. +39 (0) 2 5073271; email: imqittl@icil64.cilea.it

5-Ismes, v.le Giulio Cesare 29, 20124 Bergamo (Italy), Tel. +39 (0) 35 307773; Fax. +39 (0) 35 211191; email: psalvaneschi@ismes.it./dpina@ismes.it

6-Tecnopolis Csata Novus Ortus, strada provinciale per Casamassima Km. 3,70010 Valenzano, Bari (Italy), Tel. +39 (0) 80 8770111; email:dicapua@mailserv.csata.it/jeanrena@max.csata.it

7-IEI-CNR, v. S. Maria 46, 56126 Pisa (Italy), Tel. +39 (0) 50 554095 email: fusani@iei.pi.cnr.it

Abstract

This paper presents the approach adopted by the Qseal Consortium with respect to software product quality evaluation and certification practices. This paper aims at giving an overview of the framework for evaluation and certification and describes the whole process, the main goals, and the available techniques.

Keywords

Software product assessment, product quality, evaluation and certification, product metrics and measures.

1. INTRODUCTION

Over the past years both software engineers and users have paid increasing attention to assessing the quality of software products (Bache and Bazzana, 1993). This fact has lead many organisations to the development of practices enabling them to assess and give evidence of software quality degree that is suitable for its specified service (De Neumann and Bazzana, 1992).
Among others, many Italian companies have been involved in national and international projects (Robert, 1991), (TASQUE) concerning software quality evaluation and certification. Most of those companies increased their knowledge in real case studies and, starting from research experiences, developed proprietary measurement methodologies and apparatuses.
Due to the state of the art of software quality evaluation, each available measurement methodology and apparatus is a bit different from each other, and none of them can be considered the most suitable and credible.
In order to offer both to the developer, the customer and the user a harmonised service (measurement and apparatus) at the end of 1994 the Qseal Consortium was founded. The Consortium was constituted thanks to the effort of CIMECO (Centro Italiano MEtodologie di COntrollo), the Italian organisation for accreditation of certification bodies and testing laboratories in the IT&T sector; it is composed by Etnoteam, Cesvit, Ismes, Tecnopolis Csata acting as testing laboratories (CNR participated as well as an external partner) and by IMQ acting as a certification body.
One of the main goals of the Consortium is to keep the activities transparent both to the providers and the users and in line with all the possible evolution of the state of the art; to this end, the Consortium established a few basic principles as its basis:

- participation is open to any company or individual being interested in its initiatives;
- it operates internationally and forster participation from all countries;
- it seeks harmonisation with similar schemes world-wide and will therefore liaise with standard bodies, ECITC and other harmonisation promoting committees.

The paper deals with the methodology and the measurement apparatus defined by the Qseal Consortium, and in particular defines:

- the software quality model;
- the measurement records, including information about how and where to measure;
- the interpretation functions.

2. THE QSEAL APPROACH TO SOFTWARE QUALITY EVALUATION AND CERTIFICATION

2.1. The quality model

What does the Qseal Consortium mean by quality? The first requirement is in fact a definition of quality that can be applied to software. It is the policy of the Consortium to seek harmonisation, and evaluate, and adopt (when appropriated) International Standards: so the Consortium has decided to adopt the definition provided in the ISO/IEC ISO 9126 (ISO/IEC International Standard 9126, 1991), which express the quality of a software product as a function of six quality characteristics: Functionality, Reliability, Efficiency, Usability, Portability and Maintainability.
The characteristics are defined as follows:

- *Functionality*, that bears on the existence of a set of functions and their specified properties;
- *Reliability*, that bears on the capability of software to maintain its level of performance under stated conditions for a stated period of time;

- *Efficiency*, that bears on the relationship between the level of performance of the software and the amount of resources used, under stated conditions;
- *Usability*, that bears on the effort needed for use, and on individual assessment of such use, by a stated or implied set of users;
- *Portability*, that bears on the ability of software to be transferred from one environment to another;
- *Maintainability*, that bears on the effort needed to make specified modifications.

However, this top level definition of quality is only a start; the ISO 9126 characteristics have been subdivided and refined into more specific sub-characteristics at lower levels which are relevant to the evaluation and certification activities.
The sub-characteristics presented by the ISO 9126 are not part of the standard; they are reported in Annex A and are "*published to encourage use in practice and to collect experience for further edition*".

Then, the evaluation of a software product will be done by assessing the above characteristics, and comparing the target values of specified characteristics of software with the values actually measured.

The decomposition of characteristics, as proposed by the ISO 9126, is presented in Figure 1.

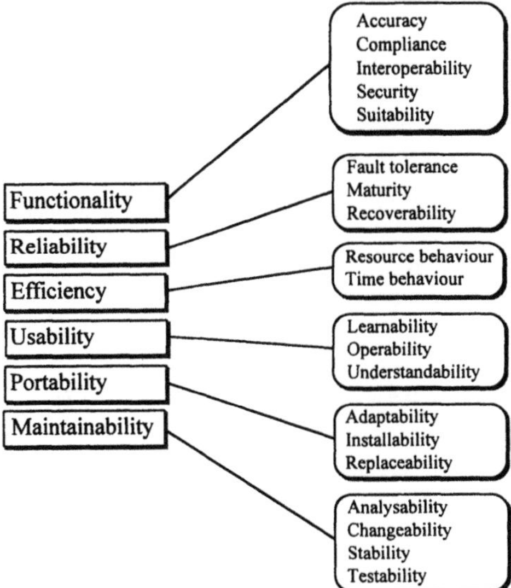

Figure 1 - Software Quality Model - ISO 9126.

2.3. Quality views

As far as evaluation and certification are concerned, one of the main problems refers to the fact that in many occasions, views of quality can be different according to the application domain; while the same general framework and the evaluation process can be applied, there are some product related aspects that can greatly differ:

- quality profiles (that is the list of quality characteristics considered relevant for the software product);
- functionalities;
- part of the measurement apparatus.

To give an answer to this point the Consortium is about to organise a set of open Fora with the main goal to constitute the platform for promoting a common understanding on quality related issues among assessors, developers, and procurers of a specific industry (Di Capua and Jeanrenaud, 1994). The Fora are directed to gather different kind of organisations with a common interest and to define the quality profiles suitable for the particular kind of products, also dealing with specific functionalities and capabilities sought after in application of a specific market sector.
One of the key task for the Fora is to establish a set of predefined quality profiles to be associated to the Qseal quality mark; those who want to obtain the Qseal quality mark must agree on one of the predefined profiles, and the evaluation process must be in line with it.

2.2. The evaluation process

The evaluation process established by the Consortium is described as a step-wise procedure, which allows to express evaluation requirements in terms of quality characteristics as defined in ISO 9126. The evaluation covers various documents which can be considered as part of software product and uses a library of measurement records.
A measurement record is a structured encapsulation of software characteristics and evaluation techniques attached together. It identifies the product parts and elements of process information it needs and defines the elementary evaluation procedure and the format for reporting the measurements resulting from the application of the techniques.

After giving the answers to a set of checklist items, a suitable integration mechanism allows to assign values in a bottom-up fashion to sub-characteristics and characteristic. The integration mechanism is the following:

1. collection of basic measures;
2. evaluation of sub-characteristic values s_j

$$s_j = \frac{\sum_i m_i}{n}$$, computed on the applicable checklist items only (n)

3. evaluation of characteristic values c_k; they are computed starting from the s_j values and combining them in different ways, using one of the *average*, *minimum* or *maximum* operators.

From a technical point of view, the evaluation process has been structured into few activities which are performed by the evaluator.
These activities, subdivided into 5 steps, are:

Step 1: analysis of the client requirements for evaluation in order to identify the purpose of the service provided and the quality profile; to release a trade mark the quality profile must correspond to one of the predefined (during the activities carried out within the Fora);

Step 2: specification of the evaluation whose aim is to identify product parts to be measured (that is documents to be provided to the evaluator), and define those characteristics to be evaluated for each part;

Step 3: design of the evaluation which shall choose tools, instruments, and techniques and plan the valuation process (costs and time schedule);

Step 4: performing the evaluation that is measuring and testing selected product parts using the applicable measurement records;

Step 5: reporting on the results generated by the measurements activities; the final report shall be delivered to the client of the evaluation and in case of certification it shall have the Qseal trade mark on it.

It is quite important that, in order to be applicable and recognised by both producers and users, evaluation and certification activities should be:

- *repeatable*: repeated evaluation of the same product to the same evaluation specification by the same testing laboratory should produce the same results;
- *reproducible*: repeated evaluation of the same product to the same evaluation specification by different testing laboratory should produce the same results.

3. The measurement records

Once the quality characteristics are identified and refined into some more specific sub-characteristics at lower levels, the evaluation activities are performed and ratings are applied to each sub-characteristics; then the various values are combined and an aggregate score obtained.

Of course, the more the evaluation is subjective, the less it is repeatable and reproducible; a mature evaluation process should be based on objective measurements, rather than individual taste. For these reasons, an agreed upon set of measurement instruments, with guidelines for usage, has been produced; the step of selecting measurement instruments represented one of the key point for the whole process.

They have been selected according to the following criteria:

- to represent the most recent evolution of the state of the art;
- to be strictly connected to the sub-characteristic/characteristic they are associated;
- to be easily understandable;
- to be objectively applicable.

Characteristics, sub-characteristics, and measurement instruments are collected into *Measurement records*, composed by the following fields (Spinelli, Pina, Salvaneschi, Crivelli and Meda, 1995):

- Id: contains the checklist item identifier;
- Lev: contains the evaluation level to which the checklist item apply;
- Characteristic: contains the quality characteristic to which the checklist item apply;
- Sub-characteristic: contains the sub-characteristic to which the checklist item apply;
- Checklist item: contains the description of the measure to carry out;
- Notes: contains possible clarification concerned to the checklist item. Clarification are inserted only when necessary and applicable;
- How: this is the most important field: it contains the description of how to evaluate the checklist item. Generally it coincides with the mathematical formula to be applied.
- Answer: contains the interpretative function, which maps the possible answers to a standard range of merit (the interval [0,1]).
- Documents: contains the documents to which the checklist item is applicable.

  Due to the characteristics of the measurement apparatus, a software product will be analysed, attributing each document available to one specific category (between parentheses some common denominations of documents in the category). The categories, reported in the following, have been subdivided according to: Development, Maintenance, and Quality assurance documentation.

•• *Development*

- **RE** Requirements (System/Software Requirement Specification);
- **AR** Architecture (System/Software Architecture);
- **DD** Detailed Design (Software Detailed Design);
- **SC** Software code;
- **MC** Machine code (Object code, Executable code);
- **QD** Qualification Documents (Test, Software qualification, System qualification requirements);
- **TD** Testing documents (Software Integration Plan, System Integrated Test Report);
- **QD** Qualification Documentation (Software Qualification Test Report);
- **AT** Acceptance testing and report (System Qualification Test Report, Acceptance Test Report;
- **SI** Software installation (Software Installation Plan);
- **UM** Software user's manuals;

•• *Maintenance*

- **PI** Post-installation data (Problem and Modification Report, Migration Plan, Withdrawal Plan);

•• *Quality Assurance*

- **QA** Quality Assurance (Quality Assurance Plan).

In selecting these documents, we started from the ISO 12207.2 standard (ISO/IEIC DIS 12207-1).

Two examples of measurement record are presented in Figure 2. The first one refers to Maintainability and the second one to Reliability.

Char	S-Cha	Lev	id	Checklist item	Notes	How	Answer	RE	AR	DD	QD	TD	AT	UM	SI	SC	QA	MC	PI
MAI	ANA	1	1,2	Is there a complete description of the functionalities performed by each high level architecture component?		X=(high level architecture components completely defined)/(n tot high level architecture components)	LIN		1										
MAI	ANA	3	3,1	Has a programming standard been established?		Inspection	YN										1		
MAI	ANA	4	4,12	Are all machine dependent units with comments?		X= number of machine dependent units with comments/ tot. numb. of machine dependent units	LIN									1			
MAI	CHA	2	2,8	Is the naming of each data item consistent throughout the component/ unit?		X= number of data item with consistent names/total number of data item	LIN			1						1			

Char	S-Cha	Lev	id	Checklist item	Notes	How	Answer	RE	AR	DD	QD	TD	AT	UM	SI	SC	QA	MC	PI
REL	FAU	2	2,4	For each data item stored in shared archives, is the admissible range defined?		X=Number of data item stored in shared archives whose admissible range is defined/Total number of data item stored in shared archives	LIN			1									
REL	FAU	2	2,15	Are specific error messages displayed when failures occur?		X=Number of failures notified with error messages/Total number of failures	LIN					1	1					1	1
REL	FAU	3	3,8	Is error checking information computed and compared with all message receptions?		X=Error checking information computed and compared/Total number of message reception	LIN			1								1	
REL	FAU	4	4,7	Are multiple entry or exit from loops/blocks/subroutines minimised?		Inspection	YN									1			
REL	REC	1	1,4	Are there back-up procedures?		Inspection	YN	1									1		
REL	REC	2	2,3	Are there duplications of data on different physical devices?		Inspection	YN			1						1			

Figure 2 - Measurement records: an example (Maintainability and Reliability).

3.1. The evaluation levels

All the selected quality characteristics and sub-characteristics need not to be evaluated with the same degree of thoroughness for all types of applications. Nobody would expect the same effort to be allocated to the evaluation of a railway signal system, and a computer game.
To ensure this flexibility, the evaluation is level-oriented.

The Consortium has defined four levels (they constitute a hierarchy), which identify the depth of the evaluation: evaluation at different levels gives different degrees of confidence in the quality of the software product.

The evaluation levels can be chosen independently for each quality characteristic.

Now the question is: which criteria have been applied to select appropriate quality levels? Table 1 gives an overview of the criteria followed in defining the evaluation levels (ISO/IEC CD 9126-6, 1993); important aspects are those related to environment, to persons, to economy and to security.

Level	Environmental	Personal	Economic	Security
1	Small damage to property	No risk to people	Negligible economic loss	No specific risk
2	Local pollution	Few people injured	Significant economic loss	Protection against error risk
3	Recoverable environmental damage	Threat to human lives	Large economic loss	Protection of critical data and services
4	Unrecoverable environmental damage	Many people killed	Financial disaster	Protection of strategic data and services

Table 1 - Guidelines for selecting the relevant evaluation levels

3.2. The evaluation functions

Evaluation function maps the possible answers to a standard range of merit: the interval [0,1].
Four evaluation functions have been selected; they are presented in the following together with their graphic explanation.

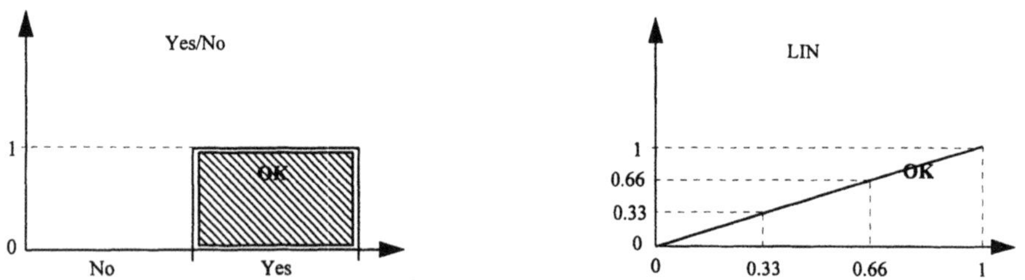

1. **Yes/No** is a function associated to checklist items whose possible answers is Yes or No. One example is: "Has a standard been established for the identification and placements of comments in the unit?". A positive result scores 1, and a negative scores 0.

2. The **LIN** function is associated to checklist items where there is a relation between two basic metrics, e.g. "Are I/O functions isolated from computational functions? (Calculate 1-(not isolated functions)/(tot. functions))". The best ratings are close to 1.

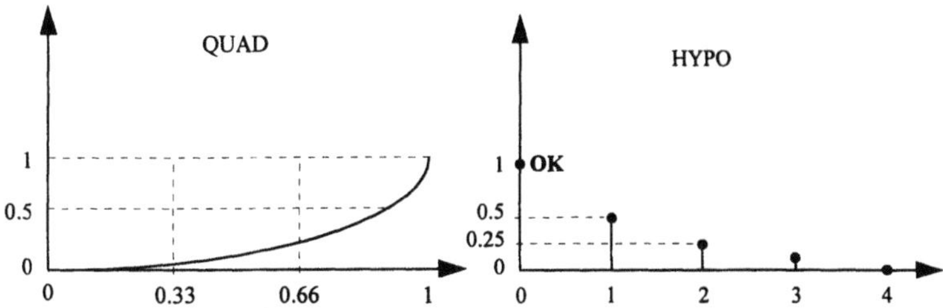

3. **QUAD** is a function similar to LIN. It differs from the previous, for it gives a worse rating to values even if they are close to the acceptable range; an example is the following "Are all components/ units independent of the source of the input and the destination of the output?" Best ratings are close to 1.
4. The fourth function, **HYPO**, is associated with the number of occurrence of a specified condition, e.g. "Is the number of loops in each component minimised?". The minimum, that is 0 scores 1; while the number of occurrences increase, the score diminish to 0.5, 0.25, and to 0. Every number of occurrences superior to 4 scores 0.

In the end, during the application of the measurement apparatus we faced a situations where constraints or technical aspects lead to have parameters which can have different values according to the specific application characteristics. We defined an other evaluation function, **PAR**, which depends on the value of one or two parameters.

One example of this function can be the following: "Is the ratio comments/statements well balanced?". As far as this checklist item is concerned, the values 0.33 and 0.66 can be suitable for an application in C language, but are meaningless for an application in Prolog.

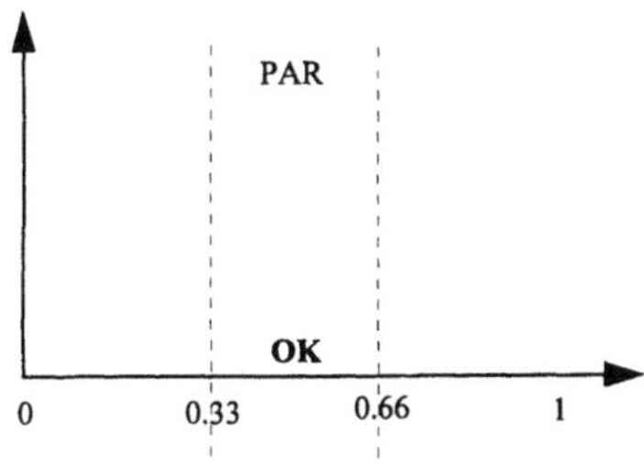

5. Conclusion

Why the Qseal Consortium approach should be a success?
We think that there are a few points that make it a success:

- the methodology and the tools take advantage of the last results in national and European research projects, and are quite close to the evolution of the normative.
- Each of the partners participated in national and European projects and the Consortium represent the effort to harmonise their experiences.
- The Consortium has, amongst its goals, to be as public as possible, in the sense that the Consortium aims at being an open organisation.
- The measurement apparatus has been designed to be as objective as possible to be easily applicable to evaluation and certification activities.
- The methodology, and the measurement apparatus have been designed to be easy to understand.

REFERENCES

Bache, R., Bazzana, G., *Software Metrics for Product Assessment*, McGraw Hill, London, December 1993

De Neumann, B., Bazzana, G., *A methodology for the assessment/certification of software,* 3rd European Conference on Software Quality, Madrid, November 1992

Robert, P., *SCOPE, Achievements and Perspectives*, Commission of the European Communities, Proceedings of Esprit Week, 1991

TASQUE - Eureka Project EU240, *Tool for Assisting Software Quality Evaluation*, TSQ/DEF/TEC-T7/10/1.2/0209/DEL

ISO/IEC International Standard 9126, *Information technology - Software product evaluation - Quality characteristics and guidelines for their use*, International Standard Organisation, December 1991

Di Capua, G., Jeanrenaud, A., *Italian perspective on IT assessment and certification agreement,* Fourth European Conference on Software Quality, Basel, October 1994

Spinelli, A., Pina,D., Salvaneschi, P., Crivelli, E., Meda, R., *Quality measurement of software products: an experience about a large automation system*, Objective Quality 1995, Firenze

ISO/IEC DIS 12207-1, *Information Technology - Software - Part 1: Software life-cycle process*, International Standard Organisation,

ISO/IEC CD 9126-6, *Guide to software product evaluation - The evaluator's guide*, International Standard Organisation, 1993

PART SEVEN

Quality Modelling

19

In Search of the Customer's Quality View

*T. Stålhane** *P.C. Borgersen* *K. Arnesen*
SINTEF - DELAB *Software Innovation AS* *Fellesdata AS*

*N-7034 Trondheim, Norway, p: +47 73593014, f: + 47 73532586 **

Abstract

This paper describes the work done in the PROFF project to get the customer's view of software product quality. The customers in this case are organizations that buy software for PCs and workstations. The main result is that the quality of service and follow-up activities are more important than the quality of the product itself. This observation should have an impact on the way we market and sell software products in the future.

Keywords

Customer quality view, product quality, service quality, price vs. quality requirements

1 INTRODUCTION

This paper describes the work undertaken by personnel working in the Norwegian software quality program PROFF, which has as its goal to improve the quality and competitiveness of Norwegian software industry.

The first activity in the project was to find the aspects of quality that are most important to the customers. In order to find an answer to this, we made a questionnaire based on the structure of the definitions of product and service quality in ISO 9126 and 9004 respectively.

This questionnaire was distributed to 1000 Norwegian companies that buy commercial software products for PCs and workstations, either off the shelf, as standard software packages or as adapted or tailor made solutions. The responders in our survey were asked to give us the relevant information for a product that they had bought recently. In this way, we hoped to get the responders to be quite concrete in their responses. In addition, this approach enabled us to also get information on price, application area and product category. Among the 90 questionnaires that were returned, six lacked all product related information, while eight only lacked information on product category. Thus, only 82 questionnaires were available for product category related analysis and 84 questionnaires could be used for analysis pertaining to product price.

The returned questionnaires were analysed and the results were presented to the Norwegian system development companies that are members of PROFF. These companies will use the results to better target their products against the market's expectations and to deliver products and services that are able to compete successfully in the European markets in the next five years.

2 QUALITY MODELS AND QUESTIONAIRE STRUCTURE

The questionnaire was structured according to the structure of the factor - criteria models used in ISO 9126 (1991) and ISO 9004 (1987). These two models are shown in figures 1 and 2 respectively. For the service quality, we removed the criteria not related to the service provided by software producers. Typical examples of removed criteria are hygiene, comfort and aesthetics of the environment. Such criteria have little relevance here since software product service is mostly provided at the customer's premises or over the telephone.

As mentioned above, we also collected information on the price of the software. This was done in order to see if there was any significant difference in the quality requirements depending on the price of the software.

For each criterion, the responders were asked to indicate how important this quality criterion was for their decision to buy or not to buy the software product under consideration. The answers were given by using a four point scale, graded as follows:

- high importance - score 3;
- some importance - score 2;
- little importance - score 1;
- no importance or irrelevant - score 0.

In addition, we asked for price information. We split the responses according to price, using the following categories:

- category 1: 0 - 10 000 NOK, or approximately 0 - 1 500 USD;
- category 2: 10 000 - 50 000 NOK, or approximately 1 500 - 7 700 USD;
- category 3: more than 50 000 NOK or approximately 7 700 USD.

The complete questionnaire - in Norwegian - can be found in Arnesen (1995).

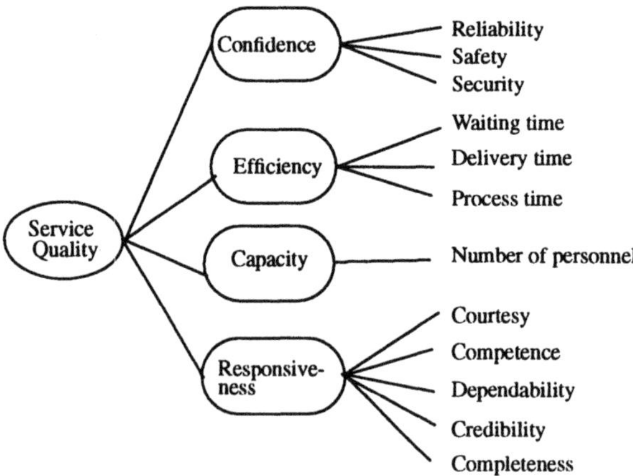

Figure 1. Reduced ISO 9004 model for service quality.

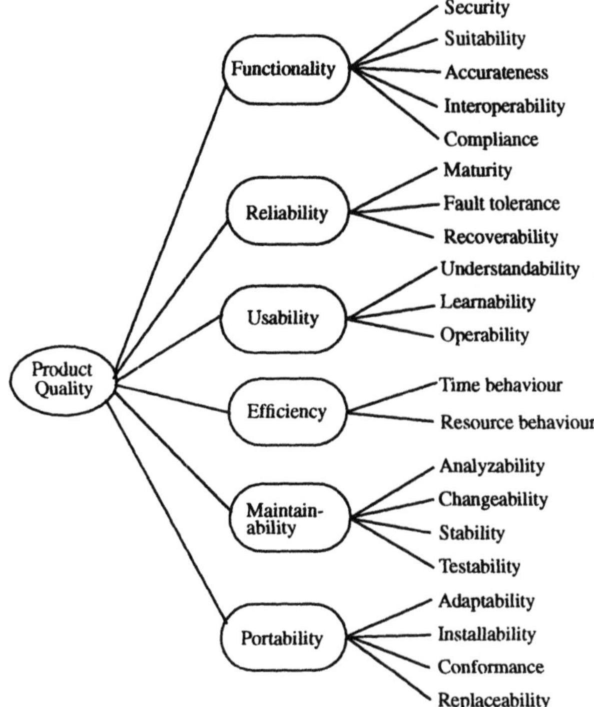

Figure 2. The ISO 9126 model for software quality.

By using the structure of the two quality models to structure the questionnaire, we got a questionnaire with the following structure:

Questions related to the software's price category, product category and application area

Questions related to product quality

1. Questions related to product quality factor 1

    Questions related to criterion 1 for factor 1
    :
    Questions related to criteria u for factor 1

2. Questions related to product quality factor 2

    :
    Questioned related to product quality factor 2

Questions related to service quality

1. Questions related to service quality factor 1

    :

m. Questions related to service quality factor m

3 MAIN RESULTS

First of all, we looked at the overall score, i.e. the ranking of the factors that we got when pooling together the responses from all price and product categories. The score for each factor was computed as the average of the scores for all criteria related to this factor. This gave the following results:

Table 1. Scores for all products pooled together

Factor	Score
Service responsiveness	2.81
Service capacity	2.74
Product reliability	2.71
Service efficiency	2.65
Product functionality	2.60
Service confidence	2.60
Product usability	2.57
Product efficiency	2.46
Product portability	2.05
Product maintainability	1.89

At first glance, it might look strange that the functionality came in fifth place. This does, however, not imply that the functionality does not matter. Instead, it implies that if the software solves the problems at hand, the details of the functionality are not that important.

What surprised us was that the reliability came in third place. We found this so surprising that we conducted a follow-up review with four of our responders. The answers that we got can be summed up as follows:

> Due to other software, such as for instance Windows, the machine crashes two to four times a week anyhow. As long as the product under consideration has a MTTF that is considerably higher than that, we do not care.

Small differences in scores in table 1 should not be used to rank one factor before another. A more detailed statistical analysis, built on the frequency of "high importance" scores is found in chapter 4.3

We the split up the responses into three product categories according to type as follows:

- COTS - Commercial Off The Shelf - software
- Standard software packages
- Customized or tailor made software products

The number of responses for each category is shown in parentheses in the heading of table 2. The factor scores were computed in the same way as for table 1. We got the following results:

Table 2. Scores according to product category

Factor	COTS (36)	Standardized software packages (27)	Customized and tailored software (19)
Product functionality	2.55	2.65	2.62
Product reliability	2.65	2.77	2.74
Product usability	2.67	2.47	2.54
Product efficiency	2.47	2.35	2.58
Product maintainability	1.68	1.94	2.32
Product portability	2.01	2.04	2.09
Service confidence	2.55	2.59	2.67
Service efficiency	2.64	2.67	2.61
Service capacity	2.69	2.74	2.84
Service responsiveness	2.82	2.83	2.76

Table 2 shows that in all cases, the producer's service responsiveness and service capacity are considered to be of most important factors while product maintainability and portability are considered to be of the least importance. The only product factor that score consistently high is product reliability.

4 DATA ANALYSIS

4.1 Hypothesis to be Tested

In order to get a more in-depth understanding of the responses, we tested the following hypothesis:

- Ha: The requirements on product and service quality have the same important for COTS, standard software packages and customized or tailor made products.
- Hb: The requirements on product and service quality do not depend on the product's price.
- Hc: The importance ordering of the service and product quality factors is independent of product price.
- Hd: The importance ordering of the service and product quality factors is independent of product type.

In order to check the first two hypotheses, we reason as follows:

If a factor is more important in one product or price category than in another, then this factor will receive significantly more top scores - the rating "highly important" - than what would be the case if this factor was not considered so important.

In order to check the last two hypothesis, we reason as follows:

The ranking of importance is described by the score as it is assigned in tables 4 and 5 below. Thus, we can use the differences between the factor ranking for each category - price or product - as a measure of the independence of the factors across categories. If the differences are not significant, then the factor ranking are not different for different categories.

4.2 Methods for Analysis.

Since our responders graded each criterion separately, we used the average number of top scores per factor for our ranking process. This value was then divided by the number of responders in each group. The reason for only using the number of top scores, instead of adding the contributions from the other scores, is that it is not possible to assign numerical values to both "highly important' and "somewhat important" in such a way that these values mirror the absolute difference between these two categories.

When selecting statistical methods for testing the hypothesis, we decided to use non-parametric methods as far as possible. The reasons for this are that:

- The data that we have collected are categorical and thus only concerned with ranks.
- It frees us from the hard-to-validate assumption that our data are normally distributed. This - often unfounded - assumption plagues too many papers where statistical methods are used in software engineering research.

We based the tests for the hypotheses Ha and Hb on the Friedman statistics, described below. See for instance Lehman (1975). The method can be described by using the following table:

Table 3. Example of Friedman's rank statistics

Factor	Category 1	Category 2	Category 3
F_1	R_{11}	R_{21}	R_{31}
:	:	:	:
F_N	R_{1N}	R_{2N}	R_{3N}
$R_{i.}$	$R_{1.}$	$R_{2.}$	$R_{3.}$

We see that if one of the categories consistently receive the best score then the rank sum for this column will be close to N, while a category which is consistently given bad scores will have a rank sum close to 3N. If there are no differences, the score for all the columns will tend to be equal. The following formulas are used to compute the Friedman rank statistics:

$$R_{i.} = \frac{1}{N} \bullet \sum_{j=1}^{N} R_{ij}$$

$$Q = \frac{12N}{s(s+1)} \bullet \sum_{i=1}^{s} \left[R_{i.} - \frac{1}{2}(s+1)\right]^2$$

Here, N is the number of rows, while s is the number of categories (columns). As an approximation, we have that Q is Chi-square distributed with s-1 degrees of freedom. We will reject the hypothesis of no inter-column difference on the α-level if $Q > c$, where c is the α-percentile in the Chi-square distribution with s-1 degrees of freedom.

The testing of the two hypotheses Hc and Hd are based on the Spearman statistics, see for instance Lehman (1975). The idea is simple, as can be illustrated by using table 3 above. The statistics on which we will base our decision of hypothesis rejection or acceptance - here called D - is computed as follows:

$$D_{i,j} = \sum_{k=1}^{N} (R_{i,k} - R_{j,k})^2$$

The indices i and j are used to mark the columns that we test, while N is the number of rows in the two columns.

We see directly that if the factors are order in the same way in the two columns, we get D = 0. Thus, small D values indicate that the ranking of the factors in the two columns are dependent while a large D value indicates column independence.

For large N, the Ds are approximately normally distributed with known mean and variance. This could be used to test the hypotheses. However, there exist tables that can be used to test the Spearman correlation for significance - for instance table N in Lehman (1975). This table is used here.

When we want to draw conclusions based on frequencies for individual quality factors, we will use a hyper-geometric model. The population is all companies that are members of DnD - The Norwegian Computer Union. If we assume that the n-sized sample we have is representative, we can estimate the population for category i as $N_i = 1000 *$ sample size $_i$ / total sample size.

As our H_0 hypothesis we will assume that the two frequencies p_i and p_j are equal. By using the normal approximation and rejecting H_0 if $\Delta = p_i - p_j$ is large we reject H_0 at the α level if

$$\frac{|\Delta|}{\sqrt{Var(p_i) + Var(p_j) + Cov(p_j, p_i)}} > u_{\alpha/2}$$

See for instance Bissell (1994)

If we compare frequencies within a single column, sample size and population size are the same for pi and p_j. By using the fact that $[p(1 - p)]^{0.5}$ is close to 0.5 for all p-values of interest and assuming independence, we obtain

$$\Delta_\alpha > u_{\alpha/2}\sqrt{\frac{N-n}{2nN}}$$

Note that this is a quite conservative limit. Even a small correlation between the quality factors will lower the Δ-value considerably.

4.3 Results from the Analysis

We used the data lay-out in the tables below to test the hypotheses. Each table entry has the format <average number of top scores / rank within table row>. Next to this, we have inserted the column rank for each factor within each category.

If two or more table entries have the same value, they are first grouped together, given consecutive ranks and are then all given the rank equal to the average of all the ranks for this group.

For the product categories in table 4, we get Q = 0.11. With an α of 0.05, we find that we can not reject the hypothesis of no difference - Ha. We can thus pool the data from all the columns. If we use the frequencies based on the pooled data, we can also group the quality factors according to importance. In order to get a clear picture of the situation, we will order the quality factors on a frequency line as shown in figure 3 below. The acronyms are explained in table 4.

SCO SE SC SR

PP PM PE PF PU PR

0.0 0.1 0.2 0.3 0.4 0.5 0.6 0.7 0.8 0.9 1.0

Figure 3. Distribution of "high importance" for quality factors

The Δ-value will in this case be 0.12. We can now group the quality factors into three groups with high, medium and low user importance respectively:

- High: service responsiveness, service capacity, service efficiency and product reliability
- Medium: service confidence, product usability, product functionality and product efficiency
- Low: product maintainability and product portability

We see that those who insist on equating product quality with product reliability have a strong case, at least from the users point of view.

Table 4. Factor importance versus product category

Factor	COTS (36)		Standardized software packages (27)		Customized and tailored software (19)		Pooled data (82)
Product functionality - PF	0.67 / 1	4.5	0.58 / 2	6	0.50 / 3	9	0.60
Product reliability - PR	0.67 / 3	4.5	0.79 / 2	2	0.81 / 1	2	0.74
Product usability - PM	0.74 / 1	2	0.51 / 3	7	0.63 / 2	6	0.63
Product efficiency - PE	0.51 /2	7	0.43 / 3	8	0.60 / 1	7	0.50
Product maintainability - PM	0.29 / 3	10	0.37 / 2	9	0.52 / 1	8	0.37
Product portability - PP	0.32 / 3	9	0.35 / 1	10	0.33 / 2	10	0.33
Service confidence - SCO	0.40 / 3	8	0.74 / 1	4	0.73 / 2	3	0.58
Service efficiency - SE	0.66 / 3	6	0.73 / 1	5	0.71 / 3	4	0.69
Service capacity - SC	0.72 / 3	3	0.78 / 2	3	0.90 / 1	1	0.78
Service responsiveness - SR	0.85 / 1	1	0.83 / 2	1	0.65 / 3	5	0.80
Average column rank	2.3	-	1.9	-	1.9	-	-

In addition to variation over product types, we were also interested in the effect of product price.

Table 5. Factor importance versus product price

Factor	Price category 1 (20)		Price category 2 (22)		Price category 3 (42)	
Product functionality	0.62 / 3	5	0.79 / 1	2	0.73 / 2	5.5
Product reliability	0.60 / 3	6	0.82 / 1	1	0.77 / 2	2
Product usability	0.70 / 1	2	0.60 / 3	7	0.64 / 2	8
Product efficiency	0.43 / 3	8	0.57 / 1	8	0.51 / 2	9
Product maintainability	0.33 / 2	9.5	0.38 / 1	9.5	0.07 / 3	10
Product portability	0.33 / 3	9.5	0.38 / 2	9.5	0.76 / 1	3.5
Service confidence	0.65 / 3	3	0.67 / 2	6	0.76 / 1	3.5
Service efficiency	0.59 / 3	7	0.72 / 2	4	0.73 / 1	5.5
Service capacity	0.75 / 3	1	0.77 / 2	3	0.81 / 1	1
Service responsiveness	0.64 / 3	4	0.71 / 1	5	0.69 / 2	7
Average column rank	2.7	-	1.6	-	1.7	-

For the price categories in table 5, we get Q = 7.4. With an α of 0.05, we find that we can reject the hypothesis of no difference - Hb. A quick glance at the table also shows that the requirements on product and service quality is much lower for the products in the lowest price category.

For the three columns used in the two tables 4 and 5 we find the following D values for the inter-column correlations:

Table 6. D values for Spearman statistics

Table number	Columns 1 and 2	Columns 1 and 3	Columns 2 and 3
Table 4 - Product category	23.10 *	96.50	26.00 *
Table 5 - Product price	82.00	101.00	68.00 *

From table N in Lehman (1975) we find that the correlations marked with an asterisk are significant at the 5% level. As we see, we can at least partly reject the two hypotheses Hc and Hd of no correlation. The correlation between neighbouring columns and the lack of correlation between the first and the third column can best be explained by the accumulation of small changes as we move from left to right in the table.

Once we had established the possible correlations, we found it fruitful to see what caused the correlation changes. In order to study this, we decide to look at which factors moved and which did not. Table 7 shows these movements over product categories. The differences shown in the table are computed as the differences between the leftmost and the rightmost categories (columns).

Table 7. Changes in relative top scores for product and price changes.

Factor	Score differences: Product categories	Score differences: Price categories
Product functionality	- 0.17	+ 0.11
Product reliability	+ 0.14	+ 0.17
Product usability	- 0.11	- 0.06
Product efficiency	+ 0.09	+ 0.08
Product maintainability	+ 0.23	- 0.26
Product portability	+ 0.01	+ 0.43
Service confidence	+ 0.33	+ 0.11
Service efficiency	+ 0.05	+ 0.14
Service capacity	+ 0.18	+ 0.06
Service responsiveness	- 0.20	+ 0.05

As we move from COTS products to tailor-made products, product maintainability and service confidence get more importance, together with service capacity. The reason for this is that customers who buy tailored software do not expect the producer to put new, improved product versions on the market, except if they have a maintenance contract. Since this is a long term commitment, the requirements on service responsiveness decreases.

As the price increases, the customers increase their requirements on product reliability and portability. At least the latter of these two effects can be seen as a result of the customers' need to protect their investment in expensive software systems. They need to be able to port expensive software so that they do not have to buy new versions when the environments are changed.

The conclusion of this discussion is that software customers behave in an economically rational manner. Thus, their behaviours and preferences can be deduced from simple economic considerations.

5 RELATED RESULTS

There are two other survey results published at about the same time that are relevant to our results. One was published in ComputerWorld Norway (1994) and the other was published by a European provider of telecommunications software. The results from ComputerWorld are related to software on mainframe computers and are summed up in the table 8 below. For the sake of comparison, we have shown the overall results from our survey in the same table. Since the ComputerWorld survey used a scoring scheme different from ours, we have only shown the factors' ranking.

Table 8. Comparison of the PROFF and the ComputerWorld surveys on quality requirements

Our survey (PC and work station systems)	ComputerWorld survey (mainframes)
Service responsiveness	Product reliability
Service capacity	Product efficiency
Product reliability	Service responsiveness
Service efficiency	Operating system functionality
Product functionality	Product capacity

We see that for mainframe users, product reliability is rated as most important, with product efficiency in second place. This reflects, in our opinion, the much higher reliability of the supporting software on a mainframe than on PCs and work stations. In this case, the product reliability will get a much higher priority. In addition, the ranking also reflects the higher degree of professionalism of the main-frame sites.

The results pertaining to the telecommunication software provider had a different focus. The questions they asked their customers were "Would you buy from this company again?" and "Would you recommend others to buy from this company?". The results are shown in the tree in figure 3.

At a first glance it is rather surprising that the only case where we get a 100% yes on the question "Would you recommend others to buy from this company?" is if the customer has complained and got a satisfactory response. In the case of no complaints this question only got 87% yes.

The conclusion seems to be that for the customers it is more important with a satisfactory service response than having no problems at all.

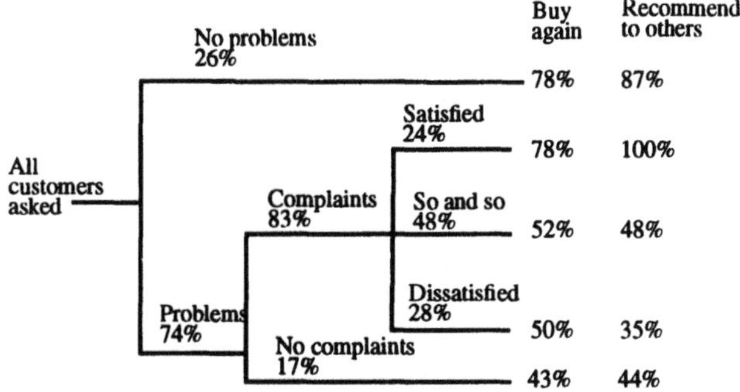

Figure 4. Customer reactions to software product problems

6 CONCLUSIONS

The conclusions are split into two parts, namely the conclusions based on the data analysis alone and the conclusions that are based on their interpretations.

6.1 Conclusions based on the Data Analysis.

The results below are based on the previous data analyses and discussions:

The first, and perhaps the most important, result of our survey is the strong focus on service quality. This can be seen already from the first summary of the results in table 1. The result is reinforced by the related surveys cited in the second half of chapter 5.

Next, we find that the customers' quality requirements increase with the price of the product. This is as should be expected - hypothesis Hb.

However, there are no significant difference in quality requirements between products of different categorise - at least not as these are defined in our survey, namely COTS, standardized software packages, customized or tailor made - hypothesis Ha. This is reasonable since theses categories describe how the product is marketed and sold and not the customers' quality needs or expectations.

Last, but not least, we found that there are a large amount of agreement over the relative importance of the quality factors between different product types and a somewhat lower degree of agreement between on the rating of the quality factors different price categories - hypotheses Hc and Hd.

6.2 Conclusions based on Interpretations of the Data Analysis

Firstly, software products are considered to be complex and having a large potential to cause problems that the average user has little competence in handling. For main-frame users this cause few problems since they have access to a competent service organization in-house. For other users, however, this has lead to a strong focus on service quality.

Secondly, maintainability and portability are not considered important for the average software customer. They consider it the producer's responsibility to provide updated and enhanced versions of the software on the platform that they need.

For the producer on the other hand, maintainability and portability are important since they use these characteristics to provide the services that the customer requires.

Thirdly, the reliability of the software product is only important if its MTTF is comparable to the MTTF of the rest of the system. As long as the system's MTTF is much larger than that of the platform, reliability is not an issue for the average user.

Fourthly, software customers behave in an economically rational way when they set priorities on quality requirements. Their preferences can be deduced from simple economic relations. If the pricing policy or market mechanisms change, so will the importance of each quality factor.

In our opinion, the customers' strong focus on service quality is an opportunity and not a problem. The advice is: Do not just sell a product; sell a product plus service, provided through personal contacts. The personnel used to provide these services must know the customer's applications and his problems and needs. In addition, he must show a genuine interest in that the customer reaps the benefits he expected from the product that he bought.

7 FUTURE WORK

The next phase of work in the PROFF project is to decide on estimators for all important factors. We have already defined estimators for the product quality factors, based on data that are observable either at the developer's site or at the customer's sites.

We will later also define estimators for the service quality factors. In addition, we will define metrics related to product and development process that will help the developers to satisfy specified customer quality requirements. We hope to have achieved most of these goals by the end of 1995.

8 REFERENCES

ComputerWorld (1994), ComputerWorld's guide to main-frames. ComputerWorld Norway, no. 30B, September 9, 1994 (in Norwegian)

Lehman, E.L. (1975), Nonparametrics: Statistical Methods Based on Ranks. Holden - Day Inc.

Bissell, D. (1994) Statistical Methods for SPC and TQM, Chapman & Hall Statistics Textbooks Series

Arnesen (1995), Arnesen, K., Borgersen P. Chr. and Stålhane, T., Final Report from the Software Quality Survey, PROFF report no. 1,(in Norwegian)

ISO/IEC 9126 (1991), Information technology - Software product evaluation - Quality characteristics and guidelines for their use, ISO

ISO/IEC 9004 (1987), Quality management and quality elements - Guidelines for services

20

Database Design for Quality

Donatella Castelli, Elvira Locuratolo
Istituto di Elaborazione dell'Informazione
Consiglio Nazionale delle Ricerche
Via S. Maria, 46
56126 Pisa, Italy,. Telephone: +39 50 593406/403. Fax: +39 50 554342.
email: `[castelli, locuratolo]@iei.pi.cnr.it`

Abstract
The approach employed to define a formal design methodology for the development of easy to use, flexible, efficient and correct database systems is described.

Keywords
Database system quality attributes, design for quality, methodological tools.

1 INTRODUCTION

Good design is always the best approach to a quality product. But what is a *good design* and how to obtain it? In our opinion, a design is a *good design* if it results in a system which meets desired quality attributes. A good design cannot be thus extemporized but it must be defined carefully using appropriate methods.

In this paper, we propose an approach to define methods for good design. This approach will be described by defining ASSO (Castelli and Locuratolo, 1994), a formal database design methodology which ensures the development of *easy to use*, *flexible*, *efficient* and *correct* database systems. The approach consists of sequence of steps. Each step is characterized by a goal, a proposed solution and a demonstration. The initial goal requires to define a database design methodology for the development of systems that meet fixed quality attributes. The proposed solution is a definition of the database design methodology, whereas the demonstration is the mean to establish if the proposed solution satisfies the goal. If the solution is correct, the proposed solution becomes the next goal of the sequence. By transitivity, the final solution, defined by a set of methodological tools integrated appropriately, satisfies the initial goal.

The quality attributes of database systems developed by ASSO are widely recognized in the database area, however the existing database design methodologies(Batini, Ceri and Navathe 1992; Rumbaugh et al., 1991; Booch, 1991; Coad and Yourdon, 1991) prioritize either easiness of use and flexibility or efficiency. Moreover correctness is often treated only partially. In order to achieve the desired quality attributes, ASSO has been designed as a methodology consisting of two stages: conceptual design and refinement. The conceptual design focuses on the construction of the conceptual schema, i.e. the specification of the database structure and behavior. An extended semantic model has been employed at this stage to guarantee both easiness in specifying the conceptual schema and flexibility in reflecting the changes occurring in real life.

The refinement stage transforms the conceptual schema into a schema acceptable by an object database management system which is nowadays considered the most promising with respect to efficiency. The conceptual and the object schemas are also represented formally as Abstract Machine models(Abrial, in press). Formality is used by the database designer to prove correctness; however, it is introduced as an orthogonal feature of the database schemas, i.e. it is completely transparent to the application user. As a consequence, correctness does not degrade the other quality attributes.

The rest of the paper is organized as follows: Section 2 lists the database system quality attributes ; Section 3 describes the approach and discusses its benefits. Conclusions are given in Section 4.

2 THE QUALITY ATTRIBUTES

The approach adopted to define ASSO assumes that the database system quality attributes to be accomplished during the database design have been established. They are considered to be all equally important, i.e., none of them is priorized. These attributes are:

easiness of use: the ability of the database system to provide a schema which can be understood easily and which can facilitate the writing of applications.

flexibility: the ability of the database system to provide a schema which permits the applications to be easily modified to reflect the changes occurring in real life.

correctness: the ability of the database system to provide a schema which satisfies its specifications expressed through the conceptual schema.

efficiency: the ability of the database system to access and store the database information using a limited amount of time and storage.

The quality attributes listed above can be classified as *external attributes* (Meyer, 1988) since they are detected directly by both the database application programmers and the database application users. The quality attributes perceptible only to the database designer are said *internal attributes* since they are the key to ensure that the external attributes are satisfied.

The approach illustrated in the next section begins taking into account the external attributes since only they really matter in the end.

Figure 1 The stepwise approach.

3 THE APPROACH

This section presents the approach which has been adopted to define ASSO, a formal database design methodology for the achievement of quality database systems. The approach consists of a sequence of steps. Each step is characterized by a goal, a proposed solution and a demonstration. The initial goals requires to define a database design methodology which meets fixed external attributes. At each step, the proposed solution is a definition of the database design methodology, whereas the demonstration is the mean to establish if the proposed solution satisfies the goal. If this is true, the proposed solution becomes the next goal of the sequence, otherwise a new solution must be proposed. In order to satisfies the goal, the solution must have a set of properties which suffices to meet the goal requirements. Step by step the proposed solution refines the previous one, i.e. new methodological tools are chosen to be integrated into the previous solution. The sequence ends when all the significant choices have been done. The final solution is given in terms of methodological tools integrated appropriately. Figure 1 illustrates this approach: each step is represented by two successive points linked by an arrow directed towards the first point. The points represent respectively the goal and the proposed solution, whereas the arrow represents the goal satisfiability. Exploiting transitivity, the solution proposed for satisfying the final goal is also a solution for satisfying the initial goal and thus it permits the development of database systems which meet the desired external attributes.

3.1 The step sequence

Let us now introduce the sequence of steps.

Step 1

Initial Goal: Goal 1
Define a database design methodology for the development of an easy to use, flexible, correct and efficient database system.

The following solution has been proposed to satisfy the initial goal:

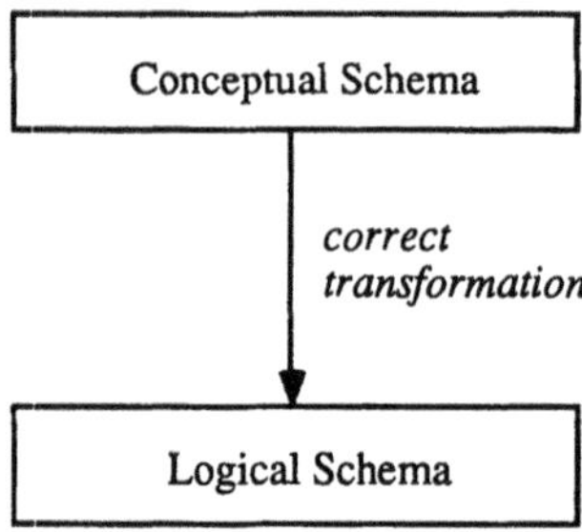

Figure 2 Solution 1.

Solution 1:
The methodology comprises

1. two modelling levels:
   (a) the *conceptual schema*, i.e. an high level description of the database structure and behavior;
   (b) the *logical schema*, i.e. a description of the database structure and behavior given in terms of a model supported by an efficient database management system;
2. a *correct transformation*, i.e. a semantic-preserving transformation from the conceptual schema to the logical schema.

This solution is illustrated in Figure 2.

Demonstration 1:
The semantic-preserving transformation guarantees that the logical schema is a correct implementation of the conceptual schema. As a consequence the applications can be written in an easy and flexible way referring the conceptual schema and at the same time they can be supported by an efficient database management system. □

Remark 1:
Although current database design methodologies use the above two modelling levels, they generally do not comprise a correct transformation to link them. As a consequence, they support a conceptual design which can be specified at an high-level description, but the database applications must be written referring the low level logical schema thus not achieving all the desired quality attributes.

Solution 1 can now be interpreted as a new goal to be satisfied.

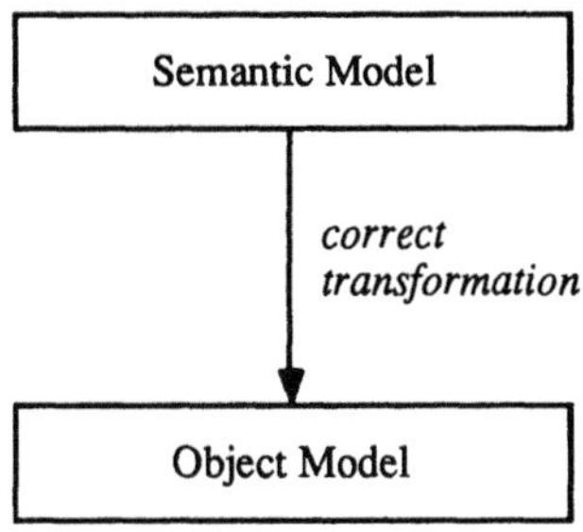

Figure 3 Solution 2.

Step 2

Goal 2:
Define a methodology which satisfies the properties expressed in Solution 1.

We propose the following solution to satisfy Goal 2:

Solution 2:
The methodology comprises

1. two modelling levels:

   (a) the conceptual schema modelled by an *extended semantic model*, i.e., a semantic data model extended with an high level behavioral model;
   (b) the logical schema, modelled by an *object model*;

2. a semantic-preserving transformation from the conceptual schema to the logical schema.

This Solution is illustrated in Figure 3.

Demonstration 2:
Semantic data models are considered to be the most appropriate models for representing the conceptual schema (Bouzeghoub and Metais, 1991) since they provides the concepts essential for supporting the application environment at a very high non-system specific level(Navathe, 1992). Extending them with an appropriate high-level behavioral model is sufficient to guarantee property (a) of Goal 2.

The object systems(Deux et al., 1990) have achieved a remarkable level of efficiency in managing information. The choice of a model which is supported by these systems suffices to satisfy property (b) of Goal 2 . □

Remark 2:

The models we have chosen for the two schemas are methodological tools frequently used within the database design methodologies. What distinguish our methodology from the others is the correctness of the link introduced between the two schemas.

We now continue by proposing Solution 2 as the new goal to be satisfied.

Step 3

Goal 3:

Define a methodology which satisfies the properties given by Solution 2.

The solution proposed at this step is the following:

Solution 3:

The methodology comprises

1. two modelling levels:
   (a) the conceptual schema, modelled by both an extended semantic model and an equivalent *formal model*;
   (b) the logical schema, modelled by both a model supported by an object system and an equivalent *formal model*;
2. a *formal* correct transformation from the conceptual schema to the logical schema.

Figure 4 shows Solution 3.

Demonstration 3:

This solution satisfies Goal 3 since it associates an equivalent formal method with each schema and specializes Property 2 of the previous solution by choosing a set of possible correctness preserving transformations. □

Remark 3:

The idea of formalizing all the phases of the software design to prove the process correctness is well consolidated in the software engineering area where several proposals exists (Wirth, 1971; Partsch, 1990, Abrial, in press). Solution 3 transfers this idea to the database area. In our proposal, formality is a mean to prove correctness, but it is not visible to the database users. This implies that correctness does not degrade the other external attributes.

Figure 4 reflects that formality is an internal attribute since it concerns only the internal components of the database design.

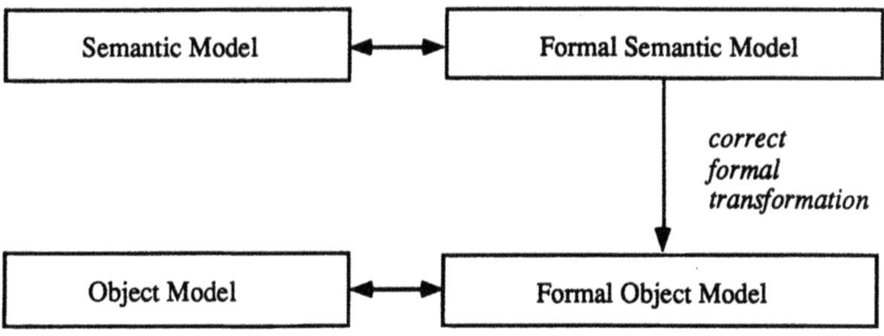

Figure 4 Solution 3.

Step 4

Goal 4:
Define a methodology which satisfies the properties expressed in Solution 3.

The following solution has been proposed to satisfy this goal.

Solution 4:
The methodology comprises

1. two modelling levels:

   (a) the conceptual schema, modelled by both an extended semantic model and an equivalent *Abstract Machine model*;
   (b) the logical schema, modelled by both a model supported by an object system and an equivalent *Abstract Machine model*;

2. a formal correct transformation from the conceptual schema to the logical schema defined by a *stepwise refinement.*

This solution is illustrated in Figure 5.

Demonstration 4:
This solution is a specialization of the previous one since it selects a particular formal model for the conceptual and logical schema formalization. Furthermore, it selects a special type of correct transformation, i.e. the stepwise refinement. It thus satisfies Goal 4. □

Remark 4:
We formalize our schemas using the Abstract Machine(AM) model.

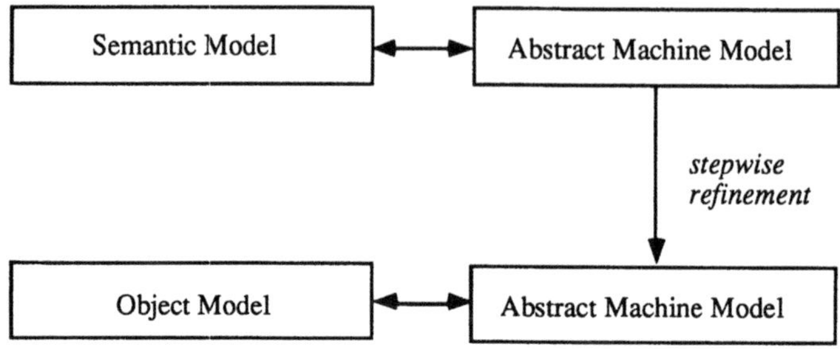

Figure 5 Solution 4.

AM is a mathematical model based on first order logic and a subset of set theory. It supports a model-based approach to the specification, i.e. a specification in which both a model of the state of a system and the operations which constitute its interface are described. This characteristic renders the AM model particularly suitable to be used for database system specifications. The AM model is employed within the B-Method (Abrial, in press), a formal method introduced in the software engineering area to construct correct programs, i.e. programs which satisfy their specifications. This method supports a design made of two stages, specification and refinement, both carried out within the same formal framework. The specification stage builds an AM incrementally. The refinement stage consists of a sequence of steps. At each step, an AM closer to an implementation is proposed and proof obligations which express the correctness of the new AM model with respect to the previous one are proved.

The stepwise refinement has been chosen for both the reasons: a) the implementation of a semantic model by means of an object model is a complex task which can be better approached with a stepwise refinement; b) the refinement supported by the B-Method is a stepwise refinement.

Step 5

Goal 5 is the last goal of the ASSO definition process. It imposes to satisfy the following requirement:

Goal 5:
Define a methodology which satisfies the properties expressed in Solution 4.

Solution 5: the final solution
The methodology comprises

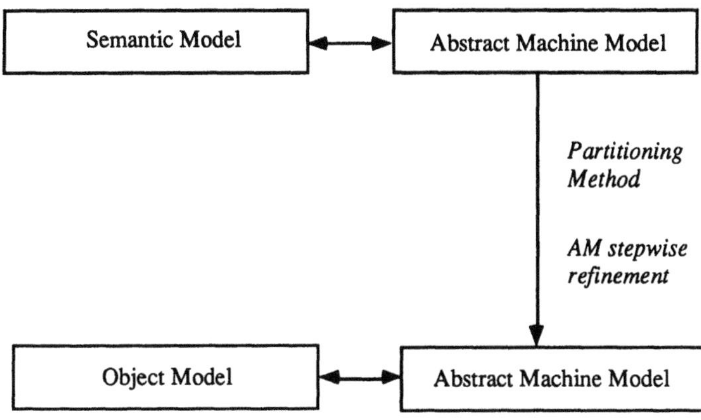

Figure 6 ASSO.

1. two modelling levels:
   (a) the conceptual schema, modelled by both an extended semantic model and an equivalent Abstract Machine model;
   (b) the logical schema, modelled by both a model supported by an object system and an equivalent Abstract Machine model;
2. a formal correct transformation from the conceptual schema to the logical schema defined by a stepwise refinement which consists of *two phases*: the *Partitioning Method* and the *Abstract Machine refinement.*

The final solution is illustrated in Figure 6.

Demonstration 5:
The stepwise refinement has been decomposed in two phases corresponding respectively to data refinement and behavioral refinement since the transformation is a complex task which can be better approached considering statics and behavioral aspects of schemas independently.

The Partitioning Method(Locuratolo and Rabitti, in press) transforms step-by-step the formal semantic schema in a schema with features of object models. These models enjoy the property that each object belongs to one and only one class. At each step, a new schema equivalent to the previous one is defined. This guarantees both the correctness of this phase and the compatibility of the resulting schema with the Abstract Machine Model.

The Abstract Machine Refinement defines a sequence of schema transformations from the output of the Partitioning Method to a formal object schema which can be translated easily into an object logical schema. At each step, the database designer proposes a new schema which reformulates the behavioral definition of the previous schema and proves first order formulas to establish the correctness of the step. By exploiting transitivity, also the correctness of this refinement phase is guaranteed. □

Remark 5:

In semantic models an object can belong simultaneously to any intersection of subclasses, whereas in object data models no object can belong simultaneously to two subclasses if one of them of them is not a subclass of the other. This characteristic of object models limits the flexibility in reflecting changes occurring in the real life. The Partitioning Method defines a link between class of objects at semantic level and class of objects at object level thus combining the useful features of both semantic and object models.

The Abstract Machine Refinement is a particular B-Method refinement. As a consequence, formulas simpler than the corresponding B-Method formulas are used to ensure the correctness of this phase.

The step 5 completes the methodology definition process. By exploiting the transitivity of the goal satisfiability, it follows that ASSO satisfies also the initial goal, i.e. it is a methodology for the development of database systems which meets the chosen external attributes.

3.2 The approach benefits

The approach demonstrates ASSO to be a database design methodology for quality; i.e. the database systems developed by ASSO achieve the chosen external quality attributes. The demonstration is organized step-by-step. As a consequence, if a proposed solution does not meet the goal properties, only a solution for this step must be given again.

At each step no specific solutions is imposed by this approach but several solutions are possible. The only constraint is that the proposed solution must have properties which suffices to meet the goal. In particular, our choices have been driven with the aim of selecting, when possible, consolidated tools whose contribution to the achievement of the fixed quality attributes is well understood. In doing so, we have turn our attention mainly towards tools typical of the database area. However, when these proved insufficient to our purposes, as for the definition of the correct transformation, we have directed our attention towards methodological tools of other areas.

Another benefit is that choices can be made gradually. At each step the attention is focused on few aspects. This simplifies the task of understanding which are the most appropriate methodological tools with respect to various factors such as tools at disposal, optimization criteria, etc..

The approach can be generalized to the case in which a goal can be decomposed in subgoal. When this generalization holds, the approach can be applied independently to each subgoal. This generalization is particularly useful for database design methodology of complex database systems.

Finally, although this approach has been described for the definition of ASSO, it is not strictly related to the database area, i.e. it can be applied to define a general design methodology.

4 CONCLUSIONS

This paper introduces a stepwise approach for defining a database design methodology for quality. It consists of a finite sequence of steps. Each step is associated with a goal, a proposed solution and a demonstration to establish if the solution satisfies the goal. This approach permits to demonstrate that the resulting methodology favors the development of database systems which achieve the following quality attributes: easiness of use, flexibility, efficiency and correctness.

A direction for future work is the generalization of this approach to the case in which the external attributes are not completely compatible. In the case a trade-off concept must be considered.

5 REFERENCES

Abrial, J., R. (in press) *The B-Book.* Cambridge Press.

Batini, C., and Ceri, S. and Navathe, S.B. 1992. *Conceptual Database Design: An Entity-Relationship Approach.* Redwood City, California: Benjamin Cummings.

Booch, G.,1991. *Object Oriented Design with Applications.* Redwood City, California: Benjamin Cummings.

Bouzeghoub, M. and Metais, 1991. E., Semantic Modelling of Object Oriented Databases. In *Proceedings of the 17th International Conference on Very Large Data Base, 1991.*

Castelli, D. and Locuratolo, E. 1994. ASSO: A Formal Database Design Methodology. In *Information Modeling and Knowledge Bases VI, Stockholm, 1994* edited by H. Jaakkola and H. Kangassalo. Finland: IOS Press, 145-158.

Castelli, D. and Locuratolo, E. 1995. Enhancing Database System Quality through Formal Design. In *4th Software Quality Conference, Dundee, 1995* edited by I.M. Marshall, W.B. Samson and D.G. Edgard-Nevill. Dundee. 359-366.

Deux, O. and et.al., The Story of O2, 1990. *IEEE Transaction on Knowledge and Data Engineering,* 3(1), 91-108.

Locuratolo, E. and Rabitti, F. (in press). Conceptual Classes and System Classes in Object Databases. *Acta Informatica.*

Meyer, B., 1988. *Object-Oriented Software Construction.* International Series in Computer Science. University Press, Cambridge: Prentice-Hall.

Navathe, S. B., 1992. Evolution of Data Modelling for Databases. *Communication of the ACM.* 35(9).

Partsch, H. A. 1990. *Specification and Transformation of Programs.* Texts and Monographs in Computer Science. Springer-Verlarg.

Rumbaugh, J. and Blaha, M. and Premerlani, W. and Eddy, F. and Lorensen, W. 1991. *Object-Oriented Modeling and Design.* Prentice-Hall.

Wirth, N., Program Development by Stepwise Refinement. 1971. *Communications of ACM.* 14. 221-227.

6 BIOGRAPHY

Donatella Castelli received her degree in computer science from the University of Pisa in 1983. Currently, she is a researcher at Istituto di Elaborazione dell'Informazione-CNR, Italy. Her interests includes database and multimedia design methodologies, formal methods, and re-engineering methods.

Elvira Locuratolo received her degree in mathematics from the University of Napoli in 1978. Currently, she is a researcher at Istituto di Elaborazione dell'Informazione-CNR, Italy. Her interests includes information modelling, database design and re-engineering methods.

Methodology assistant in a graphical design of real-time applications

R. Aubry, M. Maranzana and J.J. Schwarz
LISPI - L3I - INSA de Lyon Département Informatique - Bât. 502
F-69621 Villeurbanne Cedex, France
tel.: (+33) 72 43 81 62
fax: (+33) 72 43 85 18
e-mail: Mathieu.Maranzana@if.insa-lyon.fr

Abstract

LACATRE (**L**angage d'**A**ide à la **C**onception d'**A**pplications **T**emps **RE**el) is a graphical environment dedicated to multitasking real-time application developments. At the lowest level, it handles objects close to those supported by real-time executives (such as tasks, messages, semaphores...), and at the highest level, it manipulates applicative objects (like agencies and processes), near to the application programmer's preoccupation. Graphical programming has been used in order to obtain a documentation with a high degree of legibility and a synthetic as well as precise view of the dynamic behaviour of a real-time application.

The aim of this paper is to present the definition of a methodology assistant which takes advantage of the specificity of the Lacatre environment -behavioural axis, transformational axis, abstraction level axis, operative mode axis and graphical programming-, allowing an incremental development and providing an assistance adapted to the design context. Starting with a known, and rule based, stepwise design method, the methodology assistant can help the designer to verify the design steps and to monitor the complexity of the software components currently under construction.

Keywords

CASE tool, graphical design, real-time application, methodology, assistant, quality

1 INTRODUCTION

If the major concern in the development of real-time applications is to produce functionally correct results within given deadlines, the same holds more and more true, with respect to the quality control, trying to reach in priority the maintainability and the reliability factors.

At the outset, the aim of the Lacatre tool was to provide our students with a set of pedagogical tools for real-time multitasking learning. But, in fact the use of such a tool is not only restricted to educational purposes: a lot of industrial applications are based on the use of multitasking real-time kernels. In such cases, the tool will bring a substantial aid in the creation of programmes and their documentation. The Lacatre environment relies upon an intensive use of graphical programming and thereby inherits characteristics contributing to execute quality control in complex applications. Our idea is also to always place the designer in a situation which promotes a quality approach all along the development process.

The first part of the paper gives a short description of the Lacatre design principles relying on four different axis -behavioural, transformational, abstraction level and application phase-.

The second part will be devoted to the presentation of the Lacatre methodology and the methodology assistant. This assistant takes advantage of the Lacatre environment specificity, allowing an incremental development and providing an assistance adapted to the current context of the design.

We will introduce short examples to illustrate the Lacatre design principles and methodology and the use of an assistant.

2 DESIGN PRINCIPLES

The use of graphical tools can be very convenient for the realisation of complex real-time systems, as it is in other domains, such as mechanical or electronic engineering (Hinchey, 1994). Graphical design and programming with Lacatre provide a precise and synthetic view of the various aspects of a multitasking real-time application and produce a look-and-feel documentation with a high level of legibility. That guided us all along the definition and design of the Lacatre environment, which essentially relies on a graphical design and programming language. Such a designed application gives a set of diagrams with a well defined syntax and semantic. These diagrams are made up with graphical objects -the **Lacatre atomic objects**, images of those involved in standard industry real-time executives- and graphical links -the **Lacatre actions**, the **kernel system calls-**. Associated to this diagram, the designer can, if needed, take advantage of the textual dual form (Figure 1), which completes the documentation of the application design: it highlights the very detailed algorithmic structures of the application.

A real-time application can be analysed throughout various views and we primarily extract four main ones:

- The **behavioural axis** gives an idea of the dynamic behaviour of an application from the multitasking and communication/synchronisation points of view.
- The **transformational axis** defines how and where is done the real-time application data processing -data flow modelling- (Petit, 1994).

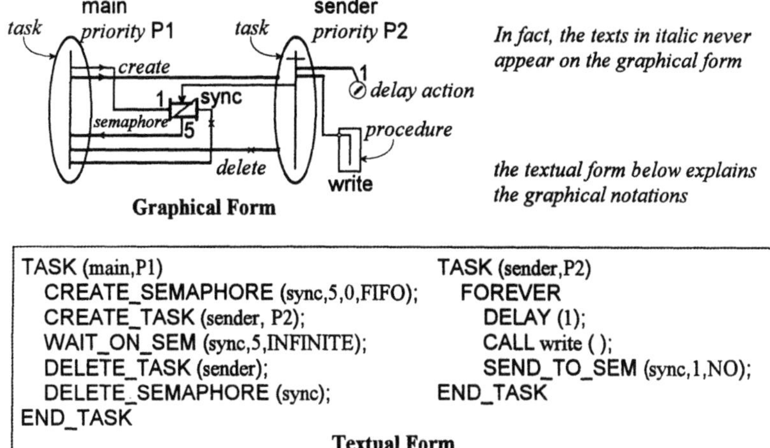

Figure 1 Diagram and textual form for a tasks synchronisation application.

- The **abstraction level axis**: the high level is closely linked with the application issues - applicative objects- and the low level defines the interface with the target computer system - Lacatre atomic objects-, executing the real-time application program. The **applicative objects**, used at the Preliminary Design step, are very general components able to express the main functionality of an application. The **atomic objects**, the designer handles at the Detailed Design step, are functionally very close to the target system possibilities: task, semaphore, interrupt, resource... Their use are straightaway dependant of the chosen target system (Schwarz and Skubich, 1993).
  This abstraction level axis will be developed and illustrated later in the paper.
- The **applicative phase axis**: several phases may be distinguished within a real-time application execution which correspond to the various steps of the application execution and which are bound with its own time constraints. One can distinguish four major phases:

1. The **initialisation phase** which launches the application by defining all the various components of the application; this phase can be purely sequential and usually is not time critical but only time ordered.
2. The **termination phase** when it exists, is symmetric to the initialisation one -takes charge of the objects deletion- and may be purely sequential too (usually not time critical); it is associated to the program shutdown.
3. The **kernel phase** describes the normal running mode of the application; it corresponds to the dynamic behaviour of the real-time application in standard situations with respect of all its constraints and in particular the temporal ones.
4. The **exception phase** deals with the exception handling that are bound to the application side effects (dynamic behaviour in non standard circumstances); according to the application complexity, this phase can be integrated to the kernel or to the termination phase and is essential in real-time applications.

The programmer separately designs these different phases, associating to each of them a design tracing with the appropriate objects and primitives. The general design document of the application is achieved by the superposition of all the basic tracings (Figure 1 and 2). Therefore, the applicative phase axis enhances the system simplification by partitioning: it is more efficient than a simple modularity -in fact, modularity can be added on each phase-.

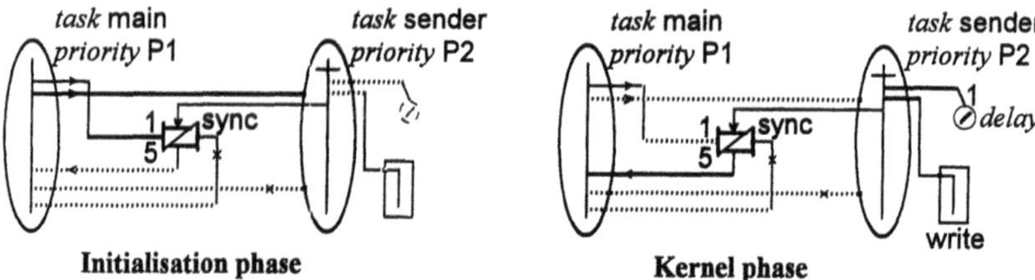

Figure 2 Two phases of the previous real-time application.

The **Lacatre atomic objects** act as an overlayer upon most of the off-the-shelves real-time executives and thanks to a modelling of such an executive, it is possible to complete the design with the target code generation (currently C language for the iRMX kernel).

The design quality of real-time applications is favoured by a strict adequation between the abstraction level and the object **resolution**: on the one hand, the higher the abstraction level is (Preliminary Design), the simpler the graphical symbolism and the connection rules are and, on the other hand, at a low abstraction level (Detailed Design), the symbolism is more detailed and the connection rules are more elaborated justifying thus to a great extent the automatic assistance given by the tool. We note that the introduction of the high level objects in the environment is a clear incitement to maintainability improvement, at a reasonable cost and promotes a coherent approach to complex systems.

This design formalism is not necessarily adapted for correctness verification which requires usually formal methods. Therefore when necessary, an automatic translation into an other formalism better suited for formal methods like for example Communicating Real-time State Machines (Shaw, 1992), can be done. This solution (CRSM) is carried out in the Lacatre environment but other translations may also be possible e.g. Petri nets.

3 LACATRE METHODOLOGY

3.1 Aim

The quality control, in CIM applications as well as in embedded systems, requires a global approach and becomes essential as soon as dependability is tackled (reliability, availability, maintainability, safety...). The development of a reliable system is based on the combined use of a set of methods (Laprie, 1989; Laprie, 1993; Laprie, 1995):

- two classes contributing to achieve quality that is, to avoid during the design and the programming, the emergency and introduction of faults (fault prevention methods) and to provide, for example thanks to redundancy, a service consistent with the specification in spite of faults (fault tolerance methods);

- and two others for quality validation that is, to reduce the occurrence (number and severity) of faults (fault elimination methods like testing) and to anticipate the faults presence (prediction methods like quantitative approaches).

The process described in this paper deals with the methods for avoiding faults (methodology approach) and with the prediction methods (quantitative measurements). It covers both the preliminary design steps and the detailed design steps with a view to an automatic target code generation. This process relies on a phases and steps chain whose aim is to minimise omissions, to avoid inconsistency, to favour reusability (atomic objects and applicative objects) and to master complexity thanks to a design based on drawings.

As the use of CASE tools with a too strong rigidity in the design process is often at the beginning of a rejection on behalf of the users (Gibson and Snyder, 1991), we have chosen a small steps chain with flexibility and adaptability. Thus, the methodology assistant has to advise, contextually and in a clever manner, the designer to incite him to reach a good design and development, and to assist him in the selection and construction of a final solution satisfying the quality constraints. During the following description of the design principles, all illustrations will be taken out from the same example: a simple monitoring of an industrial transfer system.

3.2 Description

During the preliminary design steps, the programmer defines a possible application decomposition in terms of applicative objects and theirs relations. Each object will be defined by:

- a name, image from the real world or the design step (inherited from the specification stage);
- a description of the offered services (inherited from the specification stage);
- architectural features (for instance, the applicative object is distributed or not...);
- an interface.

The initial steps includes four stages each of which is made up with operations and activities to do, with useful information for each activity, with control on the activities results, with the appropriated documentation to produce.

Context analysis

The designs starts with the enumeration of the inputs and outputs of the system. They define the connections or interface with the monitored or controlled world (Figure 3 (a)).

Architecture definition

It consists in a general architecture description of the real-time application in terms of Lacatre applicative objects (e.g. services required or provided by these objects) (Figure 3 (b)).

Definition, phase by phase, of all the relations between the applicative objects:

This step is a basic refinement of the previous one and is focusing on the communication channel between the objects (Figure 4).

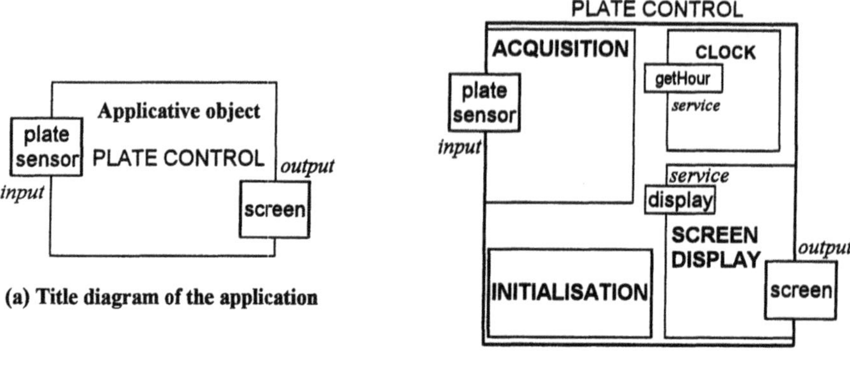

(a) Title diagram of the application

(b) General architecture of the application

Figure 3 Applicative objects of the monitoring part of a transfer system.

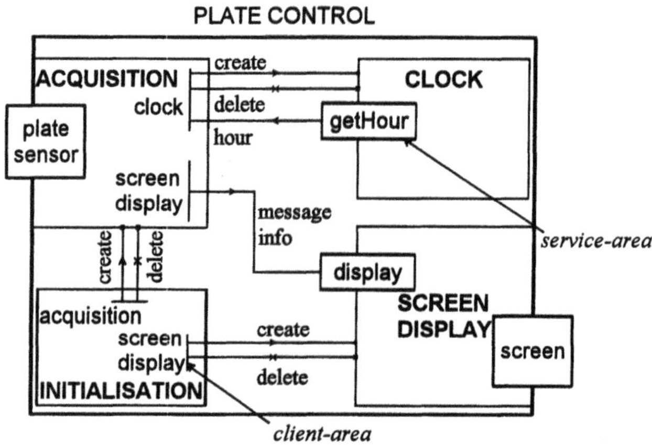

Figure 4 Definition of the communications.

It is decomposed into:

- the definition of all the relations: control flow (create, delete, suspend...) and data flow (message passing...);
- the introduction, if necessary, of connection areas (client-area, service-area in Figure 4 and import / export operators in Figure 5 and 6) in the applicative objects in order to provide anchor points for the communication channels.

Choice of the communication channel

The purpose of this step is to refine the communication between the applicative objects. The different communication possibilities the designer can use, are then proposed -or even imposed- indicating clearly the implications with regard to efficiency, reusability, embedding, distribution on a multiprocessor architecture... This choice has obviously to be guided by quality constraints. There are mainly two communication possibilities:

- Access to an applicative object through a single entry point identified by a simple procedure call. Thus, the only thing to do is to make available to the outside of the application object the name of that procedure (entry point **InitClock**).

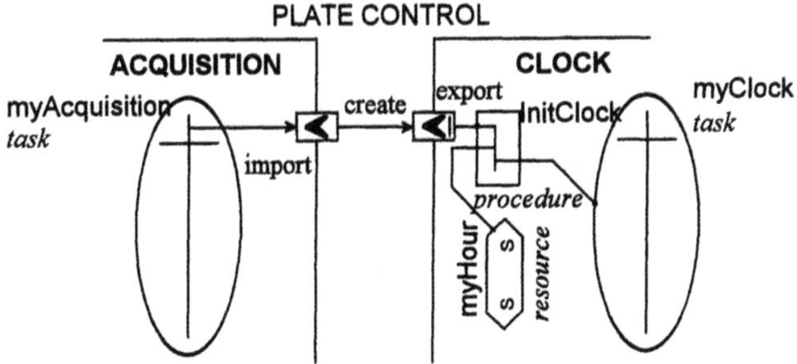

Figure 5 Communication channel through an import / export procedure entry point.

- Data flow through direct access to the atomic objects involved in the construction of the applicative objects, otherwise said, a partial inside view of the applicative object is accessible. From a dynamic point of view, the designer has a better control of the behavioural aspect of his application and thus, of the time essential in real-time applications.

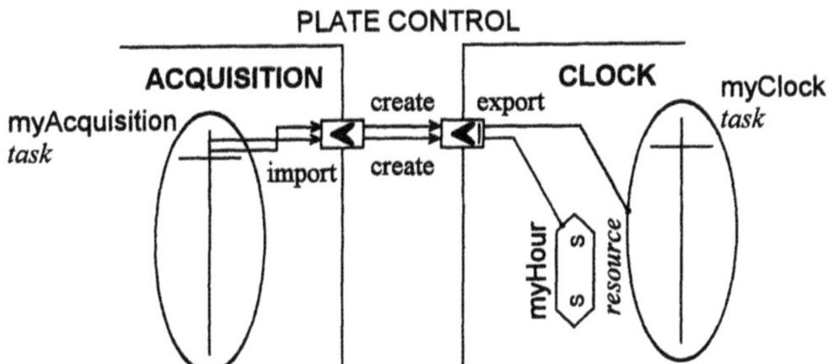

Figure 6 Communication protocol through a direct access to the atomic objects.

At this stage of the development, the application architecture is well defined. A synthetic check up can be proposed and is essentially based on:

- the list of objects to develop, with their specification and some indications about a possible reuse of already existing applicative objects (search, by name or keywords, in the object data base of applicative objects) (Aubry, 1995);
- the different views of the developed application (hierarchical, synthetic...).

Thus, during the detailed design steps, all the previous defined applicative objects, issued from the preliminary design steps, have to be designed in detail with the use of the Lacatre atomic objects and actions. The proposed method follows two specific axis:

- definition of the services between applicative objects, if necessary;
- definition or end of the definition of the applicative object itself.

The intensive use of graphical design in this step reduces the programmer's work, especially by relieving him of technical and low level detail -necessarily textual-. During this activity, he is guided by the application phase axis (kernel phase, initialisation and termination phases and possibly exception phase) (Figure 2) and by the graphical tool controls which avoid any redundancy and connection mistakes.

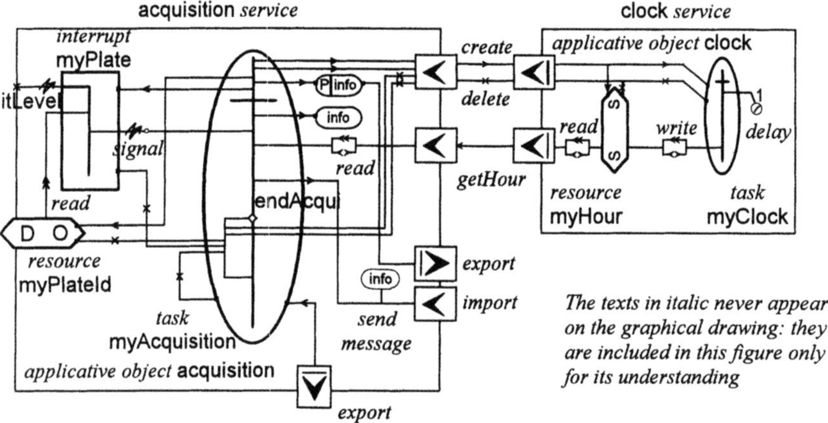

Figure 7 Applicative object acquisition and clock (detailed view).

After this step, all the various components of the application are completely defined and an automatic target code generation can take place.

Allowing incremental developments, this methodology can be well suited to very large systems construction in which the applicative objects may be designed and implemented by different groups of people. Indeed, at a given time, they may not all be at the same level of progress and a precise evaluation of each level of progress becomes absolutely necessary (step in the development methodology).

4 METHODOLOGY ASSISTANT

4.1 Main features

The Lacatre methodology, presented in the former section, applies both the Preliminary Design (software architecture) and the Detailed Design. This methodology is supported by a methodological assistant (Burlon and Tagliati, 1990). Its purpose is to help, all along the development process, the designer by providing contextual methodological advice and particular guidelines for a good respect of the methodology. It becomes one of the principle communication interfaces between the Lacatre environment and the designer.

The Lacatre methodology assistant will provide the designer with a trace of the development process he adopted for a given design. He may analyse it and/or have it in mind for the next equivalent project.

This tool provides several kinds of classical functionality (illustrated in the next section) (Burlon and Tagliati, 1990):

1. **Guidance through the method steps**:
   Thanks to this guidance, the designer is able to carry out the methodology process himself (phases and steps with the associated activities and operations for each of them). It completely defines the guideline through the development method.
2. **Methodological advice**:
   Step by step, the assistant supplies the designer with contextual advice and with information about goals and criteria to observe during the development.
3. **Information and reporting about the design**:
   A general view of the current design state is provided.
4. **Check facilities**:
   The help of the methodology assistant is also based on a set of checks to be performed in order to detect design faults.
5. **Quality assistance**:
   The assistant has also to ensure a better monitoring of the quality of the developed application (static measurement approach on the product) (Fenton, 1991). The specific attributes, defined in our assistant are the maintainability, the reliability, the reusability and the portability.

4.2 Illustration of the assistant

Some special features of the assistant will be illustrated using our transfer system.

Methodological advice

Among the constraints required by an application, the encapsulation aspect can be an important one. In such a case, the assistant will rather recommend, during the choice of a communication protocol (applicative object **CLOCK**, step 4. in the preliminary design), a procedure call (**InitClock**) than a direct access to a set of Lacatre atomic objects. The tool can produce as an output, the following control panel in answer to such a methodological advice.

Table 1 A methodological advice

Phase	*Step*	*Activity*	*Non functional requirement*	*Assistant advice*
preliminary design	step n°4	Communication channel choice	embedding	access to an applicative object through a single entry point (procedure call)

Information and reporting about actual design

At each stage of the development, the designer can obtain a general view concerning the design states of his applicative objects. In the example, the state diagram Figure 8 may be displayed for the applicative object **CLOCK** when the user is in the step n°4 **-Choice of the communication channel-** (Figure 5).

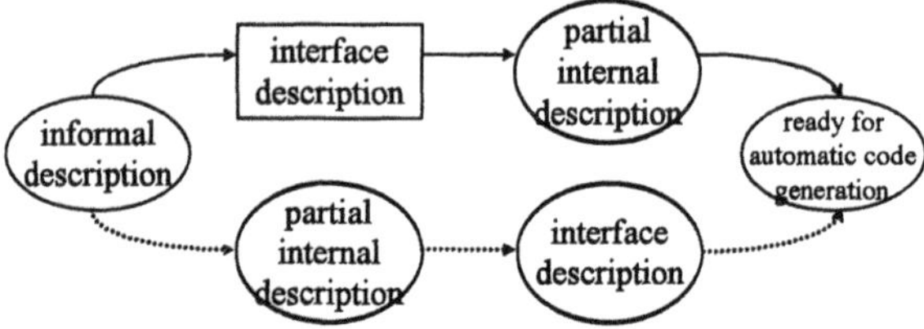

Figure 8 Simplified development states for an applicative object.

This diagram shows several possible paths to build an applicative object and illustrates the flexibility aspect of the method. The ideal way to go from the **informal description** to the final applicative object construction is given by the continuous line. An alternate way is possible via the doted line. The state, surrounded by a rectangle, indicates the current design state of the applicative object. Thus, the designer evaluates the necessary work to obtain a ready for automatic code generation applicative object. This gap is highlighted by the difference between Figure 5 and Figure 7 which completely defines the applicative object **CLOCK**. The diagram Figure 8 is a very simplified one. The complete drawing integrates the different development states corresponding to each axis of the Lacatre design principles and especially to the application phase axis (kernel phase, initialisation and termination phases and possibly exception phase). Thus, the different nodes are split.

Check facilities

The help is based on a set of coherence checks to detect design faults. For example:

- loop detection in the relationship between applicative objects;
- harmful use of some primitives in special situations for some specific real-time operating systems (e.g. during interrupt servicing);
- static validation of the correct use of the atomic objects (correct sequence of the used primitive calls: create, use, delete)...

Quality assistance

The quality assistance is based on a quality tree derived from Mc Call's and Bowen's model (with a three level hierarchy of factors, criteria and metrics) (Bowen,1985; Kitchenham, 1992).

The main preoccupation is to evaluate the design quality, according to different possible views (application, applicative objects, programmable objects) and thanks to a set of easily and classical measurable indicators (Fenton, 1991) (Mc Cabe's cyclomatic number (Mc Cabe and Butter, 1989)) but also some new and completely specific ones inherited from the hierarchical relative correctness verification (Szmuc, 1991; Szmuc, 1992; Aubry, 1995).

The Lacatre quality assistant deals with four usual factors used to estimate the design quality of complex systems (Figure 9).

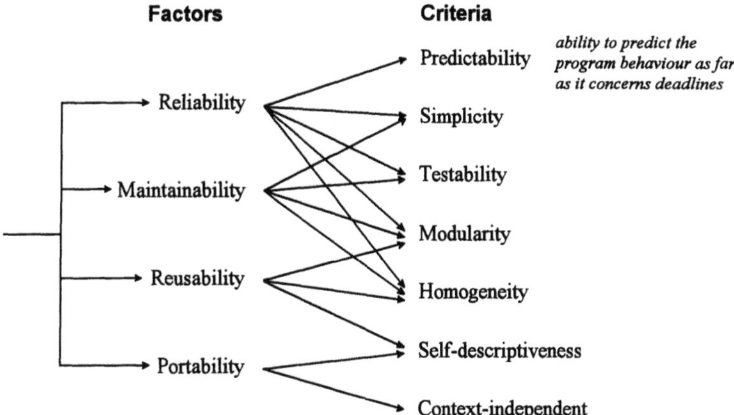

Figure 9 Lacatre quality tree (factors, criteria).

In accordance with the current progress state of the project, the quality assistant guides the user to reach, first of all, good maintainability and reliability features. The achievement of this goal is obtained by controlling the complexity of, firstly, the applicative objects and then, the complexity of the programmable atomic objects of the detailed design. For example, the applicative object simplicity can be checked with respect to thresholds set up by the project manager (Figure 10).

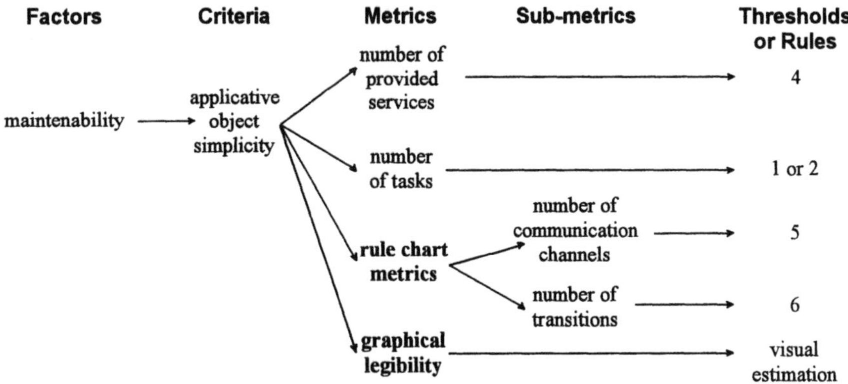

Figure 10 Maintainability factor.

The **graphical legibility** metric can be estimated qualitatively by static verification technics which are checking the respect of user friendly rules.

The **rule chart metrics** are derived from characteristics (such as communicating channels properties, transitions) defined during the correctness verification steps (Szmuc, 1992) thanks to a Communicating Real-time State Machines modelling (Shaw, 1992) of the Lacatre design.

5 CONCLUSION

The interest of a methodology assistant, which is under definition, is to contribute to the design of better quality real-time systems. It allows, step by step, to accompany the developer by giving him a view on the current design state. The use of such an assistant in conjunction with a graphical design environment and with correctness verification possibilities (Szmuc, 1991; Szmuc, 1992) contributes to reach a better quality control in the real-time applications development and to satisfy non functional requirements such as dependability. Moreover, a quality assistant is grafted to this environment to perform a static evaluation of the design quality from a Lacatre quality tree.

6 REFERENCES

Aubry, R., Maranzana, M. and Schwarz, J.J. (1995) Quality assistance for a graphical development of real-time applications. *4th Software Quality Conference*, Dundee, Scotland.

Bowen, T.P. (1985) Specification of software quality attributes. *New York: Rome Air Development Centre (RADC)*, **3**, Technical report RADC - TR-85-37.

Burlon, R. and Tagliati, M. (1990) APSIS: Knowledge based assistance for system development. *Technique et Science Informatiques, AFCET Bordas*, **9(2)**, 176-182.

Fenton, N.F. (1991) Software metrics: a rigorous approach. chapman&hall, London.

Gibson, M.L. and Snyder, C.A. (1991) Computer aided software engineering: facilitating the path for true software and knowledge engineering. *International Journal of Software Engineering and Knowledge Engineering*, **1(1)**, 99-114.

Hinchey, M.G. (1994) Visual Methods in Real-Time Programming. *19th IFAC/IFIP Workshop on Real-Time Programming*, Reichenau, Germany, June 1994.

Kitchenham, B. (1992) Development in software metrics in the last decade. *Eurometrics'92, European conference on quantitative evaluation of software and systems, practical and theoretical aspects*, Brussels, Belgium, April 1992, 17-26.

Laprie, J.C. (1989) Hardware and software dependability evaluation. *11th International IFIP Workshop*, 28 august-1 september, San Francisco, USA, 109-114.

Laprie, J.C. (1993) Dependability: from concepts to limits. *Symposium on Safety of Computer Control System (SAFECOMP'93)*, Poznan, Pologne, 157-168.

Laprie, J.C. (1995) Guide de la sûreté de fonctionnement. *Laboratoire d'Ingénierie de la Sûreté de fonctionnement (LIS)*, Cépadues Edition, Paris.

McCabe, T.J. and Butter, C.W. (1989) Design complexity measurement and testing. *Communication of the ACM*, **32(12)**, 1415-1425.

Petit, J.F., Schwarz, J.J., Maranzana, M. and Skubich, J.J. (1994) Data flow Modelling in Real-Time Multitasking Graphical Design. *IEEE Workshop on RTA*, Washington, USA.

Schwarz, J.J. and Skubich, J.J. (1993) Graphical Programming for Real-Time Systems. *Control Engineering Practice - IFAC*, 1(1), Pergamon Press.

Shaw, A.C. (1992) Communicating Real-Time State Machines. *IEEE Transaction on Software Engineering*, **18(9)**, 805-816.

Szmuc, T. (1991) Partial and total relative correctness for analysis of concurrent systems, *Journal of Applied Mathematics and Computer Sciences*, **1(1)**, 27-34.

Szmuc, T. (1992) Relative correctness for analysis of real-time programs, *IFAC/IFIP Workshop on Real-Time Programming 1992*, Pergamon Press, 173-177.

7 BIOGRAPHY

Regis Aubry is a senior lecturer of Computer Science at Institut National des Sciences Appliquées (INSA) de Lyon. His research interests include software engineering, complex system and software quality, project management and groupware. He is responsible for software engineering, quality assurance and metrology courses.

Regis Aubry is a graduate of the Computer Sciences Department at INSA and he received a doctorate in operating system. (e-mail: Regis.Aubry@if.insa-lyon.fr).

Mathieu Maranzana is a senior lecturer of Computer Science at Institut National des Sciences Appliquées (INSA) de Lyon. His research interests include compiler construction, software design, software engineering and graphical design tools and environments.

Mathieu Maranzana is a graduate of the Computer Science Department at INSA and he received a doctorate in compiler construction (e-mail: Mathieu.Maranzana@if.insa-lyon.fr).

Jean-Jacques Schwarz is a assistant professor of Computer Science at Institut National des Sciences Appliquées (INSA) de Lyon, head of the Laboratoire d'Ingénierie de l'Informatique Industrielle (L3i). His research interests are graphical design and software architectures for real-time applications, enginering and reengineering of complex computer systems.

Jean-Jacques Schwarz is a graduate of the Electronics Department at INSA and he received a doctorate in time series analysis. He is a member of the IEEE Computer Society (e-mail: Jean-Jacques.Schwarz@if.insa-lyon.fr).

PART EIGHT

Object Oriented Software

22

Using object oriented technology to measure a software process*

Amund Aarsten, Maurizio Morisio
Dipartimento di Automatica e Informatica
Politecnico di Torino
Corso Duca degli Abruzzi, 24, 10129 Torino, Italy
e-mail: {amund, morisio}@polito.it
fax: + 39 11 5647099
voice: + 39 11 5647033

Abstract

This paper reports on how object oriented concepts and technology have been applied to measure a software process in the ESSI AEFTA (Application Enabler Technology for Factory Automation) application experiment.

Measurement is considered as a full scale project consisting of 1) modelling the software process, 2) defining goals for the project, 3) formalizing goals in process measures defined on the process model, 4) designing the technological support for measures (procedures and tools, repository), 5) implementing the technological support, 6) implementing the measurement process and 7) assessing the measurement process, modifying it, if needed.

The object oriented (oo) approach has been applied to 1), 4) and 5). The process model is defined using OMT; process measures are defined using a query language to express queries on OMT object models; the repository for measures is obtained by automatic translation of the OMT process model into a set of persistent C++ classes; process measures are manually translated in C++ member functions of the persistent classes.

The advantages of applying the oo approach are discussed: sharing of tools, training, know-how and mindset with the rest of the project; ease in changing measures to adapt to changes in the process, thus the possibility of applying an evolutionary incremental lifecycle to the measurement process; lower effort in the implementation of the technological support for measurement.

Keywords

Object oriented approach, software measurement, software metrics, process modelling.

---

*This work was partially supported by the European Commission, DGIII/A, under contract ESSI AEFTA n. 10070.

1 INTRODUCTION

It is generally recognized that the best way to assess and improve a software development process is to measure it, that is to measure effort, cost, duration, faults, failures and changes (Fenton 1991, Hetzel 1993). When collected over a number of projects in the same context, these measures can be used to build prediction models for future projects (Jones 1991). Also the product must be characterized, internally (size, complexity, modularity) and externally (functionality, usability, efficiency, reliability, portability, maintainability).
The actual situation in software industry reveals a limited use of measurement. Measurement methods (such as GQM (Basili and Rombach 1988), AMI (ami 1992) and others reviewed by Roche (1994)) have been proposed to structure bare measures in a framework and propose a process to simplify their application.
Our approach to the measurement problem is that measurement should be based on a process model, and that the process model, the data repository and the whole measurement process should use object oriented concepts and technology.

1.1 The process model as a base for measurement

The issue of process modelling is receiving growing attention in the software community. The process model is seen as the starting point to analyse, improve and enact the process, but the need of strict coupling between process modelling and process measurement has not yet clearly emerged.
Basili and Weiss (1984) consider the measurement process and its validation, but do not couple the measurement process and the surrounding software process. Bache and Bazzana (1994), Hetzel (1993) cite a process model but do not define nor use it. Pfleeger and McGowan (1990) associate sets of measures with the levels of the Capability Maturity Model but do not define measures on a process model. Wolf and Rosenberg (1993) define (implicitly) a process model in terms of production of events, then collect and analyse them to assess the process. Cook and Wolf (1994) continue in the same line by defining measures of distance of sequences of real events from process model events.
Matsumoto et al. (1993) are the first authors, to our knowledge, to use a process model to define and collect process measures. The model is represented by Petri nets; duration measures are coupled with transition firing. The Petri net representation allows enacting the process and automatic collection of the measures. The drawback of this approach is in the use of Petri nets, which are not adequate to express structure and static relationships, nor to model complex systems such as a real world process model.
Our thesis is that the collection of valid measures relies on a clear, unambiguous, easy to understand and communicate definition of the process (a process model, according to the terminology of the software process community (Feiler and Humphrey 1993)). Further, the definition of measures should be integrated in the process model. Let us examine why.
Usually when measures are collected in current software engineering practice, three situations can occur.

1. The process is not defined, measures are applied and their definition is taken from the literature. A definition of a measure relies on the identification or definition of the attribute of an entity, or the entity to be measured (see Fenton's framework for

measurement in (Fenton 1991)). An entity defined in literature and the equivalent entity in the context of a process can differ, resulting in mismatches between the definition of measures and their application in the actual process context. For instance, to compute the design effort how is design defined, does it consists of the initial design only, or of rework to fix faults too? And how is a fault defined? Is an incoherence between design documents a fault or not? If the design documents are not yet validated, is it still a fault? And when is a document considered to be validated? *Standard* entities, such as design and fault, in fact rely heavily on their context. Since process measures are in many cases collected manually by different people, it is plausible that each person give a different interpretation to entities, producing unreliable measures.

2. The process is defined in natural language, process measures are applied and their definition is taken from the literature. The risk of mismatches still exists, but it is lower, since the definition of the process prescribes coherency checks. The real problem here is the complexity of the process, which is not adequately modeled in natural language, with the well known drawbacks in analysis and communication. This leads again to the risk of different interpretations by different people, producing unreliable measures.
3. The process is defined in a semi-formal or formal language. Entities are defined in a language suitable to represent them and to tackle complexity. The risk of different interpretations is greatly reduced. Now the problem lies in the separation between process definition and measures definition which can lead to incoherencies. Adding a measures-process validation task is one solution, better is to merge measures and process definition, that is to define measures as an extension of the process model.

1.2 The object oriented approach and measurement

Given the need to define measures on a process model, which is the best formalism for it ?
If "software processes are software too" (Osterweil 1987) and if measurement is part of the software process, then measurement is software, too. So why not to apply to measurement the object oriented (oo) approach, to exploit its well known advantages in this area too ?
The majority of works in the process modelling domain and all commercially available process support tools do not take this point of view and use activity or dynamics oriented formalisms such as Petri nets (see for instance Curtis (1992)). The rationale of this choice is that the model is used to enact the process. From a measurement point of view, entities and the static relationships among them are more important, thus favouring an oo view.
Our choice for the process model language was OMT (Rumbaugh et al. 1991). We preferred the general OMT over specialized process modelling languages because: it allows the description of the information part of the process along with the dynamic aspect; it allows to structure easily the model of a complex system. Last but not least, it is used in the application experiment to develop the product, therefore allowing to share tools and training.
The definition of the process model and of measures on it corresponds, in a software project, to the specification of requirements phase. Continuing in this correspondence, the design and implementation phase consist of designing and implementing tools and procedures to collect, store and analyse measures. If the object oriented approach is used, these tasks are partially automated. For instance in the AEFTA (Application Enabler Technology for Factory

Automation) application experiment, the tool used to define the OMT model supports the semi-automatic definition of the measurement database and forms on the database.

2 THE PROJECT

The AEFTA application experiment, which involves Digital Equipment Corp., Politecnico di Torino and Syco, develops a factory automation product using BASEstar (DEC 1990) and object technology. BASEstar is, in factory automation terminology, an application enabler that provides a number of basic services such as support for communication with field devices, support for building GUIs, libraries of emulators of programmable logic controls (PLC) and other field devices. Object technology means C++ and G++ (Menga 1993), which is not the gnu compiler but a homonym CASE tool supporting oo analysis and design via a modified version of OMT, a concurrency/distribution model, and generation of code.
The product now developed in object technology already exists in functional technology (C language and BASEstar). The experiment must answer to the questions: is the oo product of the same quality as the functional product, has the oo product the same functionality, how much reuse is made in the oo product, how much this reuse did cost.
To answer these questions a measurement process is defined and implemented, which uses oo concepts and technology. The measurement process is described in the following section.
AEFTA is an application experiment in the ESSI (European Software and Systems Initiative) initiative, sponsored by the European Community to advance the state of the art in software production.

3 THE MEASUREMENT PROCESS

The measurement process consists of 1) modelling the software process using OMT, 2) defining goals for the project, 3) formalizing goals in measures defined on the process model, 4) designing the technological support for measures (procedures and tools, repository), 5) implementing the technological support, 6) operating the measurement process, 7) assessing the measurement process, modifying it, if needed. In the following the first five steps, and in particular steps 4 and 5, will be described. Step 1) in section 3.1, 2) and 3) in 3.2, 4) in 3.3, 5) in 3.4. For a complete description of the measurement process see (Morisio 1995).

3.1 Modelling the software process

The first activity is the definition of the process model, since measures are defined on it. The model should be a snapshot of what actually happens, and not a model of what should be. According to Feiler and Humphrey (1993) a descriptive and not a prescriptive process model. Therefore no emphasis is given to the lifecycle used (waterfall, spiral, or else).
The process is modeled in OMT, using mainly the object model, in which activities, products and roles are modeled as classes. The dynamic model is limited to some classes having rich or complex behaviour. The rationales for these choices are explained in section 4.

Now we present and comment a reduced version of the process model (refer to (Aefta 1994) for the complete version). **Boldface** denotes classes and associations of the model.

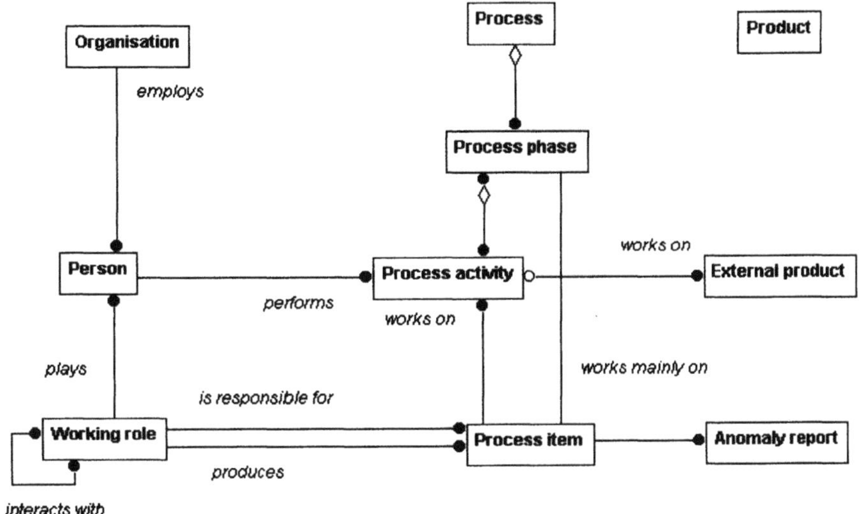

Figure 1 Process model, overview.

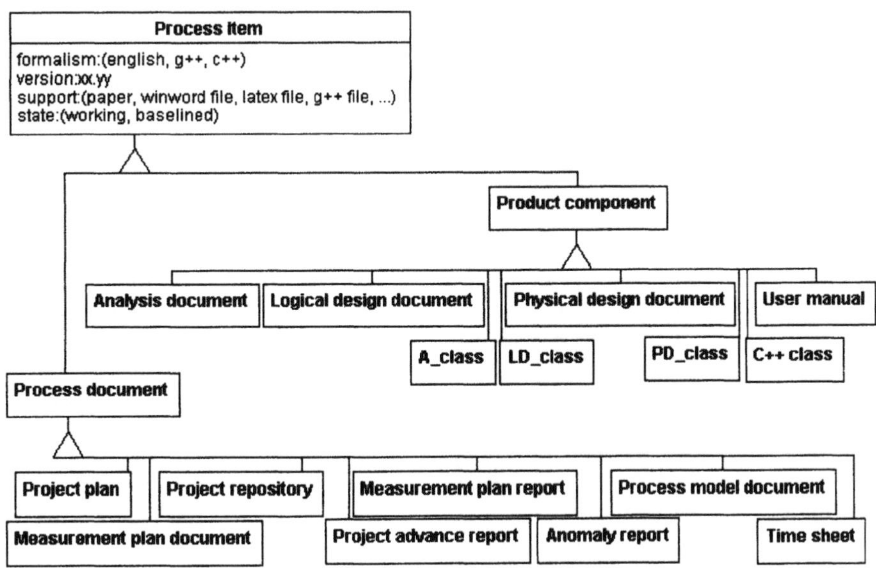

Figure 2 Process model, specialisation of **Process Item**.

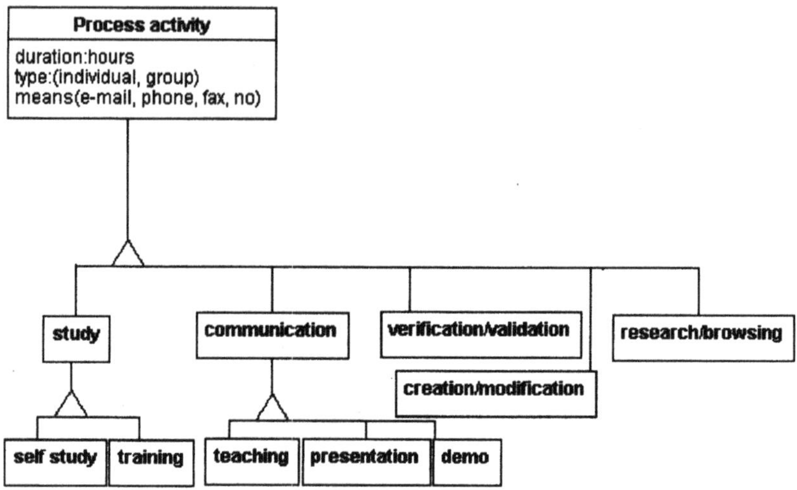

Figure 3 Process model, specialisation of **Process Activity**.

Process Item

The basic classes of the model are **Process item** and **Process activity** (see Figure 1). A **Process item** models whatever item is produced during development and specializes in **Product component** and **Process document**. A **Product component** relates to the product and can be (see Figure 2) **Analysis document, Logic Design** document, **A_class, LD_class, PD_class, C++ class**. A **Process document** can be (see Figure 2) **Process model, Measurement plan, Measurement report** and so on.

Process Activity

A **Process activity** (see Figure 3) models the time spent by one person doing something in the project under consideration. It is characterized by its duration and by the fact that the person works alone (**type = individual**) or with other people (**type = group**). Group activities are characterized by the communication means used (**means** attribute). Activities can be **creation/modification** (creative work involving modification), **verification/validation** (inspection work not involving modification), **research/browsing** (search work not involving modification nor inspection), **study** (self study or training), **communication** (teaching or oral presentation), **travelling** (displacement outside the normal working site to perform an activity in the context of the project).

Activities are neutral, since they do not specify the object on which work is done. The associations **Process activity works on Process item** and **Process activity works on External product** model this information.

Since associations are inherited too, **works on** holds between any specialization of **Process activity** and any specialization of **Process item** or **External product**. For instance some work on the analysis document is modelled by an instance of **creation/modification**, an instance of **Analysis document** and a link between them, instance of **Process activity works on Process item.**
The strong link between activity and what is acted upon is contained in the cardinality one and only one between **Process Activity** and **Process item**, that means no activity can exist without a connected process item.

Process Phase

The traditional definition of phases, such as analysis, design, implementation, testing and the like, are represented as **Process Phases**, with attributes **initiated** and **terminated**. They model the milestones of the project.
A **Process Phase** specializes in **Analysis**, **Logical design**, **Physical design**, etc.. The definition of each specialization is delegated to specializations of association **Process Phase works mainly on Process Item** (see Figure 1). For example **Analysis works mainly on Analysis Document** defines Analysis.
Process Phase is an aggregation of Process activity models that in a phase many concurrent activities happen, while activities have no concurrency inside. Since each activity **works on** an item, in a phase work is made on many items. The document that is the focus of the phase is defined by **works *mainly* on**.
The description of a phase via the document on which it works follows an oo style; (objects, such as the structure and content of documents, are privileged against functionality, such as what is made during phases) and has advantages in the definition of measures (see 3.2 for definition of measures and 4 for a discussion).

External Product

An **External product** is an object which is not developed in the software process, but used in it (association **works on** in Figure 1). Among other things, the **External products** model reuse.

Working Role

Working Role models roles in an organization, and specializes in **Project Manager**, **Software Engineering**, **Quality Manager**, etc.. A **Working Role** is responsible for one or more **Process Items**, or simply produces one or more of them. A **Person** **plays** one or more **Roles**, a **Role** is played by at least one **Person**.

3.2 Defining goals and measures

The next activity after defining the process model is the definition of measures. The well known, 'top down' Goal Question Metric approach (Basili and Rombach 1988), refined in standard IEEE1061 (1992) and in AMI (1992), is used.
The project goals were stated informally in 2. Now they are formalised in term of goals, subgoals and measures. In Table 1 we present a reduced version of the decomposition of goals relevant to process measures.

Table 1 Decomposition of goal in subgoals and measures

Goal	*Subgoal*	*Measure name*	*Measure definition* *[U of measure]*
Characterize the process	Characterise effort	effort per phase (ex. Analysis)	ΣProcess_phase {Analysis}.works_mainly_on. Process_activity.duration [person hour]
		total effort	ΣProcess_activity.duration [person hour]
	Characterise faults	faults per phase (ex. Analysis)	Cardinality(Process_phase {Analysis}.works_mainly_on. Anomaly_report) []
	Characterise reuse activities	reuse effort 1	ΣG++Library.study.duration + ΣG++Library.research /browsing.duration [person hour]
		reuse effort 2	ΣClass[derived from g++library = true].Process activity.duration [person hour]
		non reuse effort	ΣClass[derived from g++library = false].Process activity.duration [person hour]
	Characterise learning activities	oo learning effort	ΣG++.Study.duration + ΣC++.Study.duration [person hour]

Measures are defined in an OMT query language (see Morisio 1995). In this language 'Class' denotes all instances of **Class**, 'Class.attribute' selects all attributes of all instances of **Class**, 'Class.relation' selects all instances of the class linked to **Class** by the relation **relation**. 'Class[predicate]' selects all instances of **Class** that satisfy 'predicate'. 'Class{subclass}' is a particular predicate that selects all instances of **Class** that are also instances of **subclass**.
For instance in measure 'total effort' 'Process_activity' selects all instances of class **ProcessActivity**, 'Process_activity.duration' selects the attribute duration of such instances, 'ΣProcess_activity.duration' adds the duration of all activities. The measure 'effort per analysis phase' sums the duration of all activities of any type executed on instances of **ProcessItem** on which the **Analysis** phase **worksMainlyOn.**
The measure 'reuse effort 1' sums the duration of all the **study** and **research/browsing** activities executed on instances of **G++Library.**

3.3 Technological support

In this activity procedures to collect, store and analyse measures are designed and the required tools are chosen. In this section we will describe only automated procedures and the tools chosen or developed to support them.

The automated procedures are: definition of the process model, definition of measures, definition of the database for measures, elaboration of raw data into measures. The manual procedures are: collection of process data (effort, faults) through paper time sheets and fault report sheets, insertion of process data into the database, definition of the algorithms to transform raw data into measures.
The tool chosen to support the automated procedures is G++, the same tool used by the measured development process. The advantages of this choice are discussed in section 4.2.
The definition of the process model uses the OMT editor of G++, the definition of measures uses the annotation feature of the editor.
The database for measures is generated from the process model using the C++ code generation facility of the tool and the library to add persistency to classes; part of the translation is done by hand and explained in more detail in the next section.
The elaboration of raw data into measures is made in terms of C++ function members belonging to the persistent classes. The definition of these function members is done by hand starting from the definition of measures on the process model and is explained in the next section.

3.4 Implementation

This section describes in more detail the C++ implementation of the automated part of the measurement process, basically the translation of the process model and process measures into a database, queries on it and forms to input raw data.

The Process Model Classes

Most of the classes in the process model were mapped directly to persistent C++ classes. Some of the sibling classes in the hierarchy have identical structure and behaviour; for instance, the subclasses of **ProcessActivity** only serve to distinguish between different types of activities. In these cases, the class hierarchy was simplified, and the classes in question were implemented as different instances of the parent class.
The queries need to identify some of the objects by a symbolic name. The classes for these objects therefore include a dictionary to map names to instances, along with a static (i.e. class) method returning an instance from a name.
Attributes are implemented as protected member variables which can be read through public member functions ("getters".) For the classes related to the measurement, the attribute values do not change after object creation, so they are simply passed to the constructor when the object is created.
As an example, the class declaration for **ProcessActivity** follows:

```
class ProcessActivity : public Object
{ protected:    Symbol name;
                Time duration;
                char type;
                Symbol means;
  public:       ProcessActivity(Symbol& name, Time t, char type, Symbol* means=0);
                Symbol& getName();
                Time& getDuration();
                char getType();
                Symbol& getMeans();
};
```

Relations

Relations were implemented using object pointers or collections of pointers, depending on the cardinalities involved. For instance, the relation between **ProcessItem** and **AnomalyReport**, where an **AnomalyReport** concerns one **ProcessItem**, while there can be many **AnomalyReports** for each **ProcessItem**, was implemented with a pointer to the involved **ProcessItem** object in the **AnomalyReport** objects and a collection of pointers to **AnomalyReports** in the **ProcessItem** objects.

For some relations, it is not worthwhile to maintain pointers for both roles. Typically, they are maintained only when they are needed for implementing a metric query.

A special kind of relation is the containment relation between a class and all its instances. Some of the queries need this to get to all instances of a specific class; other queries need to find a particular instance by its name without having prior visibility of that instance. When required, this was implemented by the above-mentioned dictionary of instances. For subclasses, instances must also be registered in the superclass' dictionary, so that queries accessing the superclass can find them. (This possibility is actually a beneficial side effect from using oo technology, difficult to implement with traditional databases.)

The declaration of **ProcessItem** is given below as an example of relation implementation.

```
class ProcessItem : public Object
{
  protected:
    Symbol formalism;                              // attributes
    String version;
    Symbol state;
    Symbol name;
    WorkingRole * responsible_role;                // relations
    WorkingRole * produced_by_role;
    ProcessPhase * produced_by_phase;
    OrderedCltn worked_on_by;
    OrderedCltn anomaly_reports;
    static Dictionary instance_dict;               // map Symbol->instance pointer
  public:
    ProcessItem(Symbol name);                      // constructor/destructor
    ~ProcessItem();
    Symbol& getName();                             // attribute access
    Symbol& getFormalism();
    void setFormalism(Symbol);
    String getVersion();
    void setVersion(String);
    Symbol getState();
    void setState(Symbol);
    OrderedCltn *  workedOnBy();                   // relation access
    OrderedCltn *  anomalyReports();
    WorkingRole *  responsibleRole();
    void           responsibleRole(WorkingRole*);
    WorkingRole *  producedByRole();
    void           producedByRole(WorkingRole*);
    ProcessPhase * producedByPhase();
    void           producedByPhase(ProcessPhase *);
    Dictionary&   getInstanceDict();              // name->instance map access
    ProcessItem * getInstance(Symbol name);
};
```

Populating the Object Base

The database schema includes an explicit representation of the time sheet as a class, **TimeSheet**. This was done to simplify the population of the object base, since the time sheets must be entered manually. A time sheet object holds no attributes; it is simply a placeholder with pointers to the objects represented by the time sheet. The time sheet constructor takes the information from a line on a paper time sheet, creates a **ProcessActivity**, and sets up relations from the related objects. The **TimeSheet** object is filled with pointers to the objects involved, so that the **TimeSheets** can be browsed for verification against the paper sheets.

Queries

The G++ persistence framework does not include a query language, so the metrics queries had to be implemented manually. In the context of a larger project, this could surely be automated, but for the relatively small number of queries needed it was not found worthwhile to develop a query interpreter. In a larger project, however, it would be a useful addition, as it would allow experimenting with different queries to discover new metrics and to understand as early as possible which metrics are useful and which are not.

Queries are implemented by simply following the pointers that implement the relations. When following a link of cardinality N, the corresponding collection is traversed with a loop. Conditions, e.g. [type=group and means=e-mail], are translated into `if` statements that determine whether a link is followed further or not.

The innermost loop level performs the computation of the query's return value, e.g. by incrementing a counter for cardinality expressions or by accumulating a sum.

As an example, consider the metric "reuse effort 1", defined by the query ΣG++Library.study.duration + ΣG++Library.research/browsing.duration. To evaluate this query, we loop for each instance of the **GppLibrary** class, retrieving the collection of **ProcessActivity** pointers representing the relation **works on.** (**GppLibrary** inherits the collection needed to participate in this relation from its superclass **ExternalProduct**, see the process model in Figure 1.) Each **ProcessActivity** is queried for its name; if the name is "Study" or "Research/Browsing" the **ProcessActivity**'s duration is added to the sum.

The code that implements the query is given below.

```
// from ProcessActivity.h:     extern Symbol Study;
//                             extern Symbol ResearchBrowsing;
Time ReuseEffort1()
{   Time sum = 0;
    Dictionary& gppLibInstances = GppLibrary::getInstanceDict();
    DO(gppLibInstances, GppLibrary, theGppLib)
        Collection& activities = *theGppLib->workedOnBy();
        DO(activities, ProcessActivity activity)
        Symbol& activityName = activity->getName();
            if (activityName == Study ||
                activityName == ResearchBrowsing) {
                sum += activity->getDuration();
            }
        OD
    OD
    return sum;
}
```

4 DISCUSSION

In the AEFTA project measures are based on a process model.
The first advantage in basing the definition of process measures on a process model is the clear definition of entities to be measured, in the actual context of the project under examination. Without the model, misinterpretations of definitions are very likely to happen, since the collection of process measures involves people and their judgment .
If the process model is defined in a formal or semi-formal language like OMT, analysis to produce definitions and their communication are greatly improved.
Moreover, object oriented concepts and technology have been applied to measurement, defining a process model in OMT, defining measures on it via an extension of OMT, using persistent C++ classes to implement the repository of measures, deriving semi-automatically the repository for measures from the process model, using an incremental/evolutionary lifecycle for the measurement process.
The advantages and rationales of these choices are now discussed.

4.1 Object oriented process model and evolutionary lifecycle

An evolutionary measurement process is a strict, important requirement since the software process, and the measurement process, change. This is fulfilled through careful use of oo characteristics.
Two categories of things can evolve in the measurement process: the process model (to adapt to changes in the real process, or to add detail) and measures (to adapt to new goals, or to follow the process model).
Impact of changes in the process model is reduced as follows. Whenever possible entities in the process are described as classes or associations: for instance actions are objectified in classes **ProcessPhase** and **ProcessActivity.** The process model is made mainly of the object model. The dynamic model is limited to some classes having rich or complex behaviour: for instance the why and when an anomaly report has to be issued. Moreover the dynamic model acts as documentation and is not used, up to date, in the definition of measures.
Changes in the definition of measures have two aspects: 1) changes in procedures for collection, computation and analysis, 2) compatibility with older measures. The former problem impacts only clerical rework and is reduced by the semi-automatic derivation of repository and function members. The latter problem is more dangerous since measures already taken and stored in the repository can become incoherent with the changed ones. The problem is tackled by exploiting generalisation/specialisation in defining a two level process model. One level, (abstract classes **Process Item**, **Process Activity** and the related abstract associations) is designed to be very robust against changes. The other level, or concrete level (specialisations of the above classes and the related specialised associations), is designed to change (by adding classes, by modifying associations) to accommodate evolutions. Measures are defined, whenever is possible, at the abstract level (let us call them abstract measures). Abstract measures are coherent, provided abstract classes and their relationships do not change, even if concrete classes change. On the contrary concrete measures can become incoherent if changes affect the concrete classes on which they are defined.

Any type of change in the process model and in measures is easily reflected in the supporting environment, since the repository is automatically generated from the process model.

4.2 Synergy between software process and measurement process

The measurement process uses the same concepts and technology as the software process. In particular the same development tool (G++) and language (C++) are used. In addition to the evident advantage of saving resources (same hardware, same tools, same training on tools and OMT method), a definite advantage is the sharing of the same mindset for programming and measuring. Process measures are collected mainly through manual filling of time sheets by the staff, and time sheets rely heavily on the process model for the definition of terms and relationships. Since the process model is described using OMT, a staff member can understand it using the same skill (s)he uses to understand project analysis and design documents. This skill improves with time and produces more reliable measures.

4.3 Measurement effort

The use of oo concepts and the definition of a process model impact heavily the distribution of effort for measurement in phases 1, 2, 3, 4 and 5 of the measurement process. The effort for the definition of measures (3) is very low, because the hard part of the job becomes the definition of the process model and of goals for the project (1 and 2). The technological phases (4 and 5) demand low effort too, partly because the know how is shared with the software process, partly because many components from the G++ library are reused.
When this paper was written the experiment was halfway from conclusion. Measures, and in particular measurement effort, will be published at the end of the experiment.

5 CONCLUSION

Object oriented concepts and technology have been applied to measure an object oriented project. This means defining a process model in OMT, defining measures on it via an extension of OMT, using persistent C++ classes to implement the repository of measures, deriving semi-automatically the repository for measures from the process model, using an incremental/evolutionary lifecycle for the measurement process.
The advantages of this approach are: sharing of tools, training, know-how and mindset with the rest of the project; possibility to define a process model and a set of measures which evolve easily; lower effort in the implementation of the technological support for measurement.

6 REFERENCES

AEFTA consortium, (1994). Aefta project - Quality plan.
AMI, Applications of Metrics in Industry (1992) - *ami Handbook, a quantitative approach to software management*, CSSE, South Bank Polytechnic, London.
Bache R. , Bazzana G., (1994), *Software metrics for product assessment*, McGraw-Hill.

Basili V.B., Weiss M.W. (1984), A methodology for collecting valid software engineering data, *IEEE Transactions on Software Engineering*, 10(6), Nov. 1984, 728-738.

Basili V.B., Rombach H.D. (1988), The TAME Project: Towards Improvement-Oriented Software Environments, *IEEE Transactions on software engineering*, 14(6), June 88.

Cook J. E., Wolf A.L., (1994), Towards Metrics for Process Validation, *3rd Int. Conf. on the Software Process*, Reston.

Curtis B., Kellner M.I., Over J. (1992), Process modeling, *Comm. ACM*, Sept 92, 35(9).

DEC, (1990), *BASEstar Open Introduction*.

Feiler P.H., Humphrey W.S., (1993), Software Process Development and Enactment: Concepts and Definitions, *2nd Int. Conf. on the Software Process*, Berlin.

Fenton N., (1991), *Software Metrics - A Rigorous Approach*, Chapman & Hall.

Hetzel B. ,(1993), *Making software measurement work*, QED.

IEEE, (1992), IEEE 1061 Standard for a Software Quality Metrics Methodology.

Jones C. (1991) , *Applied software measurement*, Mc Graw Hill.

Matsumoto K. , Kusumoto S., Kikuno T. , Torii K., (1993), A new Framework of Measuring Software Development Processes, *Proceedings of the 1st Int. IEEE Software Metrics Symposium*, Baltimore, MD, 21-22 may 1993.

Menga G., Elia G., Mancin M., (1993), G++: an environment for object oriented design and prototyping of manufacturing systems, In *W. Gruver, G. Boudreaux, ed., Intelligent Manufacturing: Programming Environments for CIM*, Springer Verlag, 1993.

Morisio M., (1995), A Methodology to Measure the Software Process, *Proceedings of the Annual Oregon Workshop on Software Metrics*, Portland, OR, 5-7 june 1995.

Osterweil L., (1987), Software Processes are Software Too, *Proc. 9th ICSE*, April 1987.

Pfleeger S.L. , McGowan C., (1990), Software Metrics in the Process Maturity Framework, *Journal of Systems and Software*, n. 12, 1990, 255-261.

Rumbaugh J., Blaha M. , Premerlani W., Eddy F., Lorensen W., (1991), *Object oriented modelling and design*, Addison Wesley.

Roche J., Jackson M., Shepperd M., (1994), Software Measurement Methods: an Evaluation and Perspective, *3rd Symposium on Assessment of Quality of Software Development Tools*, Washington, June 1994.

Wolf A.L., Rosenbaum D.S., (1993), A Study in Software Process Data Capture and Analysis, *2nd Int. Conf. on the Software Process*, Berlin, 1993.

7 BIOGRAPHY

Amund Aarsten is a Ph.D. student at Politecnico di Torino, writing his thesis on concurrent and distributed object-oriented systems. His research interests lie in the fields of design patterns, programming languages, and software process modeling.

Maurizio Morisio is a researcher at Politecnico di Torino. His research interests include object oriented software metrics, CASE tools evaluation and selection, software process modelling, requirements specification and design formalisms. He was in charge of measuring the AEFTA project. He received a Ph.D. in software engineering from Politecnico di Torino in 1989.

23

Object-Oriented Software Testability

Jeffrey M. Voas
Reliable Software Technologies Corporation
Loudoun Tech Center, Suite 250, 21515 Ridgetop Circle, Sterling, Virginia 20166, USA, Telephone: 703.404.9293, Fax: 703.404.9295, email: jmvoas@RSTcorp.com

Abstract
This paper studies whether object-oriented systems are more likely to hide faults during system level testing. When this project began, we suspected that although object-oriented designs have features particularly supportive of software reuse, this paradigm is detrimental to system level testing for fault detection. After comparing the testability of both OO and procedural systems, this project studied ways to engender reusability, while maintaining an acceptable level of testability. By studying whether this family of programming languages and design paradigm are harmful to testability, and evaluating methods to increase testability, we provide information that should be considered before OO languages are endorsed as tools for developing safety-critical software.

Keywords
Software testing, testability assessment, information hiding, encapsulation, assertions

1 INTRODUCTION

This paper is a condensed version of a technical report that was provided to The National Institute of Standards and Technology (NIST) in December, 1994. The purpose of this NIST-sponsored project was to study whether object-oriented systems are more likely to hide faults during system level testing. When this project began, we suspected that although object-oriented designs have features particularly supportive of software reuse, this paradigm is detrimental to system level testing for fault detection. After comparing the testability of both OO and procedural systems, this project studied ways to engender reusability, while maintaining an acceptable level of testability. By studying whether this family of programming languages and design paradigm are harmful to testability, and evaluating methods to increase testability, we provide information that should be considered before OO languages are endorsed as tools for developing safety-critical software.

This project studied the impact of (1) inheritance, (2) polymorphism, (3) function overloading, (4) encapsulation, (5) information hiding, and (6) software assertions on object-oriented systems. Recommendations for how to maintain sufficiently high testability while maintaining object-oriented design (OOD) were developed. Our major recommendations were:

1. Formal methods, although capable of demonstrating dependability of objects, do not demonstrate that the manner in which the objects are linked together produces a dependable composition.
2. Assertions appear to have the greatest ability to preserve OOD while increasing testability and hence decreasing testing costs; also, we have provided a simple lemma of why software assertions cannot lower software testability.
3. Information hiding and encapsulation are detrimental to state error propagation, which is very necessary if faults are to be found via software testing.
4. Abstract data types have little impact on software testability as far as we can determine.
5. Inheritance is not necessarily detrimental to software testability; however, when it is combined with information hiding, it may become a "lethal" combination. Unit testing costs increase as the depth of inheritance increases due to the number of drivers and stubs that are necessary. As a counter argument, subclasses tend to be simpler in deep, complex inheritance trees and hence increase the ability to asses high reliability of the subclasses. This presents another related problem: *the reliable composition of reusable subclasses.*
6. Polymorphism is difficult to test, i.e., find test cases to exercise different binding scenarios. However from our previous intuition and this effort's experimentation, polymorphism, when faulty, causes the faults to be of larger sizes, and that means increased testability, and hence it is not problematic for testing.

We will now explain the testability model and experiments that we performed in building these recommendations.

2 BACKGROUND

Previous research has conjectured that procedural languages are less likely to hide faults during system level testing than are OO languages. On the other hand, object oriented languages show advantages for developing software that is highly maintainable, readable, structured, and reusable. Thus for safety critical software we have a conflict:

> *We would like to use OO languages to ease the process of reusing components but might then pay a price in terms of reliability (which for safety-critical systems we cannot afford).*

In the object-oriented paradigm, *objects* are atomic units of encapsulation, *classes* manage collections of objects, and *inheritance* structures collections of classes. Objects partition the state of computation into encapsulated units. Each object has an interface of operations that control access to an encapsulated state. The operations determine the object's behavior, while the state serves as a memory of past executions that might influence future actions. Note that procedural and object-oriented languages differ sharply in their patterns of resource sharing. Procedure-oriented languages encourage autonomy at the procedure level, while not encouraging interaction through nonlocal variables. Object-oriented languages discourage procedure autonomy, and instead organize procedures into collections of operations that share an object's state through nonlocal variables. Thus encapsulation at the level of objects derives its power by abandoning encapsulation at the level of procedures. It is our conjecture that encapsulation at the object level is very detrimental to overall system testability.

When we talk about a potential problem with the OOD philosophy and software testability, we are talking about testability assessments at the system testing level, not the unit testing level. Small objects and classes can be tested quite thoroughly in isolation, but it is at the higher levels of object composition where we suspect that there is a reduction in testability, e.g., due to capabilities afforded the developer such as **private** and **protected** data objects. There are cost benefit and reuse claims for why OO languages should be used, and we are not in disagreement with these claims. For example, given the enormous costs of software, maintenance and reuse are characteristics that OO languages support nicely. So from an economic perspective, those are advantages. But from a testing perspective, OO languages may hide catastrophic faults for longer time intervals, and if true, this makes testing such systems more difficult, and hence the benefit of these languages must be brought into question.

2.1 Our Basic Testability Approach

For clarity, we should define what we mean by the term "software testability"; our definition differs slightly from the way others commonly use the term. Until recently, the term "software testability" had been considered to be a measure of the ability to select inputs that satisfy certain structural testing criteria, e.g., the ability to satisfy various code-based testing coverages. For example, if the goal is to select a set of inputs that execute every statement in the code at least once, and it is virtually impossible to find a set to do so, then the testability ascribed would be lower than if it were easy to create this set. (For a thorough reference on the differing perspectives on software testability of OO software, see (Binder, 1994).)

In an effort to minimize the risk of performing too little testing and becoming excessively confident in the absence of faults, Voas (Voas, 1992) (Voas and Miller, 1995) (Voas et al., 1991) redefined the term software testability. Voas defines "software testability" to be a *prediction of the probability of software failure occurring due to the existence of a fault*, given that the software testing is performed with respect to a particular input distribution. Other well-known researchers have since accepted this new definition in their research initiatives (Howden and Huang, 1993). This definition says that the testability of the software is strictly related to the ability of the software to hide faults during testing when the inputs are selected according to some input selection scheme D. This definition indirectly addresses the amount of textual coverage achieved during testing. If large regions of a program are infrequently executed according to D, both of these definitions of software testability would converge, producing a lower software testability prediction. However Voas's definition of testability does not go the next step and assert that the ability to easily execute all code regions implies that faults are not hiding; it considers other factors before such a strong claim can be justified.

In Voas's definition, if we observe no failures while testing (given input selection technique D), we can boast high confidence that faults are not hiding *only* if we have a priori knowledge that the testability of the software was high. However, if after testing according to input selection technique D, we observe no failures and are told that the testability of the software is low, we gain less confidence that faults are not hiding. This view of software testability provides a way of quantifying the risk associated with critical software systems that have demonstrated successful testing. The other factors considered before this definition of testability converges with the coverage-based definition of testability is provided by a technique termed "sensitivity analysis" (Voas, 1992) (Voas and Miller, 1995) (Voas et al., 1991).

3 EXPERIMENTAL RESULTS

RST Corporation has developed an automated sensitivity analysis tool in their *PiSCES Software Analysis Toolkit*$^{(TM)}$. We examined and compared the testability of C (procedural) and C++ (object-oriented) code using this tool. For the experiment, we developed an automatic-teller machine (ATM) program in C and C++. We also developed a simple SHAPES drawing package in both languages as a second experiment.

Due to the size of this NIST-sponsored effort, the amount of experimentation was limited, and not statistically conclusive. We wish however to place the results in the public domain to encourage discussion and independent experimentation.

3.1 The ATM Experiment

We first summarize the results obtained by performing propagation analysis on both object-oriented and procedural versions of an Automated Teller Machine (ATM) simulation. The ATM system was coded in both C and C++ from a simple ASCII specification. In this experiment, we focused solely on the impact of encapsulation and information hiding. 102 test cases were developed such that all locations in the program were covered.

The Automated Teller Machine (ATM) program simulates a single ATM connected to a bank. The machine accepts ATM cards and verifies the validity of the user by accepting a PIN number and matching it with the users PIN number maintained at the bank. If the user enters three unsuccessful PIN numbers, the machine eats the card and informs

Paradigm	Minimum Inequality	Minimum Point Estimate
Object-Oriented	0.0098	0.011
Procedural	0.011	0.075

Table 1 The lowest location upper bound and point estimate propagation scores for any location in the respective versions.

Paradigm	# of Inequalities	Percentage of Inequalitites
Object-Oriented	17	16.2%
Procedural	16	14.3%

Table 2 The total number of locations for which propagation never occurred and the percentage of these with respect to the total number of locations.

the user to contact the bank. If valid, the user has access to one checking and one savings account. Possible transactions includes: withdrawls, transfers, and balance checks. A transaction is invalid if either the user tries to withdraw greater than $200 per access or attempts a transfer/withdraw that overdraws an account. Each valid transaction generates a separate receipt. All receipts are printed when the user has completed all desired transactions.

Procedural and Object-oriented versions of ATM were developed from a generic specification including information contained in the previous paragraph. The procedural version maintains a set of data structures and a set of procedures that operate on data to perform the aforementioned tasks. the object-oriented version consists of a set of classes that combine to create functioning ATM and bank objects.

Inputs·to the program take the form:

```
<atm card>
<pin number>
<transactions>*
<quit>
```

Tables 1- 3 summarize the results. The average and minimum scores in Tables 1- 3 are based on propagation estimates at the location level. In Table 1, we are showing both the minimum inequality and minimum point estimate.* In this table, it is interesting to note that the minimum point estimate is almost 7 times larger for the procedural than for the object-oriented. Although this may seem large, it should be noted that these values are of

*An inequality occurs whenever propagation never occurred; instead of providing a 0.0 propagation estimate, we place an upper bound on the point estimate, making it into an inequality.

Paradigm	Average Propagation Score
Object-Oriented	0.49
Procedural	0.57

Table 3 The average propagation point estimate score (this does not include upper bounds).

the same order-of-magnitude. Table 2 shows the number of locations (although not from identical code) that demonstrated no propagation; this was only slightly greater in the OO system than in the procedural system. But then again, it was too close to draw any statistical significance. Table 3 shows that on average, it will take 20% more test cases to test the OO code than the procedural code. Once again, this is not a large difference.

In summary, this example showed that for the same 102 test cases, the OO design with encapsulation and information hiding faired slightly worse in enforcing the propagation condition. This experiment suggests that information hiding and encapsulation are detrimental to testability, specifically propagation, which has been our suspicion for several years.

3.2 The SHAPES Experiment

SHAPES is a simple draw package that allows various shapes to be drawn, moved, and stacked on top of one another. Currently SHAPES supports three basic shapes: lines, rectangles, and a simple face (head, eyes, nose, mouth) made out of the first two shapes. The program defines a drawing space in which shapes can be manipulated by changing their x, y coordinate positions.

In this example, our OO design enforced inheritance and polymorphism, and function overloading in C++, whereas the ATM experiment enforced encapsulation and information hiding. Here, we were interested in looking at whether inheritance, polymorphism, or function overloading have an observable negative impact on testability. To draw comparisons we used a C procedural version that did not include these features.

Input values to SHAPES consist of information for creating shapes and manipulating them. A SHAPES input file is in the following format:

```
<number of shapes>
<shape type><shape position>*
<shape manipulation><parameters>*
```

All shape diagrams are output to the screen after creation or a refresh. Tables 4- 6 summarize the results of this experiment.

What this experiment suggests is that inheritance, polymorphism, and function overloading in C++ do not have a negative impact on propagation as opposed to the pro-

Paradigm	Minimum Inequality	Minimum Point Estimate
Object-Oriented	0.031	0.32
Procedural	0.033	0.20

Table 4 The lowest location upper bound and point estimate propagation scores for any location in the respective versions.

Paradigm	# of Inequalities	Percentage of Inequalitites
Object-Oriented	3	4%
Procedural	37	26%

Table 5 The total number of locations for which propagation never occurred and the percentage of these with respect to the total number of locations.

cedural version. In fact, in all categories for which we compared results, the OO version outperformed the procedural version. We are not conjecturing that these characteristics are *beneficial* to testability, but that we were surprised by the results. We have begun a close examination of the C version to determine why this occurred.

Before this project began, we expected that inheritance, in isolation from information hiding, would not be problematic. It is when information is hidden from lower methods that propagation can be thwarted. As for polymorphism and function overloading, we also expected no direct impact on testability, however in combination with other features, this could be different. This experimentation has suggested that encapsulation and information hiding are detrimental to effective fault detection with system level testing. Although this experiment can only be viewed as one data point, it does agree with the original hypothesis that was put forth several years ago (Voas, 1991). Additional research is required, but this is preliminary evidence from an actual OO system where the hypothesis was substantiated. This task has failed to conclude whether polymorphism or inheritance are detrimental to testability, given that the OO version produced better results than its procedural counterpart. Once again, this evidence must be viewed as a single data point and is not conclusive.

Paradigm	Average Propagation Score
Object-Oriented	0.729
Procedural	0.576

Table 6 The average propagation point estimate score (this does not include upper bounds).

3.3 Assertions

Given that encapsulation and information hiding are probably detrimental to OOD, we then applied one specific design-for-testability (DFT) heuristic to the aforementioned C++ code, *assertions*.

An *assertion* is a test on the entire state of an executing program or a test on a portion of the program state.† Although empirical assertions are validation mechanisms, their use in hardware testing has earned them the label of "design-for-test" mechanisms, and thus we will also consider them here as an approach to improving the design of OO software.‡ ("Observability" is the term used in hardware design representing the degree to which the inner logic of a chip can be tested.)

Typically, software testing checks the correctness of values only after they are output. In contrast, assertions check intermediate values, values that are not typically defined as output by the requirements. The benefit of checking internal states is that testers know as soon as possible whether the program has entered into an erroneous state.

Assertions can be derived at any time during the software life-cycle, however we will only use them once code is available. When developing software using formal methods, assertions are employed before code is available. Here, we are looking at applying assertions during the software assessment phase, but we wish to derive these assertions during design using measures for where they should be placed by quantifying metrics such as the DRR. Typically, assertions are used during testing (to improve testability) and removed during deployment (for efficiency and speed). The removal of assertions however can be problematic, and it is preferable that this is done in an automated fashion to lessen the probability of human error. Removing assertions after testing is analogous to compiling without the debug flag when run-time errors are no longer being experienced. (Assertions remaining in production software can be useful in detecting and diagnosing problems.) Also of extreme importance are the mechanisms used to derive the assertions from the requirements or specification; incorrect assertions can lead to a false sense of a good design process.

Assertions that are placed at each statement in a program can automatically monitor the internal computations of a program execution. However, the advantages of universal assertions come at a cost. A program with such extensive intrusive instrumentation will execute more slowly. Also, some assertions may be redundant. And the task of instrumenting the code with "correct" assertions at each location is of high risk; there is no guarantee that the assertions will be correct.

We advocate a middle ground between no assertions at all (the most common practice) and the theoretical ideal of assertions at every location. Our experiments showed that OO systems can have regions of quite high testabilities, and hence assertions are not war-

---

†The type of assertion that we are interested in is *empirical* assertions that are invoked when the code is executed; we are not talking about formal logic pre and postconditions that are used in a "cleanroom" like development process.

‡By "improving the design of OO software," we mean "forcing a more explicit and better specified design."

ranted. A plausible compromise is to inject assertions only at locations where traditional testing is unlikely to uncover software faults (Voas and Miller, 1994). For instance, we can statically detect information hiding within a design, and we can easily place assertions on encapsulated variables. By doing so, we explicitly test the validity of computations at the system and unit level that are normally tested implicitly.

We will assume that all assertions are logical and evaluate to TRUE when the internal state is satisfactory (meaning it passes the particular test in the assertion), and FALSE otherwise. When an assertion evaluates to FALSE, we consider the execution of the program to have resulted in failure, even if the specified output is correct. You can think of this as "artificially" modifying what is defined as failure:

failure is said to occur if the output is incorrect *or* an assertion fails.

In essence, this not only redefines failure, but it modifies what is defined as output.

Lemma of the Impact of Assertions on Testability

Here, we wish to give a simple lemma that the impact of an assertion on error propagation must either be: (1) negligible, or (2) positive. Error propagation is a direct factor in assessing software testability: greater error propagation implies greater testability. As you will see, this lemma is intuitive and obvious, and hence we will not belabor the point.

Lemma 1 *The impact of an assertion on error propagation must either be: (1) negligible, or (2) positive.*

Proof. Assume that for some program P, all memory that the program has access to is contained in a ten-element array: $\mathbf{a}[0]$, $\mathbf{a}[1]$, ..., $\mathbf{a}[9]$. Assume further that some percentage x of that array, $0 < x \leq 100$, is output from P, and all information that is output from P is checked by an oracle, O. And assume that each member of $\mathbf{a}$ is only ever defined with a value once. For any element in $\mathbf{a}$, there is a probability (≥ 0) that either a fault (design error) or corrupt input will cause the element to also become corrupted; we denote these probabilities: $P_{\mathbf{a}[0]}$, $P_{\mathbf{a}[1]}$, ..., $P_{\mathbf{a}[9]}$. For example, if some element of $\mathbf{a}$ is defined in unreachable code, this probability is 0.0.

If $x = 100$, then all members of $\mathbf{a}$ are currently being checked correctness by O, and if $x < 100$, then not all members of $\mathbf{a}$ are being checked. If $x = 100$, adding an assertion to check an element $\mathbf{a}[y]$ that is already being checked will not increase the likelihood of error propagation. But if $x \neq 100$, and we assert on a member of $\mathbf{a}$ that is not being checked by O, then unless this data member is dead, the likelihood of error propagation must increase.

This is true because of the basic probabilistic laws: given two events A and B,

$$\mathbf{Pr}(A) \vee \mathbf{Pr}(B) \geq \mathbf{Pr}(A)$$

$$\mathbf{Pr}(A) \vee \mathbf{Pr}(B) \geq \mathbf{Pr}(B)$$

In our notation, suppose that **a**[0] through **a**[8] are being tested by O; then adding an assertion to **a**[9] cannot decrease the likelihood of error propagation, because:

$$P_{\mathbf{a}[0]} \vee P_{\mathbf{a}[1]} \vee P_{\mathbf{a}[2]} \vee P_{\mathbf{a}[3]} \vee P_{\mathbf{a}[4]} \vee P_{\mathbf{a}[5]} \vee P_{\mathbf{a}[6]} \vee P_{\mathbf{a}[7]} \vee P_{\mathbf{a}[8]} \geq$$

$$P_{\mathbf{a}[0]} \vee P_{\mathbf{a}[1]} \vee P_{\mathbf{a}[2]} \vee P_{\mathbf{a}[3]} \vee P_{\mathbf{a}[4]} \vee P_{\mathbf{a}[5]} \vee P_{\mathbf{a}[6]} \vee P_{\mathbf{a}[7]} \vee P_{\mathbf{a}[8]} \vee P_{\mathbf{a}[9]}.$$

□

We have just shown that assertions cannot decrease software testability assessments; they can only improve testability scores or have no effect whatsoever. To better understand why this occurs, consider the two main implications that the assertion, **ASSERT(***a b c*, **x, a*b - c)**, has when triggered:

1. If the most recent expression that assigned **x** has not assigned it a value of **a*b - c** (for the most recently assigned values of a, b, and c), then the assertion will trigger and return a message that it failed; this *may* be because the expression being used to calculate **x** is incorrect, or
2. If the expression that assigns **x** does not assign it a value that is equal to **a*b - c**, then this may mean that some combination of the values referenced in that expression contain incorrect values. For debugging purposes, analysis both of the expression and the calculations for the referenced variables should be performed. This provides a way of partially checking the "goodness" of the state coming into that expression, i.e., a way of testing for whether an incorrect data state has propagated to the point in the program state where the assertion is called.

3.4 Verifying the Value-Added by Assertions

In the C++ ATM code, we have identified eight locations in the source code that are of particularly low testability. Although the procedural code did have low testability locations, we are interested in showing improved OO code testability, and so we did not inject assertions to that code. (We expect similar gains in testability had we applied assertions to the procedural code.)

For each of the low testability locations in the C++ version, an assertion was manually placed immediately following the location, and the testability analysis was rerun. Here, we did not assume that the code was correct, but we believe that the assertions were correct. Realize that after an assertion is injected, it then is a location that contributes to the output space, and hence the functional definition of what constitutes failure for the system is also modified. These assertions forced each propagation point estimate to increase to 1.0, which is a remarkable increase in the testability of the code with respect to the 102 test cases (See Table 7).

Code	Original Propagation	Propagation After Assertion
`rec->type = ret_val;`	0.00	1.0
`rec->transaction = WITHDRAW;`	0.095	1.0
`rec->type = ret_val;`	0.00	1.0
`rec->transaction = DEPOSIT;`	0.00	1.0
`ret_val = CHECKING;`	0.00	1.0
`rec->type = ret_val;`	0.00	1.0
`RecordNumber = 0;`	.156	1.0
`RECORDMAX = 30;`	0.00	1.0

Table 7 The "before and after" propagation point estimate location scores for OO-ATM.

4 CONCLUSIONS

It has been conjectured that there may be a theoretical upper bound on the testability achievable given a particular mathematical function that we wish to compute (Voas, 1991). It is unknown whether such exists, nor whether the upper bound is computable. However what it does suggest is that various program designs, implementations, and languages all contribute to the resulting testability given a fixed input distribution. Thus as a side- effect of this research, we hope to better determine whether the existence of such a theoretical upper bound is a realistic conjecture.

Assertions represent a valuable design tool for OO systems. We have produced a small lemma showing that an assertion can *never* decrease the propagation condition, i.e., an assertion can only improve or make no change to the propagation condition, which is very important for thwarting the negative impact of information hiding. Our conclusion that assertions are beneficial to testing parallels the recommendations of Osterweil and Clarke in (Osterweil and Clarke, 1992), where they classified assertions as "among the most significant ideas by testing and analysis researchers." This conclusion is also confirmed in (Yin and Bieman, 1994) and (Mueller and Hoshizaki, 1994). Propagation estimates are a means for logically deciding where assertions are needed in code regions that seem unlikely to reveal faults during testing. Current schemes for the placement of assertions are often either *ad hoc* or brute-force, placing assertions in random places or everywhere.

Intrusive assertions have costs: (1) a decrease in performance during testing, and (2) the cost of deriving assertions from the specification. Also, if the assertions are removed before the code is deployed, there will be a slight, additional cost. But for critical systems, if a value-added benefit can be demonstrated relative to cost for a scheme, the scheme cannot be automatically dismissed. Given the results of Table 7, we recommended applying them.

5 REFERENCES

Yin, H. and Bieman, J.M. (1994) Improving software testability with assertion insertion. In *Proc. of International Test Conference*, October.

Binder, R. V. (1994) Design for testability in object-oriented systems. *Communications of the ACM*, 37(9):87–101, September.

Osterweil, L. and Clarke, L. (1992) A Proposed Testing and Analysis Research Initiative. *IEEE Software*, pp. 89–96, September.

Dahl, O.J., Dijsktra, E. W., and Hoare, C.A.R. (1972) *Structured Programming*. Academic Press.

Mueller, B.A. and Hoshizaki, D.O. (1994) Using Semantic Assertion Technology to Test Application Software. In *Proceedings of Quality Week'94*, May.

Howden, W. E. and Huang, Y. (1993) Analysis of Testing Methods Using Failure Rate and Testability Models. Technical Report CS93-296, University of California at San Diego, June.

Voas, J., Morell, L., and Miller, K. (1991) Predicting Where Faults Can Hide From Testing. *IEEE Software*, 8(2):41–48, March.

Voas, J. and Miller, K. (1994) Putting Assertions in Their Place. In *Proc. of the International Symposium on Software Reliability Engineering*, November, IEEE Computer Society Press.

Voas, J. and Miller, K. (1995) Software Testability: The New Verification. *IEEE Software*, 12(3):17–28, May 1995.

Voas, J. (1991) Factors That Affect Program Testabilities. In *Proc. of the 9th Pacific Northwest Software Quality Conf.*, pp. 235–247, Portland, OR, October, Pacific Northwest Software Quality Conference, Inc.

Voas, J. (1992) *PIE*: A Dynamic Failure-Based Technique. *IEEE Trans. on Software Engineering*, 18(8):717–727, August 1992.

6 BIOGRAPHY

Jeffrey Voas is the Vice-President of Reliable Software Technologies (RST) Corp. and heads the research initiatives of the company. Voas is currently the principal investigator on research initiatives for NASA, National Institute of Standards and Technology, U.S. Air Force, and National Science Foundation. He has published over 60 journal and conference papers in the areas of software testability, software reliability, debugging, safety, fault-tolerance, design, and computer security. Voas has coauthored a text entitled Software Assessment: Reliability, Safety, Testability (John Wiley & Sons, 1995). In 1994, the Journal of Systems and Software ranked Voas 6th among the 15 top scholars in Systems and Software Engineering.

24

Applying Metrics for Quality Analysis and Improvement of Object-Oriented Software

I. Morschel
Daimler Benz Research Center
P.O. Box 23 60, D-89013 Ulm, Germany, +49 731 505 2870, morschel@dbag.ulm.Dailmer-Benz.com

Ch. Ebert
Alcatel SEL AG
Lorenzstraße 10, D-70435 Stuttgart, Germany, +49 711 821 42283, cebert@stgl.sel.alcatel.de

Abstract

Software metrics are playing an important role in analyzing and improving quality of software work products during their development. Measuring the aspects of software complexity for object-oriented software strongly helps to improve the quality of such systems during their development, while especially focusing on reusability, reliability and maintainability. It is widely accepted that more widespread use of object-oriented techniques can only come about when there are tool systems that provide development support beyond visualizing code. Distinct complexity metrics have been developed and integrated in a *Smalltalk* development support system called *SmallMetric*. Thus, we achieved a basis for software analysis (metrics) and development support (critique) of *Smalltalk* systems. The main concepts of the environment including the underlying metrics are explained, its use and operation is discussed, and some results of the implementation and its application to several projects are given with examples.

Keywords

complexity metrics, development support, object-oriented metrics, quality control, Smalltalk.

1 INTRODUCTION

Software metrics are measures of development processes and the resulting work products. In this context we will focus on metrics that are applicable to software developed in *Smalltalk*. We will further concentrate on such metrics that can be used as quality indicators during the development process, hence providing support for the developers. These metrics are often classified as product metrics because their inputs are products of the development process. We will not distinguish metrics and measures from a mathematical point of view. When referring to complexity metrics we are using this phrase for a group of software metrics that measure structural or volume aspects of products that are intuitively related to parts difficult to understand. These difficulties in dealing with such complex components have been proved to cause high error-rates, testing effort and bad maintainability (for further details on metrics see Fenton (1991). Because of the extreme subjectivity of such quality attributes per se, it is important to select metrics that can be applied to the specific objectives of a project, that have been derived from the project's requirements and can be used to prove consistency, that can be applied during several phases of the development process on resulting products (design, code, documentation, etc.), and that can be collected and evaluated automatically by the development environment in use.

Product metrics are used to supply mechanisms for: Fenton (1991), Chidamber & Kemerer (1991), Pfleeger & Palmer (1990)

- estimating effort and costs of new projects;
- evaluating the productivity to introduce new technologies (together with their methods and tools);
- measuring and improving software quality;
- forecasting and reducing testing and maintenance effort.

Based on software metrics and quality data from finished projects quality models can be derived from all work products generated during the development process. Quality models, thus, are generated by the combination and statistical analysis of product metrics (e.g. complexity metrics) and product or process attributes (e.g. quality characteristics, effort, etc.). These models are evaluated by applying and comparing exactly those invariant figures they are intended to predict: the process metrics (e.g. effort, fault rate, number of changes since the project started, etc). Iterative repetition of this process can refine the quality models, hence allowing the use of them as predictors for similar environments and projects. While currently applied quality models for the software development process are primarily focussing on product metrics of procedural source code, developers are waiting for control mechanisms based on analysis metrics, hence being applicable much earlier. The obviously shorter feedback cycles permit a direct design improvement without waiting for the source code.

Due to successful application in many projects such metrics obviously should be available for object-oriented environments. The goals might be the same, primarily indicating potentially troublesome classes that should be improved before being introduced to the class libraries. The object-oriented paradigm could directly profit from metrics as a vehicle to instruct staff who are new to this approach. Furthermore software metrics could be used to measure the problems to introduce this paradigm and its acceptance as well as to set design standards for an organization.

Traditional metrics for procedural approaches are not adequate for evaluating object-oriented software, primarily because they are not designed to measure basic elements like classes, objects, polymorphism, and message-passing. Even when adjusted to syntactically analyze object-oriented software they can only capture a small part of such software and so can just provide weak quality indication, LaLonde (1994). It is hence important to define customized metrics for object-oriented programs. Additionally the characteristics of the target language should be considered. Some languages directly support the object-oriented approach (*C++*, *Smalltalk*, *Eiffel*) and others just to some extent (*Ada*). Other factors like the size and contents of the class library and the semantics and syntactical form of particular commands should also be considered.

We will describe an programming analysis environment for *Smalltalk-80*, Goldberg & Robson (1983), because of its uniformity and elegance. The syntax of *Smalltalk* is easy to understand, it possesses a small number of operators (in contrast to *C++*), and it completely supports the notion of object, class, and inheritance. This article presents a basic set of metrics to support the development of object-oriented programs as well as a tool to automatically measure and to judge programs written in *Smalltalk*. In the next section the basic concepts of object-orientation and of *Smalltalk* will be presented. Section 3 gives an overview of related research in the area of object-oriented program analysis, quality control and product metrics. Section 4 and 5 describe the selection of metrics for object-oriented software and a tool environment called *SmallMetric*. Results from applying the analysis environment first to classroom projects and then in industrial projects are presented in section 6. A brief summary with an outlook on further work is given in section 7.

2 OBJECT-ORIENTATION AND *SMALLTALK*

Object-oriented modeling and programming is based on four fundamental concepts, namely inheritance, encapsulation, polymorphism, and reusability. for better understanding of the approaches described later, we'll try to give a rather brief summary about interesting features of object-orientation with respect to the *Smalltalk* programming language. As can easily be imagined the term "object" plays a central role in object-oriented programs. It comprehends data structures that describe its state, and methods[1] that realize its functionality. Data structures are encapsulated and provide information hiding with respect to their object which means that they do only offer access functions, called methods, but no direct use of the internal data structures. Objects communicate with each other via message passing which means that one method starts a method in another object. Mechanisms to hierarchically structure objects in classes exist in all object-oriented languages. Instances can be derived from classes and differ from other objects only on the basis of associated states.

Another important characteristic is the possibility of incrementally defining class hierarchies. This is done by the inheritance mechanism. From a superclass, a subclass inherits all its data structures and methods. In the subclass, new data structures and methods can be defined or they can be rewritten. *Smalltalk*'s inheritance mechanism for example is designed to model software evolution as well as to classify.

Smalltalk support the object-oriented concepts fully. It manipulates classes, objects and implements a single inheritance mechanism. It does not include multiple inheritance, prototypes, delegation, or concurrency in its standard version. In addition to its programming language *Smalltalk* includes an open programming

---

[1] we use in this paper the Smalltalk terminology.

environment to develop object-oriented programs. It offers a comfortable graphical user interface, several helpful tools and a vast class library. Programming language and environment coexist in a homogeneous form, where concepts at the programming level are reproduced in the environment. An example is the message passing mechanism. In *Smalltalk* programs, it means the activation of a method. The same strategy is used in the user interface to identify a selected object. This message passing consists of: an object (the receiver of the message), a message selector and optional arguments as parameters.

Object behavior is described by the mentioned methods, which have a selector and include *Smalltalk* commands. In different classes, methods with the same selector can exist. This is called polymorphism. The status of an object is captured through class and instance variables that might be accessed from outside by suitable methods. Class variables are defined at the class level and instance variables at the object level to store object's states.

3 ANALYSIS AND DEVELOPMENT SUPPORT FOR OBJECT-ORIENTED SOFTWARE

Most software developers apply quality assurance that identifies problems (as instances of poor quality) and ensures that they are resolved. Although striving to high quality standards, only a few organisations apply true quality control. Quality management includes continuously comparing observed quality with expected quality, hence minimizing the effort expended on correcting the sources of defect. In order to achieve software quality, it must be developed in an organized form including understanding of design and programming methods, associated review and testing strategies and supportive tools for analysis. The latter is accomplished through the use of metrics and statistical evaluation techniques that relate specific quantified product characteristics to some attributes of quality. The development environment provides the formal description of different work products that are analysed automatically. Multivariate analyses techniques provide feedback about relationships between components (e.g. factor analysis). Classification techniques help determining outliers (e.g. error-prone components). Finally, detailed diagrams and tables provide insight into the reasons why distinct components are potential outliers and how to improve them (see Ebert (1992) for a detailed description of such techniques).

So far there has been little work concerning the definition and use of metrics for object-oriented programs. With the broader application of this paradigm quality control, both analytic (i.e. with metrics) and constructive (i.e. by providing design and help facilities) quality control are of increasing importance.

One of the first attempts to investigate quality aspects of object-oriented programs was done by Lieberherr and colleagues, Lieberherr & Holland (1989). They defined a set of design rules that restricts the message-sending structure of methods. It was called *Law of Demeter*. Informally, the law says that each method can send messages to only a limited set of objects: to argument objects, to the *self* pseudovariable, and to the immediate subparts of *self* (self being the object or class itself). The *Law of Demeter* thus attempts to minimize the coupling between classes.

Most application of metrics for object-oriented programs are based on transforming well-known metrics for procedural programs, Karunanithi & Bieman (1993). Unfortunately such metrics do not cover completely the relevant aspects of coupling, such as inheritance or polymorphism. Other approaches suggest metrics that really focus on object-oriented descriptions, however do not offer any guidelines for using the metrics in practical projects, Bilow (1993), LaLonde & Pugh (1994). In the same context six metrics have been suggested for measuring elements contributing to the size and complexity of object-oriented design that will be used here as a base for selecting metrics, Chidamber & Kemerer (1991). An approach for estimating size and development effort of object-oriented systems based on requirements analysis has been discussed in Pfleeger & Palmer (1990). However, no metrics for distinct products have been provided. Sharble and Cohen (1993) compare two object-oriented development methods using an object-oriented brewery as example. They suggest indicators to enhance the software quality by increasing cohesion, reducing coupling, increasing polymorphism, and eliminating redundancy.

4 METRICS FOR ANALYSIS OF OBJECT-ORIENTED SOFTWARE

Goals such as quality improvement, increasing productivity or maturity certification are of growing interest in industry. Navigating the way with metrics is one important approach to ensure that a company stays on the course of achieving these goals. Though the search for underlying structures and rules in a set of observations is performed in software quality control and effective solutions to refine forecasting methods based on past data have been suggested, their applicability to object-oriented software development has been restricted.

Quality models are built on former project experiences and combine the quantification of aspects of software components with a framework of rules (e.g. limits for metrics, appropriate ranges etc.). For assessing overall quality or productivity, it is suitable to break it down into its component factors (e.g. maintainability), thus arriving at several aspects of software that can be analyzed quantitatively.

There is a growing awareness that such approaches could also support the object-oriented software development process. Anybody starting with object-oriented software rises the following questions, Lieberherr & Holland (1989), that also serve as guidelines for developing a measurement tool environment for quality control:

- What is good style in object-oriented programs?
- Are there any rules that can be applied to develop a good object-oriented program?
- Which metrics could be employed in order to determine if a program is "good" or not ?

Nevertheless, the mere definition of a metrics suite combined with statistical number crunching without intuitive backgrounds would result in the same acceptance problems procedural metrics applications ran into during the eighties, Fenton (1991). As long as the objectives of a object-oriented development process are not stated and supported with tailored methods, metrics would be of no practical help. To overcome such problems we introduce *SmallMetric*, a tool to evaluate and meliorate object-oriented programs written in *Smalltalk*. It is embedded in an environment for the learning of object-oriented programming, Morschel (1993).

5 A DESCRIPTION OF THE OBJECT-ORIENTED METRICS FRAMEWORK

SmallMetric analyses object-oriented programs by applying construction rules that distinguish between (Figure 1):

- the static and dynamic structure of a class or an object;
- the static and dynamic relationships between classes and or objects.

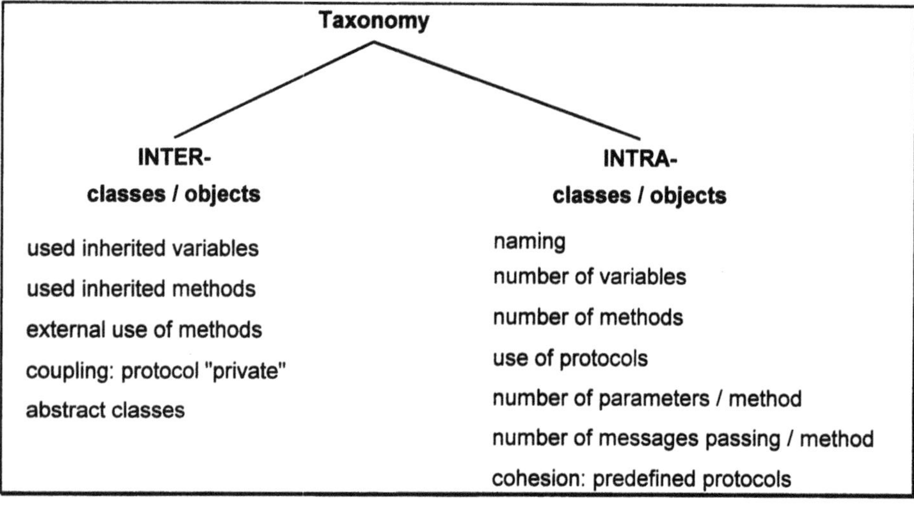

Figure 1 Taxonomy for SmallMetric.

The metrics that are presented in the following list comprehend different aspects of object-oriented software. We will describe the underlying intuition of the metrics as well as a comprehensive summary of our observations from object-oriented development projects.

Metric 1: Volume

The volume of an object is a basic size measure that is intuitively connected with the amount of information inside a class. Many empirical investigations of metrics showed relationships among size metrics and comprehensibility or number of errors. Volume thus is a potential indicator of the effort to develop an object as well as for its future maintenance. The bigger the number of variables and methods, the more specific for one application. In other words, the object's reusability is likely to be small with increasing volume. Volume can be measured by:

- Number of variables (class and instance variables);
- Number of methods (class and instance methods).

Metric 2: Method structure

The internal structure of an object based on its methods and the information that is accessed by them is an indicator of its functionality. If the methods are overloaded with information to pass back and forth, there is good reason to assume that the object or class should be broken into several objects or classes. Method metrics are used to forecast effort for debugging and testing early. Method structure can be measured by:

- Number of parameters per method;
- Number of temporary variables per method;
- Number of message passing per method.

Metric 3: Cohesion

The term cohesion is frequently used in software engineering to designate a mechanism for *keeping related things together*. Cohesion can be defined to be the degree of similarity of methods. The higher the degree of similarity of methods in *one* class or object, the greater the cohesiveness of the methods and the higher the degree of encapsulation of the object. Cohesion in *Smalltalk* means the organization of methods, which set or access the value of a class or instance variable, under predefined schemes (*protocols*). These protocols are predetermined in *Smalltalk*. The programmer can use them to manipulate variables of an object. Such methods are called *accessors*, Beck (1993). The intuitive base is that direct reference to class and instance variables limits inheritance by fixing storage decisions in the superclass that can not be changed in a subclass. Besides, modifications in the structure of these variables are not visible to other methods, just to the accessors. Hence, the effort to extend or to modify a given program is minimized.

As an example consider an instance variable instVar of an object anObject. To access the class and instance variables it is necessary to define two kind of methods:

- one method for getting the value of an instance variable

```
instVar
    ^instVar
```

- and other for setting an instance variable

```
instVar: aValue
    instVar := aValue
```

This solution forces all accesses to variables to go through an accessor method. Therefore, *information hiding* with respect to variables and methods in a class is enforced, Parnas, Clements & Weiss (1985). *SmallMetric* examines a *Smalltalk* program to find accesses to variables outside of the predefined protocols. This is called a cohesion violation of an object.

Metric 4: Coupling (Coupl)

Coupling designates the interaction between objects that are not related through inheritance. Excessive coupling between objects besides inheritance is detrimental to modular design and prevents reuse. The more independent an object, the easier it is to reuse it in another project, Fenton (1991), Chidamber & Kemerer (1991). The suggested metric is:

- Number of invoked classes.

A predefined scheme in *Smalltalk* is the protocol **private**. It comprehends methods that should only be activated inside of an object. The *Smalltalk* compiler or interpreter does not check these specific accesses. When a message from another object starts a method under this protocol, undesirable effects can occur because during development such access had not been anticipated. *SmallMetric* tries to identify such references.

Metric 5: Inheritance tree (Inh)

This group of metrics analyzes the amount of inherited variables and methods used by a class. The use of inherited methods and data in a class indicates the difficulty of changing superior classes. On a low level of the inheritance tree variables and methods available to a class could be changed in meaning several times on higher levels, thus increasing complexity even more. It is hence necessary to provide information about how many methods and variables are available to a distinct class. The metrics are:

- inherited variables used;
- inherited methods used.

In *Smalltalk*, an instance variable can be directly set by an object of a subclass. This can reduce the reuse of a class in other applications. *SmallMetric* nominates it an "*information hiding violation*" (example 1).

Metric 6: Class organization (Org)

This group of analyses captures three comprehensability indicators: naming, checking of comments and the use of predefined protocols. Naming analyzes all identifiers of a class. *SmallMetric* informs the developer about their distribution. This metric has just documentation purposes. The existence of comments within an object is also checked. In *Smalltalk*, one can define a global comment to clarify the intents and functionality of an object. *SmallMetric* warns, when there is no such comment provided. The programmer may organize the methods of an object under predefined protocols. The *Smalltalk* environment advises the developer to use these recommendations which is checked by *SmallMetric*. For novices, these protocols can help to elucidate some aspects of a *Smalltalk* program.

```
Object subclass: #Superclass
    instanceVariableNames: 'text'
    classVariableNames: ''
    poolDictionaries: ''
    category: 'SmallMetric'

Superclass subclass: #Subclass
    instanceVariableNames: ''
    classVariableNames: ''
    poolDictionaries: ''
    category: 'SmallMetric'

Subclass class methodsFor: 'instance creation'
new

    ^super new initialize
```

```
Subclass methodsFor: 'initialize release'
initialize
    text := 'This is an example of an information hiding violation !!'
```

Example 1 An information hiding violation

6 EXPERIENCES WITH *SMALLMETRIC* FOR *SMALLTALK* PROGRAM ANALYSIS

Upon starting SmallMetric a window is opened, which inquires the name of the class to be analysed. Wildcards (*) can be used. When the given class is found, a new window is created (Fig. 2). It presents the following information:

1. number and list of all variables;
2. number of methods;
3. buttons to switch between class and instance;
4. predefined protocols used;
5. naming;
6. violations of *SmallMetric* metrics.

Four buttons are provided to select a new class, to print the information of a class, to switch between different dialogue languages (now English and German) and to activate Help. The critique window of course can be adjusted to specific standards and process guidelines of an organization. It has a menu, which presents the design limits for development support.

SmallMetric comprises a basic set of guidelines for metric-based development support of *Smalltalk* applications. On the basis of the metrics above as applied to Smalltalk projects with available quality data, we extracted some *design guidelines* to enhance the quality of object-oriented programs written in *Smalltalk*. Because one of the main reasons for using object-oriented technology is reusability, we focussed our evaluations on maintainability and reusability. Such guidelines should be understood as recommendations and not as restriction of a programmer's creativity. The projects being analyzed ranged in size from few classes to 400 classes of a commercially available *Smalltalk*-based tool, thus covering effort of up to 30 person years. Our approach for extracting guidelines of metrics that can serve as indicators of poor quality is based on analyzing the classes with respect to complexity metrics and quality data. Since the metrics are applied on different scales (complexity metrics: ratio scale and quality metrics: ordinal scale) we performed non-parametric statistical methods for correlations and factor analysis. Unlike in other approaches we don't discard outliers, because it is - ex ante - unknown what classes or metrics are outliers. Instead all metrics are normalized with a quadratic approach before comparing or ranking them.

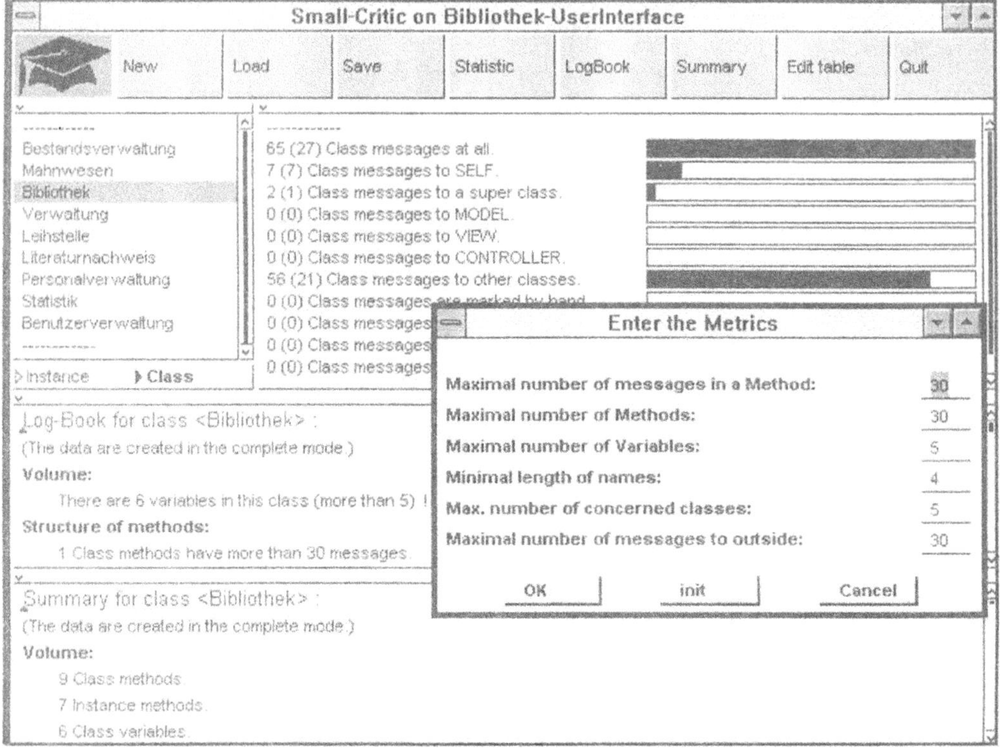

Figure 2 The user interface of *SmallMetric*.

The following suggestions usually seem to be very clear in theory - but just have a look on your latest designs ...

- **Volume**:
  Number of variables → maximum 5
  Number of methods → maximum 30
  Number of invoked classes and objects → is only numerically indicated
- **Struct**:
  Number of parameters per methods → is only numerically indicated
  Number of temporary variables per methods → is only numerically indicated
  Number of message passing per methods → maximum 30
- **Cohes**:
  Existence of an *accessor* outside of a predefined protocol
- **Coupl**:
  Number of external message passing per method → only numerically indicated
  External access of methods under the protocol private → only numerically indicated
- **Inh**:
  Violation of the *information hiding* principle → *only numerically indicated*
- **Org**:
  Number of characters of an identifier → minimum 5
  Non-existence of comment

The measured values were analyzed with respect to boundaries (minimum, maximum), intervals, deviations from the average, and nonparametric correlations between them. The interpretation was performed according to these criteria and used as follows:

- Sustain a high comprehensability level by providing a sufficient length of descriptive parts in all design objects and object names with meanings, rather than enumeration such as "class-1". The descriptions should include subclasses or inheritance relations, changes of inherited methods or variables, functionality, related objects, used data items, date, author, test cases to be performed, requirements fulfilled, management activities and staff connected with this project.
- During class and object design, the metrics and their statistical evaluation (regarding similar projects) are taken to distinguish between different designs (e.g. alternative approaches, division into subclasses).
- During reviews at the end of design and coding, the metrics are taken as indicators for weak components (e.g. inadequate inheritance hierarchy, unsatisfying object description) and as indicators for process management (timely ordered number of classes or volume metrics).

After applying such metrics to different, however similar projects, the statistical results obtained can be used to define intervals or limits for metrics in order to increase quality.

7 SUMMARY AND FUTURE WORK

Most complexity metrics have been designed without regard to the problem domain and the programming environment. There are many aspects of complexity and a lot of design decisions influence the complexity of a product. This paper presents an approach to integrate software metrics with design support for object-oriented techniques based on *Smalltalk*. A tool environment for program analysis called *SmallMetric* that incorporates metrics and guidelines for improving programs has been developed. Based on these set of metrics we investigated different projects both from industry and academia to improve the guidelines. This approach to integrate a measurement tool system into *Smalltalk* illustrates a way to minimize the efforts for implementation and maintenance of such a tool and shows how to cope with changes in future requirements for such tools and their individual interfaces. By transforming the object-oriented information representation into another language it is possible to integrate such measurement techniques into other environments as well.

With an early analysis of software products we are able to provide developers with helpful hints to improve their designs and code during the development process and not at the end when it will be much more expensive. By following the given suggestions we could actually and reproducible improve designs and achieve better programs in terms of such quality items as understandability, reusability and maintainability. Of course, much more research is necessary in order to provide complete guidelines for achieving high quality designs. The basic step, however, still is the measurement and evaluation of software complexity as early as possible: during the software development process when the most expensive faults are induced (e.g. inheritance trees). By making software engineers aware that there are suitable techniques and tools for analyzing their programs, even when they are object-oriented, this could be a small step to avoid a similar software crisis to what we are currently facing in procedural environments.

ACKNOWLEDGEMENTS

The assistance of the Landis&Gyr corporation Switzerland, to provide product and process data of object-oriented projects is gratefully acknowledged. Several discussions with A. Riegg of Debis in Stuttgart contributed to the proposed guidelines.

BIBLIOGRAPHY

Fenton, N.E.: *Software Metrics: A Rigorous Approach*. Chapman & Hall, London, UK, 1991.

Chidamber, S.R. and C.F. Kemerer: Towards a Metric Suite for Object Oriented Design. *Proc. of Conf. on Object-Oriented Programming Systems, Languages, and Applications (OOPSLA). Sigplan Notices*, Vol. 26, No. 11, Nov. 1991.

Pfleeger, S.L. and J.D. Palmer: Software Estimation for Object Oriented Systems. *Proc. Fall international Function Point Users Group Conference*, San Antonio, TX, USA, pp. 181 - 196, Oct. 1990.

Goldberg, A. and Robson, D.: *SMALLTALK-80 The Language and its Implementation*. Addison-Wesley, 1983.

Ebert, C.: Visualization Techniques for Analyzing and Evaluating Software Measures. *IEEE Transactions on Software Engineering*, Vol. 18, No. 11, pp. 1029 - 1034, Nov. 1992.

Lieberherr, K.J. and I.M. Holland: Assuring Good Style for Object-Oriented Programs. *IEEE Software*, Vol. 6, No. 9, pp. 38 - 48, 1989.

Bilow, S.: Software Entropy and the Need for Object-Oriented Metrics. *Journal of Object-Oriented Programming*, Vol. 5, Jan. 1993.

Sharble, R. and Cohen, S. The Object-Oriented Brewery: A Comparison of Two Object-Oriented Development Methods. *Software Eng. Notes,* Vol 18, No. 2, 1993.

Morschel, I.: An Intelligent Tutoring System for the Learning of Object-Oriented Programming. *Proc. EAEEIE '93*. Prague, 1993.

Beck,K.: To accessor or not to accessor? *The Smalltalk Report*. Vol. 2., Num. 8., June 1993

Parnas, D.L., P.C. Clements and D.M. Weiss: The Modular Structure of Complex Systems. *IEEE Transactions on Software Engineering*, Vol. SE-11, No. 3, pp. 259 - 266, Mrc. 1985.

LaLonde, W. and J. Pugh: Gathering Metric Information Using Metalevel Facilities. *Journ. Object Oriented Programming*, Vol. 6, pp. 33 - 37, Mrc. 1994.

Karunanithi, S. and J.M. Bieman: Candidate Reuse Metrics for Object Oriented and Ada Software. *Proc. Int. Software Metrics Symposium*. IEEE Comp. Soc. Press, New York, pp. 120 - 128, 1993.

BIOGRAPHY

Dr. I. Morschel: Majored in computer sciences at the UFRGS in Brazil (1983-1987), M.Sc. at the UFRGS (1988-1990), PhD under the supervision of the Department of Dialogue Systems at the University of Stuttgart (1990-1994) with thesis "Software Engineering - Object-Oriented Technology and Intelligent Tutoring Systems". Since 1994 employed at Daimler-Benz AG in the field of research of software engineering.

PART NINE

KBS Quality

25

Software Engineering Concepts for KBS Design and Testing for Reliability

F. Battini
IEEE Member
via L. Banfi 25, 20040 Carnate (MI), Italy, Tel: +39.2. 25075342
e-mail: battini%laben@icil64.cilea.it

Abstract

The quality of an expert system is usually measured on the goodness of unexpected advice. Although adequacy is involved rather than correctness, however a minimum of correctness should be reached. Hence, as effectiveness of a KBS implies hard predictability on its results, satisfactory testing can be assured just in an operational-like phase of the system lifecycle. Such assumption is not far away by similar assumptions made by some software reliability approaches, like the Cleanroom Approach. To generalize such parallelisms between knowledge and software engineering concepts, this article explains how to provide knowledge engineering with a complete lifecycle strategy.

Keywords

Euclidean Model, Design Principles, Cleanroom Approach

1 INTRODUCTION

KBS are designed for use in non obvious situations where only an expert can infer a sensible solution, whose a priori description is not easy to describe through an a priori analysis and shall be considered as unexpected (i.e. not following a defined and detailed model).

The quality of a KBS is then measured either on the goodness of unexpected advices, if you deal with expert systems, or on the effectiveness of the control actions facing unexpected situations, not explicitly forecasted by the knowledge design.

KBS validation shall start from matching results produced by a fixed set of test cases framing expected results in some simpler situations, whose representiveness, however, can be hardly demonstrated with reference to operations to be faced by the system.

Thus, the concept of absolute correctness should be replaced by the concept of system adequacy: what you can assume as correct by lack of evidence of the contrary, even for results you are not able to predict "a priori". That standpoint dramatically impacts on KBS validation and reliability assessment, unless you fix the following points:

1. Although adequacy is more involved in the KBS reliability rather than correctness, nevertheless a full correctness should be reached at least in simpler situations explicitly forecasted by the knowledge design (Hollnagel, 1991).
2. As a consequence, an operational-like testing is the best suitable way for verifying the KBS adequacy.
3. The goal of KBS reliability should be take into account that KBS do have unpredictable data results (i.e. not framed by a fixed algorithm or model), but must be deterministic in the behaviour of control.
4. Validation and testing are achievable at the end of a development activity, but must be clearly addressed in the earlier design activity.
5. Verification, validation and testing methodology must be framed in a developing strategy referring as most as possible to software engineering principles (Partridge,1988) (ANSI/AIAA,1992).

Our aim is to set relationships between knowledge and software engineering in order to show that reliability assessment can be approached for KBSs through a re-statement of the modularity concept to be managed by knowledge design principles.

We start from the point of view of a knowledge engineer who has not to care on validation and testing of inference engine, user interface and so on, because he is supposed either to use a commercial shell or to have already tested the A.I. tools he is dealing with. His goal is to build a test plan and validation procedures for the implemented knowledge base.

1.1 Knowledge Base as a Software Abstraction

Abstraction is the main feature in knowledge based systems (Partridge,1988). In fact, when we design a knowledge base , we actually design a software in a higher degree of abstraction than the traditional software, which is rather a device, an abstract machine.

For instance the software dealing with the inference engine is an "abstract" engine, whose control is driven by the abstract "software" of the knowledge base. Therefore, no wonder if we abstract the software engineering goals such as modifiability, efficiency, fault-tolerance and understandability as follows:

- **Modifiability** implies controlled changes in the knowledge base such that inference is affected only in the deduction line we desire to change.
- **Efficiency** implies the optimal way in which inferences are performed, pruning everything is redundant or unwanted.
- **Fault tolerance** implies meaningful inferences for every set of data you could input, providing some mechanisms of recovery from failure due to inconsistency, incompleteness or lack of data.
- **Understandability** implies a full understanding of the reasoning lines by the end user: a bridge between problem solving strategy and empirical expertise.

Besides, both software codes and knowledge bases do have primary attributes (the properties) directly felt by the user and manageable by technical principles. Hence, software properties as modularity, concision, consistency, completeness, robustness and self-documentation are still properties of a knowledge base summarized by a second level of attributes: the capabilities.

What we are showing is how to verify, validate and test such capabilities through the modularity of the knowledge base, in order to achieve the goals of fault-tolerance, efficiency and modifiability of our abstracted software: the knowledge base.

1.2 Modularity as a Knowledge Property

Unfortunately the traditional statement of modularity, related to the principles of localization and information hiding, cannot be fully applied in knowledge base design, because knowledge items (rules, frames, script or plans and so on) are strongly coupled to each other. In fact, it could be difficult to decompose a knowledge base in order to readily test it, because localization could be a poor concept in the incremental growing of a knowledge base and it could be hard to define modules cohesively strong and loosely coupled. Nevertheless modularity is just what we are looking for: a knowledge property reached through design concepts, as localization and information hiding, that allows to separate something from the general concern and to verify it without changing its behaviour "in the large". The only thing we would be able to do is to manage the strong coupling among the knowledge items, defining different clusters of related knowledge items and preventing from unwanted interferences among them, through a suitable knowledge model and suitable design principles.

2 THE KNOWLEDGE MODEL

Knowledge grows in an incremental way. Hence a knowledge base, mapping larger and larger expertise, could be thought as a succession of nested incrementing domains, rather than a collection of disjoined areas partitioning a formalized knowledge.

Even a better definition and formalization of a single expertise domain might be viewed as an upper layer of more detailed knowledge encapsulating a less defined knowledge formalization.

Moreover, goals belonging to a single domain could be sub-goals for a more general domain (or a better defined domain) embedding the first one. Hence, that nesting gets domains strongly coupled to each other.

Clusters

If we consider knowledge items sequentially fired in inferencing some conclusions, we have a deduction line. Many deduction lines correlated to the same set of conclusions set up a cluster of related knowledge items. Many deduction lines, making up a cluster, may have in common one or more pieces of their inferencing paths. Hence, a cluster is a set of knowledge items with a strong cohesion.

Module definition

First, we define a module as a cluster of related knowledge items belonging to one or more deduction lines, and not necessarily disjoined, inferencing a correlated set of conclusions and mapping an aspect of a single knowledge domain. The fact that a module has to map just one aspect of a knowledge domain reflects the incremental growing of the knowledge, in such a way you are allowed to merge your module in an outer module mapping a broader aspect, or only a better definition of the first one.

The Euclidean model

We define an Euclidean model of the knowledge, in which 2 kinds of clusters could be defined: theorems and corollaries. Theorems are Goal-driven clusters of knowledge items in backward chaining. Corollaries are data-driven clusters in forward chaining. Hence an Euclidean model of knowledge defines opportunistic reasoning toggling between backward and forward chaining. The knowledge model we defined has been called "Euclidean" because it recalls the logical structure of the Euclid geometry, moving from simpler theorems to more and more complicated deduction with the help of theorem results and corollaries.

3 VVT SUPPORTED BY THE KNOWLEDGE MODEL

The Euclidean model supplies a "natural" methodology for Verification, Validation and Testing (VVT) In fact, theorem results referenced by other theorems can be verified and validated adopting two alternative ways:

- Recursively, asking for details of the referenced theorems (that is by a clear-box testing).
- Through modularity, asking just for which hypotheses inference which conclusions (that is by a black-box testing).

Finally, to test knowledge in solving problem, we must check the correct use of corollaries and theorems referred by a piece of inference.

3.1 Validation and Testing

Validation requires an enhanced confirmability of the knowledge base towards both the understandability goal and the achievement of the right level of correctness. Validation needs a computer-environment interaction model that matches the system dynamic behaviour with reference to possible situations. So, a logically consistent module, that is statically correct, has to behave like a black-box that transforms a time succession of "modulate impulses" into an ordinate succession of meaningful responses, in a sort of convolution between present input and former deductions.

The order of the inferred conclusions becomes very important. In an expert system for instance a right advice given at the wrong time could be hardly understood, because the system is not reasoning as an expert may do. In embedded KBS, a right reaction in the wrong moment can trigger an incorrect overall system response. Therefore the behaviour has to obey to causality in concatenating deductions in the right order. That implies that two kinds of checks should be provided by KBS testing.

- A consistency check, to confirm **statically** the correct relationship between input data and expected results.
- A behavioural check, to confirm **dynamically** the correct evolution of the produced results with reference to a defined computer-environment interaction model.

The difference between the usual software engineering and the knowledge engineering is that knowledge base are continously submitted to testing even after release of modules validated on the basis of a defined test plan. In fact, only the operational use is a meaningful testbed for a knowledge base. Therefore it is no point to put emphasis on testing activities before validation (not to be eliminated, anyway), rather than to be aware that the real testing is just entered when the KBS is released.

Although that may seem awfully misleading to traditional software practitioners (see Adron, 1982), actually there exists an advanced software engineering practice that emphasizes testing on the field and get rid of most test for debugging activities: the Cleanroom Approach (Mills,1987).

Testing is then a natural consequence of the validation activity, because validation checks a limited set of computer-environment interaction situations, while testing is performed in solving real-problems impacting the knowledge base across many domains. If the validation is a minimum test of reliability, testing is a full stress-test as well as an evaluation of the goodness of the computer-environment interaction model.

3.2 The Cleanroom Approach

As KBS testing should cope with hard predictability on the expected data even if the general behavior is well fixed, thus full satisfactory testing can be assured just in an operational-like phase of the system life cycle.

Such assumption is not far away from similar assumptions made by some software reliability approaches, like the Cleanroom Approach (Mills, 1990), that emphasizes the operational testing instead of a mere debugging. Furthermore, that approach uses an incremental design to assess reliable software systems, starting from a first kernel up to successive layers of additional features: just what we should follow to increment a knowledge base.

That similarity sets a relationship between the knowledge engineering and the software engineering practice, giving a baseline in the KBSs implementation for reliability measurements, that can be assessed by a succession of incremental releases, supported by a more and more reliable growing core.

3.3 Reliability Assessment

Reliability for software is a product metrics to be assessed on the final software system after a complete integration, when the software is ready to be exercitated as in the operational use (Musa,1987): as we have seen that is the natural approach to be used in knowledge engineering as well. The measure of the reliability in software can be achieved in 2 ways (Goel, 1985):

1. By means of a continuos monitoring of the decreasing defectiveness in a **Software Reliability Growth** condition typical of integration, verification and validation phases, when the software can still be submitted to corrective maintenance.
2. In a final **qualification** phase by means of statistical models applied on direct observation of presence or absence of failures, when the software is stressed by an actual use. Here the software is frozen and cannot be changed except through a new release.

It must be noticed that testing for validation is aimed at assessing the satisfaction to stated requirements of the produced software, whereas testing for reliability must measure the statistical confidence we have on a validated software to be failure-free in any possible situation. For knowledge base engineering, validation still assesses satisfaction of some requirements that are formalized on the form of very few representative cases, whereas the qualification phase should be considered for KBS a Testing activity for reliability assessment.

Software Reliability Growth

In a Software Reliability Growth condition, the trend in the rate of fault detection and correction is observed and extrapolated in order to foresee the time of the next failure occurrence. Therefore level of the reliability shall be assessed with reference to MTTF (Mean Time To Failure) metrics. An equivalent application of the Reliability Growth Models in the knowledge engineering has been suggested by Bastani (1993), but the trouble stands in the fact that Reliability Growth Models deal with many corrections on the software which may be dangerous on a knowledge base affecting the reliability growing, because the required modularity is hard to get in KBS in order to isolate the fault zone.

Statistical Reliability Qualification

During qualification the software is frozen and its behavior can be observed by means of a statistical sampling of independent possible input classes (**sampling model**) defined following an operational profile (Musa,1993): in our case we talk about triggers and stimuli coming from the environments. By means of the sampling model, assessment of the software reliability shall be made on a statistically meaningful base of tests and again observing the failure rate as in the software reliability growth phase.

In the traditional software, however, the number of the possible observation is very close to 0 by definition, as the software as already passed all the validation steps. Therefore the reliability models used in the former phase, which need a good deal of failure data, cannot be effectively applied. Then the reliability assessment is adopting the Parnas approach (Parnas,1990), a very conservative one, where the so-called **0-failure method** and **k-failure method** are used to measure reliability. Those are an extension to the software testing of observation of a binomial distribution on the results of some Bernoulli trials.

The first method is more conservative, because qualification must restart when a failure, no matter how severe, is observed. The second one allows to keep into account a longer test history, even if some no severe failures are still observed. Then that approach seems more appropriate although:

- The actual use for a KBS is hard to be defined by the equivalent of an Operational Profile.
- According to Poore and Mills (1993) reliability assessment by 0-failure or k-failure methods are very expensive in effort, because to assess a $MTTF=\tau$ you should need at least a $2*\tau$ time of observation.

If the actual software production, however, follows an incremental development as in the Cleanroom Approach, the evolution in quality of the software along such sequential releases can be take into account. In fact, it has been observed that MTTF from a release to the next ones increases exponentially:

$$MTTF_p=MTTF_0\,(e^{h})^p \quad \text{for the } p\text{th release.} \qquad (1)$$

where $h = 1 / MTTF_0$ and $MTTF_0$ Mean Time To Failure of the starting release.

A suitable Qualification approach is able to consider such software evolution and then to qualify with less tests a software owning long MTTF, provided that the software has been delivered through p releases. That last framework, referring to the Cleanroom Approach, should be adopted for KBS.

4 APPLICATION FIELD

The described knowledge model and the related VVT methodology has been applied already in 2 real applications:

- The definition of a Test Plan for an Autonomous Spacecraft Data Management System (ASDMS) (Marradi, 1992) where the knowledge base to be validated was a set of predefined plans, fired in a real-time traditional software. In such case, the Euclidean Model supplies the required modularity through data-driven clusters (the Autonomy Plans), but strong coupling between the embedded knowledge base and the background of software processes drives to refine the different goals between the static consistency checks and the dynamic behavior checks (where also real-time concerns had been considered). Besides, according to the described methodology, Validation had been performed on a finite set of deterministic test case, and postponing the "testing" to a qualification phase made directly by the user.
- The development and validation of a production rules expert system, advising on signal processing algorithms, giving some timing and signal constraints. The description of the approach used in that field is explained as a study case in (Battini, 1993).

In the next future the described methodology is likely to be applied on a fuzzy controller where a set of rules shall be defined and validated to control the fine positioning of some actuators.

5 DESIGN PRINCIPLES

It is obvious that efficacy on the VVT techniques may be affected by the testability of the designed knowledge base. Therefore for KBS any VVT methodology should be supported by appropriate design principles able to enhance modularity or at least to manage and reduce strong coupling among different knowledge modules.

Roughly speaking, problems arise when you deal with modules and nested sub modules. To manage strong coupling among them, it is possible, in the case of a knowledge base for an expert system, to state three design principles that can be considered as a general paradigm for translation of design principle from software engineering to knowledge engineering.

Statements

Principle A: every sub module must be fired by an outer module only in these items strictly bounded with the final Goal inferenced by the module.
Desired properties: concision. It is a sort of information hiding principle
Principle B: for every choice between a Goal and one of its subgoals the inferential behaviour, related to the subgoal inference, must be invariant. Or better, the succession of the fired knowledge items must be the same with, eventually, the needed pruning according to principle A. Desired properties: completeness, consistency, modularity.
Principle C: subgoals already inferenced can be integrated and completed through knowledge items in forward chaining belonging to the final goal only.

Desired properties: completeness, modularity.
Figure 1 frames the stated principles with properties, capabilities and knowledge engineering goals.

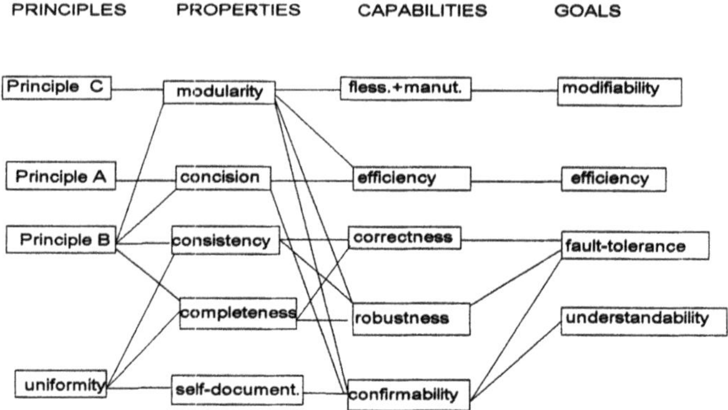

Figure 1 Relationships among design principles, knowledge base properties, capabilities and design goals.

5.2 Applicability of the Principles

To clarify the applicability of the stated design principles, let consider the following example:

- Let N a module, verifying a deduction goal "x" through 2 representation (1 and 2) of the same problem (Figure 2). Either deduction line is chosen according to the initial set S0 of the starting data.
- Nest module N into an outer module M, aimed at verifying final goal "y" through an assessment of the goal "x" inferred by N and representing an intermediate sub-goal of the whole deduction line (Figure 3).
- Suppose that the representation 1 is meaningful for the final goal "y" and that should be used.

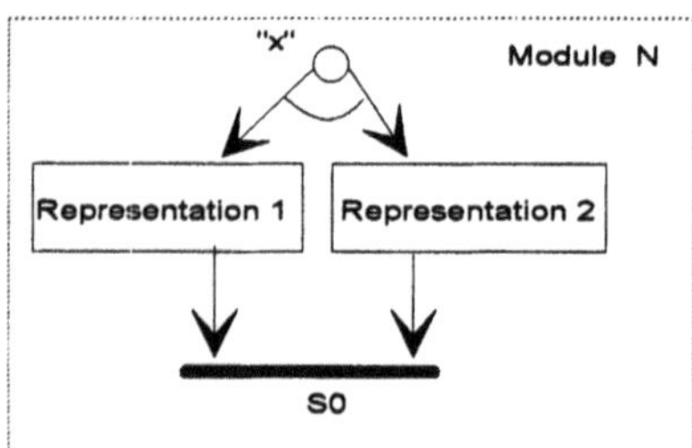

Figure 2 Module by Cluster with 2 representations.

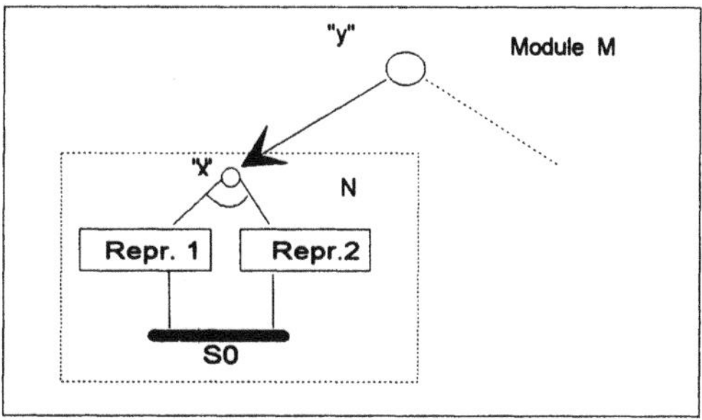

Figure 3 Module M with a nested sub module

Principle A claims that, when the nested (sub-)module N is fired by M for inferencing its final goal "y", just the meaningful deduction line (representation 1) should be scanned and the deduction of "x" should not use any items of representation 2 (Figure 4).

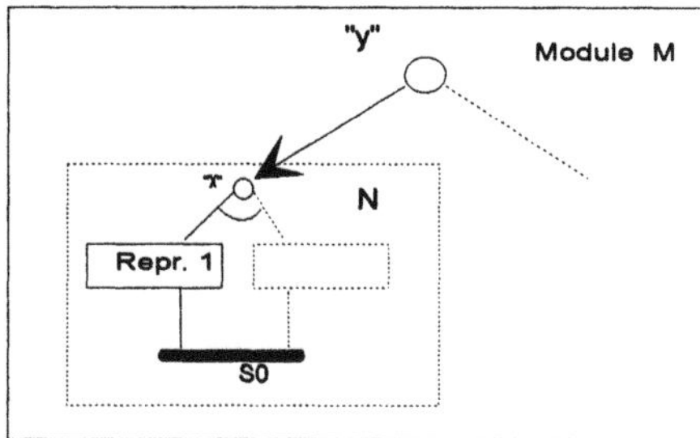

Figure 4 Design Principle A: just the meaningful deduction line (representation 1) should be fired.

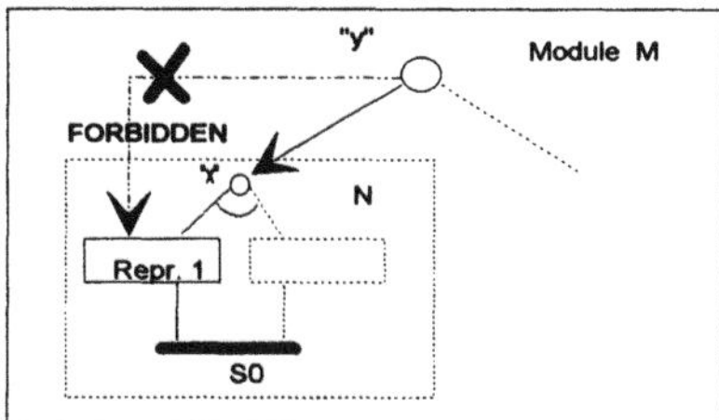

Figure 5 Design Principle B: the communication between modules should be set through sub goals only

Principle B states that no direct links should be set between the final goal "y" and any intermediate items of the representation 1 (Figure 5) to prevent from any interference in the deduction line of the module N. That allows to control coupling between modules, defining the communication mode between them. Besides, principle B states that the inferencing behaviour of the system should not change for any order in the choice between goal "y" and sub-goal "x". Consider the following case:

- First choice: goal "x" through representation 2.
- Second choice: goal "y".

What should happen ? Of course module N should not be fired again, as the sub-goal "x" has been already inferred. Principle C claims that knowledge items transposing the representation 2 into representation 1 should be owned by the outer module M as a set of corollaries and, being data-driven items, should be designed in forward chaining (Figure 6). Principle C, in addition to the module definition, plays the role of localization principle of the "usual" software engineering.

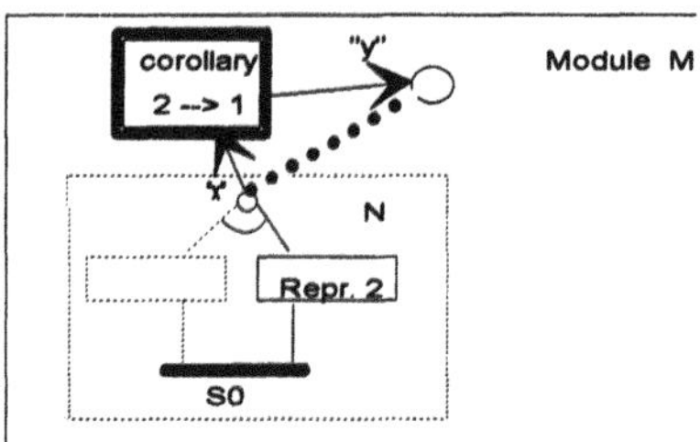

Figure 6 Design Principle C: transformation in the right representation by a forward-chained corollary.

Besides, design principles supply designers with a criterion to define which knowledge items should be chained in backward and which ones in forward.

5.3 Verification

The design principles allow to set the stated VVT methodology, acting in a separate way on every theorem-module, without introducing any trouble during the incremental growing of the knowledge. In fact:

1. cohesion comes from module definition
2. every aspect of a knowledge domain is localised:
   - in a cluster by definition of a module
   - in corollaries belonging to an outer module by principle C
3. coupling is controlled by principle B, because it forbids any link between the final Goal and any deduction line related to the subgoals, defining that the only communication way is through the subgoal.

Moreover, principle C states that every possible link with an intermediate module conclusion must be set through the discontinuity backward/forward chaining.

The result is to get a set of cluster (the theorems), that can be cut in the discontinuity between backward-chained theorems and forward-chained corollaries, holding the property of separability.

Verification is mainly a first consistency assessment in which the order of conclusions has not to be considered. Identifying a knowledge module as a Goal driven cluster of knowledge items embedded in outer clusters, you are allowed to separate a module, because the design principles (especially principle B and C) state how clusters should be coupled.

The discontinuity of the reasoning strategy among cluster links assures the invariance of the behaviour "in the large" for an isolated module. Hence, the module can be separated, applied on a set of initial facts and verified in the inference conclusions through a consistency test.

When a module infers consistent conclusions, according to the knowledge designer purpose, you are supplied with a matrix of linked hypotheses-conclusions that states the consistency, the completeness, the concision of every module.

6 CONCLUSIONS

Reliable KBSs can be assured through effective testing in an environment very close to the operational one. That drives KBS reliability assessment to be approached by a Cleanroom methodology by which successive incremental releases are produced.

As a consequence, the modularity way has to be followed in order to decompose the VVT in simpler activities. Assuming that software engineering goals are still adequate for knowledge based systems (Partridge,1988), we fit them to knowledge engineering through an abstraction.

To get a "cleanroom" product with low defectiveness for each release, a knowledge based system design has to match with:

- a knowledge model
- a computer-environment interaction model, like operational profiles are used for the traditional software

Therefore, VVT should not be thought as a separate activity after knowledge base implementation, but it has to be embedded already in the design phase. Hence the need of design principles, based on the assumed knowledge model, that allow consistency tests and behaviour tests upon more bounded domains of a knowledge base.

7 REFERENCES

Adron S. et alii (1982) Validation, Verification and Testing of Computer Software. *Computing Reviews,* **14**(2), 1982, 159-192.

ANSI/AIAA G-031-1992; *Guide for Life Cycle Development of Knowledge Base Systems with DoD-Std-2167A*.

Bastani,F. and Chen, I.R. (1993) The Reliability of Embedded A.I Systems. *IEEE Expert,* **8**(2), 72-78.

Battini F. (1993) Reliability of KBS: from Knowledge Design to a Verification, Validation and Testing Methodology. Proceedings of the 4th Symposium *Ada in Aerospace*, Brussels;8-11 November 1993.

Goel A.L. (1985) Software Reliability Models. *IEEE Transaction on Software Engineering,* **SE-11**(12), 1409-10.

Hollnagel (1991) The Reliability of Knowledge Based Systems. Proceedings on Workshop *Artificial Intelligence and Knowledge-Based Systems for Space*. ESA-ESTEC, Noordwijk, NL, May 1991 ESA WPP-025, vol.2

Marradi, L. and Battini F. (1992) Verification, Validation and Testing for Autonomous Spacecraft Systems. Proceedings on *Electrical Ground Support Equipment Workshop*, ESA/ESTEC, Noordwijk (NL), ESA-WPP-042

Mills, H.D. and Dyer, M.(1987) Cleanroom Software Engineering. *IEEE Software*.

Mills, H.D. (1990) Cleanroom: An Alternative Software Development Process; in *Aerospace Software Engineering*, (ed. C.Anderson and M.Dorfman), AIAA: Progress in Astronautics and Aeronautics, 1990.

Musa, J.D. Iannino, A. Okumoto, K. (1987) *Software Reliability*. McGraw Hill, N.Y.

Musa, J.D. (1993); Operational Profiles in Software Reliability Engineering. *IEEE Software*, **10**(2), March 1993.

Partridge, D. (1988) *Artificial Intelligence Applications in the Future of Software Engineering*. Ellis Horwood Limited, Chichester.

Parnas, D. and Van Schouwen, A.J., Kwan S.P. (1990). Evaluation of Safety Critical Software, *Communications of the ACM*. **33**(6), 636-648.

Poore, J.H. and Mills, H.D. Mutchler, D. (1993). Planning and Certifying Software System Reliability; *IEEE Software*, **10**(1), 88-99.

7 BIOGRAPHY

Ferdinando Battini was born in Milan, Italy, on October 18, 1960. He received the Master degree in Physics from Genoa University, Italy, in 1987. He was software researcher in the field of signal processing algorithms and A.I. techniques at the Naval System Division of ELSAG - Elettronica S.Giorgio in Genoa. In 1992 he joined LABEN S.p.A in Vimodrone as senior software engineer.

Now, he is supervisor of the software development for the European Photon Imaging Camera (EPIC) experiment for the next XMM spacecraft of the European Space Agency.

Member of the IEEE Computer Society, his reserach interests include Embedded Real-Time Systems, A.I. applications as well as Software Reliability Mesurements.

Assessing the Role of Formal Specifications in Verification and Validation of Knowledge-Based Systems

Pedro Meseguer
IIIA - Artificial Intelligence Research Institute
CSIC - Spanish Scientific Research Council
Campus Universitat Autonoma de Barcelona
08193 Bellaterra, SPAIN
Phone +34-3-580 95 70; FAX +34-3-580 96 61
Email: meseguer@lsi.upc.es

Alun D. Preece
University of Aberdeen
Computing Science Department
Aberdeen AB9 2UE, Scotland, UK
Phone +44 1224 272296; FAX: +44 1224 273422
Email: apreece@csd.abdn.ac.uk

Abstract

This paper examines how formal specification techniques can support the verification and validation (V&V) of knowledge-based systems. Formal specification techniques provide levels of description which support both verification and validation, and V&V techniques feed back to assist the development of the specifications. Developing a formal specification for a system requires the prior construction of a conceptual model for the intended system. Many elements of this conceptual model can be effectively used to support V&V. Using these elements, the V&V process becomes deeper and more elaborate and it produces results of a better quality compared with the V&V activities which can be performed on systems developed without conceptual models. However, we note that there are concerns in using formal specification techniques for V&V, not least being the effort involved in creating the specifications.

Keywords

Knowledge-based systems, artificial intelligence, formal specification, verification, validation, life-cycle.

1 INTRODUCTION

Unlike most conventional software, knowledge-based systems (KBS) are rarely validated and verified against an explicit specification of user requirements. Probably the main reason for this is that the tasks which these systems are required to perform are not well-understood at the outset of development, and so development proceeds in an exploratory manner — usually via prototyping — until a system is produced which is deemed to embody the implicit requirements of the prospective users. This explains why most of the early efforts to validate KBS by comparing their performance directly against the performance of human performers, rather than against any specification document (Buchanan and Shortliffe, 1984).

The problems with this approach are obvious: the validation is inherently prone to bias and, even when an "acceptable" system is deemed to have been produced, it is not clear what the system actually does (or may fail to do). Much of the work done in recent years to improve the state of verification and validation (V&V) practice for KBS has held on to the assumption that, because KBS are difficult to specify, practical V&V techniques should not depend upon the existence of detailed specification documents. This assumption is clearly seen in, for example, the work done on checking KBS for domain-independent *anomalies* such as inconsistency and incompleteness (Preece, Shinghal and Batarekh, 1992), as well as in the quantitative techniques for comparing KBS with human "experts" (O'Keefe, Balci and Smith, 1987).

Such techniques have been shown to be effective, but to a limited extent only. This paper will examine the limitations of a number of "state-of-the-art" KBS V&V techniques, and will assess how the power of the techniques can be extended when precise specification documents are available for the system. We will focus upon *formal specifications*, because informal and pseudo-formal specifications are too weak to provide a foundation for V&V.*

Therefore, the main aim of this paper is to examine the ways in which formal specification techniques can support the V&V of KBS. In doing so, two related issues naturally come under consideration. Firstly, it becomes apparent that verification and validation techniques can, in turn, support the development of formal specifications. Secondly, it becomes necessary to consider how specification, verification and validation techniques need to be applied within the whole KBS development process. This paper will touch upon these issues, although they will need more detailed consideration in their own right.

Verification and Validation of KBS

Before proceeding, it is necessary briefly to define the terms verification and validation for the purposes of this paper. *Verification* is a process aimed at demonstrating whether a system meets it's specified requirements; this is often called "building the system right" (O'Keefe, Balci and Smith, 1987), which we take to mean "checking the system against its (preferably explicit and formal) specifications". *Validation* is a process aimed at demonstrating whether a system meets the user's true requirements — often called "building the right system". Verification and validation can be viewed as a set of techniques and an associated process in which the techniques are applied, as part of the whole development process (for example, static verification of the knowledge base, followed by dynamic testing of the whole KBS (Preece, 1990)).

Formal Specification Techniques for KBS

Like V&V, formal specification techniques for KBS include a number of techniques (formal specification languages of various kinds) and processes (for example, transformation from a pseudo-formal specification to an implementation through several levels of detail). A *formal specification* for a KBS includes (Fensel and van Harmelen, 1994) (i) some specification of the I/O behaviour of the system (establishing the correct relation between data and results) and (ii) a description of how this behaviour can be made. This second element blurs the distinction between specification and design and is perhaps controversial from the standpoint of traditional software specification. However, it *is* a feature of current KBS formal specification techniques, and can be of great benefit in V&V, so we will not debate its appropriateness here.

---

*We note, however, that non-formal specifications may be *approximated* by formal specifications and employed for *partial* V&V; this is the role played by the *pseudo-formal* specifications in (Laurent, 1992).

2 VERIFICATION AND VALIDATION OF KBS

The earliest validation technique in AI was Alan Turing's proposal on how to decide if a program could be considered "intelligent", commonly known as the "Turing test" (Turing, 1950). This is a blind test where the evaluator communicates through a teletype with a person and a program; if the evaluator is unable to differentiate between the person and the program, the program is considered to be intelligent. Although many criticisms have been levelled against the Turing test as a general procedure to characterize intelligent behaviour, the idea of blind testing has remained central in KBS validation from the earliest systems on (see, for instance, the validation of the MYCIN system (Buchanan and Shortliffe, 1984) and blind testing in medical KBS (Chandrasekaran, 1983)).

In addition to testing, KBS developers realized that rule bases could be analyzed for anomalies which are indicative of errors in the construction of the KBS, and which can lead to faulty behaviour at run-time. Commonly considered anomalies included inconsistency, redundancy, subsumption, circularity, unreachable goals, and unfireable rules. Tools to detect such anomalies were called verifiers due to the logical nature of the tests. Early verifiers, performed pair-wise comparison of rules (Suwa, Scott and Shortliffe, 1982); more sophisticated techniques including the effect of rule chaining were used by Ginsberg (1988). The use of such verifiers has been widely acknowledged as being complementary to the necessity of testing. Nowadays, validators perform a combination of verification and testing methods in order to obtain maxiumum evidence as to the correctness of KBS.

It is well known that software validation cannot be delayed until implementation. Otherwise, there is too high a risk that errors will be found late which may be very expensive to correct. This principle, coming from software engineering, also applies to knowledge engineering. However, most of the validation approaches developed for KBS assume to work on an implemented system (in the context of prototyping). Several authors have made proposals to include validation during the early stages of KBS development, but this does not appear to have become common practice, and there is consequently little published evidence of the practical usability of existing techniques early in development.

2.1 Dominant V&V Techniques for KBS

Currently, the dominant techniques for V&V activities can be clustered in four main groups:

- Inspection
- Static verification
- Empirical testing
- Empirical evaluation

Inspection techniques aim at detecting semantically incorrect knowledge in the KB. Inspection is performed manually, by a human who has expertise in the application domain. During development this is usually the same expert who provided the knowledge for the KB, but at some point the KB should be inspected by an expert independent of those involved in the KBS development. (Typically, this technique can be used only infrequently due to the lack of availability of experts.). Inspection is most able to identify errors in isolated KB elements: when errors come from the interaction of several KB elements — for instance, chaining of several rules — human inspectors are usually unable to detect it "by eye".

Static verification checks the KB for anomalies. An anomaly is a static pattern in the KB structure which suggest the presence of an error in the encoded knowledge. Typically, the anomaly pattern is a counterexample of a general property which should hold in the KBS (for instance, consistency). Detected anomalies need to be analyzed to determine whether they represent an real error or just a minor defect coming from the encoding process in the selected knowledge representation. Only the most limited verification checks can be performed manually: generally this process requires computational support by automated tools. Depending on the capabilities of the verification, the checks it may perform range from a limited to an exhaustive search for anomalies in the KB. Although the properties to be checked are to a great extent domain-independent, verification tools depend on the specific semantics of the knowledge representation language used. For this reason, verifiers cannot be reused among KBS using different knowledge representation languages.

Empirical testing aims at checking KBS correctness by executing the system on sample data sets. To guarantee complete correctness, testing has to be exhaustive; that is, every potential input should be tested. This is obviously not feasible for real applications, so testing only analyzes a finite set of test data, the *test set*. The selection of the test set is crucial to the efectiveness of the testing process. Among several testing strategies, two seem to be the most effective when applied to KBS: structural and functional testing (Zualkernan, Tsai and Kirani, 1992). Structural testing aims at executing as many different KB elements as possible. Functional testing aims at checking the different KBS functions according the requirements, without considering internal structure. Real test cases are usually scarce, so test cases have to be synthesized automatically by test case generators. A final difficulty in KBS testing occurs when the application domain is so ill-defined that "correct" behaviour is not well-defined (there is no "gold standard"). In such case, it is necessary to make some definition as to what is to be considered a "correct" or "acceptable" solution for each test case; usually, the correct solution is approximated by a consensus among the opinions of several human experts.

Evaluation addresses the relation between the operational KBS and the final user. Typical evaluation issues are technical performance, acceptability, inclusion in the organization, responsibility issues, and so on. Empirical evaluation is performed by using the operational KBS either in a controlled environment (laboratory evaluation) or in the working environment (field evaluation). KBS evaluation is a human activity which is highly application-dependent.

Of these four groups, inspection and empirical evaluation methods are clearly application-dependent and they are not candidates for potential reuse across different KBS. On the other hand, verification and testing *methods* can be reused to a great extent on different KBS, even though the computational tools supporting the methods are usually bound to specific knowledge representation languages. However, even in the reusable methods, the role of human experts remain significant, because they are needed to evaluate verification and testing outputs.

2.2 Limitations of Current Approaches

While success has been achieved using the above techniques, there are still causes for concern. The presence of requirements which are hard to formalize or express without ambiguity induces different weaknesses in the V&V process. This kind of requirement is difficult to validate, and so one never knows to what extent such requirements are fulfilled. This problem becames more difficult when different requirements coming from different users are to be integrated. Here there is an extra issue: to guarantee the internal consistency of the set of requirements. In any case, there is no rigorous way to verify the correspondence between a set of requirements and its final implementation.

The absence of formal specifications limits the capacity of KBS verification, which remains constrained to assuring that some general logical properties (such as consistency, no redundancy, no cycles, no useless objects, etc) hold in the system. These properties appear as prerequisites of a correct function of a KBS, and they should be tested. However, although they are necessary they are not sufficient, they say little about the correctness of the system behaviour. Consider a (somewhat exaggerated) example comparing knowledge engineering with numerical programming: checking a rule base for consistency is analogous to checking in a numerical program that no computation arrives to overflow or underflow. Obviously, it is something useful to know but it has nothing to do with the correctness of the computation: one can have a consistent rule base (or a neither-overflowing-nor-underflowing numerical program) that performs totally incorrect computations, which nevertheless are consistent!

Results from testing indicate that the system performs adequately on a set of cases, and it is reasonable to expect that the system will behave in the same way on similar cases. If the test set is representative of the set of possible inputs (which in complex KBS hardly occurs), this may represent enough evidence for non-critical tasks. However, when a new case appears, we cannot be sure that the system will behave properly on it (except for trivial cases, or very specific applications where advanced testing techniques can be applied).

In summary, the main weakness of current V&V approaches on implemented KBS lies in the fact that they do not really bring confidence in the quality of the system as a whole and of the system parts. V&V methods should provide adequate answers to issues such as correctness, completeness, robustness, precision, safety, and so forth. Currently, many of these questions are answered only partially or by indirect evidence only. To overcome these defects V&V methods have to employ more precise information about the *task* the KBS is required to perform. Formal specifications can play a fundamental role in accomplishing this goal.

3 FORMAL SPECIFICATIONS FOR V&V

Strictly speaking, no verification or validation is possible without specifications, by the definition of verification (Section 1). While some of the existing verification techniques may *appear* to operate in the absence of any specifications, in reality they make reference to *implicit* specifications; for example, the techniques for verifying the consistency of knowledge bases make reference to some model of consistency, which can be considered a domain-independent requirement (that the KBS be free from inconsistency) (Preece, Shinghal and Batarekh, 1992). Similarly, early validation efforts comparing a KBS against human performers made implicit reference to a requirement that the KBS should emulate such human performers (Buchanan and Shortliffe, 1984).

Once the necessity for specifications is clear, it must be said that the more precise and detailed are the specifications, the more thorough will be the V&V process. At the least-desirable extreme we have the case where the sole requirement is implicit emulation of human performers. If we have informal or semi-formal statements-of-requirements for the system, then we can devise tests to determine if the system complies with these requirements; however, because the requirements are not stated formally:

- there is no way to be sure if we have tested them completely (or to what extent we have tested them);
- they may be ambiguous, incomplete and incorrect.

The most desirable case, then, is to have requirements that are specified formally (with a well-defined syntax and semantics). Such specifications are produced by formal methods and, thus, such methods clearly have a role in the V&V process for KBS.

3.1 Formal Specifications for KBS

A growing number of formal specification languages are available — and have already been used — to specify KBS. We can categorise them roughly according to the intent of their developers:

- *General purpose* specification languages, developed in the context of conventional software engineering, for the specification of any type of software system. For example, Z (Plant and Gold, 1990) and VDM (Haugh, 1988) have been used to specify KBS.

- *Special purpose* specification languages, predominately European in origin, developed for the purpose of specifying complex knowledge-based reasoning systems. Among the best known are $(ML)^2$, DESIRE and KARL, surveyed in (Fensel and van Harmelen, 1994).

For our purposes, the second category is more attractive, not merely because the facilities of the languages are well-suited to specifying KBS, but also because these languages are better-suited to the practical needs of KBS developers. Most importantly, most of the special-purpose KBS specification languages do not expect that a fully-formal specification will be developed *a priori*; rather, they expect that the specification will be developed gradually, as a refinement of informal and semi-formal descriptions of the system: see Figure 1. Here, the informal description — typically called the "conceptual model" in various methodologies — is iteratively refined to create a more precise formal specification, with ***both*** descriptions undergoing gradual modification during the process. (The informal description is kept because it may be easier to communicate with domain experts using this description.) The formal description will form the basis for the implementation: later we discuss the various ways in which this can be done.

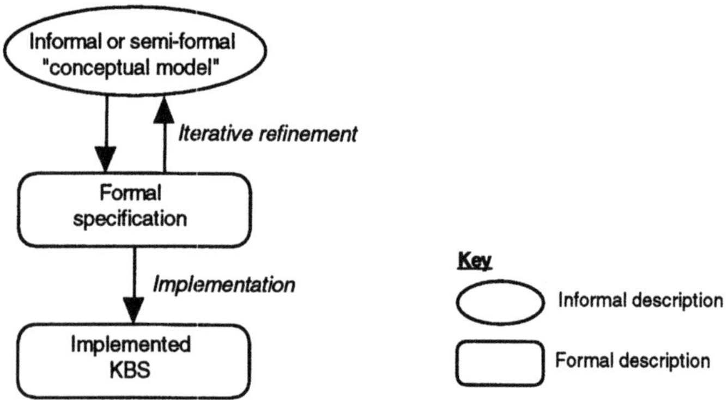

Figure 1 Using a formal specification in KBS development.

In fact, the possibilities of using formal specifications are richer than shown in Figure 1. We may want to have several formal specifications, providing different formal descriptions of the system, for example:

- At different levels of detail; for example, a specification of the system as a "black box", showing the input-output relations only, and a complementary description of the system as a "glass box", showing aspects of its required behaviour. These two views have been referred to as the *problem specification* and the *solution specification* — or as the "contract" and "blueprint" — respectively (Batarekh, Preece, Bennet and Grogono, 1991).
- Of different "models" of the system; for example, the *cooperation model* may describe how the system interacts with its users, while a separate *task model* may describe the tasks the system performs on its own (Wielinga, Schreiber and Breuker, 1992).

3.2 Formal Specifications for V&V

From an idealistic point-of-view, the goal in performing verification and validation is to deliver a KBS that is as reliable as possible; more pragmatically, the goal is to deliver a KBS that is as reliable as *necessary* — given the users' needs (Miller, 1990). The most important decision is that of *what* to verify and validate.

When formal specifications are available, they provide more opportunities for doing V&V than are available otherwise. Figure 2(a) shows what V&V can be done when the only available descriptions of the system are an informal statement of requirements, and the implementation itself.

The implementation can be verified for internal consistency and apparent completeness, and validated for (approximate) compliance with the informal requirements, using the methods described in Section 2, but that is all. The weaknesses of V&V conducted to this extent were highlighted at the end of the previous section. When formal specifications are available, however, many more V&V opportunities exist, as shown in Figure 2(b). Here, there are two typical levels of formal specification — "black box" and "glass box" — in addition to the implementation.

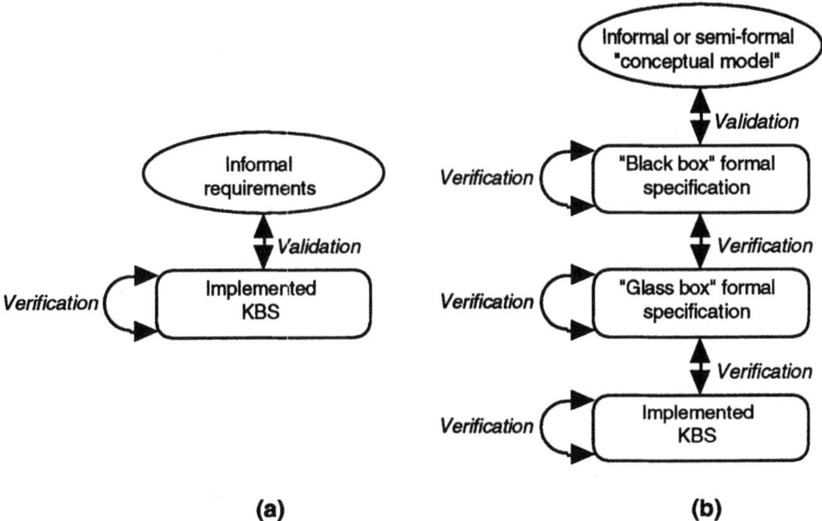

Figure 2: V&V opportunities: (a) without any formal specification; (b) with two levels of formal specification.

The availability of the multiple formal descriptions provides support for additional:

- *Intra-model V&V* (V&V of a single description of the KBS in and of itself), because the formal descriptions of the KBS can be verified and validated in and of themselves, for properties such as consistency and completeness (appropriately defined); these descriptions can also be validated manually for correctness, because the specifications are unambiguous.
- *Inter-model V&V* (V&V between different descriptions of the system), because different descriptions of the system can be verified with respect to one another; this supports validation because one level of description can be the user's requirements, made explicit.

Since the formal specifications are descriptions of the system, V&V techniques may be used to ensure the validity of the specifications themselves in the above contexts.

As described in Section 1, a formal specification provides (i) a description of the intended I/O behaviour, and (ii) a description of how this behaviour can be constructed. Some of the potential uses of a formal specification in V&V are the following:

- To give ***structure*** to the domain knowledge, providing a vocabulary of knowledge elements which can be used in V&V.
- To allow verification of the intended I/O behaviour in a "black box" manner.
- To allow verification of the way a solution is constructed by the system, in a "glass box" manner. The structure of the domain knowledge plus the specification of how the solution should be constructed must be sufficient to devise V&V techniques specific to the task performed by the system, to provide the necessary level of confidence in the reliability of the system.
- Some languages, such as KARL (Fensel and van Harmelen, 1994) produce executable specifications. They can be used to test the system against the ideal behaviour provided by the specifications.

The various V&V techniques described in Section 2 can — and in some cases must — be redefined in this context. The question of verifying the specification itself is still open, as few of the existing special-purpose KBS specification languages have well-developed proof techniques at present. If general-purpose specification languages are used, then their existing proof techniques apply, but these have been found to entail a great deal of labour when KBS are specified (Haugh, 1988). However, extended versions of the existing V&V techniques for KBS become possible: we consider each of the four techniques described in Section 2.

Inspection

In intra-model V&V, at the specification level, it is often argued that the unambiguous nature of formal specifications permits easier direct validation via inspection by customers and — in the case of KBS — domain experts. This is made difficult in practice when unfamiliar and unintuitive notations are employed for the formal descriptions, although this difficulty may be alleviated to some extent because the declarative nature of much of the specification (for example, logical rules) is more comprehensible to non-programmers than procedural descriptions. We believe, however, that it will usually be more practical to employ the the semi-formal conceptual model in this capacity as a more intelligible (though not unambiguous in and of itself) version of the specification.

The conceptual model provides an implementation-independent description of the intended task, and therefore can be inspected by domain experts without the burden of implementation details. At this level, inspection aims at evaluating the knowledge quality and completeness with respect to the intended task. If necessary — due to ill-definition or ambiguity — formal specifications can complement or substitute the conceptual model. In this case, domain experts would likely require assistance from the knowledge engineers to deal with formal languages.

In inter-model V&V, the high degree of structure provided by a formal specification can be used manually to check for the detection of corresponding structures in the implemented system. The conceptual model may play a role here also: at the implementation stage, one can check the correspondence between the conceptual model and the final implementation of the system.

Static Verification

In intra-model V&V at the specification level, if a formal specification is to be verified according to the properties for static verification (consistency, redundancy, etc), then these properties need to be defined in terms of the formal specification language. Once this is done, however, the reusability of this approach is high, because the same anomalies can be checked for in any specification written using the language. Furthermore, formal specification languages provide additional opportunities for verification by some of the techniques, as a benefit of their features. For example, the modular architecture and declaration of hierarchies of types (sorts) provided by languages like (ML)[2], permit additional properties to be checked in static verification (for example, violation of modularity, and type mis-matches).

Static verification can also be employed to detect structural nonconformances between specification levels and implementation. This provides an automatic (and hence more reliable) version of the inter-model inspectional verification discussed above. Recall that, in addition to the I/O behaviour, a formal specification describes how this behaviour can be achieved. This implies that a formal specification provides, to some extent, elements of the KBS structure. After implementation, these elements can be checked to verify whether their functionality meets their specification. This is an important step towards constructing correct and reliable KBS because (i) verification is no longer limited to general purpose properties; it can check domain-dependent properties, and (ii) verification can be made of specific parts of the KBS structure, providing evidence of correctness for these parts.

Empirical Testing

In an idealised view of the development process with formal specifications, testing is typically considered to be unnecessary, because the specifcations are intended to be self-evidently correct, and all subsequent descriptions are shown to be compliant with the previous specifications. Although the presence of formal specifications may suggest that testing is unnecessary, this view is currently too extreme and impractical, and is likely to remain so for the foreseeable future. The translation from specifications to implementation is performed manually, and some errors can be introduced. Therefore, testing is still necessary, but the existence of formal specifications can help greatly in the selection of the test set. A formal specification provides the intended I/O behaviour, so it contains all the information needed to perform functional testing. On the other hand, the level of structure in formal specifications can be used to support structural testing.

Furthermore, with the existence of formal specifications, it becomes possible to test the specifications directly; such testing can take the conventional form of running test cases on an executable specification, or can take the form of proving properties (such properties corresponding to "test cases") of the specification. In order to do this, proof techniques must have been defined for the specification language.

Empirical Evalation

This aspect of V&V would seem at first to benefit little from the use of formal specifications. However, a number of possibilities exist. For example, it is possible to use a formalised model of the required cooperation between KBS and users to check for potential system integration problems in a more principled way — and at an earlier stage in development — than would otherwise be possible. Secondly, subjective requirements such as "user friendliness" can be approximately expressed by means of pseudo-formal specifications, and then become amenable to V&V methods other than experimental evaluation (Laurent, 1992).

3.3 Outstanding Issues

While formal specification techniques offer clear benefits to V&V, there are a number of unclear issues at present.

Nature of the Development Process

One question concerns the nature of the development process incorporating formal specification with V&V. Should a transformation approach be adopted, wherein the specification is gradually refined into an implementation, as shown in Figure 3(a)? This is attractive from the V&V point-of-view because it is easier to promote and control validity throughout the process: all verification is performed directly upon the formal specification (benefitting from its well-defined syntax and semantics), and correctness is then assured by the transformation process.

However, it is harder to ensure that the implementation will be efficient when the transformational approach is taken, and the progression through successive levels of refined specification may place a heavy burden on developers. This contrasts with the more conventional approach shown previously in Figure 2(b), where an implementation is crafted with the intention that it will comply with the specification, without actually being derived from it. V&V techniques are used to establish the compliance between the descriptions.

Completeness of Formal Specifications

Another important question concerns the completeness of the specifications; that is, whether the specification should (and, in complex cases, whether it *can*) describe every aspect of the system. One approach to development is to aim towards building a formal specification which is a complete description of the KBS. This can then be transformed (as in Figure 3(a)) or constructed into an implementation.

An alternative approach is to specify different aspects of the system as independent "mini-models", against which the implemented system can be verified (Bellman, 1990) — see Figure 3(b). There may be a strong practical reason for choosing the latter approach: when the KBS is complex and ill-structured, requiring a great deal of knowledge aquisition, analysis and refinement (typically supported by exploratory prototyping) before a reasonably complete version exists. However, transformational implementation is no longer possible because the specification is not complete.

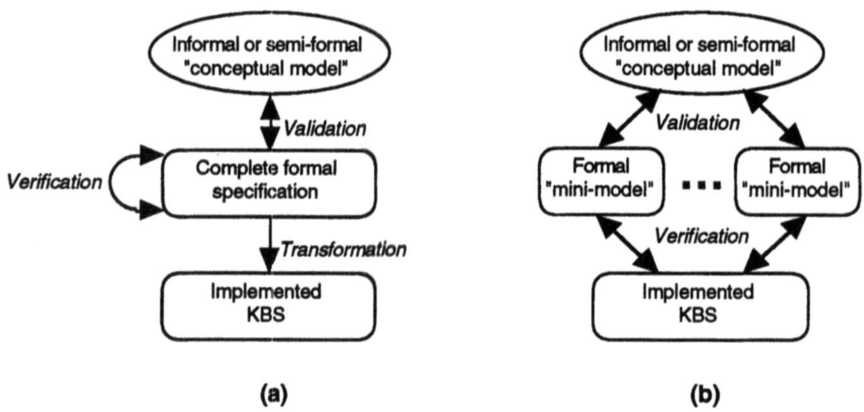

Figure 3: Using formal specifications for V&V: (a) transformation from complete formal specification; (b) use of "mini-models".

4 CONCLUSIONS

In knowledge engineering, the V&V activity is a kind of "watching eye" aimed at detecting deviations between what is intended to be built and the artifact being built. To perform this task, V&V requires information about the intended KBS. The more information that is available, and the more precise that information, the better the validation process will be. This will have a direct impact in the quality of the final KBS.

Conceptual models of the intended task appear to be essential in KBS construction. These models play a fundamental role in the validation process, because they act as the reference to compare against at any stage of KBS development. Conceptual models allow one to structure the domain knowledge, identifing domain-dependent properties which can be effectively tested. These properties can provide direct evidence of the different dimensions to be evaluated in V&V. Importantly, this checking can be made at any stage in the development process, so the difficulties to include V&V activities during KBS construction are removed by this approach.

Conceptual models can support the development of formal specifications. The presence of formal specifications eliminates one of the main weaknesses in V&V process: the use of vague or ambiguous requirements. Formal specifications can be used to verify the system, and to define precisely its boundaries (one of the classical problems in KBS validation). In addition to describing the I/O behaviour, formal specifications define how this behaviour can be achieved. This brings more information for V&V, because a formal specification provides, to some extent, elements of the KBS structure. These elements can be effectively used in the V&V process, which is no longer forced to be a "black box" testing process.

The construction of conceptual models and their translation into formal specifications is neither an easy nor currently a complete task. Some typical KBS tasks remain elusive to formal specification, and the specification construction can be a costly process. Topics for immediately-necessary future work include:

- making concrete the proposals for using formal specifications with the various V&V techniques, and evaluating the effectiveness of doing so;
- investigating the utility and practicality of different approaches to formal specification (e.g. "mini-models" versus complete specification);
- development of development processes in which all of the techniques can be applied and managed effectively;

These issues remain open in knowledge engineering, but they should not be obstacles to the development and use formal specifications for KBS construction. Their benefits will improve the quality of KBS in the near future.

5 REFERENCES

Batarekh, A., Preece, A.D., Bennett, A. and Grogono, P. (1991) Specifying an expert system. *Expert Systems with Applications*, **2**, 285-303.

Bellman, K.. (1990) The modeling issues inherent in testing and evaluating knowledge-based systems. *Expert Systems with Applications*, **1**, 199-215.

Buchanan, B. and Shortliffe, E. (1984) The problem of evaluation, in *Rule-Based Expert Systems: the MYCIN Experiments of the Stanford Heuristic Programming Project*, 571-588, Addison-Wesley, Reading MA.

Chandrasekaran, B. (1983) On evaluating AI systems for medical diagnosis. *AI Magazine*, **4**, 34-37.

Fensel, D. and van Harmelen, F. (1994) A comparison of languages which operationalise and formalise KADS models of expertise. *Knowledge Engineering Review*, **9**, 105-146.

Ginsberg, A. (1988) Knowledge-base reduction: A new approach to checking knowledge bases for inconsistency & redundancy, in *Proc. 7th National Conference on Artificial Intelligence (AAAI 88)*, vol. 2, 585-589.

Haugh, J. (1988) The application of formal specification techniques to knowledge-based system development, in *UK IT 88 Conference Publication*, 95-98, Information Engineering Directorate, London.

Laurent, J-P. (1992) Proposals for a valid terminology in KBS validation, in *Proc. 10th European Conference on Artificial Intelligence (ECAI 92)*, 829-834, John Wiley & Sons, Chichester.

Miller, L.A. (1990) Dynamic testing of knowledge bases using the heuristic testing approach. Expert Systems with Applications, 1(3):249-269, 1990.

O'Keefe, R.M., Balci, O., and Smith E.P. (1987) Validating expert system performance. *IEEE Expert*, **2**, 81-90.

Plant, R.T. and Gold, D. (1990) Increasing expert system reliability through the use of a formal specification, in *AAAI-90 Workshop on Knowledge Based Systems Verification, Validation and Testing*, AAAI, Menlo Park, CA.

Preece, A.D. (1990) Towards a methodology for evaluating expert systems. *Expert Systems*, **7**, 215-223.

Preece, A., Shinghal, R., and Batarekh, A. (1992) Principles and practice in verifying rule-based systems. *Knowledge Engineering Review*, **7**, 115-141.

Suwa, M., Scott, A. and Shortliffe, E. (1982) An approach to verifying completeness and consistency in a rule-based expert system. *AI Magazine*, **3**, 16-21.

Turing, A. (1950) Computing machinery and intelligence. *Mind*, **59**, 236-248.

Wielinga, B., Schreiber, A. and Breuker, J. (1992) KADS: a modelling approach to knowledge engineering. *Knowledge Acquisition*, **4**, 5-54.

Zualkernan, I., Tsai, W-T. and Kirani, S. (1992) Testing expert systems using conventional techniques, in *Proc. 16th Annual Computer Software and Applications Conference*, 320-325.

PART TEN

Formal Methods

27

Software Quality Improvement: Two Approaches to the Application of Formal Methods

A. Alapide, S. Candia, M. Cinnella, S. Quaranta
Space Software Italia
Viale del Lavoro, 101 -- 74100 Taranto -- Italy
Tel: +39 99 4701619 Fax: +39 99 4701777 E-mail: cinnella@ssi.it

Abstract

This paper illustrates two different approaches for the application of Formal Methods (FM): *integrated-parallel* and *after-the-fact*. In the first approach FMs have been applied integrated and in parallel with structured methods starting from the design phase. In the second approach FMs have been applied after the whole application code had already been developed, before the delivery, to derive an abstract specification of the s/w system and verify that the most critical properties hold.

Both approaches have been adopted in the development of a real application in the domain of the Air Traffic Control, whose purpose is to predict and detect potential air conflicts.

The results show that FMs can improve the quality of the software process and products. In particular the accuracy of the final documentation improves and the number of early discovered errors increases.

The paper provides general guidelines for the integration of formal and structured methods and presents the documentation outline which has been defined to comment the formal specifications, in the framework of the project applicable standards: 2167-A military standard and ESA PSS-05-0 and PSS-01-0.

Finally the paper makes an analysis of eight software quality factors, showing also the typology of the discovered errors with the two after-the-fact and integrated-parallel approaches with respect to the traditional development approaches. One conclusion is that FMs provide a real support in developing better quality software, identifying errors, which sometimes, with traditional approaches, remain undiscovered till and after the software delivery.

Keywords

Formal methods, RAISE, Ada/Teamwork, 2167-A standard, quality factors

1 INTRODUCTION

SSI (Space Software Italia) has applied the RAISE Formal Method (FM) to develop a software application in the domain of the Air Traffic Control for the Alenia Radar System Division. The overall aim in the application has been to innovate the software development

process integrating FMs with structured methods, applying them to develop a wide part of a TCA CSC (Computer Software Component), the Detector, which was critical because in charge of detecting the potential conflicts.
This approach to FM introduction was smooth. It allowed to obtain some of the benefits arising from FM adoption -- both in the product and in the process -- without overspending with respect to the effort that would have been required using a more traditional approach. Moreover it allowed, to both SSI and the customer, to learn some lessons, which can constitute the basis for ensuring a future low risk transition towards a larger scale adoption of FMs.
The project focused essentially on a few, but well defined process and product quality factors. The four most relevant key *process* factors which were considered are:

- Early error discovery;
- Effective communication with the customer;
- Easiness of maintenance;
- Compliance with the applicable process standards.

The four most relevant *product* quality factors were:

- Correctness of the final software;
- Readibility, completeness and consistency of the final documentation;
- Compliance with the applicable product standards;
- Reusability of both code and documentation.

Several approaches for the integration of structured and formal methods [5], [8], [10] have been proposed. For the development of the Detector CSC two approaches based on the ones presented in [5] have been followed: *integrated-parallel* and *after-the-fact.* After their brief description, the article presents an analysis of the two approaches, focusing on on each of the eight above mentioned quality factors. Moreover it compares the results with the ones obtained with a traditional approach for the development of the other TCA application CSCs.

2 APPLICATION BACKGROUND

The developed application is *TCA (Traffic Conflicts Alert) Analyzer*, a software system in charge of elaborating radar data and predicting potential air conflicts belonging to the following classes:

- STCA (Short Term Conflicts Alert): conflicts among planes;
- MSAW (Minimum Safe Altitude Warning): planes going lower than the minimum safe altitude;
- DAIW (Dangerous Area Infringement Warning): planes entering a restricted area.

The CSC Detector is a critical component of TCA. The development process was based on the SSI SQS (Software Quality System) for projects having a medium criticality level. SSI SQS has been accredited by ESA (European Space Agency) for the PSS-05-0 and PSS-01 series and is compliant with the Nato and the 2167-A DoD standard (required by the customer).
The RAISE FM was selected for the application development because SSI had a previous related experience on it and because the CEC (Commission of the European Communities)

sponsored the application within the LaCoS (Large Scale Correct Systems) ESPRIT II (European Strategic Programme for the Information Technology) project.

3 RAISE AND TEAMWORK/ADA

3.1 RAISE

The RAISE (Rigorous Approach to Industrial Software Engineering) FM is based on the formal language RSL (RAISE Specification Language), the RAISE method and a powerful toolset.
The *RAISE Specification Language* (RSL) [1] is provided with structuring mechanisms that allow one to build modularized specifications of complex systems with layering. It includes constructs to model concurrency and allows several specification styles at different level of detail (from *abstract* to *concrete*).
The *RAISE method* [2] allows two types of formal proofs: *inter-level* proofs and *intra-level* proofs. The former deal with proving that the specification of level i+1 is consistent with the specification of level i (static and dynamic *development relations* in fig. 1), while the latter deals with proving that the specification of level i is consistent and satisfies the stated critical requirements.
The *RAISE toolset* [3] allows to edit RSL specifications with automatic correctness checks, supports the automatic generation of confidence conditions and the automatic verification of the static development relation. It provides support to prove the dynamic relation and allows to edit and prove theories, confidence conditions and the dynamic development relations. Moreover it allows to translate automatically in Ada or C++ the RSL concrete specifications.

3.2 Teamwork/Ada

Teamwork/Ada [4] is based on the Ada Structure Graph (ASG) editor and on the Teamwork/Ada Source Builder. The former can be used for creating models of Ada application systems using graphic icons that map to the semantic of the Ada language. The latter can be used to automatically generate source code from analyzable sets of ASGs to which appropriate source code notes shall have previously been associated.

4 INTEGRATED-PARALLEL APPROACH

The integrated-parallel approach is illustrated in part (b) of fig. 1. After a requirements analysis phase in which some preliminary formal specifications of the subcomponent to develop have been derived, the real development activities started applying both Temwork/Ada and RAISE as follows:

- Teamwork/Ada was used to represent graphically the modular decomposition of the Ada software;
- RAISE was applied to specify each identified module, as a substitution of the PDL (Program Design Language) generally used in the detailed design phase.

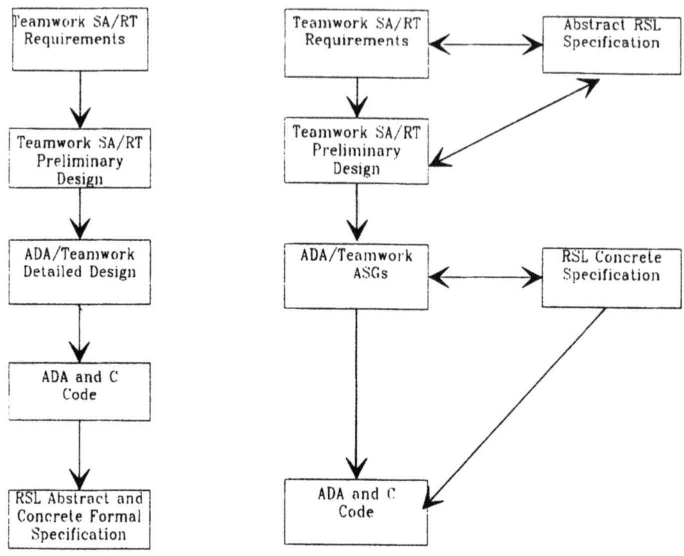

Figure 1 The after-the-fact (a) and parallel-integrated (b) approaches

5 AFTER-THE-FACT APPROACH

The after-the-fact approach is illustrated in part (a) of fig. 1. After the code development, some basic properties of the implemented alorithms were specified and verified. The specification process in itself, more than the formal proofs (which are more difficult and costly) was useful because it:

- allowed to detect some hidden errors;
- allowed to formulate the requirements in a more domain-oriented way;
- provided suggestions for reusable design as a basis for developing an Air Traffic Control software library.

5 EVALUATION OF THE QUALITY FACTORS

5.1 Early error discovery

Early error discovery is an important quality factor because, as well known, correcting an error later in the lifecycle has higher costs. One of the most severe error typology is related to misunderstanding in the requirements, because the subsequent corrections force the developer to go back to several phases of the software development.

In the TCA application, no error related to requirements misunderstaning was discovered neither in the unit nor in the SSI system test phases in the parts developed with the RAISE FM, while in the parts developed only with Teamwork/Ada a few such errors occurred. Even though direct conclusions cannot be derived from this fact, it is highly probable that the development of preliminary RSL specifications, has allowed a deeper understanding of the requirements. This conclusion is also confirmed by the fact that during the requirements analysis phase an higher number of questions arose from the specification development constituting a good basis for further clarifications with the customer.

The histogram reported in fig. 2 shows the classification of the discovered errors both for the Detector CSC, developed with formal and structured methods, and for the CSCs developed only with structured methods.

5.2 Effectiveness of communication with the customer

This quality factor, even though considered crucial to project success, because it allows to minimize misunderstanding on requirements and customer needs, could be assessed only to a minimum extent. This because:

- The design reviews normally focus on high level design choices, while in the TCA SSI application RSL was used for the detailed design of each module;
- An ad-hoc training on the specification language is required for the customer.

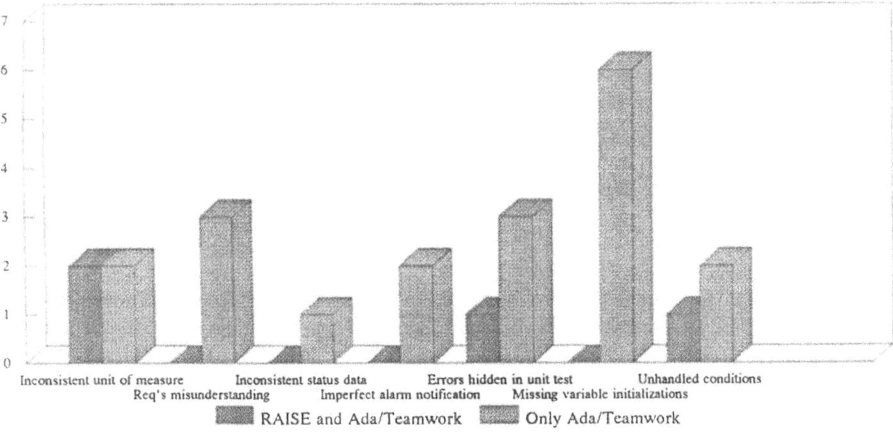

Figure 2 Error typology

5.3 Easiness in maintenance and consistency between phase products

The easiness in maintaining consistency among different lifecycle phase products is a quality factor because it provides the guarantee that the aimed consistency between detailed design and code exists. RAISE provides support to get this consistency. In the SSI application, it was generally very easy to keep consistent the detailed design and the Ada code because of the automatic Ada code generator. However the development of automatically translatable specifications requires more effort during the detailed design phase because (a) the mapping between RSL entities and correspondent Ada code has to be checked in order to be sure that the implemented translation strategy is efficient, (b) it is necessary to keep separate the modules that shall be coded manually from those that can be automatically translated.

5.4 Compliance with process standards

The compliance with process standards is a "must" for the critical projects. For the TCA development the applicable standards were: the 2167-A DoD standard and the SSI SQS with a waterfall lifecycle model. The main need was to calibrate the 2167-A standards to fit with the adoption of RAISE for what concerns the phase products to be reviewed. As the TCA application started from the requirements analysis phase, the phase products related only to the design and coding phases. However, as the requirements phase is the one in which the applications would mostly benefit from FMs adoption, adequate guidelines should be derived as well.

5.5 Correctness of final software

During the acceptance phase no functional errors were discovered in the subcomponent developed with RAISE. In the parts developed only with structured methods, some errors were discovered. Among them, a not very severe one was related to state inconsistency between air conflict information and tracks data, allowing in particular the existence of conflicts in the related database, when the corresponding tracks had already been deleted. This typology of error might have been detected sooner with a formal and rigorous approach to verification. In fact similar errors were discovered with the after-the-fact approach.

5.6 Readibility,completeness,consistency of the final documentation

The quality of the final documentation is typically measured in terms of attributes such as clarity, consistency, accuracy, reusability. The main difference of applying FMs as SSI did in the TCA application, with respect to a traditional approach, is that the specification language substitutes the PDL with the following advantages:

- The formal specifications are internally consistent (at least from a syntattical point of view)
- If the specification language is translatable, also the consinstency between design and code is guaranteed.

On the other side, as reported in [6], the automatic code is prolific in lines of code and less readible.

5.7 Compliance with the product standards

A general observation that can be made regarding this point is that the 2167-A standard does not refer to formal specifications at all, while the ESA PSS-05-0 and PSS-01-0 mention some formal specification languages. Therefore, as usual the standards are one step behind practical usage because and some guidelines are missing.

Specifically concerning the 2167-A standard two types of problems occurred:

- Tool integration for the automatic generation of the design documentation;
- Need to define a specific outline to comment the formal specifications (see appendix A to this article).

5.8 Reusability

From the TCA application development it was evident that the application of the after-the-fact approach potentially enhances the oportunities for reusability of the produced documentation because of the more abstract and property oriented formulation of the requirements, highly independent from implementation details.

6 GUIDELINES FOR THE INTEGRATION

Even though this article does not provide detailed guidelines for applying RAISE and Teamwork/Ada with a parallel-integrated approach, it intends to mention the aspects that need to be addressed when such approaches are adopted: (a) selection of the critical component to be developed with FM (b) definition of a mapping between FM and structured method entities, (c) definition of an appropriate documentation outline to comment the formal specifications, (d) preparation of unit test plans based on the formal specifications, (e) calibration of the project applicable standards to the FM to be applied, (f) training of the customer and his/her involvement in the verification process as soon as possible.

7 CONCLUSIONS

The RAISE FM has been applied to develop a CSC part of the Analyzer-TCA software. This article has illustrated the application results, focusing on the obtained benefits. The most important lessons learnt from this experience have been:

- The formal specification process cannot avoid taking into account the training and backgrounds of those who are to read and review the specifications (testers, quality assurance responsibles, customer)
- It is a good solution to integrate the formal specifications with graphical, symbolic and tabular notations to facilitate their understanding and reviews from non-experts.
- The creation of a mathematical model of the system to develop, also when it does not represent a "deliverable", allows to obtain a "mental control" of the application that is an optimum basis to develop highly correct software.

In conclusion Formal Methods can provide some benefits to the software development process and product, but it is crucial to integrate them properly into the standard project development frameworks and acquire a more mathematical mental attitude towards software development.

8 ACKNOWLEDGEMENTS

We would like to thank the SSI Technical Manager, Piero La Vopa, for his commitment to the paper underlying activities and technical advice. Moreover we would like to thank the SSI Advanced Technology Line Manager, Matteo Piemontese, and the SSI Quality Assurance Line Manager, Domenico Dininno, for their technical review of this article.

9 LIST OF ACRONYMS

CSC	Computer Software Component
FM	Formal Method

PDL	Program Design Language
RAISE	Rigorous Approach to Industrial Software Engineering
RSL	RAISE Specification Language
TCA	Traffic Conflict Alert

10 REFERENCES

[1] The RAISE Language Group (1992). The RAISE Specification Language, edited by Prentice Hall

[2] The RAISE Method Group (1994). The RAISE development method, edited by Prentice Hall

[3] The RAISE Tool Group (1994). RAISE Tools Reference Manual.

[4] Cadre Technologies Inc. (1990) Teamwork/Ada -- User's Guide

[5] Richard A. Kemmerer (September 1990) Integrating Formal Methods into the Development Process, in *IEEE Software*,

[6] A. Alapide, M.Cinnella, P. La Vopa (1992) Automatic Generation of Ada Code with the RAISE Formal Method in *Proceedings of the third Symposium Ada in Aerospace*, Wien.

[7] A. Alapide, M.Cinnella, P. La Vopa (1992) The Viability of Applying COCOMO to RAISE-Ada Projects in *Proceedings of the third Symposium Ada in Aerospace*, held in Wien.

[8] Jeannette M. Wing, Amy Moormann Zaremski (1991) Unintrusive Ways to Integrate Formal Specifications in Practice, in *Proceedings of the 4th International Symposium of VDM Europe* Noordwijkerhout, The Nertherlands, October 1991.

[9] M.Cinnella, S.Candia, A.Alapide, S.Quaranta, D.Stellacci, P.La Vopa (1995) SSI Confidential Assessment Report on the TCA Application, *SSI report for the CEC*, doc ref. LACOS/SSI/MCSCAADS/1/V3

[10] Semmens, France and Docker (1992). Integrating Structured Analysis and Formal Specification Techniques, in *The Computer Journal*, Volume 35, Number 5.

11 BIOGRAPHY

Angela Alapide is a software engineer, graduated in Mathematics, with over six years of experience in the area of the application of formal methods to the development of high quality industrial systems. Her expertise ranges from project management to training courses organization and documents reviewing.
She represents SSI in the CEC sponsored Formal Methods Europe steering committee and regularly attends events related to the Formal Methods Technology.
Mrs. Alapide works in the SSI Advanced Technologies Department. She has coordinated the SSI dissemination of knowledge and experiences on formal methods within Alenia, the SSI mother company. (e-mail: alapide@ssi.it)

Sante Candia has over six years of experience in software development of scientific applications. After university he attended a two-year specialization course in Industrial and Applied Mathematics. He acquired experience of various software development methodologies applied throughout the software lifecycle phases. In particular, he got experience in the development of software for real time applications (satellite on-board, air traffic control software), and for discrete and continuous simulation software. (e-mail: candia@ssi.it)

Maddalena Cinnella has been the project manager of the TCA application. She has experience in the management of projects applying formal methods in combination with more traditional methodologies. Her interests and expertise range from the specification and analysis of real-time systems to the management of critical software projects developed with advanced technologies.
She is now in charge for the activities related to the simulation of the Space Station Control Center for a Prototype of the Distributed Execution Level Planning.
She received a degree in Computer Science from the University of Bari and a Master in Business Administration. (e-mail: cinnella@ssi.it)

Sallustio Quaranta has over seven years of experience in software and algorithm development for industrial and scientific applications. He acquired experience with different software development methodologies from the traditional to the formal ones. He was involved in the Presentation Monitoring System project as lead engineer.
He received a degree in Phisics at the University of Bari. (e-mail: quaranta@ssi.it)

APPENDIX: OUTLINE OF DOCUMENTATION

10 Introduction

10.1 Scope and Purpose
10.2 Document Organization
10.3 References
10.4 Formal Development Strategy

20 Abstract Specifications

20.1 List of RSL constructs used in the abstract specifications
20.2 Abstract Specifications
  20.2.1 Module 1
  ..
  20.2.n Module n

30 Detailed Design: RSL Concrete Specifications

30.1 List of RSL constructs used in the concrete specifications
30.2 Concrete specifications
  30.2.1 Module 1
  ..
  30.2.n Module n

40 Proofs and Justifications

60 Basic Concepts on RAISE

70 Description of RSL constructs in the abstract and concrete specifications

80 Glossary

90 Analytical Index of the ASG entities

100 Cross reference ASGs/RSL specifications

28

Assessing the quality of specification-based testing

S.P. Allen and M.R. Woodward
University of Liverpool
Department of Computer Science, P.O. Box 147, Liverpool, L69 3BX, U.K. Tel: +44 151 794 3670 Fax: +44 151 794 3715 email: {spa,mrw}@csc.liv.ac.uk

Abstract

This paper reports an experimental investigation into the quality of sets of test expressions automatically generated from algebraic specifications. Faults were introduced into implementations in C and Fortran equivalent to the chosen specifications, manually in the case of the C versions, and using the Mothra mutation system in the case of the Fortran versions. The algebraic specifications themselves were also subject to mutation analysis. A number of test generation strategies were considered, in order to circumvent the problem of handling prohibitively large numbers of test expressions. Results show that certain test sets detected the majority of faults and appear to perform better than random test sets of comparable sizes.

Keywords

Specification-based testing, error-seeding, mutation, test experiments

1 INTRODUCTION

The bewildering variety of different testing methodologies means that software testers often rely on experience and intuition to carry out their work. With more and more programs being specified by using a formal method, it appears feasible to use these formal specifications to derive appropriate test cases. A formal specification is a description of a program or module; it only describes what has to be done to produce the required result, not how it is to be done. At present most testing techniques rely on the execution of the program to give an indication of what is happening. These methods usually require an inspection of the program to select test data that is likely to expose faults. It is felt that a testing methodology based upon the formal description of a program will provide a systematic way of generating tests that will expose a substantial number of faults.

There are many different types of formal specification notation. The model-based sequential notations of Z and VDM (Vienna Development Method) are among the most popular. Property-based sequential notations using an algebraic style are another popular approach. The specific focus of interest here is the algebraic notation OBJ, for two reasons (i) OBJ is executable and (ii) a tool is available that automatically generates test expressions from an OBJ specification. It is hoped that full advantage can be taken of these two features in this research.

The earliest work done in this field concentrated on test expression generation from algebraic specifications of abstract data types (ADTs) because these are the most understood and most mathematical aspects of a system's design. Perhaps the most widely known work in this area is the DAISTS system developed by Gannon et al (1981). Gerrard et al (1990) have done research into design time testing using algebraic specifications; they believe one of the best ways of ensuring correct specifications is being able to add unvalidated objects to correct environments. This way if a failure occurs it is straightforward to determine where the fault is located. The ability to execute the specification is an advantage in this case. Many ideas have been suggested for generating test data from specifications. Stocks and Carrington (1993) have presented a framework for generating general descriptions of test sets by specifying what constraints should be applied to the test data. The framework was applied to Z specifications. Hall (1988) has discussed the problems of automating the generation of test cases. Jalote (1989) suggested that meaningful test sets can be generated by just considering the syntactic aspect of the formal specification. Doong and Frankl (1991) though, indicate through their research, that it is very important to consider the other aspect of a specification, that is, the semantic part, as different initial values of parameters can lead to many different states. Building on the work of Bougé et al (1986), Bernot et al (1991) have conducted extensive research into generating test data from algebraic specifications by translating them into Horn clauses. A tool implemented using Prolog simulates equational resolution and provides control mechanisms for generating the test data. Very little research has been conducted on assessing the quality of test data automatically generated from specifications in terms of its effect on equivalent implementations.

This paper considers the feasibility of automatically generating test expressions from a formal specification and reports on experiments aimed at determining how good these expressions are at exposing faults in implementations. Two medium-sized OBJ specifications were selected and equivalent implementations in C and Fortran were developed. Faults were seeded into the C programs and mutants were generated of the Fortran programs and the OBJ specifications themselves. These faulty versions were used to assess the quality of test expressions generated from the OBJ specifications. In section 2 an overview of OBJ is given, as is a brief description of some of the tools that were used to perform this study. Section 3 describes in more detail the experiments carried out. Section 4 outlines the results that were achieved and some of the interesting points raised by this work. Finally section 5 summarises this work.

2 OBJ AND TOOLS AVAILABLE

Given below are brief descriptions of some of the tools that were used in assessing the quality of automatically generated test expressions.

2.1 OBJ

OBJ is an algebraic specification language a full introduction to which can be found in the work of Goguen and Tardo (1979). The version used in this study was developed at UMIST (Coleman et al, 1987). At its simplest level an OBJ specification consists of a collection of objects; an object starts with the keyword OBJ and ends with JBO. An object can consist of up to four sections: SORTS, OPS, VARS and EQNS. The SORTS section describes the abstract data type that will be used in the object. The OPS section describes the operators required in terms of the range and domain of each operator. The VARS section is for declaring the symbols needed for the EQNS section. This last section describes the behaviour of operators by means of equations which indicate their relationships with one another. An equation may hold only if a certain condition is true; this may be expressed by means of an optional *if* clause. The only built in sorts are NAT, the natural numbers, with the usual arithmetic operations being defined, i.e. +, /, -, * etc and BOOL, the booleans T and F with predefined logical operators *and*, *or* and *not*.

OBJ specifications unlike most other types of formal notation are executable. This is achieved by term rewriting. When a test expression is presented to the OBJ interpreter if the left hand side of an equation matches with elements in the expression, it is replaced by the corresponding right hand side of the equation. This continues until it is not possible to repeat the matching process and the result is returned. An example in OBJ below shows part of a specification, given by Gerrard et al (1990), which defines a List ADT.

```
OBJ   Pair / Name
SORTS pr
OPS
      < _ ; _ > : nat name -> pr
JBO

OBJ   List / Pair
SORTS list
OPS
      #     :             -> list
      _ . _ : pr list    -> list
      _ & _ : list list -> list
VARS
      p     : pr
      l,l'  : list
EQNS
      ( # & l = l )
      ( ( p . l ) & l' = p . ( l & l' ) )
JBO
```

If *aa*, *bb* and *cc* are valid names then the following expression creates a list containing three elements:

```
< 0 ; aa > . < 1 ; bb > . < 2 ; cc > . #
```

Adding a list of one element to another (empty) list, as in the following expression:

```
# & < 0 ; aa > . #
```

will produce, using the first equation for term rewriting, the result:

```
< 0 ; aa > . #
```

2.2 Test expression generator OBJTEST

OBJTEST (Woodward, 1993) automatically generates test expressions from an OBJ specification. Test expressions are generated by taking each operator in turn and substituting for the arguments in the domain each operator whose range is of the appropriate sort. Testing the List ADT described above, OBJTEST will produce, in addition to others, expressions like:

```
( < 0 ; aa > ) . #
( < 0 ; aa > ) . ( ( < 1 ; aa > ) . # )
( < 0 ; aa > ) . ( ( < 0 ; cc > ) . ( # & # ) )
```

OBJTEST has many options that can be used to help generate test expressions. The most important of these are:

- The ability to select specific modules from a complete specification to test.
- The ability to specify the nesting depth of test expressions. Here expressions are generated as described above and repeated until the depth of nesting as specified by the user has been reached.
- The ability to de-select a constant from being used to generate test expressions. This is useful because many test expressions are seen to be equivalent. For example, if for the List ADT described above, many more numbers and names were defined then all combinations would be produced using the additional values but many expressions would be essentially the same. These can be considered as symmetrical expressions.

Additionally OBJTEST has another facility, the ability to generate mutants from an OBJ specification. This is achieved by introducing minor modifications to the specification. Again it is possible to specify which modules are to be tested and what type of mutant is to be generated. The version of OBJTEST that was being used generated four classes of mutant. They were:

- Similar variable replacement. A variable is replaced with a different variable of the same type.
- Operator attribute alteration. If an operator is for example, associative and commutative, one mutation would be to remove the associativity.
- Equation removal. Each operator is defined normally by one or more equations; with this mutation each equation is removed one at a time.
- Similar operator replacement. An operator is replaced with a different operator but having the same domain and range.

An example of a mutant generated from the List ADT would be to replace l by l' on the right hand side of the second equation resulting in the following:

```
( ( p . l ) & l' = p . ( l' & l' ) )
```

Being executable, the mutant specifications can then be tested in an attempt to distinguish them from the original.

2.3 Mothra

Mothra (King and Offutt, 1991) is a mutation testing system for Fortran programs. It incorporates 22 mutation operators and the user can specify which of them are to be used. Mothra generates mutants of Fortran programs and by using test sets, supplied by the tester or automatically generated by Mothra, determines which mutants are killed by the test set.

When a test run has been completed Mothra generates comprehensive results of the mutant killing ability of the test set. It is up to the user to identify equivalent mutants, although recently some algorithms have been produced that attempt to identify equivalent mutants (Offutt and Craft, 1994).

3 ASSESSING THE QUALITY OF AUTOMATICALLY GENERATED TEST EXPRESSIONS

When designing experiments to assess the quality of automatically generated test expressions, the choice of subject programs and specifications is very important. Ideally both the program and specification should be available. Obtaining reasonable sized programs and their corresponding formal descriptions was discovered to be very difficult. For this experiment a student database system (Rolland, 1992) was used, given as a formal description in VDM and as an equivalent program in Modula-2. Also used was a nontrivial airport scheduling specification, given in OBJ by Goguen and Tardo (1979). The unavailability of large OBJ specifications made it necessary to translate the VDM specification of the student database into OBJ. It is acknowledged that this method is not ideal and was done to overcome the aforementioned problem. The equivalent implementation of the student database was translated into C and Fortran. The OBJ airport specification was used to develop implementations in C and Fortran.

3.1 Subject programs

Below is a brief description of the sample programs and specifications used.

Student Database

The student database is designed as a set of student details: name, class and the sex of each student. The OBJ specification is implemented using a Set ADT. The C and Fortran versions were implemented accordingly. There are seven operations that manipulate the database; they are: *initialise*, *addmale*, *addfemale*, *deletemale*, *deletefemale*, *findmales* and *findfemales*. Examples of typical operations allowed on the OBJ specification are:

```
addmale ( Fred , 0 , Null )
addmale ( Fred , 0 , addmale ( Fred , 1 , Null U Null ) )
findmales ( deletefemale ( June , 1 , addmale ( Fred , 0 , Null ) ) )
```

where Null is the empty set (or empty database) and U is the set union operator.

Two values each were chosen for the name and class parameters. No restrictions were placed on the length of names or the size of the class. *Fred* and *June* were chosen as the names and 0 and 1 as the class numbers. Test expressions were generated using OBJTEST together with various constraints that it was believed would provide insight into the ability of test expressions generated from an algebraic specification to expose faults in implementations. These are described in section 4.

Airport Specification

The airport specification is a much larger specification than the student database. Essentially there are three modules that deal with different aspects of scheduling airplanes, with another module that brings the other three modules together. There are additional minor modules that check the validity of the flight numbers, plane numbers and time. Typical operations may be:

```
schedule ( Fl 1, LAX, 13 hrs 45, Pl 2, DC9, create )
```

This schedules flight 1 to go to LAX at 13:45 using plane 2 which is a DC9,

```
change~time~of FL 1 to 12 hrs 34 in
               schedule ( Fl 1, LAX, 13 hrs 45, Pl 2, DC9, create )
```

This changes the time of flight 1 to 12:34.

```
cancel Fl 5 in schedule ( Fl 1, LAX, 13 hrs 45, Pl 2, DC9, create )
```

This cancels flight 5 details from the airport schedule.

Three values each for the flight number, plane number and times were chosen and only one of the plane types and destinations available were used. Also four constants were added that represented one, two, three and four flight details. The constant representing four complete flight details was called TODAY and was an example given with the original specification. Values for the times, flight numbers and plane numbers included invalid values.

3.2 Using test expressions generated from OBJ specification

The test expressions generated from the OBJ specifications described previously, were used to test the C and Fortran implementations. The test expressions were read in and translated into a form that could be used to test the implementations. There was a direct relationship between the operators of the OBJ specifications and the procedures of the C and Fortran implementations.

Table 1 Number and type of faults seeded into C programs

Subject	Fault Category	Omission	Commission
Student	Data Definition	3	6
Database	Data Handling	3	4
	Decision and processing	5	0
	Decision	4	2
Airport	Data Definition	6	12
Scheduler	Data Handling	6	6
	Decision and processing	5	6
	Decision	9	1

3.3 Assessing the quality of test expressions

To assess the quality of test expressions faults were seeded into the C programs. The intention was to make the type and number of faults as far as possible representative of the type and number of faults found in real world situations. To this end the seeded faults were modeled in type and frequency on the result of a study of industrial software by Ostrand and Weyuker (1984). This study classified faults in two ways. Faults could either be errors of omission, i.e., something was left out of the code causing it to function incorrectly, or errors of commission, i.e., something was added to the code to make the software function incorrectly. The fault detection ability of the test expressions was assessed by determining the ratio of the exposed faults to the number of seeded faults. To supplement this limited experiment, mutation analysis was also used. Using Mothra, mutants of the Fortran programs were generated and the quality of test expressions was assessed against these mutants. Additionally mutants of the original OBJ specification were generated and the mutant killing ability of the test expressions on the specification itself was assessed. It is believed that by determining how many mutants are killed by a test set, that this will provide some indication of the quality of the test set. The ratio of dead mutants to the total number of inequivalent mutants is the test data adequacy (TDA) of the test set. The same term is also used for the ratio of exposed to seeded faults with the C versions.

Test expressions were generated by OBJTEST, initially using the lowest operator nesting and minimum of parameter values. After the initial study an investigation was conducted to see how varying the number of values and other alternative techniques would affect the number of test expressions being produced and their fault exposing ability.

4 RESULTS

Faults were seeded into the C programs according to the results from the study done by Ostrand and Weyuker and details are given in Table 1. The size of the subject programs (LOC) and the number of mutants generated by Mothra and OBJTEST are given in Table 2.

Table 2 Size and number of faults inserted / mutants generated for subject programs

Subject	OBJ		C		Fortran	
	LOC	Mutants	LOC	Faults	LOC	Mutants
Student Database	159	99	171	27	263	866
Airport	264	135	489	51	594	5006

Table 3 TDA of test sets generated from student database specification

Test Set	Size	OBJ TDA	C TDA	Fortran TDA
a	324	87.1	77.8	81.9
b	2250	84.3	77.8	81.2
c	12402	92.9	81.5	87.6
d	2250	70.0	81.5	85.5
e	13770	100.0	81.5	87.6
fa	36	46.5	22.2	24.5
fb	146	77.8	63.0	67.3
fc	146	78.8	66.7	70.2
fd	146	81.8	66.7	71.7
fe	290	81.8	66.7	71.7
ra	36	46.5	22.2	25.4
rb	146	70.7	63.0	61.5
rc	146	69.7	65.6	69.6
rd	146	72.7	66.7	70.7
re	290	75.8	66.7	71.7

4.1 Student database results

The different test sets generated for the student database were:

- *a* - operator nesting level of 2, using the two names and two numbers.
- *b* - operator nesting level of 3, using two names and one number.
- *c* - operator nesting level of 3, using one name and two numbers.
- *d* - operator nesting level of 3, using two names, two numbers but expressions containing only one of the sex constants (male,female).
- *e* - operator nesting of level 3, using two names and two numbers.

The size of the test sets generated and the test data adequacy (TDA) for these test sets, *a* to *e*, for the three versions, OBJ, C and Fortran, are given in Table 3.

For some of the test sets the number of test expressions being generated was very large indeed. Many of the expressions were considered similar. For example, because a set notation was being used to represent the student database and the operations on it, test expressions were produced containing Null and the set union operator, such as:

```
addmale ( Fred, 0, Null U Null )
```

Table 4 Size of test pools for the student database and airport scheduler specification

Test category	Size	
	Student	Airport
a	10 404	3180
b	20 350	1590
c	20 350	1590
d	20 350	273
e	66 854	684

It was felt that expressions like this achieved very little beyond the equivalent expressions where union with Null (the identity for set union) is removed:

```
addmale ( Fred, 0, Null )
```

When analysing the output from Mothra it was discovered that many of the test expressions at the start of the test sets were killing large numbers of mutants and the remaining expressions were only killing a very small number each, if any at all. This led to the belief that choosing a small number of expressions from the total number of test expressions would provide comparable results. To investigate this various different strategies were tried. They were:

- Use only the first 5, 10, 15, 20, 25 test expressions generated from the major operators: *addmale*, *addfemale*, *deletemale*, *deletefemale*, *findmales* and *findmales*. Because there are six major operators taking the first 5, 10, 15, 20, 25 would produce test sets of size 30, 60, 90, 120 and 150. These sets are labeled *a5* to *e5*, *a10* to *e10* through to *a25* to *e25*.
- Use only expressions that have an operator that does not alter the state of the database outermost; these are called evaluators and for the student database these were the operators *findmales* and *findfemales*, and an *addmale* or *addfemale* operator innermost. If two expressions are similar then remove one of them; also if the test set is generated to a nesting depth of n then do not include expressions at depth less than n. Finally remove symmetrical expressions. These sets are labeled *fa* to *fe*. The test sets generated using this strategy did not include test expressions generated using any other method.

The size and the test data adequacy of these test sets are given in Tables 3 and 5. Random test data with evaluators outermost was generated to compare with the test sets *fa* to *fe*. These sets *ra* to *re* are also presented in Table 3.

The results of test sets *a5* to *e5* through to *a25* to *e25* were compared with random test data generated for each category, *a*-*e*. For each category, five names and five numbers were used and large test sets were generated. The same constraints were applied on these test sets as the initial test sets. The size of the test pools that expressions were chosen from are given in Table 4. Expressions were taken randomly from these sets in sizes comparable to the size of the original test sets. Results for the random test sets are given in Table 5.

Table 5 TDA of 'first 5, 10, 15, 20, 25' test expression sets generated from student database and random test sets

Test Set	OBJ TDA		C TDA		Fortran TDA	
	Initial	Random	Initial	Random	Initial	Random
a5	83.8	59.2	61.7	61.6	29.6	30.7
b5	57.6	66.7	67.8	47.5	37.0	39.7
c5	55.6	63.0	68.2	60.6	59.3	62.6
d5	56.6	66.7	68.1	57.6	55.6	57.5
e5	56.6	63.0	68.0	54.5	48.1	51.3
a10	84.8	63.0	61.7	73.7	33.3	33.3
b10	58.6	63.0	67.8	56.6	55.6	57.3
c10	56.6	66.7	70.8	62.6	63.0	67.2
d10	57.6	66.7	70.1	61.6	63.0	67.2
e10	57.6	63.0	69.2	59.6	63.0	67.2
a15	84.9	63.0	68.2	77.8	44.4	47.0
b15	58.6	66.7	68.3	62.6	59.3	60.9
c15	59.6	63.0	71.0	68.7	63.0	68.6
d15	59.6	70.4	72.6	67.7	66.7	69.2
e15	59.6	70.4	74.4	65.7	66.7	69.7
a20	84.9	63.0	68.2	77.8	44.4	48.6
b20	58.6	66.7	68.3	70.7	59.2	60.9
c20	59.6	63.0	71.0	70.7	66.7	70.6
d20	59.6	70.4	72.6	70.7	66.7	70.7
e20	59.6	70.4	74.4	70.7	66.7	70.7
a25	84.9	66.7	70.4	77.8	48.1	49.0
b25	61.6	66.7	71.0	71.7	63.0	66.9
c25	59.6	70.4	75.3	70.7	66.7	70.7
d25	61.6	74.1	75.9	70.7	66.7	71.1
e25	62.6	70.4	76.4	71.7	66.7	71.6

Table 6 TDA of initial test sets for airport specification

Test Set	Size	OBJ TDA	C TDA	Fortran TDA
a	186	17.8	84.3	75.2
b	93	14.8	52.9	35.4
c	93	17.0	62.7	75.1
d	66	58.5	56.8	74.5
e	112	57.0	60.8	74.6
fe	102	91.1	72.5	67.7
te	112	84.4	72.5	81.5

Table 7 TDA of random test sets for the airport scheduler specification

Test Set	OBJ TDA	C TDA	Fortran TDA
a30	15.6	60.8	34.0
b30	13.3	58.8	18.8
c30	15.6	66.7	34.4
d30	56.3	62.7	37.5
e30	62.0	66.7	43.9
a60	15.6	62.7	39.7
b60	13.3	62.7	18.9
c60	15.6	66.7	38.2
d60	57.0	66.7	37.9
e60	63.0	74.5	44.0
a90	15.6	62.7	39.7
b90	17.8	62.7	22.2
c90	20.0	66.7	38.2
d90	57.0	66.7	43.2
e90	63.0	76.5	47.0
a120	15.6	64.7	39.7
b120	17.8	62.7	22.2
c120	20.0	66.7	38.2
d120	57.0	66.7	43.2
e120	63.0	76.5	47.3
a150	20.7	64.7	60.3
b150	17.7	64.7	22.5
c150	20.7	78.4	62.8
d150	57.0	66.7	68.0
e150	67.4	76.5	51.2

4.2 Airport specification results

The test sets generated from the airport specification were produced using the following constraints:

- a - Level 2 nesting of operators with evaluators outermost.
- b - Level 2 nesting of operators with evaluators outermost. Using the same constraints as for test set *a* except for de-selection of the constant TODAY.
- c - Level 2 nesting as above but with just TODAY, i.e. not including the empty set.
- d - Level 1 nesting not just with the evaluators outermost and including TODAY and the empty set.
- e - Level 1 nesting as above but including two constants, one containing details of just one flight and the other containing details of two flights.

The size and the TDA of the described test sets are in Table 6.

Overall the results being achieved were reasonably satisfactory, but in an attempt to improve upon them additional test sets were generated. These were a test set with an extra flight number (fe) and a test set with two extra invalid time values (te). The results for these test sets are given in Table 6.

Random test sets were again used for comparison purposes. Test pools were produced for the major test sets by using extra flight, plane and time values and the constants containing flight details included or excluded accordingly. Sizes taken were 30, 60, 90, 120 and 150, with constraints as applied to sets *a*, *b*, *c*, *d* and *e*. Given in Table 4 is the size of the test pool used. The results are presented in Table 7.

5 CONCLUSION

This paper has presented an investigation into the quality of test expressions generated from algebraic specifications, using two medium-sized specifications and their equivalent implementations in Fortran and C. Faults were inserted in the C versions using as far as possible the same types and proportions as found in a study of real industrial software. Mutation analysis was used on the Fortran versions and the OBJ specifications themselves. Assessed using this method, the fault detection ability of the initial test sets generated from the student database ranged from 70.0% to 100.0% for the OBJ, 77.8% to 81.5% for the C and 81.9% to 87.6% for the Fortran versions. For the airport specification the fault detection ability ranged from 14.8% to 91.15% for the OBJ, 52.9% to 72.5% for the C and 35.4% to 81.5% for the Fortran versions. In an attempt to generate some heuristic guidelines for producing a small number of test expressions that detect a large number of faults, different techniques and strategies were investigated. Although not as effective as the initial test sets, the number of test expressions generated are significantly smaller for only a slightly worse fault detection ability than the best case. The effectiveness of these simple strategies have been evaluated against random test sets of the same size. The random test sets performed slightly worse.

It is acknowledged that for experiments of this nature to provide concrete conclusions requires more and larger specifications together with equivalent implementations and that rigorous statistical methods be applied. The experimental work conducted by Hutchins et al (1991), on comparing the effectiveness of dataflow-based and controlflow-based test data adequacy, considered that the results obtained using seven subject programs that produced 130 faulty programs was severely limited. Obtaining moderate-sized specifications and equivalent implementations that have both been produced by independent sources is a limiting factor in this research. Using smaller specifications and implementations will not produce many faulty versions that can be used to assess effectively the quality of automatically generated test sets.

The tentative conclusion seems to be that test expressions from algebraic specifications can be effective at exposing faults in implementations. Although different specifications will probably need to be treated on an individual basis, depending on the abstract data type being used to implement the operations. This is because the number of test expressions that could be generated can become extremely large and many of them may detect very few additional faults. There does not appear to be an obvious relationship between the number of specification mutants killed and the number of faults exposed in the C implementation or the number of mutants killed in the Fortran implementation. The results show that at deeper levels of nesting more faults are exposed. This was also suggested by Doong and Frankl (1991). It could be that the more operations that are applied to a data structure, the more likely it is that a fault will produce erroneous data values that are amplified by the long sequence of operations. It is also possible that many different operators appearing in a test expression will cover a large part of the implementation's functionality and thereby expose many faults. It was discovered that for a test expression to be able to kill a mutant of the specification, the expression has to be nested to at least the same depth as the operator nesting in the equation under test. The majority of equations describing the operators of the airport specification were at depth 3. This explains why the first three test sets did not kill many specification mutants at level 2 nesting. The effective depth of the remaining test sets was at least 3 or 4.

The authors look forward to building upon these experiments. Perhaps by including additional techniques that will allow better analysis of possible parameter values or by determining the quality of the formal specification, the number of faults detected can be increased and the number of test expressions can be decreased. In particular, the authors are considering ways of reducing the number of test expressions automatically generated by exploiting symmetry and other techniques.

6 REFERENCES

Bernot, G., Gaudel, M., and Marre, B. (1991), Software testing based on formal specifications: a theory and a tool. *Software Engineering Journal*, **6**(6):387-405.

Bougé, L., Choquet, N., Fribourg, L., and Gaudel, M. (1986), Test sets generation from algebraic specifications using logic programming. *The Journal of Systems and Software*, **6**(4):343-360.

Coleman, D., Gallimore, R., and Stavridou, V. (1987), The design of a rewrite rule interpreter from algebraic specifications. *Software Engineering Journal*, **2**(4):95-104.

Doong, R. and Frankl, P. (1991), Case studies on testing object-oriented programs. In *Proceedings of the Symposium on Testing, Analysis and Verification (TAV4)*, pages 165-177, Victoria, B.C., Canada. ACM Press.

Gannon, J., McMullin, P., and Hamlet, R. (1981), Data-abstraction implementation, specification and testing. *ACM Transactions on Programming Language and Systems*, **3**(3):211-223.

Gerrard, C., Coleman, D., and Gallimore, R. (1990), Formal specification and design time testing. *IEEE Transactions on Software Engineering*, **16**(1):1-12.

Goguen, J. A. and Tardo, J. J. (1979), An introduction to Obj. In *Proceedings of Specifications of Reliable Software*, pages 170-189. IEEE Computer Society Press.

Hall, P. (1988), Testing with respect to formal specification. In *Proceedings of the Second IEE/BCS Conference 'Software Engineering 88'*, pages 159-163. University of Liverpool, IEE/BCS.

Hutchins, M., Foster, H., Goradia, T. and Ostrand, T. (1994), Experiments on the effect iveness of dataflow- and controlflow-based test adequacy criteria. In *Proceedings of the 16th International Conference on Software Engineering*, pages 191-200. IEEE Computer Society Press.

Jalote, P. (1989), Testing the completeness of specifications. *IEEE Transactions on Software Engineering*, **15**(5):526-531.

King, K. N. and Offutt, A. J. (1991), A Fortran language system for mutation-based software testing. *Software-Practice and Experience*, **21**(7):685-718.

Offutt, A. J. and Craft, W. M. (1994), Using compiler optimization techniques to detect equivalent mutants. *Software Testing, Verification and Reliability*, **4**(3):131-154.

Ostrand, T. and Weyuker, E. (1984), Collecting and categorizing software error data in an industrial environment. *The Journal of Systems and Software*, **4**(4):289-300.

Rolland, F. (1992), *Programming with VDM*, chapter 5, pages 42-52. MacMillan.

Stocks, P. and Carrington, D. (1993), Test template framework: A specification-based testing case study. In *Proceedings of the 1993 International Symposium on Software Testing and Analysis (ISSTA 1993)*, pages 11-18. ACM Press.

Woodward, M. (1993), Errors in algebraic specifications and an experimental mutation testing tool. *Software Engineering Journal*, **8**(4):211-224.

7 BIOGRAPHY

Stephen P. Allen received a BSc (Hons) degree in computer science in 1993 from the University of Liverpool and is currently working towards a PhD at the same institution.

His current research interests include software testing and software specification.

Martin R. Woodward received a BSc (Hons) degree in mathematics in 1969 and a PhD degree in applied mathematics in 1972, both from the University of Nottingham in the UK.

For three years he was employed by the University of Oxford as a Research Assistant on secondment to the UK Atomic Energy Authority at the Culham Laboratory. He has been at the University of Liverpool since 1975 where he is now a Senior Lecturer in the Computer Science Department. His current research interests include: software specification, software testing and analysis, software metrics, and software development environments.

Dr. Woodward is Editor of the journal *Software Testing, Verification and Reliability* (Wiley) and is also on the Editorial Board of the *Software Quality Journal* (Chapman and Hall). He has also served on the Programme Committees of several international conferences, including recently the *International Symposium on Software Testing and Analysis (ISSTA-96)* held in San Diego, USA, in January 1996.

A tool for testing synchronous software

I. Parissis
Laboratoire de Génie Informatique, Institut IMAG
BP 53 38041 Grenoble Cedex 9, France
Phone : (33) 76 82 72 57, Fax : (33) 76 82 72 87
E-mail : Ioannis.Parissis@imag.fr

Abstract
We present a testing tool for synchronous reactive software, an interesting subclass of critical real-time software. Its aim is to provide a new means for critical software validation since formal verification techniques are often impracticable. For the particular domain of synchronous reactive software, we have designed specific testing techniques which are loosely related to techniques proposed for sequential programming languages. One of the main characteristics of synchronous reactive software is the importance of the environment behavior in the validation process. Moreover, software requirements are usually expressed by means of temporal properties. The tool comprises random testing and specification-based testing techniques which have been designed to take into account these particularities. A structure-based testing technique well adapted to data-flow languages is also described.

Keywords
Software testing, formal methods, automated validation, quality of synchronous software.

1 INTRODUCTION

With the increased use of software controls in critical real-time systems, the need for rigorous methods at each step of the development process has become clear to all companies working on trustworthy systems. The aim of such methods is to provide confidence in the critical software, for instance by ensuring that it will behave in obedience to some properties (typically safety properties).

This paper is concerned with *synchronous reactive* critical software. A reactive software continuously reacts with its environment and must satisfy temporal constraints so that it can take into account all the events issued by this environment. The *synchrony hypothesis* (Benveniste and Berry, 1991) for a software requires that every reaction of the software to a set of inputs is theoretically instantaneous. In fact, this requirement is filled by any reactive software for which it is possible to prove that its environment is invariant during every reaction.

An important feature of reactive software is that it is developed under assumptions about the possible environment behavior. When such assumptions are formally expressed they can be easily integrated in an automated software verification process.

Special programming languages have been designed for the development of synchronous software, such as Esterel (Boussinot and De Simone, 1991) and LUSTRE (Halbwachs et al., 1991a). When a software is implemented in one of these languages it is often possible to perform a formal verification of some safety properties by model-checking. This verification technique, which can be fully automated, requires the software to be portrayed as a logical model and the safety properties to be expressed as logical formulae. Then, if the formulae are true in the model, it is assumed that the safety properties hold in the software. For instance, LESAR (Halbwachs et al., 1992) is a tool dealing with LUSTRE programs allowing automatic verification of safety properties. This tool uses LUSTRE as an executable specification language (for describing the model) as well as a linear temporal logic (Pilaud and Halbwachs, 1988) (for expressing the safety properties).

The main drawback of such formal verification techniques is that they often require prohibitive memory and time amounts. When they fail (because of lacks of memory and/or time) they do not provide any information about the satisfaction of the safety properties. Thus, it is clear that new - complementary - verification and validation approaches have to be developed.

The use of rigorous software testing techniques is the approach proposed here. Testing usually requires less memory and time amounts than formal verification and, hence, it is often the only means to perform software validation when formal verification is impracticable. Moreover, testing can reveal discrepancies between the model on which formal verification is carried out and the real world.

The tool presented in this paper provides a formal framework for testing synchronous software. Although it is based on the use of the LUSTRE language, most of the facilities it offers do not require the software to be implemented in that specific language. Therefore, the tool, of which the principles have been presented in (Ouabdesselam and Parissis, 1994a) and (Ouabdesselam and Parissis, 1994b), can be used for a wide range of synchronous applications. It offers three main testing facilities : constrained random testing, specification-based testing and structure-based testing. They are respectively presented in sections 2, 3 and 4 while section 5 describes how the tool should be used.

2 CONSTRAINED RANDOM TESTING

Random software testing consists in executing the software with input values which are randomly selected from the software input domain. The input domain is usually considered to be equal to the cartesian product of the domains of the input variables of the software.

Such a definition of the input domain is not suited to the test of most reactive software since it overlooks the environment description.

Let's consider the following example of a temperature control system developed in (Atlee and Gannon, 1993). This system is composed of a heater, an air conditioner, temperature sensors and an on/off switch. For the present paper, we introduce a reactive software for controlling that system.

Table 1 SCR Requirements for the Temperature Control Software.

Current Mode	*Running*	*BelowDesired Temp*	*TempOK*	*AboveDesired Temp*	*New Mode*
OFF	@T	**f**	t	**f**	INACTIVE
	@T	t	**f**	**f**	HEAT
	@T	f	**f**	t	AC
INACTIVE	@F	-	-	-	OFF
	t	@T	**@F**	**f**	HEAT
	t	**f**	**@F**	@T	AC
HEAT	@F	-	-	-	OFF
	t	**@F**	@T	**f**	INACTIVE
AC	@F	-	-	-	OFF
	t	**f**	@T	**@F**	INACTIVE

The software has four boolean inputs and four boolean outputs :

- The input *Running* is true when the on/off switch of the device is to the 'on' position.
- The inputs *BelowDesiredTemp*, *TempOk* and *AboveDesiredTemp* are mutually exclusive signals issued by temperature sensors; they are true when the current temperature is respectively lower, equal or higher than the desired temperature.
- *OFF*, *INACTIVE*, *HEAT* and *AC* are the four mutually exclusive outputs and correspond to the current *mode* of the system. *OFF* is true when the system is turned off, *INACTIVE* is true when the system is on but neither the heater nor the air conditioner is on, while *HEAT* and *AC* are true when the heater or the air conditioner, respectively, is on and controlling the temperature.

The software specifications are given in (Atlee and Gannon, 1993) as SCR tabular requirements (see table 1). Every row in the table 1 is associated with a *transition* : the left column contains the current mode of the system, while the right column contains the new mode computed with respect to the current input values given in the central columns of the table. @T means that at the instant when the new mode is computed, the associated input value raises from false to true. Similarly, @F specifies the point in time when the value becomes false. A lower case letter 't' (resp. 'f') means that the associated input value is true (resp. false) at this instant and at the instants immediately preceding and following it. For example, the eighth row of the table 1 states that when the system is turned on, if its current mode is *HEAT* and the temperature becomes equal to the desired temperature (i.e. *TempOK* becomes true) then the new system mode is *INACTIVE*.

The input values given in bold characters do not belong to the initial specification but are computed according to the *environment constraints* : the first assumption on the environment is that (I) exactly one of the three inputs *BelowDesiredTemp*, *TempOK* and *AboveDesiredTemp* is true at the same time. The second less obvious assumption on the environment can be deduced from the requirements specification : (II) the temperature cannot raise (resp. fall) from a value below (resp. above) the desired temperature to a value above (resp. below) it

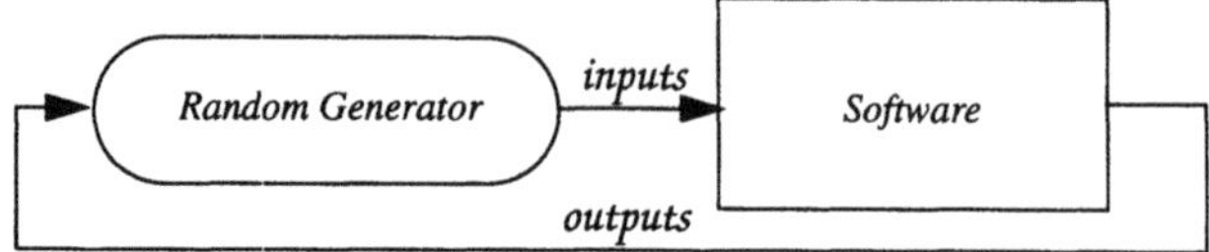

Figure 1 Random test data generator.

without reaching in the meantime the desired temperature. Indeed, no transition is specified in table 1 allowing the system to progress directly from the *HEAT* (resp. *AC*) mode to the *AC* (resp. *HEAT*) mode. As shown below, these environment constraints are easily expressed in LUSTRE, used as a temporal logic :

(I) *(AboveDesiredTemp **or** BelowDesiredTemp **or** TempOK) **and***
#(AboveDesiredTemp, BelowDesiredTemp, TempOK)

(II) *once_from_to(TempOK, BelowDesiredTemp, AboveDesiredTemp) **and***
once_from_to(TempOK, AboveDesiredTemp, BelowDesiredTemp)

where # is a built-in boolean operator ensuring that no more than one of its arguments is true at the same time, while *once_from_to(A, B, C)* is a user-defined in LUSTRE temporal operator returning a true value when the event *A* has occurred at least once between two subsequent occurrences of *B* and *C*. The definition in standard LUSTRE of such temporal operators can be found in (Halbwachs et al., 1992).

It is easy to conclude that the actual software input domain is much smaller than the cartesian product of the domains of input variables. The property (I) restricts the valid input values for *(AboveDesiredTemp, TempOK, BelowDesiredTemp)* to *(0, 0, 1)*, *(0, 1, 0)* or *(1, 0, 0)*. Moreover, the property (II) restricts the valid ***sequences*** of input values. The random generator the construction principles of which are outlined below performs a random generation of test data among all those defined by the environment constraints (e.g. (I) and (II)). It is used as a simulator of the software environment, as shown in Figure 1.

The first step of the generator construction consists in compiling the constraints into a finite state automaton. This automaton recognizes all input and output value sequences satisfying the constraints (in the same way that an automaton recognizes words from a language). Thanks to a process used by the LUSTRE compiler (Halbwachs et al., 1991b) (Bouajjani et al., 1990), the generated automaton is minimal. Moreover, only a symbolic representation of the automaton is actually generated in which states are represented by a set of variables, and transitions by boolean functions.

A state corresponds to one or more different values of the state variables. The next value of each state variable is computed from the current values of the state, input and output variables by means of the associated boolean function. The computation of the next state is based on the use of all these boolean functions.

A boolean function is also associated with the automaton. It is used to check whether the environment constraints are satisfied for a given state and a given value of the inputs and outputs. This boolean function is implemented by a binary decision diagram (Akers, 1978) (Bryant, 1986).

Such a symbolic representation of the automaton needs generally a quite smaller amount of memory than the usual representation in which states and transitions are explicitly generated.

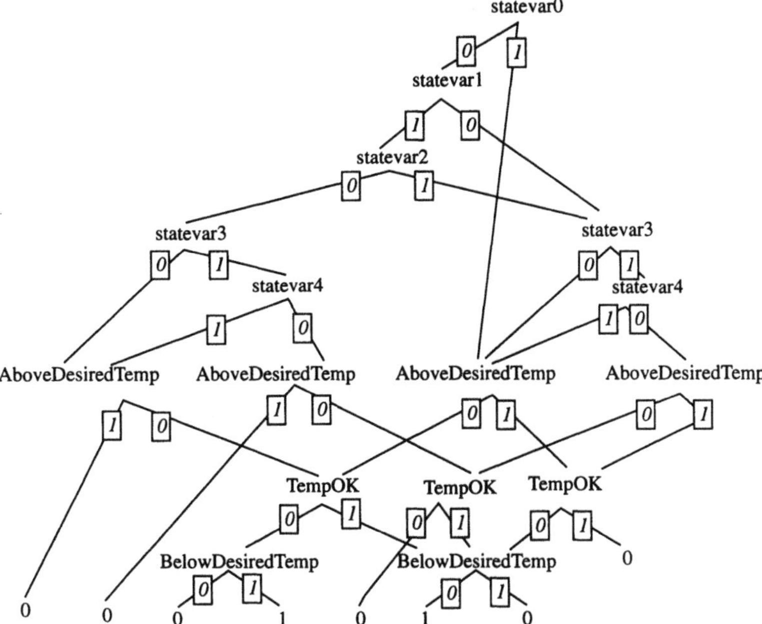

Figure 2 Binary decision diagram for the environment of the Temperature Control System.

For instance, the automaton associated with the constraints (I) and (II) of the above example has five boolean state variables. The binary decision diagram describing the environment constraints is given in Figure 2 (where *1* and *0* respectively hold for true and false). Each node of the diagram carries a variable and each of its outgoing branches is labelled with the value taken by that variable. It must be noted that the variables are ordered. The lower order variables are the state variables. They appear at the top of the diagram; for example in the diagram in Figure 2 the state variables are *statevar0*, ..., *statevar4*. Next come output variables while input variables occur at the bottom of the diagram. In the same example (Figure 2), there are no output variables.

The test data generator uses the above diagram to randomly generate input values for the temperature control software. It consists of a loop composed of the following steps :

1. Locate, in the diagram describing the environment constraints, the subdiagram corresponding to the current values of the state and the software output variables.
2. Generate a random value for the software inputs satisfying the boolean function associated with that diagram.
   (The first two steps are carried out in only one pass on the diagram)
3. Read the new software outputs.
4. Compute the next state by computing the next value of each state variable.

In other words, the generator searches in the diagram associated with the constraints a path leading to *1*. In the example (Figure 2), when *statevar0* is true, the generator will search a path in the subdiagram given in Figure 3. Possible values for the input variables

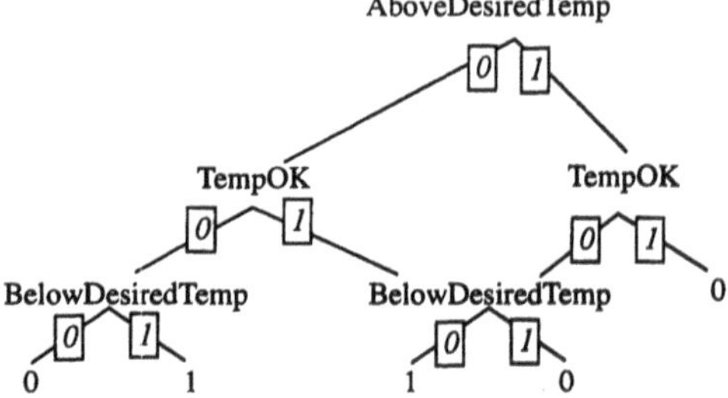

Figure 3 Subdiagram for statevar0 = 1.

(AboveDesiredTemp, TempOK, BelowDesiredTemp) are *(0, 0, 1)*, *(0, 1, 0)* and *(1, 0, 0)*. Each of these values will be generated with the same probability (*1/3* for the example of Figure 3).

3 SPECIFICATION-BASED TESTING

The test data generation technique presented in section 2 is not concerned with the problem of detecting errors occurred during the actual test operation. In the particular case of critical software, we're often interested in tracking down errors related to violation of safety properties. LUSTRE is a high level programming language which can be interpreted as a temporal logic, the most usual and natural means for specifying safety properties. In the example of the temperature control software, some safety properties supplied by the authors are :

1. *OFF ⇒ ~Running*
2. *INACTIVE ⇒ (Running & TempOK)*
3. *HEAT ⇒ (Running & BelowDesiredTemp)*
4. *AC ⇒ (Running & AboveDesiredTemp)*
5. *(Running & BelowDesiredTemp) ⇒ (HEAT∣O(HEAT))*
6. *(Running & AboveDesiredTemp) ⇒ (AC∣O(AC))*

   where *O* is the 'next state' operator : *O(A)* means that *A* will occur at the next system state.

The translation in LUSTRE of the first four properties is straightforward :

1. ***not** OFF **or not** Running*
2. ***not** INACTIVE **or** (Running **and** TempOK)*
3. ***not** HEAT **or** (Running **and** BelowDesiredTemp)*
4. ***not** AC **or** (Running **and** BelowDesiredTemp)*

On the contrary, the translation of the last two properties is more difficult because they use the 'next state' temporal operator. Indeed, in LUSTRE only references to the past values of an expression are possible by means of the ***pre*** operator, denoting the value of the expression at the previous system state. However, since only two successive system states are involved in the property, it is possible to translate the properties to equivalent LUSTRE expressions :

5. ***not pre** (Running **and** BelowDesiredTemp) **or** (**pre** HEAT **or** HEAT)*
6. ***not pre** (Running **and** AboveDesiredTemp) **or** (**pre** AC **or** AC)*

```
node TempControlOracle(
            Running,                    -- ON/OFF switch position
            BelowDesiredTemp,           -- current temp. < desired temp.
            TempOK,                     -- current temp. = desired temp.
            AboveDesiredTemp : bool     -- current temp. > desired temp.
            OFF,                        -- off mode
            INACTIVE,                   -- stand-by mode
            HEAT,                       -- heating mode
            AC: bool                    -- air conditioning mode)
returns(     PropertiesOK : bool);
let
  PropertiesOK = (not OFF or not Running) and
                 (not INACTIVE or (Running and TempOK)) and
                 (not HEAT or (Running and BelowDesiredTemp)) and
                 (not AC or (Running and BelowDesiredTemp)) and
                 (not pre (Running and BelowDesiredTemp) or (pre HEAT or HEAT)) and
                 (not pre (Running and AboveDesiredTemp) or (pre AC or AC))
tel;
```

Figure 4 Test oracle for the temperature control system.

Once the safety properties have been specified, a test oracle can be automatically constructed in a straightforward manner as a LUSTRE program of which the unique output is the conjunction of the above safety properties (see Figure 4). A violation of the safety properties (i.e. an error) is detected when this output takes a false value during the software execution.

However, the actual aim of the specification-based testing is to analyze these properties and to automatically generate relevant input values (that is, input values which are more appropriate for tracking down errors related to the violation of safety properties).

In order to illustrate the definition of relevant input values, let's consider the simple property ***not** A **or** B* (meaning $A \Rightarrow B$), where *A* is a software input and *B* is a software output, stating that the output *B* must be true every time that the input *A* is true. One can easily notice that input values setting *A* to false cannot detect a violation of the property, since in that case ***not** A **or** B* will be true for any *B*. In other words, only input values for which *A* is true are *relevant* with respect to that property. Let *R* be the predicate characterizing the relevant input values; *R(**not** A **or** B) = A*.

A similar, more complex but automated, analysis can be carried out on every LUSTRE boolean expression *E*. This is in particular true for all the user-defined in Lustre temporal operators (e.g. *once_from_to* used in section 2). It results in a new LUSTRE boolean expression *R(E)* which will be true only when the values of the input variables are relevant with respect to the property *E*.

It is then possible to automatically generate relevant input values with respect to a property *E*. The generation process is similar to the one used in section 2 for constrained random testing. Indeed, the latter consists in building a generator of input values according to a set of environment invariant properties, while the former builds a generator according to the expression *R(E)* characterizing the relevant input values for the property *E*.

Another use of the above definition of relevant input values is the assessment of the adequacy of the input values used for testing the software. Indeed, it is very easy to write a LUSTRE program counting the number of input values for which the formula characterizing the relevant ones has been true. At the end of the testing process, the ratio between the relevant and the total input values could be a useful measure of the quality of the testing process.

4 STRUCTURAL TESTING OF LUSTRE PROGRAMS

The approaches presented in sections 2 and 3 are black-box testing techniques and should be used for the detection of design errors resulting in a violation of the specifications (which are safety properties in the case of the technique of the section 3). On the contrary, implementation errors are usually tracked down by means of structural testing techniques. We consider that specifying functional features with LUSTRE is a kind of programming activity resulting in programs which are not exempt from errors. Hence, it is natural to adapt structure-based techniques to the particular case of LUSTRE programs.

Control graphs are the most common representations for programs written in sequential programming languages. Every node of the control graph consists of a sequence of successive instructions without branch statements; the latter are associated with arcs. Such a graph is a suitable representation of the control flow of the program. Structure-based testing consists in defining coverage criteria on the above graph. For instance, instruction coverage consists in running the program until all the nodes of the control graph has been executed, while branch coverage requires all the arcs of the graph to be executed (see for example (Ntafos, 1988)).

Due to the data-flow nature of the language, LUSTRE programs are represented by an operator net instead of a control graph. Indeed, a LUSTRE program (also called *node*) is an unordered set of equations defining the data flow of the program as invariant relations between inputs and outputs. Therefore, an operator net is a more natural representation of the program structure. We believe that defining structure-based criteria on such a net, by analogy with those defined on a control graph, could be useful for detecting implementation errors in LUSTRE programs.

The formal definition of such structure-based criteria can be found in (Ouabdesselam and Parissis, 1994b).

Let's consider the LUSTRE program with its associated operator net given in Figure 5.

```
node Edge(X: bool) returns(EDGE: bool);
let
  EDGE = X -> (X and not pre(X));
tel
```

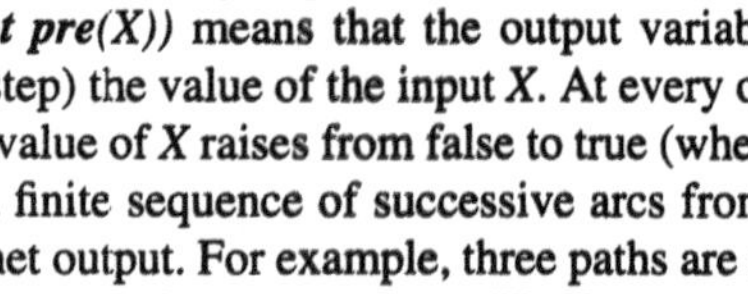

Figure 5 A node example and its operator net.

The operator -> (the "followed-by" operator) allows to set a variable to an initial value : *EDGE = X -> (X **and not pre**(X))* means that the output variable *EDGE* takes at the initial state (the first execution step) the value of the input *X*. At every other state, *EDGE* takes a true value every time that the value of *X* raises from false to true (when *X* is true and ***pre*** *X* is false).

A *path* is defined as a finite sequence of successive arcs from the net. Its first arc is a net input and its last arc is a net output. For example, three paths are defined on the net of the node *Edge* : $p_1 = (X, EDGE)$, $p_2 = (X, a_1, a_2, a_3, EDGE)$ and $p_3 = (X, a3, EDGE)$ where $a_1 = \textbf{pre}(X)$, $a_2 = \textbf{not}\ a_1$ and $a_3 = a_2\ \textbf{and}\ X$. A *path predicate at instant t* associated with a path *p*, noted *PP*(*p*, *t*), is the condition for the last arc to be computed at instant *t using* the path

p. In other words, it is the condition for the path p to be *traversed* by the data-flow when its last arc is traversed at instant t. Path predicates for the node *Edge* are :

$PP(p_1, t) = PP((X, EDGE), t) = init,$

$PP(p_2, t) = PP((X, a_1, a_2, a_3, EDGE), t) = X$ ***and not*** *init*

$PP(p_3, t) = PP((X, a3, EDGE), t) =$ ***not pre****(X)* ***and not*** *init* where *init* = ***true*** -> ***false***

Structure-based test data selection criteria can be defined on such a net. For instance the *operator coverage* is satisfied by a test data set if at least an output arc of each operator belongs to one of the resulting traversed paths (i.e the operator has been activated and its results has been used for computing the output of the path). Similarly, *arc coverage* is satisfied if every arc of the operator net belongs at least to one resulting traversed path. *Path coverage* is generally impossible to satisfy since the number of paths may be infinite. However, the number of paths is finite for a *fixed length* of the test data sequences. Note that paths are defined in such a manner that errors occurring during program execution will be propagated to the output values, even several executions cycles after their effective occurrence.

Once structural test data selection criteria has been defined, we suggest a method for computing test data in order to satisfy these criteria. This computation performs a symbolic evaluation of the associated path predicates.

The method is based on previous work made on formal verification of LUSTRE programs. A verification tool, LESAR (Halbwachs et al., 1992), has been developed, allowing to automatically prove that a property always holds on a LUSTRE program. An interesting feature of LESAR is that it provides a counter-example for properties which do not hold (i.e. an input sequence leading the program to a state violating the property). The method comprises three steps :

1. Computing a finite set of paths which must be executed in order to satisfy the criterion. Let $(p_i)_{i=1...n}$ be these paths.
2. Computing the path predicates $(PP(p_i, t_i))_{i=1...n}$ associated with the above paths where t_i has a fixed value for every path.
3. Attempting to prove with LESAR that ***not*** $PP(p_i, t_i)$ for $i=1...n$ always hold. In case of success, the path p_i is infeasible at instant t_i (another path or another instant must be chosen). Otherwise LESAR provides an input sequence which can be executed to cover the path p_i. The length of the generated input sequences will be minimal, since LESAR will search the shortest counter-example. It is however possible to generate longer input sequences. For this, consider the following LUSTRE equations : $X1$ = ***true***; and for every $n > 1$, Xn = ***false*** -> $Xn\text{-}1$ ***and pre****(Xn-1)*. In other words a variable Xn denotes a sequence of boolean values of which the $n\text{-}1$ first terms are equal to ***false*** while all the other terms are equal to ***true***. Attempting to prove with LESAR that ***not*** $(PP(p_i, t_i^0)$ ***and*** $Xt_i^0)$ always hold, where t_i^0 is the length of the required test data sequence, will result, if the path p_i is not infeasible, in an input sequence of which the length will be at least equal to t_i^0. Indeed, thanks to the definition of Xn, every property ***not*** *(P* ***and*** *Xn)* will always be true during the first $n\text{-}1$ execution cycles. Hence, the counter-example provided by LESAR, if any, will be a sequence longer than $n\text{-}1$.

It must be noted that the verification tool LESAR is used here in a quite different manner than for its original purpose which is formal verification. Indeed, when a formal verification is performed, the entire automaton (i.e. all possible states) must be explored in order to prove that properties hold at every state. On the contrary, the operation of test data generation consists in searching a counter-example of the negation of the path predicate. This is usually a very short operation (unless, of course, the path predicate is infeasible). Thus, there is no contradiction in the use of a formal verification tool for testing purposes.

5 USING THE TOOL

The testing tool includes all the testing facilities described in the previous sections. In this section we present the parameters that the user should specify for each kind of testing. We also suggest a methodology for performing test in a progressive way.

Random testing requires the user to fix at least two parameters : the environment specification as a LUSTRE boolean expression and the software to test (executable form). Other optional parameters are the number and the length of the generated input sequences.

Specification-based testing also requires two parameters : the specification of the safety properties as LUSTRE boolean expressions and the software to test. The length and the number of the generated sequences can also be specified.

Finally, structure-based testing requires the user to specify the implementation in LUSTRE of the software to test. An executable version of the software is also required. Three mutually exclusive coverage types are available : operator, arc and path coverage. The required coverage rate can be selected (the default value is 100%). If path coverage is selected, the maximum length of the paths to cover can be specified.

For any of the three kinds of testing a test oracle can be specified. Moreover, it is possible to combine the environment specification (for example the one used for random testing) with the specification-based testing or the structure-based testing. When an environment specification is provided for this techniques, the generated test data will also satisfy this specification.

At the end of any of the above testing operations the test results are stored in a file. They are composed of structured sequences of the input and output values produced during the test operation. For each input and output value the result of the oracle (if any) is also stored. The user can browse these results by listing the entire result file, by selecting specific sequence numbers or by listing sequences for which the oracle (if any) has taken a given value.

The user can choose one or more of the testing facilities in any order. However, we suggest the following methodology :

First, the test oracle and the environment specification must be written out.

Then, constrained random testing should be performed in order to get confidence in the test oracle and the environment specification. Indeed, errors detected during this stage are often caused by a bad specification of the environment constraints or by an erroneous oracle. Random testing should continue until the user is confident enough in the correctness of environment and test oracle specification.

When no more errors are discovered by random testing, specification-based testing should be performed in order to detect discrepancies between the software behavior and the specification of the safety properties. The LUSTRE expression of the safety properties of the software must be written (unless they have already been expressed for the test oracle). The environment constraints and test oracle developed for random testing are also used during specification-based testing.

Finally, structure-based testing can be performed if an implementation in LUSTRE of the software is available. Structure-based testing is useful to track down implementation errors, not necessarily related to safety properties, since is it is based on a more precise specification of the software intended behavior (the LUSTRE program).

Note that the environment constraints can be omitted if the user is interested in the software behavior in cases when the environment does not respond correctly.

6 CONCLUSION AND FURTHER WORK

We have presented in this paper a testing tool dealing with synchronous reactive software. It provides a new formal framework for critical software validation, complementary to the current formal verification techniques which are often impracticable.

Several testing techniques have been proposed in the literature, generally for sequential programming languages (see for example (Ntafos, 1988) (Dauchy and Marre, 1991)). Just a few works have been conducted in the particular domain of reactive software; they are more concerned with a testing methodology than testing techniques per se (Richardson, 1992). The techniques we have designed are specific in the sense that they deal with synchronous reactive software. Indeed, for such software the environment behavior is extremely important. Moreover, software requirements are usually expressed by means of temporal properties. Thus, specific random testing and specification-based testing techniques have been devised to cope with these particularities. Equally specific is the structure-based testing technique which is adapted to data-flow languages.

It should be noted that the last of the three proposed techniques requires the software to be implemented in LUSTRE. On the contrary, constrained random testing and specification-based testing can be applied to reactive software implemented in any programming language. Indeed, although they both use LUSTRE for the description of the environment or for the expression of the safety properties, they do not require this particular programming language to be used for the software implementation.

The extension of the proposed techniques to software with numerical inputs and outputs is the main challenge for future work. Although many reactive software handle boolean signals, such an extension would allow to enlarge the application field of the tool.

Another interesting extension of the tool that we're currently studying is the introduction of reliability estimation features. This will allow to measure the software failure probability which is the main attribute of critical software quality.

Finally, more theoretical work is needed for comparing testing with formal verification according to the required memory and time amount and the resulting software quality.

7 ACKNOWLEDGMENTS

We would like to thank Pascal Raymond of Verimag for his contribution to the modification of the LUSTRE compiler and for adapting to our needs the binary decision diagram library.

8 REFERENCES

Akers, S. (1978). Binary Decision Diagrams. *IEEE Transactions on Computers*, C-27:509–516.

Atlee, J. and Gannon, J. (1993). State-Based Model Checking of Event-Driven System Requirements. *IEEE Transactions on Software Engineering*, pages 24–40.

Benveniste, A. and Berry, G. (1991). The synchronous approach to reactive and real-time systems. *Proceedings of the IEEE*, 79(9):1270–1282.

Bouajjani, A., Fernandez, J., and Halbwachs, N. (1990). Minimal model generation. In *Workshop on Computer-Aided Verification*, Rutgers (N.J.).

Boussinot, F. and De Simone, R. (1991). The Esterel language. *Proceedings of the IEEE*, 79(9):1293–1304.

Bryant, R. (1986). Graph-based algorithms for boolean functions manipulation. *IEEE Transactions on Computers*, pages 667–692.

Dauchy, P. and Marre, B. (1991). Test data selection from algebric specifications : application to an automatic subway module. In *3rd European Software Engineering Conference*, pages 80–100, Milan, Italy. Springer-Verlag L.N.C.S. 550.

Halbwachs, N., Caspi, P., Raymond, P., and Pilaud, D. (1991a). The Synchronous Data Flow Programming Language LUSTRE. *Proceedings of the IEEE*, 79(9):1305–1320.

Halbwachs, N., Lagnier, F., and Ratel, C. (1992). Programming and Verifying Real-Time Systems by Means of the Synchronous Data-Flow Programming Language LUSTRE. *IEEE Transactions on Software Engineering, Special Issue on the Specification and Analysis of Real-Time Systems*, pages 785–793.

Halbwachs, N., Raymond, P., and Ratel, C. (1991b). Generating efficient code from data-flow programs. In *Third International Symposium on Programming Language Implementation and Logic Programming*, Passau (Germany).

Ntafos, S. (1988). A comparison of some structural testing strategies. *IEEE Transactions on Software Engineering*, pages 868–874.

Ouabdesselam, F. and Parissis, I. (1994a). Testing Safety Properties of Synchronous Reactive Software. In *7th International Software Quality Week*, San Francisco, USA.

Ouabdesselam, F. and Parissis, I. (1994b). Testing Synchronous Critical Software. In *5th International Symposium on Software Reliability Engineering*, pages 239–248, Monterey, USA.

Pilaud, D. and Halbwachs, N. (1988). From a synchronous declarative language to a temporal logic dealing with multiform time. In *Symposium on Formal Techniques in Real Time and Fault Tolerant Systems*, Warwick. Springer Verlag.

Richardson, D. (1992). Specification-based Test Oracles for Reactive Systems. In *14th Int'l Conf.on Software Engineering*, pages 105–118, Melbourne, Australia.

9 BIOGRAPHY

I. Parissis received the D.E.S.S. en Génie Informatique (Master's degree in Software Engineering) from Université Joseph Fourier, Grenoble, France in 1990 and the D.E.A. en Informatique (Master's degree in Computer Science) from Institut National Polytechnique de Grenoble in 1993. He is currently a Ph.D candidate (under a grant of the French Ministry of Research). He holds a teaching assistantship at Université Joseph Fourier and a research assistantship at Laboratoire de Génie Informatique of the IMAG Institute. His research interests include software V&V, software testing and reliability and formal methods for the development of safety critical and synchronous software.

PART ELEVEN

Quality Measurement II

30

A Case Study in Branch Testing Automation

A. Bertolino, R. Mirandola °, E. Peciola†*

* *Istituto di Elaborazione della Informazione del CNR, Pisa, Italy.*
° *Laboratory for Computer Science, Università di Roma "Tor Vergata", Italy.*
† *Ericsson Telecomunicazioni S.P.A., Roma, Italy.*

Abstract

We present a real world experience with some recent research results aimed at improving the branch testing process. The results considered consist into (i) a method for the automatic derivation of sets of paths that satisfy the branch testing criterion and into (ii) a bound on the number of test paths needed for achieving 100% branch coverage. The derivation of test path sets (point i) is based on a new method for the static analysis of the program flowgraph; the method has been implemented within a prototype tool, called BAT. The computation of the bound (point ii), called β_{branch}, considers those control flow paths with a low number of predicates, that are more likely feasible. BAT and β_{branch}, have been validated on object oriented C++ software, developed to control a new generation of telecommunications systems, within the test environment of Ericsson Telecomunicazioni. The case study regarded the basic test phase, that is the first step of the testing process and is appropriate for the application of the proposed theory, since it includes the branch testing of program units up to a prescribed coverage measure. While the experimentation is still on-going, we describe some preliminary results.

Keywords

Branch coverage, ddgraph, infeasible path, statistical test, test path, unconstrained branches.

1. INTRODUCTION

Software testing (Beizer, 1990) consists in the validation of computer programs through the observation of a meaningful sample of executions chosen from the potentially infinite execution domain.

To select an adequate set of test cases, different strategies can be followed, based either on program specification or on program structure. Whatever strategy is selected, measures of structural coverage (Rapps and Weyuker, 1985) can be used to determine how thorough the executed test cases have been. In particular, branch coverage, which requires that each branch alternative in a program is exercised at least once, is commonly accepted as a "minimum mandatory testing requirement" (Beizer, 1990).

The branch testing process involves:

i) selecting a set of test cases trying to exercise every (as yet uncovered) program branch;
ii) executing the program on the selected test cases and monitoring the branches actually exercised;
iii) evaluating the ratio between the number of executed branches and the total number of branches in the program. If this ratio reaches a predefined threshold, the test is stopped; otherwise, more test cases must be devised: the process is repeated from step i).

In this procedure, steps ii) and iii) can be mechanised, and in fact several dynamic coverage analysers are today available that instrument the program and then can probe the exercised branches as the tests are executed. The first step, that clearly involves the largest part of the test effort, is instead left to the tester's skill and creativity.

In (Bertolino and Marré, 1994), a method has been proposed that can help the tester in this task. The method derives a set of test paths that will cover every arc in the program flowgraph. Then, the task of the tester to accomplish step i) would be "reduced" to that of finding a set of test inputs that execute the suggested paths. Since the paths are statically generated, they might inevitably include infeasible paths, i.e., control flow paths that are exercised by no input data. However, to reduce the incidence of this problem, the proposed method generates "simple" paths, i.e., paths that involve a low number of predicates. Indeed, the shorter a path is, the more likely it is that such path is feasible: this is not only intuitively true, but has also been demonstrated statistically (Yates and Malevris, 1988).

The algorithm exploited in the generation of the test paths has been shown to be correct and efficient in theory (Bertolino and Marré, 94). However, its practical usefulness has yet to be confirmed. In principle, the tester task should be made easier by having at disposal the "right" set of paths. In practice, the parameters involved in a real world test process are so many and so complex that only an empirical validation of the method can be trusted upon. In this paper we describe a real world case study with the test path generation method and illustrate some preliminary results.

The described case study involved another related research result, the β_{branch} bound (Bertolino and Marré, 95). Testing activities consume a considerable fraction of the time and resources spent to produce a software product; therefore it would be useful to have a way to estimate this testing effort. Indeed, knowing in advance how much effort will be needed to test a given program is essential to the manager to plan the software process.

Now, control flow analysis can be used also to predict the number of test cases needed to guarantee a particular structural coverage. In particular, the number of test paths needed to achieve branch coverage can be regarded as a measure of the minimum mandatory effort to test a given program, regardless of the particular strategy used in the selection of test data. So, it would be useful to be able to compute a lower bound on the number of test cases needed to achieve branch coverage. This number does not correspond to the theoretical minimum number of paths needed to cover the program flowgraph: to minimise the number of paths, in fact very long and complicated paths should be considered. On the contrary, in the computation of this bound those paths containing a low number of decisions should be considered, that are more likely feasible: each path should not enter different loops and, in case a path enters a loop, then it will be iterated just once.

Following this criterion, in (Bertolino and Marré, 1995) a number, called the β_{branch}, bound, has been proposed as a metric to predict the number of test cases needed to branch test a given program. In the case study described in this paper, we have validated the performance of β_{branch} on a number of program units that have been tested according to the branch testing strategy and for which the real number of executed test cases has been collected. Besides, since the cyclomatic number (McCabe, 1976) of the program flowgraph is often used as such a bound, we have performed the same analysis on this number for comparison.

In Section 2, we provide some theoretical background. In Section 3, the real world test environment used in the case study, that is that of Ericsson Telecomunicazioni, is presented. In Section 4, the experience and the results obtained up to this point are described. Finally, in Section 5 some conclusions and future developments are briefly sketched.

2. THEORETICAL BACKGROUND

In this section we provide a short background useful to understand a little more about the path generation method and the β_{branch} bound, which were the subjects of this case study. More extensive material can be found in (Bertolino and Marré, 1994) and (Bertolino and Marré, 1995), respectively.

2.1 Unconstrained arcs

A program structure is conveniently analysed by means of a directed graph, called *flowgraph*, that gives a graphical representation of the program control flow. A program control flow may be mapped onto a flowgraph in different ways. In our approach, we use a flowgraph representation called *ddgraph*, which is particularly suitable for the purposes of branch testing. Each arc in a ddgraph directly corresponds to a program branch; thus, program branch coverage is immediately measured in terms of ddgraph arc coverage.

The following is our definition of ddgraphs.

> **Definition 1:** *Ddgraph*
> A *ddgraph* is a digraph $G=(V, E)$ with two distinguished arcs e_0 and e_k (which are the unique entry arc and exit arc, respectively), such that any other arc in G is reached by e_0 and reaches e_k, and such that for each node n in V, $n \neq T(e_0)$, $n \neq H(e_k)$, (indegree(n) + outdegree(n)) > 2, while indegree(T(e_0))=0 and outdegree(T(e_0))=1, indegree(H(e_k))=1 and outdegree(H(e_k))=0.

Ddgraph arcs are associated to program branches. A branch is here defined as a strictly sequential set of program statements. Ddgraph's nodes may correspond to a branching or to a joining in the program control flow (which may be empty, i.e., not associated to any piece of code). An example of a ddgraph is shown in the upside window of figure 1.

We exploit the *dominance* relationship (Hecht, 1977) from the graph theory, which impose a partial ordering on the nodes of a digraph. By applying dominance, and its symmetric relationship of *implication* (elsewhere known as post-dominance), to the arcs of a ddgraph, we obtain two trees (whose nodes represent the ddgraph arcs), the *Dominator Tree* (*DT*(*G*))and the *Implied Tree* (*IT*(*G*)), rooted at e_0 and at e_k, respectively. The *DT*(*G*) and *IT*(*G*) for the ddgraph given in figure 1 are shown in figure 2.

Dominance and implication allow us to identify a subset of ddgraph arcs that is very useful for branch testing: the set of *unconstrained arcs* (Bertolino, 1993). The fundamental property of unconstrained arcs is that a path set that covers all the unconstrained arcs of a ddgraph also covers all the arcs in the ddgraph; besides, the unconstrained arcs form the minimum set of arcs with that property. This property has been proved in (Bertolino, 1993).

We can immediately find the set of unconstrained arcs by using the dominator tree and the implied tree of a ddgraph G. We can obtain the set $UE(G)$ of the unconstrained arcs of G as $DTL(G) \cap ITL(G)$, where $DTL(G)$ is the set of leaves of $DT(G)$ and $ITL(G)$ is the set of leaves of $IT(G)$. This can be seen in figure 2, where the unconstrained arcs for the ddgraph of figure 1 are those that are double-circled.

2.2 Generation of branch covering set of paths

A set of paths such that each branch in a program is covered by at least one path in the set is called a branch covering set of paths. On the ddgraph G of that program, the branch covering set of paths will correspond to a set of paths that covers every arc of G (note that, due to the infeasibility problem, the reverse is not necessarily true).

The algorithm FTPS (for FIND-A-TEST-PATH-SET) is a recursive algorithm that uses $DT(G)$ and $IT(G)$ to construct a set $\pi=\{P_1,...,P_n\}$ of paths that covers every arc of a given

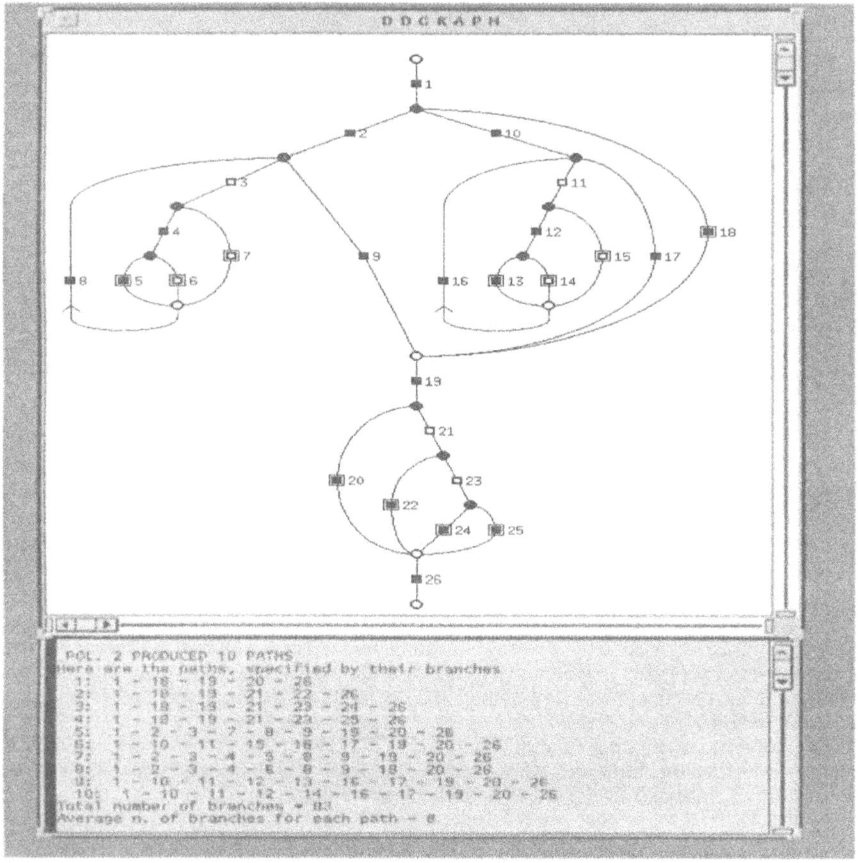

Figure 1 An example of a ddgraph.

ddgraph G . To do this, FTPS constructs a set of paths that covers all the unconstrained arcs of the ddgraph: the fundamental property of unconstrained arcs then guarantees that the path set found covers every arc.

Algorithm FTPS builds the set π of paths one path at a time. To construct each path, FTPS selects an as yet uncovered unconstrained arc e_u and then calls a recursive function FIND-A-PATH. This function constructs a path from e_0 to e_k, using arc e_u, simply by concatenating the unique path P_{DT} in $DT(G)$ from the root e_0 to the leaf e_u, with the unique path P_{IT} in $IT(G)$ from the leaf e_u to the root e_k.

The recursion is necessary since the sequence of arcs obtained by concatenating P_{DT} with P_{IT} might not be a proper path in G, because it might contain not adjacent arcs. Whenever two arcs e_i and e_j in the derived path are not adjacent arcs in G, the algorithm makes a recursive call to FIND-A-PATH and derives a path that joins the two arcs on an appropriately

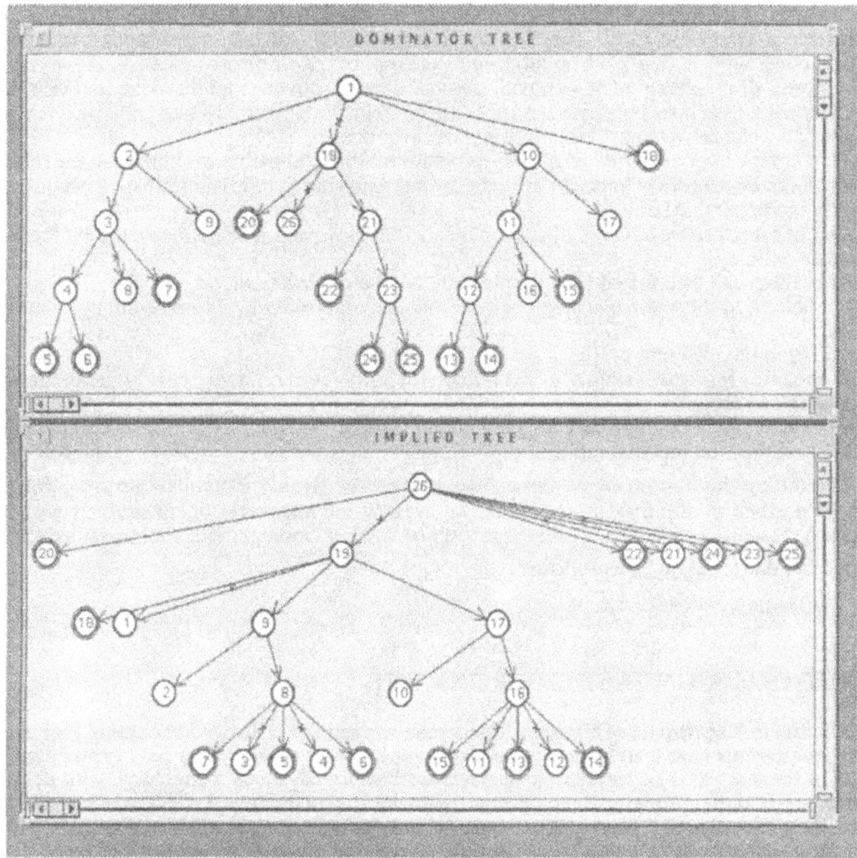

Figure 2 DT(G) and IT(G) for the ddgraph of figure 1.

derived sub-ddgraph. At each recursive iteration, another unconstrained arc e'_u must be selected: to reduce the generation of infeasible paths, the selection is made so that the resulting path will contain a low number of predicates. The paths found by the function FIND-A-PATH in this way may contain cycles (whenever an unconstrained arc within a cycle is selected) but, by construction, each cycle within each path will be iterated at most once.

Algorithm FTPS is implemented within the prototype tool BAT. Figure 1 and figure 2 are both printouts from BAT screens; in particular, in the bottom window of figure 1 the paths suggested by the tool BAT for branch testing the ddgraph in the same figure can be seen.

2.3 The β_{branch} bound

The β_{branch} bound provides a "meaningful lower bound" to the cardinality of a set of paths that is useful to guarantee branch coverage.

Let us first describe our approach intuitively: given a ddgraph $G=(V, E)$, we have seen that there exists a minimum set of arcs, the set UE of unconstrained arcs, which guarantees the coverage of every arc in G. Then, of course, the number of test cases needed to achieve branch coverage is $\leq |UE|$, where $|S|$ denotes the number of elements in a set S. However, for an arbitrary ddgraph, an entry-exit path may, in general, cover more than one unconstrained arc. Depending on how unconstrained arcs are combined together into one path, different sets of test paths can be obtained, with different cardinalities.

To combine unconstrained arcs so as to obtain meaningful paths, we introduce the relation of *weak incomparability* between arcs (Bertolino and Marré, 1995). Intuitively, two arcs are weakly incomparable if:

- either of them can be covered by a simple path, but they cannot be both covered by the same simple path, or
- one of them can be covered by a simple path, but the other cannot, or
- they belong to the same cycle and one reaches the other only by entering the cycle at least twice, or
- they belong to different cycles.

A meaningful path is thus a path that does not contain two weakly incomparable unconstrained arcs.

Obviously, for a ddgraph that does not contain cycles, two arcs are weakly incomparable if and only if they are incomparable.

Combining the notions of unconstrained arcs and of weakly incomparable arcs, β_{branch} can be defined as the maximum number of weakly incomparable unconstrained arcs in a ddgraph. Denoting by $LWI(UE)$ the largest set of weakly incomparable unconstrained arcs in G, we can define β_{branch} as follows:

$$\beta_{branch} = |LWI(UE)|.$$

3. THE ERICSSON TEST ENVIRONMENT

The Software Department of Ericsson Telecomunicazioni R&D decided about one year ago to start investments in research activity dealing with software testing, after having analysed the costs of the test phase of some projects developed using advanced technology, with iterative processes and incremental development. Considering a complete development process consisting of analysis, design, implementation and basic test, it was evaluated that the cost of basic test activity can be up to 2/3 of the total development cost (average cost of basic test of a method is inversely proportional to its amount of new or changed lines of code).

In addition, in projects with complicated test strategies and dependencies between different phases, it is a basic goal to pass milestones on schedule. The β_{branch} metric, related to the number of test paths needed to achieve 100% branch coverage, could have been a good support in the detailed estimation of expected effort of a basic test activity.

3.1 Project and methodology description

The project chosen for the case study is carried out by Ericsson Telecomunicazioni R&D in cooperation with the Headquarters in Stockholm and other Ericsson subsidiaries. It was one of the biggest projects developed in Europe using Object Oriented Technology and the first experience for Ericsson Telecomunicazioni. The project started in 1992, after a prototyping phase, and continued in overlapping development phases, with further functionalities added at each incremental step. Milestones were used to coordinate phases and steps.

The application developed in Rome consists of software controlling a synchronous triplicated switch matrix that is the core of a Digital Cross Connect System used for the new generation Transmission Network based upon the SDH technology. The software is designed following Object Oriented methodology and implemented in the C++ language using the SUN OS platform for both development and target environments.

A specific development process consisting of Analysis, Design, Implementation and Test, based on the ObjectOry methodology (Jacobson, 1992), was implemented for this project.

Due to the tough release plan from the customer, the software modelled at early phase could not be restructured and software units grew in size and complexity.

The real world testing process chosen for the case study is one step of the incremental development of this project. Analysis, design, implementation and test were performed.

3.2 Basic Test strategy

The test strategy for this project included four different test phases all of them supported by the methodology:

- Basic Test, testing the smallest module (test object) in the system. The goal is to verify design specification;
- Integration Test, testing a functional area. All modules involved in that area are integrated;
- Function Test, verifying system functions (use cases);
- System Test, verifying system performance and architectural requirements.

The basic test activity, which is the phase monitored in our case study, is a quite essential part of the testing phase: a poor basic test can never be compensated by other test activities.

The goal of basic test is to check the code against coding rules, design rules and design specification reaching a branch coverage greater then 80%. This minimum coverage range is a customer requirement. The TCAT tool (STW, 1991) is used to measure it.

The procedure used is the following: a test program is written; for each test case in the test program, input data are provided and produced output data are controlled against the expected results. Log files are produced in which the result of each test is registered. Stubs are used to simulate test object environment.

4 DESCRIPTION OF THE CASE STUDY

The objective of the case study was twofold:

1) to evaluate BAT effectiveness as a tool to improve the branch testing process. In particular, we are interested to validate the two specific aspects:
   1.a) providing the tester with a set of paths that guarantees 100% branch coverage can reduce the test effort;
   1.b) the paths derived by BAT are very likely feasible;

2) to evaluate the β_{branch} bound as a metric for the prediction of the test effort needed to obtain branch coverage.

Accordingly the case study has been conducted in two separate phases, that are described in the two following sections.

4.1 Evaluation of BAT effectiveness

In the planning of the case study, we found that the evaluation of BAT effectiveness is made difficult by the following two problems:

i) to be able to compare the testing with and without BAT, we would need to run two independent testing sessions on the same set of program units. However, if one same person is used to run both sessions, with and without BAT, of course the second session would benefit from the experience gained in the previous session, whichever of the cases is taken first. On the other side, if we use two different persons to run the two testing sessions separately, the experiment would be affected by the possible discrepancy between each tester's skill.

ii) Even admitting that we can overcome the above difficulty, for instance finding two perfectly equivalent testers, we are anyway faced with the problem that the program units that were tested are part of a real project, and so testing resources and schedule are constrained. This second difficulty resolved definitely (and negatively) the doubt whether the test of each program could be duplicated.

Before starting the testing phase, the biggest and most complex modules were selected to validate the BAT tool on them. Some adaptations were required to improve BAT performance.

Common feeling of all participants in this stage was that the tool could have been useful to fulfil the coverage requirement fixed by the customer, but if used after a first phase in which black box tests are run, derived from design specification.

Following this, the test strategy was defined. An expert tester and a beginner were chosen for the case study. Neither of them had performed coding of the modules they were going to test.

It was decided to execute the test phase according to the strategy described below:

- perform basic test in the traditional way based on test specification;
- evaluate test coverage;
- split randomly the set of program units that have not fulfilled the test coverage requirements into two groups: the STANDARD group, to be tested following the standard internal procedures, i.e., without the support of the BAT tool, and the BAT group, to be tested using the BAT tool. In particular, for the STANDARD group the tester tried manually to guess additional tests that would raise the coverage. For the BAT procedures, the tester tried to exercise the paths suggested by the tool. In both cases, the test is stopped when a given threshold of the average coverage for all the program units in a module is reached.

Modules to be tested were selected according to project priority at that time. The expert tester was planned to test two modules, the beginner performed the test of just one module. To avoid distortion of results, program units from the two groups had been alternatively tested, i.e., one from the STANDARD group and then one from the BAT group .

Identical criteria were followed in the collection of data for the tests executed with and without the tool. For each program unit: execution time, total number of executed segments and final coverage have been registered. The execution time was calculated excluding components not strictly dependent on test procedure as, e.g., compilation time or environment preparation.

The results collected up to this point do not allow us to draw significant statistical evaluations, as we could have expected given the problems i) and ii) above. We hope that adding many more results will allow us to overcome these problems. However, we can already derive some interesting conclusions.

- With regard to the use of BAT, we gained useful feedback to improve the tool interface and functionalities. More interestingly, we provided BAT with the option to suggest a set of paths that covers the branches as yet uncovered, which in practice provides a useful integration between BAT, that is static, with the dynamic coverage analyser.
- The experience with BAT confirmed the assumption that the paths derived by the tool are feasible with very good probability. All the paths suggested by the tool for the program units tested until now (cumulatively, about 60 paths for the BAT group) were feasible.
- The effectiveness of BAT is strongly affected by the tester's experience. In particular, we felt that a skilled tester can find BAT little useful, since he can derive the "right" paths immediately by his experience. In fact, an interesting observation was that, analysing the paths chosen by the expert tester for the program units in the STANDARD group, we saw, a posteriori, that he chose exactly the set of paths suggested by BAT. On the other hand, this can be considered a confirmation that BAT works fine.

  A not expert tester, instead, can find the tool useful: the beginner felt that for the program units tested with BAT he could work in a more productive way and that he could derive a lower number of test cases to reach the customer requirements. Unfortunately, the data collected up to now do not allow us to make quantitative observations on this point.

4.2 Evaluation of the β_{branch} bound

The β_{branch} bound, providing the number of complete paths needed to reach 100% branch coverage, was validated in the same test environment. The expected conclusion from the case study was that the bound is a good estimate of test effort to be used in project planning.

To this end, we have compared the theoretical (a priori) bound with the effective number of test cases used to test 55 program units. The comparison has been performed by considering both the absolute and the relative errors between the expected and the real number of test cases NT and by studying their empirical distribution. Specifically, the absolute error is given by:

$$\Delta\beta_{branch} = \beta_{branch} - NT$$

while the relative error by:

$$\varepsilon\beta = \Delta\beta_{branch} / NT$$

In order to evaluate the effectiveness of β_{branch}, we considered the relative error. Of the 55 program units considered, only 1 observation gave a relative error greater than 1. We thought that this only anomalous case could be discarded from the analysis without distorting the evaluation of results, since for all the other values the behaviour of the relative error was quite stable. From the data collected for the 54 program units analysed, we derived the histogram illustrated in figure 3. We divided the interval [-1, 1] in which the relative error was contained into 20 sub-intervals of width 0.1 and reported them on the X axis. In the Y axis we reported the number of observations within each sub-interval. As shown in figure 4, we have also derived the empirical distribution of the relative errors; i.e., the Y axis in figure 4, for each sub-interval, gives the ratio: (number of observed relative errors within the sub-interval)/(total number of observations). This ratio is the classic estimate for the probability distribution of the relative errors (Lavenberg, 1983). After the first 35 observations, we observed that the estimate for the probability distribution had reached the steady state.

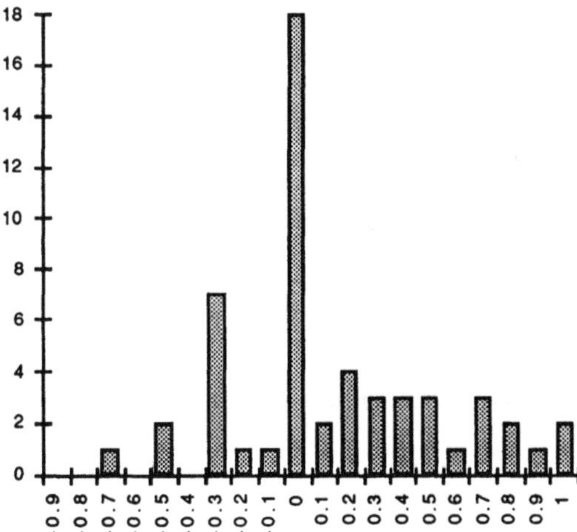

Figure 3 Observations of relative error $\varepsilon\beta$.

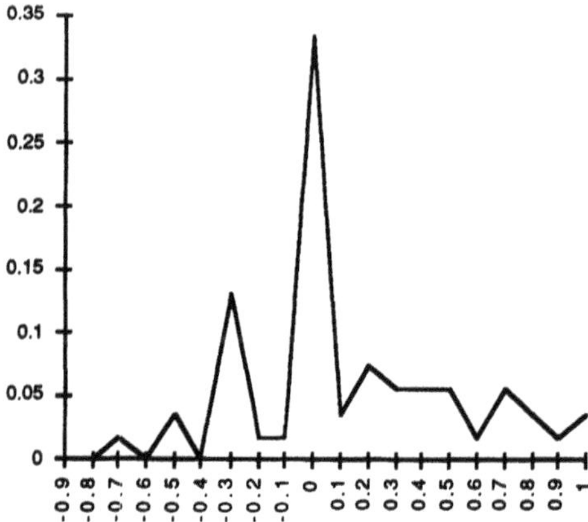

Figure 4 Empirical distribution of ε_β.

We have computed the sample mean and variance for the N=54 observations, which gave:

$$\overline{\varepsilon_\beta} = \Sigma_N \frac{\varepsilon_\beta}{N} = 0.12$$

$$s^2(\varepsilon_\beta) = \Sigma_N \frac{(\varepsilon_\beta - \overline{\varepsilon_\beta})^2}{N-1} = 0.15$$

The results confirm that the metric provides a good estimate for the test effort: 20 of the 54 observations (i.e., 37%) gave a relative error less than 10%. Let us observe that the β_{branch} predicts the number of test cases needed to reach a 100% branch coverage, while some of the tested program units reached a coverage from 80% up to 100%. Presumably, if all the program units achieved full coverage, the observed values of ε_β should be even closer to 0.

In order to generalise these results, we tried to identify a theoretical distribution underlying the empirical distribution. From figures 3 and 4, we observed that the behaviour of ε_β seems similar to that of a theoretical normal distribution. To validate this hypothesis, i.e., to check that the differences between the observed results and those relative to a normal distribution with mean $\lambda = \overline{\varepsilon_\beta}$ and with standard deviation $\sigma = \sqrt{s^2(\varepsilon_\beta)}$ are negligible, we applied the classical statistical tests χ^2 and Kolmogorov-Smirnov (Knuth, 1981). Both tests confirmed that the hypothesis was acceptable with the 94% of the confidence level.

Finally, we have compared these results with the predictions that would have been obtained by using the cyclomatic complexity (McCabe, 1976) of the program ddgraph. It is defined as:

$$\nu = |E| - |V| + 2$$

and is often used as a bound to the number of test cases needed to achieve branch coverage. In figure 5, the histogram obtained for *n* is shown. We have considered the same 54 observation used to validate the b_{branch} bound (also for ν the observation that was anomalous for β_{branch} bound gave a very high value of the relative error and was discarded). Again, 20 of the 54 observations (37%) gave a relative error less than 10%. However, of the remaining

34 observations, 8 laid outside the interval [-1, 1], and precisely between 1 and 2.67. The sample mean and variance gave respectively: 0.37 and 0.39. So, we can conclude that v is not as reliable as β_{branch} to estimate the test cases needed to achieve branch coverage. Besides, the empirical distribution for the relative error could not be approximated by a theoretical normal distribution as we have observed by applying the statistical test χ^2.

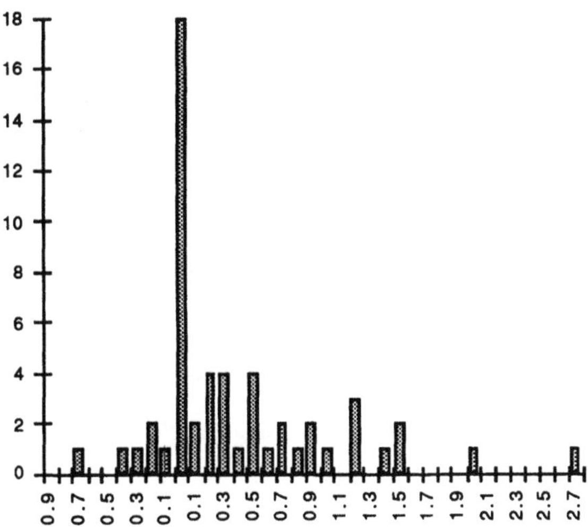

Figure 5 Observations of relative error ε_v.

5. CONCLUSIONS

We have described a real world case study aimed at evaluating a) the usefulness of a prototype tool that automatically derives a set of paths covering every branch in a program unit and b) the effectiveness of the β_{branch} bound in predicting the number of test cases needed to achieve 100% branch coverage.

For the first point we could only provide some preliminary evidence that the tool is actually useful, though only for not expert testers. Improving the automation of the basic test phase, however, was commonly felt as a positive innovation, since the testers find this phase quite tedious.

We are continuing the experimentation and we hope to be able to confirm the usefulness of the BAT tool in a more objective way. Anyway, the experience gained with the usage of the tool allowed us to make useful improvements to the tool interface and functionalities. Besides, we could confirm the effectiveness of the method used by the tool to generate the test paths, since all the paths suggested were feasible.

For the second point, the observed results confirmed that the β_{branch} bound provides a good estimate for the test effort: 20 of the 54 observations (37%) gave a relative error less than 10%. By applying classical statistical tests, we could also conclude that the empirical distribution of the relative error between the expected number of test cases and the observed number can be considered a normal distribution with λ=0.12 and σ^2=0.15 with the 94% of the confidence level.

ACKNOWLEDGEMENTS

The authors thank Andrea Baldanzi, Giorgio Morini and Giovanni My for their helpful support in the experimentation with the BAT tool.
They also wish to express their gratitude to Dr. Massimo De Sanctis, head of the Software Development Department of Ericsson Telecomunicazioni S.p.A., for his prompt availability to provide the test environment for the case study described in the paper.

REFERENCES

Beizer, B., *Software Testing Techniques, Second Edition*, Van Nostrand Reinhold, New York, 1990.
Bertolino, A., Unconstrained Edges and Their Application to Branch Analysis and Testing of Programs, *Journal of Systems and Software*, 20 (2), 125-133 (1993).
Bertolino, A. and Marrè, M., Automatic Generation of Path Covers Based on the Control Flow Analysis of Computer Programs, *IEEE Trans. on Software Engineering*, 20(12), 885-899 (1994).
Bertolino, A. and Marrè, M., How many paths are needed for branch testing?, to appear on*The Journal of Systems and Software* (1995).
Lavenberg, S.S., *Computer Performance Modelling Handbook*, Academic Press, New York, 1983.
McCabe, T. J., A Complexity Measure, *IEEE Trans. on Software Engineering*, SE 2 (4), 308-320 (1976}.
Hecht, M. S., *Flow Analysis of Computer Programs*, Elsevier, New York, 1977.
Jacobson, I., et al., *Object Oriented Software Engineering*, Addison-Wesley, 1992.
Knuth, E. D., *The Art of Computer Programming*, Vol. 2, Addison-Wesley, Reading, Massachusetts, 1981.
Rapps, S. and Weyuker, E. J., Selecting Software Test Data Using Data Flow Information, *IEEE Trans. on Software Engineering*, SE-11 (4), 367-375 (1985).
STW, Software TestWorks, Test Coverage Tools: TCAT, S-TCAT, TCAT-PATH, T-SCOPE., SR Software Research, Inc., San Francisco, 1991.
Yates, D. F. and Malevris, N., Reducing the Effects of Infeasible Paths in Branch Testing, *ACM SIGSOFT Software Engineering Notes*, 14 (8), 48-54 (1989).

Antonia Bertolino graduated cum laude in Electronic Engineering at the University of Pisa. Since 1986 she has been a researcher of the Italian National Research Council (CNR) in Pisa. Her research interests are in testing theory and techniques and in testing automation. She is an Associate Editor of the Journal of Systems and Software.

Raffaela Mirandola received the Laurea degree in Computer Science from the University of Pisa and Ph.D. degree in Computer Science from the University of Rome Tor Vergata. Her main research interests are in the areas of modelling, validation and performance evaluation of computer and communication systems.

Emilia Peciola graduated in Computer Science at the University of Pisa. She has been working in Ericsson Telecomunnication since 1985, involved in software development for telecommunication systems. Since 1993 she has been working in R&D as section manager of Object Oriented software developed for new telecommunication systems.

A Method for Software Evaluation with respect to Quality Standards

Dieter Welzel and Hans-Ludwig Hausen
GMD
53754 Sankt Augustin, Germany. Telephone: +49 2241 14-3224. Fax: +49 2241 14-3006. email: welzel@gmd.de

Abstract

Based on a set of case studies in eight European countries a method of software evaluation has been designed within ESPRIT Project SCOPE (Software CertificatiOn Programme Europe). This method deals with several types of information: software characteristics and metrics, product and process information, and evaluation techniques. In order to be applicable, the method is supported by a five step procedure which analyses the quality requirements, specifies, designs and conducts the evaluation, and finally, reports on the collection of all documents produced in an evaluation report. The thoroughness of software evaluation is expressed by evaluation levels; encapsulations of evaluation techniques, in order to measure a quality attribute and manage the whole process more easily, are described by evaluation modules. Two guides have been produced and have been submitted to the responsible ISO/IEC JTC1 sub-committee for review and inclusion in normative documents being developed for the application of ISO/IEC 9126. As terminology standards IEEE 610 and ISO 8402 were taken into consideration.This method proposed can work with customised models as well as with standards.

Keywords

software evaluation, requirements for quality, software characteristics, software metrics, evaluation techniques, verification and validation

1 INTRODUCTION

Quality of IT products is a key element of the European software industry. To be able to assess software a practical but well-founded method for software evaluation is required. With a repeatable and unbiased evaluation the quality can be improved and the productivity of the software development process can be increased. The method to be applied has to conform with international standards and to contribute to the work of the national, European and International standardisation bodies. Therefore, the ESPRIT Project SCOPE (Software CertificatiOn Programme Europe) was launched in 1989 in order to:

Table 1 Objectives stated in ISO/IEC Guide 25

Repeatability	Repeated evaluation of the same product to the same evaluation specification by the same testing laboratory gives the same result.
Reproducibility	Repeated evaluation of the same product to the same evaluation specification by different testing laboratories gives the same result.
Impartiality	Evaluation is free from unfair bias towards achieving any particular result.
Objectivity	The evaluation result is obtained with the minimum of subjective judgment.

- develop and experiment with an evaluation procedure, that is both technically well defined and cost effective,
- promote the use of modern software engineering technology for use in software evaluation and certification, and finally to
- contribute to the improvement of the European software industry.

The SCOPE consortium consisted of partners from eight European countries: Denmark, Finland, France, Germany, Ireland, Italy, Spain and the United Kingdom. The partners came from academic institutes as well as from industry. The consortium brought in European state-of-the-art technology used by software houses and testing laboratories. The project ended in June 1993 (SCOPE Consortium, 1993).

2 REQUIREMENTS FOR EVALUATION

In order to achieve the objectives of SCOPE an evaluation method was designed and applied in several case studies. The evaluation method was further refined and validated in two waves of case studies. Experimentation profited from 27 case studies in eight European countries. The procedure proposed may be applied in connection with:

- first party evaluation, i. e. internal product evaluation,
- second party evaluation, i. e. acceptance evaluation on product delivery, or
- third party evaluation, i. e. independent evaluation by, for example, a testing laboratory.

In order to develop an applicable practical evaluation procedure further objectives stated in (ISO/IEC Guide 25, 1990) have been considered (see table 1).

At the beginning of the project there was no complete description for an evaluation. Therefore, several approaches had to have a strong impact in the development of the method. The approach of GQM (Goal/Question/Metric (Basili and Rombach, 1988) supports the finding of metrics. Guidance techniques for this have been developed in the ESPRIT projects AIM and PYRAMIDE. Combined with a multi-level scheme for quality assessment (Hausen, 1989) the specifying of product-based quality models can be described. For describing the evaluation techniques to be applied in order to measure the software product or part of it a knowledge-based approach (Neusser and Hausen, 1989) was adopted, where both the features of a technique and the invocation of related methods and tools are defined in terms of production rules.

3 OBJECT OF EVALUATION

In order to perform an evaluation several types of information have to be distinguished and used in an evaluation procedure: software characteristics & metrics, product information, process information, and evaluation techniques.

Each information type is described separately in a model. The characteristics of a software product as well as of its software development process and the attached metrics define the quality model. For the software characteristics the six characteristics of (ISO/IEC 9126, 1991) are referred. They are functionality, reliability, usability, efficiency, maintainability and portability. Product and process information is defined by an information model. Requirements specification, system specification, programs or handbooks are all examples for documents containing product information; management report, quality assurance report or project file are examples for documents containing process information. The techniques and tools model embraces the evaluation techniques and tools that are to be used to evaluate software attributes. Evaluation techniques contain verification methods, validation techniques, measurement procedures and assessment methods.

Thus, an evaluation process is defined by the identified relationships between the different models. In order to reduce the variety of evaluation and to achieve a reasonable evaluation procedure standardised descriptions of the information types can either be selected or have to be developed.

Which software characteristics and metrics are evaluated is a decision of the product provider who engages, for example, a testing laboratory. To support the identification of the metrics is a fundamental concern and the first step of each evaluation. This is the reason why the method proposed is called metric-based. Two basic concepts have been developed to simplify the evaluation: the evaluation levels and the evaluation modules.

4 EVALUATION LEVELS

Evaluation levels express the thoroughness of the evaluation in terms of the evaluation techniques to be applied. Each technique determines metrics and measurements. The specification of metrics selection is supported by three steps. Environmental, personal and economic aspects of the product to be evaluated give a first selection of an evaluation level (see table 2). There are four levels where D is the lowest level and A is the highest level.

Table 3 shows to which level the evaluation techniques are attached. The '+' notation in the table indicates the additional techniques when moving to a higher level. The next step requires the agreement on the metrics and their values. The required threshold value can be defined by using table 4. Generally, the contents of all tables are not fixed. They were developed by the industrial partners of SCOPE. But before an evaluation is started, the tables should be fixed and be the subject of a contract between the provider and the testing laboratory. Product-based standardised tables will simplify the process of identifying the quality requirements.

Table 2 Guideline for selecting an evaluation level

Level	Environment	Person	Economic	Application
D	small damage to property	no risk to people	negligible economic loss	entertainment, household
C	damage to property	few people disabled	significant economic loss	fire alarm, process control
B	recoverable environmental damage	threat to human lives	large economic loss	medical systems, financial systems
A	Unrecoverable environmental damage	many people killed	financial disaster	railway systems, nuclear systems

Table 3 Guideline for selecting evaluation techniques

	Level D	Level C	Level B	Level A
Functionality	functional testing (black box)	+ inspection of documents (check lists)	+ component testing (white box)	+ formal proof
Reliability	programming language facilities	+ fault tolerance analysis	+ reliability growth model	+ formal proof
Usability	user interface inspection	+ conformity to interface standards	+ laboratory testing	+ user mental model
Efficiency	execution time measurement	+ benchmark testing	+ algorithmic complexity	+ performance profiling analysis
Maintainability	inspection of documents (check lists)	+ static analysis	+ analysis of development process	+ traceability evaluation
Portability	analysis of installation	+ conformity to programming rules	+ environment constraints evaluation	+ program design evaluation

5 EVALUATION MODULES

The concept of an evaluation module was introduced to support the structuredness and manageability for the whole process. Without an appropriate structure evaluation would quickly become intractable, unwieldy and complex. Therefore, a well-structured, encapsulated description of software characteristics and the metrics and evaluation techniques attached to them had to be identified. Such a description lists the evaluation techniques applicable for software characteristics and names the product and process information required. It also defines the evaluation procedure and the format for reporting the results of applying the metrics and techniques. In addition the information necessary for an estimation of the costs is provided.

Thus, an evaluation module encapsulates

Table 4 Guideline for selecting metrics

level	technique	threshold metric	threshold value
...	...	...	...
A	white box testing	statement coverage	100 %
		branch coverage	95 %
		...	...
		condition coverage	90 %
		expression coverage	90 %
B	white box testing	statement coverage	95 %
		branch coverage	90 %
		...	...
		condition coverage	85 %
		expression coverage	85 %
C	white box testing	statement coverage	91 %
		branch coverage	85 %
		...	...
		condition coverage	not necessary %
		expression coverage	not necessary %
D	white box testing	statement coverage	85 %
		branch coverage	80 %
		...	...
		condition coverage	not necessary %
		expression coverage	not necessary %
...	...	...	...

- the definition of one or more atomic evaluation procedures applied to the product or process information in order to measure software characteristics or sub-characteristics,
- the attachment of metrics and evaluation levels to those characteristics, - the description of the assessment procedure to be applied,
- the format for reporting the results and cost figures.

In other words an evaluation module also contains, beside the information needed, the way of how measurements can be performed on (parts of) the software product. An example of an evaluation module is given in (Hausen and Welzel, 1993b, Annex) and an example in table 5.

6 STEPS OF EVALUATION

As an example of the evaluation method proposed a five step procedure was designed within the SCOPE project. The intended use of the procedure is for actually running an evaluation (including case studies). The view of an independent testing laboratory is taken. The procedure describes the activities carried out by the testing laboratory and the interaction between the testing laboratory and the client (e. g. producer, distributor,

Table 5 Example of an Evaluation Module

EM Requirements	
scope of application:	'off-the-shelf' end-user software products
software characteristic:	ISO/IEC 9126 Usability
evaluation level:	Level D
evaluation technique:	Inspection by checklist
EM Specification	
sub-characteristics:	installability-from-scratch (INST), learnability (LRN), use-efficiency (UE), customisability of interface by the user (CUS), experienced-user-migration-ease (UME)
metrics attached to sub-characteristics:	

Metric ID.: 1.11	*related to*: INST, UME
selection constraint: new directories are automatically created	
Metric	*Value*
IF new directories are automatically created, is the user informed?	yes, in all cases – > 2 no, in all cases – > 0

aggregation of metrics:	total number of 'points' per sub-characteristic
EM Application Procedure	
how to get the information to be able to answer the questions	
EM Application Report	
document the evaluation procedure, collect all measurements and assessment results, prepare a cost report	

buyer, or user). The client is the person or institution who negotiates the evaluation specifications with the testing laboratory.

Figure 1 provides an overview. It describes the sources of input for the evaluation and the steps of the evaluation procedure.

6.1 Analysing Evaluation Requirements

The evaluation requirements are formal records of the agreement between client and testing laboratory of what has to be achieved by the evaluation process. It provides a nominal list of software characteristics which are to be evaluated at which evaluation level and identifies the source of data and evidence which might be used in the evaluation process. Software characteristics may be functionality, reliability, usability, efficiency, maintainability, portability (from ISO/IEC 9126).

6.2 Specifying the Evaluation

The evaluation specification contains the more formal description of the evaluation requirements. It includes available documents identified and received items classified into product, process and (for the evaluation process) supportive information. The classification makes use of an information model which identifies the types of information needed for an evaluation (compare figure 2).

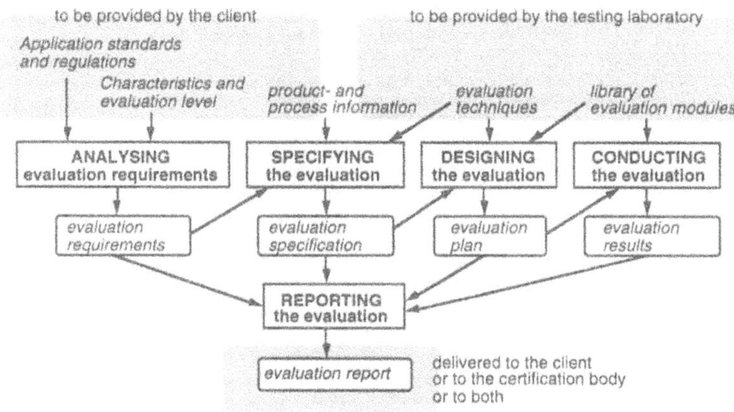

Figure 1 The Evaluation Procedure

The analysis of the product comprises two phases:

- identification of the product, and
- classification of the received items into product, process, and supportive information.

In the identification phase the following should be considered:

- document identifier
- document title
- condition of document (physical appearance, abnormalities)
- date of receipt
- legal implication of document handling (document security, confidentiality)

In the classification phase the items received are classified into the following:

- product information
- process information, and
- supportive information.

It is not required that the structure of the documentation received exactly follows the information model, but it must be possible to identify and extract the required information from the material received.The information model covers the development of a complete system which may include both hardware and software, but only the software part is subject for evaluation. In general, not all types of information are required for an evaluation. The required information depends on the selected characteristics and the corresponding evaluation levels.

The specification of the evaluation should be organised according to the quality char-

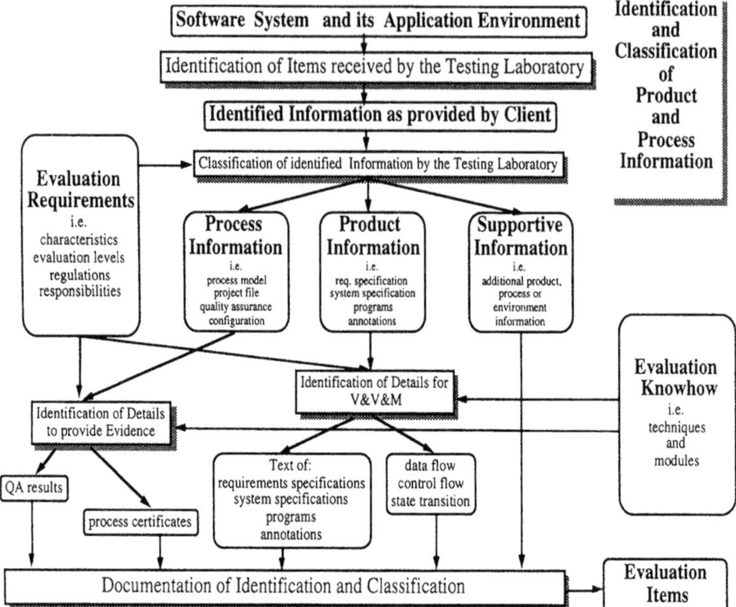

Figure 2 Specifying the Evaluation

acteristics, in this case the characteristics of ISO/IEC 9126. The evaluation specification associated with each characteristic must be formulated as a combination of the following types of statements:

- an exact reference to statements in a requirement specification document, user manual, or possibly other information, which should specify the program requirements that are to be evaluated,
- a statement about the software product which is either missing in the program specification or needs to be explained more carefully for the evaluation
- an exact reference to statements in identified standards and in regulations documents where additional program requirements are given which should also be included in the evaluation specification.

Only functional and non-functional requirements mentioned or referred to in the specification are subjects for evaluation. Therefore the evaluation specification must be detailed and complete.

Based on the classified items and the evaluation level a first feasibility study can be performed.

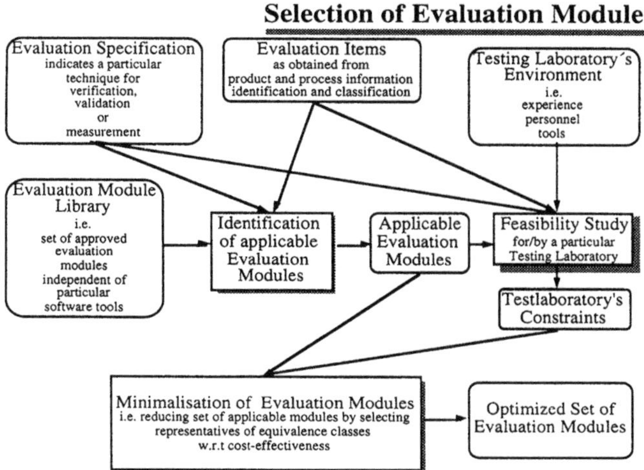

Figure 3 Selection of Evaluation Modules

6.3 Designing the Evaluation

In the design step the evaluation modules are selected from the evaluation module library. The selecting process is implied by two criteria:

- the module must be known and recognised to be useful in the evaluation of the characteristic for which it is to be used,
- the module must be applicable to the product part on which it is to be used.

However, this set of modules may not be optimal for carrying out the evaluation. Some modules may be redundant and some may be missing. It must be decided whether new modules should be developed or whether missing modules can be substituted by a combination of existing modules. The purpose is to make the final planning of these modules for the evaluation. The planning must be done in order to optimise the coverage of and the cost of conducting the evaluation.

The optimised set of modules requires product, process and perhaps supportive information as imposed by their input interface. So a refinement and adoption step may be necessary to relate the information needed by the modules to the items identified by the application of the information model.

The evaluation plan includes a list of modules to be applied. Each evaluation module includes information from which the cost of its application can be derived. Hence, it is possible to give a fairly good estimate of the cost of conducting the evaluation at this point.

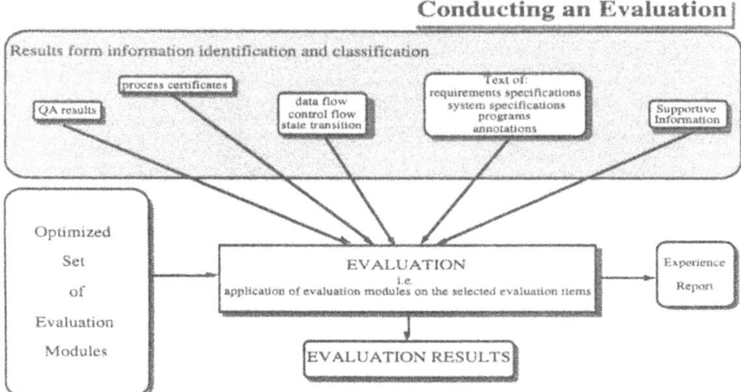

Figure 4 Conducting an Evaluation

6.4 Conducting the evaluation

Conducting the evaluation then comprises the application of the set of optimised evaluation modules on the related documents and collecting for each of them the results of validation, verification, measurement and assessment.

Measurements can be manual, computer aided (e.g. using a check list manager for applying check-lists), or automatic (e.g. measuring complexity in a source code component using a static analyser).

The main task is to collect the measurement result and also to keep any information about the measured product part that could be helpful for an acceptance decision.

The selected evaluation modules are applied according to the schedule given in the plan. The results of applying the individual modules are recorded in the evaluation report. Observations made during the process also have to be included in the evaluation report.

The application of an evaluation module comprises three steps:

- measurement according to metrics identified by the module,
- assessment by comparing measurement results with the acceptance criteria,
- recording the measurements results and results of the assessment.

Depending on the results of evaluation modules an aggregation of the module results is necessary.

6.5 Reporting the Evaluation

The final step of the evaluation is that of producing the evaluation report. The table of contents of the report follows the steps described above, and each of the steps are documented during the evaluation process.

The following table of contents is suggested for the report:

1. Preface - identification of producer and evaluator
2. Evaluation requirements - product overview, quality characteristics, evaluation level
3. Evaluation specification - identification and classification of items, detailed specification
4. Evaluation plan - selected evaluation modules, evaluation process planning
5. Evaluation results - results of applying evaluation modules
6. Conclusion of the evaluation results - including signature, responsibilities, limits of results, distribution of report

7 CASE STUDIES

The SCOPE project used 30% of its total effort to conduct case studies. This was in order to gain practical experience with the evaluation procedure produced, and also to ensure that the approach can be applied in practice. The case studies were conducted in two phases. In the first phase six case studies were carried out in an experimental fashion. They tried out different approaches to software evaluation together with different evaluation techniques. The case studies of this phase were selected based on their availability and not on any particular selection criteria. The experiences from these evaluation experiments were carefully analysed. The result of the exercise was a stepwise procedure for conducting an evaluation.

In the second phase 21 case studies were carried out. The main objective was to demonstrate the practical feasibility of the evaluation method proposed as described in the procedure. To achieve this the case studies were selected according to different criteria:

- They should be concerned with products representative of those most likely to be in need of evaluation and certification.
- Evaluation techniques, application areas, and fields of software engineering should be well covered.
- The evaluation procedure should be tested to demonstrate that it is practical and robust.

As a consequence of this careful selection process, the resulting set of case studies covered a wide range of applications including administrative and technical systems, software tools, communications protocols, and embedded systems, see table 6. In addition a wide range of commonly applied development approaches was covered. This included standard third generation life-cycles, prototypes and systems developed in 4GL. The trial evaluations covered the quality characteristics defined in ISO/IEC 9126 with a focus on functionality, maintainability, and usability. Most evaluations were at the low to medium level of stringency. That is, most case studies conducted evaluation at the C and D levels and only a few at the B and A levels. The actual distribution of case studies on levels and characteristics is shown in table 7 which reflects the actual demand of the case study providers for thoroughness of the particular evaluation.

A number of different evaluation modules were tried out. 19 out of 21 case studies used checklist-based evaluation modules. They are applicable in most cases, easy to use and very flexible. Static analysis tools were applied in 11 case studies. It is not always possible

Table 6 Case Study Application Areas

Case study product application include:	
Process control	Accounting
Electronic mail	Traffic control
Medical Application	Stock management
Phone exchange	Operating systems
Desktop publishing	Management info system
Electronic point of sale	Process monitoring
Picture generation	Message handling
Image processing	Graphical analysis
Fire alarm	

Table 7 Distribution of Case Studies on Levels and Characteristics

	Level	D Level	C Level B	Level A
Functionality	4	13	1	(1)
Reliability		1		
Usability	7	6		
Efficiency				
Maintainability	2	13	1	
Portability	3	2		

to apply such tools, but when it is possible they are thorough and efficient. A variety of other evaluation techniques were used in 7 case studies. These techniques, which often require specific application support, include Petri net analysis of software specifications and reliability modeling. An overview of evaluation techniques and evaluation modules applied in the case studies is given in table 8.

The main objective of the second phase case studies was to allow the collection of practical experiences with the evaluation procedure, and to ensure that the approach is applicable in practice. This was indeed the main conclusion in most of the case studies, each of which gave feedback on many aspects of the evaluation procedure. They identified points with a need for refinement of the procedure. These refinements were then implemented in the procedure. The efficiency and effectiveness of the evaluation method was assessed by monitoring the effort incurred from applying the evaluation modules as well as their impact on the result of the evaluation. All evaluation modules were tried out in one or more of the studies. In conclusion, the case studies successfully achieved their goals.

Essentially all the case study providers were very positive towards the evaluation process, the results, and the experience they had gained through their participation. The case studies showed that it is feasible to carry out software product evaluation according the procedure proposed.

Table 8 Evaluation Techniques and Evaluation Modules used in Case Studies

Evaluation techniques applied	Evaluation modules applied
Checklists used in 19 case studies - easy to use - subjective results - applicable in most cases	*checklists used to asses* Requirements (5 Modules), Design (9), Source code (16), Test documentation (5), User manual (10), Safety/security aspects (8)
Static analysis tools used in 11 case studies - efficient and thorough - meaning of measurement - value not clear - application not always possible	*Static and dynamic analysis* - application of Logiscope and QUALMS - measurement of structural parameters - measurement of test coverage
Other techniques used in 7 case studies - inspection, interviews, tools - each applied in one case study - application support necessary	*Petrinet Analysis* - application of Design/CPN *Reliability Analysis* - application of SW reliability modeling programs

8 RESULTS OF THE CASE STUDIES

It is reasonable to expect that the software products evaluated in the case studies were representatives of the high quality part of the software available on the market. However only about half of the evaluated products successfully passed the acceptance criteria. Many of the products had a pronounced lack of quality. Often documents necessary for the evaluation were completely missing or the contents were clearly unsatisfactory. Obtaining design documentation was especially difficult in many case studies. Other problems encountered were missing functionality and omissions in general.

These case studies which worked with their own reduced version of the evaluation procedure asked for more details and for objective decision support. Therefore it was decided to include all possible details into the an evaluator's guide.

The application of the evaluation modules also resulted in many comments. Checklist based evaluation modules were most popular in the case studies and consequently most experiences were accumulated for these evaluation modules. One conclusion was that if checklists are carefully designed with thorough explanations to each question and if the checklist includes at least 25-30 questions, then the subjectivity involved in this evaluation technique is within acceptable limits.

Static analysis techniques were experimented with in half of the case studies. This technique gives objective measures but their interpretation was considered as being difficult. However, the evaluation modules applying these techniques were very efficient for identifying program modules containing problems.

The evaluation modules applied in the case studies were not developed and documented in a common way. This resulted in confusion and misunderstandings which could have been avoided. Therefore the need for a guideline for producing evaluation modules became evident.

This ultimately led to the presentation of the guide that describes how to design, produce and maintain an evaluation module. The procedure of developing an evaluation module comprises five steps. After analysing the requirements of the module to be developed (step one) the module is to be specified (step two). The writing of the module (step three) has to follow the required evaluation module structure. A validation of the module (step four) ensures the fulfillment of its requirements . Validation comprises both a technical review to ensure that the module represents state-of-the-art and practical trials on real software products to ensure the modules' applicability in practice. Finally, the module has to be embedded into the Evaluation Module Library (step five).

The case studies stated the need of storing the experience gained in a data base in order to make them available for further investigations which could lead to an improvement of evaluation procedures or particular techniques. In order to achieve an effective evaluation process it is necessary to reflect experience gained with evaluation modules and the module library, appropriateness of levels and software characteristics, appropriateness of product representation, appropriateness of process representation, calculation of actual costs in order to improve cost estimates, appropriateness of the evaluation method.

The case studies have shown that the evaluation procedure can already be used in a wide range of contexts such as:

- *Product Certification:* Software product certification can be defined and performed in compliance with the various standards and constraints using a fully defined evaluation procedure.
- *Independent Evaluation:* Software product evaluation can be performed by an independent testing laboratory according to the Evaluator's Guide.
- *Acceptance Testing:* Departments in charge of performing acceptance testing of delivered software products could use the Evaluator's Guide to assist them when specifying and organising their activity.
- *Contractual Requirements:* Specifying a software to be subcontracted could be complemented by the technical quality requirements to be met and by appending the set of Evaluation Modules to be used for the final acceptance testing.
- *Product Ranking:* The comparison of two software products regarding quality can be performed by comparing how they behave against the results of a fixed and repeatable evaluation procedure such as the one developed.

One of the most important aspects of the resulting technology is its potential ability to adapt to the ever changing world of software engineering. Among the various foreseeable changes, we have considered, for instance

- *Evaluation Tools:* As the evaluation activity grows and matures, many new supporting (software) tools and products will appear, the integration of which within our framework will have to be as straightforward as possible while still preserving the know-how of the parties involved,
- *Evaluation Techniques:* Similarly, the overall evaluation technology itself will progress, while, hopefully, not making the fundamental results of the task obsolete,
- *Development Technology:* The need to be able to adapt to ever more programming languages or environments has been a constant driver to the design of the documents as for instance, the Evaluation Modules and their structures illustrate,

- *Harmonisation with Other Fields:* The search for quality is one of the major drivers of a lot of work in the software fields. Security and safety domains become more and more important. Thus, we must keep an eye on future harmonisation and convergence.

With this flexibility the circumstances of any testing laboratory can be taken into consideration. The testing laboratory can find out which kind of software evaluation it can offer.

What are the final conclusion form the case studies? First, an evaluation by improper qualified personnel, immature methods and without the Evaluator's Guide (or a similar guidance) produce results which are not useful for management. Therefore, both a certified procedure and a certified staff are required. Secondly, most of the evaluation tools available were immature because, amongst other difficulties, different tools produced different results for the same metric. This shows the need for well-instrumented metrics and measurements. Consequently, metrics and measurements have to be standardised. Product-type specific metrics are needed. Finally the integration of the evaluation procedure into software engineering process models (such as VORGEHENSMODELL, SSADM, MERISE) is considered as being necessary to ensure at quality assurance.

9 STANDARDISATION OF THE METHOD

With the five step procedure guidance is provided on what has to be done, how the work has to be carried out and how it has to be documented. The procedure supports planning, designing and controlling of an evaluation process tailored to specific circumstances. To help the evaluator two guides have been produced (Hausen and Welzel,1993b, and ISO/IEC 9126: Guides to software evaluation, 1993) that have been submitted to ISO/IEC JTC1/SC7 "Software Engineering" for review in WG 6 "Evaluation and Metrics" (Begh et al., 1993). They are parts of normative documents currently being produced for the practical application of the International standard (ISO/IEC 9126, 1991). They are dedicated to particular aspects:

- an Evaluator's Guide (EG), which describe the five-step procedure.
- a Guide to Developing, Documenting and Validating an Evaluation Module (GDDV), which describes how to design, create and maintain an evaluation module.

The evaluation process is defined using the EG and applies evaluation modules which are developed and documented according to the GDDV.

Although the present guides explicitly refer to ISO/IEC 9126 similar quality models can be applied without severe changes to the underlying evaluation procedure.

Figure 5 shows how the Evaluators Guide and the Evaluation Module Development Guide fit into the set of guides being discussed in ISO/IEC JTC1/SC7/WG6.

To demonstrate an application of the Evaluation Module Development Guide, an example of an evaluation module, which defines usability evaluation, was formatted along the proposed evaluation module structure and was included in the guide (Hausen and Welzel, 1993b, part 2).

Circulation of the guides through ISO/IEC provides a world-wide audience which could not have otherwise been reached. It also increases the awareness of the concept of third

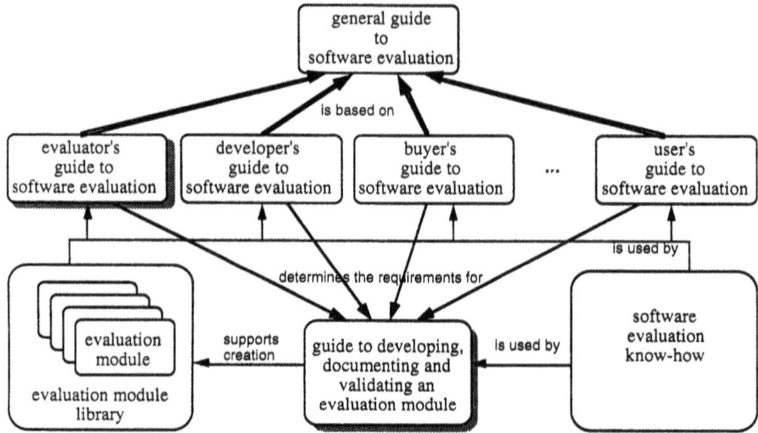

Figure 5 Guides supporting the Evaluation Method

party software evaluation and hopefully also the demand for this service similar to the situation of the ISO 9000 series of quality management standards.

10 PERSPECTIVES

The results supporting the evaluation process and the development of high quality evaluation modules, have been made available to both industry and academia. European as well as non-European industry have expressed much interest, especially in the method. Some small and medium enterprises as well as some large system integrators have adopted or are about to restructure their quality assurance with respect to the method developed. In addition, academia are considering other results, such as the way of modeling products, process and quality, for inclusion in educational circles and further research projects.

Based on the experience gained in the SCOPE project DELTA has implemented a commercial evaluation service, MicroScope, which is an instantiation of a subset of the Evaluator's Guide. The MicroScope approach (Kyster, 1993) follows closely the evaluation procedure as described, but a full set of evaluation modules is not yet available for commercial use. Therefore, commercial evaluations can only be offered for some combinations of quality characteristics and evaluation levels.

At the moment several organisations in Europe are setting up a network of testing laboratories offering harmonised software product evaluations according to ISO standards viz. the Evaluator's Guide. Feedback from the case studies showed that the software industry accepted the software evaluation concept. Furthermore the need for a certification scheme based on an approach like the Evaluator's Guide has been expressed. Such a scheme is expected to be implemented in the near future.

The evaluation method itself is specified by production rules (Hausen and Welzel,

1993a). Such a (semi-) formal description improves the possibility of using the computer itself to automate (or to assist a human in performing) some of the tasks associated with the process. Therefore, in addition, a concept of an advisory system has been designed (Hausen, 1992).

The rule-base specification allows a translation to PROLOG predicates in order to validate the evaluation method itself and to run a software evaluation. For efficiency reasons this might be implemented into an object-oriented software engineering data base system, such as the European Portable Common Tool Environment PCTE (ECMA standard 149, 1991). A feasibility study has shown that this can be achieved.

The usage of the evaluation method within a software development project is more highlighted in (Welzel and Hausen, 1994) and (Welzel, 1993). The effects to the organisational regulations of the project as well as of the whole company are still under research. The installation of the method has already contributed to process improvement (business re-engineering).

For specifying the Quality of Service (QoS) - network service - the techniques of this evaluation methods has been applied. The quality model for QoS uses characteristics of ISO/IEC 9126 and standards valid for network service (Bogen, Hausen, Worst, 1994).

REFERENCES

Basili, V.R. and Rombach, H.D. (1988), The TAME Project: Towards Improvement-Oriented Software Environments. *IEEE Transactions on Software Engineering*, 14/6, 758-73.

Begh, J., Hausen, H.-L. and Welzel, D. (1993) A Practitioners Guide to Evaluation of Software. *Proceedings of the IEEE Software Engineering Standards Symposium*, September 1993, IEEE Computer Society, p. 282-8.

Bogen, M.; Hausen, H.-L. and Worst, R. (1994) Handling of QoS Characteristics. *Computer Networks for Research in Europe*, a supplement to Computer Networks and ISDN Systems, Volume 26 (1994), Supplement 2,3, pp. 107-18, Elsevier Science Publishers B.V.

ECMA standard 149 (1991). *Portable Common Tool Environment* (PCTE), Abstract Specification, European Computer Manufacturers Association.

Hausen, H.-L. (1989) Yet Another Quality and Productivity Modeling | YAQUAPMO |. *ACM, IEEE, HICSS-22, Hawaii International, Conference on System Sciences* (ed. B.C. Shriver), Hawaii, January 1989, p. 978-987.

Hausen, H.-L. (1992) A Specification of an Assessment and Certification Advisor.*ACM, Annual Conference of the ACM* (ed. J.P. Agrawal, V. Kumar, V. Wallentine), March 1992, Kansas City, MO, 20 p.

Hausen, H.-L. and Welzel, D. (1993a) A Rule-Based Specification of Software Evaluation and Certification - Formal Model -. *SCOPE report*, SC.93/019, Version 02, GMD Sankt Augustin, May 1993.

Hausen, H.-L. and Welzel, D. (1993b) Guides to Software Evaluation (comprising: The Evaluators Guide, The Evaluation Module Development Guide). *Arbeitspapiere der GMD*, No. 746, GMD Sankt Augustin, April 1993.

Hausen, H.-L. and Welzel, D. (1994) Evaluating Software concurrently with and after its Developement. in: *Proceedings of the 11th International Conference on Testing Com-*

puter Software, Washington, DC, June 13-16, 1994.
IEEE 610, IEEE standard 610.12-1990, (1990). *IEEE Standard Glossary of Software Engineering Terminology*, Institute of Electrical and Electronics Engineers, Inc., 345 East 47th Street, New York, NY 10017, USA, December 1990.
ISO/IEC Guide 25 (1990). *General Requirements for the Competence of Calibration and Testing Laboratories*, International Standards Organization, International Electrotechnical Commission.
ISO/IEC 8402, International standard, (1990). *Quality Concepts and Terminology* Part One: Generic Terms and Definitions, International Organization for Standardization, International Electrotechnical Commission, December 1990.
ISO/IEC 9126, International standard, (1991). Information technology - Software product evaluation - Quality characteristics and guidelines for their use, International Organization for Standardization, International Electrotechnical Commission.
ISO/IEC 9126: Guides to software evaluation, International standards (1993). part 5: The evaluator's guide, ISO/IEC JTC1/SC7 N1136, July 20, 1993, part 7: Guide to Developing, Documenting and Validating Evaluation Modules, *ISO/IEC JTC1/SC7/WG6 Technical report*, July 26, 1993, International Organization for Standardization, International Electrotechnical Commission.
Neusser, H.-J. and Hausen, H.-L. (1989). Knowledge Based Handling of Methods and Tools, *ACM, IEEE, HICSS-22, Hawaii International, Conference on System Sciences* (ed. B.C. Shriver, B. C.), Hawaii, January 1989, p. 142-51.
Kyster, H. (1993). MicroScope: The Evaluation of Software Quality, DELTA, Venlighedsvej 4, 2970 Hoersholm, Denmark.
SCOPE Consortium (1993). SCOPE Technology Report, *SCOPE report*, SC.93/009, Version 03, GMD Sankt Augustin, May 1993 (revised July 1993).
Welzel, D. (1993). A rule-based process representation for software process evaluation, in: *Information and Software Technology*, Volume 35, Number 10, pp. 603-10, Butterworth Heineman, October 1993.

APPENDIX: TERMINOLOGY USED

The terminology used based on (IEEE 610, 1990) and (ISO 8402, 1990). The following terms are mentioned in order to extend and classify the terminology.

- assessment of software: Process of comparing the values obtained from the measurements with quality requirements.
- classified software: Software which is classified according to product, process and supportive information or other characteristics.
- client: Person or institution (e.g. producer, distributor, buyer, or user) who requests/ negotiates the evaluation.
- evaluation module Encapsulation of the definition of an evaluation (sub-) method applied on a product or process information in order to measure software characteristics or subcharacteristics by applying metrics, checking pass/fail criteria, delivering evaluation report and cost report.
- evaluation level: 1. Grade which is defined by a set of evaluation techniques to be applied and the thresholds of quality metrics being obtained by these techniques.

2. Identification of (subcharacteristics and) metrics and attachment of metrics to subcharacteristics and definition of acceptance criteria by selecting rating levels for each metric and reference to (sub-) evaluation method to be applied to obtain a metric.

- evaluation report: Final document of the software evaluation. It is progressively completed during the whole evaluation process and consists of four parts: - evaluation requirement, - evaluation specification, - evaluation plan, and - evaluation result.
- evaluation item: Entity being evaluated.
- identified software: Software which is identified by document identifier, title, condition, and of date of arrival as well as handling information.
- measurement: Application of a metric for product quality or process productivity.
- process information: Entities obtained during the software process.
- product information: Entities constituting a complete or part of a software product.
- software evaluation: Process which comprises validation and verification, measurement and assessment of software.
- supportive information: Entities which are not evaluated but which are necessary for an evaluation.

Authors

Dieter Welzel
received his degree in Computer Science from the University of Bonn. Since 1990 he has been working at GMD Institute for Application-Oriented Software and System Technology, Sankt Augustin. His main activities involve interface notions for concurrent systems with modular structure, process modeling and evaluation of software processes.
E-mail: welzel@gmd.de

Hans-Ludwig Hausen
received degrees in Electrical Engineering and in Computer Science from Technical University of Berlin, where he also served as a lecturer in Computer Science. At present he holds the position of a senior scientist at GMD Institute for Application-Oriented Software and System Technology, Sankt Augustin. His main interest are computer aided software engineering and software quality assurance.
E-mail: hausen@gmd.de

32

Software applications complexity evaluation in a bank environment

D. Cellino
Banksiel s.p.a.
c.so Galileo Ferraris 86 - Torino - Italy
tel. +39-11-505921 fax : +39-11-505164

Abstract

In an effort to establish a software measurement activity in a bank environment, we started considering Halstead's Software Science. We soon recognised we needed 'application metrics' more than 'program metrics' and 'user metrics' more than 'classic metrics'. This paper describes our results in validating and tailoring Halstead's Software Science in our environment and our approach in defining application and user metrics.

Keywords

Complexity measures, software applications metrics, metrics validation, bank software, McCabe metrics, Software Science.

1 INTRODUCTION

In 1994 an important Italian bank began to set up a measurement program to evaluate the quality of its software, with the objective to :

- keep track of time evolution of different metrics during the software life cycle;
- find metrics to measure applications and not only programs;
- find a way to measure not only the 'intrinsic' complexity of a software module but as part of an application;
- identify particularly complex software modules within a specific application.

My team and I began gathering data on the source programs using the McCabe's cyclomatic number and Halstead's Software Science metrics which are widely accepted and easy to evaluate. But, as the data were collected, it became quite clear that they did not portray accurately bank software quality and that, to characterise it more precisely, it should have been necessary to identify metrics more tailored on our specific environment.

This was not all that surprising since both McCabe and Halstead analyses were developed in the seventies in a completely different technical setting. After discovering, in the hard way, the drawbacks of classic metrics, we tried to find our own answers to our own software measurement problems.

We chose to focus on size and complexity of the programs and on the type of 'call statements' used*, regarding these characteristics as indicators of maintainability and readability. Since the bank was only concerned about the software developed and maintained by its own personnel, software purchased under a license agreement has not been considered in our work. The study considered a set of 617 COBOL and 64 PL/I programs belonging both to 'new' and 'old' applications, written with different techniques and affected by different amount of maintenance activity. Both 'on line' and 'batch'* programs were considered and their behaviours were investigated separately during the study.

'Copy' and 'include' statements were expanded before analysing the software to allow a complete evaluation of the programs and of the effort required to fully understand them.

The software analyser was configured to equally rate constructs which are equivalent in the two languages. For instance, the statements

- A=B
- move A to B (COBOL style assignment)

are both counted as made up of one operator and two operands.

The final result of this work has been a software application that analyses sources, evaluates several new 'customised' metrics, stores metrics history for each module and application and performs some statistical analysis to find out the acceptability ranges for modules metrics within a specific application.

2 USING CLASSICAL METRICS

The main drawback of McCabe's cyclomatic number is its lack of resolution : too many (and too different) programs have the same cyclomatic number. This occurs because this index counts the number of nodes in the graph regardless of their relative disposition, which is obviously where program complexity actually lies.

Other complexity metrics (for instance, Belady's bandwidth metric, Chen's entropy or the chunk-oriented measures) pay attention to the nesting levels and differentiate between nested decisional statements and sequential ones, allowing finer classifications; of course these metrics

---

*explicitly referring to the called module or getting its name from a program variable, thus making the program flow less obvious to understand.

* A program is 'on line' if it processes a single data item in real time (typically interfacing a video unit or a printer); it is 'batch' if it processes 'as soon as possible' (i.e. not in real time) large amounts of data typically producing a file or a printed report.

are much more difficult to evaluate.

As far as Halstead's metrics (Halstead, 1977) are concerned, some of them show a curious property which questions their usefulness (Weyuker, 1988).

For instance, one would expect the effort and time required to develop a program to be greater than those needed to develop its initial portion : the opposite would be very hard to justify, but under certain conditions Halstead's *effort* shows this peculiar behaviour.

This occurs because the effort is defined by Halstead as a monotonically increasing function of all the basic counters (total and distinct operators N_1 and n_1 and total and distinct operands N_2 and n_2) except the number of distinct operands n_2. Since the whole program will probably contain more distinct operands than its initial portion, it is not difficult to find pieces of code for which the effort decrease as the program grows.

And since Halstead's programming time is given by the Effort/Stroud number (the number of elementary discrimination per second), for such programs the time needed for developing the initial part would be greater than that needed for finishing it, which is clearly paradoxical.

We decided, before going on with a large scale measurement activity, to better investigate also some less obvious metrics proposed by Halstead.

We began working on such indicators as language level, program level, bugs number and intelligence content.

We started from the language relationship :

$$\lambda = L^2 V \qquad (2.1)$$

which is supposed to hold between the language level λ and the program level L.

To verify this relationship, we estimated the best-fit value of exponent b in the relationship :

$$\lambda = L^b * V \qquad (2.2)$$

In 9 different sets of Cobol and PL/1 programs, we found for the exponent b a set of values whose average weighed on the number of modules is 1.99 ± 0.14, in excellent agreement with Halstead's result.

On the other side, our study does not provide any indication that the product in (2.1) remains constant for a given language as suggested by Halstead : on the contrary, λ shows a great variability.

It has to be noticed that our sets contain programs using CICS, DB2 or DL/1 commands, and hence it would be more appropriate to divide them in subsets according to the kind of data communication and database they use.

For instance, considering separately time-processing (CICS) programs and batch programs, the overall agreement improves, but the standard deviation remains high.

To sum up, while it is possible to say that there is a linear correlation between the logarithms of volume and program level, it seems more difficult to sustain that L^2V tends to some constant, 'fixed' for a given language.

Other Software Science indicators that we tried to validate in our environment were the potential volume of an algorithm and its '*intelligence content*', which were supposed to be independent from the language in which the algorithm is expressed.

Combining the two different equations given by Halstead (Halstead, 1977) for the total number B of delivered bugs[*] , one gets :

$$V^* = E^{2/3} \quad (2.3)$$

which would give a simple way to obtain the potential volume V* from the effort E.

Unfortunately, in our study we could not find any convincing correlation between V* and E.

On the other side, we noticed that the intelligence content, whose complete expression is rather complicated[*], is very well approximated by the program vocabulary (number of distinct words used) : the correlation turned out to be 0.944 on the set of Cobol programs and 0.959 on the set of PL/1 program. This means that the intelligence content (and hence the potential volume V*) can be estimated by the program vocabulary.

Following the same approach, we tried to approximate the program level, the ratio between potential and real volume of the algorithm, whose value would allow to verify if the implementation of the algorithm is affected by some unnecessary complexity.

Not surprisingly the relationship between the program level and the ratio vocabulary/volume was not so good.

The correlation was still very high for Cobol (0.953), but rather low for PL/1 (0.73).

4 CUSTOMISED PROGRAM METRICS

Since our code analyser could not detect nested loops and structures, we were forced to set them aside (at least for the moment) as well as data flow complexity, live with McCabe and Halstead's counters and use them to define our program metrics.

We wanted also to obtain global indicators for application, a subject on which we were not able to find any help in the technical literature, and to set reasonable thresholds for module acceptability on the various metrics.

We learned from literature (McCabe, 1976) that 10 seemed 'a reasonable, but not magical, upper limit' for cyclomatic complexity and that exceptions should be made only for very wide case constructs (DeMarco, 1982). Unfortunately, this number is not reasonable at all in most of bank application software : just think of the programs which validate the customer data for the opening of an account or thė mortgage payment !

A recent work by 'Corpo Tecnico dell'Esercito Italiano' (Mondino, 1994), which sets the upper limit for cyclomatic number to 15, sets also the upper limit for the statements number to 50 which is ridiculously low for typical bank software modules.

It seems also questionable to compare 'absolute' values of cyclomatic complexity between two programs regardless of their size. If a program has 50 statements, 15 control nodes can really be too much : but what about a program with 15 control nodes and 1500 (or even 3000) statements ? We did not think they could be considered 'equally complex'.

We chose Halstead's program length (the number of program words, excluding declaratives) and Halstead's program vocabulary as measures of the code size. Then, we started working not directly on counters but on their normalised form : cyclomatic numbers and total operands and operators were normalised using Halstead's program length, while distinct operands were normalised using Halstead's vocabulary. Distinct operators do not need any further

---

[*] $B = E^{2/3} / 3000$ and $B = V^* / 3000$

[*] Intelligence content = $(2\, n_2(N_1+N_2) \log_2(n_1+n_2))/(n_1 N_2)$

normalisation, since they are intrinsically limited by the total number of keywords of the language used to write the code.

This normalisation allowed us to compare the different values of metrics between different releases of the same program, and to understand if a particular intervention had increased or decreased its complexity, size, and data.

Some of the metrics are not related to quality aspects, but simply reflect some aspects of 'size' : for instance, the ratio 'total operands/length' can be looked at as a 'data size', which it is not per-se related to quality even if an anomalously high or low ratio could trigger further analysis.

We did not set any threshold value for 'size' metrics acceptability, while for each 'quality metric' we set two different threshold values : a '*yellow alert*' and a '*red alert*' threshold which partitioned the programs in three sets :

- Under the 'yellow alert' threshold : **All right (60%)**
- Above the 'yellow alert' but under the 'red alert' threshold : **Could be better (90%)**
- Above the 'red alert' threshold : **Out of limits**

We set these thresholds by a statistical analysis of a subset of the bank software; for some indicators, we set different thresholds for 'on line' and 'batch' programs.

'All right' does not mean that the program has really a reasonable complexity and size : it means that its metric values are under a threshold which is satisfied by the 60% of the subset used for test. The same happens to the 10% programs 'out of limits' : they are above a threshold satisfied by the 90% of the tested subset.

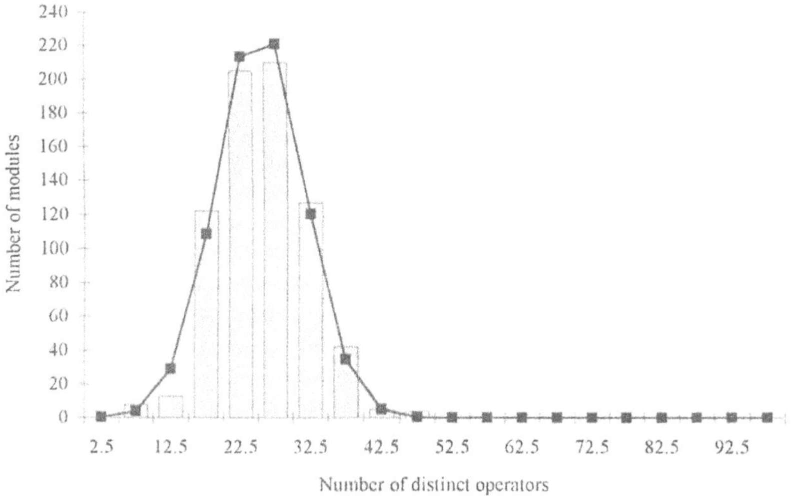

Figure 1 Frequency distribution of distinct operators (line). The bars represent the normal distribution.

It is clear that this way of setting thresholds aims at 'relative quality'; but, on the other side, we were looking for a way to focus our maintenance activity and however it would be useless to set an upper limit of 50 statements in an environment where a program with 3000 words is 'not so big'.

A few more words about the number of distinct operators n_1. On our programs sample, we never found values higher than 50. Moreover, we saw that the frequency distribution is close to normal (see Figure 1).

The value of n_1 lay in the range [20,30[for 382 programs, and in the range [15,35[for 616 programs. Only 65 programs (less than 10%) were characterised by a n_1 greater than 35.

Such programs could show some peculiar complexity (which required some special features of the language) or maybe simply display an unusual mastering of the language. But in any case they will be less obvious to understand for most programmers.

5 APPLICATIONS METRICS AND EVALUATIONS OF PROGRAMS VERSUS APPLICATIONS

Our basic assumption is that the 'computational complexity' of a program depends on the total number of operators used N_1 and on the total number of 'decisional operators' TD (including logical operators like OR, AND, NOT) : the higher the ratio 'TD/N_1', the more complex the program.

Examining a number of different software applications, we found out that there exists a relationship between N_1 and TD; more precisely (see Figures 2 and 3), the relationship is linear, and the linear term varies, in our study, between 0.09 and 0.2.

The average correlation is 0.94, which is rather good. Results are shown in Table 1.

Table 2 makes clear that parabolic regression does not lead to better results : the square terms coefficients are negligible, and the linear terms vary in the same range found for them in linear regression. Anyway, one could choose to try parabolic regression every time linear regression proves unsatisfactory.

The results are better for COBOL programs than for PL/1 programs. We have to remark, however, the smaller dimension of the PL/1 set (only 64 programs) and the lower size of its programs.

Applications whose programs show a higher density of decisional operators will be represented by regression lines with greater linear term; thus, this parameter of the linear correlation can be chosen as a measure of application complexity.

By evaluating this factor for a greater set of applications, we are now going to establish threshold for its values, in order to rate applications as 'simple', 'normal' or 'complex'.

We have called the correlation line of an application its 'computational complexity model', which is described with three values : the linear term, the coefficient of correlation and the standard deviation of the regression.

The model is considered reliable if the coefficient of correlation is higher than 0.85.*

* After analysing 14342 batch programs and 9882 on-line programs, belonging to 190 different applications, we found that 96% of the on-line applications and 84% of the batch applications shows a correlation degree greater than 0.90.

Table 1 Linear regression of TD against N_1

			Regression line			
Appl.	*Lang.*	*N. pgm.*	*Const. term*	*Linear term*	*Std. err.*	*Corr. degr.*
C1	COB	44	-2,02	0,151	5,78	0,93
C2	PL/1	36	-6,4	0,170	14,4	0,97
CTOT	Mix	80	-5,27	0,168	10,75	0,97
CM	Mix	4	32,09	0,149	42	0,87
R1	COB	10	-16,56	0,160	26,55	0,97
R2	COB	4	-0,3	0,137	1,83	0,99
R3	COB	8	-8,69	0,131	3,1	0,99
R4	COB	5	-9,98	0,126	9,76	0,99
R5	COB	14	-10,42	0,151	6,14	0,99
R6	COB	10	21,57	0,094	22,36	0,92
RB	COB	36	-10,74	0,151	16,24	0,98
RC	COB	15	10,32	0,108	21,85	0,95
R7	COB	169	-11,24	0,151	15,41	0,97
R8	PL/1	26	7,87	0,107	12,83	0,87

Table 2 Parabolic regression of TD against N_1

				Regression curve			
Appl.	*Lang.*	*N. pgm.*	*Const. term*	*Linear term*	*Square term*	*Std. err.*	*Corr. degr.*
R7	COB	169	-2,7	0,123	$1,58\ 10^{-5}$	14,98	0,97
R8	PL/1	26	4,02	0,145	$-5,58\ 10^{-5}$	12,65	0,88

We are planning to use these models during the late phases of the life cycle of an application.

During the development of a new module for an existing application, we can use the model to predict the maximum number of decisions it can contain, and therefore we can keep under control the increase of computational complexity, which means to control the number of nodes in the control graph and hence the minimal number of independent paths that should be tested (small bugs in bank software can cost big money).

We can also avoid the 'unnecessary complexity' built into a solution but not required by the basic properties of the problem : if the value of TD predicted by the model is significantly lower than the measured TD, it is possible that the program could be rewritten in a simpler way (for instance, applying distributive properties to logical operators).

The programs in an application which are not so well represented by its model are those showing an apparently odd relationship between N_1 and TD. These programs, especially if their values are higher than those given by the model, could be difficult to understand and to maintain, and more error-prone than the others.

We measure the 'oddity degree' of a program within an application in standard deviation unit, i.e. using the ratio

$$OD = (TD - TD_{model})/\text{standard deviation} \tag{5.1}$$

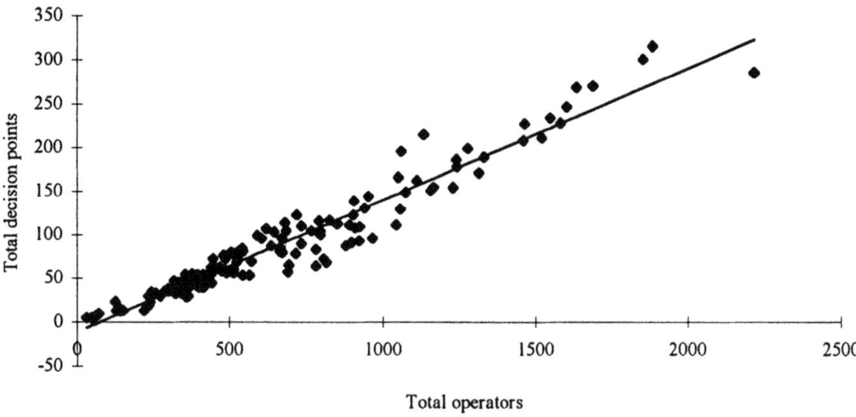

Figure 2 Total decision points against total operators for application R7 (Cobol). The chart shows the data distribution and the regression line.

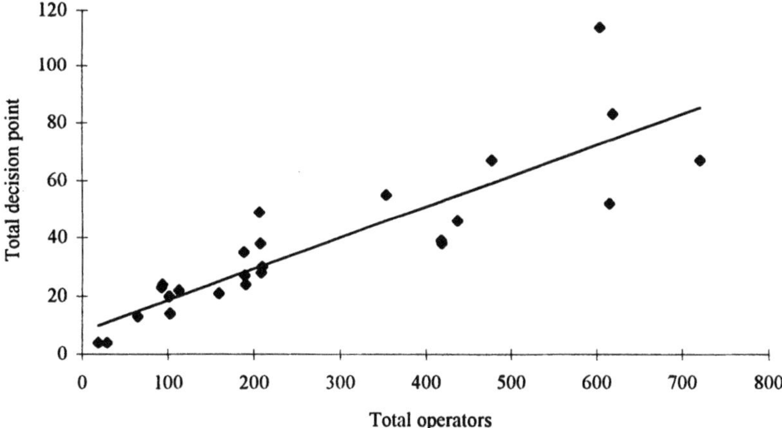

Figure 3 Total decision points against total operators for application R8 (PL/1). The chart shows the data distribution and the regression line.

The three threshold values for OD were established in a way slightly different (though almost equivalent) from the other indexes.

If the program is less complex than what predicted by the model, OD will be negative, and the program will be considered acceptable, just as if it shows positive values lower than 1 : the line parallel to the model and set at a distance equal to standard deviation is called 'acceptability line'.

Programs with values greater or equal to 1 but lower than 2 are considered as 'needing improvement'; the line as distant from the model as twice the standard deviation is called the 'improvement line'.

Programs with values greater or equal 2 but lower than 3 are considered 'critical'; the corresponding line is the 'critical line'.

Programs rated more than 3 are considered 'dangerous'; they can be placed anywhere beyond the critical line.

We defined another couple of ratios to measure the computational complexity even when the number of programs in the application is too low to reliably evaluate OD.

The first ratio is the average number of logical operators for decisional statements : it can provide an indication of the (average) complexity of the single decisional statement. A high ratio should lead the programmer to revise his code.

The second ratio is CR = TD/N_1. Since it is normalised with respect to one of the possible measures of size of the programs, it is convenient for comparison among different programs.

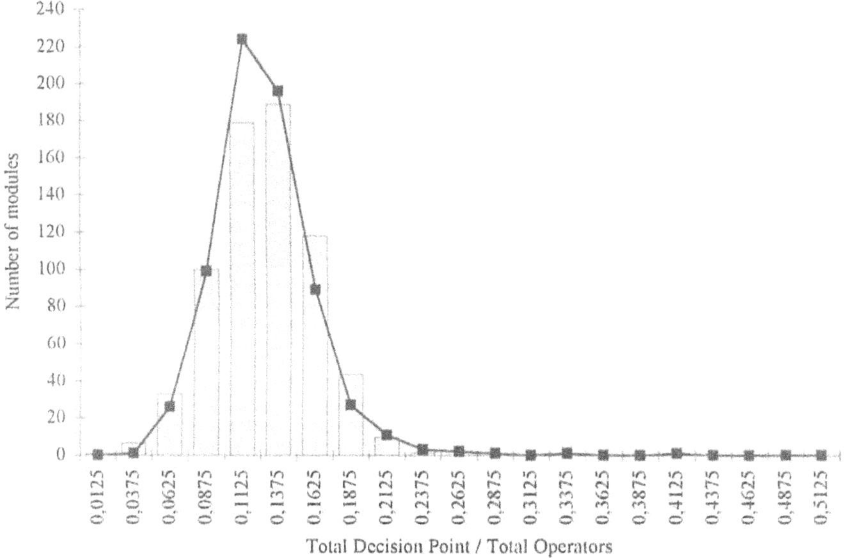

Figure 4 Frequency distribution of CR (line). The bars represent the normal distribution.

The frequency distribution of CR is rather close to normal (see Figure 4) and it shows a high concentration in the interval [0.1, 0.2[, the same of the linear term of application models.

During our study, we did not find values higher than 0.45; the 60% of the programs has a value behind 0.125 and the 50% a value behind 0.15. Thus, even if the model is not available, or if it shows a low coefficient of correlation, a program with CR greater than 0.15 should anyway be regarded as 'suspect'.

6 MANAGING QUALITY DATA : A SOFTWARE APPLICATION

We already mentioned the software written to collect and analyse data obtained from source code. Its key capabilities are :

- the evaluation of the complexity model of the applications;
- the capability to store up to 99 values of each index, thus maintaining the history of programs and applications quality;
- the availability of the statistical analysis tool for setting thresholds and evaluating the frequency distributions of indicators.

The real purpose of the application is to give users something going 'beyond numbers' : all software analysers attach numbers to software, but usually they do not help in interpreting them.

This software has been by now released to technical users (project leaders and programmers) and we are beginning to collect data on a larger scale.

This phase has already lead to some adjustments, especially to threshold values; besides, we have got a number of suggestions about new possible metrics: our users seem very interested in nested control structures sensitivity, data complexity and in spotting the use of 'prohibited keywords' such as the COBOL statements GOTO or ALTER.

7 CONCLUSIONS

We could see that :

- on line programs tend to show higher complexity and size than batch ones, essentially because of input data validation;
- most of recent written programs have a size much smaller than older ones, due to the use of functional decomposition techniques;
- objects reusing and availability of 'skeleton programs' reduces the number of distinct operators n_1;
- high values of n_1 often indicate complex mathematical evaluations or string manipulations;
- anomalously high values of OD (i.e. 15) often indicate bad coding techniques, for instance long chains of explicit tests ('if A = 24 or A = 25 or A = ...') instead of more compact and performing table searches; OD can be also high (about 6 or 8) for huge programs belonging to an application whose other programs are much smaller;

- very high values of program length (beyond 20 000 words) often indicate that the program is made up by 'copy' or 'include' statements even in the non-declarative section, or that it has been split in parts because it exceeded the maximum size allowed by the editor; this makes the source program difficult to read and to control;
- code generators and reusable software show (of course!) a very high complexity and a strong ratio of logical operators, but this software is well represented by the model (no programs with OD higher than 3.5);
- size, complexity and percentage of logical operators show rather clearly programs age.

It has to be noticed that, due to their size, extremely small programs (less than 20 operators) often result in extremely high values of CR, though they are very easy to read and to maintain.

Some of our users were a little disappointed : they observed that we rated as 'big' or 'complex' those programs which they already 'knew' to be 'big' and 'complex'. To begin with, this means that our models are reliable, and that estimation of effort and costs made using our data will probably be correct. Besides, our users did not '*know*' that the program were complex. They '*felt*' it was so. Measuring software makes possible to replace 'traditional gut-feeling guesstimate' (DeMarco, 1982) with consistent forecasting obtained using common methods and evaluation tools and based on historical data.

8 ACKNOWLEDGEMENTS

The author gratefully thanks **Dr. Ezio Ajmar** (Società Italiana Avionica, Turin) for his many helpful suggestions and the extremely accurate review.

9 REFERENCES

Belady, L. A. (1983) Complexity of large systems, in *Software Metrics : An analysis and Evaluation* (ed. A. Perlis, F. Sayward, and M. Shaw), The MIT Press, Cambridge, Massachusets.

Chen, E. T. (1978) Program complexity and programmer productivity. *IEEE Trans. Software Eng.*, **SE-4 3**,187-194.

Davis J.S. and LeBlanc R.J. (1988) A Study of the Applicability of Complexity Measures. *IEEE Trans. Software Eng.*, **14 9**, 1366-1372.

DeMarco, T. (1982) *Controlling Software Projects : Management, Measurement and Estimation.* N.J. Prentice Hall, Englewood Cliffs.

Grady, R.B. and Caswell, D.L. (1987) *Software Metrics : Estabilishing a Company-Wide program.* Prentice Hall.

Halstead, M.H. (1977) *Elements of Software Science.* Elsevier Nort-Holland, New York.

McCabe, T.J. (1976) A complexity measure. *IEEE Trans. Software Eng.*, **SE-2 4**, 308-320.

Magg. Gen. tec. Mondino, Ten. Col. tec. Mele, Magg. tec. Messina and Cap. tec. Cascella (1994) L'esercito verso il controllo dell'ambiente di produzione del software militare, in *Atti Ufficiali del CQS'94*, Etnoteam - Nomos Ricerca.

Munson J.C. and Khoshgoftaar T.M. (1992) The detection of Fault-Prone Programs. *IEEE*

Trans. Software Eng., **18 5** 423-432.
Perlis, A. and Sayward, F. and Shaw, M. (1983) *Software Metrics : An analysis and Evaluation.* The MIT Press, Cambridge, Massachusets.
Sellers, B. H. (1992) Modularization and McCabe 's cyclomatic complexity. *Comm. ACM*, **35 12**, 17-19.
Stroud, J.M. (1967) The fine structure of psychological time. *New York Academy of Science Annals*, **138(2)** 623 - 631.
Weyuker, E.J. (1988) Evaluating Software Complexity Measures. *IEEE Trans. Software Eng.*, **14 9,** 1357-1365.

10 BIOGRAPHY

Daniela Cellino received the degree in Mathematics from Università di Torino in 1982. Since then, she has been working on software development projects for insurance companies and banks. Actually, she has been the team leader of the group which designed and developed the teller support software used in front and back office activities in all branches of one of the most important Italian banks (about 10,000 workstations in the whole country). She is currently responsible for Software Engineering activities in the Turin branch of Banksiel S.p.A. (Finsiel Group), where she dealt for the past three years with software measurement activities.

33

How business relationship modelling supports quality assurance of business objects

R.A. Veryard
Texas Instruments
Wellington House, 61-73 Staines Road West, Sunbury-on-Thames, Middlesex UK TW16 7AH Phone +44 1784 212560
Fax +44 1784 212600 Email 5913301@mcimail.com

Abstract

Many claims have been made for the benefits of software reuse, in terms of enhanced quality as well as productivity. Widely reused objects are supposed to possess several desirable characteristics, such as reliability and flexibility as well as efficiency. But reusable objects may be used for unpredicted purposes in unpredicted contexts. Furthermore, in an open distributed world, technical, geographical, organizational and other boundaries, as well as significant time lags, may separate the software developer from the publisher, and the software librarian from the user. From these premises we argue that responsibility for the quality of reusable software artefacts cannot be taken by the developer (or development organization) alone, but must be shared between developer and other agents. Recent work in enterprise modelling for open distributed processing has led to new techniques for modelling responsibilities across organizational boundaries, and these techniques are introduced here as a way of determining and clarifying effective structures for the quality assurance of reusable business objects.

Keywords

Business Object, Software Reuse, Quality Assurance, Open Distributed Processing, Responsibility Modelling, Enterprise Modelling, Requirements Engineering

Acknowledgements

Some of the work described in this paper was carried out within the Enterprise Computing Project, grant-aided by the UK Government Department of Trade and Industry, involving the John Dobson, Ian Macdonald, Rob van der Linden, David Iggulden and the author. Thanks are also due to John Dodd, Aidan Ward, John Reilly, Michael Mills and Richard Gilyead.

1. INTRODUCTION

This paper introduces the techniques of business relationship modelling to reconcile an apparent mismatch between the expectations and requirements of software quality assurance on the one hand, and the expectations and requirements of reusable business objects on the other hand.

Levels of confidence in software quality vary widely, from misplaced complacency at one end of the spectrum to excessive caution at the other end of the spectrum. The purpose of quality assurance is to establish reasonable and realistic levels of confidence. Confidence is associated with predictability, stability and trust. But technology trends, especially object reuse and open distributed processing, appear to reduce the factors that lead to confidence in software quality. This is the challenge addressed by this paper.

If software users want to take advantage of unknown objects from anonymous sources, how confident can they reasonably be that these objects are fit-for-purpose? What assumptions can the users make about such objects? Frakes and Fox (1995) argue that quality concerns do not currently inhibit reuse, but they indicate that this situation may change. Meanwhile, what quality checks can and should a developer perform, before submitting an object for publication and dissemination, which may result in the object's being used in unanticipated contexts and for unanticipated purposes. What kind of systems and relationships are necessary, to attain the maximum reasonable level of confidence in software quality, without unduly restricting technological progress?

Table 1 Stakeholder concerns motivating quality assurance

User concerns	*Developer concerns*
• what evidence is there that this object is likely to work properly in my application?	• what evidence is there that this object is likely to work properly in real user applications?
• has the object been tested in a way that is relevant to my intended use?	• has the object been tested in a sufficient variety of situations?
• how much serious usage has this object had, in areas similar to my intended use?	• is the object designed for efficient performance in a reasonable range of contexts?
• what are the performance / capacity implications of using this object?	

This paper argues that full responsibility for quality can be taken neither by the developer nor by the user, nor by any intermediate party (such as a broker or software publisher). Thus effective quality assurance needs to focus on the roles and responsibilities and relationships between the various stakeholders in the object delivery chain.

The paper is in two parts. The first part states the problem: it describes quality assurance as a way of acquiring reliable knowlege about the quality of objects, and indicates how reuse cuts across our traditional ways of knowing. The second part indicates the solution: the application of responsibility modelling techniques to determine structures for the sharing of responsibilities across the object delivery chain.

The paper is derived from, and is intended to demonstrate the connections between, Texas Instruments' recent work in three separate areas:

- Software quality management
- Business relationship modelling for open distributed processing (also known as enterprise modelling)
- Business object modelling and component-based development.

2. SOFTWARE QUALITY ASSURANCE VERSUS REUSE

In this part of the paper, we describe what quality assurance is, and what makes it possible. We then describe what software reuse is, and how it potentially conflicts with the enablers of quality assurance.

2.1. Quality assurance - a process of discovery

Quality assurance is defined as 'all the planned and systematic activities implemented within the quality system, and demonstrated as needed, to provide adequate confidence that an entity will fulfil requirements for quality' (ISO 8402, 1994). (In this context, the word 'entity' may refer to an activity or a process, a product, an organization, a system or a person, or any combination thereof.) In short, therefore, quality assurance provides **knowledge** about the quality of entities.

In common with most other attempts to gain knowledge, quality assurance cannot avoid affecting the entities about which it attempts to gain knowledge. Any attempt to discover the degree of quality of an entity may bring about an improvement in the quality of that entity. Indeed, such improvement is often seen as the primary justification of quality assurance.

Conversely, any prediction of the quality of an entity should take into account the extent of quality assurance that may be applicable. In particular, if a software developer has access to quality assurance mechanisms that make the emerging quality of a software artefact visible during the development process (other conditions being favourable), this should reduce the occurrence of defects in the developed artefact.

Quality assurance can focus on three areas:

- Product certification, based on product standards
- Process assessment or audit, based on a repeatable software process
- Organizational capability and commitment, based on market regulation and/or long-term business relationships.

Although some software product standards exist, and further standards are being developed, these only address a limited subset of the desired quality characteristics.

2.2. Quality - a context-dependent property

As stated above, quality assurance provides knowledge about the **quality** of entities.

Quality is commonly (and properly) defined in 'fit-for-purpose' terms. The official ISO definition (ISO 8402, 1994) defines quality as "The totality of characteristics of an entity that bear on its ability to satisfy stated or implied needs." (This is an incomplete definition: it allows for some uncertainty about **when** the needs are stated, and **what** they may be implied by.) To be valid and useful, quality assurance must find some way of addressing the stated and implied needs. Any attempt to construct a 'pure' quality assurance, independent of user context or purpose, would necessarily fall short.

Similar arguments apply to software quality metrics. Although generic software quality measurements have been attempted, often copied from the equivalent hardware quality measurements (e.g. Mean-Time-Between-Failures, Mean-Time-To-Fail), software quality of service is often better expressed in application-dependent terms. For example, mission time, which is defined as the time during which a component is to stay operational with a precisely defined probability of failure (Siewiorek & Swarz, 1992)

Within the traditional software development paradigm (waterfall development, central design authority, fixed requirements, or what has been ironically called the 'fixed point theorem' (Paul 1993)), the evident ambiguities of the ISO 8402 definition of quality are usually glossed over. Quality assurance is carried out against a fixed set of requirements of a fixed user or user group.

ISO 9126 offers a standard framework for evaluating the quality of software products (ISO 9126, 1991). Of the six standard characteristics, four are defined in terms of stated requirements (reliability, efficiency, maintainability and portability), while the other two are defined in terms of stated or implied requirements (functionality and usability). Reusability does not appear explicitly in the ISO 9126 model, but it can probably be regarded as a special type of usability, namely usability-by-developers.

A statement of requirements is a description which an object must satisfy for its actual use, for a given purpose, in a given context. We call these the actual requirements. When developing an object for reuse, however, the developer usually does not have access to the complete set of concete requirements. Instead, the developer attempts to build reusable objects by working against an generalized statement of requirements that is hoped to cover a reasonable range of actual requirements. Carrying out QA against an generalized statement of requirements, however, begs the question: to what extent will the developer's generalized notion of the users' requirements match the users' actual requirements?

Thus the problem with restricting our notions of quality (and therefore our notions of quality assurance) to the formally stated requirements is twofold:

i it fails to reflect the practical realities of software development, namely that requirements emerge and evolve, and are never fully stated upfront, despite the insistence of theorist

ii it fails to reflect the chronology of object reuse (see Figure 1), whereby most of the uses of an object are invented after the object has been developed, thus the concrete requirements don't yet exist at the time of development.

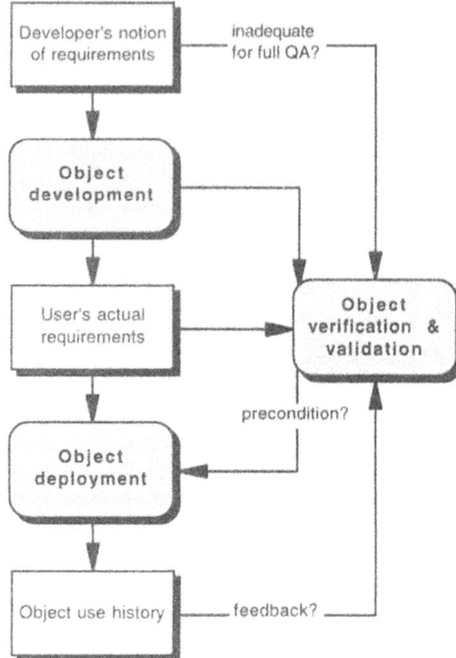

Figure 1 Chronology of object reuse.

2.3. Changing trends in information systems development

Until recently, most developers of Information and Communication Technology (ICT) systems have worked within a certain 'paradigm' - a set of assumptions about the nature of the systems they have been developing, and about the nature of the development work itself. These assumptions have included things like:

- central problem ownership, central design authority, central funding authority
- complete understanding of a given problem/situation
- permanent/final solution to a given problem
- stable or slow-moving market environments, technical architectures and policy frameworks
- life-cycle model of systems development (waterfall, spiral or whatever)

Perhaps these assumptions were never really true. But in most situations they could at least be regarded as reasonable approximations to the truth. However, this old paradigm is becoming increasingly untenable.

As requirements engineering and information systems engineering become increasingly dynamic and decentralized, quality assurance itself needs to become equally dynamic, equally decentralized. The acquisition of knowledge about quality becomes more problematic than ever: when (if ever) and from what standpoint (if any) can quality be assured? To examine these issues in more detail, let us look at two major themes in the breakdown of the traditional software development paradigm:

i object orientation and reuse

ii open distributed processing.

2.4. Object orientation and reuse

Considerable work has been done in recent years on techniques of reuse. This has been largely focused on object-oriented development methods, and on so-called 'business objects'.

The Object Management Group special interest group on Business Object Management (BOMSIG) has developed the following working definition of 'business object':

> "A representation of some thing active in the business domain, including at least its behavior, attributes, constraints (business rules), associations, a business name, and a business definition. A business object may represent, for example, a person, place or concept. The representation may be in a natural language, a modeling language, or a programming language." (OMG 1994)

A business object might be something internal to the enterprise, such as an Employee or a Department, or something external to the enterprise such as a Supplier or Tax Demand. Business objects may be conceptual, in which case we may think of them as business or design **patterns** (Alexander et al 1977), but they may also be implemented in executable software. In any case, the dividing line between conceptual objects and executable software is tenuous (Negishi 1985, Locksley 1991).

The potential benefits of software reuse are certainly considerable, not merely for enhanced productivity but also for enhanced quality. Much has been said (in passing) about the impact of object-oriented techniques on quality:

- "Reusable components ... provide products of higher quality, since components have already undergone rigorous testing before they are installed."
- "High reliability is attained because components are designed and tested as separate units, and in many different systems."
- "Object-oriented programming languages make it possible to develop reusable, modular code segments, improving the quality of the development process and of the resulting software product."

However, although the claimed productivity benefits of reuse have been extensively analysed (Veryard 91), little empirical evidence is available to support the claimed quality benefits.

The attainment of these benefits is not just a technical matter. Benefits may be lost by poor project management, or by lack of engineering discipline. This is where quality management comes in. It provides a systematic framework underpinning good management and engineering practices, thereby providing reasonable assurance to all stakeholders (including end-users and senior management) that the potential benefits of a given technology will indeed be forthcoming.

For example, it is all very well using a reusable component from a catalog or library, on the assumption that someone else has rigorously tested it. But what if they haven't? And if they have, who is to say that their testing is relevant to your intended use of the component?

An effective process of reuse relies on adequate and accurate descriptions of the objects. Indeed, where reuse crosses commercial boundaries, procurement decisions may be based solely on the description: a purchaser may only get the rest of the object after accepting certain payment obligations.

But there may be semantic subtleties or ambiguities in these descriptions. For an illustration of this, consider a business object called FIXED ASSET that implements a particular interpretation of a particular accounting convention to evaluate fixed assets. An incorrect choice of accounting convention may significantly affect the balance sheet. Therefore, a quality evaluation of a business object must address its description (or catalog entry) as well as the quality of any executable code. Quality may be improved by clarifying or extending the description. But the perfect description may never be achievable.

Various mechanisms are used in the software industry to allow the purchaser to try out a business object before committing to purchase. These mechanisms often involve giving the purchaser access to a restricted version of the object. Although these mechanisms may enable the user to verify that the object fits the user's requirements, they also introduce additional quality complications: what guarantee is there that the full version of the object and the restricted version behave identically.

The supply chain may be complex. Departmental software specialists will be using desktop tools for rapid assembly of software applications from existing components from many sources. There will be few if any software developers who develop everything from scratch; instead, even apparently original objects may contain smaller components from other sources.

2.5. Open distributed processing

Open distributed processing (ODP) is an umbrella term for a number of concepts and architectures for distributed computer systems. Architectures include the ODP Reference Model (ISO 10746, 1995), CORBA (OMG 1992), DCE (OSF 1991) and ANSA (APM 1991). For an analysis of ODP market trends, see (van der Linden, 1995). The key features of ODP are shown in Table 2:

Table 2 Key features of Open Distributed Processing

Federation	The lack of central authority over software design or configuration
Interoperability	The ability to link and reconfigure systems and services
Heterogeneity	The ability to link across different platforms and protocols
Transparency	The ability to hide complications from users
Trading / broking	The presence of intermediary agents, to promote and distribute software artefacts and services.

The relevance of ODP to this paper is that ODP further undermines the assumptions on which traditional software quality assurance is based. End-to-end knowledge and authority cannot be guaranteed; information flows must be negotiated across organizational boundaries.

2.6. Summary of changes to software quality assurance

- Patterns of (re)usage of a software artefact are not predictable
- Technical characteristics of software artefacts are hidden from the user, in the name of 'transparency'
- Individual developers may have no monopoly over supply
- Individual brokers and traders may have no exclusive control over the distribution of any given artefact
- Individual users may have no exclusive control over usage

These changes affect at least three important aspects of software quality assurance: design reviews, testing and configuration control.

The developer of a software artefact typically has incomplete knowledge of how it will be used, when, where, by whom, in what contexts, for what (business) purposes. Nobody has the complete picture: not the software tester, nor any individual end-user, nor any intermediary (planner, publisher, broker/trader, librarian, ...).

Although often there is no fixed specification of what the software artefact is required to do, some limited testing is possible, for example:

- whether the software artefact conforms to its own description
- whether the software artefact conforms to standard constraints (such as absence of side-effects)

Where testing is more difficult, and its results less conclusive, is in the compatibility of multiple objects and artefacts. This is complicated by the fact that we don't always know what compatibility is required. This is related to the problem of **feature interaction.**

3. STRUCTURING QUALITY ASSURANCE

3.1. Sharing responsibilities for quality assurance

Under the conditions described above, there is no individual standpoint from which software quality assurance can be effectively performed. The combination of partial knowledge and partial authority make it impossible for any single agent to take full responsibility for quality. Responsibility then attaches to the group, not to the individual. A 'system' of reuse is owned collectively by all the participants in the supply chain; quality assurance must be a collective responsibility.

In general, there are two approaches to organizing collective responsibilities, as shown in Table 3.

Table 3 Collective responsibility - two approaches

Homogeneous closed group stable network based on informal commitments (trust)	In some situations, responsibility can be shared by creating a stable group or team. The members of the group **identify with** the group. This has two aspects: • Each member depends on the group - personal rewards are significantly affected by the success of the group as a whole • Each member feels that the group depends on him/her - the personal contribution to the group is understood and appreciated by the rest of the group
Heterogeneous open group dynamic network based on formal commitments (contract)	In situations where stable teams cannot develop (or be built), formal structures of individual duties need to be established, to enable responsibilities to be shared. This tends to be necessary under the following conditions (Elster 1978, pp 134 ff): • High turnover of group membership, interfering with the emergence of stable relations of personal trust • High cultural / organizational diversity, increasing the barriers that have to be overcome.

Because of its tilt towards heterogeneity, open distributed processing forces us to consider the latter approach.

3.2. Business relationship modelling

Business relationship modelling (also known as responsibility modelling) is required to explicitly share the responsibility for quality across a network of interacting agents, each possessing partial knowledge and partial authority.

We define responsibility as a three-part relationship, involving two agents and a state. A state is typically a property of an entity; remember that an entity may be an activity or a process, a product, an organization, a system or a person, or any combination thereof.

Example: *The software developer is responsible to the software publisher for the thoroughness of testing.*

In this example, the software developer and the software publisher are the two agents, and thoroughness of testing is the state, which can be decomposed into a property (thoroughness) and an entity (the testing activity).

One of the reasons we are interested in the thoroughness of testing is that it is a way of gaining confidence in the robustness of the tested object(s). There are thus dependencies between states (robustness is dependent upon thoroughness), which can be represented as dependency hierarchies. The robustness of the tested object(s) is thus a state at the next level in the hierarchy.

Responsibilities can be delegated, but not escaped. Thus if the software developer delegates the responsibility for the thoroughness of testing to a third party, the software developer remains answerable to the software publisher. Meanwhile the software publisher is (let us suppose) responsible to the software user for the robustness of the tested object, which (as we have seen) is dependent upon the thoroughness of testing.

Current thinking in both ODP and quality management agrees on the fact that delegation should be (formally) 'transparent', in other words the original source(s) should be invisible to the user or customer. If I purchase an object or service from a software publisher, I don't want to have to chase up the supply chain to get satisfaction. (In practice, of course, the procurement organization does want to know about the original source, doesn't want complete transparency of supply, but this may be a consequence of incomplete trust in the vendor.)

Responsibility modelling is a technique for mapping out these delegation structures for specific responsibilities across multiple agents. Delegation structures may be informal or formal, hierarchical or contractual. Delegation structures should be reflected in contracts and agreements between agents.

Delegation structures should also be reflected in information systems. According to good delegation practice, if the software developer delegates the responsibility for the thoroughness of testing to a third party, the software developer must have some mechanism for monitoring and assessing the third party. (This is of course demanded by ISO 9000.) This means that there must be an information system (not necessarily computerized) that enables the software developer to continue to provide the necessary assurance to the software librarian, and means that the delegation can be (in principle) transparent to the users.

Previous techniques for responsibility modelling, such as RAEW analysis (Crane 1986, Texas Instruments 1990), have regarded responsibility as a two-place relation between an agent (or role) and an activity. This has proved extremely useful for identifying inconsistencies between responsibility structures and authority structures, or between responsibility structures and the distribution of knowledge. What the present approach offers in addition is the ability to model delegation structures, especially where these cross organizational boundaries.

There are many approaches to the formal division of responsibilities for quality. We shall examine three:

i Allocation of characteristics

ii Counter argument

iii Collective feedback

3.3. Allocation of characteristics

An agent takes on the responsibility towards a second agent for the possession by an artefact of a given subset of the desired characteristics.

A statement such as 'this artefact has such-and-such properties' can never be guaranteed 100%. However, the responsible agent provides a mechanism, accessible to the second agent, for corrective action.

For example, separating responsibility for the efficiency of an object from the responsibility for its functionality. Such separation of concerns will typically be based on the ISO 9126 standard.

This may be of some limited use, but fails to address the holistic aspect of quality explicitly addressed in the ISO 8402 definition.

3.4. Counter argument

A common approach is to establish a divided responsibility:

- the developers (or their representatives) attempt to prove the quality of a developed object
- a separate team of testers and/or inspectors attempt to prove the lack of quality of a developed object

Quality assurance emerges from the dialogue between two (or more) agents with clearly defined responsibilities and obligations. Responsibility modelling allows us to represent and analyse the respective duties of the two groups, as well as the necessary interactions between them, thus ensuring that the responsibilities and obligations are both clear and optimal.

3.5. Collective feedback

A more sophisticated approach is to create a collective feedback and feedforward system. This passes information from the users of an object backwards to the object source, and forwards to other users and potential users, thus establishing a self-correcting process.

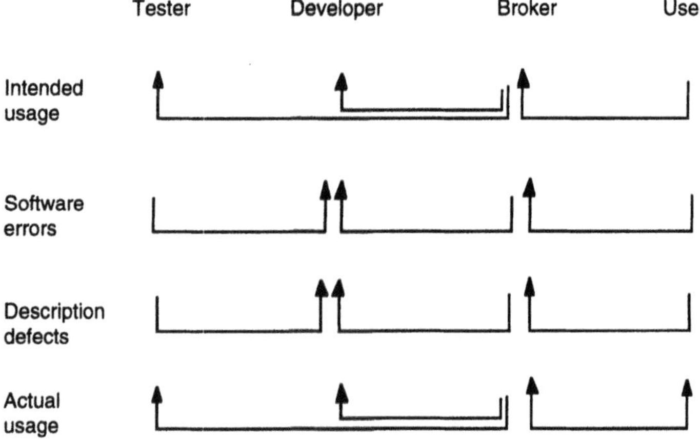

Figure 2 Feedback chains.

Intended and actual use should be fed back to testers as well as developers. Errors and defects should be fed back to the developers by the users, via intermediaries with responsibility for software distribution, such as software publishers or software brokers. They may also be fed back to the testers (since they provide some feedback on the thoroughness and relevance of the testing). Other users may want to be notified, not only of any outstanding software errors and description defects, but also of the pattern of error rates and defect rates, from which they may want to make judgements about expected future error and defect rates.

3.6. Organizational issues

One of the uses of responsibility modelling is to assess whether the organizational boundaries are in the right place. For example, does it make more sense for the development organization to employ the testers (supply-side testing) , or the procurement organization (demand-side testing). These questions need to be negotiated between suppliers and purchasers, based on a clear understanding of their implications for effective and efficient quality assurance.

The feedback chains described in the previous section usually need to work across organizational boundaries. This is likely to raise additional organizational issues. Business relationship modelling may also indicate the need for additional agents, such as independent (third party) assessors and advisors, as well as market regulators.

Detailed description of the use of responsibility modelling to support such structuring judgements can be found in the reports of the Enterprise Computing Project (Veryard 1995)

The developer or vendor may offer specific warranties, or may be subject to various liabilities, either through formal contract or through common practice. These legal aspects of the relationships need to be considered carefully.

4. CONCLUSIONS AND FURTHER WORK

Quality assurance can focus on the quality of the product, the quality of the process, or the quality of the business and organizational relationships. In an open distributed world of reusable business objects, the relationships between parts of the same organization - or between different organizations - are crucial to effective quality assurance. This paper has indicated the use of responsibility modelling as a way of supporting the organization and management of quality assurance.

The necessity of this approach has been argued on the basis of the impossibility of predicting all the uses and use-contexts of a reusable object, and the inappropriateness of unduly restricting such uses and use-contexts. This largely invalidates traditional quality assurance mechanisms.

Further development in this area may benefit from the production of support tools, as well as standards for responsibility distribution.

5. REFERENCES

C. Alexander, S Ishikawa and M. Silverstein (1977) *A Pattern Language*. Oxford University Press, New York.

APM (1991) *ANSA: A Systems Designer's Introduction to the Architecture.* APM Ltd., Cambridge UK: April 1991.

Roger Crane (1986) *The Four Organizations of Lord Brown and R.A.E.W.*. Doctoral Thesis, Kennedy-Western University.

John Dobson and Ros Strens (1994) Responsibility modelling as a technique for requirements definition. *Intelligent Systems Engineering* **3** (1) pp 20-26.

John Dodd (1995) *Component-Based Development: Principles*. Texas Instruments Methods Guide: Issue 1.0, March 1995.

Jon Elster (1978) *Logic and Society: Contradictions and Possible Worlds* John Wiley & Sons, Chichester UK.

W.B. Frakes and C.J. Fox (1995) Sixteen Questions about Software Reuse. *Communications of the ACM* **38** (6), pp 75-87.

ISO 8402 (1994) *Quality Management and Quality Assurance Vocabulary* International Standards Organization, Geneva.

ISO 9000 (1994) *Quality Management and Quality Assurance Standards* International Standards Organization, Geneva.

ISO 9126 (1991) *Information Technology - Software Product Evaluation - Quality Characteristics and Guidelines for their Use* International Standards Organization, Geneva.

ISO 10746 (1995) *Basic Reference Model for Open Distributed Processing* International Standards Organization, Geneva.

Rob van der Linden, Richard Veryard, Ian Macdonald and John Dobson (1995) *Market Report* Enterprise Computing Project.

Gareth Locksley (1991) Mapping strategies for software business, in (Veryard 1991) pp 16-30.

H. Negishi (1985) Tentative Classification of Global Software *Behav. Inf. Technol* **4** (2), pp 163-170.

OMG (1992) *Object Management Architecture Guide* Revision 2, Second Edition, Object Management Group, September 1992.

OMG (1994) Minutes of BOMSIG meeting, Object Management Group, April 7, 1994.

OSF (1991) *DCE User Guide and Reference* Open Software Foundation, Cambridge MA.

Ray Paul (1993) Dead Paradigms for Living Systems. Paper presented at the First European Conference on Information Systems, Henley, 29-30 March 1993.

D.P. Siewiorek and R.S. Swarz (1992) *Reliable Computer Systems* Digital Press.

Texas Instruments (1990) *A Guide to Information Engineering using the IEF™* Texas Instruments Inc., Plano TX, Second Edition.

Texas Instruments (1991) *Strategy Announcement: Arriba! Project*. Version 1.0, TI Software Business, Advanced Technology Marketing, January 5th, 1995.

Richard Veryard (1991) (ed) *The Economics of Information Systems and Software*. Butterworth-Heinemann, Oxford.

Richard Veryard (1994) *Information Coordination: The Management of Information Models, Systems and Organizations*. Prentice Hall, Hemel Hempstead UK.

Richard Veryard and Ian Macdonald (1994) EMM/ODP: A methodology for federated and distributed systems, in *Methods and associated Tools for the Information Systems Life Cycle* (ed. A.A. Verrijn-Stuart and T.W. Olle), IFIP Transactions, Elsevier/North-Holland, Amsterdam.

Richard Veryard, Ian Macdonald, Rob van der Linden and John Dobson (1995) *Enterprise Modelling Methodology*. Enterprise Computing Project.

6. BIOGRAPHY

Richard Veryard is a Principal Consultant in the Software Business of Texas Instruments, working within the Group Quality Department. He was one of the developers of IE\Q, which is a TI proprietary methodology for software quality management. He has been working with advanced software tools and methods for over fifteen years, and is the author of several books on information systems. He is a member of IFIP Working Group 8.6.

INDEX OF CONTRIBUTORS

KEYWORD INDEX

www.ingramcontent.com/pod-product-compliance
Ingram Content Group UK Ltd.
Pitfield, Milton Keynes, MK11 3LW, UK
UKHW022323190726
13856UKWH00001B/181

* 9 7 8 1 4 7 5 7 4 3 9 1 3 *